Professional
Active Server Pages 2.0

Alex Fedorov
Brian Francis
Richard Harrison
Alex Homer
Shawn Murphy
Robert Smith
David Sussman
Stephen Wood

Wrox Press Ltd.

Professional Active Server Pages 2.0

© 1998 Wrox Press

wrox

Published by Wrox Press Ltd,
Arden House, 1102 Warwick Road, Acocks Green, Birmingham B27 9BH, UK.
Printed in Canada
7 8 9 TRI 00 99

ISBN 1 - 861001 - 26 - 6

Trademark Acknowledgements

Wrox has endeavored to provide trademark information about all the companies and products mentioned in this book by the appropriate use of capitals. However, Wrox cannot guarantee the accuracy of this information.

Credits

Authors
Alex Fedorov
Brian Francis
Richard Harrison
Alex Homer
Shawn Murphy
Robert Smith
David Sussman
Stephen Wood

Development Editor
Anthea Elston

Editors
Jeremy Beacock
Daniel Maharry
Chris Ullman

Index
Simon Gilks
Marilyn Rowland

Technical Reviewers
Michael Corning
John de Robeck
Glen Eastman
Andrew Enfield
Richard Harrison
John Kauffman
Rick Kingslan
Srini Krishnamurthy
Richard Mario
Chris Owens
George Reilly
Steven Rice
Tom Rizzo
Kevin Roche
John Schenken

Cover/Design/Layout
Andrew Guillaume
Graham Butler

Cover photo by Sean Ellis. Supplied by Getty Images

About the Authors

Alex Fedorov

Alex Fedorov is working as an executive editor for "ComputerPress" magazine—a monthly software and hardware magazine, published in Moscow, Russia. During his work in magazines Alex has authored more that 150 articles on various programming topics, including Delphi programming, Internet programming, COM/OLE and other technologies. Alex is also the author of several books, published in Russian.

Brian Francis

Brian is the Lead Developer for NCR's Human Interface Technology Center in Atlanta, Georgia. At the HITC, Brian is responsible for prototyping and developing advanced applications that apply superior human interfaces as developed at the Center. His tools of choice include Visual Basic, Visual C++, Java, and all of the Microsoft Internet products. Brian is focused on delivering electronic commerce systems to consumers through multiple points of presence, both in the store and through the Internet. *To my wife Kristi, who makes my life complete, I dedicate this book.*

Richard Harrison

Richard is a Microsoft Certified Solution Developer (MCSD) and a senior consultant for a major global IT services company. He has recently been specializing in Microsoft Internet architectures and helping organizations to use these technologies to build mission critical Web solutions.

Alex Homer

Alex is a software consultant and developer, who lives and works in the idyllic rural surroundings of Derbyshire UK. His company, Stonebroom Software, specializes in office integration and Internet-related development, and produces a range of vertical application software. He has worked with Wrox Press on several projects.

Shawn Murphy

Shawn is currently an independent Internet developer and consultant working in the Los Angeles area where he is also studying architecture at the University of Southern California. He writes articles for IEWorld (http://www.ieworld.net) an on-line journal that is dedicated to the latest in Internet Development and Microsoft technologies. His experience in web technologies ranges from HTML to client and server-side code and web application development. He has also worked as a contractor for companies ranging from nursing homes to Microsoft's Internet Gaming Zone.

Robert Smith

Rob Smith lives in Edinburgh, where he is the Senior Consultant in charge of database and Internet development for Amethyst Group Ltd, an IT consultancy and technical training company. When the excitement of building integrated intranet systems proves too much, Rob relaxes either by causing general alarm on the local golf courses or by simply unwinding at home with his lovely wife Valerie.

David Sussman

David is a freelance developer, trainer and author, living in Buckinghamshire. He has been using Access since its first release, and now specializes in training and developing client/server solutions around Access, Visual Basic and SQL Server, and writing books for Wrox! His next project is a book on MTS/MSMQ, so watch this space!

Stephen Wood

After finishing a graduate degree in English at Clemson University, Stephen Wood landed at Microsoft by pure luck. He has been a technical and programming writer at the Microsoft Corporation for five years. He worked on the original release of Windows NT, Commerce Server 2.0, and is currently working on the second version of Visual J++ 2.0.

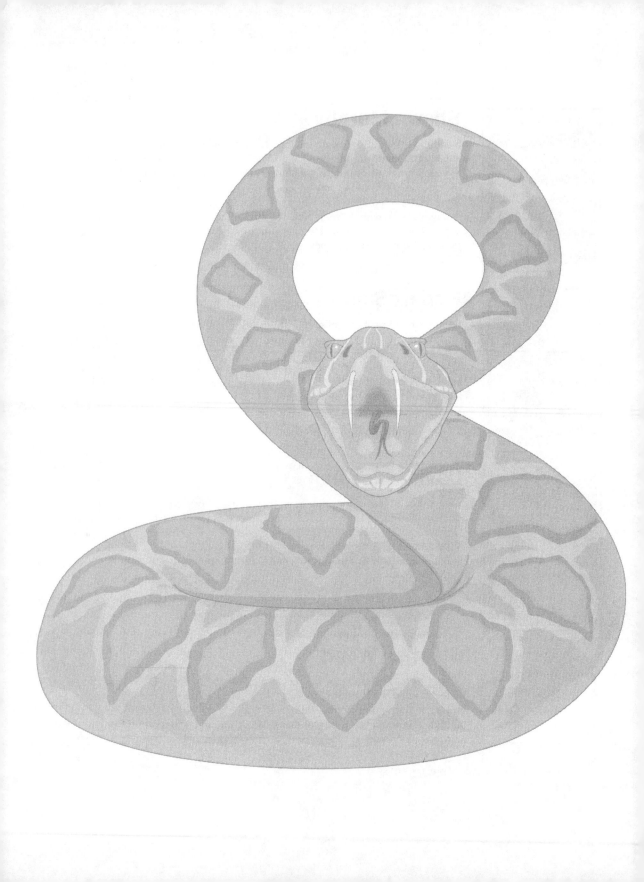

Table of Contents

Chapter 17: Message Queueing in the Electronic Commerce Case Study 601

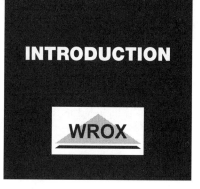

An Introduction to Active Server Pages

Active Server Pages is the latest server-based technology from Microsoft, designed to create interactive HTML pages for a World Wide Web Site, or corporate intranet. It is just part of an all encompassing concept called the Active Platform which has been developed along with Microsoft Windows NT Server, and Microsoft Internet Information Server (IIS). In this book, we start by focusing on what the Active Platform is and how the various technologies such as IIS 4.0, ASP and MTS (Microsoft Transaction Server) fit together. We also look at how you can get hold of ASP, and how to install it together with IIS 4.0 or Personal Web Server 4.0. Then we'll show how Active Server Pages fits into the grand scheme of things, how it has improved in version 2.0 and how you can use it to build really great Web sites and intranet applications.

Who is this Book for?

This is a Wrox 'Professional' series book, so we won't be wasting your time by trying to teach you everything from scratch. We appreciate that most, if not all, of the web page authors and developers who take up Active Server Pages will be reasonably familiar with ordinary HTML, basic scripting concepts, and the simple constructs of the two main scripting languages, VBScript and JavaScript. So, we're assuming that you will know about these basic concepts, and that we won't need to waste time and space by going over them. If you need a quick refresher on either scripting language, you'll be able to find comprehensive references at the back of this book. If you're already familiar with Active Server Pages and want a guide that concentrates on the new features of version 2.0, you won't be disappointed, as there are several chapters devoted to things that weren't possible in IIS 3.0.

Like all Wrox books, this one is written by programmers, for programmers. It's full of practical techniques that you can use to develop your own code. There are also plenty of solid code examples, case studies that produce real, practical, applications, and reference material both throughout and at the end of the book. This means that you can use it as a primer to learn the new techniques, and as a reference for the future- as you develop your skills and your Web sites, you can keep coming back to learn more.

What do I need to use this book?

Most importantly you'll need a copy of Active Server Pages and a web server for your platform (which must be either Windows 95 or NT 4.0). You'll also need a browser (preferably Internet Explorer 4) and a web page or text editor such as FrontPage 98 or Notepad.

Both Active Server Pages and a web server for either NT 4.0 or Windows 95 are available as part of the NT 4.0 Option Pack which is freely downloadable from Microsoft at
http://www.microsoft.com/ntserver/guide/whatisntop.asp

There are two versions of the NT 4.0 Option Pack, one for NT 4.0 and one for Windows 95. IIS 4.0 is the web server that comes with the version of the Option Pack for NT Server 4.0, while Personal Web Server 4.0 is included in the NT 4.0 Option Pack for Windows 95. Both of them include Active Server Pages 2.0 as standard, so there'll be no need to download anything extra. However, while ASP can run on Personal Web Server, this setup isn't optimal and shouldn't be used for most non-development work. In addition you'll also find parts of Transaction Server and Message Queue Server are included within the NT 4.0 Option Pack.

Nearly all of the examples use Active Server Pages and require an HTTP link to a **Web server**. You can use your own machine as a web server if necessary. As mentioned before, we recommend Windows NT4 Server or Microsoft Personal Web Server 4.0, but you can use a server from any other supplier that implements Active Serve Pages.

You may also wish to develop your pages within a specialist environment, such as Microsoft Interdev, FrontPage 98, or a similar application like HoTMetaL Pro or other Web page creation software, but you'll need to edit and write the code by hand most of the time.

Where you'll Find the Sample Code

Our prominent presence on the Web provides you with assistance and support as you use our books. Our Internet-related books (including this one) have a special site that provides examples, and allows you to download code to run on your own machine. This is at **http://rapid.wrox.co.uk**. You can also find a US based mirror of this site at **http://www.rapid.wrox.com**. Our main US-based site is at **http://www.wrox.com**, and it provides details of all our books. There is also a mirror site at **http://www.wrox.co.uk** that may be more responsive if you're accessing it from Europe.

Conventions

We have used a number of different styles of text and layout in the book to help differentiate between the different kinds of information. Here are examples of the styles we use and an explanation of what they mean:

> *Advice, hints, or background information comes in this type of font.*

Important pieces of information come in boxes like this

- ▲ **Important Words** are in a bold type font
- ▲ Words that appear on the screen in menus like the <u>F</u>ile or <u>W</u>indow are in a similar font to the one that you see on screen
- ▲ Keys that you press on the keyboard, like *Ctrl* and *Enter*, are in italics
- ▲ Code has several fonts. If it's a word that we're talking about in the text, for example, when discussing the **For...Next** loop, it's in a bold font. If it's a block of code that you can type in as a program and run, then it's also in a gray box:

```
<STYLE>
... Some VBScript ...
</STYLE>
```

 Sometimes you'll see code in a mixture of styles, like this:

```
<HTML>
<HEAD>
<TITLE>Cascading Style Sheet Example</TITLE>
<STYLE>
style1 {color: red;
    font-size: 25}
</STYLE>
</HEAD>
```

 The code with a white background is code we've already looked at and that we don't wish to examine further.

 Also you'll see that code in Professional Active Server Pages is either HTML tags, client side script or server side script (ASP). Despite being recommended in the HTML 4.0 standard that tags should be specified in lower case, for ease of reading we have chosen to display HTML tags in upper case throughout the book and all script in lower case. Server side script is surrounded by **<%** and **%>** marks. So an example might look like this

```
<BODY>
<H1>This is some HTML </H1>
<SCRIPT LANGUAGE=VBScript>
obj1 = "this is some vbscript"
<% obj2 = "this is some ASP" %>
</SCRIPT>
</BODY>
```

These formats are designed to make sure that you know what it is you're looking at. I hope they make life easier.

Tell Us What You Think

We've worked hard on this book to make it useful. We've tried to understand what you're willing to exchange your hard-earned money for, and we've tried to make the book live up to your expectations.

Please let us know what you think about this book. Tell us what we did wrong, and what we did right. This isn't just marketing flannel: we really do huddle around the email to find out what you think. If you don't believe it, then send us a note. We'll answer, and we'll take whatever you say on board for future editions. The easiest way is to use email:

feedback@wrox.com

You can also find more details about Wrox Press on our web site. There, you'll find the code from our latest books, sneak previews of forthcoming titles, and information about the authors and editors. You can order Wrox titles directly from the site, or find out where your nearest local bookstore with Wrox titles is located.

Customer Support

If you find a mistake, please have a look at the errata page for this book on our web site first. Appendix L outlines how can you can submit an errata in much greater detail, if you are unsure. The full URL for the errata page is:

`http://www.wrox.com/Scripts/Errata.idc?Code=1266`

If you can't find an answer there, tell us about the problem and we'll do everything we can to answer promptly!

Just send us an email to **support@wrox.com**.

or fill in the form on our web site: **http://www.wrox.com/Contact.stm**

A History Lesson: The Evolution of the Client / Server Model

Before we begin this book, we're going to give a quick history lesson on how the present client/server model evolved. If you're familiar with this then please feel free to skip to Chapter 1, but if not, then we recommend that you read this as we reference the concepts discussed here throughout this book.

Senior management have long recognized that an effective Information Technology strategy is required to provide productivity improvements, access to new and enhanced revenue streams, and increased customer satisfaction. For many years, businesses have exploited IT in the following three dimensions:

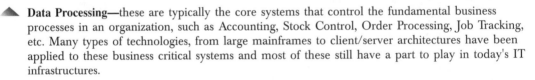 **Data Processing**—these are typically the core systems that control the fundamental business processes in an organization, such as Accounting, Stock Control, Order Processing, Job Tracking, etc. Many types of technologies, from large mainframes to client/server architectures have been applied to these business critical systems and most of these still have a part to play in today's IT infrastructures.

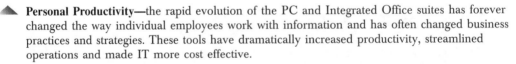 **Personal Productivity**—the rapid evolution of the PC and Integrated Office suites has forever changed the way individual employees work with information and has often changed business practices and strategies. These tools have dramatically increased productivity, streamlined operations and made IT more cost effective.

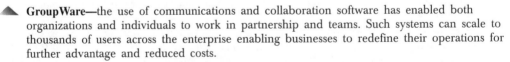 **GroupWare**—the use of communications and collaboration software has enabled both organizations and individuals to work in partnership and teams. Such systems can scale to thousands of users across the enterprise enabling businesses to redefine their operations for further advantage and reduced costs.

However, many of these benefits do not come without cost. Each of these dimensions typically has their own infrastructures and businesses have been faced with the complex problem of building 'information bridges' between the different systems and applications–building systems that span all dimensions has been historically difficult. Furthermore, having multiple different infrastructures results in additional costs for software, hardware, support and training.

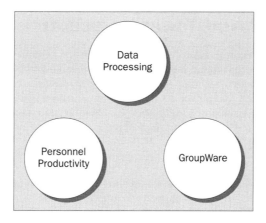

Over the years, a series of architectures have been devised in an attempt to integrate the various distributed environments within an organization. Forward-looking businesses now demanded that this integration must:

- ▲ automate the business processes to reduce costs

- ▲ provide easy access to all the organization's information (with appropriate security of course)

- ▲ provide new opportunities for marketing advantage

- ▲ remove barriers across the organization

- ▲ provide flexibility enabling the business to react quickly to change

We shall see that a distributed computing framework using client/server and Internet technologies provides the key to fulfilling these requirements.

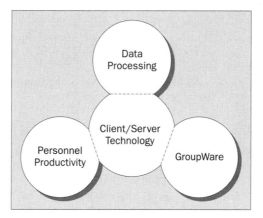

Client/Server: Moving Towards Decentralisation

Client/server computing is one of the most dominant paradigms of IT and has developed as the computer industry moved from a centralized shared logic based system to a network of workstations and servers. Client/server involves providing an application architecture that enables a computerized process to be broken up into two or more less complex tasks with a communication mechanism for these sub-processes to co-operate. The key notion of breaking up the problem is to provide designated layers of functionality that can be written and deployed across multiple machines in an optimized manner.

Typical examples of application layers are:

- ▲ **Presentation logic**—handling how the user interacts with the application; usually implemented by providing an easy to use graphical user interface (GUI)

- ▲ **Business logic**—handling the mechanics (or business rules) of the application

- ▲ **Data access logic**—handling the storage and retrieval of data; important that the integrity of the data is maintained

The development of separate layers needs careful design and an accurate definition of the distinct boundaries to ensure that logic within the different layers is not intertwined. Encapsulating the logic in this fashion ensures that future changes can be implemented with minimal impact on the other layers and enables both reusability and reliability.

Client/server is regarded as an enabling technology that can implement systems across an organization in a modular and flexible manner. It allows for the distribution of applications away from single machines located in isolated departments to an implementation across the enterprise. For example, it is now possible for one person in customer services to access all corporate systems–gone are the old days of annoying transfers between the different representatives in each department.

Many companies have rewritten old applications so they remain cost effective by taking advantage of the benefits offered by client/server environments. The investment in client/server systems has been accelerated by the rapid advances in hardware technology, the appearance of powerful client/server development tools and the decrease in prices of implementing these smaller faster platforms.

As we shall now see, there are many variations to client/server architectures. There is no greater decision, when implementing such a system, than which of these should be used.

Two-tier client/server

The first generation of client/server systems is an evolution of the file sharing applications discussed above. With these applications, the central file server is replaced with a specialized **relational database management system** (RDBMS). Such databases can offer high transaction rates at a fraction of the cost associated with mainframes. When the client (a workstation application typically using a GUI) needs to act upon data, it makes a request via the network to the database server–the database then processes the request and returns just the data appropriate the client's needs.

When compared to the file sharing application (which returned the complete file), this client/server architecture dramatically reduces network traffic. In addition, today's databases provide many features that enable the development of sophisticated multi-user applications–for example, allowing multiple users to access and update the same set of data safely.

Because the processing is split between distinct layers–the workstation and the database server–such architectures are referred to as being **two-tier client/server**.

Client - Centric Computing

The most simple and common implementation of two-tier systems is to place both the presentation and business logic on the client–making the architecture **fat client/thin server**. Database requests from the clients are typically implemented using the database query and programming language SQL. The database request is carried to the database server using a remote database transport protocol–however the programmer can be insulated from such complexities by means of database middleware such as Microsoft's **Open Database Connectivity** (ODBC).

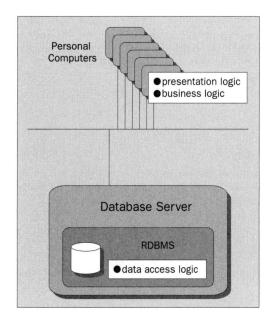

Such systems can be implemented quickly (and thus cheaply) using rapid application development (RAD) techniques and are great for small workgroup type environments. Many toolset vendors have implemented low-cost development products for creating such applications; examples include Microsoft's Visual Basic, Sybase's PowerBuilder and Borland's Delphi.

However, tightly binding the business logic into the fat client can cause some severe problems, including the following:

- the architecture imposes substantial processing on the client; this means workstations with powerful CPUs and large amounts of disk and memory may be required

- the database requests can generate large result sets; with a large user base this can cause severe network degradation

- each workstation session requires a separate database connection; this can drain resources on the database server–for example, Microsoft SQL Server requires 37K of memory for each user connection (and this is much lower than many other RDBMSs)

- deploying the business rules on the client can lead to high costs of deployment and support; if the logic changes, the effort in updating software on numerous workstations can be excessive

In practice, it is found that the performance of such two-tier architectures rapidly deteriorates as networking bottlenecks occur when an optimum number of users is exceeded. As a result, it does not provide the flexibility or scalability for large-scale applications deployed across the enterprise or Internet.

Database Server—Centric Computing

An alternative implementation is the **thin client/fat server** approach in which the business logic is pushed down to the database server using techniques such as stored procedures, triggers and constraints.

A stored procedure is business logic that is invoked by sending a request to the database server that includes the stored procedure name and any parameter values. As with the previous client-centric case, this request is transmitted using remote database transport protocols and can be implemented simply using database middleware (e.g. ODBC).

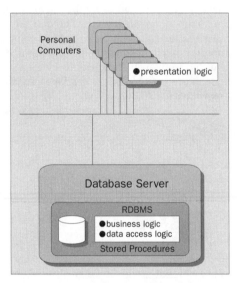

A constraint is a restriction placed on a data entered into a database. A trigger is a stored procedure that is invoked automatically on the Add/Update/Delete of items in a table. Both can be used to validate entered data and ensure referential integrity or consistency across multiple related tables in the database.

Stored procedures enable business rules to be defined and deployed across the enterprise. However, two-tier database applications can involve high development and maintenance costs since two toolsets are required–one for the client and another for the RDBMS stored procedure programming language. The proprietary nature of the RDBMS languages usually mean database vendor lock-in and reduces the possibilities for flexibility and portability–they also require specialized skills which can impact on costs.

Furthermore, as with the client-centric case, the need for the RDBMS to maintain a separate database session for each client workstation severely impacts central server resources. This makes the two-tier database server unsuitable for scaling across the enterprise or Internet. Large and complex two-tier solutions will nearly always result in failure and leave a lot of egg on the IT managers face!

Two-tier Transaction Processing

A **transaction** is a set of independent actions that are grouped together to form a 'single item of work'. The use of transactions with databases is important to ensure the following, which are often known by their acronym 'ACID':

- **Atomicity**—all updates to a database under a transaction must be either committed or get rolled back to their previous state

- **Consistency**—that the database is updated in the correct manner

- **Isolation**—uncommitted transactional results are not seen by other pending transactions

- **Durability**—once a transaction is committed, it will persist even if failures occur

Using transactions with two-tier client / server architectures is simple. Commands to be processed within a transaction must be bound by calls to functions with the RDBMS–typically these are called 'Begin Transaction' and 'Commit Transaction'. If a failure is detected, the database can be reverted to its original state by another call–typically 'RollBack Transaction' or 'Abort Transaction'. If a system crash occurs, outstanding transactions can be identified and the integrity of the database restored, when the system restarts.

Multi-tier client/server

From the problems we have encountered when discussing two-tier client server architectures, it should be no surprise to learn that this approach is now generally accepted as being a poor solution other than for small workgroup applications.

Drawing on the lessons learnt from the two-tier systems, an increase in application performance and a notable reduction in network traffic can be been achieved by implementing an alternative three-tier client/ server architecture.

Three-tier Computing

The improved architecture involves inserting an additional middle tier between a thin client and a thin server to create three tiers.

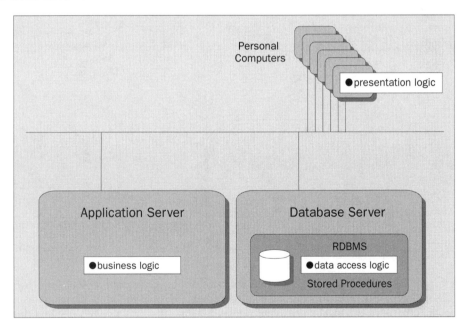

The client communicates with the middle tier using standard communications protocols such as TCP/IP. The middle tier interfaces with the backend RDBMS using standard database protocols or by means of database middleware (thus making the solution independent of the RDBMS). The middle tier provides basic message switching and contains the business rules of the application; it is responsible for:

- ▲ acting upon client requests, applying business logic and invoking database requests
- ▲ handling the database responses, applying further business logic and generating a client response

Furthermore, this approach does not require a separate database connection for each user; instead many users sessions can be funneled into just a few database connections and make considerable savings to the precious resources on the database server. This means that 1000 users simultaneously accessing an SQL Server system would not require a 37M (1000 x 37K) overhead of memory.

By creating three tiers, we have now completely partitioned the presentation logic, the business logic and the data access logic. One advantage is that any of the tiers can be enhanced or replaced without affecting the other tiers. For example, we can easily enhance a system to support new delivery channels. Let's consider a customers services based upon a three tier client/server solution. Now suppose that business reasons dictate that an interactive voice service is required so that a customer can access the system directly from their own telephone using speech recognition and text to speech play-back. Whereas a two-tier solution would need major surgery, the three-tier solution would only require the development of a new user interface (i.e. the voice handling) and could use the existing layers that contained the business logic and data access logic.

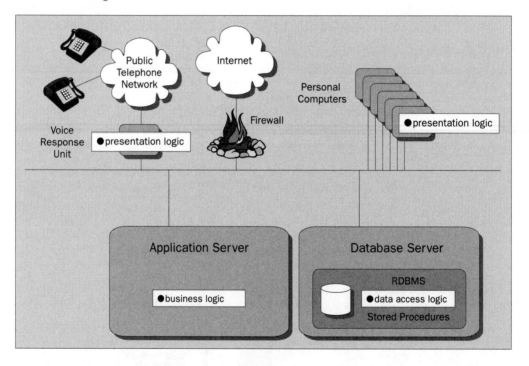

It is possible to provide both the business logic and database on the same platform—and in many cases this can provide an optimum solution. However, for it to be recognized as three-tier, distinct boundaries or interfaces must exist between the two layers to ensure the advantages of the architecture are achieved.

While two-tier systems still have their place for simple applications, three-tier client/server solutions are nowadays recognized as being the ideal choice for the enterprise since they are more maintainable and supportable, and are flexible to evolve to ever-changing business requirements.

Multi-tier Computing

A further extension to three-tier solutions is the multi-tier or, as it is sometimes called, **n-tier**. These solutions are the most flexible and scaleable and build on all the advantages of the three-tier architecture.

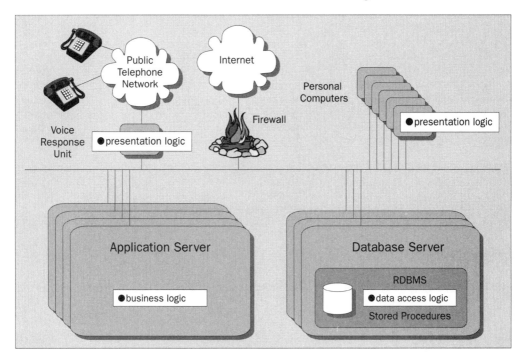

In a multi-tier client/server solution, the business logic is partitioned and distributed over several machines. As requirements change during a systems lifetime, this partitioning and deployment can be reviewed and amended with minimal impact. Furthermore, additional tiers are included to support multiple databases and other services such as message switches, legacy systems, data warehouses, communication channels and so on. By enabling the distribution of the workload over many CPUs (using either symmetric multiprocessing or massively parallel clustered technology), it is obvious how scalability–with the aim of 'no limits'–can be achieved. Sometimes the distribution of the logic over separate geographical regions can be considered to achieve optimum performance; for example, processes can be located at sites where they can limit the amount of slow network communications performed.

Drawbacks of Multi-Tier Client/Server – Where Next?

Unfortunately, three-tier and multi-tier client/server solutions are not trivial to implement. There are more tasks to undertake and complex issues to address than when building two-tier systems. A strong understanding of the multi-tier client/server development techniques and an appreciation of the potential pitfalls are vital. However with the innovation of the Internet, interest is being diverted away from client/server architectures. Demand for dynamic content on the web has transformed web computing into a new implementation of multi-tier computing, which offers solutions to many of the traditional problems of client/server. With HTML it's possible to develop an application in one language to be used on any operating system. However HTML is not without its own drawbacks, such as the static nature of the pages it creates. This is where IIS 4.0 and Active Server Pages come in...

A New Generation of Web Solutions

Without doubt, the World Wide Web is currently the major excitement in business, but the challenges that abound are also probably giving a lot of sleepless nights to many senior company personnel. The rapid changes in information processing and networking technology are compressing time–the time that is desperately needed for the business to adapt to the many opportunities offered by the new generation of Internet solutions.

While Microsoft joined the Internet game relatively late, they rapidly gained momentum and have since released an incredible range of innovative Internet products, all embracing various industry standards. These products have provided users with rich Internet experiences and organizations with the mechanisms to develop business critical Internet solutions. **Internet Information Server version 4.0 (IIS4)** is the latest release of Microsoft's leading commercial web server and is an essential component in their Internet strategy.

Fundamental to Web development with IIS4 is **Active Server Pages (ASP) version 2** and we shall see that this is a compelling technology for quickly building dynamic pages 'on the fly' by integrating the Web server with other software components, databases and legacy systems. In this book we shall study ASP in depth and see that not only is it extremely powerful, but also far simpler to implement than the traditional (and soon to become obsolete) methods used for extending web servers.

To begin, we'll discuss Microsoft's web solution that enables the next generation of business systems to exploit the convergence of computers and networking for business advantage:

- Microsoft's Internet strategy and development toolkit
- Developing solutions using software components and Microsoft's ActiveX technology for software component co-operation
- The powerful functionality available in Microsoft BackOffice which can be exploited in Web Solutions
- The architecture of IIS 4
- Where to get hold of IIS 4, PWS and ASP and how to install them

Internet Technologies: Centralized Computing With a Twist

Just as we were beginning to get used to the issues of developing multi-tier architectures, the new paradigm of **Internet Technologies** arrived to direct interest from the traditional client/server architectures.

The recent rapid expansion of the Internet has led many people to think of the Internet as a new invention. In fact, it has actually been around a number of years after starting off as a US Department of Defense project in the late 1960's. The DoD was concerned that their communications infrastructure could be wiped out by a single nuclear strike on their central systems. They decided to research into the development of a decentralized computer network such that each node is of equal importance and the resilience of the network is not affected by an unexpected malfunction or deletion of a node. Should a node be taken out of service, then the network automatically adjusts to use alternative routes to ensure that the information is delivered to its intended destination.

This network later opened up to research/education establishments and commercial organizations, and became known as the Internet, i.e. a collection of interconnected networks. It has adopted a suite of communications protocols called **TCP/IP** that enables a number of services to simultaneously operate on the network—common examples include File Transfer, Bulletin Boards and Electronic Mail. Since these early days, the growth of the Internet has been exponential with the increase in number of computer systems on the network. While no one is sure of the user base, recent estimates indicate that there are probably around 60 million Internet users worldwide.

The World Wide Web

Many people confuse the terms Internet and WWW or consider the two as equivalent but, in fact, the two are very distinct. It is important to recognize that the Web is not a network but an application that operates over networks using TCP/IP protocols. The Web architecture is based on a client/server model and uses a Web Browser (client) to retrieve documents from a Web Server which may be located on your own local network or half way around the world on the Internet.

Today's Web Browsers support the display of **multimedia** within the retrieved documents—including text, graphics, sound, video and **hyperlinks** in which items on the document are linked to other Web resources. By clicking on a hyperlink, the Web Browser automatically navigates to the target document. Furthermore— as we shall see soon—executable client logic can also be embedded in the Web page by means of scripting languages, Java applets and ActiveX Controls.

Web Directions

We shall now see how client/server underpins the evolving Web architectures.

First Generation Web Applications

The first generation of web browsers were only capable of handling text and simple multimedia such as images and sound. Information from a user could be captured by means of simple HTML forms and transmitted to the Web Server.

The functionality of Web servers could be extended by means of the **Common Gateway Interface (CGI)** which enabled the contents of a page to be generated dynamically by a program typically written in the C programming language or a scripting language such as Perl. This enabled the page contents to be personalized for the user and constructed from information stored in backend databases and applications. Unfortunately CGI programs are recognized as being a poor solution—this is because each CGI HTTP request will cause a new process to be spawned, and after the request has been handled, the process is killed. In a heavily hit site, the repetition of process creations and database opening imposes an excessive overhead on system resources.

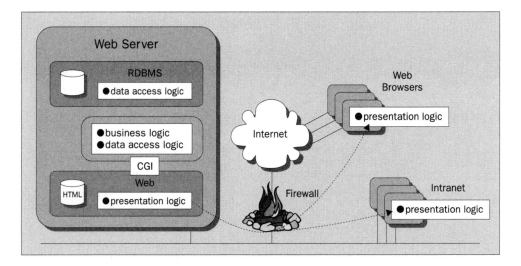

The first serious use of Web technology within business was for the implementation of intranets. Whereas the Internet is global and publicly open to all, an intranet is closed and has strict user access controls enforced or is hidden behind a firewall. Intranets take full advantage of the open Internet standards and the familiar Web browser software to provide employees, close partners and suppliers with access to corporate information and processes.

Because an intranet provides applications that are server-based, the corporate IT department does not have to deploy client-side software or configure user's machines (with the exception of the operating system and Web browser). With an intranet, users can navigate to an internal Web site and have seamless access to the application without any setup or configuration necessary. If any application is changed, perhaps due to a bug fix or enhancement, the IT department can just make updates on the server, instantly upgrading all desktops with the new functionality. This dynamic application distribution can produce considerable savings to organizations which have many hundreds of desktops distributed throughout the enterprise.

Organisations are using intranets to make it easier for their staff and partners to collaborate and locate/process information. The web browser provides a consistent operational approach and view of all company information irrespective of its format or the type of data source. To most companies, information is key and many have huge amounts of investment in existing data systems and electronic documents–mechanisms enabling the reuse of such existing information can have considerable impact on business performance.

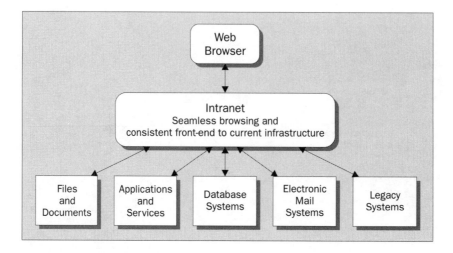

Second Generation Web Applications

These early Web pages are now often called **static pages** since they were fixed in an **.htm/.html** file and were rather dull looking, lacking the facilities for user interaction that we are accustomed to from typical PC software.

The next generation addressed these limitations by providing facilities for Active pages enabling user interaction and an architecture for distributed client/server processing. This was achieved by the new generation of web browser support for downloaded software components, scripting languages and mechanisms for the integration of existing applications.

Alternative mechanisms for developing server extensions were created which addressed the performance pitfalls of using the traditional CGI processes. For example, several Web Servers supported the Internet Server Application Programming Interface (ISAPI) that enabled the programmable logic to reside within the Web Server's process space—such logic would be loaded, once and for all, on first demand.

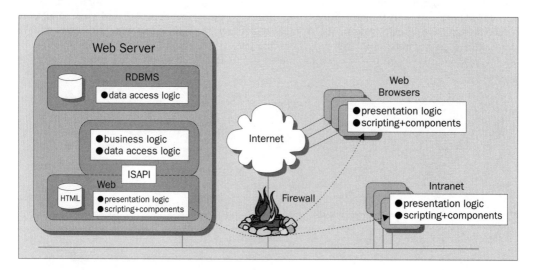

Software components embedded in Web pages could be written using high level languages such as Java, Visual C++ and Visual Basic. This enabled sophisticated functionality that was not previously possible with the relatively primitive HTML. Furthermore, such components can establish direct TCP/IP connections with other distributed components and avoid using the Web Server–thus enabling a true distributed computing environment.

The scripting languages, such as JavaScript and VBScript, that can be included within an HTML document can be viewed as the software glue that integrates the different entities within a Web page. Such items that need to interact include the HTML intrinsic controls, the objects exposed by the Web Browser and the embedded software components. This enables the client to be event driven; for example, a script can be used to detect an event being fired by one control (e.g. a button click) and as a result, invoke a method on another control (e.g. starting the playback of a video control).

Three Tiers for the Web

The demands for dynamic content has led Web computing to become a flexible and scalable implementation of multi-tier computing. And as we now fully appreciate, this results in more maintainable and supportable applications in which changes can be applied with minimal impact as business requirements change.

The client is the Web Browser and is responsible for handling the presentation logic that is defined by HTML documents and this may include script logic and software components.

The Web Server is located on the middle tier and is used to distribute the client logic and integrate the client sessions with the business logic using CGI/ISAPI. The business and data access logic should be modularized enabling it to be distributed over multiple machines.

Transaction Processing Monitors (TPM) can be used to assist with the various tasks of handling large complex database applications; this includes the coordination of transactions across multiple databases, resource sharing, dynamic load balancing and central management.

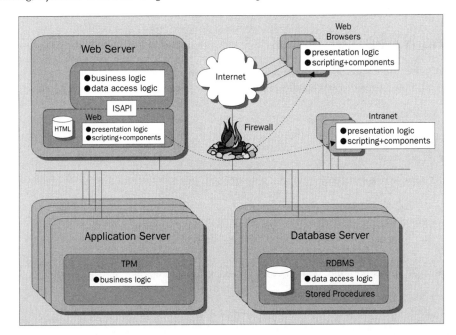

The great thing about this Web architecture is that it solves the several problems associated with traditional client/server systems. By restricting the client processing logic to HTML and a simple scripting language, it is possible to develop a single universal application that can be deployed across different types of platforms (e.g. Windows, Mac, various flavours of Unix, etc.). All client logic is centrally administered and dynamically deployed–this means that any bug fixes or enhancements will automatically be applied the next time the user accesses the application. This avoids a manual installation process on every desktop which can be very costly on a large population of users.

Microsoft and the Active Platform

When Microsoft eventually announced their Internet strategy, they declared that they would embrace Internet standards to deliver a comprehensive set of products and services that would seamlessly integrate desktops, LANs, legacy systems, GroupWare applications and the public Internet to provide a more effective computing environment for the corporate enterprise.

This strategy is to be Microsoft's trump card as they address their two recent major concerns.

Firstly, Microsoft's Windows domination of the desktop has been threatened recently by the concept of a low cost Network Computer (NC) in which any required executable logic is automatically downloaded as required in small chunks from a central application server. It is suggested that minimizing the complexity of both the NC hardware and the installed software will result in much lower administration costs.

In addition, it has been generally recognized that for Microsoft to continue its impressive growth curve, it needs to now conquer the server market. Until recent times, organizations had traditionally taken the best of breed approach for their server solutions, for example: Novell NetWare for a file & printer server, UNIX machines for communication gateways, Oracle or Sybase for relational databases, Lotus for Email & GroupWare, Sun or Netscape for the Internet, and so on. This has typically left a complex array of technologies within an organization which greatly increases the range of staff skills needed to support the enterprise and thus increases the running costs of the IT infrastructure.

Windows NT Server

The Microsoft answer for enterprise infrastructures is **Windows NT**, a single robust and high performance multipurpose network operating system that can act as the following:

- a file server
- a print server
- an application server
- a communication server
- a database server
- a workstation or client

Windows NT was first conceived by Bill Gates in 1988 when he elected that Microsoft would develop an operating system that was portable, secure, scalable, extensible, compatible and localizable.

These goals meant that Windows NT can be converted to run on a number of different hardware platforms and operate in a number of languages and character sets, all with minimal changes to the core code. In addition, it could provide support for symmetric multiprocessing (SMP) i.e. run on machines with multiple CPUs.

Windows NT extensions can be developed by writing applications that conform to a well-defined application programming interface (API) called **Win32**. In addition, support was provided for Win16/DOS, OS/2 and POSIX applications.

Strong levels of security were built into the core of Windows NT in order to meet and exceed a accepted industry security standard, the **C2** security guidelines required by the U.S. Department of Defense's security evaluation criteria. Windows NT security contrasts acutely with the thin and weak security layers that are often bolted onto the top of other operating systems. Compliance with the C2 security standard was originally only required for government organizations; however, many commercial organizations have demanding corporate security needs and recognize the value of the enhanced security that such systems offer.

To design Windows NT, Microsoft hired David Cutler who had worked at Digital Equipment Corporation on a number of operating systems that were hosted on the PDP-11 and VAX machines. After five years of development, Windows NT was released. It was delivered in two versions NT 3.1 and NT Advanced Server 3.1 with the 3.1 indicating the roots of its user interface (Windows 3.1) but that is where the similarities stopped.

In late 1994, Microsoft clarified the roles of the two versions by changing their names to give a clear indication of their purpose. Windows NT became Windows NT Workstation 3.51 and Windows NT Server 3.51. While being based on the same core code, the internal scheduling of tasks was optimized so that one functions best as a desktop operating system and the other as a robust enterprise level multi-purpose network operating system. In 1996, NT version 4.0 (Workstation and Server) was released and adopted the same acclaimed user interface from Windows 95. This included many new features including Distributed COM that we shall see later is a powerful technology for enabling distributed computing.

The ideal operating system initially dreamt by Bill Gates and David Cutler was code-named Cairo. It was originally intended as Windows NT 4.0, when the NT and Windows 95 operating systems were intended to become one. This however didn't happen and this nirvana has proven to be very difficult and tormenting and the ideas of Cairo have recently changed from being an actual product release to just a philosophy of what the ideal operating system should be.

	Windows NT Roadmap
1988 – conception	
1992 – Windows NT 3.1	
1994 – Windows NT 3.5 & 3.51	
Products renamed Server and Workstation	
Extensive bug fixes and optimisation	
1996 – Windows NT 4.0	
Windows 95 user interface	
Distributed COM	
1997 – Windows NT 4.0	
Enterprise edition	
Small Business edition	
1998 – Windows NT 5.0	
Next generation Directory Services	
Windows **D**istributed Inter**N**et **A**pplications **A**rchitecture (DNA)	
Clustering technology	
Plug and play device support	
Powerful distributed computing facilities	
21st **Century** – Cairo	

The Active Platform

The **Active Platform** is the name that Microsoft is calling the architecture that addresses their seamless integration strategy, plus the dynamic delivery of applications and rich content. This encompasses both the client (**Active Client**) and server (**Active Server**) technologies to achieve their goal. Its complete support for the ActiveX and Internet standards enables developers to integrate HTML, scripting, components, and transactions to build powerful, scalable and highly available applications that run across the enterprise. This architecture frees developers from the complexity of programming infrastructures to allow them to concentrate on delivering business solutions. The Active Platform is shown below:

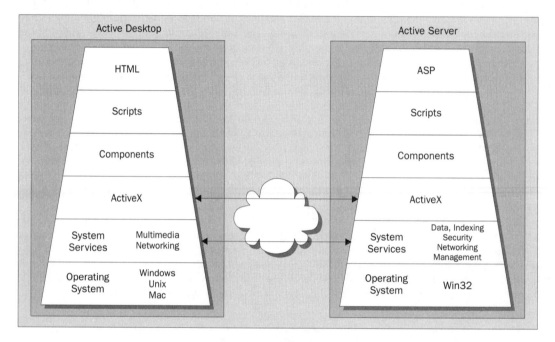

The foundation of the Active Server is Windows NT Server plus IIS4/ASP2 and the BackOffice, security, network and data components–ActiveX is the software glue that integrates these different items. This provides a great set of tools for the creation of distributed applications where different parts of a solution can reside on different machines to create the multi-tier client server architecture that–as we learned earlier–forms an optimum architectural solution.

Structuring the services into individual components means that the system is well organized, and easy to maintain and enhance. The use of Distributed COM allows the components to be deployed over multiple clients and servers.

The Active Client is Microsoft's operating system-independent client support for HTML and ActiveX technologies, and is a set of components that are included with Internet Explorer 4.0 but can easily be incorporated into any client application. Microsoft has stated that they will support the Active Client on Windows NT, Windows 95/98, Windows 3.1, Macintosh and UNIX.

ActiveX

ActiveX has to be one of the most misunderstood and ambiguously used expressions in the Internet technology arena. Many people get confused because ActiveX actually encompasses a number of technologies and is not just one thing.

When Microsoft released their first set of Internet tools in March 1996, they announced **ActiveX** technology–which in all truth was just a new marketing name for their existing **OLE** technology. ActiveX (or 3rd generation OLE technology) is a framework that allows software components to co-operate even if they have been written by different vendors, at different times using different tools, and if the objects are located in the same process, same machine or distributed over multiple machines. Put simply, ActiveX provides the *software plumbing* between software objects and insulates the component developer from such complexities.

ActiveX encompasses an ever-growing series of technologies, each of which defines the interfaces between the objects to implement the particular technology. For the Internet, examples include:

- ActiveX Scripting–enables script logic to be included in the downloaded Web page or used on the server to generate the page content
- ActiveX Controls–enables client components to be dynamically downloaded as needed and used within a Web page
- ActiveX Documents–enables the browser to support non HTML documents
- ActiveX Server Components–enables the Web Server to interface with other server software components

To most users, ActiveX is transparent and they just see the effects of these technologies–it is irrelevant to them whether it is ActiveX or 'black magic' that is operating behind the scenes. However, it is different for the developer, and we shall see later how the Internet ActiveX technologies provide a powerful environment for creating dynamic Web content.

The Need for Software Components

As discussed earlier, making effective use of information technology has become critical for companies to lower the cost of doing business and of obtaining competitive advantages. The software industry was (and, often, still is) drowning in complexity and failing to deliver many projects on time or to budget. Furthermore, organizations were finding this new generation of advanced software difficult and costly to support and make enhancements. Such code was frequently written in a monolithic fashion such that completely different bits of logic were intertwined and this made it risky to make changes–even what might appear to be a minor amendment could easily unknowingly cause severe repercussions to ripple throughout the system.

IT managers recognized that new software techniques were required to overcome the problems of complexity, increase the production rate of robust software and re-use existing proven code. **Component-based software** is the powerful new technique that is fundamental for building Microsoft Web solutions.

Component-based software is a development process that emulates the construction processes used by many more established industries. For example, the majority of today's car manufacturers build vehicles from hundreds of components parts supplied from a vast number of external companies. Each individual part would have been designed, manufactured and passed through quality checks as a separate isolated process undertaken by the part supplier. By removing many low level complexities from the car manufacturer, it enables them to concentrate on their core business—that is, designing and building cars that are more reliable and can be brought to market more quickly, thanks to a shorter development cycle.

In the early 1980s, IBM needed to quickly enter the microcomputer market to compete with powerful desktop personal computers such as Apple Macs. However, IBM did not have the experience at this low end of the computer spectrum to develop promptly from scratch its own proprietary product and so they decided to break from tradition by declaring that their new machine would adopt an open architecture. Their new 'IBM Personal Computer' would use 'off the shelf' components—such as the microprocessor, memory, hard disks, etc.—that were standard technology in the market place, and this enabled them to construct a competitive machine in a very short time period.

Unfortunately for IBM, many other vendors soon realized that they could follow suit and so numerous 'IBM PC Compatibles' become available—for example, Compaq released their first PC-compatible machine in 1983 and was a Fortune 500 company within three years.

Furthermore, a huge industry was swiftly generated to develop and manufacture these vital PC components. If you look in a PC today, you will see numerous components from a vast range of suppliers: perhaps a microprocessor from Intel, a hard disk from Western Digital, a graphics card from ATI, a CD-ROM Drive from Mitsumi, a modem from US Robotics, a sound card from Creative Labs, and a network card from 3Com. Such component suppliers are able to concentrate on their area of expertise and can develop both low cost and technologically advanced versions of their products.

This leaves the PC manufacturers the task of building machines by 'cherry picking' the most cost effective components available and integrating them together to create a computer system. Communication standards exist to ensure that the components can interact with each other or be exchanged for a similar component from an alternative vendor. The PC manufacturer can avoid the internal complexities and technologies of such components—all it needs to know is the external standards to which the component conforms.

The software industry is now at a point where it can build systems in a similar manner—that is by selecting a number of items of software, each of which performs a specific item of functionality and gluing them together to form a single integrated solution. Such components can be either developed by one's own staff or purchased from the numerous vendors who specialize in this market. The system designers and integration team must have confidence that the functionality of the component behaves as published but they do not need to worry about the complexities of the internal processing logic.

A software component can be defined as a combination of data and code which acts off that data, and together can be considered as a single unit. The data and code associated to the component defines everything that the component represents (state) and what is can do (behavior). These characteristics or *blueprint* is specified by the software component's definition. An **object**, of which there may be many, is a created instance of a component. ActiveX is the software that enables us to use components.

The software component's characteristics can be represented by the terms:

- **Properties**—these are the attributes of the object and represent the data that is encapsulated within it; sometimes properties can be accessed or changed from outside the object

- **Methods**—these are functions that can be performed internally, usually upon the encapsulated data; sometimes methods will take arguments

- **Events**—these are signals which are fired when a specific action or interesting state occurs; these signals are detected outside of the object

Properties and methods that operate together to perform a specific task are often grouped together and referred to as an object's **ingoing interface**. Events that occur are grouped in an object's **outgoing interface**. An object can support more than one interface.

Component Object Model

Underneath ActiveX is the generic **Component Object Model** (COM) which defines the binary interface between objects. The original specification of COM always allowed for co-operating objects to be located on different machines but this was not implemented until Windows NT 4.0 and was then called **Distributed COM** (DCOM). Because of this, in reality DCOM and COM are now the same animal. DCOM is layered on top of the DCE (Distributed Computing Environment) RPC (**Remote Procedure Call**) specifications. The next diagram shows how objects use COM/DCOM to co-operate even across process and machine boundaries.

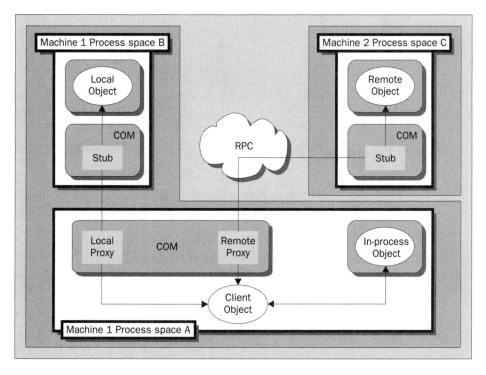

While ActiveX was not originally a committee-driven standard, it has since become an open market-driven technology that is fully published from the lowest level communications protocols to the highest level API functions. In addition, Microsoft has donated ownership of the technology's specifications to an open industry association, called **The Active Group**, (**http://www.activex.org/**) working under the auspices of The Open Group to promote the common adoption of the ActiveX core technologies. At the time of writing, it was not clear whether this independent stewardship would come to fruition or be blighted by the differing aims of the consortium members.

BackOffice 98

Providing additional value to Windows NT is a number of dynamic products and components which work together to provide a comprehensive Active Server solution. Most of these server components are grouped under the **BackOffice** portfolio of products.

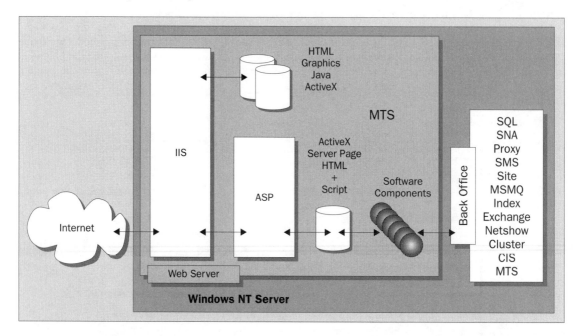

Transaction Server (MTS)	Provides facilities to share resources, manage transactions and administrate component deployment. Provides the infrastructure needed for multi-tier client server solutions.
Message Queue (MSMQ) Server	Provides assured delivery message switching. Handles network outages and heterogeneous networking architectures.
Internet Information Server (IIS)	Provides Internet services including WWW (Web-based information publishing and application delivery), FTP (file transfer), NNTP (newsgroups) and SMTP (mail).
Active Server Pages (ASP)	Provides server side scripting mechanism to implement extensions to the IIS Web services.
Index Server	Provides search engine facilities to identify documents which contain specific text
Exchange Server	Provides integrated system for email, personal and group scheduling, electronic forms, and groupware applications
SQL Server	Provides large-scale relational database management system designed specifically for distributed client-server computing.
Systems Management Server	Provides centralized management tool for software distribution, hardware/software inventory and diagnostic facilities.

SNA Server	Provides facilities for interfacing with legacy IBM and other host systems using SNA protocols.
Proxy Server	Provides secure Internet access from the corporate desktop. Provides caching of popular Web pages.
Commerce Server (formerly CIS)	Provides facilities for Internet communities, includes servers for membership, personalization, billing, white pages, chat, mail, newsgroups, user locator, content replication, information retrieval
Site Server	Provides web site environment for the deployment, implementation and analysis of electronic commerce sites.
NetShow Server	Provides streaming media services for Video and Audio broadcasting
Cluster Server	Provides clustering facilities allowing multiple NT nodes to combine to provide high availability and scalability.

This single infrastructure and the consistent approach found throughout Windows NT and these products considerably reduces training and support costs.

Internet Information Server

The foundation of Microsoft's NT Web strategy is **Internet Information Server (IIS)** which has been designed for ease of use, scalability, portability, security, and extensibility, and is recognized by many to be superior to any of the alternatives.

Today's Web sites have moved well beyond the delivery of static HTML files and users demand services which dynamically generate Web pages with content based on the identity of the user, the state of back end components/databases and any previously entered data. To enable such functionality a Web server must provide extensions allowing integration to software components, databases and legacy system. IIS supports the Common Gateway Interface (CGI), which is the industry standard that we discussed earlier, and is supported by nearly every Web server implementations. A CGI application is a program and is invoked when an HTTP request references the executable file name as part of the URL, for example:

```
http://www.wrox.com/_vti_bin/search.exe?info=Internet
```

The CGI specification details how such a program accesses any input information and generates the output HTML file. Recapping on what we learned earlier, the problem with CGI is that each invocation of a process is very resource intensive and a busy Web server could have severe performance problems.

An alternative approach adopted by IIS is the open **Internet Server Application Programming Interface** (**ISAPI**) standard. Microsoft have implemented their ISAPI extension as a Dynamic Link Library (DLL) which means it is loaded only once, on first demand, and then stays resident in the same process as the IIS Web Server. Although the development and internals of an ISAPI extension are different to those of a CGI program, the way they are referenced externally within a URL is similar, for example:

```
http://www.wrox.com/_isapi/search.dll?info=Internet
```

In addition to server extensions, the ISAPI specification also provides for Web Server **ISAPI filters**. These are used to intercept and optionally process every HTTP request. Filters can be used for such tasks as additional security measures, auditing, redirecting requests and so on. However, because they act on every message they should be used sparingly to avoid severe performance problems. The simplest method of developing ISAPI extensions and filters is to use the ISAPI Wizard supplied with Microsoft's Visual C++. This Wizard takes the developer through a number of dialogs to establish the options required and then generates the skeleton of an appropriate ISAPI application with inserted comments where the developer's code needs to be added. CGI and ISAPI are shown below:

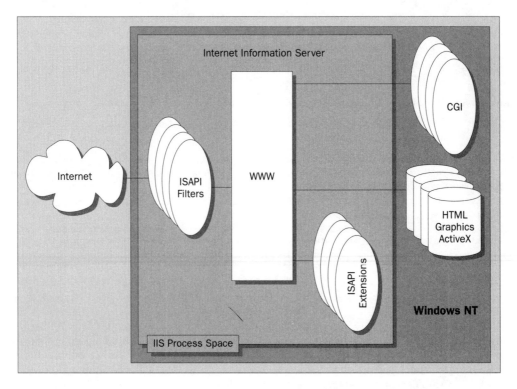

Active Server Pages

Active Server Pages (ASP) is an ISAPI extension which builds on top of the ISAPI infrastructure to provide a server-side application framework, making it even easier to build dynamic Web applications.

An ASP document can contain both HTML syntax and server-side script logic. When the Web Server receives an HTTP request for the ASP document, a 'virtual' output HTML file is generated (in memory) for the response using a combination of both the HTML static information plus any HTML that is generated by the scripting. The URL reference for an ASP page is similar to those for ISAPI and CGI, for example:

```
http://www.wrox.com/_asp/search.asp?info=Internet
```

ASP enables the scripting logic to interface to a number of ASP intrinsic objects, which automatically handle many of the menial tasks, and so simplifies the amount of development required. These objects provide ASP with the concept of a user session and allow variables to persist across Web pages, until either the session is programmatically abandoned or the Web browser is closed. Prior to ASP, the handling of user context across multiple HTTP requests was a complex process.

In addition, the real power of ASP scripting comes from its ability to interface with external COM compliant software components, including those supplied with ASP, those provided by Windows NT and other BackOffice products, and those developed by ourselves and other independent software vendors. For example, ASP is supplied with **ActiveX Data Objects (ADO)** that provides a high performance interface to databases that are **Open Database Connectivity (ODBC)** or **OLE DB** compliant.

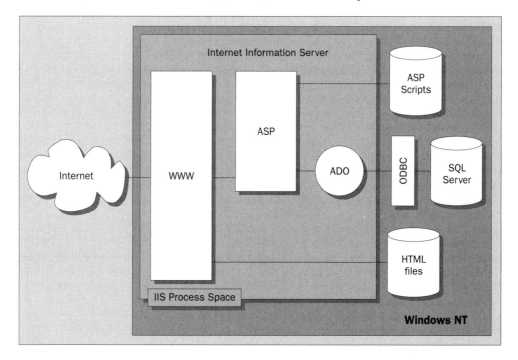

Chili!Soft Inc. (**http://www.chilisoft.net**/) have implemented an ASP scripting engine for many non-Microsoft Web Servers and they claim that this is functionally equivalent to the Microsoft implementation. This means that ASP does not force vendor lock-in and your Web applications can now be freely ported to other platforms without code change. The power and ease of use provided by ASP, along with this portability, will surely mean that ASP will quickly become the de facto Web Server programming environment.

Transaction Server

Microsoft Transaction Server (MTS) can be viewed as an object broker and uses COM to map client applications to services resident in software components (objects). It is designed to reduce the time and complexity in the development of multi-tier applications by supplying much of the infrastructure to provide a robust, scalable, high performance and distributed architecture. Future versions of MTS will work with the Cluster Server technologies to provide dynamic load balancing, scalability and high availability.

MTS insulates the developer from many of the traditional complexities by automatically handling all threading issues, the sharing of resources and the handling of transaction context across objects. This means that a developer just needs to concentrate on developing the 'business logic' as the underlying plumbing and infrastructure is handled for them.

Developing code to handle transactions is a difficult pastime and the complexity of the task grows as the number of transactions increases and becomes distributed over multiple platforms. Writing an application with COM compliant software components and installing them in the MTS environment eliminates the need to develop your own transaction processing logic. MTS monitors the transactions for any failure and if such a problem occurs, it will automatically handle the rollback. With a single component operating on a single database this would be a simple task to deal with, but MTS comes into its own when operating with a multi-tier client server application that spans multiple distributed databases.

MTS provides 'just in time' activation and 'as soon as possible' deactivation to improve performance and scalability. With standard COM, an object is released only when its reference count goes to zero. However, with MTS, clients can hold on to references to objects but the objects become 'deactivated' for the period of time when its services are not required.

Establishing database connections is a notoriously expensive operation and in large systems can result in unacceptably poor performance levels. Another advantage of MTS is that it recycles ODBC database connections in a similar fashion to the way it recycles objects. When an ODBC database connection is no longer required, MTS just deactivates the connection rather than closing the connection. When a component requires an ODBC database connection, MTS will first try to assign a connection that it has in its pool of deactivated connections. A new ODBC database connection is only established it the pool of available connections is empty.

One of the biggest changes introduced by IIS4 is the tight integration with MTS version 2. Previously, with IIS3 and ASP1, a server side script could communicate with an external component resident within an MTS environment located in another process. Now IIS4 has been totally redesigned and built as an MTS application—as a result, IIS4, ASP2, the MTS environment and the MTS software components can all be in the same process and can combine to deliver mission critical Web applications for the enterprise as shown below. In addition, Web applications can be partitioned and isolated from the main Web server process—this ensures that if a component misbehaves and causes the process to crash it will not affect the main Web service.

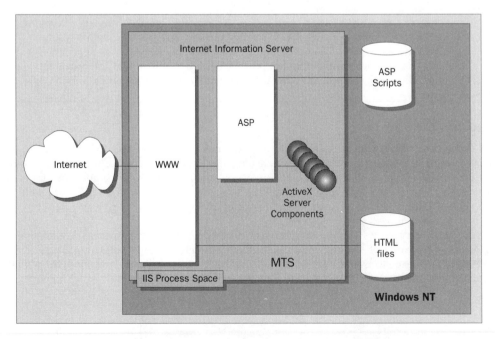

SQL Server

A major requirement for today's Internet is a secure, reliable, and scalable place to store information. **Microsoft SQL Server** provides a high-performance relational database management system specifically designed for distributed client server computing.

A Web application can easily retrieve and store information in a SQL Server database by using ASP scripting to interface with the ADO component. Alternatively, SQL server provides a Web Assistant Wizard which allows a database administrator to define a query that is automatically merged into an HTML document either on a scheduled basis or when the contents of the database changes.

Index Server

An important aspect of Internet technology is the means to quickly search through large quantities of information and identify relevant resources. **Microsoft Index Server** provides high performance search facilities using a sophisticated query language.

It provides facilities to perform full text searches on HTML and Microsoft Office (MS Word, MS Excel, and MS PowerPoint) documents–extensions also allow software vendors to provide search support for their own proprietary file formats. This means that an organization does not have to convert existing office documents to HTML in order to provide search facilities.

NetShow Server

Microsoft NetShow provides broadcasting facilities for live and prerecorded audio, illustrated audio and video over the Internet or corporate enterprise. It integrates with IIS to provide an efficient, reliable and scalable solution

It uses the new **Multicasting** and **Streaming** technologies to reduce bandwidth. Multicasting is a new open mechanism for the transmission of identical information, such as live events, to multiple users simultaneously and contrasts with the traditional TCP/IP unicasting where the server must transmit a separate copy to each user. Streaming allows users to see or hear the broadcast as soon as it arrives, as opposed to the traditional multimedia mechanisms where the entire file has to be transferred before the information can be used.

NetShow comes with a number of authoring and production tools to create high impact broadcast content.

Message Queue Server

Microsoft Message Queue Server (MSMQ) is a store-and-forward assured delivery message service that enables applications to communicate across heterogeneous networks and systems that maybe have unreliable communication links. This is an ideal solution when we need to be confident that a message will be eventually delivered but do not care when this happens or if we do not need an acknowledgement in real time.

Applications pass messages to MSMQ, which first safe stores the message contents in a '**queue**' to ensure the message is never lost and then attempts to deliver the message. MSMQ provides guaranteed message delivery, efficient routing, security, and priority-based messaging.

The NT 4 Option Pack

At the time of writing, IIS4 (and Personal Web Server 4.0) are supplied as part of the Windows NT 4.0 Options Pack. At a future date, it will be supplied as a base component of the Windows NT 5.0 operating system. It is assumed that the reader is familiar with the installation of IIS4 and the administration of Windows NT, and can follow the installation instructions that are supplied by Microsoft–we don't intend to duplicate this information here. We shall touch on the configuration aspects of an IIS4 Web site, but only to a level that introduces any concepts that we require later in the book–again, the definitive resource for administration topics is that supplied by Microsoft. But first we'll distinguish between the versions of NT 4 Option pack you can get for NT Server 4.0 and the one you can get for Windows 95.

Where do I find IIS 4.0, Personal Web Server 4.0 and Active Server Pages?

When Microsoft first released Active Server Pages, it was available as part of IIS 3.0, but also as a separate component available as a free download from their web site. It didn't come as part of Personal Web Server for Windows 95 and had to be downloaded separately. To make matters more complicated it was removed from the web site at a later point. Fortunately matters are much simplified now. All you need is a copy of the NT 4.0 Option Pack for your requisite platform which is freely downloadable from Microsoft at

```
http://www.microsoft.com/ntserver/guide/whatisntop.asp
```

There are two versions of the NT 4.0 Option Pack, one for NT 4.0 and one for Windows 95. IIS 4.0 is the web server that comes with version of the Option Pack for NT Server 4.0, while Personal Web Server 4.0 is included instead in the NT 4.0 Option Pack for Windows 95. Both of them include Active Server Pages 2.0 as standard, so there'll be no need to download anything extra. However, while ASP can run on Personal Web Server, this setup isn't optimal and shouldn't be used for most non-development work. In addition you'll also find parts of Transaction Server and Message Queue Server are also included within the NT 4.0 Option Pack.

An Overview of IIS4

IIS4 builds on the success of its predecessor to provide organizations with a powerful platform for the publishing of information and the delivery of business applications over both the Internet and the corporate intranet. The key objective of this latest version is to supply an integrated platform offering comprehensive Web services, and easy to develop and reliable Application Services.

We'll take a look at some of the new features provided by IIS4 now.

Integrated Platform

IIS4 provides the highest levels of integration with the Windows NT Server operating system and many Microsoft server products including Transaction Server, Message Queue Server, Index Server, Certificate Server and Cluster Server.

In addition, IIS4 easily integrates with the Microsoft BackOffice portfolio to leverage:

- the data storage facilities of SQL Server
- the web site life cycle management facilities of Site Server
- the messaging and groupware facilities of Exchange
- the host connectivity facilities of SNA Server

We have already spent some time discussing distributed computing and component-based systems, and seen how IIS4 can use COM to communicate with business functions dispersed across the enterprise. Suffice to say here that the reader should now appreciate that COM is fundamental to building IIS4 Web solutions.

Development

IIS4 enables the rapid application development of scalable web solutions. ASP combines HTML and script logic to enable the generation of dynamic page content and this overcomes the complexities and performance problems encountered with the traditional CGI mechanisms. Script logic can be created using VBScript, ECMAScript (JavaScript) or one of the alternative third party scripting languages, and can be easily integrated with other software components—such components can be written in any language provided that what they generate is COM compliant. The Microsoft Script Debugger enables the debugging of script logic on both the server (IIS4/ASP) and the client (IE4).

IIS4 is tightly integrated with Microsoft Transaction Server—this means that the developer of the software components that provide services to ASP only needs to concentrate on the implementation of the business rules. MTS will insulate the developer from complex infrastructure problems such as multi-threading, recycling objects, pooling database connections and transactions.

Reliability

Crash protection from misbehaving components is achieved by running Web applications as separate processes—this is called **process isolation**. Furthermore, should an application crash then it will automatically be restarted upon the next request.

IIS4 provides **Transactional Active Server Pages** which enables the logic within scripts and components to be bounded such that either all database actions are committed together or the database is reverted back to its original state. This is vital in business applications where the integrity of the database is critical. A well-used example of this is the transfer of money from one bank account to another bank account. This involves two actions: a) subtracting money from the first account and b) adding the money to the second account—with this operation it is critical that both actions are completed successfully, since otherwise money is either lost or created.

Administration

IIS4 provides Web administrators with several choices for handling management tasks. These tools can be used to administer the Web server or an individual Web site.

The mechanisms available are:

- the Windows based Internet Service Manager known as Microsoft Management Console (MMC)
- the Web-based Internet Service Manager (HTML)
- developing custom written scripts/applications to use COM to interface to an exposed set of objects called the IIS Administration Objects (IISAO)

Because IIS4 is tightly integrated with Windows NT, administrators can use several of the existing NT administration tools. These include:

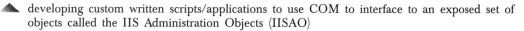 Event Viewer—for monitoring system log messages generated by the Web server

▲ User Manager for Domains–for administering users / user groups where authentication by the Web server is required

▲ Performance Monitor–for monitoring various performance counters that are manipulated by the Web server

▲ SNMP (Simple Network Management Protocol) Monitor–for monitoring the status counters controlled by the Web server

IIS4 provides great flexibility for logging information on Web site access for auditing purposes. It supports the new industry standard from the W³C called Extended Logging. This allows the selection/de-selection of 19 different items for recording on each Web site hit. Using COM, developers can create their own customized logging components for specialized requirements.

Security

The starting point for strong Internet security is the operating system of any machine connected to it. Fortunately, for organizations using IIS4, strong levels of security have been built into Windows NT in order to meet and exceed certifiable security standards, i.e. the **C2 Security Guidelines** required by the U.S. Department of Defense's evaluation criteria. Windows NT security contrasts sharply with the weak security layers bolted on to the top of certain other operating systems.

IIS4 allows web files, scripts and executables to be made available for secured access to an anonymous user or for restricted access by particular users and user groups. IIS4 is tightly integrated with the NT security subsystem and provides a single infrastructure for managing users accounts and access permissions to system resources. This contrasts to many other Web servers that are divorced from the operating system and this means the Web administrator has the additional hassle of maintaining a second database of users/ user groups.

IIS4 expands on the NT security model by including the **Microsoft Certificate Server** to provide facilities for the management and issuing of **X.509 digital certificates**–these provide a mechanism for obtaining higher levels of user authentication.

To protect confidential data that is sent over the network, IIS4 supports the industry standard **Secured Sockets Layer (SSL)** to encrypted the transferred data. SSL also prevents message tampering and enables the interrogation of the information stored in the remote party's digital certificate.

We shall discuss the implementation of secure Web solutions using access controls, SSL and digital certificates in Chapter 14.

Data Access, Indexing & Searching

Microsoft uses **ActiveX Data Objects (ADO)**–a fast, productive, and easy-to-use programmatic interface to a variety of data sources including both structured and unstructured data formats. ADO enables Web based data driven dynamic applications to be quickly developed using ASP.

IIS4 utilizes the **Microsoft Index Server** to index the contents and properties of documents available on a Web site. The Web site can provide a Search page that allows a user to specify search parameters–these values can then be submitted to Index Server for analysis and for the generation of a results page to identify any documents which match the criteria. Index server can also operate upon various non-HTML documents including those formats generated by the Microsoft Office family of products.

> The Universal Data Access mechanisms are key to business solutions using Microsoft Web technologies–we shall discuss ASP solutions using ADO in chapters 7 and 8.

Multiple Web Sites

IIS4 was designed to support various site scenarios–from single Web sites to large Web farms hosted by an Internet Service Provider. Though previous versions of IIS had support for multiple Web sites, IIS4 builds on this to offer new and enhanced functionality. In particular many options can now be set on a per Web site basis; for example, the bandwidth available can be restricted (or throttled) to each site to ensure the total available bandwidth is evenly distributed–this is called **bandwidth throttling**.

One of the problems of hosting multiple Web sites with IIS3 is that each site required a unique IP address. This problem is resolved by IIS4 using HTTP 1.1, which allows multiple Web sites to use the same IP address; the **host name** that is specified in the URL is included in the HTTP request and used by the server to map on to the correct Web site. Furthermore, IIS4 provides a solution for older Web browsers that are not compliant with HTTP 1.1–this involves the use of cookies and a menu for the first time visit.

IIS4 allows separate Web site administrators to be defined for each individual site. This means that the ISP does not get burdened down with simple administration tasks for all of the sites that they are hosting, and the web site owners do not have to rely on the ISP for any changes to be made.

Web site administrators can change those options that do not affect other Web sites or the network. This includes:

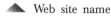 access permissions

▲ enable/disable logging

▲ change the default document

▲ specify a footer to be appended on every page

▲ content expiration

▲ content ratings

They cannot change:

▲ Web site name

▲ anonymous user name/password

▲ throttle bandwidth

▲ network configuration

▲ user accounts

Content Management

Windows NT Server includes a license for **Microsoft FrontPage**; which is a tool designed for Web site developers without programming experience. This includes:

- the FrontPage Explorer which is a Web site management tool
- the FrontPage Editor which is WYSIWYG HTML page creation editor that avoids the need for the user to understand HTML tags

FrontPage 98 includes a gallery of great looking themes and a set of wizards and templates for creating skeleton sites.

IIS4 ships with **Site Server Express**, which provides reduced functionality versions of some of the tools supplied with the BackOffice product Site Server.

The tools provided by Site Server Express includes:

- **Usage Analysis**–produces a number of predefined reports of site usage by analyzing the Web log files and assisting the identification of usage patterns
- **Content Analysis**–produces a number of predefined reports for managing Web site content and highlighting problem; also includes facilities for searching the site content for particular items.
- **Web Publishing Wizard**–a client side utility for assisting the process of updating web site content
- **Posting Acceptor**–allows IIS4 to receive Web content updates through an HTTP connection

Web site administrators can configure the content ratings using a system such as the **PICS**-based (Platform for Internet Content Selection) ratings developed by the Recreational Software Advisory Council (RSAC). This rates site content according to various levels of offensive language, sex, nudity and violence. Web browsers such as Internet Explorer 4.0 can be configured to automatically reject unacceptable content.

Internet Standards

IIS4 uses the new **HTTP 1.1** protocol standards to provide additional functionality and higher levels of performance. IIS4 will automatically fall back to an earlier version of HTTP should communication be received from an older, non HTTP 1.1 compliant, Web browser.

Specifically, HTTP 1.1 provides a performance boost, estimated as being somewhere between 50% to 100% faster than the previous HTTP 1.0, through:

- **pipelining**–allowing Web browsers to initiate multiple requests before receiving a response
- **persistent connections**–allowing a Web browser to remain connected for a period of time thus reducing the need for expensive reconnections
- **chunked transfers**–allowing responses to be broken up and sent in smaller chunks, each of which includes the chunk size

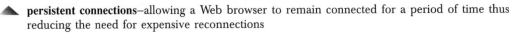

IIS4 can act as an email client allowing a Web application to send and receive messages. For example, in an e-commerce application, the stock manager could be emailed when a stock levels drop below the reorder levels. IIS4 supports email using the **SMTP (Simple Mail Transport Protocol)**.

IIS4 can also support local discussion groups using the **NNTP (Network News Transport Protocol).** These discussions can be read using any standard newsreader such as **Microsoft Outlook Express**.

Support is included for the **File Transfer Protocol (FTP)** which is an industry standard for the transferring files from one system to another.

IIS4 ships with Microsoft's **Java VM 1.1** that provides JDK 1.1 compatibility and allows for the execution of server side Java components. Furthermore, these components can be executed within the MTS environment for additional levels of reliability and scalability.

Administering IIS4

We shall now take a look at the mechanisms for managing the IIS4 Web server and its applications. IIS4 offers us the choice of using a Windows based administration utility, a Web based application or of developing our own applications/scripts to interface to the IIS Administration Objects via COM.

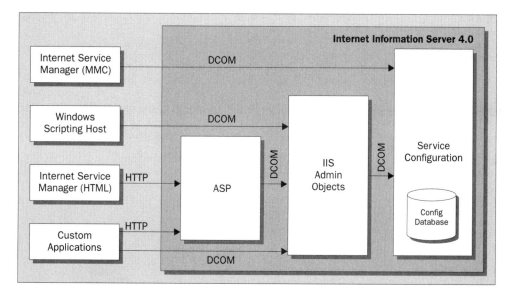

The configuration information for IIS4 is stored in a structured file called the **metabase**. This is different to IIS3, which stored the complete Web server configuration in the Windows Registry.

Windows-based Administration and the Microsoft Management Console

The **Microsoft Management Console (MMC)** provides a single application in which you can perform administration tasks for your enterprise. It allows the different management tools and system status views to be integrated into a single common management console. Senior administrators can use the MMC to provide a console to less experienced staff that only supports certain non-critical tasks.

It is the intention that all Windows NT and BackOffice administration tasks will eventually be controlled from within the MMC. In addition, other software vendors can easily develop their own administration programs to reside within this environment—such programs can interface with the MMC container using COM.

In fact MMC is not actually responsible for handling any of the administration logic. Instead it simply acts as a container for various administration programs that perform these tasks–these programs are called **snap-ins**. For example, the **Internet Service Manager**, which is used to administer IIS4, is implemented as a snap-in.

Each console in the MMC contains two panes. The left side pane is called the **scope pane** and the right side pane is called the **results pane**. The scope pane shows the hierarchy of all items that can be managed–these items are collectively known as the **namespace**. Each item in the namespace can be selected and the corresponding information in an appropriate format is then displayed in the results pane. Items in either pane can be administered using functions accessed from the toolbars, the main menu and the right click context menu.

Once a snap-in has been installed on a machine, it can be included in the namespace by means of the Console|Add/Remove Snap-in menu option. When a snap-in is added to the console, it adds items to the namespace. We can also customize the namespace by adding folders, ActiveX controls and Web links. The amended namespace definition can be saved as a management console file, which has a `.MSC` suffix–this enables a console with the customized options to be easily invoked.

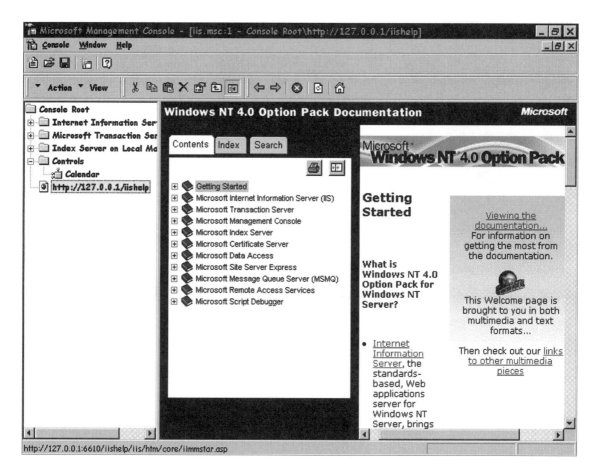

Web-based Administration

As an alternative to the MMC, IIS4 can be administered using an HTML version of the Internet Service Manager via a Web browser. This has the advantage the administration tasks can be handled remotely and so is invaluable for ISPs hosting sites for external organizations.

The Web based Internet Service Manager has a dual-screen layout displaying a context sensitive menu list of options on the left-hand side of the browser and a tree view/administration form on the right-hand side of the browser. The tree view shows the entities that can be administered. This is accomplished by clicking on an item—which then appears highlighted—and then by selecting a menu option the corresponding action is invoked. By selecting the properties option, the list of menu options is updated and an administration form is displayed on the right-hand side of the browser.

IIS Administration Objects

The IIS Administration Objects (IISAO) exposes an interface allowing IIS4 to be administered from external software components using COM. This allows developers to create their own customized administration programs either using ASP or a Windows based application. In addition, using the **Windows Scripting Host** allows command line invoked scripts to be written to automate the standard administration tasks.

The Windows Scripting Host is a low memory scripting host that conforms to the ActiveX Scripting architecture. This enables IIS4 administration scripts to be written in any ActiveX script language and as we know this includes VBScript, ECMAScript plus a number of other languages developed by third parties.

Getting Started with IIS4

Like all Web servers, IIS4 is responsible for handling an HTTP request, mapping the specified URL on to the server's file system and obtaining the data to be sent back in the HTTP response. The URL may specify the name of a file (e.g. HTML, Graphics, Java Class, etc.) in which case the file is used in the response as is. Alternatively, the URL may reference executable logic to be invoked– from, for example, an ASP page, an ISAPI extension or a CGI process–and this enables response data to be generated 'dynamically'.

We shall now see how to configure IIS4 to ensure the HTTP requests are mapped to the correct file directories. Files can only be exposed to remote Web browsers via HTTP if they appear in the directories that have been configured for Web access. There are three different types of directories:

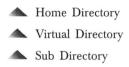 Home Directory

Virtual Directory

Sub Directory

Home Directory

An HTTP URL that contains just the domain name or an IP address actually references a document identified as the **default document**, which is located in a directory called the **home directory**. For example, the URL

    http://www.hornet.wrox.com/

would map to the default document located in the home directory on the server **www.hornet.wrox.com**. The default document is usually **default.htm** or **default.asp**, and typically provides the Web site's home page or index page.

A Web site administrator must map the home directory onto a physical file directory. For example:

    http://www.hornet.wrox.com/ might map onto c:\inetpub\wwwroot

Virtual Directory

To allow access to information that is not in the hierarchy beneath the home directory, a **virtual directory** must be configured. This is an alias that forms part of the URL and maps on to another physical file directory. For example, the URL

http://www.hornet.wrox.com/ecomm might map onto **d:\commerce server**

and since no document is specified, the browser would again access the default document. Virtual directories do not give any clues to the user of the internal physical location of the files and directories.

Sub Directory

A **subdirectory** in a URL maps onto the corresponding item in the physical file structure. Expanding on the above example, the URL

http://www.hornet.wrox.com/ecomm/stores might map onto **d:\commerce server\stores**

In contrast to previous versions of IIS, the latest version allows sub directories to have different properties to their parent directory. For example, a home directory only allowing read access could have a sub-directory called **scripts** with contents being allocated execute permissions. This greatly simplifies the configuration—in many IIS3 configurations it was common to see numerous virtual directories listed with no purpose other than to allow such attributes to be assigned.

Creating Directories

Using the MMC, we can add a new site and configure the home directory. This is done by selecting the server, right clicking and choosing the Create New | Web Site menu option, which invokes the New Web Site Wizard. The wizard dialogs request:

- the web site description
- the TCP/IP address/port number
- the physical path name for the home directory
- the access permissions

In a similar manner, we can use the MMC to configure a virtual root. This is done by selecting the Web site/directory, right clicking and choosing the Create New | Virtual Directory menu option–this invokes the New Virtual Directory Wizard. The wizard dialogs request:

- the virtual directory alias
- the physical path name for the home directory
- the access permissions

Note that sub directories do not need to be defined in the IIS4 configuration. If we create a sub directory within the physical directory it will appear in the MMC namespace. Notice in the following screen dump the different icons for a sub directory (scripts) and a virtual directory (ecomm).

Web Applications

As we have already discussed, one of the biggest improvements that IIS4 offers over its predecessors is that it offers crash protection by enabling Web applications to be configured to run in their own process space.

A **Web Application** is defined as a collection of HTML pages, server extensions (such as ASP and ISAPI) and ActiveX server components.

Application Namespace

An application is defined by flagging a directory to be the **application start point**. The application scope will then include all items within the directory and the sub directories below, within the exception of those that are included in another application. The following diagram clarifies this:

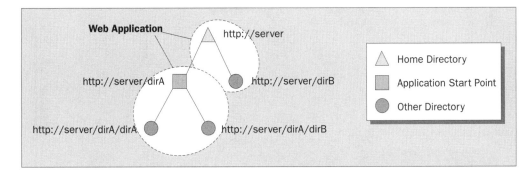

We can use MMC to create the application. This is done by selecting the directory start point, right clicking and choosing the Properties menu option. This invokes the properties dialog which consists of several sheets. Depending on the type of directory, select one of the following tabs: Home Directory, Virtual Directory or Directory. In this screenshot we've chosen to create a virtual directory.

Finally, to create the application, select the Create button in the Application Settings frame.
The following screen dump shows an application created on the ecomm virtual directory in our previous example—notice that there is a different virtual directory icon to highlight that this is an application start point.

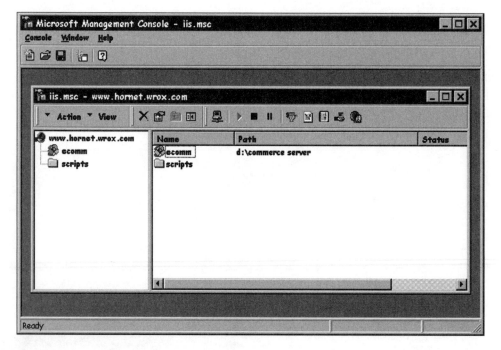

Application Process Isolation

Once an application has been created, we can optionally specify that the application must run in a separate memory space to provide the crash protection that we have already discussed.

This is done by selecting the Run in separate memory space checkbox that is located in the Application Settings frame on the Directories properties sheet.

The Web Application Manager

The goal of process isolation is achieved thanks to a subsystem called the **Web Application Manager (WAM)**. A WAM can optionally run in its own memory space and be separate from the Web server. Each application namespace has its own WAM and is responsible for loading the ISAPI Extensions used by the application. Since ASP is built on ISAPI technology, the WAM also handles any ASP logic.

A WAM is an in-process COM object that is shipped as the file **WAM.DLL**. The Web Server executable **INETINFO.EXE** normally hosts the WAMs. However, the WAMs that are responsible for applications that are process isolated are hosted in a surrogate process created by the executable **MTX.EXE**.

Each instance of a WAM is registered with Transaction Server. We can see this in the following MMC screen dump, which shows the www.hornet.wrox.com/ecomm virtual root that we configured for process isolation, residing in the IIS-{www.hornet.wrox.com//Root/ecomm} package within the MTS configuration. All WAMs that are not process isolated are configured in the default IIS In-Process Applications package.

> Don't worry yet about the details of MTS configuration—we shall be addressing this in detail later. Just appreciate that a WAM benefits from the advantages provided by MTS.

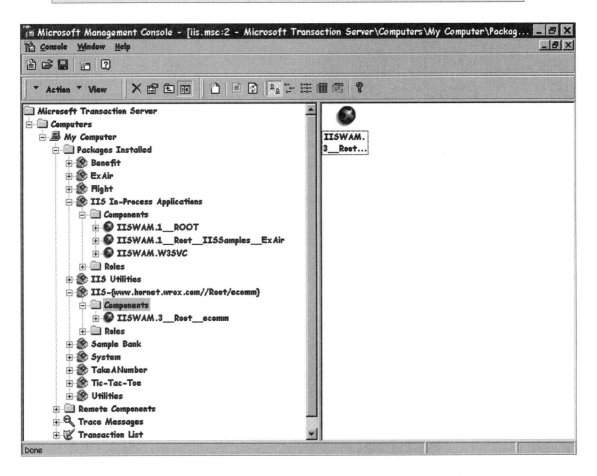

When IIS4 receives an HTTP request for a static file—such as an HTML file or graphics file—the Web Service retrieves the file and generates the HTTP response containing the file contents. Otherwise the request must be for a server extension. If the HTTP request is for a CGI extension, the appropriate executable is invoked and this is responsible for dynamically generating the HTTP response. Alternatively, if the HTTP request requires the use of an ISAPI extension, IIS4 determines from the URL the associated application namespace and checks to see if the WAM for that application has already been created. If the WAM does not exist it is created, and it is the responsibility of MTS to ensure that the WAM is created in the correct process; that is, either in **INETINFO.EXE** (if in-proc) or in a newly created **MTX.EXE** (if process isolated). Once started, the WAM processes the HTTP request and this involves loading the ISAPI extension.

A WAM and its ISAPI extensions remain loaded after being used and are then ready for subsequent HTTP requests for server extensions that are within that application. Should an ISAPI extension or another in-proc loaded COM component misbehave in the **MTX.EXE** process and cause it to crash – the next request for that application will cause a new instance of the WAM to be created. However, if any logic within the **INETINFO.EXE** crashes then the Web Server is lost for good and has to be manually restarted.

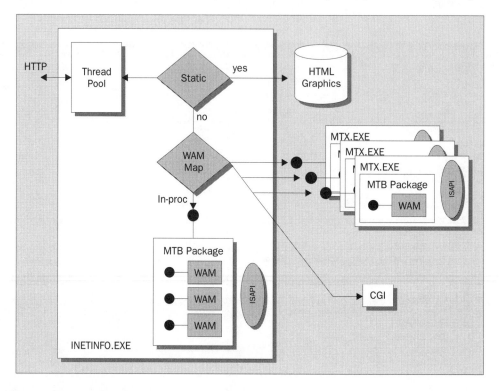

Unloading Isolated Applications

It is possible to unload the WAM using the Unload button located in the Application Settings frame on the Directories properties sheet. This enables us to update the ISAPI extensions and in-proc COM components without stopping the whole Web server.

Considerations for Isolated Applications

Applications running within a WAM located within the main Web server will be invoked slightly faster than those that reside in an isolated process. This is mainly due to the extra time taken for the inter-process communication. There is also a delay for the first application request whilst the isolated process is instantiated. Note that this is a one time cost, unlike CGI, which creates a process on every request; once created, isolated ISAPI server extensions run much faster than CGI server extensions.

Another consideration is that using isolated processes will require additional memory.

We need to take care when migrating ISAPI applications from IIS3 to IIS4 since it is now possible to have multiple copies of the same ISAPI DLL loaded in more than one process. For example, care has to be taken that the ISAPI extension does not permanently lock any resource otherwise the other instances will never be able to gain access. The WAM completes our look at IIS4.0, we'll now move on to Personal Web Server.

An Overview of Personal Web Server 4.0

Personal Web Server 4.0 is a desktop web server supplied with the NT 4.0 Option Pack that allows users to publish web pages from their own machine that runs Windows 95. If you haven't got access to a machine running NT 4.0 server, then this is the option you should try, although you might find one or two of the features of ASP with IIS 4.0 have been necessarily pruned.

> *The version of Personal Web Server that comes with FrontPage 97 bonus pack isn't version 4.0 and consequently won't have Active Server Pages.*

Administering Personal Web Server 4.0

Managing Personal Web Server 4.0 is much simpler than IIS 4.0 as there are far fewer options available. Also you'll find that FTP services are no longer available, which were in earlier versions of Personal Web Server. Personal Web Server is administered through the Personal Web Manager, which runs as an icon in your task tray. To pull up the Web Manager, just click on the icon, once Personal Web Server has been installed.

Personal Web Manager

To commence web publishing services, all you need to do is simply click on the Start button, and then this changes to Stop when the service is running. You can click on Stop to disable the service. You'll find that Microsoft have already created a home page for you on the server and a set of directories for you to store the files in.

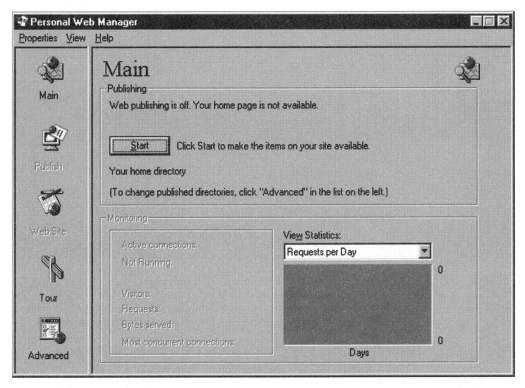

If you have any problems getting web publishing services to function then check that WinSock Proxy 2.0 has been installed on your machine, as Personal Web Server also requires this to function. It does come as part of the NT 4.0 Option Pack. If web publishing services still refuse to run, it might be wise to try and reinstall it.

Getting Started With Personal Web Server

The same set up of home, virtual and sub directories exist in Personal Web Server as they do in IIS 4.0. Indeed the directories created automatically during installation take the same structure as IIS 4.0, under the **InetPub** directory. You'll find Samples, Scripts and your default virtual root directory. We won't go through them again here, just refer back to the descriptions earlier in this chapter.

Creating Directories

To create a directory, just click on the Advanced icon on the left hand toolbar to get taken to the Advanced dialog.

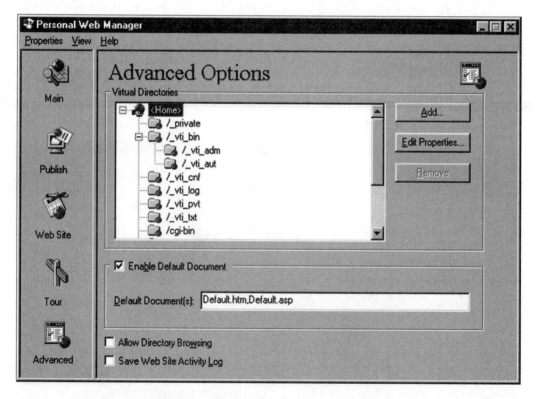

From here you can add virtual directories underneath the home directory and specify the default document a user will see when they access **http://localhost**. You can also save details of who's been visiting your home page in a log. Finally, we'll take a look at some of the development tools that you can use with IIS 4.0, Personal Web Server and ASP.

Development Tools

The Active Platform allows developers to use their familiar tools and programming languages to create the various software components–including Microsoft's Visual Basic, Visual C++, Visual J++ and Visual FoxPro plus numerous offerings from other software vendors. With staff costs being the most expensive part of any software development, it is generally accepted that the 'best' development tool is simply the one in which your organization has the most staff trained. Our view is that the choice of language is immaterial other than it must include facilities to build components with COM compliant interfaces. This then ensures that your software can readily co-operate with other components residing within the Active Platform.

Visual Studio 97 is the latest development tool release from Microsoft and includes VB5.0, VC++5.0, VJ++ 1.1 and VFP 5.0 in a single package. Also bundled in Visual Studio is a new product called Visual InterDev 1.0 that provides an environment for the development of HTML / ASP pages and doing database design / modification. An alternative for the development of HTML pages is Microsoft FrontPage 98, which is designed for Web authors who are not software developers but are involved in the visual aspects of a Web application

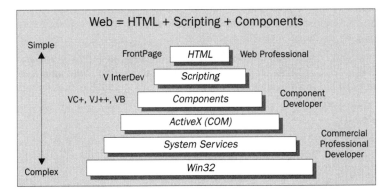

Summary

In this chapter we discussed the advantages of multi-tier client architectures and have seen how this is mapped on to a Microsoft Web solution.

The key points to this chapter are:

- The Microsoft Active Platform and BackOffice contains a wealth of functionality that can form the basis of a powerful web solution enabling us to deliver more by doing less–IIS4 is the latest version Microsoft commercial web server for Windows NT

- The Microsoft Web development approach is to fragment the solution into three distinct areas: HTML + scripting + software components

- Active Server Pages is a high performance and simple to use mechanism for enabling the dynamic generation of web content–it can integrate with other components (such as BackOffice) using COM

- Microsoft Transaction Server 2.0 is now fully integrated with IIS4/ASP2 to form a robust Web server–it enables the deployment of a multi-tier distributed architecture by managing the placement of components across multiple machines; it provides scalability and high performance by resource sharing

- IIS4 is Microsoft's latest standards-based Web application–it builds upon its predecessor to provide a powerful, scalable, reliable and secure platform for Web solutions; it can support email using SMTP, local discussion groups using NNTP and file transfer using FTP

- Personal Web Server 4.0 is available to those users who require web services to run on Windows 95.

We shall now move on to the next chapter and take a look at Active Server Pages in action.

Active Server Pages Fundamentals

In Chapter 1 we met **Active Server Pages,** which is Microsoft's compelling server-based technology for building dynamic and interactive Web pages and we saw how useful it is for programming IIS4 Web solutions. We learned that ASP solutions will probably make the older methods, such as CGI, obsolete because ASP is much easier to implement, and, because it is built upon ISAPI technology, it overcomes the traditional performance problems.

In this chapter, we will delve deeper in to what Active Server Pages is (or *are*, if you prefer to think of the rather odd name with which Microsoft has christened it as being plural). We shall look at why people often refer to Active Server Pages as software 'glue' technology. We'll see how it manages to stick together all of the useful bits (supplied as software components of course) that are rapidly falling out of Microsoft and others to form a single integrated solution.

So in this chapter we will aim to give the user an appreciation of:

- The capabilities of ASP and some different ways that we can use this technology
- How Microsoft have implemented a generic architecture for application scripting and how ASP actually works
- How to generate ASP automatically using some common Microsoft applications
- How to write your own ASP applications

We shall build on these ideas and then take a look at a few examples of ASP applications—for each, we shall disect the code in order to discuss how it works.

But, the first step is to take a look at what Active Server Pages is all about.

What are Active Server Pages?

With any new technology, the first questions you tend to ask are the obvious ones. You know the sort of thing–What is it? What can it do? Will it do what I want it to? Whose turn is it to make the coffee? Is Active Server Pages (ASP) designed for the guy who runs a Web site, or the poor IT manager who is trying to make an intranet do something (but he is not sure what)?

Put simply, an Active Server Page is a file with a `.ASP` suffix that contains a combination of HTML statements and script logic. When IIS4 receives an HTTP request for an ASP file, the final HTML response is generated dynamically from the static HTML statements plus the insertion of any HTML generated by the scripting.

So let us start now by taking a look at scripting.

Scripting

Scripting allows **script hosts** to invoke scripting services within **script engines**. IE4, ASP and the Visual Studio 97 Development Environment are examples of script hosts. The vendor of the script engine defines the script language, syntax and execution rules. This has caused compatibility problems as different vendors have defined different languages, which, unlike HTML will only work in certain environments or hosts. There are two main examples of scripting languages: the Microsoft developed **Visual Basic Script** (VBScript) which only works with Microsoft developed hosts such as Internet Explorer, and the more universal **JavaScript** which Netscape together with Sun Microsystems have developed from its predecessor Livescript. There are also several others available from third parties (e.g. Perl, Python, Awk), and if you were feeling very ambitious, you could even develop your own.

However it's only VBScript and JavaScript that need concern us. VBScript is actually a subset of the Visual Basic for Applications (as used by the Microsoft Office Products) which in turn is a subset of the popular Visual Basic. Microsoft's engineers have also developed JScript which is an implementation of the Netscape's JavaScript language–JavaScript has recently been standardized by ECMA (European Computer Manufacturers Association) after joint submissions from Microsoft and Netscape, and is now officially called ECMAScript.

The real power of scripting comes with the ability to interact with other objects. This enables the accessing of object properties, the invoking of methods and the detecting of events. Accessible objects are either:

- ▲ Intrinsic (built-in) objects exposed within the script host–often referred to as an **object model**
- ▲ External executable software components

Client Side Scripting

Client side scripting can be inserted into an HTML page using the `<SCRIPT> ... </SCRIPT>` tags pair, and so can be incorporated within minimal effort. To identify the script language, the `LANGUAGE` attribute is used, as shown next.

```
<HTML>
<HEAD>
    <TITLE>Document title
    </TITLE>
    <SCRIPT LANGUAGE="JAVASCRIPT">
            Client-side Javascript scripting logic
    </SCRIPT>
</HEAD>
<BODY>
</BODY>
</HTML>
```

The following example illustrates how events can be fired when a user selects a button by specifying the **ONCLICK** attribute. It also highlights that more than one script language can be used simultaneously in the same HTML file. Please note that, unless you have the **ActiveX plugin** for Netscape Navigator, this example will only work correctly on Internet Explorer. Client-side scripting works on *any* host that supports the scripting language.

```
<HTML>
<HEAD>
    <TITLE>Scripting
    </TITLE>
    <SCRIPT LANGUAGE="VBSCRIPT">
    sub vbs
        alert("This is VBScript")
    end sub
    </SCRIPT>
    <SCRIPT LANGUAGE="JAVASCRIPT">
    function js()
    {
        alert("This is JavaScript");
    }
    </SCRIPT>
</HEAD>
<BODY BGCOLOR=cyan>
    Select button:
    <INPUT TYPE="button" NAME="vbs"  VALUE="VBScript"
            onclick="vbs()">
    <INPUT TYPE="button" NAME="js"  VALUE="JavaScript"
            onclick="js()">
</BODY>
</HTML>
```

Clicking on the button runs the appropriate routine.

The client-side scripting can interface to all element objects in a Web page (e.g. tags, images, text, etc.), browser objects (e.g. windows, frames, history, etc.) and in a Microsoft host any ActiveX software component that has been installed on the desktop machine as well. From this, we can see that it is scripting that really enables the *Dynamic* in Dynamic HTML–with modern browsers like IE4, we can now change any part of the Web page as a user interacts with the page.

> It is important to distinguish between Dynamic HTML (DHTML) and dynamically created HTML. Dynamic HTML is a name given to HTML version 4.0, which allows the displayed page contents to be amended even after it has first been rendered on the screen. Dynamically created HTML is where the contents are generated on the fly on the server using a mechanism like CGI, ISAPI or ASP.

Server Side Scripting

We learned earlier that ASP uses server-side scripting to dynamically create HTML responses. The content generated is typically based on the user's identity, parameters in the HTTP request, and by interacting with other objects (e.g. ASP objects, multi-tier client / server business objects, middleware to access databases and legacy systems, BackOffice components, etc.). ASP provides a number of built in objects and useful components which we look at in Chapter 5. The built-in objects simplify many of the common server-side tasks such as handling the HTTP request/responses, the user's session and the Web environment.

Server-side scripting is inserted in an ASP file using either the **<SCRIPT>** tags pair or **<%** and **%>** delimiters. To distinguish client-side from server-side scripting, the latter's **<SCRIPT>** tag should include the **RUNAT="SERVER"** attribute and value. For example:

```
<HTML>
<HEAD>
    <TITLE>Document title
    </TITLE>
    <SCRIPT LANGUAGE="VBSCRIPT" RUNAT="SERVER">
          Server-side VBSCRIPT scripting logic
    </SCRIPT>
    <SCRIPT LANGUAGE="VBSCRIPT">
          Client-side VBSCRIPT scripting logic
    </SCRIPT>
</HEAD>
<BODY>
    <% Server-side VBSCRIPT scripting logic %>
</BODY>
```

Creating and Viewing ASP files

We can create ASP files simply by creating the pages in a text editor or with a tool such as Microsoft's FrontPage 98 or Microsoft's **Visual InterDev**. Of course, there's no reason why we can't create ASP files using existing web page design software, or even (as we generally do) with Windows Notepad. These products may not create the script sections, but we can use them to build the outline of the page, including the general layout and formatting, then add the ASP code later in a text editor.

> Remember to save the file as **plain text**, with the **.asp** file extension. Some editors, like Windows NotePad, insist on adding the **.txt** file extension if you forget to set the Files of type option to All Files.

To view the results that our Active Server Pages files create, however, they have to be *executed* on the server and not just sent to the browser like a normal HTML page. If we simply create a page on the server, and save it with the **.asp** file extension, the server will just download it to the browser when we reference it. This is the default action for any kind of file that it doesn't recognise. If you see this dialog, then this is what you're doing wrong. And though you can view the results with Internet Explorer or Netscape Navigator, you need to make sure that the server that you execute the code on has Active Server Pages installed, and that means it must be running either IIS 4.0 or Personal Web Server 4.0.

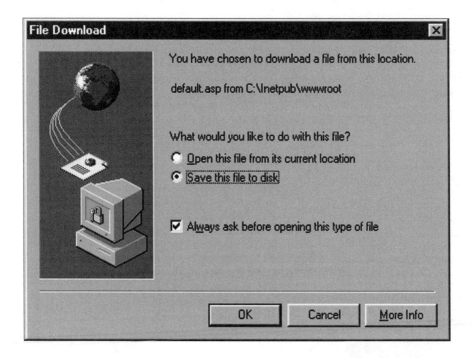

Don't panic if you don't see this dialog, but instead find yourself plunged into FrontPage 98, looking at a text version of the file. This is because some text or web page editors automatically associate themselves with .asp extensions. This is just another manifestation of the same problem.

If you're wondering why the browser doesn't recognise Active Server Pages files, remember that the ASP file itself isn't what we aim to send to the browser—it's the result, as plain HTML, after the page has been interpreted on the server by the Active Server Pages system. To force the server to execute our pages, we have to place them in a suitable existing directory, or set up a new virtual directory within IIS 4.0 or Personal Web Server 4.0 for them. Check back to Chapter 1 to remind yourself of how to do this.

Which Scripting Language Should I Use?

While there are third parties supplying alternative scripting languages, most people will use one of the two options, VBScript or JavaScript (or JScript as it's known in Internet Explorer)—but which is better? Well, the truth is that there is very little difference between the capabilities of the two. Both languages are capable of being used by those with minimal programming experience. At the time of writing, IE3/IE4 are the only browsers that support VBScript. Thus, if you are aiming for mass penetration on the Internet, using client-side scripting in addition to ASP then you should probably restrict the client side scripting to JScript or JavaScript.

If you are developing for an intranet, where you have control over the infrastructure and can enforce IE4 as the choice of browser, you can choose to use the easier VBScript. With ASP, the choice of language is less crucial—all script processing is handled on the server and the output delivered to the browser is standard, platform independent, HTML.

Most browsers assume a default script language of JavaScript. If we write code in VBScript, and do not tell the browser otherwise, it will pass it to its JavaScript interpreter and we will get an error message because the syntax requirements of the two languages are different. To use VBScript in a browser, we have to add a **LANGUAGE** attribute to the **<SCRIPT>** tag, which identifies the language we are using:

```
<SCRIPT LANGUAGE=VBScript>
```

Active Server Pages, however, works in a different way. It assumes a default language of VBScript, by setting a value in the Windows registry, and we need to tell it if we are using a different one. When we use server-side **<SCRIPT>** tags, which include the **RUNAT** attribute, we can add a language attribute in the same way, like this:

```
<SCRIPT LANGUAGE=JScript RUNAT=Server>
```

The problem arises when we use the special script delimiters **<%...%>** since we cannot include a **LANGUAGE** attribute and so the server will assume that the code is VBScript. To get round this, we can identify the **default language** for the whole page by using a special statement:

```
<%@ LANGUAGE = JScript%>
```

In this book we will be using a mixture of the two languages in our examples. We're aiming to show no favoritism as which language he/she uses is of little to concern to the ASP developer, since they can be both executed on the client side. However, it's important to note that JavaScript is now the standard scripting language (ECMAScript).

Statements That We Cannot Use

ASP code is executed on the server, so there are some things that we cannot do. There is not much point displaying a message box, for example, because the viewer could be on the other side of the world. They probably will not be very keen on popping over to your server room just to click the OK button! Consequently, some of the standard statements and functions available in VBScript and JScript are not supported in ASP. The most obvious ones are, of course, **MsgBox** and **InputBox**.

ActiveX Server Components

So we can now create pages dynamically using server side script logic, and there is almost no limit to what we can achieve. The process is more like writing an application than creating an HTML page, and so it will become more and more complex as we find exciting new effects we decide to include. This has its own dangers, and—as you will see later in the book—the pages soon grow to quite an amazing size with a mixture of text, HTML, and code.

But let's be realistic here. The code we're using is only interpreted VBScript or JScript. Once we start to create really complex routines, we will see the effects as a slowing down of server response, while it processes our code. And remember that both VBScript and JScript are limited-functionality languages. They cannot, for example, access files or other applications directly, and so we are soon likely to hit limitations when we start to write serious business applications.

The ideal solution is to minimize the amount of script and write software components in a high level language. These are then integrated with ASP using COM to provide the software plumbing. It is widely recognized that the most sensible approach is to:

- ▲ use a layered methodology to partition the business and data access logic into software components.

- ▲ restrict the ASP logic to synchronizing the information flow with the software components and handling the generation of the presentation logic (which is deployed onto the desktop for execution).

We shall see later in the book, when we discuss MTS, how this technique leads to the most scaleable of solutions.

Using Components on the Server

The use of software components with ASP is accomplished by one vital statement that's available in VBScript–**Server.CreateObject**. Using this, we can create instances of other objects on the server (or another machine), and access their methods and events directly. Fortunately, the use of COM for the inter-object communication occurs under the covers and, in most cases, the Microsoft development tools insulate the developer from most of these complexities.

Suddenly, we're freed from the limitations imposed by the scripting language. If we cannot do it in script, or it's going to take too long to execute, we just use an object written in almost any other language that supports ActiveX.

Specially created objects, designed for use in this way, are generally referred to as **Active Server Components**. There is a range of these already available and many more on the way. In later chapters, we will be taking a look at the standard ones supplied with Active Server Pages or available from Microsoft directly.

We see in Chapter 15 how easy it is to write you own Active Server Components to implement your required custom functionality.

An Example—The Active Database Object Component

One of the main reasons for using dynamic pages in a web site, and particularly on the corporate intranet, is to provide database access. This may just be retrieving values to display, such as a list of the currently available products and the up-to-date prices. Alternatively, we may also want to collect information from the user, and store this back in a database.

One of the standard Server Components that is supplied with Active Server Pages is specially designed to do just that. The **ActiveX Data Objects** (ADO) component is an important part of the Microsoft's **Universal Data Access** strategy for providing access to information across the enterprise. Today, information is key and most companies seek to leverage maximum business advantage from the data distributed throughout their organization. Universal Data Access provides high-performance along with an easy to use programming interface for accessing a variety of diverse information sources, including relational databases, office suite documents, unstructured files, message stores, directories and so on.

Universal Data Access is based on open industry specifications and is provided by a number of components including ActiveX Data Objects (ADO), Remote Data Service, (RDS, formerly known as Advanced Database Control or ADC), OLE DB, and Open Database Connectivity (ODBC). We shall discuss Universal Data Access and see a lot more about publishing information from various data sources later in the book.

Getting started with ASP

In the remainder of this book we shall get started and create our own Active Server Pages. But first we shall cheat and demonstrate two automated methods for generating ASP applications that access databases using ADO.

Active Server Pages and Microsoft Access 97

The task of generating ASP pages for Access databases has been partially automated by a wizard within Access itself. This allows us to create Active Server Pages files directly from an existing database–with almost no effort at all. It's as easy as loading up the Northwinds sample database and selecting Save As HTML from the File menu. In our example, the database contains several tables. We're going to be publishing the **products** table on our web site, so that prospective customers can see what is currently available.

The Save As HTML command starts the Publish to the Web wizard. The first couple of dialogs that it produces explain the process, and allow us to select which tables (or other objects in the database, such as forms and queries) we want to publish.

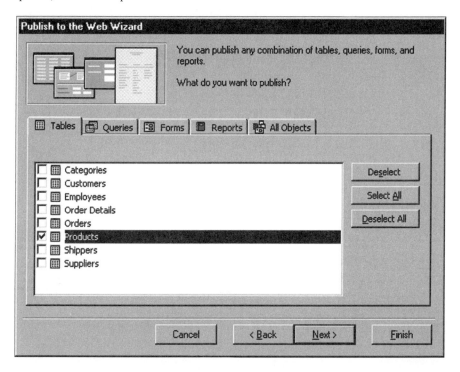

We're asked to if we want to use any document as template in the next dialog, which we don't. Then in the dialog after, we need to select what type of pages we want to create. We've chosen the Dynamic ASP option, to create an Active Server Pages file.

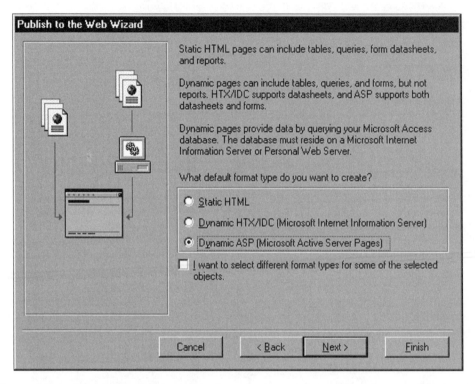

A couple more steps allow us to identify the data source name and the URL of the server, and the final location of the page.

We can even get the wizard to create a 'Home Page' to link several of our dynamic pages together. In our case, we've chosen to publish just the single table and, once the wizard has finished, we end up with a file named **Products_1.asp** containing the generated ASP code.

Here are what the results look like in Internet Explorer:

You can try this example from our web site at
http://www.rapid.wrox.co.uk/books/1266.
If you do it yourself then you will need to have created a System DSN as outlined in Appendix G.

While it looks just like a static copy of the data in the table, it's actually a dynamic page that will change as the data in the underlying table changes. Each time a visitor to our site requests this page, they'll see the latest information. Of course, it would benefit from some tidying up and perhaps some graphics, but it does show just what Active Server Pages can easily achieve.

If you use Notepad (or any HTML editor) to examine the code generated by the Access wizard, the first thing that you will notice is it actually looks a lot like a normal HTML page.

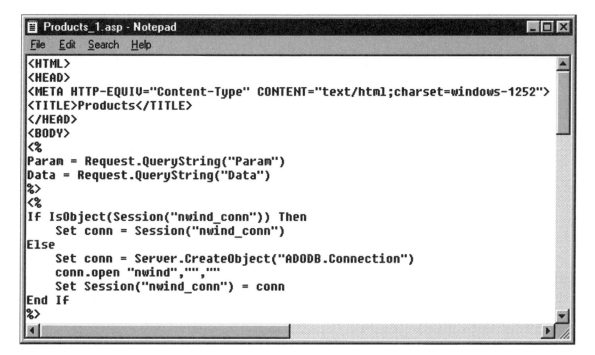

```
Products_1.asp - Notepad
File   Edit   Search   Help
<HTML>
<HEAD>
<META HTTP-EQUIV="Content-Type" CONTENT="text/html;charset=windows-1252">
<TITLE>Products</TITLE>
</HEAD>
<BODY>
<%
Param = Request.QueryString("Param")
Data = Request.QueryString("Data")
%>
<%
If IsObject(Session("nwind_conn")) Then
    Set conn = Session("nwind_conn")
Else
    Set conn = Server.CreateObject("ADODB.Connection")
    conn.open "nwind","",""
    Set Session("nwind_conn") = conn
End If
%>
```

Remember that the server side script logic is distinguished from the static HTML by being delimited by the <% and %> characters. As you can see, there unfortunately seems to be a lot of 'noise' generated by the wizard; for example, the same font information is duplicated throughout rather than being specified once at the start or in a stylesheet–but, hey, who cares: it works, and it took no brain power to create.

Active Server Pages and Microsoft FrontPage 98

Microsoft FrontPage 98 is member of the Microsoft Office family of products and enables the construction of great looking and easy to use Web sites. It provides both the FrontPage Explorer, for managing the web site; and the FrontPage Editor, which is a sophisticated HTML page editor.

The FrontPage Editor contains a Database Region Wizard that automates the construction of ASP script logic that submits SQL queries to an ODBC-compliant database and combines the results into the generated page content. The wizard is selected from the Insert|Database|DatabaseRegionWizard menu option. The first dialog requests the data Source Name of the ODBC database on which we wish to access. As an example, we shall use the Northwind Traders database.

The next dialog requests the SQL string for the query. The SQL string is used to get information from the database—you can use Access to generate SQL strings automatically, if you don't know any SQL. In our example we want details of all customers that have made an order between a set of dates and this SQL query gets details of all orders made between the 1st January 1995 and the 12th December 95. It is possible to create parameterized queries—the parameter values must be specified in the URL when the ASP is requested.

The next dialog defines all fields in the database that are to be displayed in the generated results page.

On completion of the wizard, a summary of the Database script logic is inserted into the page. Then you can save the results and view them from the browser:

If you select the HTML tag in the FrontPage Editor then you will be able to view all of the ASP generated by FrontPage wizard is as follows. Any comments that are tagged with **<!--webbot bot="** is information used by Frontpage. These are ignored by both ASP and the Web browser. Do not worry too much about understanding the actual details of the ASP script logic—at this stage, just try to get the flavor of what ASP scripting is all about.

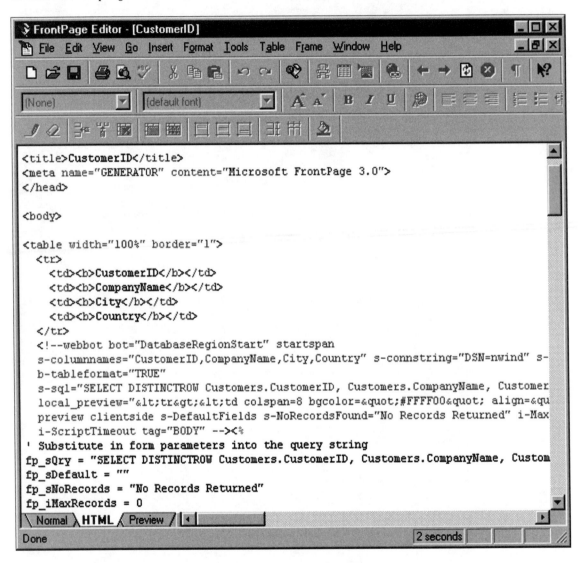

Again you will need to have installed a System DSN before you can create and run this example, although it can be run directly from our web site without installation at
http://rapid.wrox.co.uk/books/1266.

Writing Our First ASP Applications

OK. Now that we have a grasp of what ASP is all about, let's move on and write our own ASP applications.

The Polite Web Server

No, it might be our first but it isn't going to be another 'Hello World'. We are assuming that you are reasonably familiar with **VBScript** already, so we will dive straight in and create something a bit more intellectually challenging. We shall look at an example that shows how your site can offer different greetings to each visitor. This example will be in VBScript.

Here is one of the results it produces in Internet Explorer. Of course, it could be different when *you* try it–but that is the whole point!

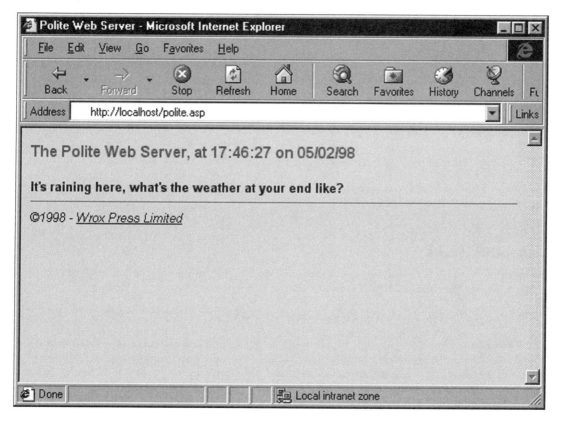

Most of the page is static HTML code, but there is some script logic executed by the server to generate a random greeting.

```
<HTML>
<HEAD>
<Title>Polite Web Server</Title>
<STYLE>  {Font-Family="Arial"} </STYLE>
<BASEFONT SIZE=2>
</HEAD>
<BODY BGCOLOR=wheat>
<FONT COLOR=Teal SIZE=3><B>
The Polite Web Server, at <% = Time %> on <% = Date %>
</B></FONT><P><B>
<% If Hour(Now) < 8 Then %>
    Don't you know what time it is? I was still in bed!
<% Else
    Randomize
    intChoice = Int(Rnd * 4)
    Select Case intChoice
      Case 0 %>
        So, where do you want me to go today?
      <% Case 1 %>
        Well, look whos back visiting us again...
      <% Case 2 %>
        Hi there, and welcome to our site.
      <% Case 3 %>
        It's raining here, what's the weather at your end like?
      <% End Select
    End If %>
</B><HR>
<CITE>&copy;1998 - <A HREF="http://www.wrox.com">Wrox Press Limited</A></CITE>
</BODY>
</HTML>
```

This example, together with all the other sample files for this book, is available from our web site at **http://rapid.wrox.co.uk/books/1266/**.

How the ASP Works

Looking at the code in the previous example shows two of the ways that we can use VBScript in our Active Server Pages. The page heading is created with the line:

```
The Polite Web Server, at <% = Time %> on <% = Date %>
```

This is the most basic format of VBScript. We are using an equals sign and the name of a variable or an expression inside the script delimiters to display information. When the page is interpreted on the server, the variable or expression is evaluated, and its value at that point replaces the entire `<%...%>` tag. In our example, the two expressions are actually built-in VBScript functions, which just return strings equivalent to the current time and date from the server's operating system. Of course, the time that is shown in the page will be the time on the server's clock. It will not be correct in a different time zone. We use the predefined Time and Date functions which are available in VBScript. A list of all function that VBScript uses can be found in Appendix A.

The second section of code is just a little more complex. Again, it uses the `<%...%>` delimiters to identify the sections that are VBScript code. We are using a standard **If...Then...Else** construct and a nested **Select Case** construct, to determine which text to include in the returned page. The VBScript function **Now** returns the current time and date, and the **Hour** function simply retrieves the hour from this as a number between **0** and **23**.

If it is before eight o'clock in the morning then the Web Server is not quite so polite.

```
<% If Hour(Now) < 8 Then %>
    Don't you know what time it is? I was still in bed!
<% Else
```

If it is after eight o'clock in the morning, we seed the random number generator using the **Randomize** statement, and then create a random number between **0** and **3**.

```
Randomize
intChoice = Int(Rnd * 4)
```

We can then use this to decide which text to include in the page. Notice in this case how we have used the `<%...%>` delimiters around the code, and left the text that will form part of the page outside them.

```
Select Case intChoice
    Case 0 %>
      So, where do you want me to go today?
    <% Case 1 %>
      Well, look whose back visiting us again...
    <% Case 2 %>
      Hi there, and welcome to our site.
    <% Case 3 %>
      It's raining here, what's the weather at your end like?
    <% End Select
End If %>
```

What Day is it?

Well, the previous example was fairly simple. Here is a more complicated one, which creates a calendar for the current month, and highlights the current day.

It looks like this in Internet Explorer:

This example, together with all the other sample files for this book, is available from our web site at
`http://rapid.wrox.co.uk/books/1266/`

Let us now look at the code. This exercise demonstrates how we can use a loop to place repeated sections of HTML or text in the returned page, and how we can include separate subroutines or functions in our pages.

```
<HTML>
<HEAD>
<Title>What day is it?</Title>
<STYLE>  {Font-Family="Arial"} </STYLE>
<BASEFONT SIZE=2>
</HEAD>

<SCRIPT LANGUAGE=VBScript RUNAT=Server>
  Function GetLastDay(datTheDate)
    intMonthNum = Month(datTheDate)       'find the month number
    intYearNum = Year(datTheDate)         'and the year number
    intResult = 28                        'start from the 28th
    For intLastDay = intResult To 31      'up to the 31st
      'create the date and see if its still in the same month
      datTestDay = DateSerial(intYearNum, intMonthNum, intLastDay)
      If Month(datTestDay) = intMonthNum Then
```

```
            intResult = intLastDay
       End If
     Next
     GetLastDay = intResult                  'return the result
   End Function
</SCRIPT>

<%
datToday = Date()                            'today's date
intThisYear = Year(datToday)                 'the current year
intThisMonth = Month(datToday)               'the current month
intThisDay = Day(datToday)                   'the current day
strMonthName = MonthName(intThisMonth)       'the name of the current month

'now get the name of the current day
strWeekDayName = WeekDayName(WeekDay(datToday), False, vbSunday)

'find the first and last days of this month
datFirstDay = DateSerial(intThisYear, intThisMonth, 1)
intFirstWeekDay = WeekDay(datFirstDay, vbSunday)
intLastDay = GetLastDay(datToday)

intPrintDay = 1   'the value of the day number to print in the page
%>

<BODY BGCOLOR=wheat>
<FONT COLOR=Teal SIZE=3><B>
What day is it?
</B></FONT><P>

<TABLE>
<TR><TH COLSPAN=7><% = strMonthName %> <% = intThisYear %></TH></TR>
  <TR>
    <TD>  Sun  </TD> <TD>  Mon  </TD>
    <TD>  Tue  </TD> <TD>  Wed  </TD>
    <TD>  Thu  </TD> <TD>  Fri  </TD>
    <TD>  Sat  </TD>
  </TR>
  <% While intPrintDay <= intLastDay %>
    <TR>
      <% For intLoopDay = 1 To 7 %>
        <% If (intPrintDay = intThisDay) AND (intFirstWeekDay <=1) Then %>
        <TD ALIGN=CENTER BGCOLOR=Red>
        <% Else %>
        <TD ALIGN=CENTER>
        <% End If %>
          <% If intFirstWeekDay > 1 Then %>
            -
            <% intFirstWeekDay = intFirstWeekDay - 1 %>
          <% Else %>
            <% If intPrintDay > intLastDay Then %>
            -
            <% Else %>
              <B><% = intPrintDay %></B>
            <% End If %>
            <% intPrintDay = intPrintDay + 1 %>
          <% End If %>
```

```
        </TD>
      <% Next %>
    </TR>
  <% Wend %>
</TABLE>

<BR>
Yes, you guessed correct - today is <% = strWeekDayName %>
<HR>
<CITE>&copy;1998 - <A HREF="http://www.wrox.com">Wrox Press Limited</A></CITE>
</BODY>
</HTML>
```

How the ASP Works

Creating a calendar is only really awkward when it comes to deciding on what actual day the first and last of the month fall. Our calendar will be laid out from Sunday through to Saturday, so we need to place day 1 in the correct column. And we need to find out how many days there are in the current month, to know when to stop.

The first part of the code is a separate **<SCRIPT>...</SCRIPT>** section, containing a function which we have written to provide the number of the last day of any month. It is pretty easy to do. We just create a series of dates using the month and year supplied in the **datTheDate** parameter, with the days from **28** to **31**.

Where we have, for example, **Year = 97**, **Month = 4** and **Day = 31**, the **DateSerial** function will automatically produce the date **1st May 1997**. All we do here is see when it 'overflows' into the next month, and use the previous value.

```
<SCRIPT LANGUAGE=VBScript RUNAT=Server>
  Function GetLastDay(datTheDate)
    intMonthNum = Month(datTheDate)       'find the month number
    intYearNum = Year(datTheDate)         'and the year number
    intResult = 28                        'start from the 28th
    For intLastDay = intResult To 31      'up to the 31st
      'create the date and see if its still in the same month
      datTestDay = DateSerial(intYearNum, intMonthNum, intLastDay)
      If Month(datTestDay) = intMonthNum Then
        intResult = intLastDay
      End If
    Next
    GetLastDay = intResult                'return the result
  End Function
</SCRIPT>
```

This function will not be executed until we call it from elsewhere in our code. Notice the **RUNAT** attribute, which prevents the script being sent to the browser. The placing of **<SCRIPT>** sections within the page is arbitrary—we just chose to put after the **<HEAD>** information.

The code that *does* run when the page is loaded comes next with the **<%...%>** delimiters. This gets the current date using the **Date()** function, and stores it in a variable named **datToday**.

```
<%
datToday = Date()                      'today's date
```

From this, it calculates the current year, month, and day numbers and the month name.

```
intThisYear = Year(datToday)           'the current year
intThisMonth = Month(datToday)         'the current month
intThisDay = Day(datToday)             'the current day
strMonthName = MonthName(intThisMonth) 'the name of the current month
```

Then, we can get the name of the current day–specifying Sunday as the first day of our week in line with the column layout we want for our calendar. Here, since there isn't a function available that does everything we want, we create our own and call it **WeekDayName**.

```
'now get the name of the current day
strWeekDayName = WeekDayName (WeekDay(datToday), False, vbSunday)
```

Next, we get the date of the first day of the month, again using the **DateSerial** function but this time with the value **1** for the **Day** argument.

```
datFirstDay = DateSerial(intThisYear, intThisMonth, 1)
```

Then the **WeekDay** function will tell us what day this date represents, where 1 is Sunday and 7 is Saturday because we have again used the VBScript built-in constant **vbSunday** as an argument to the function.

```
intFirstWeekDay = WeekDay(datFirstDay, vbSunday)
```

We get the number of the last day by calling our own **GetLastDay** function with today's date, then finally set a day counter variable to **1**–the first of the month–ready to start building the calendar.

```
intLastDay = GetLastDay(datToday)

intPrintDay = 1    'the value of the day number to print in the page
%>
```

The most obvious way to format a calendar is to use HTML tables. The next section of code creates the output we see on the browser, by using VBScript to build up the rows and columns of the table inside two nested loops. The first part of the code creates the headings for the month name / year, and the names of the days.

```
<TABLE>
  <TR><TH COLSPAN=7><% = strMonthName %> <% = intThisYear %></TH></TR>
  <TR>
    <TD>  Sun  </TD>
    <TD>  Mon  </TD>
    <TD>  Tue  </TD>
    <TD>  Wed  </TD>
    <TD>  Thu  </TD>
    <TD>  Fri  </TD>
    <TD>  Sat  </TD>
  </TR>
```

Then we use the statement **While intPrintDay <= intLastDay**, with the **<TR>** and **</TR>** tags inside it, to create a row for each week on the calendar. Each time round this loop, we use another loop, **For intLoopDay = 1 To 7**, to create the seven columns for the days.

```
<% While intPrintDay <= intLastDay %>
   <TR>
      <% For intLoopDay = 1 To 7 %>
```

Inside this second loop, we first check the value of **intPrintDay** to see if it is actually today, and if so we change the table cell's background color to red.

```
<% If intPrintDay = intThisDay Then %>
   <TD ALIGN=CENTER BGCOLOR=Red>
<% Else %>
   <TD ALIGN=CENTER>
<% End If %>
```

And now for the fiddly bit. Because the calendar starts at Sunday (**WeekDay = 1**), we have to skip columns until we get to the correct one if the first day of the month is not Sunday. We do this by checking the value of **intFirstWeekDay**, which holds the **WeekDay** number of the first day. If it is greater than **1**, we print a hyphen and decrement its value. Eventually, somewhere within the first row, we will get to a point where **intFirstWeekDay** is equal to **1**.

```
<% If intFirstWeekDay > 1 Then %>
      -
      <% intFirstWeekDay = intFirstWeekDay - 1 %>
   <% Else %>
```

Then we check to see if the value of **intPrintDay** is greater that the last day of the month. If it is, we are printing hyphens again to complete the last row.

```
<% If intPrintDay > intLastDay Then %>
      -
   <% Else %>
```

If not, we can print the day number, and increment it ready for the next column. After both loops are complete, we finish up by adding the **</TABLE>** tag.

```
<B><% = intPrintDay %></B>
         <% End If %>
         <% intPrintDay = intPrintDay + 1 %>
      <% End If %>
   </TD>
   <% Next %>
   </TR>
<% Wend %>
</TABLE>
```

Finally, we have code to print the last line using the name of the current day:

```
Yes, you guessed correct - today is <% = strWeekDayName %>
```

Again, we are using the date from the server's clock, and it might be different in another time zone.

Using ASP to interface with Databases

The next example shows an ASP script interfacing with an SQL Server database using the ADO object which is created using **Server.CreateObject**. You don't need to worry too much about understanding the ADO functionality here—we shall meet this topic in depth later. It's just useful to see how easy it is in ASP to access a database and include the results of a query in your web page.

> You must have set up the ODBC Data Source Name "NWIND" and configured it to use the Northwinds Database provided with Office 97, using the ODBC administrator program before this program will run—this is explained in Appendix G.

```
<%@ LANGUAGE="VBSCRIPT" %>
<HTML>
<HEAD>
<TITLE>Results</TITLE>
</HEAD>
<BODY BGCOLOR=yellow>

<%
SQL = "SELECT * FROM CUSTOMERS;"
SET DbObj = Server.CreateObject("ADODB.Connection")
DbObj.Open "DSN=NWIND;UID=;PWD=;"
SET oRs = DbObj.Execute(SQL)
%>

<P>Customers</P>
<TABLE BORDER=3>
<% WHILE NOT oRs.EOF %>
<TR>
<TD>        <% =oRs.Fields("CUSTOMERID").Value %> </TD>
<TD>        <% =oRs.Fields ("COMPANYNAME").Value %>      </TD>
<TD>        <% =oRs.Fields ("CONTACTNAME").Value %>      </TD>
<TD>        <% =oRs.Fields ("ADDRESS").Value %>   </TD>
</TR>
<% oRs.MoveNext %>
<% WEND %>
</TABLE>

</BODY>
</HTML>
```

If you save this file as **customers.asp** and then run the example you will get the following results:

It should be appreciated that the ASP server-side scripting logic is not exposed in the generated HTML file, whereas the client-side scripting can be inspected by simply viewing the HTML source code. This means that if you are concerned about people copying your clever code or seeing your confidential business rules then you should move your script into compiled components. In practice, you will find that both server-side and client-side scripting have specific uses and that the design of your Web application will require a combination of the two.

Databases aren't the only things that you might want to include in your pages. For example, you might want to include a straight text file and then manipulate it. We'll look at how you can do that next.

Server-side Includes

Server-side Includes (SSI) is a generic term used to describe the way that other elements can be inserted into a Web page. These are a very useful way of making your site easier to manage, and of providing extra information. We will take a brief look at the possibilities here, and you will see them used throughout this book.

Including Text Files in a Page with #include

One of the most useful techniques with SSI is to insert pre-built blocks of text into a page. As an example, let's consider the function that we created for our calendar page that calculated the last day of any month. We can save this as a text file called, say, **GetLastDay.txt**. Then, anytime that we want to use the function, we just add an include statement to the page, and call the function:

```
<!-- #include file="GetLastDay.txt" -->
...
intLastDayAugust = GetLastDay(datAugust)    'call our included function
...
```

The only point to watch out for is that if you want to include script from another file, this file must contain complete script sections. In other words, it has to have opening and closing **<SCRIPT>** or **<%...%>** tags. We cannot place part of the code section in an included file, and the rest in the main page. However, we could include half of, say, an **If...Then** construct in the file, and the rest in the main page, as long as each part was enclosed in the **<%...%>** tags. This is not likely to produce code that is easy to read or debug later, though!

Of course, the text we include does not have to be VBScript or JScript code. We can quite easily use it to include HTML or just plain text. If your site uses pages with standard footers for your copyright notice, or a standard **<STYLE>** tag to set up the text and page styles, these can be stored equally well as a separate file, and referenced with a **#include** statement.

One important point to note is that the 'including' is done **before** the Active Server Pages interpreter gets to see the page. Thus it is not possible to use code to programmatically decide which SSI **#include** directives we want to put into action. They will all be all included automatically.

Virtual and Physical File Addresses

The **#include** directive allows us to specify a file using either its **physical** or **virtual** path. For example, the file **MyFile.txt** could be in the directory **C:\TextFiles**. If this directory also had an alias (virtual path) of **/Texts** we could then reference it using either method:

```
<!-- #include file="C:\TextFiles\MyFile.txt" -->      'physical path
<!-- #include virtual="/Texts/MyFile.txt"    -->      'virtual path
```

We can also use relative paths. If the file is in the same folder, we just use the file name. If it is in the **Projects** subdirectory, we can use:

```
<!-- #include file="Projects\MyFile.txt" -->          'physical path
```

Summary

In this chapter, we have looked at the background to Active Server Pages, and taken a broad overview of what they can do. There is a lot of ground to cover yet, but we have now got a good idea of where we will be going through the remainder of this book.

The key points to this chapter are:

- Active Server Pages acts like a 'glue' technology, which can bind together various other server-based systems to help us build dynamic web sites.

- Once we have set up IIS4, our visitors can reference the ASP documents to execute the scripts they contain. This can produce far more interactive pages than most other technologies, while being simple to use and maintain.

- One of the most useful of the Server Side Include commands is `#include`, which lets us build libraries of reusable code or HTML.

- We can include script in the page that is executed on the server, as well as script that is sent to the browser for execution there. Together with Dynamic HTML, ActiveX Controls and Java applets, the returned pages can provide high levels of user interaction.

In the next chapter we'll examine in detail the Active Server Pages Object model.

The Active Server Pages Request Object

In the previous chapters, we looked at the background to the development of **Active Server Pages**, and Microsoft's **Active Server** technology in general. We saw how it allows us to include VBScript or JScript code in our pages, which is executed on the server. This is in contrast to the VBScript or JScript executed in the browser. Server execution provides us with all kinds of extra facilities when it comes to building interactive and dynamic web sites. For example, we don't have to worry about whether the browser can support the programming languages that we choose to use. Also, we can tailor our pages on the fly to suit different browsers. Active Server Pages also provides us with all kinds of other possibilities for providing customized pages to our visitors, as you'll see in the coming chapters.

In this chapter we will see how to use Active Server Pages built-in objects. Like the client browsers discussed earlier, Active Server Pages has its own object model, which is exposed for scripting languages such as VBScript. These objects run on the server and are programmed using methods, properties and collections. We will discuss each method, property and collection of the Active Server Pages built-in objects and give you several examples how to use them inside your Active Server Pages.

During our discussion we will move into the realms of client/server programming. Contrary to writing script programs, which execute on client side, we must consider where we actually execute our code, as well as how. Active Server Pages built-in objects give us the way to integrate our code with the requests sent from the browser (client), and the web pages, or responses, sent back from the server.

In this chapter and the next chapter, we're going to examine these built-in objects in detail. You'll see:

- ▲ The overall object structure that Active Server Pages provides
- ▲ How we can access and decipher the client requests
- ▲ How we provide our own responses, as customized web pages
- ▲ What we can achieve through the other parts of the object model
- ▲ How we can manipulate cookies, and use the concept of an application

But first, let's see why we need to have built-in objects at all…

Communicating with a Web site

So far in this book, we've shown you how we can use VBScript and JScript on the server to modify the content that is seen in the web browser. This allowed us to collect and display values such as the current date and time, and the values of various HTTP variables. Using this information we could make decisions about what to send the client browser, based on known quantities–such as in the calendar where we highlight the current date, as was shown in previous chapters.

This may well be *dynamic*, but it isn't *active*. The visitor to our site is a passive receptor of information. Their only input to the information path they follow is defined by which links they click in our pages. What we need to consider now is how to actually communicate with the user using Active Server Pages.

The traditional method for a web browser to communicate with the server was through **forms**, where information was sent to a server CGI program. The program could then examine this information, and produce a new HTML document on the fly to be sent back to the requesting client.

Alternatively, in some situations, the page might have contained hyperlinks that included information about the user's selections. This is often seen in Web Search pages, e.g. at **www.lycos.com**, where clicking on a link in the page sends one or more values back to the browser, by appending them to the URL to form a **query string**. This is visible in the Address box in the browser.

In both these cases, the Active Server Pages object model allows us to collect information passed with a query, and more, so that we can use it in our scripts.

The Active Server Pages Object Model

Although we can use script in an Active Server Page (i.e. **.asp** file), this itself exerts constraints on what we can actually achieve, as the scripting languages we're using have very limited functionality. However, they do have one very useful ability, namely they can act upon objects that are part of the Active Server Pages core engine, by calling their methods and setting their properties. Active Server Pages provides a distinctive set of objects that we can manipulate using scripting languages.

The Overall Object Model Structure

There are six built-in objects provided by the Active Server Pages core engine, which we can use in our server programs. Unlike other object models, such as the Browser Object Model, the Active Server Pages built-in objects don't form a hierarchy. They only relate to each other logically, not in "father-child" relationship as in "classical" object models. The Object Model provides us with a **Server** object, which has methods and properties that offer general utility functions that we can use throughout scripts. The **Server** object represents the environment in which our pages run, and the remaining five objects are used to make up an **Active Server** application. These objects are: **Application**, **Session**, **Request**, **Response** and **ObjectContext**. The last one is new to version 2.0 of Active Server Pages. The diagram below shows how these objects fit together.

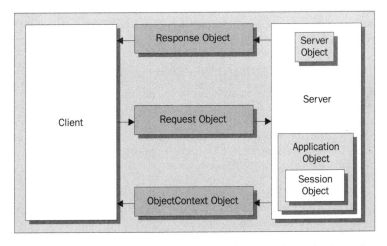

This diagram outlines some important concepts. First of all, there can be multiple applications running on a single server. **Application** consists of a set of script files, HTML documents, images, etc. that are stored in a single **virtual directory** or **virtual mapping**. This mapping points to a physical directory in our server's file system, where we store all the files that make up our application. We saw how to create a virtual directory, and provide an **alias** to access it with, in Chapter 1.

Objects Core: Applications and Sessions

As we noted above, the **Application** object represents an entire Active Server Pages application. You can use this object to share information among all users of a given application. Each **Application** object can have many sessions. A **Session** object is maintained for each user who requests a page (or document) from the application. You can use the **Session** object to store information needed for a particular user session. Variables stored in the **Session** object are not discarded when the user jumps between pages in the application; instead, these variables persist for the entire time the user is accessing pages in your application. You can also use **Session** methods to explicitly end a session and set the timeout period for an idle session.

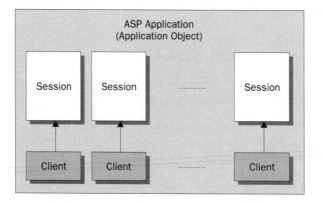

The concept of an application, and the sessions within it, is central to the concept of Active Server Pages programming, and we'll be coming back to it again later in the chapter. You'll also see it come up in most other chapters, as we take advantage of the unique way it binds all our pages and visitors together.

Session Lifetime: Requests and Responses

To be able to manage the way HTTP communications work, Active Server Pages has to be able to capture all the information from each individual request made by the client, and store it so that it can be accessed by the application, running on the server. To do this, the details of the browser, the request itself and a whole host of other information are placed in a **Request** object. The server retrieves the values that the client browser passed to the server during an HTTP request and places this information into the **Request** object. Our scripts can then use the methods and properties of this object to determine what action to take, and what kind of page to return.

To send information back to the client browser, we use the **Response** object. This object stores all the information required for the server's response to the client. Again it provides methods and properties that can be used to create and modify what is returned back to the client browser, and perform other tasks such as redirecting a request to another page.

Transactions: ObjectContext

You use the **ObjectContext** object to either commit or abort transactions managed by Microsoft Transaction Server (MTS) initiated by an Active Server Pages script. When an ASP contains the **@TRANSACTION** directive, the page runs in a transaction and does not finish processing until the transaction either succeeds completely or fails. This object implements two methods of MTS's own **ObjectContext** object. The **ObjectContext** object will be described in Chapter 4.

Now that you have a feeling for the layout of the object model and the purposes of each object, we'll look in detail at each of the objects and see how we can work with them. In this chapter we will discuss the **Request** object. In the next chapter we will look at the **Response** object, which can be treated as a counterpart to the **Request** object and after that we will move to the **Server**, **Application**, **Session** and **ObjectContext** objects. So at the end of the next chapter you'll get the picture of how all built-in objects can be used. Now, let's start with the **Request** object.

The Request Object

The **Request** object provides us with all the information about the user's request to our site or application. The following diagram and table show the interface provided by the **Request** object. This takes the form of five **collections** of variables, a **TotalBytes** property and a **BinaryRead** method.

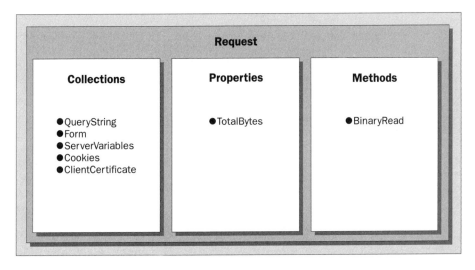

Collection	Description	Type
ClientCertificate	Client certificate values sent from the browser.	Read Only
Cookies	Values of cookies sent from the browser.	Read Only
Form	Values of form elements sent from the browser.	Read Only
QueryString	Values of variables in the HTTP query string.	Read Only
ServerVariables	Values of the HTTP and environment variables.	Read Only

Property	Description
TotalBytes	Specifies the number of bytes the client is sending in the body of this request. Read Only

Method	Description
`BinaryRead`	Used to retrieve data sent to the server as part of the POST request

A collection is a data structure, rather like an array, which can store values by linking each one to a unique key. If we know the key, we can retrieve and set values in the collection. However, in many ways it is more powerful than an array, as you'll see in a while. And in case if you haven't heard the term interface before, it simply describes the way that the values in the object can be accessed, through that object's methods and properties.

Let's take a look at the collections of the **Request** object.

The Request Object Collections

As you can see, the **Request** object provides us with a set of properties, which stores various information. Each of the properties is a **collection** of values of the same type. You'll be familiar with these if you've used Visual Basic or VBA before, or even if you've only used VBScript or JScript to program in the browser. As an example, we can access the **QueryString** collection to see if there was a value sent from the browser with the key **Answer**, like this:

```
strAnswer = Request.QueryString("Answer")
```

If we wanted to add a value to, or change an existing value in a collection, we just assign a new value using the key we want to attach it to. We can't actually do this in the **Request** object, because all the values are read-only—it doesn't make sense to be able to change the information, because it's just a copy of the request made by the browser. However, you'll see how we do it with the **Response** object later in this chapter.

So for now, we can treat these collections as similar to arrays of variable names and value pairs, although the different collections are actually implemented in subtly different ways—sometimes as a dictionary as well. A dictionary is actually a special object, provided for VBScript and JScript programs by a special library called the Microsoft Scripting Runtime, which we'll be discussing in a lot more detail in the next chapter.

Before we look at how to utilize the information in the **Request** object, we should consider just how that information gets there in the first place.

How Users Send Information

The information stored in **Request** object collections originates from the client, and is passed to the server as part of the HTTP document request. The server decodes all this information, and makes it available to Active Server Pages through the collections, which are part of the **Request** object's interface.

Apart from the normal information contained in the HTTP header parts of the request, there are basically two ways that the browser can send specific information to the server. The information can come from a **<FORM>** section on the page, or be appended directly to the end of the URL as a query string.

ASP Form 1 Example

Let's look at the following example. Suppose we have a HTML page with two text boxes and two buttons—Reset and Submit:

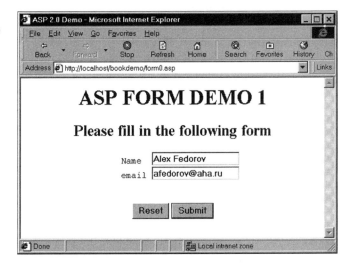

You can find the complete code for this example and all others in this chapter on the Wrox site at:
`http://rapid.wrox.co.uk/books/1266/`

The code for the form is as follows:

```
<HTML>
<HEAD>
<META HTTP-EQUIV="Content-Type" CONTENT="text/html;charset=windows-1252">
<TITLE>ASP 2.0 Demo</TITLE>
</HEAD>
<BODY>
<CENTER>
 <H1>ASP FORM DEMO 1</H1>
 <FORM NAME="userinfo" ACTION="MAININFO.ASP" METHOD="GET">
  <H2>Please fill in the following form</H2><P>
  <PRE>
   Name  <INPUT TYPE="TEXT" NAME="uname">
   email <INPUT TYPE="TEXT" NAME="mail">
  </PRE>
  <INPUT TYPE=RESET  VALUE="Reset">
  <INPUT TYPE=SUBMIT VALUE="Submit">
 </FORM>
</CENTER>
</BODY>
</HTML>
```

When the user presses the Submit button, the values of the text boxes are put into a query string along with the names of the text boxes (you define the name with the **NAME** attribute of the **<INPUT>** tag). The query string is then appended to the URL given in the **ACTION** attribute of the **<FORM>** tag after a question mark. The complete URL, which will be visible in the browser's Address box will look like this:

```
http://localhost/demo/book/MAININFO.ASP?uname=Alex+Fedorov&mail=afedorov@mail.com
```

We could get the same effect by inserting an **\<A\>** tag in the page, and appending the query string to the URL we specify for the **HREF** attribute, like this:

```
<A HREF=" MAININFO.ASP?uname=Alex+Fedorov&mail=afedorov@mail.com">Click me </A>
```

Here is a short JScript program which shows information submitted by the user:

```
<%@language = "JScript"%>
<HTML>
 <HEAD><TITLE>ASP2 Demos</TITLE></HEAD>
 <BODY BGCOLOR="#e0e0e0">
  <CENTER>
   <H1>The following information was received from user:</H1><P>
   <B>Name    = </B> <% =Request.QueryString("uname") %><BR>
   <B>e-mail = </B> <% =Request.QueryString("mail")  %>
  </CENTER>
 </BODY>
</HTML>
```

Here we use the **QueryString** collection of the **Request** object to extract information supplied by user. We will discuss **QueryString** collection in details a little bit later in this chapter.

We can use this approach when we need a set of pages to be configured and look the same way. Suppose we have a gallery of pictures. Each picture is shown on its own page together with its name and techniques. Using static pages we need to provide a separate page for each picture. Using Active Server Pages all we need is to create a template and pass it the name of the graphics file, picture title and techniques data:

```
<A HREF="PICTURE.ASP?file="pic001.jpg"&desc="Portrait"&techn="oil, canvas">Portrait</A>
```

If we add another picture to our gallery, we just add a link with appropriate data, not changing the template itself:

```
<A HREF="PICTURE.ASP?file="pic002.jpg"&desc="Still life"&techn="oil, canvas">Still
life</A>
```

Here is how the template can be implemented:

```
<HTML>
<HEAD>
<META HTTP-EQUIV="Content-Type" CONTENT="text/html;charset=windows-1252">
<TITLE>Art Gallery</TITLE>
</HEAD>
<BODY>
<CENTER>
 <H1>Art Gallery</H1><P>
 <IMG SRC=" <% =Request.QueryString("file")%>"><P>
 <H3>
 <% = Request.QueryString("desc") %>
 </H3><P>
 <H4>
 <% = Request.QueryString("techn") %>
 </H4><P>
</CENTER>
</HTML>
```

Once again we use **Request.QueryString** to get data sent to us from the browser client. Note that you can put any HTML formatting tags in this template–just leave the highlighted strings, which get data sent to us.

Sending Data Via the GET Method

Appending the query string to the end of a URL (the way the **GET** method of the **<FORM>** tag works) isn't the only way the server can receive data from the client browser. In fact, this often isn't the best way to send information at all. For a start, the values of the controls are clearly visible in the browser's address box, and could very easily be intercepted while the request is in transit over the Net.

The query string method also suffers another severe limitation. The amount of data that can be sent with the URL is limited to around 1000 characters, as part of the HTTP protocol specification. So if we want the server to collect a lot of information from a form, we're likely to find some of it is truncated in transit. But there is another way to get data…

Using the POST Method

There is a second way of sending data from the form to the server. Instead of using **GET** for the **METHOD** attribute of the form, we can use the **POST** method in a **<FORM>** tag. This buries the information inside the HTTP header, rather than adding it to the URL as a query string:

```
<HTML>
<HEAD>
<META HTTP-EQUIV="Content-Type" CONTENT="text/html;charset=windows-1252">
<TITLE>ASP 2.0 Demo</TITLE>
</HEAD>
<BODY>
```

```
<CENTER>
 <H1>ASP FORM DEMO 1</H1>
 <FORM NAME="userinfo" ACTION="MAININFO.ASP" METHOD="POST">
  <H2>Please fill in the following form</H2><P>
  <PRE>
   Name  <INPUT TYPE="TEXT" NAME="uname">
   email <INPUT TYPE="TEXT" NAME="mail">
  </PRE>
  <INPUT TYPE=RESET  VALUE="Reset">
  <INPUT TYPE=SUBMIT VALUE="Submit">
 </FORM>
</CENTER>
</HTML>
```

When this page is submitted, the names and values of the text boxes are encoded into the request header, and there is no sign of them in the browser's Address box

```
http://localhost/demo/book/MAININFO.ASP
```

But this time the values of the request can't be accessed through the **QueryString** collection. That's where the **Form** collection comes to action. This collection contains information sent from forms that use the **POST** method.

The differences between the two methods of sending data from client to server are shown on the following diagram.

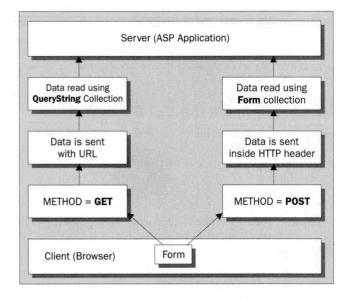

We'll look in detail at the **QueryString** and **Form** collections next, and it should now be obvious why we have these two separate collections.

So don't be fooled into thinking that just because we've received input from a **<FORM>**, that we'll actually have any values in the **Form** collection–it's all down to that **METHOD** attribute in the declaration of the form.

The QueryString Collection

To see how we can use the **QueryString** collection, let's extend the form we saw at the beginning of the chapter. Here's the new form itself:

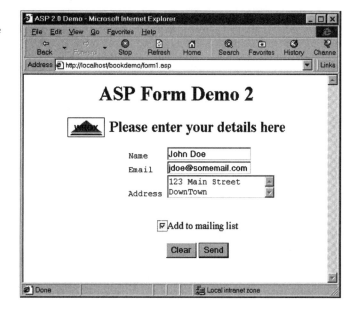

Here's the HTML code that creates it:

```
<FORM NAME="userinfo" ACTION="MAININFO.ASP" METHOD="GET">
<H2>Please enter your details here</H2><P>
<PRE>
 Name    <INPUT TYPE="TEXT" NAME="uName" SIZE=20>
 Email   <INPUT TYPE="TEXT" NAME="mail"  SIZE=20>
 Address <TEXTAREA SIZE="15,2" NAME="addrs"></TEXTAREA>
</PRE>
<CENTER>
 <INPUT TYPE=CHECKBOX VALUE=True>Add to mailing list<P>
 <INPUT TYPE=RESET   VALUE="Clear">
 <INPUT TYPE=SUBMIT VALUE="Send">
</CENTER>
</FORM>
```

What We Actually Get From Our Form

When this form is submitted, we'll expect to get all of the data about the contents back in the query string, appended to the URL, like this:

```
uname=John+Doe&mail=jdoe@somemail.com&addrs=123+Main+Street%0D%0ADownTown
```

Notice that field names and values are separated with '=', a single piece of data is delimited with an ampersand (**&**) and spaces have been converted into 'plus' signs. Other characters are referenced by their ANSI code in hexadecimal, and preceded by a **%** character–so **%0D%0A** is just return and line feed characters, **Chr(13)** and **Chr(10)** respectively. This is an example of **URL-encoding**, and you'll come across it in more detail later in this and the next chapters.

So, from looking at the query string, it would seem to be a difficult task to actually find out what the values in the form were. This, as you've probably guessed, is where our **QueryString** collection comes in. We can retrieve the value of the **uName** control (the name is set by **NAME** attribute of **<INPUT>** tag) just by referring to it in the **QueryString** collection:

```
<%
 strName = Request.QueryString("uName")
%>
```

Here we use the **QueryString** collection of the **Request** object to get the value, passed by user in the *Name* input string, which has the **uName** name inside the form. We do this by referring to it by control name and assigning the result to the **strName** variable.

Looping Through a Collection

Collections implement a very useful feature that makes it easy to get all the values from them. Each value is accessed using a unique string key, such as **uName**, and—unlike an array—there is no concept of a numeric index to each value. So it's difficult to loop (or **iterate**) through all the values in a collection using the traditional **For...Next** loop with a numeric counter variable. Instead collections support the **For...Each** construct, where we don't need to know the names of the keys up front. Using VBScript we just iterate through the whole collection, retrieving the keys and values as we go:

```
For Each member in collection
    ...
    ...
Next
```

So, if all we wanted to do was display the data sent from our form, we could use code like this to iterate through each item in the **QueryString** collection:

```
<% For Each Item in Request.QueryString %>
     Control name '<% = Item %>'
     has the value '<% = Request.QueryString(Item) %>' <BR>
<% Next %>
```

Here **Item** is a variable, which holds the value of a particular key–in each iteration we get the new key and use it to refer to the **QueryString** collection to get its value.

However, we will not see the value of our checkbox:

Control name 'uname' has the value 'John Doe'
Control name 'mail' has the value 'jdoe@somemail.com'
Control name 'addrs' has the value '123 Main Street DownTown'

The problem is that we forgot to give it a name:

```
<INPUT TYPE=CHECKBOX VALUE=True>Add to mailing list<P>
```

We just need to add a **NAME** attribute to the **INPUT** tag:

```
<INPUT TYPE=CHECKBOX NAME="chkAddToList" VALUE="True"><P>
```

Now, our query string is correct:

```
http://localhost/bookdemo/MAINVBS.ASP?uname=Johh+Doe&mail=jdoe@somemail.com
&addrs=123+Main+Street%0D%0ADownTown&chkAddToList=True
```

and we'll receive the value of the checkbox:

Control name 'uname' has the value 'John Doe'
Control name 'chkAddToList' has the value 'True'
Control name 'mail' has the value 'jdoe@somemail.com'
Control name 'addrs' has the value '123 Main Street DownTown'

As an alternative to the VBScript **For .. Each** loop, we can also use the JScript **'enumerator'** object to iterate through the collection. First, we assign our collection to a new instance of this object, then we use a **while** loop checking the end of collection with its terminator checking the **atEnd** method. In each iteration we get one item from the collection with the **item** method and move to the next item with the **moveNext** method. Here is how we can implement looping through the collection discussed above in JScript:

```
<%
// Create new Enumerator object
  items = new Enumerator(Request.QueryString)
// Loop through collection
  while (!items.atEnd()) {
// Get current item
  i = items.item()
// Show it
    Response.Write("Control name '" + i +
    "' has the value '" + Request.QueryString(i) + "'<BR>")
// Move to next item
  items.moveNext()
  }
%>
```

The Form Collection

You'll recall we discovered earlier that data is only sent to the server query string when the **METHOD** attribute of a form is **GET**, or when it's directly added to the URL in the **HREF** attribute of an **<A>** tag on the page. When the **METHOD** attribute of a form is **POST**, the data comes to us wrapped up in the HTTP headers instead. In this case, the **QueryString** collection is empty, and the values from the controls are placed in the **Request** object's **Form** collection.

Because it's a collection, like **QueryString**, we can retrieve values from it:

```
strName = Request.Form("uName")
```

and iterate through it, in the same way:

```
<% For Each Item in Request.Form %>
    Control name '<% = Item %>'
    has the value '<% = Request.Form(Item) %>' <BR>
<% Next %>
```

To iterate through the data like this also requires that all the form elements be named, just as with the query string. Or we can use **enumerator** object to iterate through **Form** collection with JScript:

```
<%
// Create new Enumarator object
  items = new Enumerator(Request.Form)
// Loop through collection
  while (!items.atEnd()) {
// Get current item
    i = items.item()
// Show it
    Response.Write("Control name '" + i +
      "' has the value '" + Request.Form (i) + "'<BR>")
// Move to next item
    items.moveNext()
  }
%>
```

Working with Control Groups

Often, we need to create forms that contain multiple groups of related information. For example, we can add two radio buttons to our form to enable us to choose between genders. We give them unique values so that we can distinguish them when we come to access the **Form** collection:

```
<INPUT TYPE=RADIO NAME=optGender VALUE="Female"> Female
<INPUT TYPE=RADIO NAME=optGender VALUE="Male"> Male
```

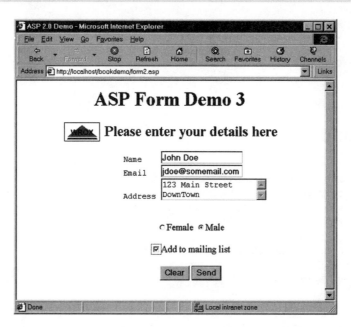

When the browser submits the page, it only includes the values of radio button and check box controls which are actually set, or selected. That's why we only received the name/value pair **optGender=Male** in the query string.

Control name 'optGender' has the value 'Male'

Radio buttons have the property of belonging to a **group**, where the user can only select one of them in that group. Clicking on one of the buttons clears the others in the same group. To tell the browser that they belong to a group, all we have to do is give them the same **NAME** attribute, but different **VALUE** attributes, as we did in the previous code.

> *This is very different from traditional Windows programming techniques, where we would put all the related controls into some type of container control, such as an option frame. In this case, the value of the option frame would be the index of the selected button.*

Collections Items with Multiple Values

To get several different groups of radio buttons to behave correctly on a single page, we have to give the buttons in each group the same name, but use different names for each of the groups. For example, if we wanted to produce a questionnaire like this:

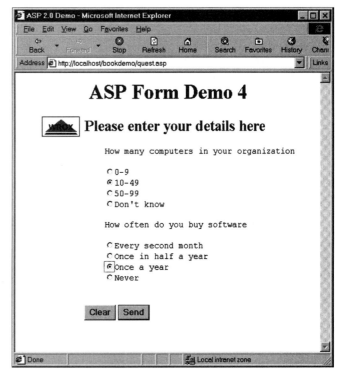

we would have to give each radio button in the column the same name, but use a different name for the other rows:

```
<FORM NAME="userinfo" ACTION="QUESTVB.ASP" METHOD="GET">
   <H2>Please enter your details here</H2><P>
   <PRE>
   How many computers in your organization

   <INPUT TYPE="RADIO" NAME="grpnumComps" VALUE="0-9">0-9
   <INPUT TYPE="RADIO" NAME="grpnumComps" VALUE="10-49">10-49
   <INPUT TYPE="RADIO" NAME="grpnumComps" VALUE="50-99">50-99
   <INPUT TYPE="RADIO" NAME="grpnumComps" VALUE="Unknown">Don't know
```

```
    How often do you buy software

    <INPUT TYPE="RADIO" NAME="grpSoft" VALUE=2>Every second month
    <INPUT TYPE="RADIO" NAME="grpSoft" VALUE=6>Once in half a year
    <INPUT TYPE="RADIO" NAME="grpSoft" VALUE=12>Once a year
    <INPUT TYPE="RADIO" NAME="grpSoft" VALUE=Never>Never
    </PRE>
    <P>
    <INPUT TYPE=RESET  VALUE="Clear">
    <INPUT TYPE=SUBMIT VALUE="Send">
    </CENTER>
    </FORM>
```

Previously, we just retrieved the name and value of the form element. However, each **NAME** now has four possible values. We can do what we did earlier, and just retrieve the **VALUE** of the selected one:

```
    strComps = Request.Form("grpnumComps")
```

This will give us the result **10-49** from the selections we made in the form. However, in some cases, the **Form** object may have to hold several values for one **member**–i.e. one control name. These values *are* available using their index, like an array, and we can retrieve them using:

```
    strTheValue = Request.Form("ControlName")(Index)
```

The only problem now, is figuring out how many values there are for each collection member. To do this, we use another useful property of a collection.

Using a Collection's Count Property

A collection's **Count** property returns the number of items in the collection. This lets us decide if there are multiple values, and provides a way to iterate through them. Again using our questionnaire, we can retrieve all the values from all the option groups, like in this VBScript code:

```
<%
  For Each Item in Request.Form
   If Request.Form(Item).Count Then
    For intLoop = 1 to Request.Form(Item).Count
%>
  <% Response.Write(Item & ": Index = " & intLoop & " Value = " _
           & Request.Form(Item)(intLoop)) %> <BR>
  <%
  Next
  Else
%>
  <% = Request.Form(Item) %>
  <%
  End If
  Next
%>
```

We're using a **For...Each** loop to iterate through all the members of the **Form** collection. Because some of the members (all in our example) may be named groups, we first check the **Count** property of that member. If it's not zero, i.e. **True**, we have a collection of values that we need to iterate through. If it's zero, then we just have a single value–this is not option in our example, but our code can be used to handle any form. For the questionnaire, we get a result like this:

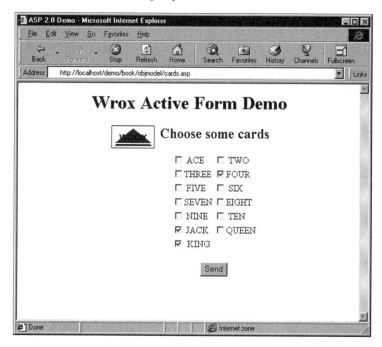

It may seem that we've gone to a lot of effort to retrieve little extra information. We still only receive one value for each collection member, because the user can only select one option for each question. In effect, what we're seeing here is just the first value in each collection member:

```
Request.Form("grpnumComps")(1)
Request.Form("grpSoft")(1)
```

Notice also, that the results don't necessarily appear in the same order as on the page in the browser.

Collections of Check Box Values

The situation with multiple-value collection members is rather different when we have a group of **check boxes** or **text boxes** on a form. Look at this group of check boxes.

These are all part of the same group–they have the same **NAME** attribute, `oneCard`, but different **VALUE** attributes.

```
<FORM NAME="userinfo" ACTION="MAINVBS.ASP" METHOD="POST">
<CENTER>
<H2>Choose some cards</H2><P>
<TABLE>
 <TR>
  <TD><INPUT TYPE=CHECKBOX NAME=oneCard VALUE="ACE">  ACE</TD>
  <TD><INPUT TYPE=CHECKBOX NAME=oneCard VALUE="TWO">  TWO </TD>
 </TR>
 <TR>
  <TD><INPUT TYPE=CHECKBOX NAME=oneCard VALUE="THREE">THREE</TD>
  <TD><INPUT TYPE=CHECKBOX NAME=oneCard VALUE="FOUR"">FOUR</TD>
 </TR>
 ...
 <TR>
  <TD><INPUT TYPE=CHECKBOX NAME=oneCard VALUE="KING"> KING</TD>
 <TD> </TD>
 </TR>
</TABLE><P>
<INPUT TYPE=SUBMIT VALUE="Send">
</CENTER>
</FORM>
```

When we send this form to the code we used with our questionnaire, we get a multiple-value member in our **Form** collection, with these three values:

This is, of course, because three of the check boxes were ticked, and they come back with index values of **1**, **2**, and **3**. Remember, however, that these are *not* the indexes of the original check boxes–just the indexes of the three values within the collection member.

Because of the way in which the browser supplies data from a form, we can never make any assumptions about the number or order of elements in the collections. However, we can use this feature to our advantage. If we want to produce an address entry form, we could give all the individual address-line text boxes the same **NAME** attribute. Then, the only data that will appear in the **Form** collection will be from text boxes where the user actually entered some text. There will be no more blank lines in the database's **Address** table!

Searching in All the Collections

When we've used the **Request** object's collections so far, we've always specified the collection name. In fact, this isn't required. If we omit the collection name, ASP will search through the collections in a pre-defined order, and return the first value it finds with a matching key. The search order is:

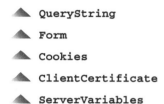

- QueryString
- Form
- Cookies
- ClientCertificate
- ServerVariables

However, this might not be what we actually want to happen. If the **QueryString** and **Cookies** collections both contain a value which has the key **ImportantValue**, and we want the cookie's value, we'll end up getting the wrong **ImportantValue**. For example:

```
strResult = Request.Cookies("ImportantValue")
```

returns the value of the cookie with the key (or name) **ImportantValue**, while:

```
strResult = Request.("ImportantValue")
```

will look in the **QueryString** and **Form** collections for a key **ImportantValue** first, and return the matching value from that collection if it finds one. It might never get as far as the **Cookies** collection.

Of course, the shorthand method ought to be faster. The actual statement is shorter, and so requires less processing by the script interpreter. However, unless the item we want is actually in the **QueryString** collection, it will probably be slower because it has to search through other collections as it goes.

Besides that, the risk of finding a value in the wrong collection means that you really ought to avoid this technique. It's one way of producing really erratic behavior in your pages, the source of which could take weeks of debugging to find!

The ServerVariables Collection

Another collection provided by the **Request** object is **ServerVariables**. Although this sounds as though it has little to do with the client request, much of the information that we've looked at with the other collections actually originates here in the **ServerVariables** collection. Any HTTP header that is sent by a client browser is available in this collection, through code like this:

```
strTheValue = Request.ServerVariables("HeaderType")
```

The standard HTTP headers are automatically defined as members of the **ServerVariables** collection. For example, when form data is sent to the server, the method by which it was sent can be determined from:

```
<% = Request.ServerVariables("REQUEST_METHOD") %>
```

This will return **GET** or **POST**, depending on how the data was sent from the browser.

We can also use the **QUERY_STRING** header to obtain the original unadulterated query string that was passed to the server from the browser. There are a great many headers available in this collection, and some have been processed for us, and presented in collections such as **QueryString**, while others have not. We've included a list of the HTTP header types in Appendix I, so we'll just show you a few examples here.

```
User's IP Address: <% = Request.ServerVariables("REMOTE_ADDR") %>
User's Logon Account: <% = Request.ServerVariables("LOGON_USER") %>
The whole HTTP string: <% = Request.ServerVariables("ALL_HTTP") %>
```

Using The HTTP_USER_AGENT Header

Using the **HTTP_USER_AGENT** header we can check the type of client browser and perform appropriate actions based on this information. For example, we can solve the common problem of determining the screen resolution of client's screen. First, we create a short ASP program:

```
<% Response.Buffer = True %>
<HTML>
<HEAD><TITLE>ASP 2.0 Demo</TITLE></HEAD>
<BODY>
  <%
  Set uAgent = Request.ServerVariables("HTTP_USER_AGENT")
   if inStr(uAgent, "4.") > 0 then
    Response.Redirect("scr40.htm")
   else
   ' put some code here to handle pre 4.0 browsers
  end if
  %>
</BODY>
</HTML>
```

Here we check the **HTTP_USER_AGENT** header from the **ServerVariables** collection to determine the version of client browser and if it is 4.0, we redirect the client to the HTML page, **scr40.htm**, which contains this short JavaScript program:

```
<HTML>
 <HEAD><TITLE>ASP 2.0 Demos</TITLE></HEAD>
 <BODY>
  <script language=JavaScript>
   s = "?w="+screen.width+"&h="+screen.height
   location.href="scrres.asp"+s
  </script>
 </BODY>
</HTML>
```

This program gets values from **width** and **height** properties of built-in **screen** object, supported both by Microsoft Internet Explorer 4.0 and Netscape Navigator 4.0 and redirects output to the **scrres.asp** file. Note how we manually build a query string for this Active Server Pages file:

```
s = "?w="+screen.width+"&h="+screen.height
```

We pass it two parameters–**w** and **h** with a proper syntax we discovered earlier in this chapter. So, for screen resolution 800 x 600 the query string will be

```
scrres.asp?w=800&h=600
```

Next comes the **scrres.asp** file:

```
<HTML>
 <HEAD><TITLE>ASP 2.0 Demos</TITLE></HEAD>
 <BODY>
  <%
    s = "Client browser resolution = "
    s = s + Request.QueryString("w") + " x "
    s = s + Request.QueryString("h")
    Response.Write(s)
  %>
 </BODY>
</HTML>
```

Here we use **Request.QueryString** method to extract values from request and output them on screen. We can store them somewhere and use throughout our program.

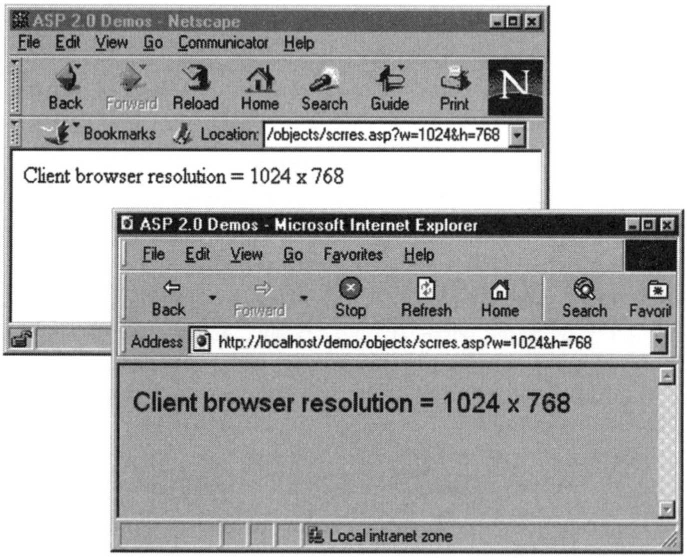

The diagram below shows program logic and the order in which files are loaded. You can find the complete code for this example at Wrox site: **http://rapid.wrox.co.uk./books/1266/**

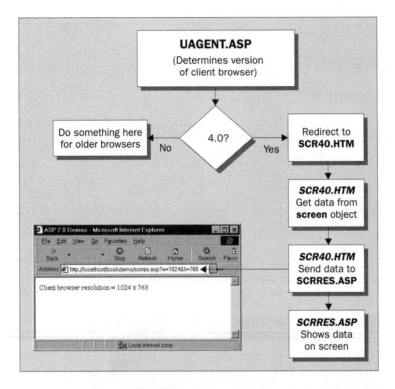

As we have seen in the example above, the **HTTP_USER_AGENT** header can be used by the server to determine the type of client browser. This technique serves as a base for the **Browser Capabilities** component, which we will discuss in Chapter 6.

Using the HTTP_ACCEPT_LANGUAGE Header

Another interesting example can be based on the **HTTP_ACCEPT_LANGUAGE** header, which will allow us to determine which (human) language is supported by the client's browser and software. For example, if the client supports the Russian language (which can be set via appropriate settings in the browser), **HTTP_ACCEPT_LANGUAGE** header will return the string "ru".

Using this information we can redirect users to international (localized) pages. For example:

```
<% Response.Buffer = True %>
<HTML>
<HEAD><TITLE>ASP 2.0 Demo</TITLE></HEAD>
<BODY>
  <%
   Set uLang = Request.ServerVariables("HTTP_ACCEPT_LANGUAGE")
   if inStr(uLang, "ru") > 0 then
    Response.Redirect("russian.htm")
   else
    Response.Redirect("english.htm")
   end if
  %>
</BODY>
</HTML>
```

One thing to note is that this will only work if the user sets appropriate language preferences in his browser. For example, in Microsoft Internet Explorer 4.0 this can be done through View | Internet Options command of the main menu and by selecting Languages button on General page. Then the proper language should be selected and added to a list of supported languages.

In Netscape Navigator 4.0 this can be done through Edit | Preferences command of the main menu by selecting Languages category.

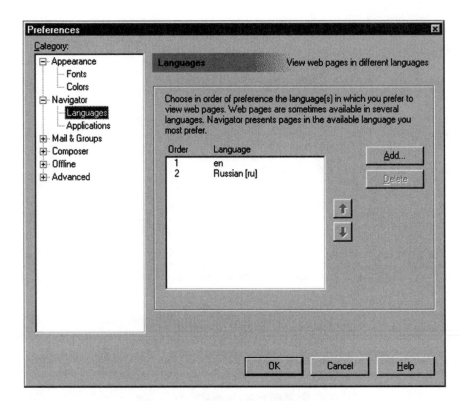

The Cookies Collection

The **QueryString** and **Form** collections that we examined earlier are only ever available in a single browser request. Each time the user requests any file from our server, the **Request** object's collections are updated with the information from that request. Occasionally we find that there's a need for more persistent data storage. To achieve this, the concept of cookies was introduced into the HTTP protocol specification, and quickly adopted by Netscape in their Navigator 2.0 browser.

A **cookie** is a packet of information that is sent by the browser to the server with each request. Data items within each cookie are available in the **Cookies** collection, and it is accessed in a similar manner to the **QueryString** and **Form** collections we've just been looking at. The cookie is stored as a file on the client machine, which means that it can be used to store information that is available the next time the browser starts.

When accessed through the **Request** object, the cookies are read-only—since the information they represent is actually held on the client browser, and not the server. We *can* change cookie information, but only by using the **Response** object. We'll come to this shortly.

In their simplest form, we access cookies as we did form data. You can use the following VBScript code to get a listing of all the members of the **Cookies** collection:

```
<% For Each Item in Request.Cookies %>
     <% = "Cookie: " & Item & "=" &Request.Cookies(Item) %> <BR>
<% Next %>
```

or using JScript:

```
<%
// Create new Enumerator object
  items = new Enumerator(Request.Cookies)
// Loop through collection
  while (!items.atEnd()) {
// Get current item
    i = items.item()
// Show it
    Response.Write("Cookie: " + i + "=" + Request.Cookies (i) + "'<BR>")
// Move to next item
    items.moveNext()
  }
%>
```

And as with the **Form** collection, each member of the **Cookies** collection can hold multiple values for that cookie name. In other words, one cookie name can have many items of data stored within it. However, cookies don't have a **Count** property. Instead, each multiple value member is said to contain **keys** to the information in that member

> *This is because the **Cookies** collection is implemented in the same way as the **Dictionary** object that we'll be meeting in Chapter 5. Just stay with us for now, and it will all become clear.*

To determine if a particular cookie is a dictionary type we need to look at its **HasKeys** property:

```
someValue = Request.Cookies("myCookie").HasKeys
```

This code will set our **someValue** variable to **True** for a cookie that is a dictionary, i.e. has multiple values for this member. To use the values stored in cookie dictionaries, we have to specify the key by name, which is similar to specifying a number for the numeric index of the **Form** collection. Again, we can iterate through the **keys** collection of the cookie dictionary with a **For...Each** loop. So, to display all the cookie information that is supplied by the browser we can use something like this:

```
<% 'Get all cookie data
   For Each Item in Request.Cookies
      If Request.Cookies(Item).HasKeys Then
         'use another For...Each to iterate all keys of dictionary
         For Each ItemKey in Request.Cookies(Item) %>
            Sub Item: <%= Item %> (<%= ItemKey %>)
                  = <%= Request.Cookies(Item)(ItemKey)%>
      <% Next
      Else
         'Print out the cookie string as normal %>
         <%= Item %> = <%= Request.Cookies(Item)%> <BR>
   <% End If
   Next %>
```

Notice that **Item** in the outer **For...Each** loop isn't actually an object variable. It's just a string used to reference the required object in the **Cookies** collection, so we use code such as:

```
If Request.Cookies(Item).HasKeys
```

If this is true, the inner **For...Each** loop will retrieve the values of each of the sub-keys.

A cookie can also have attributes that describe its lifetime and availability, but we'll leave this discussion to the **Response** object, where we can actually set these values using script, rather than just being able to read them

The ClientCertificate Collection

Security is currently a big issue on the Net. If you're concerned about security in your electronic transactions, then some thought and planning needs to be applied to your web site. One feature that is becoming increasingly available in browsers is access to the **secure sockets layer** (**SSL**). When a browser is using the SSL3.0/PCT1 protocol, the requested URLs are prefixed by **https://** instead of the more usual **http://** protocol. Private Communication Technology (PCT) is an efficient and secure upgrade to the SSL protocol.

The SSL/PCT protocols provide secure data communication through data encryption and decryption. An SSL/PCT-enabled server, such as Microsoft Internet Information Server, can send and receive private communication across the Internet to SSL/PCT-enabled clients, such as Microsoft Internet Explorer. In the Open Systems Interconnect (OSI) model, SSL/PCT are protocol layers between the TCP/IP transport/ network layer and the application layer where HTTP operates. SSL provides server authentication, encryption, and data integrity. Authentication assures the client that data is being sent to the correct server and that the server is secure. Encryption assures that the data cannot be read by anyone other than the secure target server. Data integrity assures that the data being transferred has not been altered.

When SSL is in use, the browser sends the server **certificates** that identify the client. If we want to make use of this information in our web pages, to assure ourselves that we're sending out information to only those users who are authorized to receive it, we can use the **ClientCertificate** collection of the **Request** object. We also need to include the **cervbs.inc** file in our scripts to declare the appropriate constants used with client certificates. There are actually only two constants defined in this particular file:

```
Const ceCertPresent = 1
Const ceUnrecognizedIssuer = 2
```

We could, of course, just declare these ourselves, but it makes things clearer if we use the appropriate server-side include in our ASP files for this:

```
<!--#include file="cervbs.inc" -->
```

for VBScript, or

```
<!--#include file="cerjavas.inc" -->
```

for JScript. These files are installed in the **\Inetpub\ASPSamp\Samples** directory. To use them we can copy it to our application directory, or map path to above mentioned directory and use **#include virtual** directive instead.

Accessing the information in the **ClientCertificate** collection follows a similar pattern to the one we saw with the other **Request** object collections. We reference the collection, then a **key** to the item of information we require. Two of the keys, **Subject** and **Issuer**, have sub-fields for which we can state more specific information, although this is accessed a little differently to the way we have previously seen. The following table summarizes the available keys.

Key	Meaning
Certificate	A string containing the entire certificate content in ASN.1 format.
Flags	Flags that provide additional certificate information. The following are available: **ceCertPresent** and **ceUnrecognizedIssuer**.
Issuer	A string containing a list of sub-field values which hold information about the certificate issuer. If requested without specifying a sub-field it returns a comma-separated list such as **"C=US, O=Verisign, ..."**.
ValidFrom	A date specifying when the certificate becomes valid. This date follows scripting formats, and varies with the international settings. For example, in the US it could be **1/31/97 11:59:59 PM**.
ValidUntil	A date specifying when the certificate expires.
SerialNumber	A string containing the certification serial number as ASCII representations of hexadecimal bytes separated by hyphens (-). For example, **"04-67-F3-02"**.
Subject	A string containing a list of sub-field values which hold information about the owner of the certificate. If specified without a sub-field, it returns a comma-separated list of sub-fields, in a similar way to **Issuer**.

If we intend to verify that our users are who they say they are, we first have to check for the presence (or absence) of a **certificate**. If a certificate is present, the length of the string returned when we retrieve the **Subject** key will be greater than zero:

```
<% If Len(Request.ClientCertificate("Subject")) = 0 %>
     You did not present a client certificate.
<% End if %>
```

Once we've determined the presence of a certificate, we can check various aspects of it before finally letting the client have the information they requested. For example, we may want to check the organisation that the user belongs to. In this case we refer to the **SubjectO** key. No, this isn't a spelling error! Where there's sub-field information available in the certificate, we just append the sub-field identifier character(s) to the key to get the specific information, rather than a comma-separated list. The following table lists all the sub-field identifiers we have access to.

Identifier	Meaning
C	Specifies the name of the **country** of origin.
O	Specifies the company or **organization** name.
OU	Specifies the name of the **organizational unit**.
CN	Specifies the **common name** of the user. Only used with the **Subject** key.

Identifier	Meaning
L	Specifies a **locality**.
S	Specifies a **state** or province.
T	Specifies the **title** of the person or organization.
GN	Specifies a **given name**.
I	Specifies a set of **initials**.

One of the benefits of this level of information becomes apparent when we think about commerce on the Internet. Assuming that certification is available, we could provide the user with an accurate price for their request based on the State they are registered in—this code assumes that we have declared a constant **CALIF_SALES_TAX** for the sales tax rate in California:

```
<% If Request.ClientCertificate("SubjectS") = "CA" Then
      Cost = Cost * (1 + CALIF_SALES_TAX)
   End If %>
```

In case you're wondering just why we have had to bother with the **include** file, it's all to do with the **Flags** key. We can use the value of **Flags** combined logically with the constants defined by the included file to make decisions about the requesting client. For example, the following code could be used to determine whether the issuer of the certificate is known:

```
<% If Request.ClientCertificate("Flags") and ceUnrecognizedIssuer Then
      Your certificate is not form a recognized issuer.
<% End If %>
```

These simple examples of using the **ClientCertificate** collection will give you some idea of how we can add security features to our web site.

Getting everything from the client – the BinaryRead Method

As we're talking about getting information from the client, we should mention the **BinaryRead** method, which retrieves data sent to the server from the client as part of a **POST** request. This method retrieves the data from the client and stores it in an array, which contains information about the number of dimensions and the bounds of its dimensions.

This method is used for low-level access to the raw data sent by the client as part of a **POST** request, as opposed to, for example, using the **Request.Form** collection to view form data sent in a **POST** request, described earlier. Once you have called **BinaryRead**, referring to any variable in the **Request.Form** collection will cause an error. Conversely, once you have referred to a variable in the **Request.Form** collection, calling **BinaryRead** will cause an error. Remember, if you access a variable in the **Request** collection without specifying which subcollection it belongs to, the **Request.Form** collection may be searched, bringing this rule into force. Here is a short VBScript example of how to use this method

```
<%
  dim binRead
  dim byteCount
  byteCount = Request.TotalBytes 'get the size of request
  binRead   = Request.BinaryRead(byteCount) ' get raw data
```

```
        Response.Write(CStr(byteCount) + " byte(s) received from client.")
%>
```

The **Request.BinaryRead** method can be used, for example, to read binary data that is posted to the server, such as a file upload. You rarely need to use this method and it is mentioned here mostly for completeness.

Using Collections to Debug Your Forms and Pages

The technique we've seen for displaying all the members of a collection, including the values of multiple-value collection members, is a handy way of debugging our forms or pages when we come to work with the data that they return to our server.

Microsoft have an Active Server Pages debugging script (called **DEBUG.ASP**) that you can download from their web site **http://www.microsoft.com/iis**, or as part of IIS Software Development Kit, but we can easily create our own to achieve the same result. To examine all the data coming from the browser, we just need to look at the five collections maintained by the **Request** object:

```
<H3> QueryString Collection </H3>
<% For Each Item in Request.QueryString
        For intLoop = 1 to Request.QueryString(Item).Count %>
            <% Response.Write(Item & " = " & Request.QueryString(Item)(intLoop)) %> <BR>
    <% Next
    Next %>
<H3> Form Collection </H3>
<% For Each Item in Request.Form
        For intLoop = 1 to Request.Form(Item).Count %>
            <% Response.Write(Item & " = " & Request.Form(Item)(intLoop)) %> <BR>
    <% Next
    Next %>
<H3> Cookies Collection </H3>
<% For Each Item in Request.Cookies
        If Request.Cookies(Item).HasKeys Then
            For Each ItemKey in Request.Cookies(Item) %>
                Sub Item: <% Response.Write(Item) %> (<% Response.Write(ItemKey) %>)
                        = <%= Request.Cookies(Item)(ItemKey)%>
        <% Next
        Else %>
            Response.Write(Item) %> = <% = Request.Cookies(Item)%> <BR>
    <% End If
    Next %>
<H3> ClientCertificate Collection </H3>
<% For Each Item in Request.ClientCertificate
        For intLoop = 1 to Request.ClientCertificate(Item).Count %>
            <% Response.Write(Item & " = " & Request.ClientCertificate(Item)(intLoop)) %>
<BR>
    <% Next
    Next %>
<H3> ServerVariables Collection </H3>
<% For Each Item in Request.ServerVariables
        For intLoop = 1 to Request.ServerVariables(Item).Count %>
            <% Response.Write(Item & " = " & Request.ServerVariables(Item)(intLoop)) %>
<BR>
    <% Next
    Next %>
```

Here's part of the results we get when we submit the form we've been using earlier to it. If you scroll down the page you'll see it displays a huge amount of information from the **ServerVariables** collection.

```
ASP 2.0 Demo - Microsoft Internet Explorer                          _ □ ×

 File   Edit   View   Go   Favorites   Help

 ⇦        ⇨         ⊗       ⊡        ⌂       ⊕        ⊡        ⊕         ⊡         ⊠      Ⓐ
 Back    Forward    Stop   Refresh   Home   Search  Favorites  History  Channels  Fullscreen  Mail  Font

 Address  🔗  http://localhost/demo/book/objmodel/DEBUG.ASP                            ▼

 QueryString Collection

 Form Collection

 uname = John Doe
 chkAddToList = True
 mail = jdoe@somemail.com
 addrs = 123 Main Street DownTown
 optGender = Male

 Cookies Collection

 ScriptLanguagePreference = JScript
 ComponentPreference = VB5

 ClientCertificate Collection

 ServerVariables Collection

 ALL_HTTP = HTTP_ACCEPT:*/* HTTP_ACCEPT_LANGUAGE:ru
 HTTP_CONNECTION:Keep-Alive HTTP_HOST:localhost
 HTTP_REFERER:http://localhost/demo/book/objmodel/form2.ASP
 HTTP_USER_AGENT:Mozilla/4.0 (compatible; MSIE 4.01; Windows 95)

 🔗 Done                                          🔒 Local intranet zone
```

We've included this page in the samples that you can download from our site at **http://rapid.wrox.co.uk/books/1266**.

Summary

In this chapter we've taken a tour around the built-in objects exposed by Active Server Pages. We've briefly mentioned all of the objects available and described the purpose of each of them. Then we spent almost all of the chapter discussing one particular built-in object–**Request**. It provides us with a set of properties, which stores the information passed from the user and the client browser.

The main points of this chapter are:

- Active Server Pages provides an **object model** that we can manipulate using scripting languages. This gives us a structured way of accessing all kinds of information, and producing dynamic content for our site.

- The **Request** object contains all of the information about the client's request for a file.

- To access data sent through a form we can use the **QueryString** or **Form** collections of **Request** object

- To get the values of HTTP and environment variables we can use the **ServerVariables** collection of the **Request** object

- The **Cookies** collection of the **Request** object allows us to get values of cookies sent from the browser

- To get client certificate values sent from the browser we can use the **ClientCertificate** collection

As we mentioned at the beginning of this chapter, there are six main built-in objects provided by Active Server Pages. We will cover the other five objects–**Response**, **Server**, **Application**, **Session** and **ObjectContext**– in the next chapter.

The Active Server Pages Server Objects

In the previous chapter we started to discuss the Active Server Pages object model and spent nearly an entire chapter taking a look at the properties, methods and collections of just one of the six objects– **Request**. We also covered a lot of groundwork there and that means that the objects discussed in this chapter–**Response, Server, Application, Session** and **ObjectContext**–will seem quite familiar as you meet them.

In this chapter we will continue to investigate the Active Server Pages object model and will see the following topics:

▲ How we provide our own responses, as customized web pages

▲ What we can achieve through other parts of the object model

▲ How we can manipulate cookies, and use the concept of an application

The Response Object

The second main object in the hierarchy is the **Response** object. Whereas the **Request** object is totally concerned with what is coming to our server from the browser, the **Response** object, not surprisingly, handles all the stuff we want to send back to it.

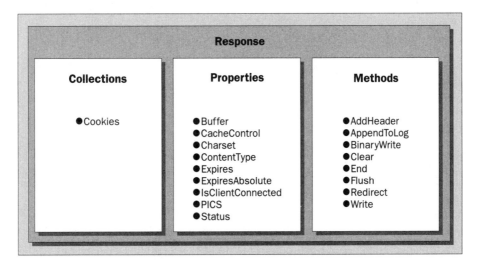

Response		
Collections	**Properties**	**Methods**
● Cookies	● Buffer ● CacheControl ● Charset ● ContentType ● Expires ● ExpiresAbsolute ● IsClientConnected ● PICS ● Status	● AddHeader ● AppendToLog ● BinaryWrite ● Clear ● End ● Flush ● Redirect ● Write

This is what the interface of the **Response** object looks like:

Collection	Description
cookies	Values of all the cookies to send to the browser.

Properties	Description
buffer	Indicates whether to buffer the page until complete.
cachecontrol	Determines whether proxy servers are able to cache the output generated by ASP
charset	Appends the name of the character set to the content-type header
contenttype	HTTP content type (i.e. **"Text/HTML"**) for the response.
expires	Length of time before a page cached on a browser expires.
expiresabsolute	Date and time when a page cached on a browser expires.
isclientconnected	Indicates whether the client has disconnected from the server
PICS	Adds the value of a PICS label to the **pics-label** field of the response header.
status	Value of the HTTP status line returned by the server.

Methods	Description
addHeader	Adds or changes a value in the HTML header.
appendtolog	Adds text to the web server log entry for this request.
binarywrite	Sends text to the browser without character-set conversion.
clear	Erases any buffered HTML output.
end	Stops processing the page and returns the current result.
flush	Sends buffered output immediately.
redirect	Instructs the browser to connect to a different URL.
write	Writes a variable to the current page as a string.

As you can see, the **Response** object implements a single collection, **cookies**, five properties, and eight methods. Excluding the **appendtolog** method, all **Response** interface elements can be divided into following groups:

Description	Response Items
Inserting information into a page.	`write`, `binarywrite`
Sending cookies to the browser.	`cookies`
Redirecting the browser.	`redirect`
Buffering the page as it is created.	`buffer`, `flush`, `clear`, `end`
Setting the properties of a page.	`expires`, `expiresabsolute`, `contenttype`, `addheader`, `status`, `cachecontrol`, `PICS`, `charset`
Checking the client connection	`isclientconnected`

The **appendtolog** method adds a text string to the web server's log file, if logging is enabled. The string can be up to 80 characters long, but must not contain any commas:

```
response.appendtolog "Adding this additional information to the log file"
```

Inserting Information into Pages

The most obvious requirement for the **Response** object is for it to be able to send back a page containing text, graphics and other interesting 'content' that our visitors would expect. As we've seen in Chapter 2, we can insert the values of variables or the results of calculated expressions into our returned pages using this syntax:

```
This is the value: <% = strSomeValue %>
```

Sometimes, however, this becomes unwieldy. Instead of having to bracket each block of code separately, and use the **<% = ... %>** syntax to insert values, we can take advantage of the **Response** object's **write** method instead. All it does is insert a string into the HTML stream that the browser receives. For example:

```
response.write("This is the value: " & strSomeValue)
```

This is just like real programming. We can construct strings in code and **write** them to the page. It also makes our code look tidier in some situations, especially when we have a loop or conditional test to perform. The following two VBScript examples produce exactly the same output:

```
<!-- Example 1 -->
<% For intLoop = 1 to 6 %>
    The number is: <% = intLoop %> <P>
<% Next %>
```

```
<!-- Example 2 -->
<% For intLoop = 1 to 6
    strOutput = "The number is: " & intLoop & "<P>"
    response.write(strOutput)
  Next %>
```

The code of example 2 will produce the following output:

As we create more complex scripts, we find that the ratio of script to HTML increases–and using the **write** method helps make our code a lot more readable.

The **write** method automatically converts the text to an appropriate character set when it is sent. If we need to prevent this conversion, we can use the complementary **binarywrite** method instead. The **binarywrite** method also can be useful for writing nonstring information such as binary data required by a custom application.

At this point, it should be said that we can use any HTML tag with **write** method. For example, the same loop above can be 'formatted' like this:

```
<% For intLoop = 1 to 6
      strOutput = "<B>The number is<B>: <U>" & intLoop & "</U><P>"
      response.Write(strOutput)
   Next %>
```

Which produces the following output:

Sending Cookies to the Browser

When we looked at the **Request** object in Chapter 3, we saw how cookies can be accessed on the server when a request is received from the browser. Cookies store information on the client machine, and are sent to the server with each request for information. The server can set or change the cookie's values, and the **Response** object provides an interface for just this purpose. Like the **Request** object, it holds a **cookies** collection–but this time we *can* use it to write values to the cookies that are sent back with our page.

This code adds a cookie to a client's cookie set, or changes the value of this cookie if it already exists:

```
<% response.cookies("independentcookie ") = "4th of July" %>
```

All modifications to cookies with the **Response** object cause HTTP headers to be sent to the client, and so they must be done *before* any text or HTML is written to the client. An attempt to modify them in an ASP file after any text or HTML code will cause an error. We will take a look at how to avoid such errors later in this chapter.

Cookie Lifetime and Availability

Cookies can also have properties relating to their lifetime and availability. If we don't set these explicitly, any information stored in them will be lost when the user shuts down their browser. If we want to store some information about the user that is still available weeks later, we can set an expiry date for it. Our **independentcookie** can be set to expire after the fourth of July quite simply:

```
response.cookies("independentcookie").expires = #7/5/1998 00:00:00#
```

We can also set various other properties of a cookie, to restrict which servers can gain access to information stored in it. In other words, we can prevent other web sites gaining access to the information we store in our cookies. These properties are **domain**, **path** and **secure**.

Setting the **domain** to **/rapid.wrox.co.uk/** would mean that only pages existing on that particular network would receive the cookie from the browser. We can also be more specific by setting the path to, say, **/Books1266**. The final attribute, **secure**, indicates that the cookie should only be transmitted to the server over a Secure Sockets Layer connection. That means that we can store some private information and get it back from client without worrying about it being stolen along the way. Here is an example of setting values of attributes:

```
response.cookies("independentcookie").expires = #7/5/1998#
response.cookies("independentcookie ").domain = "/rapid.wrox.co.uk/"
response.cookies("independentcookie ").path = "/Books1266"
response.cookies("independentcookie ").secure = True
```

Multiple Value Cookies

If we needed to produce a cookie dictionary, where a cookie has several values, we just have to specify a key along with the cookie name. As an example, we can create a **CleaningNeeds** cookie dictionary like this:

```
<% response.cookies("CleaningNeeds")("item1") = "Soap"
   response.cookies("CleaningNeeds")("item2") = "Water"
   etc.
   ...  %>
```

When dealing with cookies, we have to take some care that we don't overwrite existing information. Whenever we set a cookie value, any previous information is lost—there are no warnings that a cookie dictionary is about to be replaced by a single value, for example. So if we made a mistake in the code above, and wrote the second line as:

```
response.cookies("CleaningNeeds") = "Water"
```

we would replace the entire dictionary of values with a single value **Water**. To prevent errors, it's wise to check the **haskeys** property of that cookie, like we did with the **Request** object, to determine whether we're dealing with a dictionary of several values or a single value.

Why Use Cookies?

Of course, one question remains with cookies. Why use them at all? We could store the same information in a database, or file of some other type, on the server's disk. In fact, it would be more flexible using a database, since it can handle data other than text.

However, there will always be an overhead associated with accessing an external data source on the server, as we'll see later in this book. Using a cookie is a very fast and convenient way of storing small amounts of information. There are limits of course—we shouldn't store more than twenty cookies for any one domain—but with a little thought this resource can be put to great use in our web sites. One of the most popular uses of cookies is storing user information—you enter it once and then the server uses it many times without future assistance from your side. This is the foundation for many personal preference features, implemented on many sites like the Microsoft site.

Redirecting the Browser

A particularly useful method of the **Response** object is **redirect**. This can be used to refer users to alternative web pages. When they load a page that specifies a redirection, their browser loads the new page, which we specify in the **redirect** method, nearly immediately–actually the moment of redirection depends of the contents of ASP file itself–the actual redirection will occur as soon as redirection line will be interpreted by ASP core engine.

Consider a multinational corporation, *BigCorps*, which has web servers based in France, Australia, and the United States. The corporation runs a global Internet marketing campaign, where a single URL is plastered over hundreds of advertisements on sites all over the world. So when a potential customer clicks on an advertisement, we could be sending the response to anywhere around the globe. What we want to do is automatically redirect them to our nearest server, optimizing the use of resources both on our servers, and the Net as a whole.

Redirection Headers

The first thing to note about redirection: it's bound up with the HTTP protocol. When the client makes an HTTP **Get** request, they expect to get back headers informing the browser what is actually coming from the server. One of the things that they can receive is a **redirection header**, which tells the browser to go and get the information elsewhere. If we use this header, we can't also send other headers. What this essentially means is that, like the **cookies** collection, our Active Server Page must carry out the task before we supply any other headers, as well as any text or HTML for a page.

The following VBScript code will allow *BigCorps* to redirect their visitors to the nearest server. All it does is take a look at the **REMOTE_HOST** HTTP variable, using the **Request** object's **servervariables** collection. This provides the visitor's text URL, and an examination of the final two characters will reveal a country code if they are outside the United States:

```
<% 'Determine where in the world client originates and redirect
   Dim strRemHost  'The human readable address of the client computer
   Dim strCountryCode
   strRemHost = Request.servervariables("REMOTE_HOST")
   strCountryCode = UCase(Right(strRemHost, 2)) ' CCITT country code
   Select Case strCountryCode
      Case "AU", "JP": 'Australia and Japan
        response.redirect("http://BigCorps.co.au/MirrorSite/MyApp.asp")
      Case "FR", "DE", "IT", "UK", "IL": 'Some Europeans
        response.redirect("http://BigCorps.co.fr/MirrorSite/MyApp.asp")
      Case Else:  'The rest of the world
        response.redirect("http://BigCorps.com/MirrorSite/MyApp.asp")
   End Select %>
```

Avoiding Errors

Note that this page should include the following directive at of the start the page to be able to work:

```
<% response.Buffer = True %>
<html>
...

Rest of the page comes here
```

otherwise you'll get the following error message:

Response object error 'ASP 0156 : 80004005'

Header Error

/demo/objects/demo000.ASP, line 7

The HTTP headers are already written to the client browser. Any HTTP header modifications must be made before writing page content.

Buffering the Page

Another useful feature that we can take advantage of with the **Response** object is **buffering**. Buffering allows us an extra degree of control over *when* a client receives information, as well as *what* they receive. The **buffer** property can be set to **true** to indicate to the server that all of a page's script must be executed before any data is sent back to the requesting client. When it is **false**, the default, the server streams the page to the client as it is created.

Setting the **buffer** property alone gives us no advantage. However, by setting it to **true**, we have access to the auxiliary methods of **clear**, **flush** and **end**–attempting to use these methods when the **buffer** property is **false** gives an error.

Now the page is created as before, but held on the server until we issue a **flush** or **end** command in our code. This means we get to select which parts of the page are sent while it's being created. It also means that we can change our mind halfway through, and issue a **clear** command that empties the buffer without sending the page to the client.

To use buffering, we need to set the **buffer** property before the opening **<HTML>** tag in our source ASP files:

```
<%@ LANGUAGE="VBScript" %>
<% response.Buffer = True %>
<HTML>
```

Why Use Buffering?

Here are a couple of examples of when buffering might be useful. In our first example, imagine there's a quiz, where the questions and answers are stored in a text file or database on the server's disk. Accessing the file each time can produce a sluggish response. To make the application appear faster we can use buffering to send parts of the results early.

For example, our page may have to do three things–display the score so far, display the next question, and display a list of answers to choose from. Stages two and three will require the access to the file, and can be expected to take longer than stage one. So we could send just the results of stage one early, by including a **flush** command to send the current contents of the output buffer to the client browser:

```
<% 'Display current score
   ...
   response.flush
   'Continue with stage 2
   ... %>
```

We would then do a similar **flush** at the end of stage two. Stage three would not require a call to the **flush** method, since when we reach the end of the page the remaining contents of the buffer are sent automatically. Also the buffering is the only solution to avoid errors while we use cookies and redirection. Remember to set buffering to true at the top of the ASP file.

Trapping Errors by Buffering

A second possible use of buffering is the potential to handle data access or other errors in our pages. In the script that accesses the database to retrieve the question information, we can check for errors and modify the output of the page as appropriate. For example:

```
<%  ... 'If an error has occurred
response.clear 'Clear the current buffered output without sending it
response.write("<H1> There has been an error : please try again </H1>")
response.end  'Stop processing the page and send the new buffer contents
...  %>
```

Buffering can also be utilized in our general quest for dynamic content. For instance, if some large report were being created from a database or other external source, we may want to **flush** the contents to the browser at regular intervals. That way the client can at least start to digest the information, while our script continues to produce the rest.

Setting the Page's Properties

Each page we send to the client's browser has a set of properties, which we can specify values for in our scripts. In most cases, there's no real need to do this, but it does come in handy now and then. For example, we've seen how we can redirect a browser to a different page, by sending a redirection header. There are a lot of other kinds of headers that we can specify, and change the default values of.

Headers and Status

The **Response** object gives us access to the **headers** that are sent as part of the HTTP stream that makes up the page on the client's browser. They are used to determine how the browser should translate the information that follows in the main body of the page. Each header has a unique number. For example, the **redirect** method sends a header of value **303** to the browser. The value of the header is also known as the **status code**, and is available through the **status** property of the **Response** object.

> *There are too many different headers and status codes to discuss individually here. A full list can be obtained from Appendix J. You can also download the full HTTP 1.1 specification from the World Wide Web Consortium's site at:*
> **http://www.w3.org/pub/WWW/Protocols/rfc2068/rfc2068.txt**.

However, you'll have seen many of them before, no doubt: **404** (*Document not found*) will at least be familiar. All codes consist of three digits and a phrase explaining the status. For a normal document response this will be **200 OK** . The first digit of the code represents the type of response:

First Digit	Type of response
1	Information
2	Success
3	Redirection
4	Client Error
5	Server Error

To change or set the status code we use the **status** property of the **Response** object.

Creating Headers

We can add our own header information using the Response object's **addheader** method, supplying two string parameters, one for the **name** of the header and one for its **contents**. We can use standard HTTP headers or create our own. The main rule for new headers is that the name should not contain any underscore (_) characters. The **servervariables** collection interprets underscores as dashes in the header name. For example, the following script causes the server to search for a header named DEMO-HEADER.

```
<% Request.servervariables("HTTP_DEMO_HEADER") %>
```

As an example of **AddHeader** method usage, we can instruct the client to modify the contents of its cookies using the **Set-Cookie** header. The following code produces a cookie dictionary containing the same **CleaningNeeds** items we previously used in the **cookies** collection to create:

```
response.AddHeader "Set-Cookie","CleaningNeeds=item1=Soap&item2=Water"
```

Alternatively, we can create some headers using other properties of the **Response** object, rather than with the **AddHeader** method. For example, we can set the **contenttype**, to tell the browser what type of information to expect. For normal HTML pages, this is **"text/HTML"**, and for pictures it could be **"image/GIF"** or **"image/JPEG"**.

```
response.contenttype="text/HTML"
```

Setting Content Type

The browser will generally cache our pages locally when it loads them. Let's look at some examples of how we can use **contenttype** property to show an image, stored in a BLOB field in a database. This can be done by setting the appropriate MIME type in an HTTP header, i.e. **image/GIF** or **image/JPEG**. For example:

```
<%@ LANGUAGE="VBSCRIPT" %>
<%

    ' Clear out the existing HTTP header information
    response.Expires = 0
    response.Buffer = TRUE
    response.Clear


    ' Change the HTTP header to reflect that an image is being passed.
    response.contenttype = "image/gif"


    Set cn = Server.CreateObject("ADODB.Connection")
    ' The following open line assumes you have set up a System DataSource
    ' by the name of myDSN.
    cn.Open "DSN=myDSN;UID=sa;PWD=;DATABASE=pubs"

    Set rs = cn.Execute("SELECT logo FROM pub_info WHERE pub_id='0736'")
    response.BinaryWrite rs("logo")
    response.End
%>
```

This script only displays an image on the screen. If you wish to display an image from an HTML file or ASP program, you must refer to this script in an image tag. For example, if you wish to display this image with a caption describing it, you can use the following HTML file:

```
<HTML>
<HEAD><TITLE>Display Image</TITLE></HEAD>
<BODY>
This page will display the image New Moon Books from a SQL Server 6.5
image field.<BR>
<IMG SRC="SHOWIMG.ASP">
</BODY>
</HTML>
```

Note that this technique can be applied to any other type of binary data, not just graphics. We just specify what type of content is being presented by specifying the proper MIME type in the **response.contenttype** property. For example, if we want to view a Microsoft Word document, we can set the following value of the **contenttype** property:

```
response.contenttype = "application/msword"
```

You can find a list of common MIME Types and file extensions in Appendix K.

The expires and **expiresabsolute** properties control when the page cached on the browser will expire either after a period of time or after a specific time respectively. The browser will then load a fresh copy from our server.

```
response.expires=180       'in minutes, i.e. in 3 hours time
response.expiresabsolute=#7/5/1997 00:00:00# 'after the 4th of July
```

As with the **cookies** collection, redirection, and buffering, we must add headers before the server parses the **<HTML>** tag in our Active Server Pages.

To allow proxy servers to cache output, generated by our ASP pages, we can use the **cachecontrol** property. This property can have two values—**public** or **private**. If the value of this property is **public**, the output will be cached by proxy servers. If a proxy server caches the page, other users can get it more quickly—from the proxy server, not from the original site.

To append the name of the character set (for example, ISO-LATIN-7) to the content-type header in the response object we can use the **charset** property. This can solve some internationalization problems, which can occur if the character set is not known for client browser – specifying the right one we tell the client browser to use the appropriate code page. In the ASP page that did not include the **response.charset** property, for example, the content-type header would be:

```
content-type:text/html
```

If the same **.asp** file includes

```
<% response.charset("ISO-LATIN-7") %>
```

the content-type header would be

```
content-type:text/html; charset=ISO-LATIN-7
```

PICS Property

Using the **PICS** property we can add a value to the **PICS-Label** field of the response header.

> *PICS stands for Platform of Internet Content Selection - an infrastructure for associating labels (metadata) with Internet content. It was originally designed to help parents and teachers control what children access on the Internet, but it also facilitates other uses for labels, including code signing, privacy, and intellectual property rights management. PICS is a platform on which other rating services and filtering software has been built. One of the current standards provided by RSACI - Recreational Software Advisory Council on the Internet and it rates sites by violence, sex and nudity. For more information visit W3 site at* **http://www.w3org/PICS** *or RSACi site at* **http:// www.rsac.org**.

You set the value of **PICS** supplying the specially formatted **PICS-Label**, with will be appended to the **PICS** label field in the response header. Usually this header is presented in HTML document itself, in the **<HEAD>** section inside the **<META>** tags:

```
<META http-equiv="PICS-Label" content='(PICS-1.1 "http://www.rsac.org/ratingsv01.html"
l gen true comment "RSACi North America Server" " for "http://www.foobar.org" on
"1996.04.16T08:15-0500" r (n 3 s 3 v 3 l 2))'>
```

Just in case you need to dynamically supply the **PICS** label for current page, you use the **PICS** property:

```
<%
response.PICS("(PICS-1.1 <http://www.rsac.org/ratingv01.html> labels on " & chr(34) &
"1997.01.05T08:15-0500" & chr(34) & " until" & chr(34) & "1999.12.31T23:59-0000" &
chr(34) & " ratings (v 0 s 0 l 0 n 0))")
%>
```

This adds the following header:

```
PICS-label:(PICS-1.1 <http://www.rsac.org/ratingv01.html> labels on "1997.01.05T08:15-
0500" until "1999.12.31T23:59-0000" ratings (v 0 s 0 l 0 n 0))
```

Note that the **PICS** property inserts any string in the header, whether or not it represents a valid **PICS** label. If a single page contains multiple tags containing **response.PICS**, each instance will replace the **PICS** label set by the previous one. As a result, the **PICS** label will be set to the value specified by the last instance of **response.PICS** in the page. Because **PICS** labels contain quotes, you must replace each quote with " **& chr(34) &** ".

Checking the Client Connection

The last of the **Response** object's properties is **isclientconnected**. This is a read-only property that indicates if the client has disconnected from the server since the last **response.Write**. It allows us greater control over circumstances where the client may have disconnected from the server. For example, if a long period of time has elapsed between when a client request was made and when the server responded, it may be beneficial to make sure the client is still connected before continuing to process the script:

```
<%
'check to see if the client is connected
If Not response.isclientconnected Then
  'get the sessionid to send to the shutdown function
  shutdownid = Session.SessionID
'perform shutdown processing
  Shutdown(Shutdownid)
  End If
%>
```

In this example we use the **Session** object, which will be discussed later in this chapter.

The Server Object

We now come to the important **Server** object, which provides some basic properties and methods that are used in almost every Active Server Page that we create. First, we'll take a look at its interface:

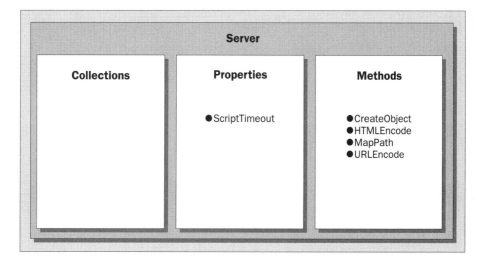

Property	Description
scripttimeout	Length of time a script can run before an error occurs.

Method	Description
createobject	Creates an instance of an object or server component.
HTMLencode	Applies HTML encoding to the specified string.
mappath	Converts a virtual path into a physical path.
URLencode	Applies URL encoding including escape chars to a string.

We'll start with a look at the single property, then move on to the methods available for use in our code.

The ScriptTimeout Property

Active Server Pages allows us to create HTML dynamically, using scripting language code. This means we can now produce pages that, just like a real programming language, have bugs. If our script enters an infinite loop, the server will eventually terminate the script to protect itself from being overloaded by running processes. The delay before script will be terminated (including ones with no errors) is defined in this property, which is set by default to 90 seconds–a long time for the user to be staring at the screen waiting for something to happen.

We can read and change the timeout period ourselves, using the **scripttimeout** property. For example, this code just inserts the current value into an HTML page:

```
<%
    response.write("Script Timeout = " + server.scripttimeout + " sec.")
%>
```

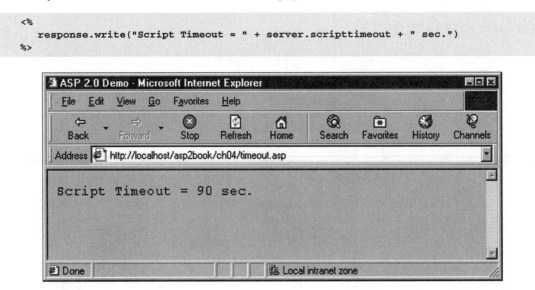

The HTMLEncode Method

Have you ever had to write a document in HTML about HTML? Look again at the previous example. Suppose we want to add the following string:

```
This output was produced by <% = server.scripttimeout%>
```

To get this displayed as part of the page on the browser, rather than having it executed on the server, we have to replace the angle-brackets (and other special characters) with an **escape** sequence which the browser can understand. An example escape sequence would be **<** (*less than*).

Fortunately, the server object can help us out. The **HTMLencode** method takes a string of text, and converts any illegal characters it contains to the appropriate HTML escape sequence. For example, to produce the text <TABLE> in our page, without it being interpreted as an opening table tag, we could use:

```
<% = Server.HTMLEncode("<TABLE>") %>
```

In the HTML page, the result is <TABLE> and this produces what we actually want to see. You might quite reasonably think that this is how we created the page above, but unfortunately it isn't that easy. The following produces an error message, because the server recognizes and translates the closing **%>** within the string as ASP code, and then it can't find the closing quotation mark:

```
<% = server.HTMLEncode("<%=server.scripttimeout%>")%>
```

To make this work, we have to cheat a little, and escape the closing angle-bracket by preceding it with a backslash character:

```
<% = server.HTMLencode("<%=server.scripttimeout %\>")%>
```

Here is our new version of the example from previous section:

```
<%
    response.write("Script Timeout = ")
    response.write(Server.ScriptTimeout)
    response.write(" sec.<BR>")
    response.write("This output was produced by " +
      Server.HTMLencode("<% = Server.ScriptTimeout %\>"))
%>
```

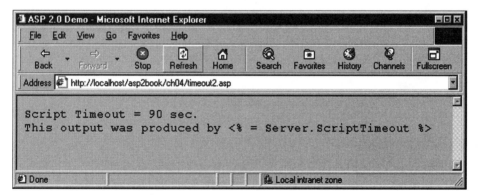

The URLEncode Method

The **Server** object's **URLencode** method is similar to **HTMLencode**, but takes a string of information and converts it into URL-encoded form rather than HTML. All the spaces are replaced by plus signs (**+**), and certain other characters are replaced by a percent sign and their ANSI equivalent in hexadecimal. We saw this earlier in the chapter, when we looked at the query string returned from a form.

So **URLencode** can translate a string into the correct format for use in a query string, but why would we want to do that? Well, it could be that we want our Active Server Page to have hyperlinks to other script pages, or even some old CGI programs. These can, in turn, take information from the query string. If we're creating hyperlinks in our code, we can use **URLencode** to ensure that they are correctly formatted:

```
<H1> What is half expressed as a percentage? </H1>
Is it: <BR>
<A HREF="Checkit.asp?Answer=<%=server.URLencode("33%")%>"> 33% </A> <BR>
```

```
<A HREF="Checkit.asp?Answer=<%=server.URLencode("50%")%>"> 50% </A> <BR>
<A HREF="Checkit.asp?Answer=<%=server.URLencode("75%")%>"> 75% </A> <P>
```

This produces the following HTML code when viewed in the browser:

```
<H1> What is half expressed as a percentage? </H1>
Is it: <BR>
<A  HREF="Checkit.asp?Answer=33%25">  33%  </A></BR>
<A  HREF="Checkit.asp?Answer=50%25">  50%  </A></BR>
<A  HREF="Checkit.asp?Answer=75%25">  75%  </A><P>
```

To see why, you only need to understand that the percent (**%**) sign itself can't be sent as text within a query string, because this character is used to indicate URL-encoded characters. In other words, **33%** has to be sent as **33** followed by something that represents a percent sign. Using the rules we discovered earlier, we need the ANSI code of the percent character, which is **25**, preceded by a percent sign–in other words the complete string is **33%25**. This is used within the query string, as **?Answer=33%25**. However, because we can use the **URLencode** method we don't have to worry about looking up each code by ourselves.

The MapPath Method

You can use the **Server** object's **mappath** method to provide file location information for use in our scripts. Its purpose is to translate the logical path information that might be used by a client browser, into a physical path on the server. For example, if a script needs to know the actual physical location on disk of the application's virtual root, in order to create a new document, we could get the information with this code:

```
<% 'Application virtual directory has the alias '/ObjModel'
   Dim strAppRoot
   strAppRoot = server.mappath("/ObjModel")
   ... %>
```

The result in **strAppPath** could be something like **C:\InetPub\Demo\ObjModel**. We could then go on to use this information to create or modify documents on the fly–perhaps using the **Filesystemobject** and **Textstream** objects, which we'll come across in the next chapter.

mappath will accept either relative or absolute virtual paths. In the example above, we used the absolute path **/ObjModel**, which is a **virtual directory** (or **alias**) on our server. If we omit the leading '**/**' or '****', the path will be treated as a **relative** path from the location of the page that is currently being executed.

> Note that the mappath **method does not check whether the path it returns is valid or exists on the server.**

Because the **mappath** method maps a path regardless of whether the specified directories currently exist, you can use the **mappath** method to map a path to a physical directory structure, and then pass that path to a component that creates the specified directory or file on the server.

Let's look at some more examples. We can map the physical path (i.e. get the full name of the current file starting from Web root directory) of the current file with **PATH_INFO** server variable:

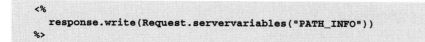

```
<%
    response.write(Request.servervariables("PATH_INFO"))
%>
```

This will produce the following output:

/asp2book/ch04/mappath1.asp

while the URL of the file is

http://localhost/asp2book/ch04/mappath1.asp

To get the full file name—starting from the root of the drive, we use **server.mappath** method:

```
<%
    response.write(server.mappath("mappath1.asp"))
%>
```

which produces:

C:\Inetpub\wwwroot\asp2book\ch04\mappath1.asp

for the same URL as above.

Next we can use **server.mappath** method to get only the directory for the current program:

```
<%
    response.write(server.mappath("."))
%>
```

this will produce

C:\Inetpub\wwwroot\asp2book\ch04

or we can find the parent directory:

```
<%
    response.write(Server.mappath(".."))
%>
```

This will give us

C:\Inetpub\wwwroot\asp2book .

The CreateObject Method

The last of the **Server** object's methods is certainly the most useful for creating interesting applications. The Active Server Pages environment can be extended by the use of **server components**. Some of these components are supplied 'out of the box' with ASP, and we shall be looking at them in detail in Chapter 6.

To actually use the components in our scripts, we need to be able to **instantiate** them—in other words create instances of the objects they contain, so that we can use their methods and access their properties. This is where the **Server** object's **createobject** method comes in. Every component that is correctly installed on our server has a programmatic identifier (**ProgID**) to reference it by. We pass this to the **createobject** method, and it creates an object of the appropriate type for us to use in our script.

Since the number of available components will only increase with time, **createobject** is potentially the most useful method that you'll ever use. For example, one of the components supplied with Active Server Pages is the **Browser Capabilities** component. This code shows how we could create and use it in our pages:

```
<%
  set objBrowser = server.createobject("MSWC.BrowserType")
%>
The <% =objBrowser.browser%> <% =objBrowser.Version%> browser supports? <P>
<UL>
  <LI>Tables   = <% =objBrowser.tables   %>
  <LI>Frames   = <% =objBrowser.frames   %>
  <LI>Cookies  = <% =objBrowser.cookies  %>
  <LI>VBScript = <% =objBrowser.vbscript %>
</UL>
```

Here, we've created an instance of the **Browser Capabilities** object, using its **progID** of **MSWC.browsertype**. Notice the use of the **set** keyword to assign it to an object variable. We can then use this new object's methods—viewed in Internet Explorer this code produces the results you can see here. Don't worry too much about what it's actually doing, that's coming in the next chapter.

As you'll see in more detail through later chapters, we need to be sure that we can actually create the object, and that there were no errors encountered doing so. One obvious way is to 'turn off' the built-in error handling in the code by using **On Error Resume Next** statement, then use the VBScript's **IsObject()** function to check that we did manage to create the object successfully:

```
<% Dim objBrowser               'define an object variable
   On Error Resume Next         'ignore any errors that occur
   Set objBrowser = Server.CreateObject("MSWC.BrowserType")
   If IsObject(objBrowser) Then  'check that we've got an object
   ...
   'use the object
   ...
Else
   response.write ("Error creating the object.")
End If %>
```

Now that we've taken a look at the other objects in the overall Active Server Pages object model, we need to consider how an application built with ASP fits together. As we saw at the beginning of this chapter, each server can have many applications running on it. An application comprises all the files that can be referenced through a single virtual mapping, or aliased directory, on your web server.

The Application Object

In coming chapters we'll be taking a look at building applications with Active Server Pages, and we'll be exploring in depth how we can use both the **Application** and the **Session** objects. In the meantime, though, we'll look briefly at what they offer. The **Application** object can store information for use by script files, process requests, and even respond to **events**. This is the interface of the **Application** object:

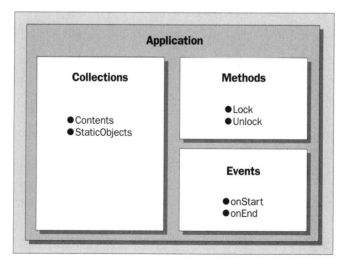

Collection	Description
`contents`	Contains all of the items added to the Application through script commands
`staticobjects`	Contains all of the objects added to the Application with the <OBJECT> tag

Methods	Description
`lock`	Prevents other clients from modifying application properties.
`unlock`	Allows other clients to modify application properties.

Events	Description
`onstart`	Occurs when a page in the application is first referenced.
`onend`	Occurs when the application quits, after the **Session_OnEnd** event.

The first thing to note is that an Active Server Pages application has a lifetime, just like any other program that might be run on a computer. When the application starts the **onstart** event occurs, and when an application finishes the **onend** event occurs.

Application Event Handlers

If we need to write code to be run when the application either starts or finishes, we need to put it into an appropriate **event handler**. In VBScript, an event handler takes the form:

```
Sub <ObjectName>_<EventName>(<ParameterList>)
   ...
End Sub
```

Since this sort of script requires a home, we place it in a particular file in the root directory of the virtual mapping, called **global.asa**. As its name suggests, this file contains information, routines and variables that are globally available to all of the pages in the application. So, if we need to do some processing at the beginning or end of an application, we can put some code in the **global.asa** file:

```
<SCRIPT LANGUAGE="VBScript" RUNAT="Server">
Sub Application_OnStart
   'Insert script to be executed when the application starts
End Sub

Sub Application_OnEnd
   'Insert script to be executed when the application ends
End Sub
</SCRIPT>
```

How Long Do Applications Live?

What isn't obvious about an application in ASP is just when it starts, and when it terminates. For a regular program running on your computer this is easy to answer–the program starts when you ask the operating system to run it, and it ends when you close the window or click an Exit button.

For an Active Server Pages application, the timing is a little different. Because what we are doing is creating dynamic and interactive web content, our application has to be based around the client machines' requests for pages from our server. Since our application is defined as all the documents contained in a single virtual mapping on the server, the application starts the first time any client requests a document from that virtual mapping.

Now that we know how an application *starts*, all we need to consider now is how it *ends*. Web servers are supposed to give continuous access to information all the time, so generally speaking we don't want our application to end while there are people out there who might want to use it. Only when the web server is stopped by the operating system does our application stop, and the script in the **onend** event handler runs. If the server actually crashes for some reason, however, the application still ends–but the **onend** script won't run in this case!

Application Variables

When creating event handlers for **application_onstart** and **application_onend**, the important question is 'What information are we going to manipulate?' The answer is absolutely anything that we might want to use in our scripts in other parts of the application, which consequently needs to be Global or Public. One obvious value is the time that the application started.

Storing Global Information

To store global information in the **Application** object, we just dream up a name for it and assign it to that name. The name becomes the key by which we access that value in future. You can think of it as being a custom property of the object. To store the time that the application started, we can add code to the **application_onstart** event in the **global.asa** file:

```
<SCRIPT LANGUAGE="VBSCRIPT" RUNAT="SERVER">
 sub Application_OnStart
  Application.Value("DateTime") = Now()
 end sub
</SCRIPT>
```

Here's part of an example page, **AppObj.asp**, which uses this stored time value, and also creates a global value of its own. You can find this among the samples available from our web site at **http://rapid.wrox.co.uk/books/1266**:

```
<H1>Application Started at:
  <% response.write(Application("DateTime")) %>
</H1>
The <B> Foo </B> value does not really exist until the button
below is clicked.<BR>
Trying to get its value gives us: <% =Application("Foo")%> <P>
<FORM ACTION="SETFOO.ASP" METHOD="GET">
 <INPUT TYPE="HIDDEN" NAME="FOO" VALUE="5">
 <INPUT TYPE="SUBMIT">
</FORM>
```

> Note that this sample will work only if you have the same global.asa file as shown above.

Here are the results it produces. The time value that's displayed is the one we set in the application's `onStart` event:

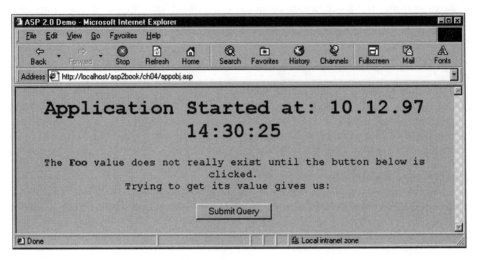

This page also makes a second use of the **Application** object, to access a variable named **Foo** and retrieve its value:

```
Trying to get its value gives us: <%=Application("Foo")%>
```

The first time the **AppObj.asp** page is requested after the application starts, **Foo** will not have been saved and so nothing is returned, as in the previous screenshot. Notice that referencing a nonexistent property doesn't cause an error. It just returns an empty value–which can have an important impact on debugging your application, since spelling errors in variable names will not be easy to find.

When we click the Submit button, we reference another ASP file, called **SetFoo.asp**. This contains the following code:

```
<% response.Buffer = TRUE %>
<HTML>
<HEAD>
<TITLE>ASP 2.0 Demo</TITLE>
</HEAD>
<BODY>
 <%
  Application.Lock
  Application("Foo") = Request.QueryString("Foo")
  Application.Unlock
  response.Redirect("appobj.asp")
 %>
</BODY>
</HTML>
```

This takes the information from the **<FORM>**, where the **HIDDEN** control named **Foo** has the value **5**. This is stored as a global value in the **Application** object, and the browser is redirected to the original **AppObj.asp** page. This time **Foo** will be a valid variable containing the value **5**. So we get the same page displayed, but this time **Foo** has a value:

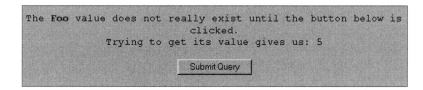

Using the Lock and Unlock Methods

You'll have noticed that the previous example used the **Lock** and **Unlock** methods of the **Application** object. Since the **Application** object is global to all the clients that may be visiting our site, it's possible that two clients could try to access the same data at the same time. To prevent the value being corrupted in this situation we have to use **Lock** and **UnLock** access to the object. When the **Lock** method is invoked, no other scripts can change the information stored in the **Application** object until the **UnLock** method is called.

Application Collections

The Application object has two collections–**Contents** and **StaticObjects**–which allow us to browse through objects and variables, created at the Application scope.

The Contents collection

The **Contents** collection contains a group all of the items that have been added to the application through a script command. We can use the **Contents** collection to obtain a list of items that have been given application scope, or to specify a particular item to be the target of an operation. The **Application.Contents** collection contains those items that have been declared at the application level without using the **<OBJECT>** tag. This would include both objects created with **Server.CreateObject** as well as global variables established through an **Application** declaration. For example:

```
<%
 Application("oneK") = 1024
%>
```

This sets a global variable **oneK** and assigns its value to 1024. We can also create instances of objects, which will have a global scope. For example:

```
<%
 Set Application("objASPEXT") = Server.CreateObject("ASPEXT.BrowserType")
%>
```

As with other collections we can iterate them either with VBScript's **For...Each** and **For...Next** statements, or with JScript **enumerator** object, described in the previous chapter. For example:

```
<%
   For Each Key in Application.Contents
    response.Write(Key + " = " + CStr(Application.Contents(Key)) + "<BR>")
   Next
%>
```

The StaticObjects collection

The **StaticObjects** collection contains all of the objects created with the **<OBJECT>** tags within the scope of the **Application** object. You can use the collection to determine the value of a specific property for an object, or to iterate through the collection and retrieve all properties for all static objects. For example, this code gives us a list of all the objects that have global scope, i.e. all the objects that are available to all the pages within our application:

```
<HTML>
<HEAD>
<TITLE>ASP 2.0 Demo</TITLE>
</HEAD>
<BODY>
 <CENTER>
 <H2>Objects with Global Scope</H2>
 <%
    For Each Key in Application.StaticObjects
     response.Write(Key + "<BR>")
    Next
 %>
</BODY>
</HTML>
```

The **Application** object will be the main topic of discussion in Chapter 10, so we'll leave it there for now. However, like all the other objects in the ASP object model, you'll be meeting it regularly throughout this book.

To finish off the object model, we just need to consider the **Session** object and the **ObjectContext** object.

The Session Object

Before we look at the **Session** object, we need to introduce the concept of **scope**, which is where data is either made available to all pages of an Active Server Pages application, or just localized to certain pages. This is actually demonstrated by the **Application** object. You can use it to store both simple data values, and—as you'll see later in this book—references to objects such as database connections. These become global to the whole application, and are available in any of its pages.

However, when we have data that needs to be shared between different pages, but not necessarily between different *clients*, we can make use of the **Session** object. Each client that requests a page from our application is assigned a **Session** object. A Session is created when the client first makes a document request and destroyed, by default, twenty minutes after their last request was received.

The interface to the **Session** object is shown here:

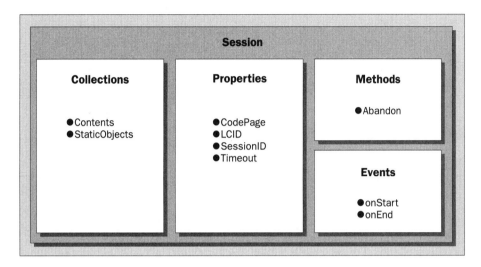

Collection	Description
contents	Contains all of the items added to the Session through script commands
staticobjects	Contains all of the objects added to the Session with the **<OBJECT>** tag

Method	Description
abandon	Destroys a **Session** object and releases its resources.

Property	Description
codepage	Sets the codepage that will be used for symbol mapping
LCID	Sets the locale identifier
sessionID	Returns the session identification for this user
timeout	Sets the timeout period for the session state for this application, in minutes

Events	Description
onstart	Occurs when the server creates a new session
onend	Occurs when a session is abandoned or times out.

Session Event Handlers

The two **session** object events, **onstart** and **onend**, are similar to those of the **Application** object. **onstart** occurs when a client browser first requests a document from the application's virtual directory. Since these events occur outside of any particular script, we need to create the event handler routines within the **global.asa** file, along with those for the **Application** object:

```
Sub Session_OnStart
    'Insert script to be executed when a session starts
End Sub

Sub Session_OnEnd
    'Insert script to be executed when a session ends
End Sub
```

Session Variables

Like the **Application** object, we have access to a **value** property that can be used to store information for a session. However, unlike the application, this information is maintained on an individual client basis. It becomes global to that client, but is not available to other clients who are using our application concurrently.

When we store information in the **Session** object, the client that owns that session is assigned a **sessionID**, which can be used in our pages to identify them while they are browsing our site. The **sessionID** is assigned by the server, and is only available to us as a read-only property.

> *The actual **sessionID** information is stored as a **cookie** with no expiry date set, so that it expires when the client browser is closed down.*

Storing Local Information

To see how we can use local values stored in the **Session** object, here's a simple script. It retrieves the current user's **sessionID**, and the current setting of the session **timeout**, and displays them in the page. Then it retrieves the value of a session-wide variable **IntSessionObjVisit** and displays this. Finally, it increments the stored value, so the page shows the number of times it has been opened from the server during the current session:

```
<H3>sessionID = <%=session.sessionID%></H3>
<H3>timeout = <%=session.timeout%></H3>
<P>You have visited this page
<%=session("intSessionObjVisit")%> times this <B>Session</B>.</P>
<% session("intSessionObjVisit") = session("intSessionObjVisit") +1 %>
```

When Do Sessions Start and End?

Although we generally consider that a session starts when a client's browser first requests a document from the application's virtual directory, this isn't the whole story. Active Server Pages will only start a session for that client automatically if there is a **session_onstart** routine in the **global.asa** file. This means that you can build applications that don't implement individual sessions for each client—saving resources if this feature isn't actually required.

However, the code in a page can store values in the **Session** object—even if it hasn't already been established when the user requested the page. At this point a session is automatically created. There will also be a session created if the **global.asa** file contains an **<OBJECT>** tag which creates an instance of an object with **session-level scope**, i.e. by including the **SCOPE=session** attribute:

```
<OBJECT RUNAT=server SCOPE=session ID=objAdRot ProgID="MSWC.Adrorator">
```

*You'll see how we create objects using an **<OBJECT>** tag like this in Chapter 6, when we come to look at Active Server Components in detail.*

There are two ways in which a session can end. The most direct is by use of the **Session** object's **abandon** method. This ends the session immediately, and frees the resources it uses. Any code in the **session_onend** event handler runs when the session ends.

Alternatively, looking at the sample above, you'll notice that we're referencing the **timeout** property. If the client that owns the session doesn't make a request from the application within this time period (in minutes), the server will destroy that **Session** object and release its resources. The default value is twenty minutes, but we can alter this on a per-session basis by changing the value of the **session.timeout** property in our code.

If we were expecting a lot of hits on our site, and needed to conserve resources, we could reduce this value so that clients will be 'logged off' more quickly. In an environment where the application has less users, and very sporadic document requests, we could consider increasing this value. At the end of the day, the needs of the application must be balanced against server resources to get the best results.

Session Collections

As with the **application** object described above, the **Session** Object has two collections—**contents** and **staticobjects**, which allows us to browse through objects and variables, created at the session scope.

The **session.contents** collection contains all of the items that have been established for a session without using the **<OBJECT>** tag. The collection can be used to determine the value of a specific session item, or to iterate through the collection and retrieve a list of all items in the session:

```
<%
Dim Item
For Each Item in Session.Contents
  response.Write(Item & " = " & Session.Contents(Item) & "<BR>")
Next
%>
```

The **session.staticobjects** collection contains all of the objects created with the **<OBJECT>** tag within the scope of the **Session** object. The collection can be used to determine a the value of a specific property for an object, or to iterate through the collection and retrieve all properties for all objects:

```
<%
Dim staticItem
For Each staticItem in Session.staticobjects
  response.Write(staticItem & " = " & Session.Contents(staticItem) & "<BR>")
Next
%>
```

Being International : CodePage and LCID properties

The **Session** object contains two properties, which allows us to create international sites—the **codepage** property, which determines the codepage that will be used to display context and the **LCID** property, which determines the location identifier that will be used to display dynamic content.

A *code page*, specified by the **session.codepage** property—is a character set that can include numbers, punctuation marks, and other glyphs. Different languages and locales may use different code pages. For example, most West European languages use code page **1252**, while in Russia code page **866** is used for DOS and **1251** for Windows.

> *You can find a list of some common code page numbers in the Appendix K.*

A code page can be represented in a table as a mapping of characters to single-byte of multibyte values. Many code pages share the first half of the ASCII character set for characters in the range 0x00–0x7F. To specify code page for an Active Server Pages, we can use the **session.codepage** property or the **@CODEPAGE** directive (which give us the same result):

```
<%@ CODEPAGE = 1251 %>
```

or

```
<% session.codepage = 1251 %>
```

As the Active Server Pages engine processes the content and script on the page, it uses the code page we have specified to determine how to convert characters from our script's character set into UNICODE. UNICODE is a 16-bit fixed-width character encoding standard used internally by the Active Server Pages engine.

When you temporarily change a code page for a portion of your script–to produce some foreign letters sentence, for example, you should restore it to its original value. For example:

```
<%
' Save current code page
 session("CurrentCP") = session.codepage
' Set new one
 session.codepage = 1252
'

' Set back the orginal code page
 session.codepage = session("CurrentCP")
%>
```

Locale identifier, specified by **session.LCID** property, is a standard international abbreviation that uniquely identifies one of the system-defined locales. This is a set of user preference information related to the user's language. The locale determines how dates and times are formatted, how items are alphabetically sorted, and how strings are compared. The *locale identifier* (LCID) is a 32-bit value that uniquely defines a locale. Active Server Pages engine uses the default locale of the Web server unless you specify a different locale for a particular script:

```
<%
  ' Set LCID for standard US english (0x409)
  session.LCID = 1033
%>
<H3>session.LCID = <% =session.LCID %> </H3>
 Now is: <% =Now() %>
 <BR>
<%
 ' Set LCID for Russian (0x419)
 session.LCID = 1049
%>
<H3>session.LCID = <% =session.LCID %> </H3>
 Now is: <% =Now() %>
```

You can find a list of all predefined Locale IDs (LCID) in the Appendix K.

```
ASP 2.0 Demo - Microsoft Internet Explorer
File  Edit  View  Go  Favorites  Help

 Back    Forward    Stop   Refresh   Home     Search  Favorites  History  Channels  Fulls

Address  http://localhost/asp2book/ch04/session3.asp


Session.LCID = 1033

Now is: 12/10/97 7:36:47 PM

Session.LCID = 1049

Now is: 10.12.97 19:36:47


 Done                                          Local intranet zone
```

The ObjectContext Object

The last object we'll take a look at in our discussion of Active Server Pages object model is the **objectcontext** object. We can use this object either to commit or to abort a transaction, managed by Microsoft Transaction Server (MTS), that has been initiated by a script contained in an ASP page. When an ASP contains the **@TRANSACTION** directive, the page runs in a transaction and does not finish processing until the transaction either succeeds completely or fails.

The interface to the **Objectcontext** object is shown here:

```
                         ObjectContext

    Collections          Properties            Methods

                                             ● SetComplete
                                             ● SetAbandon


                                               Events

                                             ● onTransactionCommit
                                             ● onTransactionAbort
```

Method	Description
`setcomplete`	Declares that the script is not aware of any reason for the transaction not to complete. If all components participating in the transaction also call **SetComplete**, the transaction will complete. Overrides any previous `setabort` method that has been called in a script
`setabort`	Aborts a transaction initiated by an ASP

Event	Description
`ontransactioncommit`	Occurs after a transacted script's transaction commits
`ontransactionabort`	Occurs if the transaction is aborted

The **Objectcontext** object implements two methods of the MTS **Objectcontext** object. The `setabort` method explicitly aborts the transaction. This causes MTS to prevent any updates to resources that were contacted during the first phase of the transaction. When the transaction aborts, the script's `ontransactionabort` event will be processed.

Calling the `setcomplete` method does not necessarily mean that the transaction is complete. The transaction will only complete if all of the transactional components called by the script call `setcomplete`. In most instances, you will not need to call `setcomplete` within the script, as the script is assumed to be complete if it finishes processing without calling `setabort`.

Objectcontext exposes six methods in addition to `setabort` and `setcomplete`. These other methods are not available to ASP scripts, however, they are available to components called by the script.

Summary

In this and the previous chapter we've taken a tour around the object model exposed by Active Server Pages. We've seen how to write script that can access the objects and their collections, methods, events, and properties–both to store and retrieve information. We've taken a close look at how information is passed from the client's browser to our application, and we've used this and the server's own methods and properties to create dynamic content.

We've also looked at some of the ways we can control document retrieval using the redirection capabilities of the **Response** object, as well as some of the other HTTP header-based manipulations that can be achieved. And we've seen how to use cookies to give our sites access to persistent data from day to day.

We finished up with a quick tour of the **Application**, **Session** and **Objectcontext** objects. These are fundamental to building real applications with Active Server Pages, so we've left a lot of the detail to later chapters, where you'll see them in use in more realistic situations. The main points of this chapter are:

 Active Server provides an **object model** that we can manipulate using scripting languages. This gives us a structured way of accessing all kinds of information, and producing dynamic content for our site.

▲ The main communication between the client's browser and our server is through two objects. The **Request** object contains all the information about the client's request for a file, and the **response** object contains the details and content of the page we're sending back from the server.

▲ We can control which documents the client receives, or even buffer output and control which sections of the document are sent. We can also add headers to the documents, which can change the document itself, how long it is cached, or even redirect the browser to a different document or site.

▲ We can store information locally, using the **Application** and **Session** objects, or remotely on the client's machine using **cookies**. We can use either method to exchange information between different active documents.

▲ By the script contained in our Active Server Pages, we can either commit or abort a transaction, managed by Microsoft Transaction Server (MTS)–this functionality is provided by **ObjectContext** object.

The Active Server Pages object model can also be extended by using **built-in scripting objects** and add-in **server components**. In fact, these are the subjects that we'll be covering in detail in the next two chapters.

The Active Server Pages Scripting Objects

In the previous chapter, we saw how Active Server Pages can use already defined instances of objects on the server, and take advantage of the methods and properties that they provide. These objects are part of the **Active Server Pages Object Model** and they are only available to scripting programs, running on the server. Its counterpart is the **Browser Object Model** that provides objects, which are only available to client programs.

The objects we'll take a look at in this chapter are the objects, which are only available on the server, but these objects are provided by a special library file—**Microsoft Scripting Runtime** (implemented in **SCRRUN.DLL**), which exposes the **Scripting object**. They can be used in various tasks and can work together with **Active Server Components**, which will be covered in the next chapter. They come as part of Active Server Pages. However, we'll also take the time to look at the VBScript only **Err** object.

Also in this chapter we'll talk about fixing your applications with a new tool from Microsoft—**Microsoft Script Debugger**—which can be used to debug script programs, running both on the client (inside the browser) and on the server (inside Active Server Pages).

In this chapter then, we'll see:

▲ How we can use the scripting objects like **Dictionary**, **FileSystem** and **TextStream** from VBScript and JScript programs

▲ How we use the built-in VBScript **Err** object

▲ How to debug programs with Microsoft Script Debugger

Scripting Objects

In the previous two chapters, we introduced the **object model** for Active Server Pages. This is basically a way of understanding how the various parts of the system are related together, and provides us with a structure that we can use to manipulate the different elements in the HTTP requests and responses, and the whole ASP environment. For example, we saw how we can find out the values of any cookies sent from the browser by looking in the **Cookies** collection—which is part of the **Request** object.

The scripting languages we use also have an object model, but for the objects that they provide, as opposed to the objects provided directly by the Active Server Pages system. Plus, Microsoft provides us with **Microsoft Scripting Runtime**—a special Dynamic Link Library (DLL), which exposes the set of objects, available from scripting languages. Among these are the **Dictionary** object, the **FileSystemObject** object, the **TextStream** object. You shouldn't be confused by the various objects available in Active Server Pages. We can divide all those available into two groups:

▲ **Built-in Active Server Pages Objects:** Objects that comprise the Active Server Pages object model. Their names are **Application**, **Session**, **Server**, **Request**, **Response** and **ObjectContext**. We discussed these in Chapters 3 & 4.

▲ **Scripting Objects:** Objects available through the Scripting object implemented in **scrrun.dll**. These include **Dictionary**, **FileSystem** and **TextStream**.

We will also cover the **Err** object, provided by the VBScript scripting engine. Let's now take a closer look at how the scripting objects are related to each other.

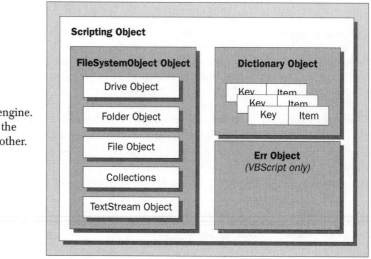

While the **Dictionary** and **Err** objects are separate, the **TextStream** object is part of the **FileSystemObject** object. This object also provides us with a set of objects to work with file system and several collections. In the next few sections, we'll look at each of these objects and collection in turn, and see how they can be used.

The Dictionary Object

In many other languages, including Visual Basic, we can use a feature called a **collection**. This is an object-oriented way of storing data, using a key with which it can be retrieved. We can think of a collection as being like an **array**, but with its own built-in intelligence that looks after the basic tasks of storing and manipulating the data. We don't have to worry about which row or column the data is in, we just access it using a unique key.

VBScript and JScript both offer a similar object (known as the **Scripting Dictionary** or **Dictionary** object) that acts like a two-dimensional array, holding the key and the related item of data together. However, in true object-oriented fashion, we can't just access the data items directly. We have to use the methods and properties supported by the **Dictionary** object instead. As an example, using VBScript, we can create an instance of the **Dictionary** object like this:

```
Set objMyData = CreateObject("Scripting.Dictionary")
```

In JScript we can create an instance of the **Dictionary** object like this:

```
var objMyData
objMyData = CreateObject("Scripting.Dictionary")
```

Once we've got a new (empty) dictionary, we can add items to it:

```
//
// VBScript example
//
objMyData.Add "MyKey", "MyItem"          'add items to the dictionary
objMyData.Add "YourKey", "YourItem"
```

And we can retrieve and remove them again:

```
//
// VBScript example
//
blnIsThere = objMyData.Exists("MyKey")   'True because the item exists
strItem = objMyData.Item("YourKey")      'retrieve an item from dictionary
strItem = objMyData.Remove("MyKey")      'retrieve and remove an item
objMyData.RemoveAll                       'remove all the items
```

Here's the full list of methods and properties for the **Dictionary** object.

Method	Description
`Add key, item`	Adds the key/item pair to the **Dictionary**.
`Exists(key)`	**True** if the specified key exists, **False** if not.
`Items`	Returns an array containing all the items in a **Dictionary** object.
`Keys`	Returns an array containing all the keys in a **Dictionary** object.
`Remove(key)`	Removes a single key/item pair.
`RemoveAll`	Removes all the key/item pairs.

Property	Description
`CompareMode`	Sets or returns the string comparison mode for the keys. This property is not supported in Jscript.
`Count`	Returns the number of key/item pairs in the **Dictionary**. Read Only.
`Item(key)`	Sets or returns the value of the item for the specified key.
`Key(key)`	Sets or returns the value of a key.

> **An error will occur if we try to add a key/item pair when that key already exists, remove a key/item pair that doesn't exist, or change the comparison mode of a Dictionary object that already contains data.**

Changing the Value of a Key or Item

We can change the data stored in a **Dictionary**, by either changing the value of the key or the item of data associated with it. To change the value of the item with the key **MyKey**, we could use:

```
objMyData.Item("MyKey") = "NewValue"
```

If the key we specify (**MyKey**) isn't found in the **Dictionary**, a new key/item pair is created with the key as **MyKey** and the item value as **NewValue**. One interesting aspect is that, if we try to retrieve an item using a key that doesn't exist we not only get an empty string as the result (as we'd expect) but also a new key/item pair is actually added to the **Dictionary**. This has the key we specified (**MyKey**), but with the item left empty.

To change the value of a key, without changing the value of the corresponding item, we use the **Key** property. So, to change the value of an existing key **MyKey** to **MyNewKey**, we could use:

```
objMyData.Key("MyKey") = "MyNewKey"
```

If the specified key (**MyKey**) isn't found, a new key/item pair is created with the key **MyNewKey** and the item left empty.

Setting the Comparison Mode

The **CompareMode** property of a dictionary allows us to define how the comparison is made when comparing string keys. The usual values are:

VB Constant	Value	Description
vbBinaryCompare	0	Binary comparison–i.e. matching is case sensitive.
vbTextCompare	1	Text comparison–i.e. matching *is not* case sensitive.
vbDatabaseCompare	2	Comparison is based upon information contained in the string. Values greater than **2** can be a Locale ID (**LCID**).

> Note that the **CompareMode** property is currently supported only in VBScript.

Iterating Through a Dictionary

There are two methods and a property that are of particular interest when dealing with a **Dictionary**. These allow us to iterate, or loop, through all the key/item pairs stored in it. The **Items** method returns all the items in a **Dictionary** as a one-dimensional array, while the **Keys** method returns all the existing key values as a one-dimensional array. To find out how many keys or items there are, we can use the **Count** property.

For example, we can retrieve all the keys and values from a **Dictionary** called **objMyData** using the following code. Notice that although the **Count** property holds the number of key/item pairs in the **Dictionary**, and VBScript and JScript arrays always starts at index zero.Therefore we have to iterate through the array using the values **0** to **Count - 1**:

```
...
   strKeysArray = objMyData.Keys           'get all the keys into an array
   strItemsArray = objMyData.Items         'get all the items into an array
   For intLoop = 0 To objMyData.Count -1   'iterate through the array
     strThisKey = strKeysArray(intLoop)    'this is the key value
     strThisItem = strItemsArray(intLoop)  'this is the item (data) value
   Next
...
```

A Real Use for the Dictionary Object

In the previous chapter, where we looked at the object model of Active Server Pages, we found that we can retrieve the values of fields on a form submitted from the client's browser. However, we had to know the names of the fields (the controls on the form) for this to be possible. In theory we'll know these names, because we create the forms as well as the Active Server Pages that process them. However, a **generic form handler**, which will accept *any* form, is a popular application with web site developers. We can quite easily create a page to do this, using VBScript and Active Server Pages together.

The point is that we don't know the names of the fields, or how many there will be. This makes the **Dictionary** object an ideal tool for storing the values, rather than creating a dynamic array, or counting the number of fields first. The first question, then, is how do we actually get the values from the fields on the form?

Using the Request Object's Form Collection

In the previous chapter, you saw how we use the individual elements of the **Form** collection to get a list of their contents. Even when we don't know how many controls there are on a **<FORM>**, or their names, we can still retrieve them using the collections with the **For Each...Next** construct. There's another way we can work with the Form object–the statement **Request.Form** with no arguments returns the complete query string, sent back from the form, in **URL-encoded** format. For example, if our form has two controls, **txtName** and **txtEmail**, we could get a result that looked like this:

```
txtName=Alex+Homer&txtEmail=alex@stonebroom.com
```

Notice that the controls and their values form the standard name/value pairs, with the control name and its value separated by an equals sign (**=**). You'll have seen this format before if you've used other languages to create server-based form handling applications. Each name/value pair is separated from the next by an ampersand (**&**). You can also see that spaces have been replaced by plus signs (**+**), and so plus signs would then need to be replaced by something else–certain non-alphanumeric characters are encoded with a percent sign followed by their ANSI character number.

Coping with URL Encoding

So before we can do anything with the string of values, we have to be able to decode them. Though Active Server Pages helpfully provides a function to encode strings, it doesn't provide one to decode them. Here's one we've written ourselves, and we've stored it in a separate text file named **URLDecode.txt**. We can make it available in any of our pages by using a Server-side **Include** tag, which simply inserts the text into the page as the server loads it into memory.

```
<SCRIPT LANGUAGE=VBScript RUNAT=Server>
Function URLDecode(strToDecode)
  strIn = strToDecode
  strOut = ""                     'the result string
```

```
    intPos = Instr(strIn, "+")     'look for + and replace with space
    Do While intPos
       strLeft = ""
       strRight = ""
       If intPos > 1 Then strLeft = Left(strIn, intPos - 1)
       If intPos < Len(strIn) Then strRight = Mid(strIn, intPos + 1)
       strIn = strLeft & " " & strRight
       intPos = Instr(strIn, "+") 'and then look for next one
       intLoop = intLoop + 1
    Loop
    intPos = Instr(strIn, "%")     'look for ASCII coded characters
    Do While intPos
       If intPos > 1 Then strOut = strOut & Left(strIn, intPos - 1)
       strOut = strOut & Chr(CInt("&H" & Mid(strIn, intPos + 1, 2)))
       If intPos > (Len(strIn) - 3) Then
          strIn = ""
       Else
          strIn = Mid(strIn, intPos + 3)
       End If
       intPos = Instr(strIn, "%") 'and then look for next one
    Loop
    URLDecode = strOut & strIn
End Function
</SCRIPT>
```

The Generic Form Handler Code

Now we have a way of decoding the string of values sent from the browser, so we need to split them up, and add them to a **Dictionary** object. Here's the complete code for the page. It first creates the **Dictionary**, and then reads the Request object's **Form** property to get the string of name/value pairs. Then it parses the string, looking for the ampersands that divide the name/value pairs from each other and the equals signs that separate the name from the value within the pair. Each pair is decoded and added to the **Dictionary** with its **Add** method, using the name as the **Key** and the value as the **Item**. Lastly, it iterates through the values stored in the **Dictionary** object just as we saw earlier, and puts them into the page with a **Response.Write** statement.

```
<!--#include file=URLDecode.txt-->

<%
'First we create a Dictionary object to hold the results
Set objResult = CreateObject("Scripting.Dictionary")

'Then we get the complete query string for the FORM
strQuery = Request.Form

'Now we can parse the query string and fill the Dictionary
intSep = Instr(strQuery, "&")
Do While intSep                              'split the string into
   strKey = ""                               'remove the last key we found
   strValue = ""                             'remove the last value we found
   strNVPair = Left(strQuery, intSep - 1)    'name/value pairs.
   strQuery = Mid(strQuery, intSep + 1)
   intEqu = Instr(strNVPair, "=")            'separate the name and value.
   If intEqu > 1 Then strKey = URLDecode(Left(strNVPair, intEqu-1))
   If intEqu < Len(strNVPair) Then strValue = URLDecode(Mid(strNVPair, intEqu+1))
```

```
    objResult.Add strKey, strValue          'and add to the dictionary.
    intSep = Instr(strQuery, "&")
  Loop
  strKey = ""                               'lastly, we have to handle
  strValue = ""                             'the remaining name/value pair.
  intEqu = Instr(strQuery, "=")
  If intEqu > 1 Then strKey = URLDecode(Left(strQuery, intEqu-1))
  If intEqu < Len(strQuery) Then strValue = URLDecode(Mid(strQuery, intEqu+1))
  objResult.Add strKey, strValue

  'Now we can loop through the Dictionary and output the results
  strKeysArray = objResult.Keys             'get the keys into an array
  strItemsArray = objResult.Items           'get the items into an array
  For intLoop = 0 To objResult.Count -1     'iterate through the array
    strThisKey = strKeysArray(intLoop)      'this is the key value
    strThisItem = strItemsArray(intLoop)    'this is the item (data) value
    Response.Write strThisKey & " = " & strThisItem & "<BR>"
  Next
%>
```

We've supplied a sample of this code that you can try. The file **GenForm.htm** contains a simple **<FORM>**, whose **ACTION** attribute is the ASP file **GenForm.asp**. You'll find them on our web site at **http://rapid.wrox.co.uk/books/1266/** or you can use the code we've shown above with any of your own pages that contain a **<FORM>** section.

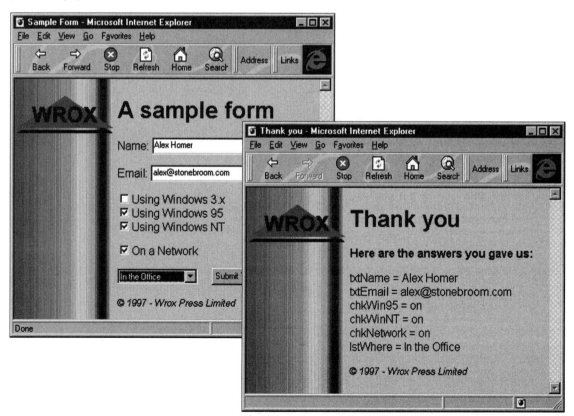

In the next section we will take a look at the **FileSystemObject** object, which is available only for server scripting programs (contrary to the objects described above) and provides us with a set of methods and properties to access the computer's file system.

The FileSystemObject Object

The **FileSystemObject** object provides access to the computer's file system, allowing us to manipulate text files, folders and drives from within our code. It's part of the **Scripting object**, supported by the Scripting Runtime Library, and we can create an instance of **FileSystemObject** in VBScript using:

```
Set objFSO = CreateObject("Scripting.FileSystemObject")
```

or in Jscript using:

```
var objFSO
objFSO = CreateObject("Scripting.FileSystemObject")
```

Also, **FileSystemObject** provides access to another scripting object——**TextStream**——which we will describe later in this chapter.

The **FileSystemObject** object contains one property, **Drives**, which returns a collection consisting of all **Drive** objects available on the local machine. Here is the code in VBScript which produces a list of drives on server along with drive types and volume names:

```
<HTML>
<HEAD><TITLE></TITLE></HEAD>
<BODY ALIGN=center>
 List of drives on server<br>
 <TABLE BORDER>
   <%
   Dim fs, d, dc, s, n
   Set fs = CreateObject("Scripting.FileSystemObject")
   Set dc = fs.Drives
   For Each d in dc %>
   <TR><TD><% =d.DriveLetter %></TD><TD>
     <%
     If d.DriveType = 3 Then
       s = "Remote"
       n = d.ShareName
     Else
       s = "Local"
       n = d.VolumeName
     End If
     %>
     <% =s %></TD><TD><% =n %></TD></TR>
   <% Next %>
 </TABLE>
</BODY>
</HTML>
```

This is what it looks like when run on a machine with a disk drive, a CD ROM and several network drives.

> Please note that if you don't have a disk in your disk drive, or a CD ROM in your CD drive, then you will experience a Disk Not Ready Error.

In real life we wouldn't want to reveal to users how many drives we have on the server—this is just an example of how we can use the **Drives** collection.

The Drive Object

As noted below, each item of the **Drives** collection is a **Drive** object. You'll not create instances of this object—you only use it through the **Drives** collection of **FileSystemObject**. Here is a list of properties and methods of the **Drive** object:

Property	Description
AvailableSpace	Returns the amount of space available on specified drive
DriveLetter	Returns the drive letter for the specified drive
DriveType	Returns the value indicating the type of specified drive. Can have one of the following values: 0 Unknown 3 Network 1 Removable 4 CD-ROM 2 Fixed 5 RAM Disk

Property	Description
`FileSystem`	Returns the type of file system for specified drive. Return types include *FAT, NTFS* and *CDFS*.
`FreeSpace`	Returns the amount of free space available on specified drive
`IsReady`	Returns boolean value indicating if drive is ready (true) or not (false)
`Path`	Returns the path for specified drive
`RootFolder`	Returns the **Folder** object representing the root folder of the specified drive
`SerialNumber`	Returns a decimal serial number used to uniquely identify a disk volume
`ShareName`	Returns the network share name for the specified drive
`TotalSize`	Returns the total space (in bytes) of the specified drive
`VolumeName`	Sets of returns the volume name of the specified drive

As you can see we can get enough information from the **Drive** object properties to create a sophisticated utility – a lesser Web-based version of Norton Utilities.

The Folder Object

The **RootFolder** property of the **Drive** object gives us another scripting object—**Folder**, which provides access to the file system on a specified drive. We can use the **Folder** object to traverse directories on a particular drive or just to get all the properties of a specified folder. Here are the properties, methods and collections of the **Folder** object:

Property	Description
`Attributes`	Returns the attributes of folder. Can be combination of the following values: 0 Normal 16 Directory 1 Read Only 32 Archive 2 Hidden 64 Alias 4 System 128 Compressed 8 Volume
`DateCreated`	Returns the date and time that the specified folder was created
`DateLastAccessed`	Returns the date and time that the specified folder was last accessed
`DateLastModified`	Returns the date and time that the specified folder was last modified
`Drive`	Returns the drive letter of the drive on which the specified folder resides
`IsRootFolder`	Returns boolean value indicating if the specified folder is the root folder (true) or not (false)
`Name`	Sets or returns the name of the specified folder
`ParentFolder`	Returns the **Folder** object for the parent of the specified folder
`Path`	Returns the path for specified folder
`ShortName`	Returns the 8.3 version of folder name

Property	Description
`ShortPath`	Returns the 8.3 version of folder path
`Size`	Returns the size of all files and subfolders contained in the folder
`SubFolders`	Returns a **Folders** collection consisting of all folders contained in a specified folder

Method	Description
`Copy`	Copies the specified folder from one location to another
`Delete`	Deletes a specified folder
`Move`	Moves a specified folder from one location to another

Collection	Description
`Files`	Collection of all files within a folder. Has **Count** and **Item** properties.
`Folders`	Collection of all folders within a folder. Has **Count** and **Item** properties and an **AddFolders** method.

Let's create a short example, which will show us how to use the **GetSpecialFolder** method of **FileSystemObject**:

```
<%@ language = JScript %>
<HTML>
<HEAD><TITLE></TITLE></HEAD>
<BODY>
 <CENTER>Locations and size for special folders
 <TABLE>
 <TR><TD>Folder</TD><TD>Size</TD><TD>Parent</TD><TD>Name</TD></TR>
   <%
    fs = Server.CreateObject("Scripting.FileSystemObject")
   %>
   <%
    for (i=0; i < 3; i++)
    {
     f  = fs.GetSpecialFolder(i)
   %>
   <TR>
   <TD><% =f %></TD>
   <TD><% =f.size %></TD>
   <TD><% =f.parentfolder %></TD>
   <TD><% =f.name %></TD>
   </TR>
   <% } %>
 </TABLE>
 </CENTER>
</BODY>
</HTML>
```

This JScript program shows information about three special folders—**WINDOWS**, **WINDOWS\SYSTEM** and **WINDOWS\TEMP**:

We'll take a look at the **GetSpecialFolder** method of **FileSystemObject** in a couple of minutes—here we use some properties of the **Folder** object to obtain the information—**Size**, **ParentFolder** and **Name**.

Having looked at the collections and properties of the **FileSystemObject** object, let's now take a look at its methods.

FileSystemObject Object Methods

The **FileSystemObject** object provides us with a set of methods, which can be used to copy, delete and move files and folders, check for the existence of files, folders and drives and collect some other useful information about the computer file system. Two methods of **FileSystemObject**—**CreateTextFile** and **OpenTextFile**—allow us to use the **TextStream** object, which can be used to manipulate with text files; we'll talk about it a little bit later.

The methods of the **FileSystemObject** object can be divided in several categories as shown in the following table .

Category	Methods
File Manipulation	`CopyFile, CreateTextFile, DeleteFile, FileExists, MoveFile, OpenTextFile`
Folder Manipulation	`CopyFolder, CreateFolder, DeleteFolder, FolderExists, MoveFolder`
Path Manipulation	`BuildPath`
Information	`GetAbsolutePathName, GetBaseName, GetDrive, GetDriveName, GetExtensionName, GetFile, GetFileName, GetFolder, GetParentFolderName, GetSpecialFolder, GetTempName`

Several of the methods of **FileSystemObject** can be used to get other objects. The **GetDrive** method returns the **Drive** object for a specified path, **GetFile** returns the **File** object, while **GetFolder** and **GetSpecialFolder** return the **Folder** object. For example, we can get the **Drive** object for a specified drive and then use its properties:

```
<%@ language = JScript %>
<HTML>
<HEAD><TITLE></TITLE></HEAD>
<BODY>
 <CENTER>
  Information for C: drive on local machine
    <%
    fs = Server.CreateObject("Scripting.FileSystemObject")
    d  = fs.GetDrive("c:")
    Response.Write("Free space on C: = " + d.freespace)
    %>
 </CENTER>
</BODY>
</HTML>
```

In this example we can detect the amount of free space available on the C: drive:

159

Note that **FileSystemObject** itself provides several methods which duplicate the functionality of some of the methods of corresponding objects. For example, **CopyFolder** corresponds to the **Folder.Copy** method, **DeleteFolder** to **Folder.Delete** and so on. The only difference is that you should get the appropriate object first to use **Folder** object methods, while the **FileSystemObject** method works with any folder. The same is true for file manipulation methods and the **File** object. Let's take a look at this object.

The File Object

The **File** object provides access to all the properties of a file. We can use it as is or as part of the **Files** collection, which is part of the **Folder** object. We have several properties and methods to manipulate a file. Here are its properties.

Property	Description
Attributes	Returns the attributes of file. See description of **Folder** object above
DateCreated	Returns the date and time that the specified file was created
DateLastAccessed	Returns the date and time that the specified file was last accessed
DateLastModified	Returns the date and time that the specified file was last modified
Drive	Returns the drive letter of the drive on which the specified file resides
Name	Sets or returns the name of the specified file
ParentFolder	Returns the **Folder** object for the parent of the specified file
Path	Returns the path for specified file
ShortName	Returns the 8.3 version of file name
ShortPath	Returns the 8.3 version of file path
Size	Returns the size of the file
Type	Returns information about the type of a file

Here is how we can get the **File** object from the **FileSystemObject.GetFile** method and access some of its properties:

```
<%@ language = JScript %>
<HTML>
<HEAD><TITLE></TITLE></HEAD>
<BODY>
 <CENTER>
  Information for AUTOEXEC.BAT
   <%
   fs   = Server.CreateObject("Scripting.FileSystemObject")
   auto = fs.GetFile("c:\autoexec.bat")
   %>
   <TABLE>
   <TR>
    <TD>Size</TD><TD><% = auto.size %></TD>
  </TR>
```

```
    <TR>
    <TD>Type</TD><TD><% = auto.type %></TD>
    </TR>
    </TABLE>
  </CENTER>
</BODY>
</HTML>
```

This provides details about the file, we have specified:

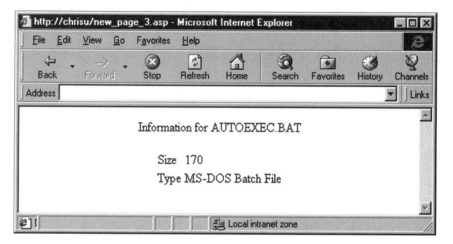

The methods of the **File** object allow us to copy, delete and move a file and to open it as a text stream. These methods are listed in the following table.

Method	Description
Copy	Copies a specified file or folder from one location to another
Delete	Deletes a specified file or folder
Move	Moves a specified file or folder from one location to another
OpenAsTextStream	Opens a specified file and returns a **TextStream** object that can be used to read from, write to, or append to the file

One of the methods of the **FileSystemObject** object—**GetSpecialFolder**—returns the **Folder** object for three special folders: **WINDOWS**, **WINDOWS\SYSTEM** and **WINDOWS\TEMP**. You can use this ability for several different tasks: storing temporary files, finding ActiveX controls to be inserted into a client browser and so on. To get a special folder location you supply its index as a parameter of the **GetSpecialFolder** method:

Folder	Index
WINDOWS	0
WINDOWS\SYSTEM	1
WINDOWS\TEMP	2

Let's go back to two methods of the **FileSystemObject** object which allows us to manipulate text files. Once we've got a **FileSystemObject** object, we create **TextStream** objects using its methods:

Method	Description
CreateTextFile	Creates a file and returns a TextStream object used to access the file.
OpenTextFile	Opens a file and returns a TextStream object used to access the file.

The CreateTextFile Method

The **CreateTextFile** method creates a new text file, or overwrites an existing one. It returns a **TextStream** object that we can use to read from or write to the file. We first create a **FileSystemObject** object, as we saw above, then use it to create a **TextStream** object, like this (VBScript version):

```
Set objFSO = CreateObject("Scripting.FileSystemObject")
Set objNewFile = objFSO.CreateTextFile("C:\TextFiles\MyFile.txt")
```

or in JScript:

```
var objFSO = CreateObject("Scripting.FileSystemObject");
var objNewFile = objFSO.CreateTextFile("C:\TextFiles\MyFile.txt");
```

The full syntax of **CreateTextFile** is:

[*object.*]**CreateTextFile**(*filename*[, *overwrite*[, *unicode*]])   where:

object	Name of a FileSystemObject
filename	Full physical path and filename for the file we want to create or overwrite.
overwrite	**True** to indicate we can overwrite an existing file or **False** if it can't be overwritten. Optional argument–if omitted existing files will be overwritten.
unicode	**True** to indicate that the file should be created as a Unicode file, **False** as an ASCII file. Optional argument–if omitted an ASCII file is created.

> If the overwrite argument is False, and a file with the same filename already exists in the specified directory, an error occurs.

Unicode files use two bytes to identify each character, removing the ASCII limitation of 256 available characters.

The OpenTextFile Method

The **OpenTextFile** method opens an existing text file. It returns a **TextStream** object that we can use to read from or append data to the file. Again, we first create a **FileSystemObject** object, then use it to create a **TextStream** object, like this (VBScript version):

```
Set objFSO = CreateObject("Scripting.FileSystemObject")
Set objNewFile = objFSO.OpenTextFile("C:\TextFiles\MyFile.txt")
```

or in JScript:

```
var objFSO = CreateObject("Scripting.FileSystemObject");
var objNewFile = objFSO.OpenTextFile("C:\TextFiles\MyFile.txt");
```

The full syntax of **OpenTextFile** is:

[*object.*]**OpenTextFile**(*filename*[, *iomode*[, *create*[, *format*]]]) where:

object	Name of a FileSystemObject
filename	Full path and filename for the file we want to open.
iomode	Either **ForReading** or **ForAppending**. Optional argument–default **ForReading**.
create	**True** to indicate we can create a new file or **False** if it must already exist. Optional argument–if omitted a new empty file is not created if it doesn't already exist.
format	Format for the file. Optional argument–if omitted the file is opened as ASCII. A value of **TristateTrue (-1)** opens the file in Unicode format. A value of **TristateFalse (0)** opens the file in ASCII format. A value of **TristateUseDefault (-2)** opens the file using the system default.

> If the *create* argument is False or not provided, and a file with the same filename *does not* already exist in the specified directory, an error occurs.

Note that **iomode** values are not defined in JScript. You can use integer equivalents as shown below or define appropriate constants in your code:

```
// iomode constants for OpenTextFile
ForReading   = 1;
ForAppending = 8;
```

The File.OpenAsTextStream Method

As we mentioned above, the **File.OpenAsTextStream** method opens a specified file and returns a **TextStream** object that can be used to read from, write to, or append to the file. It provides the same functionality as the **OpenTextFile** method of the **FileSystemObject**. In addition, the **OpenAsTextStream** method can be used to write to a file. First we create a **FileSystemObject** object, then a new file and use the method **GetFile** to get a **File** object and open it with **OpenAsTextStream** method, like this (VBScript version):

```
Set objFSO = CreateObject("Scripting.FileSystemObject")
objFSO.CreateTextFile "mytest.txt"
Set objF = objFSO.GetFile("mytest.txt")
Set objTxt = objF.OpenAsTextStream(ForWriting, TristateUseDefault)
```

The full syntax of **OpenAsTextStream** is:

[*object.*] **OpenAsTextStream** ([*iomode*[, *format*]]) where:

object	Name of a File object. Required.
iomode	Either **ForReading**, **ForAppending** or **ForWriting**. Indicated input/output mode.
format	Format for the file. Optional argument–if omitted the file is opened as ASCII. A value of **TristateTrue (-1)** opens the file in Unicode format. A value of **TristateFalse (0)** opens the file in ASCII format. A value of **TristateUseDefault (-2)** opens the file using the system default.

Once we have created the **TextStream** object we can use its properties and methods to work with text files. This is the subject of the next section.

The TextStream Object

So we can create a new text file, or open an existing one. Once we've done this, we have a **TextStream** object reference to it, and we can manipulate the file using the methods and properties of the **TextStream** object. For example, once we've created the file using a **CreateTextFile** or **OpenTextFile** method, we can write to it and close it with (VBScript version):

```
objNewFile.WriteLine("At last I can create files with VBScript!")
objNewFile.Close
```

Here's a full list of the properties and methods available for the **TextStream** object. We'll look at the important ones in detail shortly. Notice that all the properties are *read-only*:

Method	Description
Close	Closes an open file.
Read(*numchars*)	Reads *numchars* characters from a file.
ReadAll	Reads an entire file as a single string.
ReadLine	Reads a line from a file as a string.

Method	Description
`Skip(numchars)`	Skips and discards *numchars* characters when reading a file.
`SkipLine`	Skips and discards the next line when reading a file.
`Write(string)`	Writes *string* to a file.
`WriteLine([string])`	Writes *string* (optional) and a newline character to a file.
`WriteBlankLines(n)`	Writes *n* newline characters to a file.

Property	Description
`AtEndOfLine`	**True** if the file pointer is at the end of a line in a file.
`AtEndOfStream`	**True** if the file pointer is at the end of a file.
`Column`	Returns the column number of the current character in a file, starting from **1**.
`Line`	Returns the current line number in a file, starting from **1**.

> **The** `AtEndOfLine` **and** `AtEndOfStream` **properties are only available for a file that is opened with** *iomode* **of** `ForReading`**. Referring to them otherwise causes an error to occur.**

A Real Use for the TextStream Object

When we looked at the **Dictionary** object earlier in the chapter, we saw how we can use it to store name/value pairs being sent from a **<FORM>** section on a page on the client's browser. The next question is, then, what do we do with them once we've got them? Well, the combination of the **FileSystemObject** and the **TextStream** object means that we can easily store the values in a file on disk.

As an example, we'll add the values to a log file called **MyLog.txt**, which is stored in the **C:\Logfiles** directory on our server. If you want to try this example yourself, you'll have to create this directory on your server and use **NotePad**, or another text editor, to create an empty file named **MyLog.txt** first. The actual opening, writing to, and closing of the file is done by a separate function **WriteToLogFile**, which accepts the string to write and returns **True** on success, or **False** otherwise. We've also included the **On Error Resume Next** statement so that it will not halt our code if something goes wrong:

```
<SCRIPT RUNAT=SERVER LANGUAGE="VBScript">
  Function WriteToLogFile(strLogMessage)
    On Error Resume Next    'prevent the code from halting on an error
    WriteToLogFile = False  'default return value of function
    Set objFSO = CreateObject("Scripting.FileSystemObject")
    Set objLogFile = objFSO.OpenTextFile("C:\Logfiles\MyLog.txt", 8)
    objLogFile.WriteLine(strLogMessage)
```

```
      objLogFile.Close
      WriteToLogFile = True
   End Function
</SCRIPT>
```

*Notice that we've used the explicit value **8**, instead of the **ForAppending** constant in our code. We found that the constant may not be recognized implicitly by some releases of VBScript.*

This function is stored as a separate text file **WriteLog.txt** on the server, and we use another **#include** statement to insert it into our page:

```
<!--#include file=WriteLog.txt-->
```

The other changes to the **GenForm.asp** page, we used earlier just to create a string **strToLog** containing the control names and its values, including the **vbCRLF** constant that adds carriage returns in the appropriate places. Once we've got this string, we can send it to our **WriteToLogFile** function and check the result. If it fails, by returning **False**, we place an error message in our page:

```
'Now we can loop through the Dictionary and output the results
strToLog = "Results received from FORM on " & Now() & vbCRLF
strKeysArray = objResult.Keys            'get the keys into an array
strItemsArray = objResult.Items          'get the items into an array
For intLoop = 0 To objResult.Count -1    'iterate through the array
  strThisKey = strKeysArray(intLoop)       'this is the key value
  strThisItem = strItemsArray(intLoop)     'this is the item (data) value
  Response.Write strThisKey & " = " & strThisItem & "<BR>"
  strToLog = strToLog & strThisKey & " = " & strThisItem & vbCRLF
Next
strToLog = strToLog & "--------------------------- " & vbCRLF

'Lastly, we write the results to the file, and put a message in the page
If WriteToLogFile(strToLog) Then
  Response.Write "Results successfully logged."
Else
  Response.write "Error in " & Err.Source
  Response.write "<BR>" & Err.description & "<P>"
End If
```

If you try this code yourself, without creating the log file first, you'll get an error. This is because we've used the **OpenTextFile** method in the **WriteToLogFile** function without setting the **create** argument to **True**. The reason is that it better demonstrates how we have to consider errors that can arise, and find ways of handling them gracefully. This is the subject of the next section.

The Err Object

In several of the earlier sections, we've noted occasions where an error will occur if certain conditions arise when using the built-in scripting objects. OK, so we should always try to make sure that errors can't occur, by checking values entered by the user or resident in the operating system. However, as you've just seen, there will be times when it's very hard to predict exactly the state of the environment in which our code is running.

For example, the **FileSystemObject** object and **TextStream** objects can create an error if we try to open a file that doesn't exist, or create a new file with the same name as one that already exists. VBScript doesn't include advanced file manipulation commands like **Dir**, which you can use in Visual Basic to see if a file exists. To prevent an unceremonious collapse of the script in our page, and the rather embarrassing error page being returned to the user, we can trap errors in our code and recover gracefully from them. To do this, we use the **On Error Resume Next** statement we first met in Chapter 2.

Using an On Error Statement

In Visual Basic, there are several different ways of using the **On Error** statement to control how our code should react to any errors it encounters. Unfortunately, VBScript–even in its latest incarnation–only contains one of these. By placing the statement **On Error Resume Next** at the beginning of our code routines, we instruct the script interpreter to ignore any errors it encounters, and carry on chugging through our code.

Then, once we've completed the processing we need to do, we can check to see if an error actually did occur. While there's not much we can do to change the result, we can at least provide a custom message to the user or load a different page. If they are submitting values from a form, we might even decide to give them a chance to try again with different values.

Using On Error Resume Next

The **On Error Resume Next** statement causes execution to continue with the statement immediately after the one that caused a runtime error. If the error is in a subroutine or function that we have called from elsewhere in our code, however, this subroutine or function is terminated immediately and execution continues with the line in the main body of the code after the one that called it. Of course, if the subroutine or function has its own **On Error Resume Next** statement, execution of *its* code continues after an error. Once execution leaves a subroutine or function, the **On Error Resume Next** statement within that routine is deactivated. You can think of it as being local to the routine.

This corresponds to a system referred to as the **call chain**. When our code calls another procedure (subroutine or function), this can itself call other procedures, creating a call chain. As each one completes, control passes back down the call chain to the procedure that called it. When an error occurs in a procedure which doesn't have an **On Error Resume Next** statement, control passes back down the call chain to the first one that does.

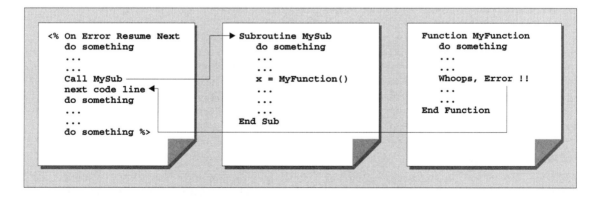

```
<% On Error Resume Next          → Subroutine MySub          Function MyFunction
   do something                     do something                do something
   ...                              ...                         ...
   ...                              ...                         ...
   Call MySub ──────────────        x = MyFunction()            Whoops, Error !!
   next code line ◄                 ...                         ...
   do something                     ...                         ...
   ...                              ...                         End Function
   ...                            End Sub
   do something %>
```

However, if none of the routines have an **On Error Resume Next** statement, the default error page is created and sent back to the user–and our code stops altogether. At this point, we've lost control. Therefore, we should always consider using **On Error Resume Next** at least in the main body of our code, so that we can trap an error that occurs in any of the other procedures we call.

Checking for an Error

Right, we've now trapped any errors that might have left our pages in a heap on the server-room floor. The problem is that our code might still be executing, even if an error did occur. Before we tell the user that they've got four million dollars in their checking account, we should make sure that there wasn't an error in the calculation. This is where the **Err** object comes in.

The **Err** object stores information about runtime errors, and you can use it to create an error. Why would we want to do this? Well, there are times when we might want to pass a custom error message back to the user. We can set the properties of the **Err** object to any value we please, then call its **Raise** method to raise this error. This stops execution of the code, and passes the error back to the Active Server Pages system. Here's a list of the available methods and properties:

Method	Description
`Clear`	Clears all current settings of the **Err** object.
`Raise`	Generates a runtime error.

Property	Description
`Description`	Sets or returns a string describing an error.
`Number`	(Default) Sets or returns a numeric value specifying an error.
`Source`	Sets or returns the name of the object that generated the error.

If a runtime error occurs, the properties of the **Err** object are set to values that uniquely identify the error. When an **On Error Resume Next** statement is executed, or when control passes back to a routine from a procedure it called, the properties are reset to zero or empty strings again. We can also reset the values on the **Err** object ourselves, using the **Clear** method.

So, to check for an error, we only need to examine the value of the **Err.Number** property after our call to **On Error Resume Next**, and before we exit from the routine. If it's zero, we know that an error hasn't occurred *in that routine*. However, remember that it is reset when we leave a subroutine or function, so we also need to check it here if we want to protect ourselves from incorrect information being returned. One of the easiest ways to use the object is to make sure that functions only return a value if they successfully run to completion. Remember, if an error occurs and we haven't used an **On Error Resume Next** statement in the function, execution immediately passes back to the code that called it.

Raising Our Own Errors

There are times when something goes wrong, and we need to pass custom details back to the routine that called our code. For example, we may be trying to open a text file that has been deleted. Normally, the VBScript interpreter will set the values of the **Err** object to the standard error code and description when this happens. By using **On Error Resume Next**, and examining the **Err** object, we can decide what kind of error occurred, and raise an appropriate message.

Here are some more modifications we've made to the code that was used in the generic form handler example, which has gradually been assembled throughout the previous sections of this chapter. Notice how we use the constant **vbObjectError** to make sure that the error number we select doesn't conflict with an existing error number. By adding our own randomly selected number to the constant, we can be more certain that we will not affect existing error numbers.

```
Function WriteToLogFile(strLogMessage)
   WriteToLogFile = False   'default return value of function
   On Error Resume Next
   Set objFSO = CreateObject("Scripting.FileSystemObject")
   Set objLogFile = objFSO.OpenTextFile("C:\Logfiles\MyLog.txt", 8)
   Select Case Err.Number
      Case 0              'OK, do nothing
      Case 50, 53         'standard file or path not found errors
        'create custom error values and raise error back to the system
        intErrNumber = vbObjectError + 1073       'custom error number
        strErrDescription = "Log file has been deleted or moved."
        strErrSource = "WriteToLogFile function"
        Err.Raise intErrNumber,  strErrSource, strErrDescription
        Exit Function
      Case Else        'some other error
        'raise the standard error back to the system
        Err.Raise Err.Number, Err.Source, Err.Description
        Exit Function
   End Select
   objLogFile.WriteLine(strLogMessage)
   objLogFile.Close
   WriteToLogFile = True
End Function
```

We've assumed that if we can successfully find and open the file, we'll be able to write our string to it and close it again. Obviously, we could extend the error handling to cover these actions in the same way. You can download the complete example, **LogForm.htm** and **LogForm.asp**, from our web site to try yourself. Here are the results, both when the file exists and when it doesn't:

```
 MyLog.txt - Notepad
File  Edit  Search  Help
Results received from FORM on 1/30/97 9:06:23 AM
txtName = Alex Homer
txtEmail = alex@stonebroom.com
chkWin95 = on
chkWinNT = on
chkNetwork = on
lstWhere = In the Office
------------------------------
```

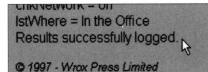

chkNetwork = on
lstWhere = In the Office
Results successfully logged.

© 1997 - Wrox Press Limited

chkNetwork = on
lstWhere = In the Office
Error in WriteToLogFile function
Log file has been deleted or moved.

© 1997 - Wrox Press Limited

> For the data to be successfully logged, there must already be a text file by the name of `Mylog.txt` present under the path `C:\LogFiles`.

Having seen how we can use the **Err** object to handle error conditions in VBScript, let's look how we can debug our programs to avoid some errors before user can get it.

Microsoft Script Debugger

In Chapter 4 we saw how we can use the **Response.Write** method in conjunction with collection iterators to produce output which can help us to make sure that some variables in our program contains appropriate values and to control the flow of our Active Server Pages application.

This technique can be used in small programs, or to debug various pieces of code. When we come to more complex applications that handle more real-life tasks, we will need a more powerful tool to debug our Active Server Pages applications. Usefully, we have **Microsoft Script Debugger**—a debugging tool that allows us to debug script programs on client and on server. Microsoft Script Debugger can be used to debug programs written on any ActiveX-enabled scripting language, including Visual Basic for Scripting (VBScript) and JScript. We can also use Microsoft Script Debugger to debug calls to Java applets, Java Beans and ActiveX components.

Before we take a look at the tool itself, let's make some introductory notes. Our Active Server Pages application can consist of two types of scripts, client scripts and server scripts. **Client scripts**, which consist of VBScript or JScript statements that appear on the HTML page. These scripts are executed inside the client browser (Microsoft Internet Explorer) either when the document is loaded or in response to some event, such as button click. On the server side we use **Server scripts**—VBScript or Jscript code that appears inside an **.asp** file. This script is executed by IIS when the page is requested by the browser, but before its contents are sent to the client. In this discussion we will take a look at server script debugging—the way we can debug our Active Server Pages applications.

Debugging on the Server Side

To debug server scripts we run Microsoft Script Debugger on the same computer that is running some version of IIS. Before we can use Script Debugger we must enable debugging. To maximize performance, debugging is not enabled by default for ASP-based applications.

> Please note, *never* enable debugging for an application in production, that is, a site being used by others since debugging slows down the whole application.

To enable debugging call application's Properties page and click the Configuration button. Under the Application Debugging tab, select Enable ASP server-side debugging check box. Then click the Ok button. Now we are ready to debug our application.

How Server Scripts are Processed

Scripts in an ASP-based application are not event-driven, unlike client-side scripts. Instead, when the client requests a page from a server, the server reads the page and processes all the server script (everything inside `<% %>` and `<SCRIPT RUNAT SERVER></SCRIPT>` tags) from top to bottom. This includes script that is inline with HTML text. The processing flow is shown on the following diagram.

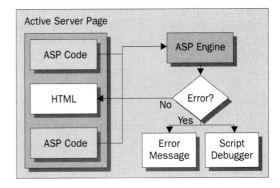

All scripts in the ASP file are processed as soon as the page is requested, so both syntax and runtime errors are caught by the ASP Engine immediately. So when the script debugger is enabled, we'll see a prompt to view our code in the debugger, if not—just an error message.

Here is a list of tasks you can perform while debugging is enabled:

- From the Start menu, choose Microsoft Script Debugger.

- When the Script Debugger is started, the Running Documents window should display. If it does not, select Running Documents from the View menu. Active Server Pages should appear as one of the entries in the Running Documents window.

- Expand the tree under the Active Server Pages entry until you find the `.asp` file that you requested. When you double-click the file, Microsoft Script Debugger will display the source for the `.asp` file.

- To set a breakpoint, click on a line in your source file (either HTML or script), and press F9 (the shortcut keystroke for Toggle Breakpoint). The nearest debuggable line in your `.asp` file should now display a red background.

- To have your breakpoint hit, request your `.asp` file using your browser. The Script Debugger should automatically get focus when the line with the breakpoint is reached. Congratulations! You are now debugging. F8 is the keyboard shortcut that you use most for Step Into, which executes the next executable block in your `.asp` file.

Now we know how to enable the debugger, how to perform tasks with it and how we can get into it. Let's look at the types of errors we can encounter and how to avoid them. Since every error should warrant a special approach, we will just outline common script errors and provide you with some thoughts how we can use the debugger to deal with them.

Common Script Errors

There can be two general kinds of errors in our ASP application—**Syntax errors** and **Runtime errors**. In either case, the ASP Engine stops processing the current page and starts the debugger (if one is enabled, as described above). If there is a syntax error, no content is sent to the client browser. If there is a runtime error, only the portion of the content up to the error is sent to the client browser.

Syntax Errors

Syntax errors occur if you mistype a keyword, forget to close a multi-line command (such as **do ... loop**), or introduce a similar syntax error. If your script includes a syntax error, the script will not execute and an error message is generated. The result of a syntax error depends on what type of debugging you are doing:

- If the syntax error is in a server script and if debugging is enabled for the ASP-based application, document processing stops. The server starts the script debugger, which displays the error message. If the browser that requested the document is on a different computer, the browser displays an error indicating that the document could not be found.

- If the syntax error is in a server script, but debugging is not enabled for the ASP-based application, error text is passed through and displayed in the client browser instead of the requested page.

- If the syntax error is in a client script, the document loads, but the script in which the error occurs does not run properly. The exact behavior of the script at that point will depend on where in the script the error occurs. Each time the script is run, the error message appears again.

Runtime Errors

A runtime error occurs when a command attempts to perform an action that is invalid. For example, a runtime error occurs if you try to perform a calculation using a variable that has not been initialized.

The conditions that result in runtime errors depend on the language you are scripting with. A condition that might cause a runtime error in VBScript might not cause an error in JScript. For example, attempting to divide by zero results in a runtime error in VBScript, but not in JScript.

- If there is a runtime error in a server script and debugging is enabled for that application, the server starts the debugger, which displays an error message.

- If a server script contains a runtime error and debugging is not enabled for that application, the error message text will appear in the client browser.

- If a runtime error occurs in a client script, you might see an error when the document is loaded into Microsoft Internet Explorer:

The result of a runtime error is similar to that of a syntax error: if you are debugging on the server, an error message appears in the script debugger on the server. Otherwise, error text appears in the client browser.

Depending on the language you are using, you might be able to include statements in your scripts to trap runtime errors and run your own error procedures. For example, in VBScript, you can use the **ON ERROR** statement to establish error trapping, as we have seen elsewhere in the book.

Debugging Tips and Tricks

Here is a list of tips that can help you find errors in your scripts more easily while you are using Microsoft Script Debugger.

- If you are debugging server scripts, enable the Script Debugger for the ASP application they appear in. If the debugger is not enabled on the server, error messages are passed as text to the client browser, but you cannot use the Script Debugger with your server scripts.

- Remember to disable debugging when your application is ready—else you'll see server performance degradation

- When the Script Debugger is enabled for one or more ASP applications, all server errors are passed to the debugger. Therefore, you should not enable the Script Debugger for an ASP application unless you can work on the server itself.

- If you are working in a client browser that is not on the server and if an error is displayed on the page, there is an error in the server script. If an error message is displayed in a dialog box, the error is in a client script.

- If there is a syntax or runtime error in a `.asp` file and if debugging is enabled for that ASP application, the client browser will not display the syntax error (unless the browser is running on the server). Instead, the client browser displays an error indicating that the browser cannot open the page and eventually times out

- When looking at line numbers in error messages note that if there is an error in the server script, the line number displayed in the error message points exactly to the error in the `.asp` file.

- If there is an error in a client script of a `.asp` file, the line number does not point to lines in the `.asp` file. Instead, it points to a line number in the HTML output of that `.asp` file. To see the line where the error has occurred, view the source of the HTML file in the client browser. Do not view the `.asp` file.

- Error codes for VBScript and JScript are listed in Appendix A and Appendix B respectively.

Summary

In this chapter, we have looked at how Active Server Pages can take advantage of several objects, offered by scripting engines and provided by a special library—**Microsoft Scripting Runtime**—through the Scripting object. We saw:

- How we can use the scripting objects **Dictionary**, **FileSystem** and **TextStream** from VBScript and JScript programs to add extra functionality to our Active Server Pages applications

- How we use the built-in VBScript **Err** object to trap some run-time errors

- How to debug programs with Microsoft Script Debugger

In the next chapter we will take a look at **Active Server Components**. In many ways, they are like ActiveX Controls, but are designed for execution on the server rather than being sent as an object to the browser. This has many advantages, as you'll see in the next chapter.

Active Server Components

CHAPTER 6

In the previous two chapters we saw three different types of objects–objects that are part of the **Active Server Pages Object Model,** built-in objects, provided by scripting engines, and scripting objects, supported by Microsoft Scripting Runtime. Now we'll take a look at the **Active Server Components**. In many ways, these are like ActiveX Controls, but they have been designed for execution on the server rather than being sent as an object to the browser. This has many advantages, as you'll see in this chapter.

The obvious question is, then, where do these components come from? Some are provided as part of the Active Server Pages installation, while others are available free or as a bought-in product. In this chapter, we'll show you just how useful the various components available from Microsoft are. Once you're familiar with using these components, you'll have no trouble slotting other supplier's products into your pages. We'll even show you how to build your own components later in the book. At the end of this chapter you'll find a list of third-party components, which you can use with your programs.

There's one standard component that we won't be covering in this chapter, however. One of the principal uses of dynamic web site technologies is to publish information direct from some type of database management system. This, and the need to collect data and store it in a database, led to the original development of server-side programming. To achieve these tasks using Active Server Pages, we'll take advantage of a special, but general-purpose component, called the **ActiveX Data Objects**. This is too large a subject to do justice to in one chapter together with all the other components, so we'll give it a whole chapter of its own later in the book.

In this chapter, therfore, we'll see:

- ▲ How we use the standard components supplied with Active Server Pages
- ▲ Other Microsoft components that are being developed, and how they are used
- ▲ How to create your own server components
- ▲ Third-party components you can use with your programs

Scripting Objects vs. Server Components

Having seen the various scripting objects, available for VBScript and JScript at work, we'll move on to look at how these are used with other components. It's important not to confuse the issue here when referring to server components and built-in script objects. The **Scripting objects**, like **TextStream** and **Dictionary**, are part of the **scripting environment**, which is implemented by a DLL as part of the Active Server Pages system. In Chapter 1, we saw how we can use different scripting languages with Active Server Pages if we want to. These other languages, and their associated scripting objects, are implemented in a similar way, using a different DLL.

Server components are separate from the scripting language DLLs. They are implemented within their own DLL. For example, the Content Linking component you'll see later in this chapter is implemented within the file **Nextlink.dll**. Once this is installed and registered on the server, the object is available within any scripting language that Active Server Pages is set up to support.

Active Server Pages Environment

Scripting DLLs

VBScript DLL

JScript DLL

Other Languages

Server Component DLLs

Other System or Add-in DLLs

As you'll see, some of the server components use the capabilities of the built-in scripting objects we've already looked at. Before we look at individual ones, however, we'll take an overview of the way we use server components in general.

An Overview of Server Components

In Chapter 3, we briefly saw one way of making use of the components supplied with the Active Server Pages package. We created an instance of the **Browser Capabilities** component using one of the methods of the **Server** object:

```
'
'VBScript Code
'
Set objBCaps = Server.CreateObject("MSWC.BrowserType")
```

This creates a reference to the object in the variable **objBCaps**, and we can then work with the object in our script. In other words, we can manipulate its properties and call its methods from code as required. In this section we'll be looking more closely at the ways we can create instances of components like this, the different components that are available, and the functions they offer.

Most of the standard components are aimed at specific kinds of tasks you need to accomplish in your web site or company intranet. What you want to achieve with Active Server Pages will, obviously, depend on the kinds of information you want to publish, and the overall aims of your site. However, using pre-built components can, as you'll see, provide a headstart when you come to getting the show on the road.

Creating Instances of Components

With VBScript or JScript we can make use of the **Server** object's **CreateObject** method, as you saw earlier to create an instance of a component. Alternatively, we can assign a reference to the object directly to a variable for use later in our code.

Reacting to CreateObject Errors in VBScript

One common source of errors is attempting to create an instance of an object that isn't properly installed, or using the wrong identifier for the object. Active Server Pages will create an error page and return this to the browser in the usual way. However, if we're using an **On Error Resume Next** statement in our page, we won't pick up this error automatically, and often the first we see of the error is when we try to use one of the object's methods, or refer to one of its properties.

An easy way to guard against this problem is with the **IsObject()** function. This returns True only if the parameter we supply is a valid reference to an object. For example:

```
'
'VBScript Code
'
On Error Resume Next
Set objMyObject = Server.CreateObject("MSWC.NotInstalled")
If IsObject(objMyObject) = False Then ...  'CreateObject method failed
```

Using an <OBJECT> Tag

Alternatively, we can use a normal **<OBJECT>** tag to create an instance of an object in our Active Server Pages, in the same way as we would when creating an object instance in a web page on the browser. Active Server Pages supports a special implementation of the HTML **<OBJECT>** tag, and we can use this to place an object in our pages. To define an instance of a component or scripting object in a normal .**asp** file, we use the syntax:

```
<OBJECT RUNAT=Server ID=ObjectReference PROGID="ObjectIdentifier">
</OBJECT>
```

ObjectReference is the name, such as **objMyObject**, by which we'll refer to the object in our code when we come to work with it. *ObjectIdentifier* is the name of the object or component in the Windows Registry; for example, **MSWC.Adrotator**.

So we can declare an Ad Rotator object with the code:

```
<OBJECT RUNAT=Server ID=objAdRot PROGID="MSWC.Adrotator">
</OBJECT>
```

Notice the **RUNAT** attribute, which must be set to **Server**. The **PROGID** is a text string which uniquely defines the component or object, in the form [*Vendor.*]*Component*[*.Version*].

Alternatively, we can use the **CLASSID** of the object instead of the 'friendly name' **PROGID**:

```
<OBJECT RUNAT=Server ID=objAdRot
  CLASSID="Clsid:0ACE4881-8305-11CF-9427-444553540000">
</OBJECT>
```

Setting an Object's Scope

When used in a normal **.asp** file, there will generally be no difference in the performance of the page between using **CreateObject** or an **<OBJECT>** tag. The real difference is the point at which the object is actually instantiated, or created. The **CreateObject** method creates the instance of the object as soon as it is called. However, an object defined within an **<OBJECT>** tag isn't actually created until it is first referenced. This allows us to minimize resource use or increase performance on the server, where the object isn't actually defined in the **.asp** page but in the **global.asa** file.

We met **global.asa**, and the notion of **Session** and **Application** objects, in the previous chapter, and we'll be coming back to it in a lot more detail later in the book. In the meantime, we only need to appreciate that we can create instances of objects in this file, and they then have a scope that is defined by the **Session** or **Application**, rather than just the lifetime of the reference variable in the .**asp** page. We do this by including the **SCOPE** attribute within the **<OBJECT>** tag:

```
<OBJECT RUNAT=Server SCOPE=Session ID=objAdRot PROGID="MSWC.Adrotator">
</OBJECT>
```

The valid values for **SCOPE** are **Session**, **Application**, or **Page**. If we use an **<OBJECT>** tag in a normal **.asp** file, we have to use **Page**, or omit the **SCOPE** attribute altogether. However, if we place the **<OBJECT>** tag in **global.asa**, we create an object that is available throughout the current session, or globally throughout the application. This has specific performance implications when we come to use the database component, as you'll see in later chapters.

Component Methods and Properties

The whole reason for using components in our Active Server Pages is to benefit from the extra functionality they provide. This functionality is either unavailable, inefficient or difficult to achieve, using just a scripting language. Once the object instance is available, and we have a reference to it, we can call its **methods** and manipulate its **properties** to achieve the effects we require.

Each component has its own particular methods and properties, so we need to know what these are, and (in the case of methods) the exact syntax and arguments each one supports. For example, the **Content Linking** component has a method called **GetNextURL**, while the **Advertisement Rotator** component has a **GetAdvertisement** method. In the next section, we'll look in detail at the standard components, plus a few of the others that are available as well.

Many component methods return a value. In most cases this will be something that we want to actually work with, such as the URL returned by the Content Linking component `GetNextURL` method. Others just accept a value, such as the **Append** method of the User Properties component. However, many of these methods also return **True** or **False** values that we can use to make sure that the operation was successful. For example:

```
'
'VBScript Code
'
If objProp("shirts").Append("Hawaiian") = TRUE Then ...   'it worked OK
```

The Standard Components

Active Server Pages includes eleven standard server components. We'll be covering the ActiveX Database Objects (ADO) component in the next chapter. In the remainder of this chapter, we'll see how we can gain extra functionality for our web site or intranet using the other ten. You'll see:

The **Ad Rotator** component
The **Browser Capabilities** component
The **Content Linking** component
The **Content Rotator** component
The **Page Counter** component
The **Permission Checker** component
The **Counters** component
The **MyInfo** component
The **Tools** component
The **Status** component

> At the time of writing several of these components (including the Content Rotator and Page Counter) weren't available as part of ASP in IIS 4.0 and were still in beta. They did however come complete as part of ASP with PWS 4.0. To obtain them for IIS 4.0, you needed to download them separately. If you find that you can't create the object within your own code and IIS 4.0 then you might still need to download them. Go to the following URL for more details:
>
> `http://www.backoffice.microsoft.com/downtrial/moreinfo/iissamples.asp`

The Ad Rotator Component

The **Ad Rotator** component allows us to display a different graphic on our pages, each time the page is referenced from a browser. Hence, the first time you access the site you may see a graphic advertising holidays, the next time you return to the page it might be for pizzas. In fact, this technique is often used in sites that display advertisements, hence the component name. Every time the page is opened or re-loaded, Active Server Pages uses the information in a **rotator schedule file** to select a graphic, and insert it into the page. However, the Ad Rotator component can do more than this. We can arrange for the image to be a hyperlink rather than a static picture, and even record how many users click each one of the advertisements.

Of all the components we're looking at in this chapter, the Ad Rotator is probably the most complicated to use because it involves several different files. Before we start to look at each file in detail, an overview of the process might help you to see how it all fits together. The visitor sees an advertisement on the page, usually a graphic that is also a hyperlink. Each time they load our page, however, a different one may be displayed from a fixed selection. Clicking on the graphic loads a **redirection file**, which itself sends the user off to the advertiser's site.

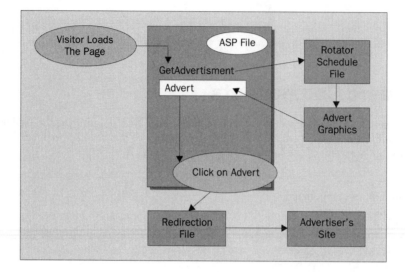

We'll now go about creating a simple example in VBScript which loads up one of two graphics. There are three steps involved:

- Creating the Component Object
- Creating the Ad Rotator Schedule file
- Creating the Redirection File

We'll start with the component itself.

Creating the Component Object

To create an instance of the Ad Rotator component, we've used the **Server** object's **CreateObject** method:

```
'
'VBScript Code
'
<%Set objAdRot = Server.CreateObject("MSWC.AdRotator")
```

Once we've got our **objAdRot** object, we can work with its properties, and the single method it provides. The first step is to decide on the width of the image border, the frame where we want the graphic to be displayed, and whether it accepts mouse clicks from the user.

```
'
'VBScript Code
'
objAdRot.Border=0                  'no border
objAdRot.Clickable=TRUE            'is a hyperlink
objAdRot.TargetFrame="fraAdFrame"  'load into frame named fraAdFrame
```

Then, we need to insert the HTML for the graphic into the page that will be returned to the user. The **GetAdvertisement** method creates this, by getting details of the next advertisement to display from the rotator schedule file. We then have to place the HTML code into the page:

```
'
'VBScript Code
'
StrHTML = objAdRot.GetAdvertisement("AdFiles\MyAdFile.txt")
Response.Write(strHTML)     'put the HTML into the page%>
```

The argument for the method is the location of the rotator schedule file relative to the current directory. For example, if this file is stored in the **AdFiles** directory within the current directory, we use **AdFiles\MyAdFile.txt**.

Methods and Properties of the Ad Rotator Component Object

Here is the single method that the Ad Rotator component supports:

Method	Description
GetAdvertisement	Gets details of the next advertisement and formats it as HTML.

Here are the properties that the Ad Rotator component supports:

Property	Description
Border	Size of the border around the advertisement.
Clickable	Defines whether the advertisement is a hyperlink.
TargetFrame	Name of the frame in which to display the advertisement.

> *The* **TargetFrame** *can also be set to one of the standard HTML frame identifiers such as* **_top**, **_new**, **_child**, **_self**, **_parent**, *or* **_blank**.

The Rotator Schedule File

The Ad Rotator component depends on the rotator schedule file to specify the advertisements, or graphics, which are to be displayed. This includes the name of the image files, the size they are to be displayed at, and the relative percentage of times each one should be displayed. It's divided into two sections, which are separated by a line containing only an asterisk (*).

The first section is optional, and sets the default values that apply to all the advertisements in the schedule. This provides us with another way of setting these values, without using the object's parameters directly as we did earlier. If we omit one or more of these optional parameters, and don't set the properties explicitly, the object will use its own default values. If we omit all of these parameters, we still have to include the asterisk as the first line of the file.

```
REDIRECT   URL
WIDTH   width
HEIGHT   height
BORDER   border
*
adURL
adHomeURL
text
impressions
```

Parameter	Description
URL	Virtual path and name of the program or ASP file that implements the redirection.
width	Width in pixels of the advertisement on the page. Default is **440**.
height	Height in pixels of the advertisement on the page. Default is **60**.
border	Border width around the advertisement, in pixels. Default is **1**, use **0** for no border.

The second section, after the asterisk, must exist in the file. It provides details of the individual advertisements, and is repeated for each one:

Parameter	Description
adURL	Virtual path and filename of the advertisement image file.
adHomeURL	Advertiser's home page URL. A hyphen indicates there is no link for this ad.
text	Text for display if the browser doesn't support graphics.
impressions	A number indicating the relative display time for the advertisement.

*If the file contains three advertisements, with their **impressions** set to 2, 3, and 5, the first is included in 20 percent of the returned pages, the second in 30 percent, and the third in 50 percent. It doesn't indicate the actual time that the advertisement will be displayed in the browser.*

An Example Rotator Schedule File

So, let's see what a rotator schedule file looks like in practice. Here's a simple one containing only two advertisements, which will be displayed an equal number of times. It depends on the virtual directory path **/ASP1266**, which we've created on the server, to be able to find the files it lists:

```
REDIRECT /ASP1266/AdRot/AdFiles/AdRot.asp
*
/ASP1266/AdRot/AdFiles/AdPics/wrox.gif
http://www.wrox.com
Better books from Wrox Press
10
/ASP1266/AdRot/AdFiles/AdPics/lunar.gif
http://www.wrox.com
Acme Lunar Boost Supplies
10
```

When we call the **GetAdvertisement** method, it returns HTML code that we can insert into our page to create the advertisement. For the first advertisement in our file, we'll get this:

```
...
<A HREF="/ASP1266/AdRot/AdFiles/AdRedirect.asp?url=http://www.wrox.com&image=/ASP0723/
AdRot/AdFiles/AdPics/wrox.gif">
<IMG SRC="/ASP1266/AdRot/AdFiles/AdPics/wrox.gif" ALT="Better books from Wrox Press"
WIDTH=440 HEIGHT=60 BORDER=0>
</A>
...
```

You can see that it has placed the image inside a normal **<A>** tag. The **HREF** attribute is set to the name of our redirection file, **Adrot.asp**, with the advertiser's home page URL and the image we used appended to it with a question mark. Therefore, our redirection file will be loaded and executed on the server when the user clicks on the advertisement. Here's what our example looks like:

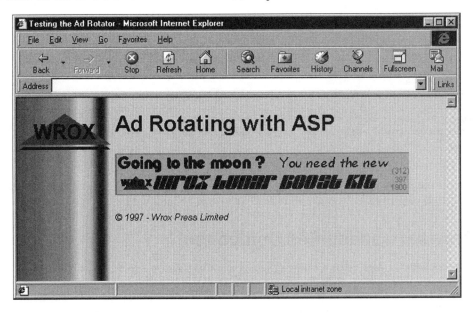

The Redirection File

The redirection file can be (either/or–one of two, not three or more) an ASP page, an ISAPI DLL, or a CGI application, all of which accept the advertiser's home page URL and the image name parameters sent to them. It can examine these and decide what to do next; for example, it will usually redirect the user to the URL associated with the advertisement. This is easy to do, using the VBScript code:

```
Response.Redirect(Request.QueryString("url"))
```

However, the redirection file provides us with the opportunity to do more than this. For example, we can count the number of users that have clicked on each advertisement–which is particularly useful if we're getting paid according to the number of redirections we achieve. We could do this with the **WriteToLogFile** function we used earlier:

```
'
'VBScript Code
'
...
If Instr(Request.QueryString("url"), "wrox.com") Then
   'this is a jump to the Wrox Press site
   strToLog = "Wrox Press on " & Now() & vbCRLF
End If
...
...
blnOK = WriteToLogFile(strToLog)
Response.Redirect(Request.QueryString("url"))
```

As the query string contains the name of the image file, we can also refer to this in our script. If the same advertiser had three images in the rotator file, we could combine the number of responses for all three:

```
'
'VBScript Code
'
...
If Instr(Request.QueryString("image"), "wrox") Then
   'this is an image with 'wrox' in the name, so it must be a jump to them
End If
...
```

As a standard component of Active Server Pages **Ad Rotator** component is implemented in **ADROT.DLL** and has a CLSID of 1621F7C0-60AC-11CF-9427-444553540000.

The Browser Capabilities Component

One of the problems we face when creating all kinds of web pages, not just dynamic ones that use Active Server Pages, is deciding which of the increasing range of tags and techniques we should take advantage of. While it's great to be able to use all the latest features, such as Java applets, ActiveX controls, and the most recent HTML tags, we need to be aware that some visitors will be using browsers that don't support these. All they might see of our carefully crafted pages is a jumble of text, images, and–even worse–the code that makes them work.

This isn't a discussion on how you should design pages to support different browsers, we'll look at an example of that in Chapter 19. However, using a special server component called the **Browser Capabilities** component we can determine which of a whole range of features a browser supports, at the point when it actually references one of our pages.

When a user requests a page from the server, the HTTP header includes details of the browser they are using. In HTTP-speak it's called the **user agent**, and is a string defining the browser software name and version. This is effectively mapped to the Browser Capabilities component, which then adopts a range of properties equivalent to the user's browser features. Hence, at any time while the page is being executed, the Browser Capabilities component can provide details of which individual features are or are not supported. Note that we can get the contents of user agent filed from HTTP header with **Request.ServerVariables** method. This is described in more detail in Chapter 4.

```
User Agent: <% =Request.ServerVariables("HTTP_USER_AGENT") %>
```

The Browscap.ini File

The Browser Capabilities component consists of a single DLL **Browscap.dll**, plus a text file **Browscap.ini** that must be in the same directory as the DLL. **Browscap.ini** contains the information about each known browser, and there's also a default section of the file, which is used when the browser details don't match any of the ones more fully specified in the file. So adding new information about browsers, or updating the existing information, is as easy as editing the **Browscap.ini** file.

We'll look at the format of this file first. All of the entries in **Browscap.ini** are optional, however it's important that we always include the default section. If the browser in use doesn't match any in the **Browscap.ini** file, and no default browser settings have been specified, all the properties are set to **"UNKNOWN"**.

```
; we can add comments anywhere, prefaced by a semicolon like this

; entry for a specific browser
[HTTPUserAgentHeader]
parent = browserDefinition
property1 = value1
property2 = value2
...

[Default Browser Capability Settings]
defaultProperty1 = defaultValue1
defaultProperty1 = defaultValue1
...
```

The **[HTTPUserAgentHeader]** line defines the start of a section for a particular browser, and the **parent** line indicates that another definition contains more information for that browser as well. Then, each line defines a property that we want to make available through the Browser Capabilities component, and its value for this particular browser. The **Default** section lists the properties and values that are used if the particular browser in use isn't listed in its own section, or if it is listed but not all the properties are supplied.

For example, we may have a section for Internet Explorer 4.0. This has no **parent** line, and so the only properties it will have (other than those defined in the default section) are those we explicitly define:

```
[IE 4.0]
browser=IE
Version=4.0
majorver=4
minorver=0
frames=TRUE
tables=TRUE
cookies=TRUE
backgroundsounds=TRUE
vbscript=TRUE
javascript=TRUE
javaapplets=TRUE
ActiveXControls=TRUE
Win16=False
beta=False
AK=False
SK=False
AOL=False
crawler=False
cdf=True
...
```

Now, we can add the definition for another browser. For example:

```
[Mozilla/2.0 (compatible; MSIE 4.01; Windows 95)]
parent=IE 4.0
version=4.01
minorver=01
platform=Win95
```

Here, we've specified **IE 4.0** as the **parent** for this browser. The properties we've explicitly provided replace, or add to, those values in its parent's definition–but it will also assume any other property values there, which aren't explicitly listed in its own section. Then, lastly, we add the default browser section:

```
[Default Browser Capability Settings]
browser=Default
Version=0.0
majorver=#0
minorver=#0
frames=False
tables=True
cookies=False
backgroundsounds=False
vbscript=False
javascript=False
javaapplets=False
activexcontrols=False
...
```

This assumes a 'worse case scenario', where the browser supports almost nothing at all. However, it's up to us to define the actual values we want to use as this base. But we need to appreciate that if we've defined some of the default properties as **TRUE**, and we *do* get a visit from someone running a green-on-black, text-only browser on a Unix terminal, they might not see our page to full effect.

Maintaining Browscap.ini

Keeping **Browscap.ini** up to date with new browsers as they are released, and adding older or specialist ones that we may have to contend with, is obviously important. To make life easier, a reasonably comprehensive version of **Browscap.ini** is supplied with Active Server Pages and updated ones can be downloaded from Microsoft's web site. The full address where you can find this file is:

http://www.backoffice.microsoft.com/downtrial/moreinfo/bcf.asp

> A company called cyScape, Inc. maintains a list of browscap.ini files, which is sometimes more up to date than even the Microsoft web site. You can find the newest one at their Web-site:
>
> http://www.cyscape.com/browscap
>
> or subscribe to a mailing list and automatically receive the newest version of the file. To do so you should send e-mail to the address:
>
> **browcap-request@cyscape.com**
>
> entering "subscribe" in message body. Subscribers will receive new browscap.ini files automatically as they are released.

To help with recognizing very similar versions of a browser, we can use the asterisk (*****) wildcard in the **HTTPUserAgentHeader** line. Then:

```
[Mozilla/2.0 (compatible; MSIE 4.0;* Windows 95)]
```

will match:

```
[Mozilla/2.0 (compatible; MSIE 4.0; Windows 95)]
[Mozilla/2.0 (compatible; MSIE 4.0; AOL; Windows 95)]
 ... etc.
```

However, wildcard matches are only used if the user agent string sent by the browser doesn't fully match an **HTTPUserAgentHeader** which does *not* include an asterisk. Only if this test fails will it attempt to match with wildcard **HTTPUserAgentHeader** values, and it will use the first one it finds in the file that does match.

Using the Browser Capabilities Component

Having grasped how the **Browscap.ini** file can provide customizable properties containing information about a particular browser, it's time to actually see the Browser Capabilities component in use. This is relatively simple–we just create an instance of it, and refer to its properties. We'll do this in VBScript. Notice that to avoid having the **Browscap.ini** file accessed every time we read the value once and assign it to a variable:

```
'
'VBScript Code
'
<%Set objBCap = Server.CreateObject("MSWC.BrowserType")
blnVBScriptOK = objBCap.vbscript  'save the value in a variable
```

```
If blnVBScriptOK Then
Response.Write "This browser supports VBScript"
Else
Response.Write "This browser doesn't support VBScript"
End If%>
```

This checks to see if the browser supports VBScript, or not and displays the appropriate message. You could imagine this could be modified to direct the user to different pages depending on the response given by the browser.

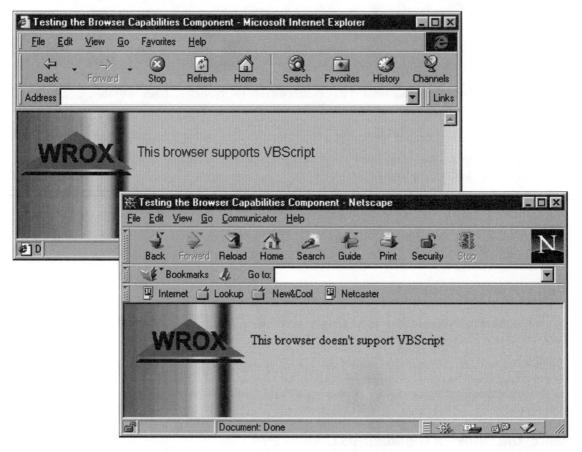

Of course, we can use the properties to do other things. One favorite technique is to load a different index page for a site, depending on what features the browser supports. If our site has a set of pages using frames, and a different set using only simple text, we can check the browser's ability to display frames when it first hits our site, and redirect it to the appropriate index page.

As a standard component of Active Server Pages **Browser Capabilities** component is implemented in **BROWSCAP.DLL** and has CLSID of 0ACE4881-8305-11CF-9427-444553540000.

The Content Linking Component

The **Content Linking** component is a very useful tool for sites that provide contents pages, or pages that contain a list of links to other pages on the same site. It automatically matches the URL of the currently displayed page to a list of pages stored in a text file on the server, and can allow users to browse through the list of pages in forward or reverse order. In other words, even after the visitor has clicked on a link in the contents page, and is viewing one of the pages in the list, the component can still tell whereabouts that page is within the list.

And because all the details are stored in a text file, maintaining the site–and the links between the pages– becomes a matter of just editing the text file. For example, we can change the order that the pages are displayed in just by rearranging them in the content linking list file.

The Content Linking List File

The **Content Linking List file** contains a simple list of page URLs, in the order they are to be displayed. We also supply matching descriptions, which are displayed in the contents page, and we can add comments to each one if required. These help identify the links later, and aren't visible to visitors. The file contains one line of text for each page. Each line consists of the URL, description and comment, separated by *Tab* characters (not spaces, otherwise it won't work) and ending with a carriage return. For example:

```
newline.htm New additions to our site    we update this weekly
offers.htm  Special Offers for this week  we only update this monthly
register.htm        Registration for new users
main.htm    The main forum and chat area  must be registered first
index.htm   Back to the contents page
```

> *URLs must be specified as a virtual or relative path, such as* **forum\enter.htm**. *URLs that start with* **http:, //,** *or* **** *can't be used.*

Using the Content Linking Component

Once we've created our content linking file, we can add the component to our pages. We can use the standard **CreateObject** syntax, or an **<OBJECT>** tag. In the examples in this chapter, you'll mostly see **CreateObject** being used:

```
'
'VBScript Code
'
Set objNextLink = Server.CreateObject("MSWC.Nextlink")
```

Then, we can use the methods it provides to manipulate the list, and create our pages:

Method	Description
GetListCount(*list***)**	Number of items in the file *list*.
GetListIndex(*list***)**	Index of the current page in the file *list*.
GetNextURL(*list***)**	URL of the next page in the file *list*.

Method	Description
`GetNextDescription(list)`	Description of the next page in file *list*.
`GetPreviousURL(list)`	URL of the previous page in the file *list*.
`GetPreviousDescription(list)`	Description of previous page in file *list*.
`GetNthURL(list, n)`	URL of the *n*th page in the file *list*.
`GetNthDescription(list, n)`	Description of the *n*th page in the file *list*.

> **The index number of the first item is 1. If the current page isn't in the Content Linking List file,** `GetListIndex` **returns** 0, `GetNextURL` **and** `GetNextDescription` **return the URL and description of the last page in the list,** `GetPreviousURL` **and** `GetPreviousDescription` **return the URL and description of the first page in the list.**

Creating a Contents Page

We've created a simple example in VBScript that uses pages describing some of our other books. You can download it from **http://rapid.wrox.co.uk/books/1266/** and try it out yourself. It creates a table of contents, using a Content Linking List file named **contlink.txt**. This code is in the main page, **content.asp**:

```
'
'VBScript Code
'
<UL>
   <% Set objNextLink = Server.CreateObject("MSWC.NextLink")
   intCount = objNextLink.GetListCount("contlink.txt")
   For intLoop = 1 To intCount %>
     <LI>
       <A HREF="<%= objNextLink.GetNthURL("contlink.txt", intLoop) %>">
         <%= objNextLink.GetNthDescription("contlink.txt", intLoop) %>
       </A>
   <% Next %>
</UL>
```

Inside the normal **<UL>** and **</UL>** tags, the code creates a Content Linking object. The correct reference for this, as stored in the ProgID key of Windows Registry, is **MSWC.NextLink**. Then it uses the object's **GetListCount** method to find out how many links there are in the Content Linking List, and loops through them. For each one, it places an **<LI>** tag in the page, followed by an **<A>** tag. The **HREF** is retrieved from the list file using the **GetNthURL** method, and the description with **GetNthDescription**. The Content Linking List file **contlink.txt**, and the results it produces, look like this:

```
wh20.asp    Beginners C++ Programming
wh21.asp    Visual C++ Masterclass
wh30.asp    Beginners Guide to VB
wh40.asp    Instant VBScript
wh50.asp    Beginner's Guide to Access
```

Here our content list file is in the same folder as the ASP page. If it wasn't, we could provide either a relative physical path, or a full virtual path, to it:

```
'
'VBScript Code
'
intCount = objNextLink.GetListCount("links\contlink.txt") 'physical path
intCount = objNextLink.GetListCount("/demo/contlink.txt") 'virtual path
```

Each item on the page is a hyperlink. Selecting View Source in the browser shows that we've just created an unordered list. Each list item is the **Description** from the content linking file, enclosed in an **<A>** tag that uses the URL as the **HREF**.

```
<UL>
  <LI>
    <A HREF="wh20.asp">
        Beginners C++ Programming
    </A>
    . . .
    . . .
</UL>
```

All pretty standard stuff, but we can do better than this....

Browsing Through the Pages

When we create an instance of the Content Linking component and access one of its methods, it matches the *current* page's URL with the entries in the Content Linking List file we specify in that method call. We can use it not only to create a contents list (as we've just seen), but also to navigate between pages in the list while we've got one of them open in the browser.

This means that we can use hot links or buttons to move to another page from one of the listed pages. For example, we can add Next and Back buttons to a page, because we can tell which is the next or previous item in the list by using the **GetNextURL** and **GetPreviousURL** methods. Alternatively, we can jump to any other page in the list, using the **GetNthURL** method. And, of course, we can tell where we are in the list at the moment using the **GetListIndex** method.

Here's the code that adds Next and Previous buttons to our pages. All we have to do is place it in each of the pages listed in the Content Linking List file or attach it with **include** directive:

```
'
'VBScript Code
'
<% Set objNextLink = Server.CreateObject("MSWC.NextLink")
strListFile = "contlink.txt"
intThisPage = objNextLink.GetListIndex(strListFile)
If intThisPage > 1 Then %>
  <INPUT TYPE=BUTTON VALUE="< Back"
  ONCLICK="location.href='<% = objNextLink.GetPreviousURL(strListFile) %>';">
<% End If %>
<INPUT TYPE=BUTTON VALUE=" Home " ONCLICK="location.href='content.asp';">
<% If intThisPage < objNextLink.GetListCount(strListFile) Then %>
  <INPUT TYPE=BUTTON VALUE="Next >"
  ONCLICK="location.href='<%= objNextLink.GetNextURL(strListFile)  %>';">
<% End If %>
```

The first step is to create the Content Linking component, and then put the name of the list file into a variable. We need to do this if we want to use it in the JScript code later in the page (see below). Besides, it makes the page easier to maintain, because we only have to change it in one place if we want to use a different filename.

Now we can see where we are within the Content Linking List. The **GetListIndex** method provides the line number, starting from **1**. If the current page has an index greater than **1**, we know we can go back–so we include the HTML to create the Back button in the page. Similarly, if the current page's index is less that the number of items in the list, we can include a Next button. We always include a Home button, so that the visitor can get back to the contents page easily at any time.

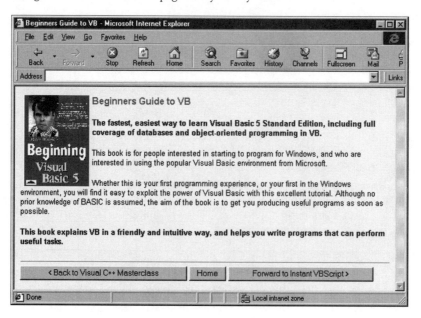

The screen shot above shows the three buttons, on a page in the middle of our list. If we browse to the end of the list, however, the index of the current page **intThisPage** is no longer less than the number of lines in the file **objNextLink.GetListCount(strListFile)**. In this page, we don't get a Next button:

Jumping with JScript

You'll see that our navigation buttons use JScript (rather than VBScript) statements to load the new page. For example, the Back button contains the attribute:

```
ONCLICK="location.href='<% = objNextLink.GetPreviousURL(strListFile) %>';"
```

When the HTML version of the page is created by ASP, the expression inside the **<%...%>** tags is replaced with its value, so the page sent to the browser could look like this:

```
ONCLICK="location.href='wh21.htm';"
```

You can also see why we chose to use a variable to hold the name of the Content Linking List file—it's cumbersome to have to try to include a third level of nested quotes inside a single statement.

> *Remember, the default language in the browser is JavaScript or JScript, not VBScript. By using JScript, we avoid having to provide a LANGUAGE argument in the* **OnClick** *code, and anyway it makes a change.*

Going to Usability Extremes

Before we leave the Content Linking component, we'll just see how two other methods can be used to go to the extreme in usability. By changing two lines of our VBScript code, we can actually display the description of the next and previous pages in the buttons or hyperlinks on the current page:

```
<% Set objNextLink = Server.CreateObject ("MSWC.NextLink")
strListFile = "contlink.txt"
intThisPage = objNextLink.GetListIndex (strListFile)
If (intThisPage > 1) Then %>
  <INPUT TYPE=BUTTON
  VALUE="< Back to <%= objNextLink.GetPreviousDescription(strListFile) %>"
  ONCLICK="location.href='<%= objNextLink.GetPreviousURL (strListFile)  %>';">
<% End If %>
  <INPUT TYPE=BUTTON VALUE=" Home "
  ONCLICK="location.href='content.asp';">
<% If (intThisPage < objNextLink.GetListCount(strListFile)) Then %>
  <INPUT TYPE=BUTTON
  VALUE="Forward to <%= objNextLink.GetNextDescription(strListFile) %> >"
  ONCLICK="location.href='<%= objNextLink.GetNextURL (strListFile)  %>';">
<% End If %>
```

This uses the **GetPreviousDescription** and **GetNextDescription** methods in the same way as we used **GetPreviousURL** and **GetNextURL**. Of course, this time we get the description from the Content Linking List file, rather than the URL. And remember—all these links are dynamically created just from the

Content Linking List. Simply changing the list automatically changes which buttons or hyperlinks appear, and sets the correct captions. This has got to be a hot choice for many intranet-related tasks, where you need to provide regularly changing pages of information for your users.

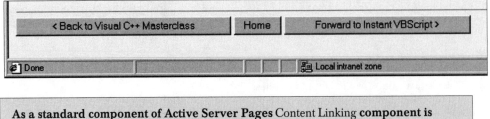

> As a standard component of Active Server Pages Content Linking **component is implemented in** NEXTLINK.DLL **and has CLSID of** 4D9E4505-6DE1-11CF-87A7-444553540000

The Content Rotator Component

The **Content Rotator Component** is like a simplified version of the **Ad Rotator** component we looked at earlier in this chapter. We provide a **Content Schedule File**, which is just a text file containing different sections of text and HTML code. The Content Rotator component automatically displays one of them in our pages. We can include almost any number of text content entries in the schedule file, and specify the weighting that will control how often each one is included in the returned page.

Using the Content Linking Component

To create the component instance in the page, we use:

```
<%Set objMyContent = Server.CreateObject("MSWC.ContentRotator")
objMyContent.ChooseContent("mycontent.txt")
Response.Write(objMyContent.ChooseContent("mycontent.txt"))%>
```

To get a specific section of text and HTML from the schedule file, we use the object's **ChooseContent** method. It simply retrieves an entry. To insert it into the page we need to use the **Response.Write** method or alternatively we could use the **=** construction:

```
<% =objMyContent.ChooseContent("mycontent.txt") %>
```

This uses a schedule file in the same directory as the page. If it's stored elsewhere, we have to supply the path of the schedule file, which can either be a relative physical path or a full virtual path, for example:

```
objMyContent.ChooseContent("\content\mycontent.txt")   'relative path
objMyContent.ChooseContent("/demo/ mycontent.txt")     'full virtual path
```

If we need to get all the content strings from the Content Schedule File, we can use the object's **GetAllContent** method. As with **ChooseContent** method we have to supply the path of the schedule file, for example:

```
objMyContent.GetAllContent("mycontent.txt")
```

This will insert all the content of Content Schedule File into client page. Now let's look at how the Content Schedule File is organized.

The Content Schedule File

The **Content Schedule File** for the Content Rotator component is much simpler than the equivalent Ad Rotator's schedule file in structure. We just supply a list of the individual text strings we want to use, separated by a line that starts with two percent signs (%%). To set the relative weighting of each, which determines how often each will appear in the return page, we add a number to this line, and we can also append comments to it using a pair of forward slash characters(//):

```
%% 3 // This is the first line of the schedule text file
For more information, mail us at <A HREF="mailto:feedback@wrox.com">Wrox Press</A>

%% 4 // This is  a multi-line text string
<H2>Wrox Press</H2>
  <UL>
    <LI> Language Primers
    <LI> Advanced Programming
    <LI> Systems and Databases
  </UL>
<HR>

%% 2
Visit us on the <A HREF="http://www.wrox.com">World Wide Web</A>
```

This example shows three different text strings which will all be used in our page. The weightings are 3, 4 and 2, so the pages will be shown in three out of nine, four out of nine, and 2 out of nine pages overall.

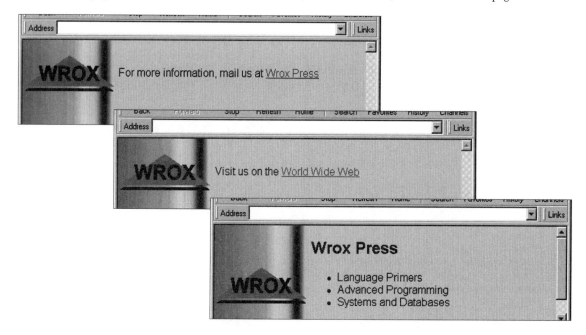

Notice however, that (like the Ad Rotator component) the actual occurrence of each individual string is determined at random, then modified to achieve the weighting. If you load the page nine times, you may not get exactly these results. When we come to look at creating applications, we'll see ways of using these components in an application-wide scope. This improves the accuracy of the weightings.

As a standard component of Active Server Pages **Content Rotator** component is implemented in **CONTROT.DLL** and has CLSID of `B4E90802-B83C-11D0-8B40-00C0F00AE35A`

The Page Counter Component

The **Page Counter** component is used to count how many times our page was hit. This component saves its data in a file—**Hit Count Data file**, so in case of server shutdown, the data will not lost.

We create an instance of Page Counter component with **Server.CreateObject** method using JScript code this time:

```
<%
//
// JScript Code
//
  var numHits = Server.CreateObject("MSWC.PageCounter")
%>
```

Then we can use **Hits** method to get number of hits and **Reset** method to reset counter if needed. Hits method has an optional parameter, which can specify the page in **/VirtualDirectoryName/ PageName.ASP** format. If this parameter is not specified, the Hits method shows the number of hits for the current page.

Let's look at the following example. Suppose we have a main page, which stores some introductory stuff— welcome message, news and so on. Also we have a downloads page, where we provide users with some free stuff. It's possible that some web surfers will skip our main page and bookmark only our downloads page. So we need to check the hits count for our main page and for our downloads page to get a track on how many hits we actually get.

Here is a brief JScript example of how we can use Page Counter component inside our page and check if current user is one of the 10th users:

```
<%
//
// JScript Code
//
  var numHits = Server.CreateObject("MSWC.PageCounter")
%>
<P align=right>
Number of hits: <B><% =numHits.Hits() %></B>
<!--
Check if current surfer in a lucky one. We treat every 10th user
as a winner of our draw.
-->
<%
```

```
  if (numHits.Hits() % 10 == 0) {
   Response.Write("<BR><FONT COLOR=RED>You're the lucky one</FONT>")
   Response.Write("<BR><A HREF='winner.asp'>Go to our winners page</A>")
  }
%>
```

As a standard component of Active Server Pages **Page Counter** component is implemented in **PAGECNT.DLL** and has CLSID of `EF88CA72-B840-11D0-8B40-00C0F00AE35A`

The Permission Checker Component

The **Permission Checker** component is used to determine whether a web user has been granted permissions to read a file. This component uses the password authentication protocols provided in Microsoft Internet Information Server. We can use this component to customize an ASP-based page for different types of users. Three types of password authentication supported by this component:

- Anonymous
- Basic
- Windows NT Challenge/Response (NTLM)

We can check permissions with **HasAccess** method and if current user does not have the proper permissions, we can change the page contents, or even supply a server error message; 401 - Unauthorized.

As a standard component of Active Server Pages **Permission Checker** component is implemented in **PERMCHK.DLL** and has CLSID of 1BE73E22-B843-11D0-8B40-00C0F00AE35A

The Counters Component

This component is used to create, store, increment and retrieve any number of individual counters. Not to be confused with the Page Counter Component, this component can be used to count some values, not only page hits (if the page with a counter is hit, it does not increment its value–you should do this manually).

A counter contains an integer value, which can be manipulated with **Get**, **Increment**, **Set** and **Remove** methods of the Counters component. We use **Set** method to set the specific value of the counter and **Get** method to retrieve it. To increase counter value by 1 we use **Increment** method and to remove counter– **Remove** method.

All counters are stored in a text file **Counters.txt**, which can be found in the same directory as the **Counters.dll** itself. Usually, this is **windows\system\inetsrv** folder for Windows 95 and **winnt\system32\inetsrv** for Windows NT. Note that you should not edit this file manually–it is maintained by the Counters component.

We create an instance of Counters object with **Server.CreateObject** method:

```
Set myCounter  = Server.CreateObject("MSWC.Counters")
```

Note that an instance of a Counter component is already instantiated in PWS for Windows 95 (through the **Global.asa** file) and you should not create another instance of it.

While **Page Counter** component described in this chapter serves to count hits on your site, you can use Counters component to track how many requests were made to download some particular file, in shopping application to count individual items selected or how many users send you an e-mail.

After we created an instance of Counters object, we can use it. First, we need to initialize our Counter:

```
<%
 var mailHits
 myCounter.Set(mailHits, 0)
%>
```

then we can use **mailHits** to count how many e-mails were sent through our page:

```
<%
    Counter.Increment (mailHits)
%>
You are a person # <% = Counter.Get (mailHits) %> who sends me an e-mail
```

Since counters are not limited in scope, once created our **mailHits** counter can be used on any page of our Active Server Pages application.

We can use the same instance to start another counter–in fact, as many counters as we need. Just to remember, that we use a *single instance* of Counters component–not a new instance for each counter.

> **As a standard component of Active Server Pages** Counters **component is implemented in** COUNTERS.DLL **and has a CLSID of** 89B9D28B-AAEB-11D0-9796-00A0C908612D

The MyInfo Component

The **MyInfo** Component can be used to keep track of personal information, provided by the server administrator.

This information is stored in the text file **MyInfo.xml**, which is located in the **windows\system\inetsrv** directory for PWS for Windows 95 and in the **windows\system\inetsrv** directory for Internet Information Server.

Let's have a look how this works with Personal Web Server for Windows 95 (PWS). When you run the Personal Web Server Setup utility for the first time, you can create a customized home page with a special wizard, implemented in **Windows\System\inetserv\iisadmin\website\template.asp** file. This is a long form, where you set the parameters of your Web server home page–Title, Mail, e-mail, personal information about yourself, etc.

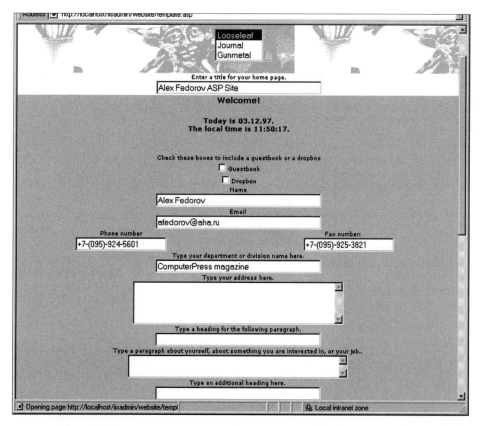

After you complete this form, you press Enter new changes button, which creates a new home page for your web server. The data you supply in the form will be used to generate a new page and will also be stored in **MyInfo.xml** file. This file contains pairs of **<property>**/**<value>** tags and may look like this:

```
<XML>
<ranWizard>-1</>
<Theme>gunmetal</>
<guestbook>0</>
<messages>0</>
<insRec>0</>
<delRec></>
<publish>-1</>
<dropStr></>
<descrip></>
<updRec>0</>
<Showtext>0</>
<numRecords>0</>
<addDisplay>1</>
<strFull></>
<strDisplay></>
<title>Alex Fedorov ASP Site</>
<Name></>
<Email>afedorov@aha.ru</>
<checkEmail></>
<intUrl>1</>
<Phone>+7-(095)-924-5601</>
<faxPhone>+7-(095)-925-3821</>
```

You can access all the fields through the properties of the **MyInfo** Component. For example, if you want to produce your e-mail address somewhere on the page, you can use **EMail** property of **MyInfo** Component as shown by the following JScript example:

```
<%
    var ref = '<a href="mailto:'
    Response.Write(ref+MyInfo.EMail+'">'+'Drop me a mail'+'</A>')
%>
```

This will produce the **<A> </A>** reference to mailto:

```
<a href="mailto:afedorov@aha.ru">Drop me a mail</A>
```

If you later change your e-mail address or other parameter, such as the fax number or description, you will not need to change anything on your page or pages, since the contents is taken from **MyInfo** Component.

You can also add your own **<property>**/**<value>** tags to **MyInfo** component and use them through your pages. For example:

```
<%
 MyInfo.FavoriteColor = "Red"
 MyInfo.WifeName = "Irina"
%>
...
...
...
```

```
<%
  Response.Write("Do you know my favorite color? It's " + MyInfo.FavoriteColor)
%>
```

Just like "built-in" properties, if you change your favorite color, or your wife changes her name, or you even change your wife, the code remains intact, thanks to **MyInfo** component.

> As a standard component of Active Server Pages MyInfo **component is implemented in** MYINFO.DLL **and has CLSID of** 4682C82A-B2FF-11D0-95A8-00A0C92B77A9

The Tools Component

The **Tools Component** provides utilities that enable us to add some functionality to our Active Server Pages. An instance of this component is already created for PWS and Windows 95. It is stored in the default virtual directory. Consequently, we can use this component directly instead of creating an instance of it. In other environments, such as PWS for Windows NT Workstation and Internet Information Server, we use the **Server** object's **CreateObject** method:

```
Set Tools = Server.CreateObject("MSWC.Tools")
```

and follow it with one of the following methods:

Method	Description
FileExists	Checks for the existence of a file
Owner	Checks if the current user is the site owner (*Macintosh only*)
PluginExists	Checks the existence of a server plug-in (*Macintosh only*)
ProcessForm	Processes an HTML form
Random	Generates a random integer

Using the Tools Component

Let's look at some examples of the **Tools Component** in action. Using the **Tools.FileExists** method we can check if some file exists on our site. The URL parameter is the relative URL for a file.

```
<% @ language = JavaScript %>
<% Response.Buffer = true %>
<HTML>
<HEAD>
<TITLE>ASP 2.0 Demo</TITLE>
</HEAD>
<BODY>
  <%
    var tools = Server.CreateObject("MSWC.Tools")
    var bc    = Server.CreateObject("MSWC.BrowserType")
```

```
    if (bc.browser == "IE")
      {
      if (tools.FileExists("ie_css.css"))
        {
        Response.Redirect("iestyle.asp")
        }
      else
        {
        Response.Redirect("common.asp")
        }
      }
  %>
  </HTML>
```

In the example above we check the client browser type with a **Browser Capabilities** component to see if it is Microsoft Internet Explorer, and then try to load a special page for it, implemented in **Iestyle.asp** file. First, we need to check for the existence of this file with **FileExists** method of the **Tools** component. If the file exists, then we redirect the page, otherwise we use the common page–**Common.asp**.

> Note that we set **Response.Buffer** property to true–neither redirection will not work. The **Response** object was discussed in Chapter 4.

Sometimes we need a random number to perform some tasks–redirect pages, choose colors and show quotes. This is where **Tools.Random** method comes in use, as it produces an integer value between -32768 and 32767. When producing a random number, you'll find that taking one number from a 64K set of values is not very practical. A better way to do it is to shorten the amount of possible values. For example, to produce positive integers from 0 to 20 we can use **Math.abs** method of the built-in **Math** object and take a modulus of it. Here is an example in JScript:

```
<%
  var Tools = Server.CreateObject("MSWC.Tools")
  var rndValue = Math.abs(Tools.Random()) % 20
  Response.Write("Random value in 0..20 = " + rndValue)
%>
```

in VBScript we can use built-in functions:

```
<%
  Set Tools = Server.CreateObject("MSWC.Tools")
  Set rndValue = Abs(Tools.Random) Mod 20
  Response.Write("Random value in 0..20 = " + rndValue)
%>
```

Here is an example in JScript of how we can generate a reference to random quotes file with **Tools.Random** method:

```
<!-------------------------------------------------------------
  To make this sample work at the top of file (above <HTML> tag)
  you should include the following directive:

  <% Response.Buffer = true %>
  ------------------------------------------------------------->
<%
```

```
var Tools = Server.CreateObject("MSWC.Tools")
var qFiles = "quote"
var qExt   = ".asp"
var qFile
var rndValue = Math.abs(Tools.Random()) % 20
qFile = qFiles + rndValue + qExt
Response.Redirect(qFile)
%>
```

Each time the user loads this page he will get the contents of a different file–from **quote0.asp** to **quote20.asp**.

> As a standard component of Active Server Pages Tools component is implemented in TOOLS.DLL and has CLSID of 64D9163F-BA0F-11D0-979C-00A0C908612D

The Status Component

The Status component creates a **Status** object that has properties that contain server status information. Currently this server status is only available on Personal Web Server for Macintosh. For all Windows platforms, the properties of the **Status** component currently all return the string 'unavailable'.

> As a standard component of Active Server Pages Status component is implemented in STATUS.DLL and has CLSID of 4682C81B-B2FF-11D0-95A8-00A0C92B77A9

Microsoft Sample Components

Microsoft's Internet Information Server site contains a selection of sample components that you can download and use directly, or as a basis for developing your own components. Each one has the source code included, and they are written in a variety of languages such as C++, Java, and Visual Basic. We'll be covering how you can create your own components later in the book. To download these samples from Microsoft, go to *IIS Samples, Components & Utilities* page at

`http://backoffice.microsoft.com/downtrial/moreinfo/iissamples.asp`

ASP2HTML Component

The **ASP2HTML** component represents a very thin layer over Java's **URL** and **URLConnection** (in Java's **java.net** package) classes. This component works in the following way: given a URL, the **ASP2HTML** object will connect to the location and retrieve its properties, exposing the properties to the Active Server Pages program. The document at the given URL can also be saved to a local file.

A typical use of this component can be downloading ASP pages from your own server, let the server-side scripting occur, and save the resulting HTML files. The HTML files can then be published on your web site.

To create the component instance in the page, we use:

```
Set objASP2HTM = Server.CreateObject("IISSample.Asp2Htm")
```

Then we can download specified page:

```
objASP2HTM.URL("http://localhost/default.asp")
```

and save it to local file:

```
if objASP2HTM.GetData() then
   objASP2HTM,WriteToFile("c:\myhtml\default.htm")
end if
```

Methods of ASP To HTML Component

The `ASP2HTML` component exposes a set of methods, which are listed below:

Method	Description
Body	Retrieves the body of the HTML document
ContentEncoding	Retrieves the content-encoding header field of the document
ContentLength	Gets the length of the content in the document
ContentType	Gets the type of content in the document
Date	Gets the sending date of the URL
Expiration	Gets the expiration date of the document
File	Retrieves the name of the file at the given URL
GetData	Retrieves the necessary data about the URL
Host	Retrieves the host of the URL
LastModified	Gets the last date of modification for the document
Port	Retrieves the port number of the URL
Protocol	Retrieves the protocol of the given URL
Ref	Retrieves the anchor of the given URL
Server	Gets the server name from the document
Title	Retrieves the title of the HTML document
URL	Sets the URL to connect to
WriteToFile	Writes the retrieved document to the given file

Registry Access Component

The **Registry Access** component provides access to the registry on a local or remote computer. Using this component you can retrieve, set, add, delete, modify and copy registry keys and names values.

For security reasons only methods that do not modify the registry (for example, **Get** and **GetExpanded**) will work by default. To enable the other methods of this component you should get administrator permissions.

To create the component instance in the page, we use:

```
Set myReg = Server.CreateObject("IISSample.Registry")
```

Once we got an instance and appropriate administrator rights, we can use methods of **Registry Access** component to retrieve, set, add, delete, modify and copy registry keys and names values. For example, we can find the location of Java class files:

```
Path2Java = myReg.Get("HKLM\Software\Microsoft\JavaVM\Classpath")
```

And use this path to dynamically load Java classes.

Methods of Registry Access Component

The **Registry Access** component exposes a set of methods, which are listed below:

Method	Description
CopyKey	Copies a registry key
DeleteKey	Deletes a key and all its subkeys and named values from the registry
DeleteValue	Deletes a named value from a registry key
ExpandString	Expands a string by replacing environment variables
Get	Retrieves a named value from a registry key
GetExpand	Retrieves a named value from a registry key, expanding any embedded environment variables
KeyExists	Returns a boolean value that indicates if the specified key exists in the registry
Set	Sets a named value in a registry key
SetExpand	Sets a named value in a registry key as data type REG_EXPAND_SZ
ValueType	Returns the data type of a registry value

Text Formatter Component

This is a very simple component, but one that may be useful if you use a lot of forms or tables in your pages. Its sole purpose is to format a single string of text into fixed-length lines. This is handy where you want to display the text in a **TEXTAREA** control, or when you want to control the width of individual columns in a table.

There are different language versions of the control supplied, and each is defined by a subtype to the **ProgID**, when it's created in the page. The three versions are:

```
Set objTextFormat = Server.CreateObject("IISSample.TextFmt.VB")
Set objTextFormat = Server.CreateObject("IISSample.TextFmt.C++")
Set objTextFormat = Server.CreateObject("IISSample.TextFmt.Java")
```

Once we've created an instance of the appropriate component, we can use its **WrapTextFromFile** method to insert the text into the page. The text itself is stored in a text file on the server, and we specify the full physical path to it. The second parameter is just the maximum number of characters for each line:

```
objTextFormat.WrapTextFromFile("C:\Demo\TxtFiles\ThisFile.txt", 35)
```

Don't forget that we can use the **FileSystemObject** object and **TextStream** objects to dynamically create the text file if required, either from the same or another ASP file. This concludes the server components available with ASP. We'll now look at how you can create your own.

Creating a Server Component

Earlier in this chapter we stated that server components were really nothing more than ActiveX Controls that have some ability to interact with Active Server Pages code. Any tool that can be used to create ActiveX controls, can be used to create server components. Until recently, this meant a tool such as Visual C++ or Delphi. Earlier versions of Visual Basic had some ability to create OLE DLLs, which are very similar to ActiveX controls. However, these still required the overhead of the Visual Basic runtime DLLs, which were interpreted rather than compiled. Now, with the advent of Visual Basic 5.0, we have a development tool that allows us to quickly and easily create the type of ActiveX object that can be used with Active Server Pages.

A server component can be used for a variety of tasks and, as we have seen, Active Server Pages ships with several different server components. A component can just encapsulate functionality that we *could* code directly using VBScript in our pages, or it might be able to do things that aren't possible with VBScript at all. We'll look at some of the advantages briefly now.

Encapsulating Scripting Language Functionality

By creating a server component to encapsulate script functionality, we can achieve a number of improvements in our application architecture:

 Our code is encapsulated in an object, and doesn't need to be replicated as script in a page each time it is used.

 Our actual source code is not visible when using the object, allowing us to keep proprietary code private, yet allowing its functionality to be used by all.

 We can modify the behavior of an application in future by changing the component, without having to change all the instances where that behavior occurs.

Let's look at an example of the type of simple server object that can be created, and how it shows all of the improvements specified above.

An Imaginary Commission Component

Imagine we are building an Intranet site for a company that has commissioned sales people. The commission schedule is reasonably straightforward, however it isn't static. The head of the sales department is constantly changing the schedule by which the commissions are calculated. Also, the company wants to make sure that the commission calculation is being done correctly, so only we are trusted to write the code. Let's look at how encapsulating the computation of the commission can increase the efficiency of the program and the programmer.

Improvement	Results in Commission Application
Code Encapsulation	We have stored all of the critical commission code in one place. Each page that needs to use the code now calls the same function.
Hidden Source Code	When the completed commission object is distributed for use, none of the source code is delivered with it. Only the object interface needs to be specified.
Ease of Change	Since all of the commission calculation is encapsulated in the object, and we are the sole owner of that source code, it becomes very easy to make changes to the commission calculation, and then distribute the updated object. And since there is only one place where the code is deployed, on the server, all changes become immediately available to all users.

To begin to create this simple server component, let's look first at the tools that we will be using. The ideal tool for creating most server components is Microsoft Visual Basic 5.0. VB5 has the ability to create both in-process and out-of-process ActiveX Servers, which can be accessed by Active Server Pages. The only restriction that exists right now is the inability to create session -scope or application-scope objects. These objects require **both** threading model, and VB 5.0 only supports the **apartment** model. These models are discussed in Chapters 13 and 16, we don't need to understand them at the moment.

Visual Basic 4.0 will also allow us to create an OLE server that can be accessed by Active Server Pages. As this example progresses, we'll point out where the differences between VB4 and VB5 come into play.

Create the Project

When we start VB5, we're asked what kind of project we want to create. For this example, as for the majority of server components, select ActiveX DLL.

Name the Project

In the Project window, select the first line Project1 (Project1). The Properties window will now display the properties for the project, which in this case is only the name. Change it to Sales.

Create the Commission Class

When we selected ActiveX DLL as the type of project we wanted to create, VB5 created a default class for us. For this component, we'll name this class Commission. In the Properties window, change the **(Name)** property to **Commission**. By default, VB5 sets the **Instancing** property **MultiUse**, which is required for a server component.

Create the Commission Calculation Function

Now comes the time to calculate the commission. In this example, we'll be using a very simple formula. The commission will be based on the total *value* and *number* of sales made. These two values will be the input parameters to the commission calculation function. In a real-world application, the calculation would probably be quite a bit more involved, and require more input parameters.

In the **Commission** class module, create the following function:

```
Public Function CalcComm (totalSales As Single, salesEvents As Integer) As Single
    CalcComm = totalSales * 0.025 + (totalSales / salesEvents) * 0.05
End Function
```

The function is created as **Public** so that is can be called by applications instantiating this object. It calculates the commission by using the two parameters, and then returns the result to the calling application.

Save the Project

Now we save our project. Visual Basic will generate a default file name for our class module called **Commission.cls**, and a default for the project of **Sales.vbp**. Accept both of these defaults.

Create the Server Component

When we started VB5, we selected an ActiveX DLL as the type of project that we wanted to create. VB5 set up all of the project parameters to make our life easy. From the File menu, select Make Sales.dll... and save the new component to a directory on the server so that it can be accessed in ASP.

A good place to store components is to the **\INETPUB\IISSAMPLES\COMPONENTS** directory. However, Windows uses registry to locate the control, so using this location is not essential. It just makes managing all of our components easier if they are in one directory—with the components that ship with Active Server Pages.

After the component is created, it automatically notifies the operating system that it is available for use. This process is called **registering the control**, and VB5 and VB4 take care of it automatically. However, if we need to move the component to a different directory afterwards, we will need to manually re-register the control.

To do this, open a DOS Command Prompt window, and change to the directory where the component has been placed. Type **RegSvr32 Sales.DLL** and press *Return*. A dialog box will either confirm that the DLLRegisterServer in Sales.DLL succeeded, or will indicate any problems.

Test the Server Component

Now that we've created our new server component, we can begin to use it from inside our Active Server Pages. This control was designed to be part of an Intranet application. For testing purposes, however, we'll just create a simple form that submits values to an Active Server Page, which will use these values to calculate the amount of commission due.

The Submission Form

Here is the HTML file, **testComm.html** that will be used to gather the data to pass to the ASP that contains the new object:

```
<HTML>
<HEAD>
   <TITLE> ASP Simple Component Test </TITLE>
</HEAD>
<BODY>
<FORM ACTION="testComm.asp" METHOD=POST>
  <BR>Total Sales: <INPUT TYPE="TEXT" NAME="TotalSales" VALUE="" SIZE=40>
  <BR>Number of Sales: <INPUT TYPE="TEXT" NAME="NumSales" VALUE="" SIZE=33>
  <P><INPUT TYPE="SUBMIT" NAME="" VALUE="Calculate Commission">
  <INPUT TYPE="RESET" NAME="" VALUE="Clear Values">
</FORM>
</BODY>
</HTML>
```

The Results Form

Now, let's create the ASP file **testcomm.asp** that will accept the values from this page, calculate the commission, and display the value to the user:

```
<HTML>
<HEAD> <TITLE> ASP Simple Component Test </TITLE> </HEAD>
<BODY>

<% 'get the values from the form
totalSales = Request.Form("TotalSales")
numberSales = Request.Form("NumSales") %>

Total Sales: <% = FormatCurrency(totalSales) %> <BR>
Number of Sales: <% = numberSales %> <P>

<% 'create an instance of our new component
Set tstComm = Server.CreateObject("Sales.Commission") %>
```

```
<% 'calculate the result and print it in the page
commAmt = tstComm.CalcComm(csng(totalSales), cint(numberSales))
Response.Write("The commission payable is : " + FormatCurrency(commAmt)) %>

</BODY>
</HTML>
```

> The `totalSales` and `numberSales` variants have to be converted into Single and
> Integer types, as when they are taken from the form, they are brought in effectively
> as strings.

If everything goes well, we should get back a valid response showing the amount of the commission for
the amounts entered in the text boxes:

If It Doesn't Work...

If we don't get a value returned for some reason, or even error message, then one of a few things may
have gone wrong. Check back over our steps to make sure you didn't miss anything.

Make sure that all of the VB runtime DLLs are available on the machine where the Web server is running.
The easiest way to achieve this is to install a minimal version of Visual Basic. This will also allow you to
perform debugging easier, and to quickly make changes to the components.

And when it does work, well, wasn't that easy! Of course, this object doesn't do very much. But we have
now seen the basics to creating Server Components. In Chapter 16, we will see how to add much more
functionality to them, and allow them to have a more involved interaction with the Active Server Page
being processed in our Electronic Commerce case study, but for the time being this is all we need to
know.

Third-party Server Components

In this section we will briefly outline several free third-party server components which you can use with your **Active Server Programs**.

Ads and Commerce ASP Components

ADMAN

The **ADMAN** component can be used to manage your banner ads automatically and configure them through a web interface. You can download this component from **http://www.overseas.com.tw/adman/**.

Credit Card Verification

This component, created by ActiveHelp, can be used to verify if a credit card is valid with Mod10 validation, AMEX, Visa, Mastercard and Discover cards types supported. You can download this component from **http://activehelp.tornet.com/components/ccard**.

E-Mail ASP Components

JavaPOP3.Mailer

This Active Server Pages component is written in Java by Simon Fell/Zak Solutions and can be used for reading POP3 email accounts. You can download this component from:
http://zaks.demon.co.uk/code/.

OCX Mail/ASP

This component, developed by Flicks, can be used to reading SMTP mail with attachments. You can download this component from: **http://www.flicks.com/ASPMail**.

Web Essentials Listcaster

This component, developed by Mustang, is a mailing list server and SMTP/POP3 server with Active Server Pages based setup and administration. You can download this component from:
http://www.download.com/PC/Result/TitleDetail/0,4,0-28163,501000.html

File Upload, Download and Management

AspExec 2.0

Developed by Steven Genusa this component allows you to execute DOS and Windows apps. DOS programs which return results via studio can be executed and the results are returned as a string. You can optionally set a timeout to wait for either DOS or Windows applications. You can download this component from **http://www.serverobjects.com/comp/Aspexec.zip**

AspProc 1.0

AspProc component developed by Steven Genusa, allows you to get a variant array of process IDs and process names, and to terminate a particular process by process ID. This component only works under NT 4.0. It will not work on WinNT 3.5x and Win95 systems. You can download this component from: **http://www.serverobjects.com/comp/aspproc.zip**

Content Link Generator 1.0

Content Link component developed by Steven Genusa, will generate content links across subdirectories. You can download this component from **http://www.serverobjects.com/comp/contlink.zip**

File I/O Component

The **File Component**, developed by Tarsus, lets you perform Directory Scans (GetFirst, GetNext), Read/Write INI files, Create/Delete Directories, Create Unique File, Delete/Rename Files, Read File Date/Time/Size, File Exists Test, File HTML Document Test, and Read HTML Title from Web Documents. You can download this component from **http://www.tarsus.com/asp/io/**

LastMod Component

The **LastMod** component, developed by Steve Genusa, gets a file's last modified date/time from Active Server Pages. You can download this component from **http://www.serverobjects.com/comp/lastmod.zip**

WaitFor 1.0

This component allows you to pause your Asp app for a specified time, wait until a file exists or wait until the component can get exclusive read/write permissions to a file. You can download this component from **http://www.serverobjects.com/comp/waitfor.zip**

Networking Components

AspInet 2.0

This component, developed by Steven Genusa, allows you to remotely GET and PUT files via FTP from Active Server Pages. You can download this component from:
`http://www.serverobjects.com comp/AspInet.zip`

ASPLogin

The `ASPLogin` component by OceanTek provides basic security for any `.asp` web page or collection of pages. The Windows NT user database is not used, so there is no risk of system passwords being intercepted. Instead, ASPLogin uses a table or users and passwords stored in any ODBC data source. When a user first loads any page protected by ASPLogin, they are asked for their user ID and password. Once authenticated, they can access any ASPLogin protected page until their session is terminated, or times-out. ASPLogin needs you to add a single server-side-include at the top of each protected active server page. You can download this component from `http://www.oceantek.com/asplogin/`

AspPing

The `ASPing` component, developed by Steve Genusa, allows you to execute **ping** command (i.e. check the connection with URL through echo protocol) inside Active Server Pages. You can download this component from `http://www.serverobjects.com/comp/aspping.zip`

DNS Component

The `Tornet DNS` component, developed by ActiveHelp, allows DNS and Reverse DNS lookup from Active Server Pages. You can download this component from:
`http://activehelp.tornet.com/components/dns/`

Trace Route component

The `Trace Route` component, developed by ActiveHelp, allows us to determine what IP addresses and domains a particular request passes through before arriving at its final destination. You can download this component from `http://activehelp.tornet.com/components/tracer`

Miscellaneous Components

MD5 Checksum

The `MD5 Checksum` component, developed by Ambrasoft, compute MD5 checksum from ASP pages. The algorithm takes as input an input file of arbitrary length and produces as output a 128-bit (16 bytes) checksum represented by a string of hexadecimal values. RSA-MD5 is believed to be collision-proof. You can download this component from
`http://www.ambrasoft.lu/external/developer/freesoft/default.asp`

AspBible 1.0

The `Bible Component`, developed by Steven Genusa, allows you to dynamically generate texts from the Bible. You can download this component from:
`http://www.serverobjects.com/comp/Aspbible.zip`

AspCrypt 1.0

The **AspCrypt** component, developed by Steven Genusa, duplicates the one-way algorithm used by Crypt on Unix. You can download this component from:
http://www.serverobjects.com/comp/Aspcrypt.zip

GUIDMaker 1.0

Developed by Steven Genusa, the **GUIDMaker** component will create GUIDs from Active Server Pages. You can download this component from: **http://www.serverobjects.com/comp/guidmakr.zip**

Text2HTML

The **Text2HTML** component, developed by Patrick Steele, converts URL and e-mail addresses that are plain text to HTML anchors. It also converts Access memo fields to line-break properly when outputting to a HTML page. You can download this component from: **http://www.msen.com/~psteele/asp/**

Strings Component

Developed by Tarsus this component contains everything to manipulate strings! It includes such tools as Add Strings, Set String by Index, Get String by Index, Delete String by Index, Clear/Sort/Reverse Collection, Word-Wrap Collection, and search for Match/Begins/Ends/Contains. Also supports Filtering out HTML Tags, Filter out specific test (like profanity), Prepare strings for inclusion in SQL (quotes problem solved), Format Date/Time/Number Strings. You can download this component from:
http://www.tarsus.com/asp/ts/

How to install components

Once you download the component, you need to install it to be able to use it from your Active Server Pages. Some components come with install utilities, which do the job, others provided in **.zip** files, sometimes with source code, but with no installation programs. In this situation you need to unzip the appropriate archive file, save its contents in some folder, for example, in **\windows\system\inetserv\addons**, and run **REGSVR32.EXE** program, with the name of the dynamic link library, containing the component. For example, suppose we got a new version of the **Browser Capabilities** component from somewhere on the Web. Unpacking **BROWSCAP.ZIP** gives us two files: **BROWSCAP.DLL** and **READ.ME**. We need to run **REGSVR32.EXE**:

```
C:\WINDOWS\SYSTEM\INETSERV\ADDONS>REGSVR32.EXE BROWSCAP.DLL
```

If everything is Ok, **REGSVR32** will produce a confirming message and the component will be registered in the registry.

After that we can use it in our programs to create an instance of it with `Server.CreateObject` or with `<OBJECT>` tag, as described elsewhere in this chapter.

> Note that with this utility we can unregister previously registered component using the /u command line option. After that this component will no longer be available.

Summary

In this chapter we've looked at how Active Server Pages can take advantage of various components, which can be used to add extra features that aren't otherwise available. We saw:

- ▲ How components can be added to the Active Server Pages environment. Several instances of these components can exist in a single page, for a whole session, or permanently as part of the application.

- ▲ Several standard Active Server Components in action: Ad Rotator, Content Linking, Page Counter, Counters and others.

- ▲ A brief list of some extra components provided by Microsoft.

- ▲ A list of third-party components, which are available for free.

- ▲ How components can be installed with the help of the `REGSVR32` utility.

The one component we haven't mentioned so far, however, is probably the most important. It's likely that the major requirement for dynamic pages on your site is the need to interface with data in existing systems, especially in a company intranet, rather than the global Internet, situation. We've devoted the next couple of chapters just to this topic. You'll first see the basic applications of the ADO (ActiveX Data Objects) component, then we'll move on to some real-world situations.

The Database Access Component

In previous chapters, we've learned how we can use **Active Server Pages**, and the overall **Active Server** technology, to make our web pages more dynamic–and more useful in today's increasingly competitive environment. On the Internet, or your own company's intranet, ASP gives you new ways of making sure that the content is always up to date, while reducing the costs involved in maintaining the site as a whole.

We looked at the basic ways of using Active Server Pages, and then moved on to incorporate some of the standard Server Components into our pages. However, the topics we've covered so far have really only been the icing on the cake. In the real world, the driving force behind the development of dynamic web sites is to link the pages with a database of some kind.

Under Windows NT and Internet Information Server (IIS), this has generally been accomplished with an existing technology called the **Internet Database Connector** (IDC), but this always had some limitations. Even though it gained more features in each release of IIS, there was always something you wanted to do that was difficult, or even impossible, using just IDC. The result was that often you had to go back to a 'real' programming language of some kind, and work with the **Common Gateway Interface** (CGI) or **Internet Server Application Programming Interface** (ISAPI) directly.

So you'll be pleased to know that Active Server Pages ends all that. It's supplied with a component called the **Database Access Component**. This provides us with a whole hierarchy of objects–collectively known as the **ActiveX Data Objects** (ADO)–which is the 'missing link' between your web pages and almost any kind of stored data. In this and the next chapter, we'll be showing you how this important component can be used to bring all the benefits of a truly dynamic web site.

In this chapter you'll see:

What the **ActiveX Data Objects** (**ADO**) are, and what they allow us to achieve

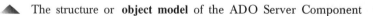 The structure or **object model** of the ADO Server Component

The How we use ADO methods to manipulate databases, and build dynamic pages

Some useful techniques for writing your own dynamic ADO pages

In this chapter, we're aiming to build an understanding of the ActiveX Data Objects in general, and give you a background in using it with the Database Access Component that is supplied with Active Server Pages. Then, in the next chapter, we'll be putting our knowledge into practice with some real-world examples. So let's start with an overview of the ActiveX Data Objects.

ActiveX Data Objects Overview

The ActiveX Data Objects (ADO) is really a connection mechanism that provides access to data of all types. The most common use is with data stored in a relational database, accessed from a client application. In the context of Active Server Pages, this allows us to write code in a scripting language such as VBScript or JScript that can interact with a database. With the flexibility already available in the form of ASP, ADO allows us to create client-server applications that run over the Internet, and are not specific to any make of client browser.

In this chapter, you'll see how ADO is powerful enough to achieve excellent results with a minimum amount of work. We'll be extending the basic use of ADO in the next chapter, and seeing how you can use it when building industry strength applications. For now though, let's have a look at ADO in general.

The ADO Data Interface

ADO is designed, in its simplest form, to interface with relational databases through **Open Database Connectivity** (**ODBC**). You can use it with any data source for which an ODBC driver is available. This means not only 'proper' database applications, like SQL Server, Oracle, Access, etc., but spreadsheet files like Microsoft Excel and text, or other, plain format data files.

However, ADO is actually built on top of another technology called **OLE DB**. This provides a uniform data interface through the methods and properties it maintains internally. ODBC data is one kind of data that ADO and Active Server Pages can access, but it isn't the *only* kind. For example, it can also access Windows NT Directory data–at present this technology is called Active Directory Services Interface (ADSI).

The Data Provider

Because ADO is built upon another layer, OLE DB, we also need to be able to specify another layer of connectivity in our links to a data source. In other words, it's no longer sufficient to think of just the **driver** software (such as ODBC), we need to consider what the actual **provider** of the data is. ODBC is just the most popular of the OLE DB providers, formally known as MSDASQL.

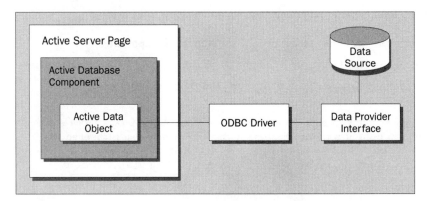

ADO capabilities vary widely based on the capabilities of the OLE DB provider. Some objects may work differently, properties may be missing, or certain objects may not exist or be usable.

ADO capabilities when using the ODBC provider vary widely also, based on the capability of the ODBC driver. Most ODBC drivers don't provide all the cursor types, for example. However, don't get confused between the cursor types that ADO will let you use and ODBC cursor types. When using the ODBC Provider, ADO doesn't use ODBC cursors – it will allow the use of its own cursors on the client or server based cursors if the server supports them (SQL Server 6.5 does, but Oracle does not). Also SQL Server and Access ODBC provide the **AbsolutePage** property, while most other ODBC database drivers do not.

Our Provider/Driver Combination

So you can see that what's actually going on 'under the hood' with ADO is less than simple to grasp. Fortunately, although it's good to appreciate what's under there, we don't need to be a mechanic to drive the car. In most cases, you'll be using a supplied ODBC driver for your database system, which will support almost all of the standard techniques we'll be seeing in this chapter.

In fact, for this chapter, we'll specifically be using Microsoft Access for the examples. In some areas, especially stored procedures, Access ODBC allows us to use a syntax that will not work with many other relational database ODBC drivers. However, it is compact, simple to set up, and more universally available for you to experiment with as you learn the basics of ADO. In the next chapter, we'll move on to see how you can use SQL Server and other database systems with ADO. For now, though, we'll start with a look at how you use the main objects in the ADO hierarchy.

The ADO Object Model

ADO is an altogether simpler and clearer mechanism for providing database access than those included in Microsoft Access, and other object-based applications. For instance, the hierarchy has only three main objects, **Connection**, **Recordset**, and **Command**, and several collections of subsidiary objects, **Parameters**, **Properties**, and **Errors**.

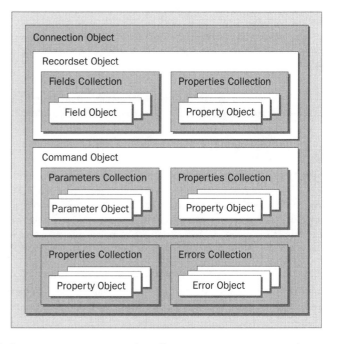

Using the **Connection** object, we can establish an active connection that allows us to gain access to data stored elsewhere–generally in a database. To obtain records from this data source, execute SQL queries, or manipulate the data directly, we can use the **Command** object. The **Recordset** object gives us access to the data that is returned from executing an SQL query, a stored procedure, or by opening a table.

The **Connection**, **Command**, and **Recordset** objects each have a collection of **Properties**, just like many of the objects we've looked at in earlier chapters. The **Connection** object also maintains a collection of **Error** objects, detailing the errors that occur as we use the objects. Finally, the **Recordset** object contains a **Fields** collection. Each member of this collection is, as you might expect, a **Field** object—which contains information about the individual fields in the recordset. Don't worry about exactly what all these terms mean for now, we'll discuss each one as we come to use them in our examples.

As well as a much simpler object hierarchy, ADO provides greater flexibility for developers than most other mainstream database applications. So even though the **Connection** object appears at the top of the diagram, we aren't forced to use it when creating a recordset. In fact, we can use the objects on their own without having to follow a hierarchy. We'll show you how this is done a little later in the chapter.

First, however, let's look at how we go about connecting to a data source and manipulating the data. We'll begin with a look at the three main objects that ADO provides.

The Connection Object

Defining a connection to a database is a straightforward process. The first step is to create an instance of the **Connection** object. This is just one of the objects implemented by the Database Access Component, whose ProgID is A**DODB**. Here's how we set up a **Connection** object that is capable of referencing a data source:

```
Set oConn = Server.CreateObject("ADODB.Connection")
```

By using the **CreateObject** method of the **Server** object, we can instantiate a variable to hold a reference to the newly created **Connection** object, just as we did with other components in the previous chapter.

> *Notice that this is different from the way we would define a variable of type* **Database** *in Visual Basic. Because VBScript deals with* **Variant** *data types, we can't declare a variable of the appropriate type directly.*

Setting the Connection Scope

We can create this connection every time we want to access a data source, or we can create it once in the page and use it repeatedly. Alternatively, we can create it with **Session**- or **Application**-wide scope, and use it in several pages. When we're performing several operations with the database, it is usual to maintain active connections, even though we could use a different connection for each one.

By maintaining one connection, the database access is improved because a lot of validation occurs during the connection phase. We can do this by placing the **Server.CreateObject** statement in either the **Session_onStart** or **Application_onStart** routines in **global.asa**, or by using an **<OBJECT>** tag.

To create an **Application**-wide instance of the connection, we can use:

```
Sub Application_onStart()
    Set oConn = Server.CreateObject("ADODB.Connection")
    Set Application("oConn") = oConn
End Sub
```

or:

```
<OBJECT RUNAT=Server Scope=Application ID=oConn ProgID="ADODB.Connection">
</OBJECT>

Sub Application_onStart()
    Set Application("oConn") = oConn
End Sub
```

However, you should be aware that creating database objects with an application scope can impair scalability.

To create a **Session**-wide instance of the connection, we can use:

```
Sub Session_onStart()
    Set oConn = Server.CreateObject("ADODB.Connection")
    Set Session("oConn") = oConn
End Sub
```

or:

```
<OBJECT RUNAT=Server Scope=Session ID=oConn ProgID="ADODB.Connection">
</OBJECT>

Sub Session_onStart()
    Set Session("oConn") = oConn
End Sub
```

However, ODBC version 3.0 includes a feature called **connection pooling**, which manages connections across multiple users. When using connection pooling it's best to open and close the database connection in each page that uses it, which allows ODBC to manage the connections most efficiently. In the next and subsequent chapters, we'll look into this subject in more depth. For the purposes of this chapter, because we're using ODBC 3.0 with Microsoft Access 97, we'll create each connection once at the start of a page, and use it throughout that page.

Connection Object Methods and Properties

The **Connection** object provides methods and properties that allow us to work with it. These fall into three groups: opening and closing a connection, executing a command on the data source specified by the connection, and controlling transactions. We'll look at each group and what it does in turn, but first here's a list of all the ActiveX Data Objects methods and properties:

Method	Description
Open	Opens a new connection to a data source.
Close	Closes an existing open connection.
Execute	Executes a query, SQL statement or stored procedure.
BeginTrans	Begins a new transaction.
CommitTrans	Saves any changes made and ends the transaction. May also start a new transaction.
RollbackTrans	Cancels any changes made and ends the transaction. May also start a new transaction.
OpenSchema	For server side scripts, allows the view of database schema, such as tables, columns, etc.

Property	Description
Attributes	Controls whether to begin a new transaction when an existing one ends.
CommandTimeout	Number of seconds to wait when executing a command before terminating the attempt and returning an error.
ConnectionString	The information used to create a connection to a data source.
ConnectionTimeout	Number of seconds to wait when creating a connection before terminating the attempt and returning an error.
CursorLocation	Whether the cursor is located on the client (**adUseClient**) or on the server (**adUseServer**)
DefaultDatabase	Sets or returns the default database to use for this connection.
IsolationLevel	Sets or returns the level of isolation within transactions.
Mode	Sets or returns the provider's access permissions.
Provider	Sets or returns the name of the provider.
State	Returns whether the connection is open or closed. For open connections **adStateOpen** is returned, and **adStateClosed** for closed connections.
Version	Returns the ADO version number.

Opening a Connection

Once we've created an instance of the **Connection** object, using the **Server** object's **CreateObject** method, we're ready to start using it. However, it doesn't actually refer to anything yet. The next step is to use the connection to open our data source, so that we can access and manipulate the data in it. This is achieved using the **Open** method that the **Connection** object provides. The general form of the **Open** method for the connection object is:

```
connection.Open  ConnectionString, User, Password
```

The **ConnectionString** parameter is a string that specifies a data source either as a **data source name** (**DSN**), or by specifying a detailed connection string made up of individual *parameter=value* arguments separated by semicolons, and containing no spaces.

> *It's generally easiest to create a System Data Source Name, using the ODBC Administrator program on your server, and this is what we've done for this chapter. Full details are included in Appendix G– refer to this if you haven't done it before.*

If we provide a detailed connection string, instead of a System DSN, ADO recognizes five standard parameter names. Any **ConnectionString** containing an equals sign is interpreted as a detailed connection string.

Parameter	Description
Provider	Name of the provider to use for the connection.
File Name	Name of a file containing provider-specific preset connection details.
Data Source	The source name or filename of the data source, that is, an SQL Server database register with ODBC, or the filename of an Access database.
User	User name to apply when opening a connection.
Password	Password to apply when opening a connection.

Any additional parameters we include aren't interpreted by ADO, and are just passed through to the provider. Note also that we can specify either the **Provider** or the **File Name** parameters, but not both. Once we open the connection, the **ConnectionString** is available as a read-only property.

For extra security, you can specify a **UserName** and **Password** as parameters, along with the **ConnectionString**. If we're using a System DSN as the **ConnectionString**, this is the only way that we can specify them on a per-connection basis.

Here's a simple example of opening a connection, using a System DSN called **Contacts**:

```
Set oConn = Server.CreateObject("ADODB.Connection")
oConn.Open "Contacts"
```

Alternatively, we can use the detailed form of the **ConnectionString**, like this:

```
Set oConn = Server.CreateObject("ADODB.Connection")
oConn.Open "DATABASE=pubs;DSN=Publishers;UID=sa;Password=;"
```

We can set the **ConnectionTimeout** property of the **Connection** object to determine how long to wait (in seconds) for a connection to be opened. By default the value is **30**. If the value is set to **0**, ADO will wait indefinitely until the operation has completed.

Executing Commands with the Connection

Having created and opened a connection to our data source, we can begin to use it. Later in the chapter, you'll see how we can return information as a recordset. For now, we'll just confine ourselves to executing commands that *change*, but don't actually *return*, any data.

Having to carry out commands that change the data in our data source, we use the **Connection** object's **Execute** method. This can accept a string containing an SQL statement, the name of a stored procedure, or the name of a table in the data source. The last of these, a table name, simply returns a recordset containing all the data in that table, and you'll see how this is used when we come to look at recordsets in detail later on.

A **stored procedure** is a command or procedure that already exists in the source database system, such as an Access query. These often consist of one or more SQL statements, and provide efficient ways of updating the data because only the instruction to run the procedure needs to pass across the network. Stored procedures can return information, or just update existing data. In this case, we're going to assume that they don't return any data.

To use ADO successfully, you really need to be reasonably conversant with **Structured Query Language** (**SQL**). To learn more about it, look out for Joe Celko's book Instant SQL Programming (ISBN 1-874416-50-8), from Wrox Press of course. You can also use the Query Builder in Microsoft Access to help you create SQL strings.

Here's an example that uses an SQL string directly:

```
Set oConn = Server.CreateObject("ADODB.Connection")
oConn.Open "Contacts"
oConn.Execute "DELETE * FROM Contact WHERE State = 'LA'"
```

If we have a stored procedure in the database, such as an Access query named **DeleteAllLA**, we can execute it using:

```
Set oConn = Server.CreateObject("ADODB.Connection")
oConn.Open "Contacts"
oConn.Execute "DeleteAllLA"
```

If we were using SQL Server, or most other databases, the string for the **Execute** argument could well be different—remember it will have to match the syntax requirements of the provider not ADO, because ADO just passes it directly back to the provider to execute. For example, in SQL Server, we would need to use:

```
Set oConn = Server.CreateObject("ADODB.Connection")
oConn.Open "Contacts"
oConn.Execute "[call DeleteAllLA]"
```

Being able to use stored procedures (or queries) gives us flexibility—we don't need to recreate the SQL queries for our ASP scripts. However, even though this method is fine for simpler cases, we can optimize database operation by providing extra information.

Specifying the Command Type

We've used the simplest form of the **Execute** statement so far, by just specifying the query or procedure we want to execute. We can improve the efficiency of the operation by using other, optional parameters:

*Connection.*Execute *CommandText*, *RecordsAffected*, *Options*

What we've been using up to now is the mandatory *CommandText* parameter. We can also specify a value for the *Options* parameter, which tells ADO what *type* of instruction we actually want it to carry out.

Because the *CommandText* parameter can be one of three different types of command, ADO has to query the data source to find out what to do with it, slowing down the whole process. If we supply one of the following values for the *Options* parameter, ADO will use the *CommandText* option as that type of command. This technique makes the whole thing more efficient, and you'll see it used in several places with ADO.

Constant	Value	Description
adCmdUnknown	0	Unknown. This is the default if not specified.
adCmdText	1	A text definition of a command, such as an SQL statement.
adCmdTable	2	The name of a table from which to create a recordset.
adCmdStoredProc	4	A stored procedure, or query, within the data source.

To use the constant names in your code, instead of specifying the actual values, you need to include a constants definition file in the page using a Server-side Include (SSI). These files are supplied with ASP, and installed by default in the IISSamples/ISSamples directory on the server. For VBScript you use Adovbs.inc. For JScript, use Adojavas.inc. For example, using VBScript:

```
<!-- #include virtual="/IISSamples/ISSamples/Adovbs.inc" -->
```

You can copy the file into the application directory instead, and include it using:

```
<!-- #include file="Adovbs.inc" -->
```

The other parameter in the **Execute** method is *RecordsAffected*. We can provide the name of a variable for this parameter, and ADO will attempt to set it to the number of records that were affected by the query or stored procedure.

Here's the two examples we used earlier, but now optimized by specifying the type of command being used, and supplying a variable, **lngRecs**, to hold the number of records that are affected by the query or stored procedure:

```
'Using a text SQL query definition directly
oConn.Execute "DELETE * FROM Contact WHERE State = 'LA'", lngRecs, adCmdText
```

```
'executing a stored procedure
oConn.Execute "DeleteAllLA", lngRecs, adCmdStoredProc
```

We can set the **CommandTimeout** property of the **Connection** object (or the **Command** object, although the **Command** object does not inherit the **CommandTimeout** properties of the **Connection** object) to determine how long to wait (in seconds) for execution of the query to finish. By default the value is **30**. If the value is set to **0**, ADO will wait indefinitely until the operation has completed. Notice this is different from the **ConnectionTimeout** property, which defines how long to wait while the data source connection is opened.

Closing the Connection

Once we're done using the database, we can close the active connection. This doesn't actually free the resources that the object is using. To do this, we have to set the object variable to **Nothing** as well:

```
oConn.Close
Set oConn = Nothing
```

We don't have to explicitly do any of this, although it is generally recommended to do it. Active Server Pages will do it automatically once the reference variable (in our case **oConn**) goes out of scope. Our example **Connection** object was created in the page that is executing, so it will be destroyed once that page has been completed and sent to the browser. Of course, if we create the connection object in **global.asa**, it will only be destroyed when the appropriate **Session**, or the entire **Application**, ends.

Using Connection Transactions

The final subject we need to look at before we leave the **Connection** object is how we use **transactions**. You may be familiar with this subject from other databases you've worked with. The principle is that when we need to perform a series of updates on a data source, we can improve efficiency by getting the system to store up all the changes, and then commit them in one go—rather than writing each change individually to the records.

This generally has another advantage: because the changes are not committed until we've completed them all, and we've informed ADO that we're done, we can always change our mind up to that point—before we actually commit the changes. This is called **rolling back** the changes, and is used most often where an error occurs. Rather than having an undetermined number of changes to the data, we know that we can roll back all of them so that the data isn't changed at all. Only if all the operations complete successfully do we actually commit the changes to the database.

We'll be looking in detail at how transactions are used in later chapters. For now, here's some code that shows how it all fits together:

```
On Error Resume Next

Set oConn = Server.CreateObject("ADODB.Connection")
oConn.Open "Contacts"
oConn.BeginTrans                          'start the transaction

oConn.Execute "DELETE FROM Contact WHERE State = 'LA'"

oConn.Execute "DELETE FROM Names WHERE State = 'LA'"

oConn.Execute "DELETE FROM Phones WHERE State = 'LA'"

If oConn.Errors.Count = 0 Then
    oConn.CommitTrans          'everything worked, keep the changes
Else
    oConn.RollbackTrans        'something went wrong, abandon the changes
End If
oConn.Close
Set oConn = Nothing
```

You can see that we only commit the changes to the database with **CommitTrans** if all the queries execute without an error. If any one fails, we abandon all the changes with **RollbackTrans**.

> *The* **Connection** *object's* **Attributes** *property can be set so that either* **CommitTrans** *or* **RollbackTrans** *automatically starts a new transaction.*

The Command Object

So far, to query or update a data source, we've used the **Connection** object to execute commands which run a stored procedure or an SQL query. Instead, however, we can use the **Command** object directly, providing that we specify a connection string for its **ActiveConnection** property.

In this case a connection is still established, but no intermediate connection variable is maintained, as it was when we created a **Connection** explicitly in the last section. This is really only efficient if we need the data from all the operations at the same time. If we're using the same connection for several operations, then we should really create a separate **Connection** object, and perform successive operations with it.

Command Object Methods and Properties

We create a **Command** object and define its scope as we did with the **Connection** object, by using the **Server.CreateObject** method or with an **<OBJECT>** tag. The **Command** object provides methods and properties we use to manipulate individual commands. These are:

Method	Description
CreateParameter	Creates a new **Parameter** object in the **Parameters** collection.
Execute	Executes the SQL statement or stored procedure specified in the **CommandText** property.

Property	Description
ActiveConnection	The **Connection** object to be used with this **Command** object.
CommandText	The text of a command to be executed.
CommandTimeout	Number of seconds to wait when executing a command before terminating the attempt and returning an error.
CommandType	Type of query specified in the **CommandText** property.
Name	Allows a name to be assigned to a command
Prepared	Whether to create a prepared statement before execution.
State	Identifies whether the current command is open or closed. For an open command **adStateOpen** is returned, and **adStateClosed** for a closed command.

Creating an Active Connection

The first step in using the **Command** object is to specify the **ActiveConnection** we want to use it against. If we've previously created a **Connection** object we can use that, or we can supply a **ConnectionString** as we did in the **Connection** object's **Open** method:

```
Set oCmd = Server.CreateObject("ADODB.Command")
oCmd.ActiveConnection = "Contacts"
```

or:

```
Set oCmd = Server.CreateObject("ADODB.Command")
oCmd.ActiveConnection = "DATABASE=pubs;DSN=Publishers;UID=sa;Password=;"
```

Executing a Query

Once we've established the active connection, we can use the **Command** object in a similar way to the **Connection** object. And we don't need to explicitly open the data source, or close it afterwards—we just use the **Execute** method directly.

However, the different properties of the **Command** object mean that we can specify some parameters outside the **Execute** method, and get more control over the operation. For example, we can set the **CommandText** and **CommandType** first, instead of specifying them in the **Execute** statement. We can also tell the data provider to create a temporary stored representation of the query. This may be slow for the first execution, but the compiled form of the query is then used in subsequent executions, which speeds up command processing significantly:

```
Set oCmd = Server.CreateObject("ADODB.Command")
oCmd.ActiveConnection = "Contacts"        'the system DSN for the data source
oCmd.CommandText = "DELETE * FROM Contact WHERE State = 'LA'"
oCmd.CommandType = 1                       'an SQL query.
oCmd.Prepared = True                       'compile the statement...
oCmd.Execute                               '...and then execute it
Set oCmd.ActiveConnection = Nothing        'release the resources used
```

Again, we can set the **CommandTimeout** property first, to determine how long to wait for the command to execute. By default the value is **30**. If the value is set to **0**, ADO will wait indefinitely until the operation has completed.

Using Parameters

If our query requires parameters, then we can either supply them by adding them to the **Command** object's **Parameters** collection first, or by creating them 'on the fly' as we execute the query. The syntax of the **Command** object's **Execute** method is subtly different from that of the **Connection** object, because it contains an argument for the parameters to be used in the query:

command.Execute *RecordsAffected*, *Parameters*, *Options*

The *RecordsAffected* and *Options* parts are the same as those of the **Connection** object, but we use the *Parameters* part this time to specify an array of parameters that are to be used while executing the query. The individual parameters in this array correspond by position to the values in the **Parameters** collection (which we'll come to next) and to the parameters required by the query. To specify three parameters, we could use:

```
oCmd.Execute Array(Parameter1, Parameter2, Parameter3)
```

If we don't specify a value for any of the parameters, the existing values in the **Parameters** collection are used instead:

```
oCmd.Execute Array(Parameter1, , Parameter3)
```

For example, our earlier stored procedure example, which deletes records for the State of LA could be replaced by a stored parameter query—where the table name and the State are parameters:

```
Set oCmd = Server.CreateObject("ADODB.Command")
oCmd.ActiveConnection = "Contacts"
oCmd.CommandText = "DeleteStateQuery"    'name of the stored procedure
oCmd.CommandType = 4                     'a stored procedure
oCmd.Execute Array("Contact", "NY")
Set oCmd.ActiveConnection = Nothing
```

The Parameters Collection

The **Parameters** collection holds all of the parameters for a query executed by a **Command** object. Instead of specifying parameters to a query 'on the fly', in the call to the **Command** object's **Execute** method, we can add them to the **Command** object's **Parameters** collection first. Here are the methods and properties of the **Parameters** collection:

Method	Description
Append	Adds a parameter to the collection.
Delete	Deletes a parameter from the collection.
Refresh	Updates the collection to reflect changes to the parameters.

Property	Description
Count	Returns the number of parameters in the collection.
Item	Used to retrieve the contents of a parameter from the collection.

Creating and Adding Parameters to a Collection

Each member of the **Parameters** collection is itself a **Parameter** object, and has a set of properties of its own:

Property	Description
Attributes	The type of data that the parameter accepts.
Direction	Whether the parameter is for input, output or both, or if it is the return value from a stored procedure. Refer to the **ParameterDirectionEnum** in Appendix E for a complete list.

Property	Description
`Name`	The name of the parameter.
`NumericScale`	The number of decimal places in a numeric parameter.
`Precision`	The number of digits in a numeric parameter.
`Size`	The maximum size, in bytes, of the parameter value.
`Type`	The data type of the parameter. Refer to the **DataTypeEnum** values in Appendix E for a complete list.
`Value`	The value assigned to the parameter.

To add a new parameter to the **Parameters** collection, we must first create an instance of a **Parameter** object, then set its property values, and finally use the **Append** method of the **Command** object. To create a new parameter object, we use the **Command** object's **CreateParameter** method:

Set *parameter* = *command*.CreateParameter(*Name*, *Type*, *Direction*, *Size*, *Value*)

For example, we can create a new parameter and append it to the **Parameters** collection like this:

```
...
Set oParam = oCmd.CreateParameter("State", 129, 1, 2, "NY")
oCmd.Parameters.Append oParam
...
```

This uses the specific numeric values for the *Type*, *Direction*, and *Size* arguments, and creates the parameter in one go. Alternatively, we can set each argument separately, and use the pre-defined constants. In this example, we're taking the parameter value from a text box on a form, submitted to our ASP page in the **Request** object's **Form** collection:

```
Set oCmd = Server.CreateObject("ADODB.Command")
oCmd.ActiveConnection = "Contacts"
oCmd.CommandText = "DeleteStateQuery"
oCmd.CommandType = 4
strValue = Request.Form("txtState")        'as submitted from a form
Set oParam = oCmd.CreateParameter("State") 'the parameter name only
oParam.Type = adChar                       'a string value
oParam.Direction = adParamInput            'a query input parameter
oParam.Size = Len(strValue)                'the size of the string
oParam.Value = strValue                    'the string value
oCmd.Parameters.Append oParam              'add it to the collection
oCmd.Execute
Set oCmd.ActiveConnection = Nothing
```

Of course, we're not just limited to using parameters in stored procedures. We can also use them in SQL statements in Access, where parameters are indicated by being placed in square brackets within the statement. This provides an alternative method for building up SQL statements with the appropriate **WHERE** clause dynamically.

Referencing Collection Objects

Once we've got our parameters into the collection, we can refer to them either by using the **Item** property, or directly because **Item** is the default property for the collection. We can also use the index within the collection, or the parameter name:

```
oCmd.Parameters.Item(0)          'all these refer to the same parameter
oCmd.Parameters(0)
oCmd.Parameters.Item("State")
oCmd.Parameters("State")
```

The **Parameters** collection is also the default collection for the **Command** object, so we can even omit the collection name. However, this makes understanding the code more difficult, and should generally be avoided:

```
oCmd(0)
oCmd("State")
```

Setting the Parameter Size and Type

One thing to note is that if we want to specify a parameter that stores a variable length value such as a **string** (as defined by the *Type* argument), we must also specify the *Size* argument–otherwise an error will be generated.

The same applies to **numeric** values, but this time we specify values for the **Precision** and **NumericScale** properties of the **Parameter** object instead. **Precision** determines the number of digits that are to be stored, and **NumericScale** indicates the position of the decimal place. To store a number like **173.25**, we would need to set **Precision** to **5** and **NumericScale** to **2**.

Reading, Refreshing and Deleting Parameters

As you've seen in earlier chapters, we can use a **For...Each** loop to iterate through all the members of a collection. We can do this with the **Parameters** collection, but first we need to make sure that all the parameters are up to date. The **Refresh** method of the **Parameter** object instructs the provider to fill the parameters collection with parameters from the query specified in the **CommandText** property of the **Command** object.

Here's an example of how we can use these concepts to output the names and values of all the parameters in the **Parameters** collection. It places them in the current page using **Response.Write**:

```
...
For Each oParam In oCmd.Parameters
    Response.Write "Parameter name = " & oParam.Name & "<P>"
    Response.Write "Parameter value = " & oParam.Value
Next
...
```

If the need arises, we can also **delete** a parameter from the **Parameters** collection. To delete the parameter named **State** from our collection, we can use the parameter name or its index:

```
oCmd.Parameters.Delete "State"
oCmd.Parameters.Delete 0
```

The Recordset Object

Up to now, we've only looked at queries which add, update or delete existing records in our data source. Of course, in many cases we'll actually want to return some records via ADO, so that we can put some values into our page. For queries that return values, we must assign the results to a **Recordset** object. This is like a table in memory, holding records (or rows of data) which are subdivided into individual fields (or columns).

Both of the methods we've looked at for executing a query, that is, those of the **Connection** object and the **Command** object, can create a recordset containing the data returned from that query. We can even create a recordset directly, without having to open a connection or execute a command first.

Recordset Object Methods and Properties

To begin with, here's a table of the more common methods and properties of the **Recordset** object. There are many more than this, but we won't be using them all in this chapter. You'll find a full list in Appendix E:

Method	Description
AddNew	Creates a new record in an updatable recordset.
CancelBatch	Cancels a pending batch update.
CancelUpdate	Cancels any changes made to the current or a new record.
Clone	Create a duplicate of the current recordset.
Close	Closes an open recordset and any dependent objects.
Delete	Deletes the current record in an open recordset.
GetRows	Extract a number of rows into an array.
Move	Moves the position of the current record.
MoveFirst, MoveLast, MoveNext, MovePrevious	Moves to the first, last, next or previous record in the recordset, and makes that the current record.
NextRecordset	Move to the next recordset in the query.
Open	Opens a cursor on a recordset.
Requery	Updates the data by re-executing the original query.
Resync	Refreshes the data, but does not re-execute the query. This allows updates to be seen but not new rows.
Supports	Determines whether the recordset supports certain functions.
Update	Saves any changes made to the current record.
UpdateBatch	Writes all pending batch updates to disk.

Property	Description
AbsolutePage	The ordinal position of the current page.
AbsolutePosition	The ordinal position of the current record.
ActiveConnection	The connection object to which the recordset currently belongs.
BOF	True if the current record position is before the first record.
Bookmark	Returns a bookmark that uniquely identifies the current record, or sets the current record to the record identified by a valid bookmark.
CacheSize	The number of records in local memory.
CursorLocation	Whether the cursor is located on the client (**adUseClient**) or on the server (**adUseServer**)
CursorType	The type of cursor used in the recordset.
EditMode	The editing status of the current record.
EOF	True if the current record position is after the last record.
Filter	Sets or returns a data filter for the recordset.
LockType	The type of locks placed on records during editing.
MarshalOptions	Sets or returns which records are to be marshaled back to the server when using client side recordset.
MaxRecords	Sets or returns the maximum number of records to return in the recordset.
PageCount	The number of pages in the recordset.
PageSize	The number of records in a page.
RecordCount	The number of records currently in the recordset.
Source	The source for the data in the recordset, that is **Command** object, SQL statement, table name, or stored procedure.
State	Returns whether the recordset is open or closed.
Status	Returns the status of the current record in respect to a bulk operation.

Getting Back a Recordset

We can create a recordset as the result of executing a query, either an SQL statement, a stored procedure, or by just specifying the name of a table in the data source. This can be from either the **Command** or the **Connection** object. You'll recognize these as being similar to the way we execute a query that doesn't return any records. The only difference is that we **Set** the result to refer to a recordset object, and we enclose the parameters in parentheses:

```
Set recordset = connection.Execute(CommandText, RecordsAffected, Options)

Set recordset = command.Execute(RecordsAffected, Parameters, Options)
```

Creating Recordsets with a Query

As an example, here we're using the **Connection** object, and just specifying the **CommandText** argument. This time the SQL query is a **SELECT** query which should return records from the data source:

```
Set oConn = Server.CreateObject("ADODB.Connection")
oConn.Open "Contacts"
Set oRs = oConn.Execute("SELECT * FROM Contact WHERE State = 'LA'")
```

If we want to know more about the results, and be more specific when supplying the **CommandText**, we can supply a variable for the **RecordsAffected** argument and set the **CommandType** for query in the **Options** argument:

```
Set oConn = Server.CreateObject("ADODB.Connection")
oConn.Open "Contacts"
strSQL = "SELECT * FROM Contact WHERE State = 'LA'"
Set oRs = oConn.Execute(strSQL, lngRecs, adCmdText)
```

Alternatively, we can use the **Command** object to create our recordset:

```
Set oCmd = Server.CreateObject("ADODB.Command")
oCmd.ActiveConnection = "Contacts"
oCmd.CommandText = "SELECT * FROM Contact WHERE State = 'LA'"
oCmd.CommandType = adCmdText
Set oRS = oCmd.Execute
```

And, of course, we can still supply a variable for the **RecordsAffected** argument and a list of **Parameters**. This time we've put the **CommandType** in the **Execute** method call as well:

```
Set oCmd = Server.CreateObject("ADODB.Command")
oCmd.ActiveConnection = "Contacts"
oCmd.CommandText = "SELECT * FROM Contact WHERE State = 'LA'"
Set oRS = oCmd.Execute(lngRecs, Array("Contact", "LA"), adCmdText)
```

The **RecordsAffected** argument only receives a value with expressions that change data. It receives –1 when viewing data, for example via a **SELECT** statement.

Creating Recordsets from a Table

One way of using the **Execute** method that we haven't seen so far, because it can only return data and not update it directly, is to specify a table name. This works for either the **Connection** or the **Command** object. For the **Connection** object:

```
Set oConn = Server.CreateObject("ADODB.Connection")
oConn.Open "Contacts"
Set oRs = oConn.Execute("Contact")     'the name of the table
```

Of course, we can supply the **CommandType** argument to improve processing efficiency:

```
Set oConn = Server.CreateObject("ADODB.Connection")
oConn.Open "Contacts"
Set oRs = oConn.Execute("Contact", , adCmdTable)
```

And, finally, we can use the **Command** object in a similar way:

```
Set oCmd = Server.CreateObject("ADODB.Command")
oCmd.ActiveConnection = "Contacts"
oCmd.CommandText = "Contact"          'the name of the table
oCmd.CommandType = adCmdTable
Set oRS = oCmd.Execute
```

Creating Recordsets Directly

For a single access to our data source, where we don't need to maintain a connection for several operations, it's possible to create a recordset directly, without going through the **Connection** or **Command** objects. The **Connection** is still created in the background automatically, just as it was when we used the **Command** object without specifically creating a **Connection** object first.

To create a recordset directly, we first have to create an instance of a recordset object, using the **Server.CreateObject** method or with an **<OBJECT>** tag. Then we can use the **Open** method of the **Recordset** object to fill the new recordset with values from the data source. The syntax of the **Open** method is:

recordset.Open *Source, ActiveConnection, CursorType, LockType, Options*

Argument	Description
Source	A **Command** object, SQL statement, table name or stored procedure.
ActiveConnection	An existing **Connection** object.
CursorType	The type of **cursor** to use when opening the recordset: **adOpenForwardOnly** (**0**–*the default*), **adOpenKeyset** (**1**), **adOpenDynamic** (**2**), or **adOpenStatic** (**3**)
LockType	The type of **locking** to use when opening the recordset. See Appendix E for a full list.
Options	The type of query or table represented by **Source**.

> *Remember that, to use the constant names in your code, instead of specifying the actual values, you need to include a constants definition file in the page using a Server-side Include (SSI). For example, using VBScript:*

```
<!-- #include virtual="/IISSamples/ISSamples/Adovbs.inc" -->
```

The ***Source*** argument indicates where the data will come from. If we already have an active connection string, we can use this as the ***ActiveConnection*** property, and supply a table name for the ***Source*** argument:

```
Set oRs = Server.CreateObject("ADODB.Recordset")
oRs.Open "Contact", "Contacts", , , adCmdTable
```

Alternatively, we can follow the same principles as with the **Command** object, by setting the properties first and then calling the **Open** method:

```
Set oRs = Server.CreateObject("ADODB.Recordset")
oRs.Source = "Contact"              'the name of the table
oRs.ActiveConnection = "Contacts"   'the DSN to use for the connection
oRs.Options = adCmdTable            'the type of query/table to assume
oRs.Open                            'and open the recordset
```

Recordset Cursor Types

There are four **cursor types** available when opening a **Recordset** object. The different cursor types have their own merits, and each one lends itself to particular uses. In our examples, we've assumed the default cursor type of **adOpenForwardOnly**. Here's a summary of the different types:

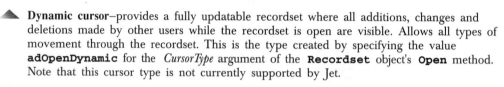

▲ **Dynamic cursor**–provides a fully updatable recordset where all additions, changes and deletions made by other users while the recordset is open are visible. Allows all types of movement through the recordset. This is the type created by specifying the value **adOpenDynamic** for the *CursorType* argument of the **Recordset** object's **Open** method. Note that this cursor type is not currently supported by Jet.

▲ **Keyset cursor**–provides an updatable recordset, like a dynamic cursor, except that it prevents access to records that other users add after they were created. Allows all types of movement through the recordset. Created by specifying **adOpenKeyset** for the *CursorType* argument (or by using **1** instead of the constant).

▲ **Static cursor**–provides a static non-updatable copy of a set of records, useful for retrieving data. Changes to the records made by other users while the recordset is open are not visible. Allows all types of movement through the recordset. Created by specifying **adOpenStatic** for the *CursorType* argument.

▲ **Forward-only cursor**–(*the default*) provides a recordset identical to a static cursor except that it only allows us to scroll forward through the records. With Access this recordset is also non-updateable. This improves performance in situations where we need to make only a single pass through the recordset. This is the type of recordset created either by specifying **adOpenForwardOnly** (or 0 instead of the constant) for the *CursorType* argument, or by omitting this argument from the **Open** method.

You can see that we'll get a forward-only cursor from our earlier examples of the **Open** method, because we didn't specify a *CursorType* value. If we want to be able to edit the records, or even move around the recordset at will, we need to specify a different, more appropriate, type. You'll see more of this in a while.

The reason for using different cursor types is that it provides ways of making the access to the data source more efficient. ADO and the data provider have to do a lot more work to maintain dynamic and updateable recordsets. Even static recordsets that allow full movement require several accesses to the database to allow the user to scroll up as well as down. It's far more efficient if ADO knows whether locking is required, or whether the recordset will need to move back through the records.

Closing a Recordset

Once we're finished using a recordset, we can close it with the **Close** method, then release any resources it was using by setting its variable reference to **Nothing**:

```
oRS.Close
Set oRS = Nothing
```

Again, ADO will do this automatically when the variable referencing the recordset goes out of scope.

Using Recordsets in ADO

When we create a **Recordset** object and fill it with data, we'll generally want to use it for something. We may want to move around from one record to another, edit existing records and add new ones to it, and extract data from the records. In order to do this, we need to consider several aspects of how recordsets work, and look at the **Fields** collection which the recordset object implements.

It's likely that your main use of Active Server Pages, at least to start with, will be to display the contents of a data source, such as an Access, SQL Server, Oracle or other database system. So the first step is to look at how we get the information from the recordset onto the web page.

Moving Around within a Recordset

After all the esoteric descriptions of creating objects, connections, and commands, you'll find this section easy going—especially if you've programmed using Microsoft Access or the Visual Basic Jet database methods before. We're now at the point where we've got a recordset, and we can actually start to do something with it.

It's often convenient to regard the **Recordset** object as having the same structure as a table; in other words it consists of rows (each of which is a complete record) and columns (each of which represents a field). We can move from one record to another, making it the **current record**, and access the individual fields within this current record. There are five main methods we can use to move around a recordset, and we'll look at these now.

The Move Method

The **Move** method moves a number of records in either direction, relative to the current record, and makes the record to which it moves the new current record. We can specify positive or negative numbers for the argument, to move forward or backward.

Bear in mind the limitations imposed by the type of the recordset—the **cursor type**. In a recordset opened with the default cursor type of **adOpenForwardOnly**, we can only move forward. If we want to be able to move around in a recordset, we need to open it with a cursor type of **adOpenStatic** (or a dynamic cursor type of **adOpenDynamic** or **adOpenKeyset**) instead. The **adOpenStatic** type is still very efficient, because it's only a 'snapshot' of the contents of the data source at the point it was created.

> *ADO caches records as it creates the recordset. Even in a recordset created with the* **adOpenForwardOnly** *cursor type, we can still move backwards within the cached records; however this isn't really good practice.*

Here are some examples of the **Move** method:

```
oRs.Move 7        'move forward seven records
oRs.Move -4       'move backward four records
```

There are a couple of other things that we can do to move around a recordset in a random manner like this. We can establish the number, or position, of the current record within a recordset using the **AbsolutePosition** property of the **Recordset** object. This returns either the ordinal position of the current record within the recordset, or one of these values:

Constant Name	Value	Description
adPosUnknown	-1	No current record
adPosBOF	-2	Before the first record
adPosEOF	-3	After the last record

So if we know we are on the ninth record, and we want the seventeenth, we just:

```
oRs.Move 8
```

Using a Bookmark

In Access and SQL Server we can also use a **bookmark** to identify a record in a recordset, although other database systems may not support them. A bookmark does what it says–it marks a record so that we can come back to it later. We can use a ***StartBookmark*** argument with the **Move** method to move relative to that bookmark, instead of relative to the current record:

```
varMyBookmark = oRs.Bookmark    'save the bookmark of the current record
oRs.Move 3                      'move around the recordset
oRs.Move -7
oRs.Move 1, varMyBookmark       'move to the record after the bookmarked one
```

Other Ways of Moving

ADO provides four other related **Move** methods. Each one moves to another record and makes it the current record. The four methods are **MoveFirst**, **MoveLast**, **MoveNext**, and **MovePrevious**. As you'll no doubt have guessed, these move to the first or last record in the recordset, or the next or previous one. The most useful of them is **MoveNext**, which we can use to move through a recordset examining records one at a time, and putting the contents into our page–after all, that's often the whole purpose of the exercise.

The only other consideration when we use the **Move** methods is how do we know when we get to the end of the recordset? If the current record is the last one in the recordset, calling **MoveNext** will generate an error. While we could trap the error and stop moving, there's a far better way.

The Beginning and End of a Recordset

Although it seems a strange concept, the current record pointer in a recordset doesn't actually have to point to a 'real' record. It can indicate a point before the first record, or after the last one. In some cases, it can even point to a record within the body of the recordset that doesn't exist. This can happen if we have a dynamic or keyset driven recordset, which reflects the actual contents of a table in the data source. If another user deletes the record that is the current one in our recordset, our pointer is pointing to a deleted record. This is one reason why there is an 'unknown' value **adPosUnknown** that can be returned by the **AbsolutePosition** property.

However, the situation we're most likely to come across is when we use the **MoveNext** or **MovePrevious** methods, and we need to know when we get to the end or the beginning of the recordset. The **Recordset** object provides two properties, **BOF** and **EOF**, which represent 'Beginning Of File' and 'End Of File'. This goes back to the days when we used to think of recordsets as being individual files on a disk that, together, made up a database—in fact some databases still work in this way.

> *You have to speculate whether, if we were naming the properties afresh now, they'd be called **BOR** and **EOR** instead!*

The BOF and EOF Properties

The **BOF** property of a recordset is **True** when the current record pointer is positioned before the first record in the recordset, and the **EOF** property is **True** when the current record pointer is beyond the last record. If there are no records in the recordset, then both **BOF** and **EOF** are **True**.

When **BOF** is **True**, any attempt to move backward in the recordset will produce an error, as will any attempt to update the record. Similarly, when **EOF** is **True** any attempt to move forward in the recordset will generate an error. It's always a good idea, therefore, to inspect the **BOF** and **EOF** properties when we first open a recordset, to ensure that there is at least one record in it before any operations are attempted.

Checking for an Empty Recordset

When we first open a recordset as a forward-only cursor type, the current record position is always set to the first record (if there is one). For the other types of recordset, the **MoveFirst** method should be used explicitly as soon as we open it. In fact, it doesn't do any harm to get used to using it every time we open a recordset.

The other **Move** methods will create an error if the recordset is empty, so it's a good idea to check the **BOF** and **EOF** properties are **False** first, to ensure that we aren't trying to move to a nonexistent record.

Checking How Many Records We've Got

We can find out the number of records in a recordset using the **RecordCount** property. Note, however, that for forward only recordsets the **RecordCount** property returns –1.

You may decide to use this property to iterate through a recordset, using a **For...Next** loop. This is a bad habit to get into—if the recordset is a dynamic one, the number might change while you're looping through the records, and you'll get an error. A better way, is to use the **EOF** property, or the **BOF** property if (for some reason) you decide to iterate through the records in reverse.

Iterating Through a Recordset

To iterate through the records in a recordset, we generally use the **MoveNext** method. Combining this with a **Do While** loop, and examining the **EOF** property each time, means we will access every record in turn:

```
Set oConn = Server.CreateObject("ADODB.Connection")
oConn.Open "Contacts"
Set oRs = oConn.Execute("Contact", , adCmdTable)
  oRs.MoveFirst            'not actually required, but good practice
  Do While Not oRS.EOF     'while not at end of file
    ...                    'do something with the record
    oRS.MoveNext           'and move to the next one
  Loop
```

When we have no more records to read, the **EOF** property returns **True**. In this case, our **CurrentRecord** reference is actually *beyond* the last record, and so attempting to read data would cause an error. We've used a **Do While** loop because there may not be any records in the recordset when it's opened, and in this case we'll never want to perform the **MoveNext** method or access any records.

The Find Method

The ability to find records is provided by the **Find** method, allowing us to move to a record that matches the criteria. The syntax is:

recordset.Find *Criteria, SkipCurrent, SearchDirection, Start*

Argument	Description
Criteria	A string representing the record to find. Equivalent to a **SQL WHERE** clause without the **WHERE**.
SkipCurrent	A boolean value indicating whether the current record should be skipped as part of the search. This defaults to **True**.
SearchDirection	Whether to search forwards or backwards. This defaults to forwards.
Start	A bookmark indicating the position to start the search from. This defaults to the current record.

Only the first argument is required, the latter three taking their default values. If performing successive finds you would generally want to set *SkipCurrent* to **True**, so as not to include the currently found record in the next find.

For *SearchDirection* you can use one of the constants shown:

Constant Name	Value	Description
adSearchForward	0	Search forward from the current record.
adSearchBackward	1	Search backward from the current record.

If the record is not found, either **BOF** or **EOF** is set depending upon the direction, as shown below:

```
Set oRs = Server.CreateObject("ADODB.Recordset")
oRs.Open "Contact", "Contacts"

oRs.Find "Name = 'Le Bistro'", 0, adSearchForward

If oRs.EOF Then
    Response.Write "'Le Bistro' was not found<P>"
Else
    Response.Write oRs("Address") & "<P>"
End If

oRs.Close
Set oRs = Nothing
```

Working with the Fields Collection

While this proves a useful way of getting at each record in the recordset in turn, it doesn't do much towards extracting the data from it. That's the job of the **Fields** collection. Every **Recordset** object has a **Fields** collection, which contains the data and other information about each field in the current record.

Property	Description
Count	Returns the number of fields in the collection.
Item	Used to retrieve the contents of the fields in the collection.

Method	Description
Refresh	Updates the collection to reflect changes to the field values.

This is a relatively simple collection, containing the single method, **Refresh**, and the two properties **Count** and **Item**. We saw how to use the **Item** property to reference members of the collection when we looked at the **Parameters** collection earlier in the chapter:

```
oRs.Fields.Item("State")        'all these refer to the same field
oRs.Fields.Item(0)
oRs.Fields("State")
oRs.Fields(0)
```

The **Fields** collection is also the default collection for the **Recordset** object, so again we can omit the collection name. In this case (unlike the **Command** object, where this was true of the **Parameters** collection) it *does* make sense now. In fact, there's another way of referencing a member of the default collection that is even more 'readable':

```
oRs("State")                    'all these refer to the same field
oRs(0)
```

The Field Object

Each member of the **Fields** collection is itself a **Field** object, and has a set of properties of its own:

Property	Description
ActualSize	The actual length of the field's current value.
Attributes	The kinds of data that the field can hold.
DefinedSize	The size or length of the field as defined in the data source.
Name	The name of the field.
NumericScale	The number of decimal places in a numeric field.
OriginalValue	The value of the field before any unsaved changes are made.
Precision	The number of digits in a numeric field.
Type	The data type of the field.
UnderlyingValue	The field's current value within the database.
Value	The value currently assigned to the field, even if unsaved.

Method	Description
AppendChunk	Appends data to a large text or binary field.
GetChunk	Returns data from a large text or binary field.

So now, we have a way of referencing each field in the current record. Let's use it in a real example.

A Simple Contact Tracking System

Here's a simple example that demonstrates how we can use ADO to view data from a data source. The example collects together many of the techniques we've seen so far in this chapter.

The Active Server Page **RecordsetMethods.asp** displays a list of all the contacts from our database, nicely formatted into a table.

There are three versions of our example, **RecordsetMethods.asp**, **SQLMethods.asp** and **GetRowsMethod.asp**, described in the text. The first makes use of the **Recordset**'s **Field** collection, the second uses SQL statements, and the third uses the **GetRows** method of the **Recordset**.

Here's what the page looks like:

ContactID	Name	Address	Town	State	ZipCode	Phone
1	Aardvark Limited	All Saints Street	Athens	OH	39812	216-376-1298
2	Burger Queen	Constants Avenue	Houston	TX	30517	713-771-6727
3	Education Dept.	The Offices, City Square	Chicago	IL	10745	312-712-8567
5	Cummings Intl.	124th Street West	Pittsburgh	PA	17265	412-455-6104
6	J.R. Higgins	The Market	Green Bay	WI	61733	414-831-8812
7	James Builders	2131 New Street	Phoenix	AZ	78034	602-281-3318
8	Jonahs Boats	The Quay	Stocksville	FL	16734	305-711-8855
9	Le Bistro	Rue Francais	Vancouver	WA	41322	206-133-8294
10	Major Records	Third Avenue	Stocksville	FL	10015	305-711-7851
11	Martha's Bar	Top Street	Clarksville	NY	54876	
14	Miracle Supplies	18th Avenue	Oakland	CA	10593	415-671-6633
15	Pedro Mana	Calle Sebastione	St. Paul	MN	65109	612-401-1350
16	Union Records	712 Main Street	Tampa	FL	51267	813-167-3520

You'll find this example among the samples available from our web site at:
http://rapid.wrox.co.uk. *You'll have to setup a System DSN for* **Contact.mdb** *called* **Contact** *first however, see Appendix G for details.*

How It Works

The code in the page is quite simple. It opens a recordset on the **Contact** table in our data source, for which we've previously defined a System DSN named **Contact**. Then it uses the **Count** property of the **Fields** collection to find out how many fields there are in the recordset, and creates a table with that number of columns.

This same value is then used in a **For...Next** loop to create the **<TH>** heading cells for the table. Into each cell is placed the field name, retrieved by referring to the field in the **Fields** collection by its ordinal position–and specifying its **Name** property.

```
...
<% Set oRs = Server.CreateObject("ADODB.Recordset")
   oRs.Open "Contact", "Contacts", , , adCmdTable
   oRs.MoveFirst %>
   <TABLE BORDER=1 COLS=<% = oRS.Fields.Count%>>
      <TR>
         <% For Each oField In oRS.Fields %>
            <TH> <% = oField.Name %> </TH>
         <% Next %>
      </TR>
   ...
```

Note that we must include the **Adovbs.inc** *file to provide the constant* **adCmdTable** *as we mentioned earlier.*

Now we've created the headings for the table, we can retrieve the values from the records. We use a **Do...While** loop to iterate through all the records, and for each one we include a **<TR>** tag in the page to define the start of a row. Within the main loop, we have a second loop—this time a **For...Each** loop which iterates through all the **Fields**:

```
   ...
   <% Do While Not oRS.EOF %>
      <TR>
         <% For Each oField In oRS.Fields %>
            <TD ALIGN=RIGHT>
               <% If IsNull(oField) Then
                     Response.Write " "
               Else
                     Response.Write oField.Value
               End If %>
            </TD>
         <% Next
            oRS.MoveNext %>
         </TR>
   <% Loop %>
   </TABLE>
<% oRs.Close
   Set oRs = Nothing %>
   ...
```

For each field in the recordset, we include an opening **<TD>** tag, then we need to get the value. Recordsets based on a database table, and some other data sources, can include the special value **Null**, which indicates that there's no data for that field. We can't include a **Null** in our page, so we use the **IsNull** function to check for this first. If the field does contain **Null**, we include the non-breaking space character instead. This provides the nice beveled edge to the cell, which would otherwise appear flat.

If the value of the field is not **Null**, we retrieve it and place it in the page, followed by a closing **</TD>** tag. Once we've done all the fields in the **oRs.Fields** collection, we **MoveNext**, add a closing **</TR>** tag, and go back to the **Do...While** condition. Once all the records are listed, we close the table with a **</TABLE>** tag, **Close** the recordset and set the recordset variable we were using to **Nothing**.

> *If the scripting language that we're using doesn't support iteration through collections with* **For...Each**, *we can still access the members of the collection using their ordinal number in a* **For...Next** *loop.*

Adding a User's Details

At the foot of the page, we've provided a hyperlink so users can jump to a page where they can add their own details to the table:

```
<H2>
   Add yourself to our mailing list by clicking
   <A HREF="Getdetails.htm">Here</A>
</H2>
```

Here's the Posting Page, **GetDetailsRS.htm**, where the user enters their details. It's created with a single form and normal HTML **TEXT** controls, plus a **Submit** button labeled Finished:

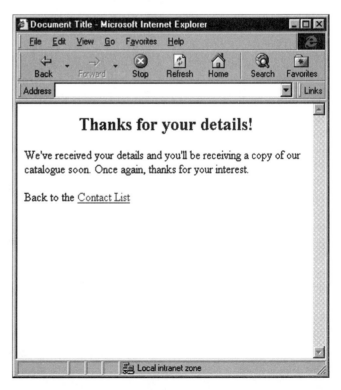

Once the user has entered their details, so that every field has some entry, and clicked the Finished button, the form is submitted to the Active Server Pages **ProcessUserRS.asp** (or **ProcessUserSQL.asp** in the second version). This is responsible for updating the database, and returning a 'thank you' message with a hyperlink back to the contacts list page (which may need refreshing to show the changes that you've made to the database):

So, from the `<FORM>` section of the Posting Page, we can get the values entered by the user for their contact details. Notice the `#include` statement that allows us to use the named constant values in our code. We also explicitly convert the values into strings with the `CStr()` function, because that's the data type we need for our database:

```
<!-- #include file="Adovbs.inc" -->
   ...
<% strName = CStr(Request.Form("txtName"))
   strAddress = CStr(Request.Form("txtAddress"))
   strTown = CStr(Request.Form("txtTown"))
   strState = CStr(Request.Form("txtState"))
   strZipCode = CStr(Request.Form("txtZipCode"))
   strPhone = CStr(Request.Form("txtPhone"))
   ...
```

The next step is to add them to our database. It's time to consider how we can update records in a recordset, and add new ones.

Updating the Source Data with a Recordset

We can only achieve so much by dynamically creating HTML, based on data taken from a recordset. What we really want to do is capture data that is sent from users of our applications, and submit this to the database.

There are two main ways of updating a database using ADO. We can run SQL statements against the data using the `Execute` method of the `Recordset`, `Command` or `Connection` objects, and we can manipulate the individual records within a recordset directly. We'll now have a look at both of these techniques.

Using SQL to Update Records

We saw early on in this chapter how the `Execute` methods of the `Command` and `Connection` objects accept SQL statements that can delete records in our data source. We can also use this method to run `INSERT` and `UPDATE` queries as well.

In our Contact Tracking application we've got the details of a new contact stored in string variables. We can use an SQL `INSERT` statement to get them into our `Contact` table, as you can see in `ProcessUserSQL.asp`:

```
   ...
<% Set oConn = Server.CreateObject("ADODB.Connection")
   oConn.Open "Contacts"        'the database's System DSN
   strSQLStatement = "INSERT INTO Contact " _
                   & "(Name, Address, Town, State, ZipCode, Phone) " _
                   & "SELECT '" & strName & "' AS Name, '" _
                   & strAddress & "' AS Address, '" _
                   & strTown & "' AS Town, '" _
                   & strState & "' AS State, '" _
                   & strZipCode & "' AS ZipCode, '" _
                   & strPhone & "' AS Phone;"
   oConn.Execute(strSQLStatement)
   oConn.Close
   Set oConn = Nothing %>
   ...
```

This is a quick and easy way to add or update records in a database. If you're using Microsoft Access, you can create the queries using the graphical Query Builder tool then copy the SQL statement into your ASP code.

Using Recordset Methods to Update and Delete Records

Using SQL statements to update the database is very convenient, but it's often not the optimal way of performing multiple individual updates. Using **recordset methods**, we can modify the data in individual fields in individual records. To do this, we use the **AddNew** and **Update** methods of the **Recordset** object.

We also have to open the recordset with a dynamic cursor type of **adOpenDynamic** or **adOpenKeyset**, so that the changes we make are actually passed back to the data source. Remember that the static and the default forward-only recordsets are not updatable. Here's how we handle the recordset in outline:

```
Set oRs = Server.CreateObject("ADODB.Recordset")
oRs.Open "Contact", "Contacts", adOpenKeyset, adLockPessimistic,
                                  ➥ adCmdTable

...
'do something with the records
...
oRS.Update    'save the changes to the records
oRS.Close
Set oRS = Nothing
```

Once we **Open** the recordset, we automatically have read/write access to all the relevant fields in the current record. Using the **Fields** collection we met earlier, we can get at the contents of the individual fields. The example **ProcessUserRS.asp** page updates the contents of the current record to the values submitted from the Posting Page form we looked at earlier:

```
Set oRs = Server.CreateObject("ADODB.Recordset")
oRs.Open "Contact", "Contacts", adOpenKeyset, adLockPessimistic,
                                  ➥ adCmdTable
oRS.Fields("Name") = strName
oRS.Fields("Address") = strAddress
oRS.Fields("Town") = strTown
oRS.Fields("State") = strState
oRS.Fields("ZipCode") = strZipCode
oRS.Fields("Phone") = strPhone
oRS.Update
oRS.Close
Set oRS = Nothing
```

> *Remember that the* **Fields** *collection is the default collection of the* **Recordset** *object, so you can use* **oRS("Name")** *instead of the full syntax of* **oRS.Fields("Name")** *if you wish.*

Once we've finished editing the records, we use the **Update** method to save the changes to that record. If we move to another record or close the recordset before calling **Update**, we lose the changes. We can also choose to abandon any changes explicitly by calling the **Recordset** object's **CancelUpdate** method.

We can always tell if there are any changes waiting to be saved by examining the **EditMode** property of the **Recordset** object. It will be **adEditInProgress** when there are change waiting, and **adEditNone** when they've been saved. Finally, we can delete the current record using the **Recordset** object's **Delete** method.

Adding New Records

Of course, when we collect a new contact's details, we don't want to overwrite an existing record with them—we want to add a new record to the database containing them. To add a new record, we use the **Recordset** object's **AddNew** method:

```
Set oRs = Server.CreateObject("ADODB.Recordset")
oRs.Open "Contact", "Contacts", adOpenKeyset, adLockPessimistic, adCmdTable
oRs.AddNew
oRS.Fields("Name") = strName
oRS.Fields("Address") = strAddress
oRS.Fields("Town") = strTown
oRS.Fields("State") = strState
oRS.Fields("ZipCode") = strZipCode
oRS.Fields("Phone") = strPhone
oRS.Update    'save the changes to the records
oRS.Close
Set oRS = Nothing
```

Once a new record has been added with **AddNew**, the **EditMode** property of the recordset is **adEditAdd**. Again, we can choose to abandon any changes with the **CancelUpdate** method, where the record that was current prior to the **AddNew** call becomes the current record again. Once the **Update** method has been executed, **EditMode** goes back to **adEditNone**.

We can also use the **AddNew** method to set the values of the fields in the new record, instead of specifying them individually afterwards. For example, this code sets the value of the **Name** field as we add the new record:

```
varName = "David Sussman"
oRs.AddNew "Name", varName
```

We also create a **Variant** array of field names, and another **Variant** array of values, and specify these in the **AddNew** method:

```
varFields = Array("Name", "Address", "Town", "State")
varValues = Array("David Sussman", "Wrox Press Ltd.", "Chicago", "IL")
oRs.AddNew varFields, varValues
```

In this case, we don't have to use the **Update** method to save the changes, as ADO does it automatically. When the **AddNew** parameters are arrays like this, they must have the same number of members, otherwise an error occurs. The order of field names in the first array must also match the order of field values in the second one.

Updating Records in Batch Mode

We can add or update records in two different operating modes—**immediate mode** and **batch mode**. In the previous examples, we've specified **adLockPessimistic** for the *LockType* property in the **Open** method call. This means that the data provider will lock the records so that they can't be changed by another user while we have them open for editing. As soon as we call the **Update** method for each record, while it is the current record, the changes are passed back to the data source. This is **immediate mode** updating.

Rather than writing changes to individual records back to the data source separately, we can add and update data in **batch mode**. This means that we can make multiple changes to different records, then flush these to the database in one go when we're finished. The changes to all of the records in the recordset are saved up until we call the **UpdateBatch** method, or cancel the update using the **CancelBatch** method.

To tell ADO that we want to use this mode, we open the recordset with the value **adLockBatchOptimistic** for the *LockType* parameter:

```
Set oRS = Server.CreateObject("ADODB.Recordset")
oRS.Open "Contact", "Contacts", adOpenKeyset, adLockBatchOptimistic, adCmdTable
...
'update several records here
...
oRS.UpdateBatch
oRS.Close
Set oRS = Nothing
```

Some Tips on Updating Recordsets

You need to remember that all these methods of updating data, whether with an SQL statement or by using recordset methods, will only succeed if the provider allows the update to take place. The data integrity rules of the database, or the properties of the fields in the tables, may prevent certain updates and generate an error. For example, a field marked as **Required** may not have been given a value, or a related record in another table may be required before a new record can be added.

When the **Update** method is called, the new data items are kept in the ADO cache. We can call the **UpdateBatch** method of the **Recordset** object, which propagates all changes back to the underlying data source. This update can also be canceled by using the **CancelBatch** method.

Changes to the original tables may not always be visible in the recordset. For this reason, ADO provides us with the **Requery** method. Calling this updates the data in the **Recordset** object by re-executing the query on which the recordset is based.

That about covers the **Recordset** object–the last main object in the ADO hierarchy. However, there are a couple of collections that we need to look at briefly before we move on to the next chapter. These are the **Properties** and the **Errors** collections.

The Properties Collection

All three of the main objects in ADO, the **Connection**, **Command**, and **Recordset**, implement their own **Properties** collection. These collections house a set of **Property** objects, but the actual member objects are different for each parent object.

Method	Description
Refresh	Updates the collection to reflect changes to the property values.

Property	Description
`Count`	Returns the number of properties in the collection.
`Item`	Used to retrieve the values of the properties in the collection.

The Property Object

Within the **Properties** collection, as you will by now have come to expect, the members are **Property** objects. And again, the **Property** objects have their own properties:

Property	Description
`Attributes`	Indicates when and how the value of the property can be set. See the **PropertyAttributesEnum** values in Appendix E for a list.
`Name`	The name of the property.
`Type`	The data type of the property.
`Value`	The value of the property.

One of the most difficult concepts to grasp is the difference between the ADO **built-in properties** and the **dynamic properties** which come from the data provider.

Built-in properties are automatically defined by ADO for objects as they are created. These properties are available directly from the parent object, such as the **CommandType** property of a **Command** object. The values of these properties are retrieved and set (where they are not read-only) by referring to that object directly–that is, **oCmd.CommandType**. Because built-in properties are provided in this way, they don't appear as **Property** objects in an object's **Properties** collection, and they are always available– independent of the provider being used.

In addition to these built-in properties, many data providers expose additional object properties to the ADO, known as **dynamic properties**. These properties are generally specific to the provider, and are used to indicate additional functionality that is available. For instance, a property specific to the provider may indicate if a **Recordset** object supports transactions. Any additional properties of this nature will appear in the **Properties** collection of the relevant object.

How to Determine Dynamic Properties

It's easy to find out which provider-specific properties are available from a particular object. If we want to find the dynamic properties available for a standard **Recordset** object for a specific provider, we can iterate through the **Properties** collection. This is what we'll do next. In **PropertyObjects.asp**, we'll create two different types of recordset, and pick out the **Property** object's **Name** and **Value**:

```
Set oConn = Server.CreateObject("ADODB.Connection")
oConn.Open "Contacts"                'the database's System DSN
Set oRS = oConn.Execute("Contact")    'the name of a table

'first the default recordset type
Response.Write "<I> Default recordset: </I><BR>"
```

```
For Each oProp In oRS.Properties
  Response.Write "Name = " & oProp.Name & " : "
  Response.Write "Value = " & oProp.Value & "<BR>"
Next
oRS.Close

'now using a different recordset type
oRs.Open "Contact", "Contacts", adOpenKeyset, adLockBatchOptimistic,
                                      ➡ adCmdTable
Response.Write "<I> Keyset recordset with optimistic batch locking: </I><BR>"
For Each oProp In oRS.Properties
  Response.Write "Name = " & oProp.Name & " : "
  Response.Write "Value = " & oProp.Value & "<BR>"
Next
```

You'll find this page among the samples available for this book. When we run it, we get around twenty-five lines of properties for each recordset type. Here we've picked out part of the results, and you can see that the values of two of the properties have changed:

```
Default recordset:
Name = ODBC Concurrency Type : Value = 14
Name = BLOB accessibility on Forward-Only cursor : Value = True

Keyset recordset with optimistic batch locking:
Name = ODBC Concurrency Type : Value = 11
Name = BLOB accessibility on Forward-Only cursor : Value = False
```

Handling Runtime Errors

Even with the most careful coding, we can be sure that runtime errors are bound to occur, especially in a multiuser environment. Even with the most stringent testing, errors can occur in any application that we create. When they do, we need to be able to detect them, and recover in as graceful a way as possible.

Detecting and Handling Errors

There are mechanisms available in ADO to help us detect and handle errors. We can use the VBScript **On Error Resume Next** statement, or the equivalent in other scripting languages. In addition, we can inspect either the **Connection** object's **Errors** collection, or the built-in scripting object **Err**. Often, a combination of the methods is used—we use **On Error Resume Next** to ensure that our code continues to execute when an error occurs, rather than throwing up an error message and stopping, then we inspect the **Errors** collection or the **Err** object to see what went wrong.

When we build applications that will include error handling, it's not necessary to create an explicit **Connection** object, just so that its **Error** objects can be inspected. If we use an implicit **Connection** object (that is, allow a **Command** or **Recordset** object to create it automatically), we can access the **Error** objects like this

```
oRs.ActiveConnection.Errors.Count
```

Consider this simple example, from **Error_1.asp**:

```
Set oConn = Server.CreateObject("ADODB.Connection")
oConn.Open "Contacts"
Set oRS = oConn.Execute("Contact")   'a table in the database
oRS.AddNew
Response.Write "Won't reach this far"
oRS.Fields("Name") = "John Doe"
oRS.Update
```

You'll notice that we're attempting to add a new record to a non-updatable recordset. This produces an error, and the script terminates. We must stop this because, even if we can't complete the update, we still want the script to run to completion. By simply adding **On Error Resume Next**, the script will run to completion, as is shown by the output message in this example:

```
On Error Resume Next
Set oConn = Server.CreateObject("ADODB.Connection")
oConn.Open "Contacts"
Set oRS = oConn.Execute("Contact")   'a table in the database
oRS.AddNew
oRS.Fields("Name") = "John Doe"
oRS.Update
Response.Write "Will reach this far now"
```

Of course, the only problem now is that we have no way of knowing if the update actually succeeded. To remedy this, we have to use the **Errors** collection or the **Err** object.

The Errors Collection

The **Errors** collection holds all the **Error** objects for a specific **Connection**. It has one method, and the usual two collection properties:

Method	Description
`Clear`	Removes all of the errors in the collection.

Property	Description
`Count`	Returns the number of error objects in the collection.
`Item`	Used to retrieve the contents of the error objects in the collection.

Generally, if an operation being performed by ADO encounters an error, one or more new **Error** objects are automatically created and added to the **Errors** collection. These are the result of just *one* operation not completing successfully–a single database operation can create several errors.

Detecting Errors and Warnings

By examining the **Error** objects that were created, our code can determine more precisely what went wrong, rather than just relying on vague error codes generated by the scripting language. However, some method calls and property accesses don't create **Error** objects in the **Errors** collection when they fail. An example of this is the **AddNew** method, which will raise an error in VBScript, but can't be detected by inspecting the **Count** property of the **Errors** collection. This is because the error is raised by VBScript and not by the data source. In this case, we have to examine the **Err** object. The key is that **Errors** are returned by the data source and **Err** objects are created in at compile or runtime by VBScript or by an automation object (like ADO).

In addition to critical errors, which stop script execution, some properties and methods return warnings that appear as **Error** objects within the **Errors** collection. Warnings do not stop execution of the script, but may indicate a subtle problem such as implicit data conversion, which can compromise the accuracy of results stored. For this reason, in larger applications, it's a very good idea to explicitly test the **Count** property after any ADO operation:

```
On Error Resume Next
Set oConn = Server.CreateObject("ADODB.Connection")
oConn.Open "Contacts"                   'the database's Systm DSN
Set oRS = oConn.Execute("Contact")      'the table in the database
oRS.Fields("Name") = "John Doe"  'update the 'Name' field
If oConn.Errors.Count > 0 Then          'errors or warnings occurred
   Response.Write "<B> Cannot update the 'Name' field </B><P>"
   ...
   'code to display and handle the errors
   ...
Else
   oRS.Update
End If
```

The **Errors** collection can contain warnings that didn't halt the code, and so may be left from a previous operation. We can remove these by calling the **Errors** collection's **Clear** method before executing the operation.

The Error Object

Each **Error** object within the **Errors** collection is itself an object, with its own properties:

Property	Description
Description	A description of the error.
HelpContext	Context, as a **Long** value, for the matching help file topic.
HelpFile	The path to the help file for this topic.
NativeError	The provider-specific error code number.
Number	The ADO error code number. Refer to Appendix E for a list.
Source	Name of the object or application that generated the error.
SQLState	The SQL execution state for this error.

After an ADO operation fails and adds one or more **Error** objects to the **Errors** collection, we can use these to get a better idea of what went wrong. You'll find this code, **ErrorHandling.asp**, among the samples for this book available from our web site:

```
On Error Resume Next
Set oConn = Server.CreateObject("ADODB.Connection")
oConn.Open "Contacts"
Set oRS = oConn.Execute("Contact")
oRS.Fields("Name") = "John Doe"
If oConn.Errors.Count > 0 Then
    Response.Write "<B> Cannot update the 'Name' field </B><P>"
    For intLoop = 0 To oConn.Errors.Count - 1
        Response.Write "Error Number: " & oConn.Errors(intLoop).Number
        Response.Write " - " & oConn.Errors(intLoop).Description & "<P>"
    Next
Else
    oRS.Update
End If
```

The **Errors** collection in the current version of ADO is not fully implemented–as the above code returns a blank form. If, however, you comment out the **On Error Resume Next** line, an error is flagged up. However, this sample should work under ADO 2.0.

The Err Object

We looked at the **Err** object in detail in Chapter 5, so we won't go over it all again. However, you'll recall that an error in your code will set the **Number**, **Source** and **Description** properties of the **Err** object, and we can use these in the **Error_2.asp** code in a similar way to the **Errors** collection:

```
On Error Resume Next
Set oConn = Server.CreateObject("ADODB.Connection")
oConn.Open "Contacts"
Set oRS = oConn.Execute("Contact")
oRS.Fields("Name") = "John Doe"
If Err.Number > 0 Then    'an error occurred
    Response.Write "<B> Cannot update the 'Name' field </B><P>"
    Response.Write "Error Number: " & Err.Number
    Response.Write " - Source: " & Err.Source
    Response.Write " - " & Err.Description & "<P>"
Else
    oRS.Update
End If
```

Preventing Errors

Of course, the best way to deal with errors is to make sure that they don't arise in the first place! There's no way to prevent *all* runtime errors; some are unavoidable, such as when the database is unavailable for some reason, or the network between web server and database has gone down. Often, however, we can avoid having to use specific error handling by pre-empting the causes of errors. One example would be when we try to perform an illegal operation on an object.

Imagine that we've already got a **Recordset** object available, created from an existing **Command** object. We may want to move to the previous record using the **MovePrevious** method. This will generally cause an error if the recordset was opened with a forward-only cursor. We can check what kinds of operations are supported by the recordset using its **Supports** method:

```
...
If oRS.Supports(adMovePrevious) Then oRS.MovePrevious
...
```

The **Supports** method of the **Recordset** object can provide a range of information about that recordset and the functions it supports, such as whether **AddNew**, **Delete**, and **UpdateBatch** are available, if **Bookmarks** can be used, and whether **AbsolutePosition** is supported. Look for the **CursorOptionsEnum** values in Appendix E for a full list.

Summary

In this chapter, we've introduced the ActiveX Data Objects and talked about the individual objects that make up its hierarchy. We've shown you the most widely used methods and properties of those objects, and how you can use them to fulfill your data processing needs.

Of course, there are many more ways that you can use ADO, and you'll see some of these in the next chapter, and throughout the remainder of the book. In particular, three of the case studies in Part 4 of the book use ADO to great effect. In the meantime, the most important points of this chapter are:

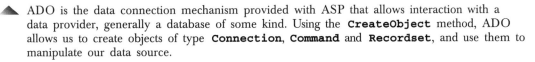

- ADO is the data connection mechanism provided with ASP that allows interaction with a data provider, generally a database of some kind. Using the **CreateObject** method, ADO allows us to create objects of type **Connection**, **Command** and **Recordset**, and use them to manipulate our data source.

- The **Connection** object is used to provide an active link to the data source through a Data Source Name (DSN), or with a DSN-less connection string. By explicitly creating a **Connection** object, we can use it to perform multiple database operations on the database connection.

- The **Command** object is used to perform execution of SQL queries and statements, table record resolution, and stored procedures. We need to create an explicit **Command** object if we want to access the **Parameters** collection.

- The **Recordset** and **Field** objects give us access to the rows of data contained within the database. We can manipulate the underlying tables at the record level using **Recordset** methods.

- In larger applications, we must provide error handling so that our scripts run to completion, and never leave the database in an unstable state.

In the next chapter, we continue to look at the ADO–but in a wider context. Now that you've got a good grounding in the ways ADO can be used, you'll see ways that we can extend this and perform more complicated types of operations. We'll also be looking at using a data source other than Microsoft Access– in particular, how the data can be moved into more enterprise-oriented systems such as SQL Server.

Advanced Database Techniques

In the last chapter, we spent a lot of time looking at the basic structure of the **Database Access Component**. This was intentional because, while it isn't as complex as many other Microsoft database engines, it's important that you are comfortable with the way that it's used before we go on to look at more complicated techniques. As you've seen, ADO follows the example of earlier database systems in being built around a defined object structure. This means that working with it requires a structured approach, but it brings many benefits.

For example, we've seen that there are several different ways of creating a **Recordset**, and directly updating the database. ADO is very flexible, and a great deal more complicated than any of the other Server Components we looked at in earlier chapters. However, while the techniques we used in the previous chapter are fine for databases such as Microsoft Access, in the real world we often have to connect our Web site to one of the more commercially-oriented systems. This might be Microsoft's SQL Server, Oracle, Sybase, DB2 or any of the other enterprise-based systems.

We also need to investigate some of the more advanced ways that the Active Database Component can be used. Rather than the simple examples you saw in the previous chapter, you'll now see how some real-world problems can be solved. For example, we need to consider how our pages might affect the security of our data, and take steps to protect our database systems.

So, in this chapter, we'll be looking at:

- How the ActiveX Data Objects links to different databases
- Techniques for manipulating enterprise-oriented databases
- Real-world problem-solving techniques with the ActiveX Data Objects
- How we can maintain security when linking a database to the Web

Manipulating Enterprise Data

So far we have assumed that the data source used to supply data to our Web page was an Access database. However, Access is not designed to handle really large volumes of data, or high transaction rates from multiple users. As we begin to look at developing an Internet or Intranet site, we need to consider the potential number of simultaneous visitors we might have to cater to. Hundreds or thousands of users might visit a typical Internet site in any given day, potentially dozens at the same time. In this environment, Microsoft Access would quickly overheat. So let's take a step beyond Access, and look at how ADO can be used with other stores of data, including enterprise database systems such as Microsoft SQL Server.

Expanded Data Access

ADO is a collection of objects that expose a standard set of properties and methods that our applications can use when accessing data. Like many of its predecessors, such as DAO and RDO, ADO relies on an underlying layer of software to actually interact with a given data source. As we saw in the last chapter, **OLE DB** is this underlying layer.

OLE DB technology is being positioned as the cornerstone to Microsoft's component database architecture. It is a set of OLE interfaces that provide applications with a standard means of accessing data stored in various information stores. These standard interfaces support specific elements of the data access functionality that are appropriate to the data source, enabling it to share its data.

The benefits of component DBMS's can be seen in the success of the **Open Database Connectivity** (ODBC) database access interface. ODBC is provided as a means of accessing relational data from a diverse set of sources, using a standard series of functions and commands, the idea being that the programmer is shielded from having to code to each specific data source's SQL requirements, thus vastly increasing productivity.

OLE DB takes ODBC a step further, towards a truly standard means of accessing data from diverse sources. Whereas ODBC is designed around accessing relational data sources using Structured Query Language (SQL), OLE DB is focused on providing access to *any* data, anywhere. The first OLE DB provider was the Microsoft OLE DB Provider for ODBC. This allowed connection to existing ODBC data source from ADO. However this is really only intended as a stop gap, and true OLE DB providers are the ones you should be using, since they will provide greater functionality and better performance than the ODBC provider. Microsoft have providers for SQL Server, Oracle, Microsoft Exchange, Microsoft Active Directory Services, Microsoft Index Server, Jet, AS/400 and VSAM, and the Com Transaction Integrator for CICS and IMS currently in development, and they should be available by the time this reaches you. Other OLE DB Providers are also being developed by third parties.

In addition to simplifying the programmer's job, the OLE DB interface layer provides the developer with a means of accessing data which may not be stored in a traditional DBMS format. As we all know, there is a large amount of mission-critical data stored in systems that are not classified as a DBMS, for example Web servers or Mail systems such as Microsoft Exchange. One of the most significant limitations of the ODBC approach to data access is that it is difficult for non-relational database vendors to support. Building a data provider layer means exposing the data via SQL. For a non-SQL data provider, such as an Excel file or a Mail system, this requires the equivalent of a SQL engine within the ODBC driver.

OLE DB simplifies the development of access methods for simple tabular data providers by only requiring them to implement the functionality native to their data source. At a minimum, an access provider must implement the interfaces necessary to expose data in a tabular form. This requirement allows for the development of query processor components, such as SQL query processors, that can work with tabular information from any provider that exposes its data through OLE DB. In essence then, OLE DB provides an interface layer that is consistent despite its having an underlying data structure that may be very diverse.

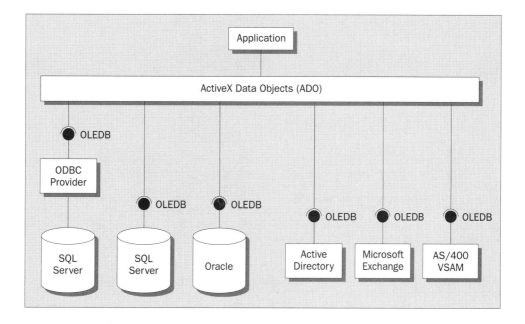

OLE DB and ADO

As we have seen, OLE DB is a collection of components that work together to provide data access capabilities to an application. These components are loosely grouped into two classes, **consumers** and **providers**. Consumers are the components that submit requests for data. Providers service these requests by accessing the data sources, and retrieving the information requested. In these terms, ADO is an OLE DB consumer. In other words, it makes requests to a provider. The name of the provider that will service a request is supplied either as a part of a **connection string**, or as the **Provider** property of the **Connection** object.

In this example, we supply the name of the Microsoft OLE DB provider for ODBC, **MSDASQL**, as a parameter to the **Provider** method, and creating and ADO **Connection** object.

```
Set DBConn = Server.CreateObject("ADODB.Connection")
DBConn.Provider ="MSDASQL"
DBConn.Open "DSN=SQLForum;UID=sa;PWD=;"
Set Session("DBConn") = DBConn
```

> *Be careful not to include a **Provider Name** as both a part of the connection string, and as the **Provider** property of the **Connection** object. If you do, the result is unpredictable. **MSDASQL** is the default Provider.*

Providers, like any other OLE object, must be defined in the registry before the OLE DB layer can use them. They are identified by the OLE DB Provider sub-key, under the class ID of the provider. Within the HKEY_CLASSES_ROOT key, providers must have the following sub-keys and values for the programmatic identifier (**ProgID**):

```
ProviderProgID = FriendlyDisplayName
ProviderProgID\CLSID = ProviderCLSID
```

The entries for the **MSDASQL** ODBC provider are shown here–the CLSID value is a unique key that identifies the provider installed:

```
MSDASQL = Microsoft OLE DB Provider for ODBC Drivers
MSDASQL\CLSID = {c8b522cb-5cf3-11ce-ade5-00aa0044773d}
```

Under the HKEY_CLASSES_ROOT\CLSID sub-key, providers must have the following sub-keys and values:

```
ProviderCLSID = FriendlyDisplayName
ProviderCLSID\ProgID = ProviderProgID
ProviderCLSID\VersionIndependentProgID = VersionIndependentProgID
ProviderCLSID\InprocServer32 = ProviderDLLFilename
ProviderCLSID\InprocServer32\ThreadingModel = Apartment | Free | Both
ProviderCLSID\OLE DB Provider = Description
```

Again, the entries for the **MSDASQL** ODBC provider are:

```
{c8b522cb-5cf3-11ce-ade5-00aa0044773d} = MSDASQL
{c8b522cb-5cf3-11ce-ade5-00aa0044773d}\VersionIndependentProgID = MSDASQL
{c8b522cb-5cf3-11ce-ade5-00aa0044773d}\InprocServer32 = MSDASQL.DLL
{c8b522cb-5cf3-11ce-ade5-00aa0044773d}\InprocServer32\ThreadingModel =
                                                          ⤷ Both
{c8b522cb-5cf3-11cc-adc5-00aa0044773d}\OLE DB Provider - Microsoft OLE DB
                                      ⤷ Provider for ODBC Drivers
```

In addition, the ODBC provider entry references a second key that points to another OLE object, which is used for error processing. Other providers are identified in the registry in this same way. Thankfully, the installation of ADO provides all the registry entries required, but you'll find the information here useful if you need to delve into the registry yourself, however, you rarely need to do this sort of thing.

Connecting to a Data Source

Let's take a moment to look at how we connect to various data sources. ADO provides a number of ways of actually establishing a connection to a data source. Each has its advantages and disadvantages but, underneath the covers, each is limited by the ability of the provider to service the connection. As we walk through various examples, keep in mind that some of the features discussed may only be appropriate for the provider being used in that example.

The Connection Object

In the previous chapter, we reviewed how the **Connection** object is used to create a connection between an ASP page and a data source. Now let's look in more detail at the **Connection** object and at some of the more advanced options we can make use of when connecting to and working with various data sources, including SQL Server.

The **Connection** object appears to be the parent object in a hierarchy of several other objects including the **Errors** object, **Command** object and **Recordset** object. It only appears to be the parent object, but as you'll see later you can create **Command** and Recordset objects directly and an implicit **Connection** is created for you. The **Connection** object can be used to create a new connection to a data source, by providing the connection object with a connection string or connection information. This connection can then be referenced by each of the other objects in the hierarchy to interact with the described data source.

```
Set DBConn = Server.CreateObject("ADODB.Connection")
DBConn.Provider="MSDASQL"
DBConn.Open "DSN=SQLForum;UID=sa;PWD=;APP=Forum;WSID=MAINFRAME;
                                    Database=Forum"
Set Session("DBConn") = DBConn
```

However, unlike the DAO and RDO libraries, ADO doesn't require you to work your way down a hierarchy of objects in order to instantiate the one you actually require. The **Command** and **Recordset** objects can be called independently of any **Connection** object, allowing these objects to create a new **Connection** directly and interact with the database through it:

```
Set oRS = Server.CreateObject("ADODB.RecordSet")
oRS.Open "Select * from Message", "DSN=SQLForum;UID=sa;PWD="
Response.Write "<B> Records Found: </B><P>"
Do While Not oRS.EOF
   For intCount = 0 to oRS.Fields.Count -1
      Response.Write oRS.Fields(intCount).Value & " - "
   Next
   Response.Write "<BR>"
   oRS.MoveNext
Loop
```

In this example, we create a simple listing of each record in the **Message** table. You will notice that no **Connection** object is explicitly created, we simply create a **Recordset** with the **Open** method of the **Recordset**, using a SQL query and a connection string. Behind the scenes, ADO creates a **Connection** object and associates it with the **Recordset** we just created. When the **Recordset** goes out of scope or is set to **Nothing**, the **Connection** object is released.

Let's take another example. Here we need to call a SQL Server Stored Procedure only once per session. Rather then opening a **Connection** object, and passing a reference to it to a **Command** object, we can take advantage of the **Command** object's ability to create a **Connection** object for us automatically in the background:

```
Set oCmd = Server.CreateObject("ADODB.Command")
oCmd.ActiveConnection = "dsn=SQLForum;database=Forum;uid=sa;pwd=;"
oCmd.CommandText = "{call myproc}"
oCmd.Execute
```

In the above example, we supply a connection string to the **Open** method of the object. The connection string is passed directly to the underlying ODBC driver, which in turn uses it to attach to the specified data source. Here a connection object is created for temporary use and destroyed when the **oCmd** object variable goes out of scope, or is set to **Nothing**.

Connection Tips

When defining connections, here are a few simple guidelines that are useful to follow:

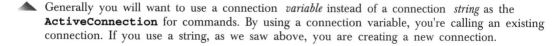 Generally you will want to use a connection *variable* instead of a connection *string* as the **ActiveConnection** for commands. By using a connection variable, you're calling an existing connection. If you use a string, as we saw above, you are creating a new connection.

▲ Make sure you explicitly close a connection when it's no longer needed. Although a connection is closed when it goes out of scope, it's better to make sure it is closed when you think it is. You can proactively call **Close** and set the variable to **Nothing** when you know that you will no longer need a connection. This frees up resources before it actually goes out of scope. For example

```
oRs.Close
Set oRs = Nothing
```

When working with a SQL Server data source, consider that with forward-scrolling, read-only cursors (also known as **firehose** cursors) against SQL Server, you will not be able to start a new transaction on that connection. This is because the connection is dealing with the cursor and needs to complete what it's doing (i.e. get to the end of the cursor and close it) before continuing.

Connection Pooling

In each of the examples we've discussed, we've created a new **Connection** object for each session, and then done something with it. However, consider a site where the number of simultaneous users is in the hundreds. In this environment, creating a new **Connection** object for each and every user can be very resource intensive. To help alleviate this problem, ADO can take advantage of a feature provided with ODBC 3.0 and 3.5 and ASP known as **connection pooling**. This is a resource manager for connections, maintaining the open state on frequently used connections, and thereby avoiding the need to continuously create new connections.

A connection remains in the pool for a default of 60 seconds, and then the connection is closed. You can alter this from the following registry entry:

`\HKEY_LOCAL_MACHINE\SOFTWARE\ODBC\ODBCINST.INI\driver-name\CPTimeout = timeout`

For example, the entry for SQL Server is:

`\HKEY_LOCAL_MACHINE\SOFTWARE\ODBC\ODBCINST.INI\SQL Server\CPTimeout = 60`

If you find that you are repeatedly creating connections over this period, for example every two minutes, you may wish to increase this value so that connections remain pooled for longer.

Connection pooling is a standard feature of ODBC 3.0 and 3.5 and cannot be disabled through the registry, however, on a driver by driver basis it can be disabled, simply by removing the CPTimeout registry key as described above. Be aware, however, that performance will most likely suffer if you do remove connection pooling. There is also no way to control the number of ODBC connections in a pool.

Creating a DSN 'on the Fly'

So far, each of our connections has assumed that we have previously defined a **Data Source Name** (DSN). The DSN describes a data source, and the standard settings to be used when attaching to it. However, this can be limiting in some circumstances–especially when attaching to data sources that are dynamic in nature.

For example, let's take a situation where the user connects to several servers, depending on the information they need. We could setup an ODBC Data Source Name definition for each server and selectively attach to it. A better way is to create the connection 'on the fly', without using a DSN:

```
ServerName = Request.QueryString("ServerName")    'from the submitted page
DBConn.Open "Driver={SQL Server};Server=" & ServerName & _
    ";UID=sa;PWD=;WSID=MAINFRAME;Language=us_english;Database=Forum;DSN=;"
...
```

In this example we create a definition on the fly, using the server name from a form submitted by the user to determine which SQL Server to attach to.

Expanding the Connection Object

The **Connection** object is responsible for more than just the initialization of communication between the server and the application. It is also used to manage transactions, submit SQL statements directly to a provider, and set provider-specific attributes.

Let's look at an example of using several of the advanced features of the **Connection** object to update our database. Typically, when working with ADO, you might assume that to update a record in a table we would open a **Recordset**, use **AddNew** to add a new record, change the data for the fields in the **Recordset** and then **Update** the fields in the **Recordset**:

```
Set rsAddMessage = Server.CreateObject("ADODB.Recordset")
rsAddMessage.Open "Message", Conn, adOpenKeyset
rsAddMessage.AddNew
rsAddMessage.Fields("FromMsg") = strFrom
rsAddMessage.Fields("Email") = strEmail
rsAddMessage.Update

rsAddMessage.AddNew
rsAddMessage.Fields("FromMsg") = strFrom
rsAddMessage.Fields("Email") = strEmail
rsAddMessage.Update

rsAddMessage.Close
Set rsAddMessage = Nothing
```

This is fine for adding a single record, but how about multiple records? You would have to call **AddNew** and **Update** for each record, resulting in data being sent back to the server for every record as well as being longer and more cumbersome to type. Instead you could use the **UpdateBatch** method which batches together changes and only sends them to the server once.

```
Set rsAddMessage = Server.CreateObject("ADODB.Recordset")
rsAddMessage.Open "Message", Conn, adOpenKeyset, adLockBatchOptimistic
rsAddMessage.AddNew
rsAddMessage.Fields("FromMsg") = strFrom
rsAddMessage.Fields("Email") = strEmail
rsAddMessage.AddNew
rsAddMessage.Fields("FromMsg") = strFrom
rsAddMessage.Fields("Email") = strEmail
rsAddMessage.Updatebatch
```

```
      rsAddMessage.Close
      Set rsAddMessage = Nothing
```

This uses the **adLockBatchOptimistic** on the recordset Open to tell ADO that batch mode is in operation. Multiple changes can then be made to the records and the **UpdateBatch** method called when all changes are done, sending everything to the server in one hit.

Now, let's take a look at a piece of code that does the same thing, using a different tactic:

```
      ...
      SQLQuery = "INSERT INTO Forum.dbo.Message " _
              & "( FromMsg, Email, Subject, Body, WhenMsg, MsgLevel, " _
              & " PrevRef, TopRef ) " _
              & " VALUES ( '" & strFrom & cDlm & strEmail & cDlm & strSubject _
              & cDlm & strBody & cDlm & CStr(Now()) & "', " & intNewMsgLevel
              & ", " & lngPrevRef & ", " & intNewThreadPos & " )"
      oConn.Execute SQLQuery, lRecs
      ...
```

Here we build an **INSERT** statement to apply the data stored in a number of variables to the records. The SQL Statement is syntactically compatible with **Transact-SQL** (TSQL), the native SQL language of SQL Server. You can also do this with other data stores too, such as Access, but you use the SQL statements appropriate to the data store you are connecting to. For example, there are minor differences between SQL Server transact-SQL and Access SQL.

The SQL statement is then submitted to the provider using the **Execute** method of the **Connection** object. Notice that an **lRecs** variable is supplied as a parameter to the **Execute** method call. This variable will contain a count of the number of records affected by this statement after it is submitted.

One of the advantages of the direct SQL approach is that it simply requires fewer steps. More importantly, it provides us with the ability to supply **batches** of SQL to the server. In the above example, we use a single **INSERT** statement. Consider, however, the need for multiple inserts or updates–or perhaps additional data validation that might occur during, or as a part of, the submission.

Batch and Transaction Management

Perhaps the most compelling reason to use a batch SQL approach is the need for a finer level of **transaction** control. When using an Access database with a single user, transaction management is a minor concern at best. However, when multiple users are accessing a data source, with the potential of simultaneous updates, transaction management can have a huge impact on the performance and reliability of SQL Server.

> A **transaction** is simply some set of actions that must all be completed or none completed. For example, in banking a transfer from one account to the other must be run as a transaction, so that the debit from one account and the credit to the other account are both completed. If either isn't completed, then the other half of the transfer must be undone, and both accounts left in the state they were before the transaction started.

In the previous example, the transaction is committed to the server–i.e. the changes are actually applied to the data–as soon as it is executed. In many cases this is perfectly acceptable. However, if we need a finer level of control over when a transaction is committed, either for performance reasons or due to dependencies between records, we can choose to define the beginning and the end of each transaction.

We looked briefly at transactions in the previous chapter. To define the beginning and end of transaction, we use the **BeginTrans** and **CommitTrans** methods of the **Connection** object:

```
Conn.BeginTrans
Conn.Execute SQLQuery, lRecs
Conn.CommitTrans
```

Here we explicitly define the beginning of a transaction. By doing so, the underlying ODBC provider will no longer automatically commit a transaction. To apply changes to a database, the **Connection** object's **CommitTrans** method is called. If an error occurs, the **RollbackTrans** method is available. **RollbackTrans** will 'undo' any changes made as a result of the SQL that has been submitted since the last **CommitTrans** was called.

Things to Consider when Using Transactions

To get the maximum performance when using transaction statements to process database records, we need to structure them well. The following is a list of guidelines that may be helpful as you experiment with transactions:

 Keep the transaction processing blocks as short as possible. Remember that as long as a transaction is open on a series of records (especially in the case of an update), other people cannot access or change them. For example:

```
Conn.BeginTrans
    Statement1...
    Statement2...
    Statement3...
    Statement4...   '*** If you have a number of statements,
                    '*** you could slow processing and increase
                    '*** the chance of errors occurring.
Conn.CommitTrans   (or RollbackTrans)
```

In fact it is possible to allow other people to read your records whilst you are in the middle of a transaction, and this is known as the **Isolation Level**, which can be set using the **IsolationLevel** property of the **Connection** object. For example, setting **IsolationLevel** to **adXactReadUncommited** (256) allows you to read uncommitted changes in other transactions. The default is **adXactCursorStability** that only allows you to view changes in other transactions once they have been committed. This is the safest option and should always be used unless you have a specific need not to.

When working with transaction statements, don't create a new connection or perform further database processing until the transaction is complete. Jumping out of an open transaction can lead to contention and lockout conditions:

```
Conn.BeginTrans
    Statement1...
    Statement2...

    '*** Don't create a new transaction within an open tranaction

    Set RS = Server.CreateObject("ADODB.RecordSet")
    RS.Open "select * from Message", DBConn, 3, 1, 2
    If NOT RS.EOF Then
        Statement3...
```

```
        Statement4...
    End if
Conn.CommitTrans  (or RollbackTrans)
```

> ▲ When working with a **Recordset** object, don't refresh the object in the middle of a series of transactions. Doing so will create the Attempt to Commit or Rollback without BeginTrans error:

```
Conn.BeginTrans
    Statement1...
    If UserReset Then
        Rs.Refresh   '*** Can cause an error
    End If
    Statement2...
    Statement3...
Conn.CommitTrans  (or Rollback)
```

> ▲ When using transactions to control server updates, don't execute a **Close** on the **Connection** object in the middle of a transaction. This can lead to problems when attempting to commit the transaction:

```
Conn.BeginTrans
    Statement1
    If Error
        db.Close   '*** Commit will fail after this
    End If
    Statement2...
    Statement3...
Conn.CommitTrans  (or Rollback)
```

As you can see, we can now specify when and under what conditions data is applied to our data server. In addition, and perhaps more importantly, we can undo these changes at any point in the process.

Connection Attributes

Depending on the **Connection** object's **Attributes** property, calling either the **CommitTrans** or **RollbackTrans** methods may automatically start a new transaction. If the **Attributes** property is set to **adXactCommitRetaining**, ADO automatically starts a new transaction after a **CommitTrans** call. If **Attributes** is set to **adXactAbortRetaining**, ADO automatically starts a new transaction after a **RollbackTrans** call. This could be useful if you know that you are going to be making several sets of changes to records and you automatically wish for transactions to be created for you. Setting the **Attributes** for a **Connection** to 0 indicates that transactions are not automatically started after a **CommitTrans** or **RollbackTrans**.

Take care to note what state the driver is in. The ODBC provider for ADO does not support multiple simultaneous transactions within a single connection. As such, if we attempt a **BeginTrans** and the previous **CommitTrans** automatically created a new transaction, an error will result.

> *Note that once you start a transaction yourself, rather than having it started automatically, you will have to manually manage transactions until the connection is closed and reopened.*

The Command Object

The Command object is used to obtain records and create **Recordset** objects, as well as to execute bulk operations or manipulate the structure of a database. Depending on the functionality the provider exposes some collections, methods, and properties of a **Command** object may not be available. Refer to your provider's documentation to verify a command feature is available before attempting to use one.

In previous chapters we looked at how we could use the **Command** object. Now let's take a closer look at one of its most appealing capabilities, especially when working with SQL Server.

Using Stored Procedures

Stored procedures provide an alternative to executing batches of SQL statements in ADO. We looked briefly at how we can call a stored procedure earlier. Let's take a look at how to get values back out of a stored procedure. Here's a simple code sample showing how to call a stored procedure with a single output parameter.

```
Set cmd = Server.CreateObject("ADODB.Command")
oCmd.ActiveConnection = "dsn=SQLForum;database=pubs;uid=sa;pwd=;"
oCmd.CommandText = "{call recordcount(?)}"
'now specify parameter info
oCmd.Parameters.Append oCmd.CreateParameter("cnt", adInteger, adParamOutput)
oCmd.Execute
Response.Write "RecordCount = " & oCmd(0)
```

In this example, we have a stored procedure called **recordcount**, which accepts one integer parameter and returns the number of records in our table. Alternately we can use this approach with the same stored procedure:

```
Set oCon = Server.CreateObject("ADODB.Connection")
Set oCmd = Server.CreateObject("ADODB.Command")
oCon.Open "SQLForum", "sa", ""
Set oCmd.ActiveConnection = oCon
oCmd.CommandText = "{? = call recordcount}"
'now specify parameter info
oCmd(0).Direction = adParamReturnValue
oCmd.Execute
Response.Write "RecordCount = " & oCmd(0)
```

The Recordset Object

The **Recordset** object is the real heart of ADO. It's the primary mechanism we use to interact with a database. In previous chapters we've introduced the **Recordset**, and seen what it has to offer. In this section, we'll consider some of the things we must take into account when creating **Recordsets**. Then we'll look at how we go about retrieving **Binary Large Object** (BLOB) data using a **Recordset**.

A **Recordset** is in essence a **cursor**. A cursor is a subset of a database, organized and sorted in accordance with a SQL query. Cursors are powerful tools within a relational database engine. They allow developers to retrieve a subset of data, position that data in rows and columns, and then navigate the result set–both forward and backward (depending upon the cursor type)–updating and changing the data as required. The following are some things to consider when creating and working with **Recordsets**.

Tips for Working with Cursors

Some providers, such as SQL Server, implement a forward-scrolling, read-only (or 'firehose') cursor mode, meaning that they can efficiently retrieve data by keeping a connection open. When working with such providers, the connection could be blocked by another user's transaction. The following examples demonstrate scenarios that result in errors.

▲ Example 1

```
dbConn.Open "DSN=SQLForum;UID=sa;PWD=;"        'Example 1
dbConn.BeginTrans
RS.Open "SELECT * FROM Message", dbConn
Set dbCmd.ActiveConnection = dbConn
```

The problem is that the command object's **ActiveConnection** is being set to a connection that is forward-scrolling and in 'firehose' mode. This is the same connection involved in the batch mode. The error from the provider will only appear in the **Err** object, and it will return as unspecified. For example, with the ODBC Provider, you will get an Unspecified error.

▲ Example 2

```
dbConn.Open "DSN=SQLForum;UID=sa;PWD=;"        'Example 2
RS.Open "SELECT * FROM Message", dbConn
dbConn.BeginTrans
```

The problem here is that the connection is forward-scrolling and in firehose mode, so it cannot be put into transaction mode. The error returned in the **Errors** collection from the provider will indicate that it is operating in firehose mode, and can't work in transaction mode. For example, with the ODBC Provider against Microsoft SQL Server, you will get the error "Cannot start transaction while in firehose mode".

▲ Example 3

```
dbConn.Open "DSN=SQLForum;UID=sa;PWD=;"        'Example 3
RS.Open "SELECT * FROM Message", dbConn
Set dbCmd.ActiveConnection = dbConn
dbConn.BeginTrans
```

The problem here is that the connection is in forward-scrolling firehose mode, so it cannot also be involved in a batch mode. The error returned in the **Errors** collection from the provider will indicate that the transaction could not be started. For example, with the ODBC Provider against Microsoft SQL Server, you will get the error Cannot start transaction because more than one hdbc is in use. This is a feature of the SQL Server ODBC driver which only allows one query to be executed at any single time.

Working with the CacheSize Property

When dealing with cursors, especially those created by ODBC, it is important to control how much data is cached by ODBC in client memory. ASP assists in this area considerably, as the actual ADO processes are executed on the Web server. As such, cached data is stored in the server's memory, as opposed to the actual end-user or client machine. However, this can also have a downside as we scale up our server. If our default **Recordset** cache is large, and our server incurs a large volume of traffic, we can quickly run into resource issues.

The **CacheSize** property of the **Recordset** object is used to control how many records our underlying ODBC driver keeps in its memory buffer, and how many to retrieve at one time into local memory. For example if the **CacheSize** is set to **10**, the ODBC driver retrieves the first ten records into a local cache as soon as a **Recordset** object is opened. As we navigate through the **Recordset** object, the ODBC driver then retrieves data from the data source and puts it into the cache as required, for example as soon as we move past the last record in the cache, it retrieves the next ten records from the data source.

Typically, for a read-only forward-scrolling **Recordset**, we only want to cache one record at a time, and **CacheSize** is set to **1**. Because we can't move backward or change the data, caching records on the client isn't efficient. Bringing them into memory as they are read is all that is needed.

However, when data is being updated, or we create a **Recordset** that supports forward and backward navigation, a larger **CacheSize** may be appropriate. In the case of updates, when the cache size is **1**, the recordset will need to go back to the server for each changed record. With a recordset that allows backward as well as forward navigation, it has to go back to the server to retrieve the same data many times, especially as we move upwards (**MovePrevious**) in the recordset.

The value of the **CacheSize** property can be adjusted during the life of the **Recordset** object, but changing this value only affects the number of records in the cache after subsequent retrievals from the data source. To force the cache size to be adjusted immediately, we can **Resync** the **Recordset**. However, we cannot set the cache size to **0**—if we do an error will result.

Binary Data

The **Recordset** is an extremely flexible object. In addition to working with data of various types, it supports the retrieval and manipulation of raw binary data stored in a database. This can be especially valuable if our database contains items such as graphical or sound data.

It's important to note that although BLOB (Binary Large Object) data can be retrieved from a database, it is not wise to store all of the graphical images on the Web site in the database. SQL Server, or Access for that matter, was not designed to process and work with this type of data. Typically it's far more efficient to store BLOB information as normally, as **.gif** or **.wav** files, along with our Web pages.

BLOB data manipulation comes in handy when we have graphics that are supplied from other sources, and are typically dynamic in nature. For example, a workflow imaging system may track document images across various users, and we may need to display some of these images within a dynamic Web page. To do this, the **GetChunk** method of the **Field** object is used. Let's take a look at an example:

```
ID = Request.QueryString("ID")
BlockSize = 4096
```

```
Response.ContentType = "image/JPEG"
strQuery = "SELECT * FROM Blob WHERE Blob_ID = " & ID
Set oRS = oConn.Execute(strQuery)    'oConn is a Session level object
oRS.MoveFirst
Set Field = oRS("Blob")
FileLength = Field.ActualSize
NumBlocks = FileLength \ BlockSize
LeftOver = FileLength Mod BlockSize
Response.BinaryWrite Field.GetChunk(LeftOver)
For intLoop = 1 To NumBlocks
  Response.BinaryWrite Field.GetChunk(BlockSize)
Next
oRS.Close
```

*Make sure the BLOBs are the last things in your **SELECT** statement. Currently they don't work if they are not the last field(s).*

In this example, a **jpeg** image has been stored in an **Blob** field within our SQL Server database. We're retrieving it from the database, and displaying it on our Web page. SQL Server supports several binary data types. Two of these, **Binary** and **VarBinary** are limited to a maximum of **255** characters. In addition, SQL Server supports an **Image** type that stores data as **2KB** increments of binary information. This type meets our need for this example.

Our first step is to obtain a key that references the binary object in which we are interested. Here, we will use an **ID** that is selected by the user on a previous page. In a real world scenario, the previous page would include a number of "thumb nail" pictures, that when selected would call this page and pass the appropriate **ID** for the image required.

A **BlockSize** value is used to determine how much data will be read from the data source at one time. Take care when setting this value. It is best to use a value that is a multiple of the field increment size to avoid an excessively large or small leftover chunk. It may seem logical to read the whole image as a single chunk, but keep in mind that we need to move this data from our server to our Web site in a single transaction, a process that can be very resource intensive with large files.

The next step is to define the type of data that will be displayed on the page. This is done using the **ContentType** property of the **Response** object, which is an object of IIS itself. Then, with our initial values set, we can define a query to retrieve the data. Using the **Execute** method of the **Connection** object, we submit the query and return a **Recordset** containing the query results. To verify that the data set is populated, we call the **MoveFirst** method of the **Recordset** object.

Now we are ready to actually read the data from our **Recordset**. To do this we define an object variable representing the **BLOB** field. In this example we use:

```
Set Field = RS("BLOB")
```

The object variable **Field** now has a reference to the actual binary data. Our next step is to calculate how much data we need to retrieve in terms of the block size defined earlier. We do this by retrieving the actual size of the object (using the **ActualSize** property as you might guess), and then dividing that value by our block size variable to determine the number of chunks our data can be retrieved in. As our block size may not be evenly divisible by the size of the image, a **LeftOver** value is calculated to determine any partial chunk of data that needs to be retrieved:

```
FileLength = Field.ActualSize
NumBlocks = FileLength \ BlockSize
LeftOver = FileLength Mod BlockSize
```

Using the **BinaryWrite** method of the **Response** object, we can output a chunk of the data read from the data source with the **GetChunk** method. **GetChunk** is design to read an unstructured binary data stream from an object of a given size. Here, we initially retrieve the extra bytes (if any), and then read blocks of data of the size defined, and write them to the Web page:

```
Response.BinaryWrite Field.GetChunk(LeftOver)
For i = 1 To NumBlocks
   Response.BinaryWrite Field.GetChunk(BlockSize)
Next
```

Using Recordset Filters

At the risk of sounding repetitive, a **Recordset** object works with a result set of data. We can think of a result set as a table that is a subset of the original table from which the **Recordset** retrieved its data. Consider the need to retrieve further subsets of this result data. We have two options—either create a new **Recordset** with the additional filtering criteria, or apply the filtering criteria to the existing record set.

Creating a new **Recordset** introduces a great deal of overhead and processing time, as well as the need to cache data that may be duplicated. To avoid this the **Recordset** object supplies a filtering method: **Filter**.

A **Filter** can be a string that provides filtering information to the **Recordset**, or an array of bookmarks on specific records in the record set. Keep in mind however, that ADO must do the filtering work itself, and incur the processing overhead it entails. With a large recordset, this overhead can exceed the effort of simply creating a new recordset with the same filtering criteria applied.

Let's take a look at how a string of filtering criteria might be applied. A **criteria string** is made up of values in the form *FieldName Operator Value* (for example, **"LastName = 'Smith'"**). We can create compound clauses by joining individual clauses with **AND** (for example, **"LastName = 'Smith' AND FirstName = 'John'"**). The following lists some guidelines for creating filter strings:

- *FieldName* must be a valid field name from the **Recordset**. If the field name contains spaces, we must enclose the name in square brackets.

- *Operator* must be one of the following: **<, >, <=, >=, <>, =, LIKE**.

- *Value* is the value with which we will compare the field's values (for example, **'Smith'**, **#8/24/95#**, **12.345** or **$50.00**). Use single quotes with strings and hash signs (**#**) with dates. For numbers, we can use decimal points, dollar signs, and scientific notation. If *Operator* is **LIKE**, *Value* can include wildcards. Only the asterisk (*****) and percent sign (**%**) wild cards are allowed, and they must be the last character in the string. *Value* may not be **Null**.

The filter property also allows us to supply a number of constants that affect the way in which the filter is applied to the data, and the results it produces. The constants that can be applied are:

Constant	Value	Description
`AdFilterNone`	0	Removes the current filter and restores all records to view.
`AdFilterPendingRecords`	1	Allows you to view only records that have changed but have not yet been sent to the server. Only applicable for the batch update mode.
`AdFilterAffectedRecords`	2	Allows you to view only records affected by the last `Delete`, `Resync`, `UpdateBatch`, or `CancelBatch` call.
`AdFilterFetchedRecords`	3	Allows you to view records in the current cache, that is, the results of the last fetch from the database.

Beyond Microsoft Access

In the previous sections, we've looked at the workings of OLE DB and ADO in detail. It's time to put some of it into practice. We'll take an example database, and move it from Access to the SQL Server platform. This is a surprisingly straightforward process. With some thought as to the differences between the two platforms, and some good up-front design work, we can create and develop an ASP application using Access, then **upsize** it to SQL Server for use in an enterprise-oriented, high volume environment.

Upsizing to SQL Server

Since release 2.0 of MS Access, an add-on tool has been available from Microsoft that can greatly simplify moving an Access database into the SQL Server environment. This tool is called the **Upsizing Wizard**. It is available from a variety of sources, including the Microsoft web site at **http://www.microsoft.com/ AccessDev/ProdInfo/AUT97dat.htm**

Upsizing Wizard consists of two tools. The first is the wizard itself, which takes a Microsoft Access database and creates an equivalent database on SQL Server—with the same table structure, data and most (but not all) of the attributes of the original Microsoft Access database.

The second tool supplied as part of the Upsizing Wizard package is the **SQL Server Browser**. This allows the developer to view, create, and edit SQL Server objects, including tables, views, defaults, rules, stored procedures and triggers. SQL Server Browser can be used to manage both a SQL Server database created by the Upsizing Wizard, and any existing SQL Server objects.

Upsizing Design Issues

Before we can upsize an Access database to SQL Server, there are several important design issues we need to consider. Ideally, we would design our database from the very beginning with Web deployment in mind. As we'll see, the design of a database optimized for access from the Internet, or on an intranet, is very different to that of a typical single-user database. If you have an existing database that was not built with Web access in mind, you're likely to have to redesign certain aspects of it to take advantage of the upsizing process. We'll look at these aspects first.

Design Tips from the Client Side

Throughout this book, we're looking at how to build Active Server Pages. Let's take a moment to recap on some of the things we should take into account when designing a Web page that accesses data using ADO. These can have an enormous impact on the performance of our site.

▲ Use `Recordset` objects of the **static cursor** type if the result set contains relatively few columns, doesn't contain `OLE Object` or large `Memo` fields and when you don't need to update the server tables. If you are simply presenting data, and bi-directional scrolling is not required, use the `adOpenForwardOnly` cursor type. This makes a single pass through the request table to present the results, incurring a minimum overhead.

▲ Minimize the number of items in server-populated combo boxes, list boxes and other selection controls. Use **static cursor** type `Recordset` objects to populate these controls wherever possible. Don't let the selection lists get too big–keep in mind that you have to pump all this data across to the user's Web browser. Anyway, from a design perspective, a selection list with too many items quickly becomes unwieldy.

▲ Adhere to server-based naming restrictions from the beginning. Upsizing Wizard can correct many common errors in this regard, but not all of them. It's best to adhere to SQL Server restrictions from the beginning, in order to assure a painless migration. SQL Server field names must be `30` characters or less. The first character must be a letter or the symbol `@`. The remaining characters may be numbers, letters, or the symbols, `$`, `#` and `_`. No spaces are allowed.

Design Tips from the Server Side

On SQL Server, we also need to take into account some basic design issues. Addressing these before we start the process can save us the difficulties associated with having to start again.

▲ To make upsizing go as smoothly as possible, you should make sure that you have sufficient access permissions on the SQL Server you want to upsize to. The permissions you need will vary according to what you want to accomplish. At minimum, you must have `CREATE TABLE` permission. If you want to build a new database from scratch, you must have `CREATE DATABASE` permissions. Finally, if you want to create new devices, you must be a member of the Admin group.

▲ Calculate how much disk space upsizing will require, by multiplying the size of your Microsoft Access database by two, and make sure you have enough free. This will ensure that Upsizing Wizard has enough space to upsize your database and leave it some room to grow as well. If you expect a lot of data to be added to the database, you should allow more space.

▲ If your server has more than one physical hard disk, you may want to place your database on one disk, and the log for the database on a different disk. In the event of a disk failure, the likelihood of recovering will be much greater.

Upsizing the Sample 'Contacts' Database

In the previous chapter we used the Contacts database as a data source, but this was in Access. Consider the prospect of developing your ASP pages using Access as a development test, and then having to migrate to SQL Server. Fortunately this can be achieved in a simple step.

Upsizing Wizard allows us to create a new SQL Server database or if we have previously upsized our Access database (or just want to add Microsoft Access tables to an existing SQL Server database) we can upsize to an existing database. Typically, we will have created a database beforehand, as opposed to having the wizard create it. By creating the database up front, we are assured that it is created with the attributes and permissions required.

The next step is to install and select **Upsize to SQL-Server** from the Access **Tools | Add Ins** menu. Note that you must install the Wizard and restart Access before this becomes available.

Here we will be using a database that has already been created. Clicking Next brings up a **Data Source** dialog requesting the name of the data source to upsize to. This list reflects the ODBC data sources defined on our system–in our case we select a **Data Source Name (DSN)** which we previously defined using the **ODBC Administrator** for the SQL Server we are upsizing to. If we hadn't already created the DSN, we can define it at this point.

Using the DSN we selected, the wizard will attempt to connect to the SQL Server specified. Once connected, it presents a list of the tables stored in the Access database. We simply select the tables we want to be upsized.

Now things get a bit more interesting. Although Access and SQL Server have many common characteristics, there are several significant differences in the way data is structured, and the indexes maintained. The wizard goes a long way in trying to simplify the conversion from Access to SQL Server, but we need to give it a bit of guidance. First, we need to decide what attributes we want to upsize. The wizard can convert **indexes**, **validation rules**, **Access defaults** and **relationships** to SQL Server.

Indexes

Indexes in SQL Server and Microsoft Access are very similar. If we choose to have the Access indexes upsized, the wizard will convert primary keys to SQL Server clustered, unique indexes named `aaaaa_PrimaryKey`. In an Access database, a primary key does not have a user-assigned name. However, SQL Server requires a name for all objects, including the unique index created to represent the Access primary key.

All other indexes retain their names, except where they contain illegal characters–which are replaced with an underscore. Unique and non-unique Access indexes become unique and non-unique SQL Server indexes. SQL Server doesn't support ascending or descending indexes, and so this attribute is ignored.

Default Attributes and Validation Rules

Default attributes are directly supported by the SQL Server catalog, and as such are ported directly between the two platforms. However, **validation rules** are by necessity treated differently. Validation rules and referential integrity, in Access, are part of the data dictionary and are enforced at the engine level. SQL Server validation rules and referential integrity are not part of the data dictionary, and are enforced through code bound to a table (stored procedures and triggers). This can lead to difficulties if a validation rule cannot be implemented as a stored procedure. The wizard is very good at making this conversion, but it is always a good idea to check the procedures generated for accuracy.

*A **data dictionary** is a repository of information concerning the structures in the database.*

Relationships

When we create a **relationship** between two Access tables, a new index on the foreign key in the relationship is created automatically. These system-generated indexes do not appear in the Access index editor. Access names these relationship-indexes Reference and, if the index name is not unique within a database, adds a suffix. Because an index named Reference could also be created by a user, Upsizing Wizard exports all indexes, and does not distinguish between system-generated and user-created ones. System-generated relationship indexes improve performance when tables are joined. However, if we end up with two identical indexes, one user-created and the other system-generated, we can drop one of them.

Relationships can also be enforced in SQL Server 6.5 through **Declarative Referential Integrity** (DRI) as opposed to triggers. Upsizing Wizard for Access 97 allows us to enforce the relationships defined in our Access tables using DRI in SQL Server. DRI can be easier to administer, better performing, and more flexible then referential integrity enforced through triggers. If you are upsizing to SQL Server 6.5 you should select this option. You should only clear this option when backward compatibility is required or if there is something that cannot be done with DRI.

> For more information on SQL Server 6.5 and DRI see Professional SQL Server 6.5 Admin (ISBN 1-874416-49-4), published by Wrox Press.

Timestamp Fields

By default, Upsizing Wizard creates additional new columns, with the **timestamp** datatype, in SQL Server tables generated from Access tables that contain floating-point (single or double), memo or OLE fields. A **timestamp** field contains a unique value, generated by SQL Server, which is updated whenever that record is updated. Access uses the value in **timestamp** fields to see if a record has been changed before updating it.

Allowing Upsizing Wizard to create **timestamp** columns is most often used when Access Tables will be attached to the corresponding SQL Server. In this instance, Access will use these **timestamp** columns to determine if data in a table has changed, without having to scan the whole table. Upsizing Wizard can also attach the upsized tables to an Access database. This can be of value in a system where Access databases will provide local storage. In our case, this would not be practical.

When we reach the final screen of the Upsizing Wizard, it offers to create an Upsizing Report. This documents the objects that the wizard has created in SQL Server. It includes information about any databases that were created, as well as a complete explanation of how each Access object that was upsized maps to a SQL Server object. After upsizing is complete, we can view this report on screen, or print it for future reference.

Differences between Access and SQL Server

As we mentioned earlier, Access and SQL Server are not 100% compatible. These differences, as well as design decisions made by Upsizing Wizard, mean that much of the Microsoft Access data dictionary cannot be mapped directly to SQL Server constructs. The following table summarizes how objects are mapped from Microsoft Access objects to SQL Server:

Microsoft Access object	SQL Server object
Database	Database
Table	Table
Indexes	Indexes
Field	Field
Default	Default
Table validation rule	Update and Insert triggers
Field validation rule	Update and Insert triggers
Field Required property	Update and Insert triggers
Relations	Update, Insert and Delete triggers

Database and Table Objects

An Access **mdb** file maps directly to a SQL Server database. A Microsoft Access table, excluding much of its data dictionary, maps to a SQL Server table. Access maintains this information as a part of the **mdb** database. Upsizing Wizard replaces illegal characters with the _ symbol. Any names that are SQL Server keywords, for example **FROM** and **GROUP**, have the _ symbol appended to them, resulting in the names **FROM_** and **GROUP_**.

However, this does not always avoid problems, as some keywords do not get converted correctly. A Field Name of **when**, for example, does not have the _ symbol appended, which causes the Upsizing Wizard to fail. Therefore it's always a good idea to check your field names first before upsizing.

Also, we need to keep in mind that the data types supported by SQL Server differ from those supported by Access. Upsizing Wizard will convert our Access data types to the nearest matching SQL Server types. The conversions are made as follows:

Access Data Type	SQL Server Data Type
Yes/No	Bit
Number (Byte)	Smallint
Number (Integer)	Smallint
Number (Long Integer)	Int
Number (Single)	Real
Number (Double)	Float
Currency	Money
Date/Time	Datetime
Counter	Int
Text(n)	varchar(n)
Memo	Text
OLE Object	Image

The Upsizing Report indicates whether the Upsizing Wizard was successful in converting all the field names and creating the new tables.

Using the SQL Server Browser

The second of the Upsizing Wizard's two tools is the **SQL Server Browser**. It's essentially a database container integrated into the Access development environment. It allows us to view, edit and modify SQL Server objects, including **Tables**, **Views**, **Rules**, **Defaults** and **Stored Procedures**. This allows the developer to take advantage of their understanding of Access when developing against a back-end database.

Just like Upsizing Wizard, the SQL Browser requires an ODBC definition to create the connection to SQL Server. It provides an "Access-like" view of SQL Server:

A developer familiar with Access should have no difficulty interacting with the SQL Server database using this utility. By using Upsizing Wizard and the SQL Server Browser, moving from an Access data source to a SQL Server data source can be relatively painless.

Database MAP Example

With our database now in SQL Server, let's take a look at some techniques we can use to access it. In this example we'll use many of the techniques we've already discussed to pull catalog data from our new data source. So far, we have seen how to get data from a data source using various objects. In this example we'll take a look at retrieving information concerning the data source itself.

The **MAP** Example is designed to present us with a listing of all the tables it finds in a SQL Server database we specify. We then have the option of selecting a table, and seeing its structure. The source code for this example is available for download with the other samples, from our Web site at:
http://rapid.wrox.com/books/1266/.

> *If you wish to use these on your own web site, then you can just copy them into a directory and set this directory as a virtual root. There is a default html page giving you a simple menu of examples.*

The Login Page

To start things off, we are presented with a screen where we enter the information that will connect us to our SQL Server. This is **SQLServerMAP.htm** (the first option on the default page), and is created with a single form containing normal HTML **TEXT** controls and a **SUBMIT** button:

The Database Mapper

Server name: Tigger
Database Name: Contact
Login: sa
Password:

Login

The Server name, along with a Database Name, Login ID and Password, are used to locate and attach to a SQL Server database. A straightforward HTML page produces this screen. When we click the Login button an ASP page **List.asp** is executed, which will actually attempt the connection.

The Table List Page

To start things off, we define a number of variables that will be used throughout this page:

```
Dim oServer
Dim sServerName
Dim sUid
Dim sDatabase
Dim sPassword
```

Of interest, as you will soon see, is the **oServer** variable. It will be used to hold a reference to the SQL Server OLE Object–in this first part of our sample, we have to take a step beyond ADO. Why? Well, we want catalog information concerning what structures are actually maintained by the SQL Server, and typically this information would be gathered from the ODBC provider.

However, at the time of writing this, the ODBC/ADO provider supplied for SQL Server does not include catalog level functionality. As such, we need to find an alternative method. The alternative is to create a reference to the SQL Server OLE Object directly. SQL Server 6.5 client utilities provide a number of OLE Objects that can be used to access SQL Server services. These OLE objects take advantage of the underlying SQL Server network libraries in order to communicate with the server.

First off, we use the same **CreateObject** method to create an instance of the SQL Server Object, **sqlole.sqlserver**, within ADO:

```
Set oServer = Server.CreateObject("sqlole.sqlserver")
```

With this reference created, we now have an access mechanism we can use to talk to a SQL Server. Before we can establish a connection, we will need the information supplied by the user on the main page. To do this we use:

```
sServerName = Trim(Request.Form("ServerName"))
sDatabase   = Trim(Request.Form("DatabaseName"))
sUid        = Trim(Request.Form("Login"))
sPassword   = Trim(Request.Form("Password"))
```

Then, with this information, we call the OLE Object's **Connect** method to establish a link to the server specified by the user:

```
OServer.Connect sServerName,sUid,sPassword
```

An important point to note here is that, because we are accessing the SQL Server via its OLE Object libraries, we are bypassing ODBC completely. Any previous ODBC definitions have no impact on this connection.

With a connection established, we are ready to retrieve the catalog data needed. In this case, we want a list of all the tables that exist for the selected database. This can be done using the catalog functions that are provided via the SQL OLE interface. First we display a confirmation of the login details, then retrieve the information we want by querying the **Database** object's **Tables** object. The name of each table found is used to populate a drop down list box:

```
<SELECT NAME="TableNames" SIZE="1">
<% Set oSQLdb = oServer.Databases(sDatabase)
   For Each oSQLTable In oSQLdb.Tables
      Response.Write "<option value=""" & oSQLTable.Name & """ > " _
                     & oSQLTable.Name & "</option>"
   Next %>
</SELECT>
```

And here's the result:

Please Select A Table Name from the List Below:

Given the following data, I will display a map of the Table you select.

Server Name	Database Name	Login ID	Password
Tigger	Contact	sa	

Table Name

[Contact ▼]

[Submit]

Now we can select a table on which to gather additional information, and click the Submit button to bring up our final ASP page **Map.asp**. This will display all of the fields in the selected table, along with their type, size, precision etc.

To do this, ADO does provide the functionality we need. To begin, we create a read-only, forward-scrolling **Recordset**:

```
Set oRS = Server.CreateObject("ADODB.recordset")
oRS.Open "SELECT * FROM " & sDatabase & ".dbo." _
         & Request.Form("TableNames"), "Driver={SQL Server};Server=" _
         & sServerName & ";uid=" & sUid & ";pwd=" & sPassword _
         & ";Database=" & sDatabase & ";DSN=;"
```

Note that in this instance, the use of a forward-scrolling **Recordset** is very important. If you remember earlier, we indicated that the default **CacheSize** setting for this type of cursor is one. As such, even though we are doing a **SELECT** * SQL command, only a single record will actually be retrieved. You may also notice that this recordset is created without using a DSN. This is because we do not know what the connection will be defined as until the user of the application provides us with a server name. We define the connection 'on the fly'.

With a cursor in place, we are ready to retrieve information about the fields in our table:

```
iRow = RS.Fields.Count
For iCount = 0 to (iRow - 1)
   Set Fld = RS.Fields(iCount)
   response.write "<TR>"
   response.write "<TD> " & Fld.Name & "</TD>"
   response.write "<TD> " & Fld.Type & "</TD>"
   response.write "<TD> " & Fld.ActualSize & "</TD>"
   If Int(Fld.Precision) >= 255 Then
      response.write "<TD> 0 </TD>"
   Else
      response.write "<TD> " & Int(Fld.Precision) & "</TD>"
   End If
   If Int(Fld.NumericScale) >= 255 Then
      response.write "<TD> 0 </TD>"
   Else
      response.write "<TD> " & Int(Fld.NumericScale) & "</TD>"
   End If
   response.write "</TR>"
Next
```

Here we use the number of **Field** objects in the data source's **Fields** collection to control how many cells are created in the output table. We then populate each cell with data from each **Field** object. The end result is a presentation of each **Field**, along with its attributes:

Here is your Table

Table Name: Contact

Field Name	Type	Length	Precision	Scale
ContactID	3	4	10	0
Name	200	255	0	0
Address	200	255	0	0
Town	200	255	0	0
State	200	255	0	0
ZipCode	200	50	0	0
Phone	200	255	0	0

Database Schemas

A Database Schema is just a description of the database and its contents. Now that you've seen the hard way to do database schemas, the easy way is to use the **CreateSchema** method of the **Connection** object. The above method has been shown because it's useful to know how SQL Server works underneath, and how to use SQL OLE. Let's revisit this MAP Example using the new method.

The Login Page uses **SQLServerSchema.htm** (which you can select from the default page), which differs from the first example only by the script it calls to view the table names. The Tables Page is similar, and the changes are outlined below:

```
Set oConn = Server.CreateObject("ADODB.Connection")
sConn = "DRIVER={SQL Server};"
sConn = sConn & "SERVER=" & sServerName & ";"
sConn = sConn & "DATABASE=" & sDatabase & ";"
sConn = sConn & "UID=" & sUid & ";"
sConn = sConn & "PWD=" & sPassword & ";"
oConn.Open sConn
```

This replaces the creation of the SQL OLE object and the connection to it. Now we are building a dynamic data source from the details the user entered on the Login Page, and opening a normal ADO Connection object.

To fill the combo box with table names we have some different code:

```
Set oRs = oConn.OpenSchema (adSchemaTables)
While Not oRs.EOF
  Response.Write "<option value=""" & _
  oRs("TABLE_NAME") & """ > " & _
  oRs("TABLE_NAME") & "</option>"
  oRs.MoveNext
Wend
```

This time we call the **OpenSchema** method, passing in **adSchemaTables** (defined in **adovbs.inc**) to identify that we want a list of tables returned. This returns a standard recordset which can be iterated through to find the table names.

For the Table Page the code again differs, and instead of using SQL to find the fields, we use another **OpenSchema** option. Firstly a connection is made, as before:

```
Set oConn = Server.CreateObject("ADODB.Connection")
sConn = "DRIVER={SQL Server};"
sConn = sConn & "SERVER=" & sServerName & ";"
sConn = sConn & "DATABASE=" & sDatabase & ";"
sConn = sConn & "UID=" & sUid & ";"
sConn = sConn & "PWD=" & sPassword & ";"
oConn.Open sConn
```

Then we actually return a recordset of the columns:

```
Set oRs = oConn.OpenSchema (adSchemaColumns)
oRs.Filter = "TABLE_NAME = '" & sTable & "'"
```

Notice that we apply a filter to restrict this recordset to just the table requested by the user. The recordset now contains a row for each field in the database, so we can loop through this extracting the ones we need:

```
While Not oRs.EOF
    response.write "<TR>"
    response.write "<TD> " & oRs("COLUMN_NAME") & "</TD>"
    response.write "<TD> " & oRS("DATA_TYPE") & "</TD>"

    select case oRS("DATA_TYPE")
    case sqlBinary, sqlChar, sqlImage, sqlSysname, sqlText, sqlTimestamp,
sqlVarBinary, sqlVarChar
            sLength = oRS("CHARACTER_MAXIMUM_LENGTH")
    case sqolDateTime, sqlSmallDateTime
            sLength = oRS("DATETIME_PRECISION")
    case else
            sLength = 0
    end select

    response.write "<TD> " & sLength & "</TD>"
    sLength = oRS("NUMERIC_PRECISION")
    If sLength >= 255 or IsNull(sLength) Then
        response.write "<TD> 0 </TD>"
    Else
            response.write "<td> " & sLength & "</td>"
    End If
    sLength = oRS("NUMERIC_SCALE")
    If sLength >= 255 or IsNull(sLength) Then
        response.write "<TD> 0 </TD>"
    Else
            response.write "<TD> " & sLength & "</TD>"
    End If
    response.write "</TR>"
    oRs.MoveNext
Wend
```

Now you'll notice some interesting things here. The **DATA_TYPE** returns a number just like the **Fld.Type** from the previous example, but we've added these to an include file (**adosql.inc**) just to make things clearer in the code. The reason is that the schema doesn't return a generic length field, only a length for character or binary type data. The results look like this:

Here is your Table

Table Name: Contact

Field Name	Type	Length	Precision	Scale
ContactID	3	0	10	0
Name	129	255	0	0
Address	129	255	0	0
Town	129	255	0	0
State	129	255	0	0
ZipCode	129	50	0	0
Phone	129	255	0	0

Something even more interesting here is the **Type** column. You'll notice that for some of the fields the type is slightly different than that returned from the previous example. Why? Another one of life's little mysteries! It seems that the **Field** object returns a different number than the **Schema** field type column. You'll just have to make sure you use the correct set of constants if you need to refer to the types.

Some Components, Tips and Methods

Once you come to use ADO regularly, you'll find that there are lots of ways to achieve the same thing, and all kind of things that you can't easily achieve with other dynamic Web page technologies. Here are a few useful tips, which may help to expand your outlook, and make different kinds of task that bit easier. It's a mixed bag of components, add-ins, and methods.

The HTML Table Formatter Component

In our previous example, and in examples you saw in the last chapter, we've come up against the need to display data from a table in our Web pages. This is a regular requirement and is, of course, the main reason that HTML sports the **<TABLE>** tag and the wide range of formatting options it offers.

However, we still have to manually create the **<TR></TR>** and **<TD></TD>** tags to get the layout right. There are tools that help to do this, but a sample component that is now available from Microsoft can do it all automatically. You can get the component from: **http://backoffice.microsoft.com/downtrial/default.asp**. Follow the links to the IIS Samples, Components and Utilities page.

It's written in Java, so you'll also need to install the latest Java Virtual Machine (VM) from Microsoft, as well as the component, and the easiest way to do this is to install Microsoft Internet Explorer 4. Because it's a sample, rather than part of ASP, you need to install it separately, but full instructions are included in the distribution file.

So what can it do? Well, it has four properties, and one method. The best way to learn about it is to see how we use it:

```
' Create a connection, and open it using the System DSN 'MyDatabase'
Set oConn = Server.CreateObject("ADODB.Connection")
oConn.Open "MyDatabase"

' Create a recordset containing the records from the table 'MyTable'
Set oRs = oConn.Execute("MyTable")

' Create an instance of the HTML Table Formatter Component
Set oTblfmt = Server.CreateObject("IISSample.HTMLTable")

' Now set its properties for the borders, caption, style and headings
oTblFmt.Borders = False
oTblFmt.Caption = "Displaying my data"
oTblFmt.CaptionStyle = "ALIGN=CENTER VALIGN=BOTTON"
oTblFmt.HeadingRow = True

' And insert the formatted table into the page
oTblFmt.AutoFormat(oRs)
```

The **AutoFormat** method takes a recordset and formats it into an HTML table for you.

If you are into creating components, you'll find the download worth it just to see how it's done—all the source code is included. And it certainly saves a lot of coding, and keeps the actual size of the page down as well!

Converting from IDC to ASP—IDC2ASP

If you've already got a Web site or corporate Intranet bulging with data that is supplied via the Internet Data Connector (IDC) there is help available. IDC is an interface supplied with IIS that allows quite complex data retrieval from ODBC data sources, for use in a Web page. We discussed it briefly in Chapter 1, and we have no intention of covering it in depth. ASP is not only more powerful and efficient, but is also a lot easier to work with as well.

However, that doesn't help you to convert existing IDC scripts and templates into ASP format. What does help, is the IDC2ASP tool that is available free of charge from Microsoft. Again, this can also be downloaded from **http://backoffice.microsoft.com/downtrial/default.asp**

IDC2ASP.EXE is a command-line utility that will convert IDC files into ASP form automatically. There are a series of command-line switches available that control all kinds of aspects of the conversion, and it leaves the original files intact so that you can test the new ones before committing yourself fully to the new technology.

Alternatively, there is an active server component version of IDC2ASP, which can be instantiated within an ASP page, just like any other component. All that's needed then is to set its properties and call the **Convert** method.

> *IDC2ASP carries the IntraActive name, and is not supported by Microsoft. However its potential usefulness makes it worth a try if you have a lot of IDC files to convert.*

Using Arrays and the GetRows Method

We'll often find ourselves wanting to repetitively scan through a recordset searching for different sets of data. This can easily be achieved using dynamic cursor recordsets or multiple SQL queries, but both are less that ideal in the efficiency stakes. There is a far more efficient method at our disposal. ADO provides us with a method that enables us to easily convert a **Recordset** object into an array—which can then be scanned efficiently using ordinary code. This is the syntax:

variantarray = *recordset*.**GetRows**(*NumberOfRows*)

The **GetRows** method takes a **Recordset** object and converts it into the equivalent multi-dimensioned array. Just as we'd expect, a recordset consisting of three fields and ten records is converted to a 3 x 10 array—think of the first dimension being horizontal and the second vertical, just as a normal table is displayed in Access or SQL Server. The *NumberOfRows* argument is optional, and specifies the number of records to retrieve. This argument is frequently used on ordered recordsets, where the record ordering has been set by a defined table index, or an **ORDER BY** clause in the SQL query.

Using Multiple Recordsets

One other nice method available for the **Recordset** object is **NextRecordset**. So far, we've only talked about a **CommandText** property as containing one SQL query. We can provide multiple SQL queries as long as they are separated by semicolons, in the form **SELECT * FROM Table1; SELECT * FROM Table2;** etc. Normally, when we open a recordset from a query like this, it's only the first set of results that are available. To retrieve the next set of records we just call the **NextRecordset** method. We can also supply the name of a variable that will be set to the number of records affected by the query, though this is optional:

Set *recordset* = *recordset*.**NextRecordset** (*RecordsAffected*)

When we use the **NextRecordset** method, we're provided with a new **Recordset** variable that is one of the following:

- If a row-returning command returns no records, the **Recordset** object referenced by the variable will be empty. We can test for this case by inspecting the **BOF** and **EOF** properties, which will both be **True**.

- If a non row-returning command completes successfully, the **Recordset** referenced by the variable will be closed. We can test for this case by ensuring that the **Recordset** object variable is not equal to **Nothing**. In this case, inspecting the **EOF** property will generate an error.

- When there are no more statements, the **Recordset** variable returned will be set to **Nothing**.

Note that the **NextRecordset** method will continue to return **Recordset** objects as long as there are additional SQL statements in our **CommandText** parameter.

Using multiple recordsets can be quite useful if you know in advance what data you are going to need, and you want to minimize the number of recordsets you create. For example, imagine that you have a table with records that are grouped by a certain item (sales figures and sales region perhaps). If you wished to show this data one region at a time you could do it two ways. Firstly by selecting the whole recordset and then while stepping through the recordset using **If** statements to see if the current region is the same as the previous. Just a little tedious perhaps. Using a recordset for each region obviates the need for this sort of code, as you can treat each region independently and simple move to the next recordset when you want to change region. This does involve slightly more work on the server as it has to perform multiple queries, but you may find this offset by the ease of handling the data later.

ADO and OLE DB in the Real World

In response to the increased capacity of personal computer software tools, and their extended accessibility to external and remote data, businesses have a growing need to provide solutions that span desktop, midrange, mainframe, and Internet technologies. The expanding diversity in structure and complexity of business data creates the need for a universal data access middleware that enables a new class of solutions to be easily built and managed.

ADO can bridge the gap. As we've discussed in these two chapters, ADO is a higher level interface to OLE DB. It provides the programmer with a very usable interface both for client server, Internet and intranet applications–allowing standardized access to almost any data provider. This doesn't just mean Active Server Pages programming. ADO can provide a translation layer for use with other tools and applications as well.

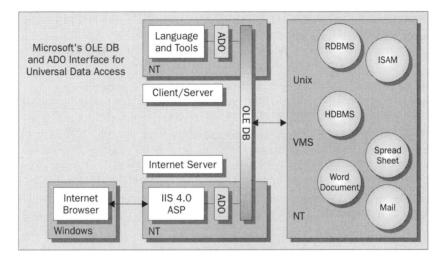

We haven't covered the real core of OLE DB in these two chapters because, as an ASP programmer, you really don't need to know what's happening 'over the fence'.

ADO and SQL Server Security

Security is a growing concern in the Internet/intranet development community. It is a constant trade off between access to services and data, and protection of those services and data. This is really the heart of the security dilemma–if your site is *too* secure it could lose its value. On the other hand, without appropriate security measures, you might find someone corrupting your database for you, or selling your company's secrets to your competitors.

Security issues can be addressed at three different levels–the features offered by the Web server, those offered by the operating system, and those offered by the data source being accessed. In the Microsoft world, the operating system and the Web server are tightly coupled, as are the security features they offer.

Internet Information Server (IIS) supports advanced security facilities, such as a Secure Sockets Layer (SSL) which provides a security scheme for bulk-encrypting data between the server and its clients, when private communication is required. In addition, IIS completely integrates with the object-level and user-level security services provided by Windows NT. This can be used to protect a specific area of your site, such as DSN definition files, to which you don't want people to have access. In Chapter 14, we'll be looking at Web site security in a lot more detail.

However, as powerful as these facilities are, they will generally need to be supplemented with additional security measures that can be used to protect the data accessed by your site. In this section we will take a brief look at SQL Server security, and see what features and capabilities are available in this product. Then we will apply these features to accessing a SQL Server from an ASP page. Finally, we will take a look at a few simple steps you can take to protect your site and its data.

Security and Web Access

IIS has different security modes, and which one you use can have an impact on your data access, so let's have a quick look at them:

- ▲ **Anonymous Authentication**. This isn't really an authentication system, rather what happens when you don't authenticate. When no authentication system is in place all users accessing your web site are logged in as an anonymous or guest user.

- ▲ **Basic Authentication**. With basic authentication IIS will prompt the user for a user name and password before allowing access to your site. This is not a widely used security system since the user details are transmitted in an unencrypted form.

- ▲ **Windows NT Challenge/Response Authentication**. This uses the NT logon information to validate the user, and the user details are never actually transmitted. If the NT user information is not available then Basic Authentication is used. This is a popular security system on Intranets where the client and server are in the same NT domain.

- ▲ **Client Certificate Authentication**. This is an advanced security feature that uses digital certificates to validate users accessing your web site.

We are not going to deal with the above in detail but you need to know the different types so that you can plan you data access security in conjuction with you web access security.

Security and Data Access

The level of security actually required is dependent on the level of access needed by our clients. If our database is servicing a small group of individuals, with information that requires minimal protection, then a very open security framework could be put into place. Essentially, we just need to allow our users to access the data they need, while protecting them from accidentally destroying or damaging it. However, if our database is servicing a public forum, much more stringent controls must be built. Not only do we need to protect the data from accidental damage, we need to verify that those accessing it have the right to do so, as well as protect it against those that do not—or who might intentionally damage it.

SQL Server supports several powerful security features that can be applied to each of these scenarios. SQL Server security options determine a server's login security mode, what auditing is done, and what objects, resources and data a user has access to. In the next section, we will take a high-level look at some of the security features offered by SQL Server.

SQL Server Security Modes

SQL Server 6.5 offers three login security modes. The mode we choose will significantly effect how the server handles security. Let's take a look at each of the options available, and how these options affect our environment:

- ▲ **Standard Security Mode**: This is the default security mode. In standard mode, SQL Server manages its own login validation process for all connections (except client applications that explicitly request integrated security over trusted connections).

▲ **Windows NT Integrated Security Mode:** This mode uses Windows NT authentication mechanisms for all connections. Only trusted connections are allowed into SQL Server. SQL Server always ignores the login name and SQL Server password submitted in the login request from an Open Database Connectivity (ODBC) client application. Network users, who were assigned user-level privileges to SQL Server, log in using their network username or the default login ID (if their network username is not found in `syslogins`).

▲ **Mixed Security Mode**: This mode allows both trusted and non-trusted connections, and is a combination of integrated and standard modes. For trusted connections, SQL Server examines the requested login name as specified by the client ODBC application. If this login name matches the user's network username, or if the login name is null or spaces, SQL Server first tries the Windows NT integrated login rules as described above. If this fails, SQL Server uses the standard rules. If the requested login name is any other value, the user must supply the correct SQL Server password, and SQL Server handles the login using the standard rules described above. All login requests from non-trusted connections, such as people not logged onto the network, are handled using the standard rules.

Integrated and mixed security modes are best utilized in an intranet environment. In this environment, user IDs and privileges are defined in the Windows NT domain, and subject to domain security. The user ID can be retrieved from the client system directly, and authenticated against the domain master list. Here, the user is never required to provide authentication information.

In the big wide world of the Internet, a domain-based authentication model would not be realistic. Here, security must be tightly controlled and access provided only as is necessary.

User Groups

Creating a Login is just the first level of security associated with SQL Server. A Login ID does not permit the user to access any of the objects in a database. Access to a database and the objects within it are granted to individual users or groups of users.

SQL Server security is based on a detailed hierarchy of **groups**, which include **users**. Both groups and users are defined as having specific access to, and control over, services and data. In SQL Server, permissions for services and data can be controlled at a very granular level. For example, access to an individual object can be controlled, and then the actions that are possible on that object can also be regulated.

A group is simply a means of organizing the users of a database. Permissions are assigned to the group, as opposed to individual users. Users in the group have access to any resources available to the group as a whole. This simplifies the administration of users and objects in an SQL Server environment.

There is a built-in group, public, in every database. Each user automatically belongs to public and can be added to only one other group. A user cannot be removed from the public group. If a group is deleted (or 'dropped'), all users in that group are automatically removed from the group, although you can't drop the public group. However, dropping a group does not drop its users. Users who were members of the dropped group are still valid users in the database and members of the public group.

Database and Object Owners

SQL Server is organized around databases. Each one contains **objects**, such as tables, stored procedures, rules etc. Each object has an **owner**, who has full authority over that object. SQL Server recognizes two types of owner–the database owner (DBO) and database object owner.

The **database owner** is the creator of a database, and has full privileges over it. However, beyond simply having the ability to manipulate the object itself, the DBO has the option of granting access to the database to other users or groups. In summary, the DBO can:

- Allow users access to the database.
- Grant users permission to create objects and execute commands within the database.
- Set up groups.
- Assign users to groups and add guest accounts, which give users limited access to a database.

Just like any other user, the database owner logs into SQL Server by using an assigned login ID and password. In their own database, the user is recognized as DBO; in databases which they haven't created, the user is just known by their database username.

As we said earlier, a database contains objects. The user who creates a database object is the **database object owner** for that object. In order for a user to create an object within a database, the database owner must first grant that user permission to create that particular type of object. Just as the database owner can grant permissions for their database to other users, the object owner can grant permissions for their object.

Database object owners have no special login IDs or passwords. The creator of an object is automatically granted all permissions to it. An object owner must explicitly grant permissions to other users before they can access the object. Even the database owner cannot use an object unless the object owner has granted the appropriate permission. The distinction between the database owner and the owner of a database object is quite a subtle one, although in most cases they will be the same user. The database owner is the owner of the whole database (usually the administrator) and will grant permissions to other users. One of these permissions can allow users to create their own objects (temporary tables, user queries, etc), and in this case the owner of the object will be the person who created it.

As you can see, database and database object privileges are assigned at a very detailed level. Let's take a look at what privileges (referred to as **permissions**) can be granted to users and groups.

Security Permissions

SQL Server has two categories of permissions: object and statement. Some statement permissions (for the **SELECT**, **UPDATE**, **INSERT**, **DELETE** and **EXECUTE** statements) are handled as object permissions because these statements always apply to database objects that are in the current database.

Object permissions regulate the use of certain statements on certain database objects. They are granted and revoked by the owner of the object. Object permissions apply to the following statements and objects:

Statement	Object
`SELECT`	Table, view, columns
`UPDATE`	Table, view, columns
`INSERT`	Table, view
`DELETE`	Table, view
`REFERENCE`	Table
`EXECUTE`	Stored procedure

Statement permissions are not object-specific. They can be granted only by the system administrator (often referred to as the **sa**) or the database owner. Statement permissions allow the user to create new objects within a database. The following are examples of these statements:

▲ **CREATE DATABASE** (can be granted only by **sa**, and only to users in the master database)

▲ **CREATE DEFAULT**

▲ **CREATE PROCEDURE**

▲ **CREATE RULE**

▲ **CREATE TABLE**

▲ **CREATE VIEW**

Each database has its own independent permissions system. In other words, being granted permission to perform a given task in one database has no effect in other databases.

Now that we have had a chance to take a brief look at SQL Server Security, let's look at a few tips that will help us design our next database.

Security and ODBC

ODBC has the ability to provide user information on each data source, which can be either NT authentication or SQL Server authentication. The former uses the network login ID to automatically connect to the data source, ignoring any user id and password passed in to the connection. The latter requires a user id and password for each connection to the data source.

IIS and SQL Security

Now that you've seen the different aspects of SQL Server security you have to consider how best to use it in conjunction with your web server. There are several points to consider depending upon which mode you are using:

SQL Server Location

If your SQL Server is on a different physical server from IIS and you are using named pipes, then you might receive connection failures, as IIS attempts to connect to the SQL Server anonymously. The anonymous user is defined on the Directory Security tab of the Web Server options, and is usually `IUSR_MachineName`, where *MachineName* is the name of the NT server.

To enable this form of connection you can do three things:

- ▲ Create a local user account on the SQL Server machine that corresponds to the user details from the anonymous user details.
- ▲ Make the anonymous user a member of the SQL Server domain.
- ▲ Map the IIS anonymous user account to a SQL Server Guest account.

ODBC Server Name

If using NT Integrated Security with SQL Server and Integrated security on the ODBC data source you have to beware of what you enter for the Server Name in the ODBC data source. If using IIS on the same server as SQL Server then you should use the Local Server (it often shows up as (local) in the Server list). If you enter the server name then IIS makes a network connection to SQL Server (despite the fact that it's on the same machine) and does not pass over the user details, passing a blank username and password instead. This often results in the following error:

Microsoft OLE DB Provider for ODBC Drivers error '80004005'
[Microsoft][ODBC SQL Server Driver][SQL Server]Login Failed- User: _ Reason: Not defined as a valid user of a trusted SQL Server connection

Notice that there appears to be no user name, and looking at SQL Trace output for this attempted connection confirms this. Setting the server to **(local)** however cures this problem. This error is also seen when trying to connect to a remote SQL Server using Integrated security.

Security Tips

When designing a database in the SQL Server environment, which will be accessed by public sources, here are a few guidelines to keep in mind:

- ▲ Take advantage of the Guest default login. The Guest login is a special login defined by default in SQL Server. Guest has no rights to any object in the server aside from the ability to login. The Guest login can be granted **read** access to the specific views, tables, or objects needed for your Web site. The Web site can then use this account when attaching to SQL Server objects, minimizing your site's exposure.

- ▲ Use stored procedures where possible for updates and insertions. Coding static SQL in your ASP page is perhaps the most straightforward way to provide dynamic data content. However, keep in mind that not only can your Web site see this code, but so might a really clever hacker. To minimize this exposure it is often better to call a stored procedure, which in turn performs the required updates or inserts. A stored procedure can be granted permissions to access and modify objects and data that the ID calling the stored procedure cannot. This provides a shield between your site and the actual data being changed.

- ▲ When tables are scanned for data, views can serve as security mechanisms. Through a view, users can query only the data provided by the view. The rest of the database is neither visible nor accessible. Permission to access the subset of data in a view must be granted or revoked, regardless of the set of permissions in force on the view's underlying tables. Data in an underlying table that is not included in the view is hidden from users who are authorized to access the view but not the underlying table.

Don't expose more then you have to. In most cases, you will want to retain the majority of your data behind the 'firewall', and supply a mechanism to access this data. Always keep in mind that any security can be compromised and, as such, preventative measures must be in place which assume that this will occur. One recommendation is to store only high-volume transactional data on the SQL Server that is directly accessed from a Web site. Supportive information can be maintained on a separate secured system, and retrieved as needed using Remote Stored Procedures, or other similar technologies. For more information on this you should consult the SQL Server documentation.

Summary

In this chapter we have had the opportunity to review a wide variety of techniques and technologies that we can bring to bear when developing Active Server Web sites. ASP is a very powerful tool. Its ability to access data via ADO only scratches the surface of the many features that are made available by this exiting new product. The issues that we have addressed here provide you with a good introduction into the many features and capabilities of ASP and ADO.

The main points of this chapter are:

 Connecting to a data source: In this section we examined the hows and whys of connecting to a data source, and then went beyond the basics to take a look at the flexibility built into the **Connection** object.

 With an understanding of the **Connection** object under our belts, we dug into the workings of ADO, looking at expanding the **Recordset** object and accessing binary data.

 With the fundamentals behind us, we took a look at moving our Access database into the SQL Server environment using the upsizing tools available for Access.

 With a lot of information behind us, we took a look at a 'real' example of how to make some of this stuff to work for us. The MAP example goes outside ADO, and walks through pulling more then just data from the database.

 In the end, we had to consider the nature of things on the wild and woolly Internet. A brief introduction to SQL Server security provided some insight as to how we can protect our data.

In the next chapter we are going to consider the what tools you can use for managing your data on SQL Server, and how you go about using components on your pages.

Managing Enterprise Data

CHAPTER 9

In the previous chapters we discussed ADO and its use for accessing data from databases. We also looked at upsizing Access databases to SQL Server to give greater performance and scalability. What we need to consider now are the facilities we have available as web developers to manage this newly scaled data.

The first half of this chapter will be based around Visual InterDev, and how a web developer can use it to smooth development. Visual InterDev is part of the Microsoft Visual Studio, which is gradually becoming the cornerstone of all of their development products. The aim is to have a central studio in which you can develop with a range of products. As you start to use more tools, these can be included in the studio enabling you to work in a familiar environment, thus you can have your web editor, database manager, and reference tools all to hand, without having to launch separate applications.

In the latter portion of the chapter we will concentrate on some issues of scalability–how to ensure that your web database can cope with a large number of users.

In this chapter we are going to look at

- How to use Visual InterDev as a database development tool.
- How to use Visual InterDev with design time controls.
- Enterprise Scalability.

Visual InterDev and SQL Server

Although SQL Server comes with an excellent management tool, that's exactly what it is–a management tool. It's not really designed for quick viewing of data or for interacting with other design tools. Visual InterDev, on the other hand, adds functionality that makes it a great client development tool.

Creating a new database project

To work with SQL Server from Visual InterDev you need to create a new Database Project from the File/New dialog:

The example shows the project will be called **pubs**—the sample database that is installed with SQL Server. In this case it's called the same as the database, but it doesn't have to be the same name. You are then asked to select an ODBC data source or create a new one, and log into the database. Appendix G shows you how to create an ODBC data source. The workspace is then broken down into three panes; File View which shows the files available in your workspace, Data View which shows the data available in the file you have selected, and Info View which shows the reference material. Since we are looking at SQL Server, we'll concentrate on the Data View.

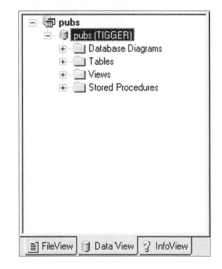

You might think that this looks very similar to the Enterprise Manager as installed with SQL Server, and you'd be right, but the Data View differs in some very important areas. First of all, there are no database devices, backup devices, databases or users. Remember this is viewed through an ODBC data source, so you are looking at a single database only–you cannot create or delete databases, add users, or set permissions (except through executing SQL commands). In fact, the facilities you have are like a cross between Enterprise Manager and the Access Query grid.

Viewing Data

You can expand the outline view to show the tables and the column names, and unlike Enterprise Manager you can also view the data easily without resorting to SQL statements. Just double-click on a table and a data grid appears.

Not only does this give you quick access to the data, but you also have full edit ability. You'll notice that the toolbar looks similar to Microsoft Access, and you have very similar facilities.

Toolbar Icon	Description
	Show Diagram Pane. Shows the tables and joins.
	Show Grid Pane. Shows a grid of the columns sort order and selection criteria.
	Show SQL Pane. Shows the SQL string for the query.
	Show Results Pane. Shows the result pane, where the query output is seen.
	Create Select Query. This query will be a select query, just selecting data.

Toolbar Icon	Description
	Create Insert Query. Allows the query to append data to a table.
	Create Update Query. Allows the query to update existing data.
	Create Delete Query. Allows the query to delete rows from a table.
	Verify SQL Syntax. Validates the SQL string without running the query.
	Run. Execute the query.
	Remove Filter. Removes any filters applied to the query.
	Sort Ascending. Sort the data in ascending order.
	Sort Descending. Sort the data in descending order.
	Properties. Show the properties for the query.

Show Diagram Pane gives you a table diagram where you can see the table and select the columns you wish to appear. You can even drag tables from the workspace window to create multi-table queries:

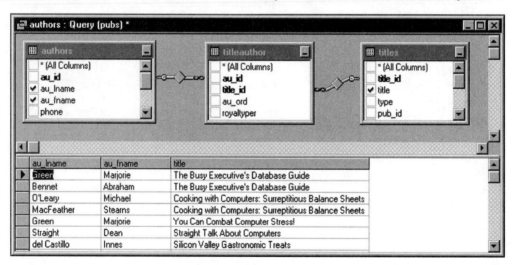

Holding the cursor over the table joins tells you the join type and a right mouse click gives you the option to edit the join type.

Show Grid Pane gives you a criteria grid, for filtering and sorting the results:

Column	Alias	Table	Output	Sort Type	Sort Order	Criteria	Or...
au_lname		authors	☑	Ascending	1		
au_fname		authors	☑			LIKE 'M%'	
title		titles	☑				

au_lname	au_fname	title
DeFrance	Michel	The Gourmet Microwave
Green	Marjorie	The Busy Executive's Database Guide
Green	Marjorie	You Can Combat Computer Stress!
O'Leary	Michael	Cooking with Computers: Surreptitious Balance Sheets
O'Leary	Michael	Sushi, Anyone?

All of the above also applies to views, and these act in the same way as a table.

Once you've created your query you can save the details as a local query definition, allowing you to call up the query at a later date.

Database Diagrams

Something that has never been possible in Enterprise Manager is the ability to view database diagrams (or Entity-Relationship diagrams as they are often called). Many developers have used Access as a front-end tool for SQL Server, by linking their tables into Access and using the Relationships diagram. With the introduction of Visual InterDev you can now do this directly with SQL Server tables.

To create a new diagram you right-mouse click on the Database Diagrams item (in the Data View) and select New Diagram. This gives you a blank canvas upon which you can drop your tables. You can drag them directly from the Data View Workspace, and the table relationships are added automatically.

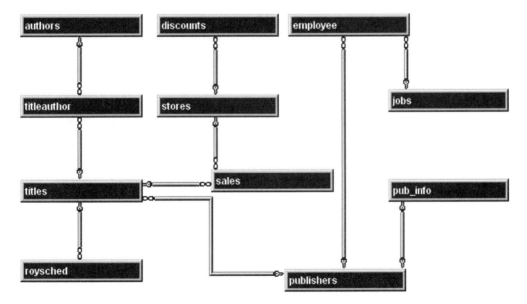

The diagram above shows just the table names, but another mouse click allows you to select whether to show column names, the key columns, or full column properties. Since you can have more than one diagram you can create ones like the one above for an overview, and others with more detail.

Creating Relationships

If you need to create new relationships between your tables you can drag columns from one table to another to create the join:

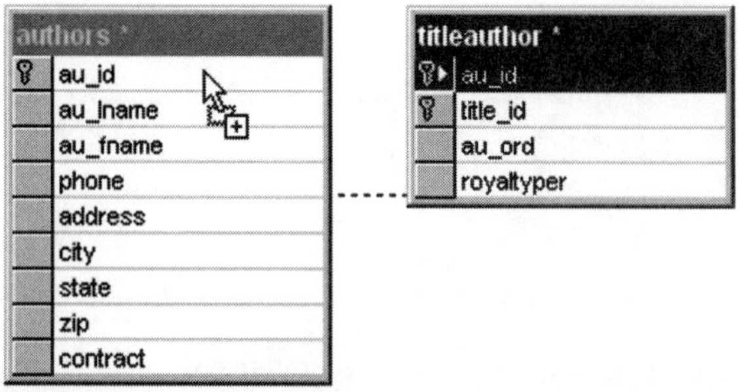

In fact you can drag any field since the Create Relationship dialog gives you the opportunity to change which fields are included in the table relationships. This dialog is automatically shown when you drag one field onto another to create the relationship:

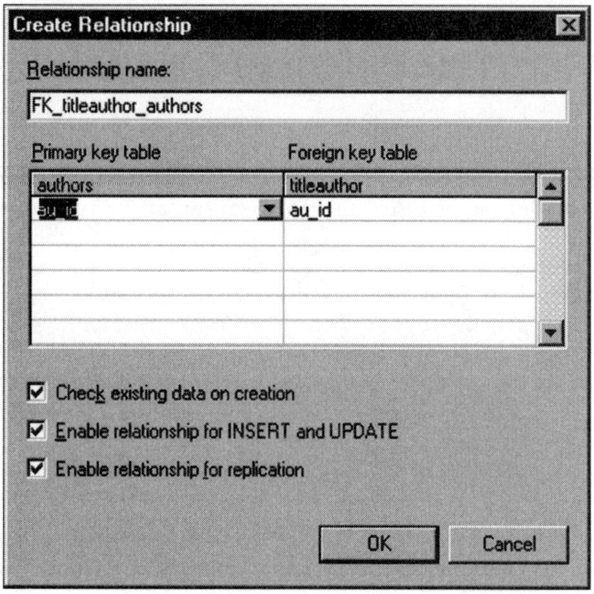

Managing Tables

It's all very well having a great query grid and nice pictures, but what about actually managing the database. As with other options, a right-mouse click on a table gives you the option to create a new one or edit an existing one. There is no difference between the two modes.

authors										
Column Name	Datatype	Length	Precision	Scale	Allow Nulls	Default Value	Identity	Identity Seed	Identity Increment	
au_id	id (varchar)	11	0	0						
au_lname	varchar	40	0	0						
au_fname	varchar	20	0	0						
phone	char	12	0	0		('UNKNOWN')				
address	varchar	40	0	0	✓					
city	varchar	20	0	0	✓					
state	char	2	0	0	✓					
zip	char	5	0	0	✓					
contract	bit	1	0	0						

This is in fact more flexible than Enterprise Manager for table alteration, as you can modify both the column name and the data type. Enterprise Manager doesn't allow you to change the data type of an existing column, or add columns that can't contain null data. Another right mouse click gives you the option to edit the table properties, such as constraints, relationships, indexes and keys.

Saving Changes

One thing that is really good about Visual InterDev is that you can defer your database changes to a later time by creating a script. The Table toolbar appears when you are designing tables, and has a Save Change Script button which allows you to save the changes to a SQL script file, which can then be run at a later time. This is particularly useful for when you need to modify the database but not implement the changes, and then later run all of your changes in at once. This scripting method is, in fact, very thorough as it creates temporary tables and copies data for you if necessary, allowing you to do database changes that would normally take several stages.

For example, without Visual InterDev, changing the data type of a column in the authors table means you would have to create a new table and copy the data into it. Now you can do the change and save the script for later:

Save Change Script

Do you want to save this change script to a text file?

```
BEGIN TRANSACTION
SET QUOTED_IDENTIFIER ON
GO
SET TRANSACTION ISOLATION LEVEL SERIALIZABLE
GO
COMMIT
BEGIN TRANSACTION
ALTER TABLE dbo.authors
        DROP CONSTRAINT DF__authors__phone__03D09CBB
GO
CREATE TABLE dbo.Tmp_authors_1
        (
        au_id id NOT NULL,
```

Yes   No

If you scroll through this window you notice that a large amount of work is being done. A new temporary table is created, the data copied from the old table, the old table dropped and the new one renamed. All of the constraints and permissions are also restored to the new table.

Managing Stored Procedures

Stored procedures are a great way to not only increase the readability and structure of your code, but also increase the performance at the same time. A stored procedure allows you to compile together some SQL statements under a single name, and they can all be run together just by calling the procedure name.

You can create a stored procedure by right mouse clicking on the Stored Procedures item in the Workspace Data View and selecting New Stored Procedure. This gives you the stored procedure window:

```
Untitled : Stored Procedure (pubs)

Create Procedure /*Procedure_Name*/
As
       return (0)
```

This is where the cleverness of Visual InterDev wears off as you have to type in the SQL yourself. You simply replace /*Procedure_Name*/ with the name you wish to give the procedure and add the SQL after the As statement. If you are unsure of, or just learning, SQL, then you can create the query you want by opening the table, modifying the criteria, and viewing the SQL. You can then copy it from the SQL window and paste it into the stored procedure window. Saving the stored procedure automatically compiles it ready for running, which you can do by clicking the right mouse button and selecting Run. The results are shown in the results pane.

Parameters

If the stored procedure has parameters then you can see these in the Data View:

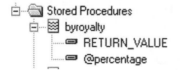

When you run this procedure you are prompted for the values:

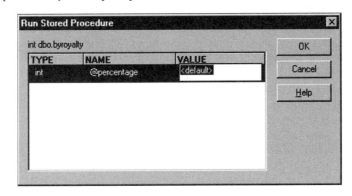

and the results pane shows the value of the parameter as well as the results and return value:

```
Running Stored Procedure dbo.byroyalty ( @percentage = 25 ).
au_id
-----------
724-80-9391
899-46-2035
(2 row(s) affected)
Finished running dbo.byroyalty.
RETURN_VALUE = 0
```

Managing Views

Views are a bit of an exception in Visual InterDev because you can't create them automatically, and this seems an odd omission since it could be handled in a similar way as stored procedures. You can, however, create views by using SQL directly, by creating a local query and typing in the required commands and pressing the run button on the query toolbar. One of the easiest ways to create a local query for temporary use is to double click any one of the tables as though you were just opening it to look at the data. Then press the SQL button and type in your own SQL. When you have run the query you can close the window and say No when asked if you want to save the changes:

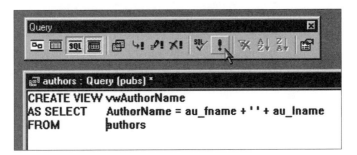

The view will then appear under the Views and can be used as though it were a table.

Managing Triggers

Triggers are managed better than views, but not in an obvious way, as they don't appear to have a place of their own. However, once you realize that triggers are bound to tables it becomes clear where triggers are situated. Select a table and a right-mouse click gives you New Trigger option. As with stored procedures you have to type in the SQL yourself:

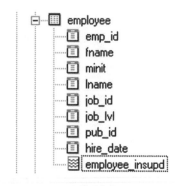

Once created, triggers appear as an item under the table to which they belong. The one shown here is one that already exists in the database:

Design Time Controls

The design time controls are a set of ActiveX controls giving you greater freedom in the Visual InterDev environment, and making database development easier. They are available when you are in File View, editing an HTML or ASP file.

Any of these controls can be inserted like normal ActiveX controls from within Visual InterDev, by selecting the Design Time tab from the Insert ActiveX Control dialog and picking your required control. This can be shown by right-mouse clicking when editing the HTML page, and then selecting Insert ActiveX Control from the menu.

Include Control

The simplest, and perhaps most superfluous, of these controls is the Include control, designed to make the addition of server side includes easier. Although it is primarily intended for inclusion of layout files (**.alx**) it can be used to include any file in an HTML document. Adding this control gives the following:

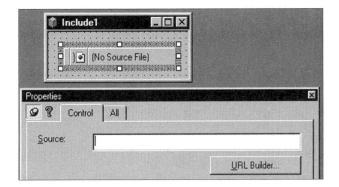

Notice that even though this is just a design time control it still has a real visible control, although you can't do anything with it. Its only purpose is to provide an interface for the properties. You now have the opportunity to type in the path of the include file, or you can select the URL Builder:

The left window gives a view of all of the web projects within the current workspace, and the right shows the files within the selected project. The URL Type allows you to specify where the included file will actually reside on the web server:

- ▲ Doc Relative. The included file is relative to the referring file, for example, **layout.alx**.

- ▲ Absolute. A fully qualified URL, for example, **http://piglet/pubs/layout.alx**.

- ▲ Root Relative. The included file is relative to the web server root directory, for example, **/ pubs/layout.alx**.

You can also specify Extra Info, such as a bookmark, which will be appended to the URL. When the properties sheet and control are closed, the include details are added to your file:

```
PubsInclude.htm *

<!--METADATA TYPE="DesignerControl" startspan
    <OBJECT ID="Include1" WIDTH=151 HEIGHT=24
        CLASSID="CLSID:F602E725-A281-11CF-A5B7-0080C73AAC7E">
            <PARAM NAME="_Version" VALUE="65536">
            <PARAM NAME="_ExtentX" VALUE="3986">
            <PARAM NAME="_ExtentY" VALUE="635">
            <PARAM NAME="_StockProps" VALUE="0">
            <PARAM NAME="Source" VALUE="layout.alx">
    </OBJECT>
-->
<!--#INCLUDE FILE="layout.alx"-->
<!--METADATA TYPE="DesignerControl" endspan-->

</BODY>
</HTML>
```

While not providing a great deal of added benefit, this does mean that you can graphically find your include files, and the path will be created for you.

Data Connections

Data connections allow the three data controls shown above to bind to an ODBC data source, and the project must have a Data Connection before any of them can be used. To use the data controls you first need to open or create a Web Project, by selecting **Web Project Wizard** from the **Projects** tab of the File/New dialog. You can then enter the project name and the web server name to which the project will connect, and this will either connect to an existing web directory or create a new one for you.

Once you have created a web project you can add a data connection by right-mouse clicking on the project name or the global.asa file and selecting **Add Data Connection**.

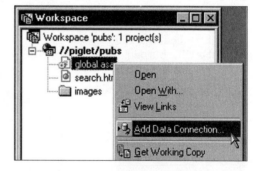

You can then pick your ODBC data source from the standard ODBC dialog, and the connection is added to the project.

This has the effect of adding the following lines to your global.asa file.

```
</SCRIPT>
<SCRIPT LANGUAGE=VBScript RUNAT=Server>
Sub Session_OnStart
    '==Visual InterDev Generated - DataConnection startspan==
    '--Project Data Connection
            Session("pubs_ConnectionString") =
"DSN=pubs;SERVER=(local);UID=IUSR_PIGLET;APP=Microsoft (R) Developer
Studio;WSID=PIGLET;DATABASE=pubs;Trusted_Connection=Yes"
            Session("pubs_ConnectionTimeout") = 15
            Session("pubs_CommandTimeout") = 30
            Session("pubs_RuntimeUserName") = "IUSR_PIGLET"
            Session("pubs_RuntimePassword") = ""
    '==Visual InterDev Generated - DataConnection endspan==
End Sub
</SCRIPT>
```

As you can see this sets the connection details for the session, and then these can be referenced later in the other data controls in other pages of the project..

Data Command Control

The Data Command Control creates the code necessary to run an ADO Command against the database, giving you a graphical method to select the properties.

The first screen you get when adding this control allows you to name the control and select the data connection to which it belongs. You can then pick the Command Type from SQL, Stored Procedure, Table or View, and the Command Text will show the appropriate items in the database. If you choose SQL the Visual InterDev SQL window appears and you can create your SQL query, in the same manner as shown earlier. Copy Fields allows you to select the fields from the database object (or SQL) and copy them to the clipboard, where they can be pasted into your code as the following:

```
<%= DataCommand1("AuthorName") %><BR>
<%= DataCommand1("title") %><BR>
```

The Advanced tab allows you to choose the different cursor and record locking types:

The great thing about this is it saves you from having to remember (or even look up) the ADO constants. The Parameters tab allows you to set any parameters for a stored procedure and shows you the return value.

The upshot of all these fancy screens is a chunk of code that is added to your ASP file when you close the command windows. The first section of code is used by Visual InterDev to set the properties of the Data Command Control.

```
<!--METADATA TYPE="DesignerControl" startspan
    <OBJECT ID="DataCommand1" WIDTH=151 HEIGHT=24
    CLASSID="CLSID:7FAEED80-9D58-11CF-8F68-00AA006D27C2">
        <PARAM NAME="_Version" VALUE="65536">
        <PARAM NAME="_Version" VALUE="65536">
        <PARAM NAME="_ExtentX" VALUE="3986">
        <PARAM NAME="_ExtentY" VALUE="635">
        <PARAM NAME="_StockProps" VALUE="0">
        <PARAM NAME="DataConnection" VALUE="pubs">
        <PARAM NAME="CommandText" VALUE="dbo.&quot;usp_AuthorsTitles&quot;">
        <PARAM NAME="CommandType" VALUE="1">
        <PARAM NAME="ParamCount" VALUE="1">
        <PARAM NAME="Param0" VALUE="Return Value,,4,4,4">
```

```
        </OBJECT>
-->
```

The second set of code is the VBScript code created for the Command.

```
<%
Set pubs = Server.CreateObject("ADODB.Connection")
pubs.ConnectionTimeout = Session("pubs_ConnectionTimeout")
pubs.CommandTimeout = Session("pubs_CommandTimeout")
pubs.Open Session("pubs_ConnectionString"), Session("pubs_RuntimeUserName"),
Session("pubs_RuntimePassword")
Set cmdTemp = Server.CreateObject("ADODB.Command")
Set DataCommand1 = Server.CreateObject("ADODB.Recordset")
cmdTemp.CommandText = "dbo.""usp_AuthorsTitles"""
cmdTemp.CommandType = 4
Set cmdTemp.ActiveConnection = pubs
Set tmpParam = cmdTemp.CreateParameter("Return Value", 3, 4, 4)
cmdTemp.Parameters.Append tmpParam
DataCommand1.Open cmdTemp, , 0, 1
%>
<!--METADATA TYPE="DesignerControl" endspan-->
```

As you can see all this does is create a Command object and run that command. You might wonder why you couldn't have just typed this in directly, and the simple answer is that you could. However, what it offers is a visual method of creating the code, without having to remember the syntax and options.

If you wish to edit the control again you can right-mouse click within these code sections and selected Edit Design-Time Control, which brings up the properties window. It is important to note that if you make any changes to the pre-prepared code and then invoke the design time control again, your changes will be lost.

Data Range Controls

The Data Range Header and Footer controls work together to create the code for extracting data from a database to a web page. They bracket together a section of code that will be repeated for each record in the selected recordset. Imagine a report with a header section, some detail lines, and a footer section, and you get the general idea. The page created can have two different modes depending upon the options you select. If you don't select record paging then you will get standard page, but selecting record paging gives you a navigation bar to allow stepping through the pages.

If you use both controls what you get is two sections of code, and a gap in the middle where you can show the records. Here is some example header code created by the Header Control:

```
<!--METADATA TYPE="DesignerControl" startspan
    <OBJECT ID="DataRangeHdr1" WIDTH=151 HEIGHT=24
    CLASSID="CLSID:F602E721-A281-11CF-A5B7-0080C73AAC7E">
      . . .
-->
<%
      . . . ' ASP Code for Header Control and start of loop

    Do
%>
<!--METADATA TYPE="DesignerControl" endspan-->
```

This is the code for the detail lines–you enter this yourself:

```
. . . ' ASP Code for showing the records from the recordset
```

And this is some example footer code created by the Footer Control:

```
<!--METADATA TYPE="DesignerControl" startspan
    <OBJECT ID="DataRangeFtr1" WIDTH=151 HEIGHT=24
    CLASSID="CLSID:F602E722-A281-11CF-A5B7-0080C73AAC7E">
      . . .
-->
<%
Loop
      . . . 'ASP code for navigation bar
%>
<!--METADATA TYPE="DesignerControl" endspan-->
```

Data Range Header Control

The Data Range Header is very similar in look to the Data Command, and the only areas where the property window differs are a section on the Control and Advanced tabs.

On the Control tab you can select whether paging is going to be in effect, and if so where the navigation bar should be placed.

You can also select the way in which you would like the data to be shown, by changing the Range Type. If this is Text or Table, then when you copy the fields to the clipboard the following syntax is used:

```
<%= DataRangeID("FieldName") %><BR>
```

If Form is selected, then the following is used:

```
<INPUT TYPE="Text" SIZE=25 MAXLENGTH=60 NAME="FieldName" VALUE="<%=
DataRangeID("FieldName") %>"><BR>
```

The Advanced tab has an optimization option that allows you to set the caching for this command.

When set to No Caching, the cache size on the web server is set to the Page Size. When set to Caching, the Session object caches the recordset and consumes more server resources.

If you pick the paging option then the code produced by this control is quite large, mostly concerned with setting the page options, etc. If you are not paging then the code is much smaller, just setting a few options, connecting to the database and executing the command. In either case the code added ends in a loop statement, but only provides the start of the loop. If this sounds a little confusing then just think of how this will work. You will have a header, where all of the initial set-up is done, and headings printed. You then have a loop where all of the details are printed, and a footing for summary lines etc. This first part of code you have created is the header part and contains the start of this loop for the detail lines, and it's up to you to enter the detail lines, which is where copying the fields to the clipboard becomes useful.

If you have copied fields to the clipboard and paste them into your HTML page they look like this initially:

```
<%= DataRangeHdr1("au_lname") %><BR>
<%= DataRangeHdr1("au_fname") %><BR>
<%= DataRangeHdr1("address") %><BR>
<%= DataRangeHdr1("state") %><BR>
<%= DataRangeHdr1("zip") %><BR>
```

Although this is not formatted very well at least it saves a little typing.

Data Range Footer Control

The Data Range Footer Control is designed to provide the end of the loop that the header control started, and the navigation bar if you are using paging. If you are not using paging you can ignore this control and simply end the loop created in the header yourself.

With just a little addition of HTML you can have a very functional form:

Last Name	First Name	Address	State	ZIP
Johnson	White	10932 Bigge Rd.	CA	94025
Marjorie	Green	309 63rd St. #411	CA	94618
Cheryl	Carson	589 Darwin Ln.	CA	94705
Michael	O'Leary	22 Cleveland Av. #14	CA	95128
Dean	Straight	5420 College Av.	CA	94609
Meander	Smith	10 Mississippi Dr.	KS	66044
Abraham	Bennet	6223 Bateman St.	CA	94705
Ann	Dull	3410 Blonde St.	CA	94301
Burt	Gringlesby	PO Box 792	CA	95428
Charlene	Locksley	18 Broadway Av.	CA	94130

Address: http://piglet/1266/Chapter%209/Paging.asp

Page: 1

Even if you don't want much of the extra code that the Data controls create, the above example gives a good example of how to use the paging properties of ADO recordsets, and is worth looking at. The only code that has been manually typed in was the creation of the table—everything else was done by the design time controls.

HTML Layout Control

The Layout Control is not one of the controls that shows up under the Design Time Controls, but it is a control you use at design time, and is used to create HTML Forms, and lay out the controls on them. The great beauty of this is that it creates an HTML file (with a suffix of **.alx**) full of those awful **<OBJECT>** commands, relieving you of this tedious task. But remember that this will only work in browsers that support ActiveX controls.

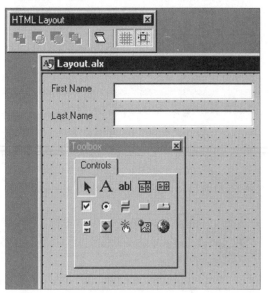

To create a new layout you select HTML Layout from the Files pane of the File/New dialog, where you are presented with a form and toolbox of controls:

This now works like a standard form designer and you can layout your controls visually. When saved you get a file full of **<OBJECT>** tags. For example, the above layout produces the following tags:

```
<DIV ID="Layout1" STYLE="LAYOUT:FIXED;WIDTH:400pt;HEIGHT:207pt;">
    <OBJECT ID="Label1"
     CLASSID="CLSID:978C9E23-D4B0-11CE-BF2D-00AA003F40D0"
STYLE="TOP:8pt;LEFT:8pt;WIDTH:74pt;HEIGHT:17pt;ZINDEX:0;">
        <PARAM NAME="Caption" VALUE="First Name">
        <PARAM NAME="Size" VALUE="2611;591">
        <PARAM NAME="FontCharSet" VALUE="0">
        <PARAM NAME="FontPitchAndFamily" VALUE="2">
    </OBJECT>
    <OBJECT ID="txtFirstName"
     CLASSID="CLSID:8BD21D10-EC42-11CE-9E0D-00AA006002F3"
STYLE="TOP:8pt;LEFT:66pt;WIDTH:132pt;HEIGHT:16pt;TABINDEX:1;ZINDEX:1;">
        <PARAM NAME="VariousPropertyBits" VALUE="746604571">
        <PARAM NAME="Size" VALUE="4657;564">
        <PARAM NAME="FontCharSet" VALUE="0">
        <PARAM NAME="FontPitchAndFamily" VALUE="2">
```

```
    </OBJECT>
    <OBJECT ID="txtLastName"
     CLASSID="CLSID:8BD21D10-EC42-11CE-9E0D-00AA006002F3"
 STYLE="TOP:33pt;LEFT:66pt;WIDTH:132pt;HEIGHT:16pt;TABINDEX:2;ZINDEX:2;">
        <PARAM NAME="VariousPropertyBits" VALUE="746604571">
        <PARAM NAME="Size" VALUE="4657;564">
        <PARAM NAME="FontCharSet" VALUE="0">
        <PARAM NAME="FontPitchAndFamily" VALUE="2">
    </OBJECT>
    <OBJECT ID="Label2"
     CLASSID="CLSID:978C9E23-D4B0-11CE-BF2D-00AA003F40D0"
 STYLE="TOP:33pt;LEFT:8pt;WIDTH:50pt;HEIGHT:8pt;ZINDEX:3;">
        <PARAM NAME="Caption" VALUE="Last Name">
        <PARAM NAME="Size" VALUE="1764;282">
        <PARAM NAME="FontCharSet" VALUE="0">
        <PARAM NAME="FontPitchAndFamily" VALUE="2">
    </OBJECT>
</DIV>
```

So this has performed the entire layout for you, and you can include this layout file in your standard HTML or ASP files.

You can find more information about other features of the Layout Control in Michael Corning's article in the April 1998 Issue of Smart Access (published by Pinnacle Publishing).

Script Wizard

The layout editor also contains a script wizard to help you create you client side VBScript code. A right-mouse click when designing the layout will offer you a Script Wizard option:

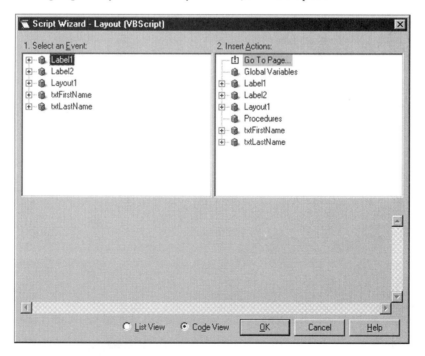

The left pane shows you the objects on the form. In this case there's the actual layout itself, two labels and two text boxes. On the right you can select the methods and properties for the objects, and the bottom is where the code goes. So if you want to run some code when the user exits from the FirstName field, you expand txtFirstName and double-click the Exit event:

```
1. Select an Event:
  ⊟  🎲  txtFirstName                              ▲
        ◇  AfterUpdate
        ◇  BeforeDragOver
        ◇  BeforeDropOrPaste
        ◇  BeforeUpdate
        ◇  Change
        ◇  DblClick
        ◇  DropButtonClick
        ◇  Enter
        ◇  Error
        ◇  Exit
        ◇  KeyDown                                 ▼

Sub txtFirstName_Exit(Cancel)

```

You can select methods and properties from the right pane to have these added to your code. For example, suppose you wanted to set the background color of the surname to red when the first name field was entered.

```
1. Select an Event:                    2. Insert Actions:
  ⊟  🎲  txtFirstName          ▲          ⊞  AutoTab
        ◇  AfterUpdate                    ⊞  AutoWordSelect
        ◇  BeforeDragOver                 ⊞  BackColor
        ◇  BeforeDropOrPaste              ⊞  BackStyle
        ◇  BeforeUpdate                   ⊞  BorderColor
        ◇  Change                         ⊞  BorderStyle
        ◇  DblClick                       ⊞  CanPaste (r)
        ◇  DropButtonClick                ⊞  CodeBase
        ◆  Enter                          ⊞  CurLine
        ◇  Error                          ⊞  CurTargetX (r)
        ◇  Exit                           ⊞  CurX
        ◇  KeyDown         ▼              ⊞  DragBehavior

Sub txtFirstName_Enter()
txtLastName.BackColor = htmlRed
```

The code created is placed at the top of the layout file:

```
<SCRIPT LANGUAGE="VBScript">
<!--
Sub txtFirstName_Enter()
txtLastName.BackColor = htmlRed
end sub
-->
</SCRIPT>
```

You can also create new procedures by a right-mouse click in the action pane. Selecting New Procedure creates a blank procedure for you, and New Global Variable creates global variables. These are also added to the script section of the layout file.

While this doesn't do all of the coding for you it does give you a full list of the events, methods, and properties of the objects, and so is an invaluable tool. In the future we might see a more integrated editor where you get QuickTips like Visual Basic, but for now the Script Wizard provides a very good interface.

Database Scalability

You may think that database scalability is not something you need to worry about. After all, it's for really big databases isn't it? Not at all. Scalability concerns how your database will cope with an increased workload, whether it is a larger amount of data to be stored, or an increase in the number of users.

Why Scale?

Companies grow. That's a fairly sure fact, and as they grow so do their demands. One of the things that databases have brought to companies is the ease with which data can be accumulated, correlated, and analyzed, so the increased demand for information is fueling the increase in data. It's a vicious circle.

There are several types of growth that need to be accommodated:

- **Users**. This doesn't necessarily mean an increased number of people in the organization, but an increase in the number accessing the database. As information becomes more available and easier to access, more people are going to want to access it.

- **Data**. This will always accumulate at a rate far greater than you think. Having data in an easily obtainable format often leads to more data being stored.

- **Complexity**. As the demands for information increase so do the methods required to produce the information in the desired format.

With this increased growth come other areas that need to be considered:

- **Manageability**. As the database becomes larger and more complex, its management will also increase.

- **Availability**. As the data becomes more and more important to a company, it's vital that the data is always available.

- **Accessibility**. Making sure the data is accessible from varying locations.

- **Security**. With more users and increased accessibility comes the security of the data. It's important to ensure that only those people who have permission are allowed to see the correct data.

So you can see that scaling a database can be quite a complex issue and has many factors that involve planning.

How to Scale

Now you understand why you might have to scale your databases, but what exactly can you do? Is it simply a question of buying a bigger and faster machine so that everything will run quicker? Obviously that will have an impact, but it's not the first thing you should think of.

Database Design

People very often don't realize that the design of the database can have an impact on how it will scale. This isn't going to be an extensive discussion on database design, but there are a few areas that can make a difference, and although some are standard performance enhancement techniques, they are equally valid here.

Scalability isn't just about supporting more data and more users, but improving performance too. The quicker your database can do something, then the more times it can do it, and the more users it can support. Consider an ASP page that fetches data from a database and displays a table of the results. While this provides you with up-to-date figures you may find that this isn't necessary. Would yesterday's figures do? Or even hourly updates? Would you consider replacing this with a static HTML page that was automatically constructed hourly? SQL Server has automated tasks that can create HTML pages, and if they can be used to improve the response time then they should be used. For more information about these tasks you should look at the SQL Server Web Assistant which is installed with SQL Server.

You could also consider using un-normalized temporary tables, rather than performing complex multi-table joins. Admittedly the data wouldn't be current, but that may be acceptable. Temporary tables in stored procedures can be used to break down complex joins too.

Using stored procedures will improve the efficiency of SQL Server to service data requests, therefore they should be used where ever possible.

Hardware

Throwing more hardware at the problem is valid as long as it's done in a planned way. SQL Server, for example, can benefit in a number of areas.

 Memory. SQL Server works better when given more memory, and given the relatively cheap price of memory at the moment, there is very little excuse for not putting in as much as you can. 128Mb is a good start for a large database server. Memory is important because it allows the server to hold more data in cache where it can be accessed faster.

Disks. This can have a big impact on databases. When the data you are trying to retrieve is not in memory SQL Server has to get it from disk, therefore the faster the disks, the faster the data is returned. Since disks are quite cheap too many small servers start with EIDE disks, and a move to SCSI disks, and especially **RAID** systems will bring a large performance increase. A RAID system also gives fault-tolerance.

Processor. This actually has less impact than you might realize. The processor does a small proportion of the actual work, so the processor type and speed are less important than good disks and memory. However, a multi-processor system can have big benefits. SQL Server is extremely well integrated with NT Server and the load sharing of CPU's is very good, so a two processor system will service more users, and faster, than a single processor system.

Another often-overlooked way to increase scalability is to move SQL Server to a separate machine, especially one that isn't a Windows NT Domain Controller. If the NT Server doesn't have to do anything else, then SQL will perform better.

Clustering too, is somewhere that will have an impact. Although this is still an immature technology as far as NT is concerned, the possibilities look good. The ability to have several NT Servers linked together and sharing resources should give good performance as well as fault-tolerance should one of the servers fail.

RAID stands for Redundant Array of Inexpensive Discs, and allows several disc drives to be used together, and the data stored on them is spread around the discs. So if one disc fails, the data can be recovered from the information stored on the others. The failed disc can be replaced with a new one and the data rebuilt. Some systems allow this to happen whilst the machine is still active.

Clustering allows several machines to be linked together and share resources and has several useful features. The first allows a single set of discs to be used between machines. Then there is the ability to share processing—so if one machine is busy the task can be offloaded onto the other. Failure of one machine can also be handled with the tasks it was processing being handled by the other machine. All in all it provides fault tolerance and greater reliability.

Software

The software aspect can be broken down into two areas. At one end there is the server and database software, and at the other the application software being used to access the SQL database. It's no good having one tuned to work well if the other is not performing well. It's really important to ensure that both the server software and the application program are written well. So let's examine these a little to see what you should look at to ensure that they are working at optimum performance.

Databases

You've already seen how easy it is to use a database within ASP pages, but what if you suspect the database is not performing well. There are a number of things you can do:

- If using Microsoft Access, compact your database regularly if you are deleting records at all. When you delete a record in Access it doesn't get physically deleted from the database, but is only marked as being deleted. Compacting removes these marked records, reduces the size of your database, and thus improves performance.

- Use prepared queries with parameters. On Access this is just creating a query, and on SQL Server it is stored procedures. The advantage of these is that the database server works out in advance how the query will be executed. This execution plan is then used when the query is run.

- Make sure the database has enough memory. With Access you can't control this but you can make sure the machine has enough memory. With SQL Server you can allocate memory to certain areas of SQL Server. For example, how much of the machine's memory it uses, how much is allocated to the data cache (where frequently accessed data is stored) and how much is allocated to the procedure cache (where frequently accessed stored procedures are stored).

- Make sure your database machine is not doing other intensive tasks that are taking time away from the database server.

If you are using Access and find that despite all of the above tests your database is slow, you may find that for the size, complexity and use, Access just isn't good enough. In this case you should consider upsizing to SQL Server. SQL Server is designed as a database server and will naturally give better performance, and given that within ASP you work through an ODBC connection you shouldn't have to change any of your code during this upsizing exercise. This makes a move from Access to SQL ideal as the first step towards an enterprise wide database solution. The forthcoming OLE DB providers for SQL Server will be even faster that the ODBC ones.

If you are gravitating towards a large-scale enterprise solution you might also like to consider SQL Server Enterprise Edition. This is designed to work closely with NT Server Enterprise Edition and provides better support for high-end systems with multi-processor servers, giving better scalability and support.

Applications

Application software is a bit more of a problem concerning scalability and web applications. There is currently a huge focus on ASP and ADO (and rightly so), but do these have an impact on scalability and database performance? Well yes, but perhaps in way that you might not have thought of. We know that the IIS server has to cope with an increase in the number of users accessing your site, but imagine if all of the pages being accessed used ADO, with scripts running on the server. This will use more resources, especially if the IIS Server and SQL Server are situated on the same physical machine.

To get large-scale enterprise performance from your application you need to consider how it is structured and what it is doing:

- Is it a large application, using lots of memory on the client machine? If so consider breaking it down into smaller units that can work quicker.

- Are your ASP pages doing a lot of database access? Would it be possible to cache some of the database data locally on each client machine? This is not such a bad attitude—consider lookup tables that don't change very often. If these were stored locally then you can avoid the connection to the remote database. Building client-side scripting to handle these would be simple.

You might also like to consider rewriting your application. Sure, you have neither the time nor the money, but how far ahead do you want to look. Many businesses quite rightly focus on the immediate future, and too few focus on long term goals. Redesigning an enterprise application would take time and cost a lot, but the long-term benefits could pay off. If an application takes a year to write, but from then on is error free, easily maintainable, and scales well, then it might be worth the cost.

One way to rewrite your application is to base it around the Microsoft Distributed interNet Applications (DNA) architecture. Now don't jump back in horror as another client/server architecture leaps at you, as this is really just a foundation for a lot of sensible ideas. Building an application from components, and organizing them so they each do their own task is a sensible way to develop. The underlying foundations of DNA are Microsoft Internet Information Server, Microsoft SQL Server, Microsoft Transaction Server, and Microsoft Message Queuing Server. These are designed to provide a structure for handling component-based applications in a fault-tolerant and scalable manner. We briefly touched upon these in Chapter 1 and there is too much involved in these technologies to discuss them here, but they should be considered.

You can find out more about MTS and MSMQ in detail from our forthcoming book Professional MTS and MSMQ Programming, ISBN 1-861001-46-0.

Summary

This chapter has really covered two areas that are very loosely linked. To start with we examined Microsoft Visual InterDev and how it can be used to manage your enterprise database. Although some of the features cross over with the SQL Enterprise Manager, Visual InterDev is much more of a development tool, and is focused less on the database management issues. We've seen that Visual InterDev can be used as a serious development tool, not only to aid the management of your data in your database, but also to easily create database access code for your ASP pages. The next version of Visual InterDev (2.0) promises to make this development environment even better.

The latter part of this chapter has looked at database scalability. This is always a controversial subject since so many people think it involves acquiring huge database servers and the staff needed to maintain them, but this isn't necessarily so. Making your database more scalable can simple be just optimizing it, that is, making it perform better given the tasks it has to do. Of course there may well come a time when you have to move to a larger database, but you will generally find that the cost and effort involved is justified. If your customers have to wait too long for their data, they may not be your customers much longer.

Getting into Client/Server

This chapter begins a broader exploration of Active Server Pages. Now that you are familiar with the individual techniques, we'll move on to look at how they can be combined with existing technologies available on the client's browser—and implemented from a client/server point of view.

Developing a client/server application is never a simple task. The key benefits of the Web and the Active Server platform in designing such applications are universal access, richer content and easier creation. Active Server Pages doesn't trivialize the process, but it does simplify the distribution of server code and client code. In this part of the book, we'll learn how to start building client/server applications that can be used in business critical situations.

But first we need to understand the background to client/server as a whole. If you're coming to ASP from a web site developer's point of view, the term client/server may well carry threatening overtones. So we'll use this chapter to augment the history of client/server solutions first addressed in Chapter 1 and then move on to discuss how you can easily get into the client/server world using Active Server Pages.

Specifically, we'll be looking at:

▲ The thinking behind client/server solutions

▲ How client/server can be applied to Active Server Pages

▲ How we go about designing a client/server application

▲ How we integrate server-side components and database connections

The Theory of Client/Server

In the introduction to this book, we took note of the evolution of the client/server computer to the position of de facto standard for the implementation of a company intranet. Client/server has become the buzzword that every new product, be it hardware or software, must support, feature and advance. In its very simplest form, we can use this definition: Client/server computing is the splitting of a computing task between client and server processes.

Getting More Specific

This literal definition is very vague. Previously, we have approached the client/server architecture as the derivation of data access, presentation and business logics into separate entities on the system. Of course, this is not the only way to approach the problem—just one of several.

To illustrate this point clearly, we'll now look at a different client/server design model. This time, consider the presence of four layers within the typical client/server system, each of which may combine with one o more of the others to form one discrete section. The diagram below illustrates this model.

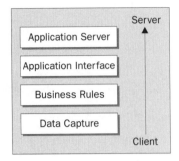

The Data Capture Layer

The first layer is called **Data Capture**. This means that the data is captured and converted from a human representation to a computer representation. The previous sentence could be more easily termed as punching in the data. However, using that type of definition implies that the user has something that they can actually punch–such as a keyboard. The more precise definition is better, because it sums up all possibilities. For example, in the future, input devices could use voice, gesture, or neural transmitters. Coming back to reality, current input devices may be a mouse, keyboard or virtual reality interface device. The only limit is human imagination. This layer could also be called the "human interface" to the system.

The reverse of input is output, and the statement also applies in this context. Examples of output devices are monitors, printers, or tape drives. Programming operations that are acceptable in this layer would be filling or reading the contents of a list box or a combo box, and then packing the data into a pre-defined structure.

However, it's important to note that this layer is only responsible for the translation of the data from one form to another, human to computer or vice-versa. The actual contents of the data aren't verified for correctness or accuracy at this point.

The Business Rule Layer

This layer is responsible for applying the **Business Rules** to the data captured in the first layer. It is responsible for converting the data to a business context, and adding information about the business rules. The user doesn't interact with the software in this layer at all. However this layer is critical because it validates the data to make sure that it is in the correct form–and is applied to the data that is both coming from or going to the server. **The business rules must only be rules—they must not process the data.**

Consider, for example, the implementation of a mortgage loan application. The business rule layer would filter the input first for completeness, then apply any other validation. A valid rule would be granting loans only to people who are at least 18 years old. However, a rule that denied a mortgage application just because the applicant did not earn enough for the property at a specific price would not be a valid business rule. In reality, denial of a mortgage is more complicated than a simple rule could cover. And while rules like this could be expressed in computer terms, they tend to contain too many ands, ifs, and buts.

A business rule should nest within other business rules, otherwise this layer becomes too fat, and requires too much processing. It shouldn't depend on any data coming from higher layers and needs to be self-supporting in all cases. In programming terms, the rules should be able to be stored in a small local file or, even better, coded within an application component.

The Application Interface Layer

The third layer in the model acts as translator between user and application. This is responsible for converting the data from a business context to a technology context, the latter being whatever the **Application Server** (the final layer) requires.

Going back to the mortgage example, the application interface might convert the request and associated data into a SQL statement, and then pass that to the final layer. By convention you would not to put any business logic into this layer, to allow for future expandability.

The Application Server Layer

The final layer is called the **Application Server** layer. This layer has the task of processing the data, which is now in a technology context, and the processing is not dependent on the actions of the user interface. The processing doesn't need to be logical in human terms either. This layer is all about the storing and retrieval of data and calculation of results.

For example, the equation $y = x / b$ is a mathematical reality, and can be computed for all values where b isn't zero. However, when b is zero, the results are undefined in mathematical terms and an overflow error occurs. Yet in our own human terms, the result still has sense of reality–it's just a very big number. The point is that in this layer the data is manipulated as something only mathematics, science or computers can fully understand. Our conceptions of the result will often be wrong.

As another example, take a SQL statement that we generated in the previous layer. While we would understand the plain English definition of the query, and probably have a good idea of what the SQL statement actually meant, we would have no conception of what actually went on inside the database while the query was being processed. It is considered to be a 'black box'.

Reconciling The Two Client/Server Models

As you can see, the client/server model we have just detailed is not so different from the one we met earlier in the book. The two approaching the same problem from slightly different angles, one model being just a lateral jump from the other.

Obviously the most direct correlation between the two lies with the business rules layer which corresponds directly with the business logic tier in our first model. The data capture layer is a cruder abstraction over the concept of presentation logic, except that the former allows us to consider the devices on which the latter may manifest itself. It also considers the retention of user input——via keyboard, mouse, VR, the internet or voicemail system——which the logic construct does not consider. By default, this means that the Application Server and Application Interface layers correspond to the data access logic tier in our first model. This they do, but, like the data capture layer, they also abstract over the physical aspects of data access in a client/server architecture above and beyond the logic they also encapsulate.

The four layers form a definition of client/server computing in a nutshell, and are of interest to anyone who needs to develop corporate solutions. But they prompt the questions 'Why do we really care about these layers at all?' and 'Why don't we just create programs and let the layers sort themselves out?'.

Partitioning a Client/Server System

In fact, the whole purpose of the layer definitions is to help us understand how we divide up, or **partition**, our client/server applications. We ultimately have to define the split between the client and the server, or servers. In other words, we have to decide which layers will be on which side of the network connection, and what layers will execute on what machines. This is the subject of a great deal of industry debate. Past history has seen this model implemented mostly in a client-centric fashion with all but the Application Server located on the client machine. However, as mentioned before, the classic fat client/thin server approach is plagued with problems of poor performance, complex maintenance and high running costs.

Client/server Middleware

A second problem with corporate client/server architecture, running on the company network, has always been how the client and server communicate with each other. The technical term for this is **middleware**– the software that makes it simple to abstract the communication. Every vendor has a solution, and these aren't always compatible with each other. This causes many network headaches, and solving it would make client/server development that much easier.

However, we won't be delving into the details of which other architectures are acceptable and workable in this book, but instead we'll focus on the single architecture that interests us–web client/server. The Web solves the communication layer problem because the HTTP protocol it uses provides a common base for all applications. What we do need to do is decide how we're going to partition our applications in this environment.

Partitioning a Web-Based Application

To end our look at the theory of client/server computing, we'll go through how a typical application would be partitioned under the web client/server architecture. Layer one is the human-to-computer interface—typically an HTML based browser. There may be some client-side controls or scripts to add richness to the user interface, but this is purely optional.

Layer two is the business rule layer, and is generally handled on the client by the scripts and controls in the HTML page. However, no parts of the rules are hard-coded into the browser, they only exist in the pages themselves. There's an argument that this can pose a security risk because the rules then need to pass across the network. The risks involved here though can be reduced by the use of Secure Sockets Layers (or Secure Channel Services). We'll be discussing all these topics in Chapter 14. So in some cases, either to enhance security, or because a rule requires features that aren't available on the client, all or part of the business rules layer may reside on the server.

Layer three, the conversion from a business context to a technological context, occurs on the server. It could be that an HTTP request triggers a routine that creates a structure of data, or that ASP converts it to a new representation ready for the final layer.

Layer four, the application server layer, is again located on the server, and is the 'back end' that actually does the processing and produces the results. This may be a database or other business object, and the result might be retrieval of information for return to the client, or just storage of data sent from it.

So, in our Web based model, layer one is on the client machine, layer two has parts on both the client and the server, and the server contains layers three and four. We now have a more balanced and better performing system, with one exception–the middleware.

Middleware on the Web

At the time of writing there was no standard middleware based on the HTTP protocol. Microsoft is hard at work on a version of the Distributed Component Object Model (DCOM) that can be tunneled over HTTP. There is new software that is showing some promise of being accepted, however, for it to become reality a standard method of **tunneling protocol** needs to become freely available.

> Tunneling is the process of securely embedding one protocol within another, so that information can be sent directly from one client/server layer to another across the Net, within the HTTP packets.

This ends our theoretical and perhaps rather dry look, at client/server. However, it should have indicated that there is more to the subject than just script and components. We need to think seriously about how we design our applications to conform to the accepted standards, and to get the best performance—in terms of processing, usability, and security. The remainder of this chapter looks at different aspects of designing an application that will combine Active Server Pages and some relevant other technologies. At the same time, we'll be setting the scene for the remainder of this part of the book and the case studies that follow.

Applications, Sessions, and State

Traditional network based applications have always had one major advantage—the automatic maintenance of **state** by the network itself. The previous lack of this feature within HTTP has tended to limit the development of true Web based applications. What do we mean by state? In a traditional local or wide area network, the software (such as Novell, Banyan, or Microsoft's own protocols) combined with features of the operating system in such a way that once a user logged into the network, they could be automatically recognized by all the applications on it.

Bringing State to HTTP

On the Web, with previous applications based on technologies such as CGI, the problem has always been that, when a client submits a request, the server just produces a response and returns it. When another request is received from that user, the server has no idea if there was a previous request. This is because the HTTP 1.0 protocol is **stateless**. Building client/server programs with a stateless protocol can become very complicated. One of the new features of IIS 4.0 is its support of the HTTP 1.1 protocol. This protocol addresses some of the issues with regard to state, and will be discussed later in this chapter.

Why Do We Need State?

To understand why we need state, imagine building a traditional application in, say, Visual Basic. You design a form with a dozen or so command buttons, and write a piece of code that runs when each button is clicked. Since the button has a state which identifies itself, VB knows which button was clicked, and so runs the correct code routine for that button. Now imagine that VB was designed like HTTP. Instead of each button having a state to identifying itself, all that VB would know is that some button somewhere was pressed. VB could not tell which specific button was pressed and would run the same block code regardless. You can see how this would, to say the least, make building applications difficult.

The Global.asa File

In the same way as the button has a state which identifies itself, so too must an application. However, rather than just a unique identifier that a button might have to maintain its state, we regard the **state of an application** as the collection of variables which uniquely identify both the application itself and the period during which it is being used (the session).

Fortunately, the Active Server Pages object model caters for these requirements by providing us with the **Application** and **Session** objects, both of which we briefly examined in Chapter 4. These two allow us to steer the user through the application with much greater ease than if they were not present. They also enable us to track a users travels through our site.

In order to make **Application** and **Session** work in ASP, we use a single file named **global.asa** for each 'application'. **Global.asa** contains t he state of the application via the **Application** and **Session** object properties and any global code the 'application' requires to alter it. This file resides in the directory on the server that is the root of that application—where the files that make up the application are located. Any subdirectories of the main application directory are also part of the application, and the **global.asa** file applies to their contents as well. This means you need to be aware of the possibility of overlap between applications, and should generally create separate directories for each one. For example:

Physical directory	Virtual directory	Application
`C:\InetPub\WWWRoot\`	`/`	
`C:\InetPub\WWWRoot\Demo\`	`/DemoApp`	`Demo`
`C:\InetPub\WWWRoot\Demo\Images\`		`Demo`
`C:\InetPub\WWWRoot\Main\`	`/MainApp`	`MainApp`
`C:\InetPub\WWWRoot\Main\Test\`	`/TestApp`	`TestApp` *and* `MainApp`

So when we talk about an application in ASP, we are actually talking about all the files in the same directory as **global.asa**, and any of its physical subdirectories.

A Word Of Caution

It cannot be emphasized more strongly, however, that you must be very careful how you structure your applications on your server and how you set up your virtual roots. Bad structuring may lead to the wrong **global.asa** being called at the wrong time and the state of the application being lost. It's worth adhering to these simple rules to avoid confusion.

- If **/** contains the **global.asa** file while **/DemoApp** and **/MainApp** do not, then the same **global.asa**–the one in the root–will be used for both applications.

- Inversely, if **/** does not contain **global.asa** while **/DemoApp** and **/MainApp** contain different versions of the file, the **global.asa**'s in each root will execute different code. So depending on the URL's you request, a different **global.asa** will be executed, a different application state will be created, different object variables will be called and different deletions made.

- As an addition to this last rule, be aware that if **/DemoApp** and **/MainApp** relate to physical directories which share a common parent directory, as in the above example, then this rule holds. However, if **/DemoApp** and **/MainApp** relate to physical directories where one is the parent of the other, as **/MainApp** and **/TestApp** are, this rule may not hold for either application.

Also if you find that you are getting Type Mismatch errors, then this is quite likely caused by your server not being able to read the variables in your **global.asa** file. The result is that as your variables aren't defined, when you come to use a variable supposedly defined in **global.asa** in your application, the server will try and allocate a value to variable that hasn't been defined, thus causing this error. To cure it you will need to reposition **global.asa**.

Creating State with Cookies

So we now have a file which contains all the information we need to have to maintain the state of an application—**global.asa**. However, it is stuck on the server and we need to share the state information with the client browser. Conversely, when the client requests a new page, the state will change and the server will need to be informed.

To get around this problem Netscape developed the concept of a **cookie**. A cookie is purely a small informational text string that is stored on the user's hard disk—we looked at them in some depth back in Chapter 4.

> *Many people worry that cookies can be dangerous. While they can be used in all kinds of ways by server-based applications, they pose no risk to you as a user. Cookies, as they are documented, will not format your disk, send back information about your system, or put you on a mailing list. What they will do is allow the website to better know who you are, and present a more focused and compelling presentation of information to you. If that sounds dangerous, then maybe you've been reading the alt.paranoia USENET group too long.*

Typically, when the client makes a request for a document from a specific virtual directory on a server (which can include the **root** directory), the server returns a cookie—or token of information. When the user returns to the same virtual directory or one of its subdirectories, the browser sends that cookie back, as part of the HTTP request.

If we were building CGI-based applications, we would use the cookie information to check who the user was and collect other information regarding their interaction with our application. Working with cookies directly can be fun and interesting for about 30 seconds. As we saw in Chapter 4, ASP does make the task a lot easier through the **Cookies** collections of the **Request** and **Response** objects.

The big advantage is that the Active Server Pages framework provides an automatic mechanism for maintaining state in our applications, without having to directly manipulate cookies ourselves. One caveat to this is that ASP requires the browser to support and accept cookies in order to function properly. If the user refuses to accept cookies through settings in their browser's security options, or if their browser doesn't support cookies, this automated mechanism will fail.

Using Applications and Sessions

We looked briefly at what the **Application** and **Session** object are in Part 1 of this book, and had a brief glimpse at the way they could be used. When we come to build Web based client/server applications, it is now easier to see why these two objects now assume a far greater importance that we've previously credited them with. They allow us to connect all the various parts of our application.

We can store and maintain the values of (state) variables for each user, as well as globally for all users. In this section, we'll explore some of the possibilities in detail.

Application and Session Events

We talked about the events that **Application** and **Session** can fire back in Chapter 4. However, we'll summarize these briefly in the context of state, and then move quickly on to look at how we can use them in our applications.

The Application_onStart and Session_onStart Events

Both of these events are to be used to initialize state, by setting up variables that are global for the application or for a specific user. When the first user accesses a file in our application, the **Application_onStart** event is triggered. This is used to initialize any application-wide global variables. When the user begins a session for the first time, the **Session_onStart** event is triggered. This is used to initialize user-specific information.

The power of the **Session** object comes from the fact that it can store variables that are global to just that specific user, and so each user can have their own individual value for that variable. **Session** objects aren't always created automatically for every user when they enter our application. However, storing or accessing a variable in the **Session** object will create it, and fire the **Session_onStart** event. We can force new sessions to always be created as soon as a visitor enters our application by writing code in **global.asa** to respond to this event.

When responding to the **Application_onStart** event, we must not under any circumstances use code specific to any one particular user. In this event, we would typically create global objects, such as a server side component that needs to be shared and available to every visitor.

> *Session and Application events only happen when a client retrieves an ASP page—they are not triggered when an HTML page in the application is requested. Therefore, if you have additional server-side applications such as ISAPI or CGI scripts, make sure that they don't depend on specific events having occurred within an ASP page. Otherwise the ISAPI or CGI script may crash and cause the web server to hang.*

The Session_onEnd and Application_onEnd Events

The **Session_onEnd** event occurs either when a current **Session** is abandoned by using the **Session.Abandon** method, or when it times out. By default this is 20 minutes after the last request for a page from the application, though this can be changed either by setting the **Session.Timeout** property or by editing the registry.

Something we need to consider is if we have objects that themselves contain timeouts. If, for example, we create a database connection in a **Session**, and the connection timeout is less than the **Session** timeout, it's possible for corruption of the object to occur. If the database connection times out after ten minutes, and the **Session** times out after twenty minutes, the database connection will not be valid, even though the object in the **Session** still is.

The **Application_onEnd** event can be used to clean up all of the global objects and variables. This event is fired when the application is unloaded from the web server. The Microsoft Management Console with the Internet Information Server snap-in, otherwise known as the Internet Service Manager, allows you to manage the properties and state of your web application.

If the application is configured to run in its own process space, then this dialog box allows you to explicitly shutdown an application by using the Unload button. Pressing this button will cause the **Application_onEnd** event to be fired. Once the event was finished processing, the application will be unloaded from memory on the server. Any objects that were allocated would be deleted. In the future, it seems likely that the developer can specify that the **Application_onEnd** event be triggered once the last **Session_onEnd** event occurred. This would occur when the last session ends and there are no current application users.

Session Properties and Methods

The **Session** object has a number of properties that provide more information about the current user. These properties can be examined and their values used to dynamically change the information that is being presented to the user, as well as changing how the information is visually represented. The **Session** object also provides a method that allows the developer to force a session to end, regardless of the timeout value.

CodePage property

The **CodePage** property of the **Session** object is used to determine which codepage is used to display the content that is generated by the ASP script. A codepage is the Windows term for a language-specific character set. Different languages and different locales may use different code pages. For example, American English, along with most European languages has a codepage value of 1252. The codepage itself consists of a table that maps physical characters to single byte or multi-byte values. As a developer, you can use this property to ensure that users in different places around the world will see the content in their proper, local character set.

SessionID property

The **SessionID** value is a long value that uniquely identifies this session amongst all other sessions running on the same system. This value could be used as an identifying value for each user as they are using the system. A word of caution is that the **SessionID** is only guaranteed unique within this current instance of the application. If the application is stopped and restarted, there is a chance that the **SessionID** value could be a duplicate value of one that had been used previously.

Timeout property

The **Timeout** property is the time in minutes that the session can remain idle before it is terminated by the system. A session is considered idle as long as there are no new page requests, nor any requests to refresh the current page. The default value for this property is 20 minutes. The developer depending on the needs of the application can adjust this value. If the application is a high volume site, then the developer may want to set this number rather low, to prevent resources from being consumed by users who have moved on to other sites. If an application requires user login, and holds that information in session-level variables, then a shorter timeout period may be beneficial from a security point-of-view.

Abandon Method

If a developer wishes to force a session to end before its timeout value has been reached, then they can use the **Abandon** method of the **Session** object. This method will destroy all of the objects that were allocated by the session and release their resources. When this method is called, the current script that is being processes will continue to be processed to completion, as if nothing had happened. When the current script finishes, the **Session_onEnd** event is fired. One way of triggering this is to design the user interface so that there is an explicit end to the interaction, and the user is told to press a Logout button to complete their interaction with the site.

A change in this new version of ASP (version 2.0)is that all session-level variables remain available until **Session_onEnd** completes processing. This now makes calling **Session.Abandon** have the exact same effect as the session timing out. In the previous version, if the session was explicitly abandoned, then all of the session-level variables were deleted **before Session_onEnd** was fired.

Disabling Session State

Just because we can use sessions in our applications doesn't mean that we always have to. When a user first enters a site, there may be entire sections of the site that have no need to track user session information. It may only be once the user reaches a certain part of the site that it becomes important that the web application maintain state for that user.

But if this is all built in to ASP, and very easy to use, why would we *not* want to use it all the time. ASP pages that have the session state disabled can often improve the performance of your website by not performing potentially time and memory consuming session activity. In fact, Microsoft consultants are now recommending achieving scalability by not storing state in a session object. Rather, the application should store state on disk or in a personalization server. ASP executes session requests in a sequential order, and can only execute one at a time. This means that if your request has multiple session requests, the server can only perform one request at a time. Each request will have to wait until all of the ones before it have finished before it can execute.

If some of these requests can be written without needing session state, then they can execute at the same time as the session requests are being carried out. This multi-tasking will increase the perceived throughput of the web server.

To mark a page as sessionless, you need to add this to the first line of the ASP script file:

```
<%@ EnableSessionState=False %>
```

To mark a page as supporting session state, simply omit this line from your ASP script.

When the session state is disabled for a page, ASP does not perform the following functions:

▲ Any **Session_onStart** procedure in the **global.asa** file is not executed.

▲ The cookies that are used to identify a session to the browser are not sent.

▲ Session objects are not created.

▲ The built-in session objects and session scope objects created with the **<OBJECT>** tag cannot be accessed.

An advantage of sessionless pages is that execution is NOT serialized with other session requests. For example, when dealing with multiple simultaneous requests, like in loading the multiple pages of a **<FRAMESET>**, the browser will open multiple simultaneous HTTP sessions with the server to download the various pages to fill the frames. However, some web browsers may serialize the requests to the server themselves. In this case, sessionless pages offer no performance advantage over pages with session state.

Is the Client Still Connected?

All of the features of the **Application** and **Session** objects allow us to help maintain state in an environment where state has very intrinsic support. Even so, the web is basically still a connectionless environment, where a browser connects, gets its info, and then disconnects. This can sometimes make maintaining state a bit tricky. For example, what if while processing a page, the user hits the stop button, or shuts down the browser. ASP will go on its merry way, continuing to process the page, even if there is no one there to receive the results.

This can make for unnecessary processing. It can also cause session-level objects to be left with nothing to do until the timeout value is reached. This will begin to place a drain on system resources, with all of these objects hanging around with nothing to do, just waiting to timeout. With the **Session.Abandon** method, a developer can force a session to close. What they need is some type of indication that the client is no longer there.

The **Response** object provides a property, **IsClientConnected** that, when queried, will indicate if the client is still listening, at least since the last **Response.Write** command. The developer can query this value to determine if it should continue processing the page. If the client is gone, as in the case if they hit the stop button or selected another bookmark before the page loaded, then the application can end processing immediately, call **Session.Abandon** to instantly free up the resources of the session, then continue on to the next task. This value can also be used to check to see if a client is still waiting for a response after a lengthy server task.

Application and Session Variables

The **Application** and **Session** objects can be used to store values that are global either to a particular user (the **Session**) or to all users (the **Application**). Within the **onStart** events, we can initialize these variables. We can also store new variables, or change existing values, in the code inside any other ASP page.

Initializing variables is very important, especially with a language like VBScript that uses **Variants**. Imagine the following code in a page:

```
Response.Write("The current value is: " & Session("MyValue"))
```

This places the contents of the **Session** variable **MyValue** in the page. The only problem with this code is if the variable hasn't been initialized. In such a case what we get is:

```
The current value is:
```

Any **Variant** (the only data type available in VBScript) that hasn't been assigned a value is said to be **Empty**. Because we're dumping the variable as its default type, we get nothing. The best way to solve this type of problem is either assign a default value to it, or examine the variable using the **IsEmpty()** function. Here's how we could use **IsEmpty()**:

```
varTheValue = Session("MyValue")
If IsEmpty(varTheValue) Then varTheValue = "* Undefined *"
Response.Write("The current value is: " & varTheValue)
```

Alternatively, we can set any default value we like in the **Session_onStart** event, so that we have a value ready for access in that session:

```
Sub Session_OnStart
  Session("MyValue") = 42
End Sub
```

Counting Sessions

An immediately obvious use of this technique is to count how many sessions have occurred during the current application. All we do is use a variable stored in the **Application** object, which is then available to all sessions:

```
Sub Application_OnStart
  Application("NumVisitors") = 0
End Sub
```

Now, in **Session_onStart**, we can increment the value for each new session:

```
Sub Session_OnStart
  Application.Lock
  Application("NumVisitors") = Application("NumVisitors") + 1
  Application.Unlock
End Sub
```

Then we can drop it into the 'welcome' page with a few lines of code:

```
<% Application.Lock %>
<H3> Your are visitor number <% = Application("NumVisitors") %> </H3>
<% Application.Unlock %>
```

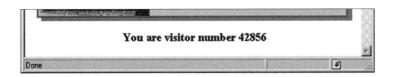

Storing Array Variables

In ASP, we have a problem when storing arrays in a **Session** or **Application** object. All Session-level and Application-level variables are stored as **Variants**. There is no way to store an array of variants. So we have to instead use a variant array, and store all of our values in there. The following example shows how we can get around this limitation:

```
'Create and initializing the array
Dim MyArray()
ReDim MyArray(5)
MyArray(0) = "hello"
MyArray(1) = "some other string"

'Store the array in the Session object
Session("StoredArray") = MyArray
```

```
'Now retrieve the array from the Session object
LocalArray = Session("StoredArray")
LocalArray(1) = "there"
...
'and then store the updated one back again
Session("StoredArray") = LocalArray
...
```

We create the array **MyArray()** and **ReDim** it to hold five elements. Then we assign strings to the elements **0** and **1**, and simply assign the array directly to a variable **StoredArray** in the **Session** object. We've effectively converted our array of strings into a **variant array**, and stored it in a single **Variant** in the **Session**.

Later in the same script–or in another request in the same session–we can retrieve the array using **LocalArray = Session("StoredArray")**, then access it as normal using the indexes. You might be tempted to believe that instead of assigning the array to a single **Session** variable, we could access it using **Session("StoredArray")(1) = "there"**, but this is *not* the correct method. It will result in loss of data.

The **Application** and **Session** objects' variables are implemented as collections, but should only be accessed using the **Contents** collection. This collection contains those items that have been declared without using **<OBJECT>** tags. This includes objects created by **Server.CreateObject**, and through variables stored in session or application level variables.

It is not possible to store references to any of the Active Server Pages built-in objects. The statement **Set Session("MyRequest") = Request** is not legal, for example.

Reference Counting with the Application Object

You'll recall we suggested earlier that the **Application_onEnd** event might not be fired until the application is explicitly unloaded in the Microsoft Management Console (MMC), or the web server is stopped. So what happens to the global objects that are stored within the **Application** object? They are kept alive and available all of the time. If you have a resource that you don't want to be kept in memory for days on end, when the application isn't in use; the following code solves the problem, and demonstrates some of the ways of using **Application** and **Session** objects:

```
Sub Session_OnStart
  Application.Lock
  If IsEmpty(Application("Object")) Then
    Set Application("Object") = Server.CreateObject("global.connection")
    Application("ObjectCount") = 0
  End If
  Application("ObjectCount") = Application("ObjectCount") + 1
  Application.Unlock
End Sub
```

```
Sub Session_OnEnd
  Application.Lock
  Application("ObjectCount") = Application("ObjectCount") - 1
  If Application("ObjectCount") = 0 Then
    Set Application("Object") = Nothing
  End If
  Application.Unlock
End Sub
```

The technique we use in this code is called **reference counting**. Notice that the **Application** *events* aren't used, but the **Application** *object* is. All the events are those that occur for each **Session**. The technique, however, is simple enough. At the start of each **Session**, we only create an instance of the object we want (in this case a fictitious **"global.connection"**) if it doesn't already exist. At the end of each **Session** we destroy the object if no one else is using it. This works because **Session_onEnd** is always fired. If you like, it's the old 'last one out turn off the lights' trick.

> *In Chapter 13, when we look at application components, you will see some of the caveats relating to storing objects as application-level properties. Basically, the object needs to be marked as Both threaded for optimum performance. If this is not possible given the development tool, the apartment threaded is the only other reasonable choice. These threading terms will be more fully explained in Chapter 13.*

How It Works

This code works by keeping a count of the number of users that are using the application at any one time, storing this count in a global variable called **ObjectCount**. If this is zero, or doesn't exist, the **Session_onStart** code creates the object and stores the reference to it in the **Application** object as a variable called **Object**, and it's then available to all users. At the same time, it sets the value of **ObjectCount** to zero, in case it didn't actually exist––in other words if this was the first ever session to use the application.

The next step is to increment the value of **ObjectCount**, so that it reflects the number of current sessions. If the object already exists when a **Session** starts, and the **Object** variable does reference an object when this session begins (i.e. it's not **Empty**), the code will just increment **ObjectCount** without creating a new instance of the object.

The **Session_onEnd** code, which runs for each **Session** as it ends, just has to decrement the value of **ObjectCount**. It can then tell how many other sessions are still active. If this is zero it can destroy the object by setting its reference variable to **Nothing**.

Notice that we've again used the **Application** object's **Lock** and **Unlock** methods before changing the values of any of its variables. Failing to do this can cause all kinds of problems by allowing more than one session to access the values at the same time. This concept is called **concurrency**, and we'll look at the implications that arise from it next.

Application Concurrency Issues

As we've already seen, the purpose of the **Application** object is to be able to store information that is globally used among all application users. These could be object reference variables or other values that all application users require access to. However, the problem is that, because they are shared, we can come up against concurrency problems. Consider the following example:

```
Application("NumberOfSales") = Application("NumberOfSales") + 1
```

This line of code in an ASP file could be used to count the number of users who had ordered goods from our site. It maintains the count in the **Application** variable **myData**. However, if two users access this variable at the same time corruption is likely to occur, because the single **Application** object has global scope and is visible to all. User **A** reads the value of **NumberOfSales** at the same time as user **B**. Both instances of the ASP page get the same value, they both increment it, and they both store it back in the **Application** object. The result is that it only gets incremented once. It might even corrupt it altogether if both writes occurred at the same moment.

Locking the Application Object

To solve the problem, we just change the code to read:

```
Application.Lock
Application("NumberOfSales") = Application("NumberOfSales") + 1
Application.Unlock
```

> *You don't need to use **Lock** and **Unlock** in the **Application_onStart** event because this event can only be called once—by the single session that starts the application. The **Application_onStart** event is called before the first **Session_onStart** event, which is called before the ASP page is actually processed. However, we do need to call it in the **Session_onStart** event.*

Read-Only Session and Application Variables

You may think that with a simple assignment like the one we've just looked at, the chances of corruption are remote. That may be true for a single-processor computer, but with SMP multiprocessor machines this assumption isn't safe under all circumstances. One useful trick, where appropriate, is to make variables read-only for all sessions by checking the value first–as shown here:

```
Sub Session_OnStart
  Application.Lock
  If IsEmpty(Application("myData")) Then
     Application("myData") = strTheValue
  End if
  Application.Unlock
End Sub
```

This code only sets the value of the variable if it hasn't been set before, giving it–in effect–a default value. Once the variable has been assigned a value, and isn't **Empty**, it can't be changed. However, any other code can read the value as required, and with no fear of corruption:

```
Application.Lock
MyVar = Application("myData")
Application.Unlock
```

> *This does not prevent the developer from locking the application object and assigning a new value to the application-level variable. There is no way to make the variable TRULY read-only.*

Using Global Values and Object References

While the previous example solves the concurrency problem, it brings with it new ones. In a very busy site, the code to read the value could be called thousands of times a day. Locking the application just to read a value could drastically hit server performance. The situation is even worse when we come to store references to objects, which could be required by all users.

If we only need to read the value of a variable as it stood at the start of a session, we could copy it from the **Application** object into that user's **Session** object. Then, each ASP page could reference the **Session** version. This has a downside, however, in that the value will not keep up with changes to the value in the **Application** object automatically–but it all comes down to what we actually use the values for.

```
Sub Application_OnStart
    Application("myData") = "Initial Value"
End Sub

Sub Session_OnStart
  Application.Lock
  Session("myData_SessionCopy") = Application("myData")
  Application.Unlock
End Sub
```

Connection Pooling with ADO

When we come to use objects like the ActiveX Data Objects (ADO), we often need to access a single instance of it several times in a page, and across our application. For example, we use the **ADODB.Connection** object to create a database connection. Instead of doing it on every page, we might consider just opening a single database connection once (in **Session_onStart**, or even in the **Application_onStart**) and then using that connection throughout the entire session or application.

> *The new direction coming from Microsoft is that ADO logic should not be put in ASP. It should be stored in Business Objects that are controlled by Microsoft Transaction Server (MTS). We will examine MTS and Business Objects in great detail starting in Chapter 13.*

Database applications designed for a multi-user audience will generally run on something like SQL Server, or another high-end database. While reusing a connection stored in the **Session** or **Application** object might be an efficient way to work with low transaction volume databases like Microsoft Access, this method loses its attractiveness as the number of users of our application increases.

You might recall from Chapter 8 that ODBC 3.0 includes a feature called **connection pooling**, which manages connections across multiple users. When using connection pooling it's best to open and close the database connection on each page that uses it—this allows ODBC to manage the connections most efficiently. Without it, there could be ten users logged onto our application not actually doing anything, which could cause ten idle connections that decrease performance and consume server and database resources.

So, with Access, you should consider a **Session_onStart** instantiation of connections—while for other databases it may well be wiser to use local connections in each page. The *Accessing a Database* topic of the IIS Documentation can provide you with more detailed information about connection pooling.

Global Object Reference Problems

When we come to create global references to objects, however, we can't just shuffle the values around between the **Application** and **Session** objects. This is because we run the risk of creating problems as the object's own internal state changes. Instead, we need to make the decision as to where we actually want to use the object. We saw ways of creating and destroying an object at global **Application** level earlier. We can, of course, create **Session** level objects in **Session_onStart**, and destroy them in **Session_onEnd**. In this case, we don't have to worry about concurrency, and we know they will not hang around in server memory when the session ends.

Creating objects at **Session** level is generally the best solution. If we do need a global object for the whole application, we have to take some extra care when using it. Have a look at these two extracts of code:

```
Sub Application_OnStart
    Application("myObject") = Server.CreateObject("game500.player")
End Sub
```

This is in **global.asa**, and it creates the global instance of the object that will manage a multi-user card game. In one of the ASP files that are used as part of the game, we call the **SetData** method of this object to change the game state at that point.

```
Application("myObject").SetData(Request.QueryString("txtUser"))
```

If there are multiple players in the game that are trying to call this method simultaneously, then there could be a data concurrency problem. Part of this data concurrency problem is handled by ASP itself, in the way it handles different types of objects. In Chapter 13, we will look at the issues surrounding the threading model that an object uses, and how that affects the operation of the rest of the application. In this case, one threading model will allow multiple users to access the object at one time, in which case the object itself must deal with data concurrency. Another threading model, known as single threaded, will serialize the access to the object, solving the concurrency problem for us. This discussion will be looked at in greater detail in Chapter 13.

When State Doesn't Look After Itself

The whole concept of **Applications** and **Sessions** requires the browser to accept and implement cookies. If it doesn't, then ASP is unable to maintain state information of any kind. In that case, we have to resort to the older methods of CGI programming.

How State Works in ASP

As we said earlier, the HTTP protocol is inherently stateless, and relies on cookies to be able to manage and recognize requests, and match them to the users. When ASP wants to establish a session, it sends the **Set-Cookie** HTTP header to the browser, to establish a unique user session ID and the path of the application it corresponds to–i.e. where the appropriate **global.asa** file resides:

```
Set-Cookie: ASPSESSIONID=LRUSDYXQMWRTNWEB; path=/TestApp
```

From our discussions of cookies in Chapter 4, you'll realize that this one doesn't expire until the browser is shut down. In theory, if the browser was to be left running for weeks on end, the cookie will remain current. But the **Session** object has a default **Timeout** of twenty minutes, and at that point the **Session** is marked as having ended and any variables in it are destroyed.

The Un-expired Cookie Problem

The fact that a user's **SessionID** cookie may not have expired, while the matching **Session** on the server has already expired, raises an interesting question. What happens if that user comes back to our site again? The server will check the **sessionID** in their cookie against the currently active sessions, and if it doesn't match will just create and initialize a new **Session**. The user then effectively 'goes back to the start'. The new **Session** will be created with the same **sessionID** as the old **Session**. However, the data from the original session will no longer be available.

Of course, this assumes that the **sessionID** will be unique for every user. If this isn't the case, the application might find itself with two users sharing a **Session**. ASP will ensure that all **sessionID** values within an application are unique for that instance of the application. If the application is unloaded and restarted, or if the server itself is stopped and restarted, then ASP could conceivable produce duplicate **sessionID** values. If a browser has a cookie that has not expired yet, and goes to access the server, there is a very, very small chance that they could inadvertently get another user's session.

When the Cookie Jar is Empty

One problem that Microsoft can't prevent is the situation where the **sessionID** cookie our server sends isn't supported by the browser, or is not accepted by the user. Or more critically, it's possible for the server administrator to turn off the ability to maintain sessions altogether by editing the registry. Now, the automatic state mechanism isn't going to work, so we need an alternative plan.

We could use a system originally implemented in ASP (but then removed again) which added parameters to all the hyperlinks in the pages that served to pass on the `sessionID`. We could emulate this, or just shunt the user off to a separate version of our site that worked without requiring state information. We could even throw them out altogether, though this may tend to discourage future visits.

Checking for Cookie Acceptance

But before we can do any of this, we need a way of determining whether the browser can support cookies, without causing havoc. Easy enough. We just use a default opening page that gets sent to *every* user when they first enter the application. We could include a 'Welcome' graphic, like a real application's splash screen, or possibly some introduction to the site:

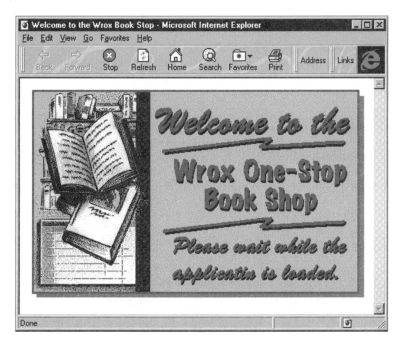

Here's the code that creates this page, with the important lines highlighted:

```
<HTML>
<HEAD>
<META HTTP-EQUIV="REFRESH" CONTENT="5; URL=hellotest.asp">
<TITLE>Document Title</TITLE>
</HEAD>
<BODY>
<CENTER><IMG SRC="Welcome.gif"></CENTER>
<% On Error Resume Next
   Session("TestBrowser")="Hello" %>
</BODY>
</HTML>
```

The ASP code first turns off error checking, then stores a value in a **Session** level variable named **TestBrowser**. If the browser doesn't support cookies, or if they're turned off, there will be no **Session** object and the code will fail–however, there won't be an error message because of the **On Error Resume Next**. The real key to this page is the first highlighted line:

```
<META HTTP-EQUIV="REFRESH" CONTENT="5; URL=hellotest.asp">
```

Once the page has finished loading, the browser waits five seconds and then loads the page **hellotest.asp**–which contains this code, placed before the **<HEAD>** section:

```
<% On Error Resume Next
   If IsEmpty(Session("TestBrowser")) Then
     Response.Redirect "NoCookie.asp"
   Else
     Response.Redirect "AllowCookie.asp"
   End If %>
<HTML>
<HEAD>
   . . .
```

All it does is check the value of the **TestBrowser** variable. If it's **Empty** we know that the browser, for one reason or another, doesn't have the ability to use a **Session**–which is likely to be because it can't (or won't) support our **sessionID** cookies. If this is the case we just redirect the visitor to a page that is intended for non-session ASP users. Otherwise it's business as usual, and we redirect them to the main menu of our application. Notice that it's necessary to wrap the **If** statement in another **On Error Resume Next**, in case the **IsEmpty** test fails. If it does, the next statement to be executed still sends them to the non-session area of the site.

Using Document Redirection

The code we've seen in the previous section is an excellent example of the way that we can redirect users to a different page at will. We can often take advantage of this method to route users through an application, depending on the current state for that user, or the application as a whole.

For example, we might allow them to choose goods they want to purchase, in a kind of virtual shopping trolley. Each time they click the Yes, I Want One button, we add the details to our **Session** object, using an array as we saw earlier:

```
Sub cmdYesIWantOne_onClick
   'Retrieve the array and current item count from the Session object ...
   LocalArray = Session("BoughtItems")
   intNumberOfItems = CInt(Session("ItemCount")) + 1
   LocalArray(intNumberOfItems) = strItemCodeNumber
   'then store the updated values back again.
   Session("BoughtItems") = LocalArray
   Session("ItemCount") = CStr(intNumberOfItems)
End Sub
```

When they've finished shopping, and click the All Done Now button, we only need to route them to the virtual checkout if they've actually bought anything. It's easy using document redirection:

```
    If CInt(Session("ItemCount")) > 0 Then
      Response.Redirect "cashdesk.asp"
    Else
      Response.Redirect "thankyou.asp"
    End If
```

Redirecting from Within a Page

Doing a redirection like the last example is only possible from the header of a document, before any content has been sent to the browser. If we attempt it after that, we get a Buffer not empty error. Remember (Chapter 4) that if we want to provide an opportunity for redirection to occur part way through a page, we need to turn on **buffering**, and clear the buffer:

```
<%@ LANGUAGE="VBSCRIPT" %>
<% Response.Buffer = True %>
<HTML>
<HEAD><TITLE> Document Title </TITLE></HEAD>
<BODY>
<H1>Welcome to our site</H1><P>
<% If Session("TestCondition") = True Then
      Response.Clear
      Response.Redirect "anotherpage.asp"
   End If %>
   . . .
   rest of page
   . . .
</BODY>
</HTML>
```

HTTP/1.1 Protocol

IIS 4.0 now supports the new **HTTP/1.1** protocol. HTTP stands for **HyperText Transfer Protocol**, and it defines how web servers and web browsers communicate. The earlier versions of this protocol, 0.9 and 1.0, were what gave the web its stateless and connectionless attributes. Some of the new features that are now supported in version 1.1 are:

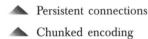 Persistent connections

 Chunked encoding

Caching

Of course, since the protocol defines both client **and** server, the browser must also support HTTP/1.1. Internet Explorer 4.0 is one of the next generation of browsers to support this protocol, and all of the features it adds.

Persistent connections

One of the techniques that browsers use to increase performance is to open multiple connections with a server when downloading a page. This way, one connection can be downloading the text of the page, another the background graphic, and even more for the other graphics or objects. This means, in effect, that the server has to deal with many times more connections than actual users. Since each of these connections is made using the TCP protocol, each one is subject to the lengthy startup time that a TCP connection is *in*famous for.

To get around this problem, HTTP/1.1 uses persistent connections between the server and the browser. This means that the connection only needs to be opened once, incurring that TCP connection establishment only once. The connection is held open, and multiple requests can be passed through it. This also allows the browser to send multiple requests to the server at once, without requiring a response from one before sending another. The server will respond to each request in order.

Chunked encoding

In earlier versions of HTTP, the server and browser did not specify how long the response was that was sent back to the client. Since the connection was closed at the end of each response, the server would close it when it was done sending data. The browser would see that the connection had closed and know that all the data had been sent. But now, with persistent connections the connection is left open at the end of the response. So now, the server must tell the client how much data it can expect by using the **Content-Length** header at the beginning of the response.

This is quite easy to compute when working with static HTML files. All the server has to do is ask the OS for the length of the file, then put that value in the **Content-Length** header before sending the file. But what happens when the server is trying to return an ASP page. In a dynamically generated page, its length is not known until the end. One way would be to completely generate the page at the server, compute its length, and then send it to the client. But this would seriously impair perceived performance, since nothing would appear at the browser until the page was completely done.

This problem is solved in HTTP/1.1 through the use of **chunked encoding**. This is a method of sending back the response using chunks of data, each of which includes its size as part of the data. The chunks that are sent back for a particular response can be of different sizes, since each carries its own size with it. When all of the data has been sent, the server sends a chunk with a size of 0. When the browser reads this chunk, it knows that it has received all of the data for this response.

Caching

In general, since ASP pages are dynamically generated, the client should not cache them. The developer can use the **Expires** property of the **Response** object to explicitly state how long the client should cache the page for. Setting the value of the property to **0** will cause the browser to ask for a new page from the server every time this page is accessed. This can be used to reduce the load on the server. For example, the server knows that the data will change only once an hour. It can compute the time until the next data change, and then tell the client that it can cache the page until then. This way, if the user wishes to view the page within the hour, the browser will know to show the one from cache, and not even bother contacting the server.

In addition to browsers performing their own caching, clients who access the Internet through proxy servers may have information cached at the proxy server. Networks such as AOL will cache popular web sites in their proxy servers, which will provide a faster response time for their clients. In previous versions of the HTTP protocol, there was no way for IIS and ASP to tell proxy servers how to, or if to, cache dynamically generated pages. All pages were marked as non-cacheable.

The caching model in HTTP/1.1 provides a much richer set of options when dealing with determining how items are cached. One of these options will allow proxy servers to cache dynamically generated information. If a developer wants an ASP page to be cached, they can set the **CacheControl** property of the **Response** object to "**Public**". As long as the proxy sever supports the HTTP/1.1 protocol, which not all of them do, it will cache the page for all clients that are behind it.

Making use of State Information

We've now established the ways that Active Server Pages can provide us with the state information we need to create working client/server applications. We have a unique **Session** object for each user and we can store values and object references in it. These will remain valid while that user is working with the application. In this section, we'll look at ways that we can use this information, then move on to considering how it might influence the design of our site, and the pages it contains.

Logging Users into an Application

One of the primary reasons that we use state information is to identify each user. They are already identified within ASP by a **sessionID**, but this tends not to be very useful. What we will generally want to do is change the behavior of our application based on the user's absolute identity, i.e. a **UserID** or **nickname**. This follows a similar practice to a normal, non-Web-based client/server application.

It's possible to identify users through advanced communication methods, when using **Secure Channels** or **Challenge/Response Authentication**–subjects that we will cover in Chapter 14. However, often we'll need to implement a standard log-on type of dialog, and then use the information the user provides within our application.

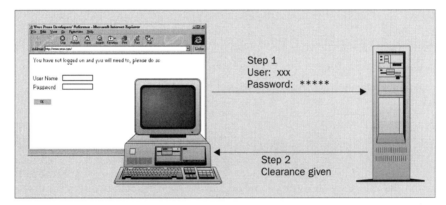

The user supplies a user name, a password and clicks the Submit button. All we need to do is respond to the request by checking these details. It makes sense to use the **POST** method for the form so that the information isn't sent attached to the URL in the query string, but at least partly concealed within the HTTP header. Of course, we should really use some type of secure transmission as well, to ensure maximum privacy.

Using the User's Information

Having received the request at the server, we can examine the values the user entered:

```
txtUserName = Request.Form("txtUserName")
txtPassWord = Request.Form("txtPassWord")
```

The question now is what do we do with it? We can use it in our code in a minimalist way, like:

```
Welcome <% = txtUserName %> to our site
```

and even to redirect users, or control access to the pages:

```
If txtUserName = "Admin" And txtPassWord = "secret" Then
    Response.Redirect "AdminPage.asp"
ElseIf txtUserName = "Manager" And txtPassWord = "reports" Then
    Response.Redirect "SalesReports.asp"
Else
    Response.Redirect "UserMenu.asp"
End If
```

Even so, this doesn't really provide a foundation for 'proper' application design. We need to be able to log users in, verify their passwords against a central list, and decide what further action to take. For example, we might want to deny access to users who don't have an existing user name (i.e. not accept new users), or we might want to automatically add them to our user list and give them certain default access permission. And if they have been here before, do we have any user preferences we need to set, like the background and foreground colors of their pages?

Verifying the User

Generally, the first step will be to verify who the user is, and decide if we already know them. Then, if we do know them, we can check to see if they've supplied the correct password. This process involves three basic steps, and we'll normally be taking the information from a database of some kind. In the following example we'll work through the steps, which are:

- See if the user name exists in the database
- If it does, check that the password is correct
- If it doesn't, add the user to the database if appropriate

Does the User Already Exist?

To see if the user already exists in our database, we just need to search for their user name in the appropriate table. Assuming we have a table **UserDetails** with **UserName** and **UserPword** fields, we can use an SQL query to extract the details. However, we may need to ensure that the length of the database fields and the validation are identical, depending on how the database actually stores text fields.

The database system may offer two types of text field **varChar** and **char**. If the field is of type **char** and length **10**, we would need to pad out the string to **10** characters first, to ensure that we get a match. Using **varChar**, or a normal **Text** field in Access, avoids this problem.

So, we can use the normal ADO object methods in our page to find out if the user exists. Here, we're using a **connection string** that we previously stored in the **Session** object, so that we can retrieve it as required:

```
'create SQL string using the value in the txtUserName control on the form
strSQL = "SELECT UserName, UserPword FROM UserDetails WHERE _
    (UserName = '" & Request.Form("txtUserName") & "')"

'create the database connection and open a recordset with the results
Set oConn = Server.CreateObject("ADODB.Connection")
oConn.Open Session("Logon_ConnectionString"),
Set oUsers = Server.CreateObject("ADODB.Recordset")
```

```
oUserRs = oConn.Execute(strSQL)

'now check if there is a record
If oUserRs.BOF AND oUserRs.EOF Then              'we didn't get any records
    Response.Write("User name does not exist")
    ...
```

Once we've got the **recordset**, we just need to see if there was a record in it. There will only be one at most, because the user name would need to be unique, and defined this way in the database tables. We might try using the **RecordCount** property, but this requires a move to the last record first (see Chapter 7 for more about how this works). And if we do this with an empty **recordset**, it only causes an error. The easier way is to do what we do here, and check the values of **BOF** and **EOF**. Only if the **recordset** is empty will they both be **True**.

Does the Password Check Out?

If this first check discovers a record, then the user exists in the database, so we can now compare the password. The **recordset** we retrieved contains the password field as well. If the password is stored in the clear, then it's just a matter of a straight comparison. If the password is encoded in some manner, then the value that the user submitted can be passed through the same encoding, and that value compared against the one in the database

```
    ...
    Else
        If Request.Form("txtPassword") <> oUserRs.Fields("UserPword") Then
            Response.Write("You did not enter the correct password")
            ...
```

The usual option here would be to allow them another attempt, by displaying the login form again. It's quite possible to do this in the same page, and in the next few chapters you'll see how we can achieve this.

Adding New Users to the Database

If the user name check fails, in other words the user doesn't already exist, we need to decide if we want to add them to the database as a new user. Again, an SQL statement can do this. We know that the username they have supplied is unique compared to the existing ones, because we didn't get a record returned. All we need is an appropriate SQL **INSERT** statement:

```
    ...
    'add the user to the database
    strSQL = "INSERT INTO UserDetails (UserName, UserPword) VALUES ('" _
            & Request.Form("txtUsername") & "','" _
            & Request.Form("txtPassword") & "')"
    oConn.Execute(strSQL)
    ...
```

Ensuring Concurrency during Log-on

There's just one problem. If we're going to add records to a globally accessible database, we need to make sure that we don't upset any other logons that are being performed concurrently. For small sites this risk is marginal, but consider what would happen if two new users specified the same user name. The **recordset** we retrieved would be out of date by the time we came to add the new record, and the original could by now already contain the user name we're trying to add.

We could get around this in several ways. Firstly by making sure the database table design specified unique values—and then trapping the error that would arise. However, this approach isn't ASP-centric, so instead we'll try one that makes use of the features available in ASP. What we need is a concurrency model that controls access to an item during the process, preventing two sessions accessing it at the same time.

Locking the Connection

Here's one possibility. Having decided to add the user, we do another database search for this user name in case it has been added meanwhile, by another visitor. However, we first lock the **Application** object while we read the connection string, and keep it locked until we've finished the whole process. Now, no other session can create a connection, and upset our code. While the application is locked, this session will be the only one that is processed. We do need to be careful as keeping the application locked for too long will degrade the performance of the web site. Notice also that we only need to extract the user name and not the password as well. And the result we want is to *not* find a record this time

```
'create SQL string using the value in the txtUserName control on the form
strSQL = "SELECT UserName FROM UserDetails WHERE UserName = '" _
        & Request.Form("txtUserName") & "')"

'create the database connection and open a recordset with the results
Application.Lock
Set oConn = Server.CreateObject("ADODB.Connection")
oConn.Open Session("Logon_ConnectionString"),
Set oUsers = Server.CreateObject("ADODB.Recordset")
oUserRs = oConn.Execute(strSQL)

'now check if there is a record
If oUserRs.BOF AND oUserRs.EOF Then       'we didn't get any records
   strSQL = "INSERT INTO UserDetails (UserName, UserPword) VALUES ('" _
           & Request.Form("txtUsername") & "','" _
           & Request.Form("txtPassword") & "')"
   oConn.Execute(strSQL)
Else
   Response.Write("Error accessing database, please try again")
End If
Application.Unlock
```

We could, of course, have just locked the **Application** originally. This would have saved the second search through. It all depends on whether you expect to get more existing users than new visitors, or vice-versa.

Making Use of the Logon Information

Having identified our users as they log onto the application, what are we actually going to do with the information? This is open to the design of your applications, and it's not possible to lay down criteria, methods, or examples that are going to be relevant to every individual's needs. However, there are a few obvious details that we should consider.

Setting User Preferences

Recall that when we logged an existing user into our application, we extracted the single record from the **UserDetail** table in our database that contained their user name and password. This record could just as easily contain a great deal more about the user, such as their department, workgroup, page color preferences, or even the name of their dog. All we need to do is change the SQL query to include all the fields in the **recordset**, and then capture the other details in **Session** level variables ready for use while the user is touring our site:

```
strSQL = "SELECT * FROM UserDetails WHERE UserName = '" _
         & Request.Form("txtUserName") & "')"
...
...
Session("BackColor") = oUserRs.Fields("BackColor")
Session("FontColor") = oUserRs.Fields("FontColor")
Session("DogsName") = oUserRs.Fields("DogsName")
...
```

Now, we can really make them feel at home:

```
<HTML>
<HEAD>
<TITLE> Welcome to the Wrox Pets Supermarket </TITLE>
</HEAD>
<BODY BGCOLOR=<% = Session("BackColor") %>>
 <FONT FACE=Arial COLOR=<% = Session("FontColor") %>>
 <CENTER><IMG SRC="welcome.gif"><CENTER><P>
 <H3> Great News... </H3> We now have a new variety of Scrummy<BR>
 <I><B>the dog food for champions</B></I><BR>
 available from the new products page.<P>
 Why not take some home for<B> <% = Session("DogsName")%> </B>- we
 <I>guarantee</I> it will be a hit!
</BODY>
</HTML>
```

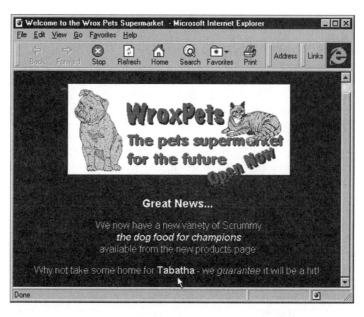

Checking the Success of Object Creation

One thing we regularly do in the **Application_onStart** and **Session_onStart** events is to create instances of objects that we need to use throughout the application. In our logon example, we're also creating objects to check the user's identity–database connections and recordsets. If any of these processes fail, the state of our application is invalid. In this case, taking the login page as our example, we must be sure to set the 'logged on' status to **False**.

The easiest way is to examine the object variable that is now supposed to be referencing the object instance. We can use either **IsEmpty()** or **IsObject()** for this, or compare it to the standard value **Nothing**. It depends on whether we're referring to the object itself or a variable that holds a reference to it. In both cases, for it to work, we have turn off error checking with an **On Error Resume Next** statement first:

```
On Error Resume Next
Set oConn = Server.CreateObject("ADODB.Connection")
If IsObject(oConn) Then
  '... success, OK to continue
Else
  '... error, could not create object
End If
```

```
On Error Resume Next
Set Session("MyConnection") = Server.CreateObject("ADODB.Connection")

'now check if it failed
If Session("MyConnection") Is Nothing Then
  '... got an error
```

Or we can use this method:

```
If IsEmpty(Session("MyConnection")) Then
  '... got an error
```

Designing for Client/Server

We spent some time early in this chapter looking at what client/server really is, and how we need to build applications to a structure that makes sense for the environment in which they are used. In our case, whether on the Internet or an intranet, we're looking to share processing as evenly as possible between the client and the server. This involves moving the business rules, wherever appropriate, to the client–and leaving the server to do the actual processing work.

The browser (our client) can no longer be just the dumb terminal that we've been assuming all the way through this book so far. It has to do its share of the work where appropriate, and to achieve this we need to extend our application's processing across the network. We need to be able to program the client. Much of the rest of this book details how we can do this, and how we integrate the processing at both ends of the wire into a seamless application.

To finish off this chapter, we'll look briefly at the methods available to do this, and consider how this affects the design of our applications. We'll be considering three main areas:

▲ Designing to match the Business Rules

▲ Different ways to use a browser

▲ Client-side scripting and components

Designing to the Business Rules

The key to developing successful client/server applications is to develop the objects within it using the business rules. Allowing a programmer to create their objects as they go along, without understanding the ultimate needs of the application and the business it must support, leads to long term maintenance and expansion problems. Any team developing client/server applications, or any other programs, needs to talk to the business team, so that they are aware of the problems they face and the solutions they need.

As an example, imagine building a house. If it were built according to the *builder's* needs, i.e. speed, ease of construction, and minimum cost, the house would be functional and not overly complex. However, the people who actually live in the building may find it confining, unsuitable for their domestic requirements, and when it comes time to redecorate they may find it too expensive to realize their wishes.

But didn't the team leader at your last project meeting say that the current main aims of the project were speed, ease of construction and minimum cost?

Use Good Design Techniques

This is an absolute requirement. You must begin by designing your application and not launch straight away into building parts of it to see what happens. Grab a book on client/server systems design, read and analyze the examples, and then develop your design for the final application. Good design, which matches the needs of the business, will ensure that the application will be maintainable and expandable. Plus as a by-product the debugging requirements will fall dramatically.

The key to good design is developing the application as components, be they individual pages, HTML files, or compiled standard or custom components. Active Server Pages allows even script code to be built into modules and used as required. Remember the Server-side Include command **#include**? We can use this to insert any file into an ASP file, and it's an ideal way of storing functions and subroutines as text files that are used by several other pages:

```
<!-- #INCLUDE FILE="MyFunction.inc" -->
```

By defining and maintaining the same interface, (i.e. names and parameters of the routines it contains) we can update them as required, without affecting the pages that use them.

Use Small and Efficient Techniques

Active Server Pages has a relatively simple debugging environment, and they are still interpreted at run-time. So it makes sense to move much of the standard functionality into server components where possible. Using small well-defined components can speed up the entire development process, and the execution speed of the application. It has other advantages as well, as we'll discuss in the case study that follows in the next few chapters. For example, we can update the component, and all the pages that use it will automatically take advantage of the changes. It also gives us the opportunity to encapsulate secret business rules inside the component, rather than as script in a page.

The question is, how do we define a small component? In reality, what we want is the minimum code and the optimum functionality–based on a business rule or business object. Remember, we may have many instances running at a time if they are created at page or session level.

A Sample Page Counter Component

We saw how we can use the **Application** object and VBScript code to maintain a count of visitors to our site, by counting new sessions. There is, however, a problem with this. The contents of the **Application** object are lost when it is destroyed, i.e. when the application ends. This may be when the Web server is stopped, or in the future when all active sessions have ended. So we need to consider some more solid way of saving the data.

The IIS ships with a sample **page counter component** (which we looked at in chapter 6) that neatly demonstrates the principles of component design. It's written in C++, and is reasonably compact in code terms. It also has added functionality in that it can maintain a count of accesses to almost as many different pages as we like. The details of the 'hits' to each page are stored in a text file on the server's disk. Before the server shuts down and at undetermined intervals while it is running, the component updates this file from a memory-based cache of hit counts.

The component is instantiated on any page for which a count is required–it can't be created at session or application level like most other components because it uses the URL of the current page, which can be derived from the HTTP Server variables, to identify the page:

```
Set MyCount = Server.CreateObject("IISSample.PageCounter")
```

This is all that's required to maintain the hit count. Each time the page is accessed by the server, the count is incremented. To get the count for the current page, we just use the **Hits** method:

```
Response.Write("You are visitor number " & MyCount.Hits)
```

To reset the counter for the current page, we just call its **Reset** method. So this is a simple but highly efficient component, packaged up and available to be dropped into a page easily. You can get a copy from:

http://backoffice.microsoft.com/downtrial/moreinfo/iissamples.asp

Different Ways to Use a Browser

In a client/server situation, the browser is going to become a lot more than just a way of viewing static pages. It actually becomes part of the application, and so we need to be aware of some of the other ways it can be used. For example, we can embed the browser inside another application, or use a special control called the **Web Browser Control** that comes as part of the Internet Explorer controls installation.

Alternatively, we can embed other applications within the web browser, although this gives us only limited opportunity for adding extra features to our applications. We can even use a control called the **Internet Transfer Control**, (available from Microsoft as part of Visual Basic 5) that allows us to retrieve pages from the server without actually displaying them–but we can then get at the information in the HTTP stream, the HTML code, and the text contents.

Embedding a Browser within an Application

Typical web browsing involves either surfing from one site to another, or searching for specific information. In many situations, the user simply types in a URL, or clicks on previously defined bookmarks. While this is simple enough, it isn't the most user-friendly method. And if you have a set of predefined sites that the users go to regularly—such as the technical catalogue menu on your intranet or a shares value monitor on the Net as a whole—how do you keep the lists up to date?

Microsoft's Internet Explorer is actually an object, and the program **IExplore.exe** that we run to start it is just a shell. We can create our own instances of the **InternetExplorer** object in code in Visual Basic, or most other languages. By embedding the browser within another application like this we have the ability to create a lightweight shell, and yet maintain dynamic content within that shell.

This has many advantages. For example, it can give us a standard corporate interface with pop-up forms, and extra features. The regularly used sites can be catalogued and controlled by the application, even allowing the server administrator to shift all of the users from one site to another, without the clients even realizing that it is happening. Selecting certain sites could be entirely automatic, and the server can control the whole process. Of course, all these techniques are really intranet-bound, in an environment where you can specify the client software directly.

Using the InternetExplorer.Application Object

Creating and controlling the browser in code is easy, and can be done from any application that supports Visual Basic for Applications and can control automation objects, or most other programming languages. Here's an example that uses VBA:

```
Dim TheBrowser as SHDocVw.InternetExplorer
Set TheBrowser = New "InternetExplorer.Application"
TheBrowser.Visible = True
```

Once we've got the browser instance, and made it visible, we just use its methods and properties like any other object. Here are a few examples:

```
TheBrowser.Navigate URL:= "http://www.wrox.com
TheBrowser.Top = 100                    'set the browser in the top
TheBrowser.left = 100                    'left of the user's screen
TheBrowser.StatusBar = True              'display the status bar
TheBrowser.GoSearch                      'open the default Search page
TheBrowser.GoHome                        'open the default Home page
TheBrowser.Refresh                       'refresh the current page
TheBrowser.Quit                          'close the browser
```

Running an Application within the Browser

The browser will quite happily download and display different kinds of documents, as well as the usual defaults of **.htm** pages, **.txt** files, and **.jpg** or **.gif** images. However, if the user has Office 97, or the Office viewers, installed on their machine, Internet Explorer will also handle standard office documents, like Word **.doc** files and Excel **.xls** spreadsheets. Because Internet Explorer is a COM Container, it can provide in-place viewing and editing capabilities to a document whose application supports COM.

Here, we've used Word 97 to create a document, and saved it in Word's standard **.doc** format. The template contains custom macros that manipulate the Office Assistant character and produce a user guide:

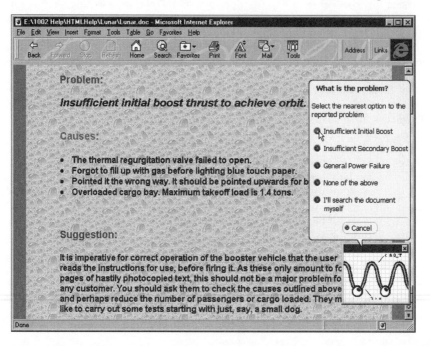

This is really only useful in an intranet environment, because of the size of the documents. And the user can't normally edit the original, only the copy that is downloaded to their own browser. However, by maintaining local copies of templates, and loading files directly over the network (using the syntax **HREF="file://C:\Documents\Lunar.doc"**, for example) we can achieve a great deal this way.

Client-Side Scripting and Components

Before Active Server Pages came along, there were web browsers that could interpret script code embedded in the HTML, and host Java or ActiveX components. ASP is a very powerful environment that enables quick and easy creation of a huge variety of web pages. However, there are times when the fact that ASP can only execute script and use objects on the web server creates limitations, such as we've discovered with client/server applications. Quite often, these limitations can be overcome by using client-side code and a range of special objects, in tandem with pages generated by ASP.

Why use Client-Side Features?

Since this book is primarily about the server side of web application development, we will not spend too much time looking at the ways you can do client-side programming. You can check out the case studies later in the book for some examples of using client-side programming. For an in-depth look at the power of client side programming, take a look at *Professional IE4 Programming* from WROX–*ISBN 1-861000-70-7*.

As just a simple example of the power that client-side programming can provide, think back to the task of performing validation of data entered on a form like our earlier logon code. If the user is supposed to supply a six-character user name, and they enter only four characters, verification is bound to fail.

However, it still involves a bandwidth-consuming trip across the network to the web server, and back again, just to inform them that they didn't enter enough characters. Client-side code can do this validation, and inform the user of their mistake, before the form is actually submitted to the server.

But we know that it's generally much easier to perform complicated computations and tasks on the server and send back a completed page consisting solely of HTML, than it is to send a page and attempt to perform many of the same tasks via HTTP (especially with today's technology). And since we know the kind of browser our page will be viewed on, we can modify our page so that it suits that browser well. So there are two sides to the argument.

Sharing the Processing Load

To decide how you split the processing in your applications, keep in mind the different layers of the client/server model, and the arguments for and against client-side programming in your particular environment. We saw earlier that the business rules should exist on the client-side where possible, and the length of an acceptable user name is a valid business rule. However, as we've seen earlier, actually processing the user name is a server-side job—to maintain security, concurrency and efficiency.

There are also the concerns of browser compatibility. Hopefully, the approved HTML 4.0 standard will move the two major browsers, Internet Explorer 4.0 and Netscape Navigator 4.0, closer to being compatible. The tremendous increases in flexibility on the client side that **Dynamic HTML**, a **Scriptable Object Model**, and **Cascading Style Sheets** provide make the use of these technologies very compelling. For example:

- Need to display data in a format more robust and interactive than allowed by HTML? Take a look at the power provided by Dynamic HTML in creating interfaces that are far more robust than plain HTML.

- Need to provide immediate feedback to someone entering text on a form without requiring that they send another request to your server? Use client-side code to validate their input. Even better, Remote Scripting allows you to call a method on the server without going through the standard HTTP request.

- Want to show some snazzy animation or graphics, but don't know how to do it in HTML? The multimedia controls and visual effects and filters of IE4 allow you to create a very rich and interactive experience without the penalties of Java or ActiveX.

The MSN Investor page at **http://investor.msn.com** shows an excellent example of how client- and server-side code can be combined to produce a really interactive web page. It uses an ActiveX control that communicates with a server application to track your portfolio and provide current information on stocks.

New Things to Learn Client-Side

Based on all we've seen up to now, you might be wondering exactly how we can accomplish these wonderful new tricks. How does the browser know what to execute as script code? How exactly does the script code interact with the browser, and with objects on the page? How do objects get from the server to the client in the first place? We will be discussing these topics and putting the techniques to use with ASP throughout the rest of this book.

Fortunately, there are a lot of similarities between client-side and server-side scripting, and experience working with Active Server Pages code makes it easy to pick up the new topics that we'll be introducing. In many cases, the script language you're using with ASP at the moment can be used inside a browser.

And because you're used to using objects with ASP, you won't have to learn a completely new way to use objects within HTML.

The Undefined Programming Platform

The major change is the platform or computer system our code will be running on. If we're using ASP, we know a lot about our system: it has certain software packages (like database management systems) installed, it's running a Microsoft operating system, and so on. In other words, it's a relatively constant environment that we have some measure of control over. The client system is a completely different ballgame.

People viewing our pages may be doing so from a variety of operating systems, with many different browsers, different screen resolutions and color depths, and with different software installed. If you've used the Browser Capabilities component we introduced in Chapter 6, you've had some experience with the differences in browsers. Some support Java applets, others support Java applets and ActiveX controls, and others support no objects at all.

The same thing occurs for scripting languages: the browser may be able to interpret VBScript and/or JavaScript, or it might not even know what a script is. In fact, it's possible that our pages may be accessed by browsers that understand different dialects of these languages. For example, the version of JavaScript in Navigator 4.0 differs from both the versions in Internet Explorer 4.0 and Navigator 3.0. With ASP, we've been using VBScript version 3.0 but many of our Internet Explorer 3.0 users may only have version 1.0. While the difference between these languages is often minor, it illustrates how different browsers can be, and how this must be a consideration when we design pages with client-side functionality.

In fact, it's a bit like writing a program in Fortran and then giving it to someone else, who may know nothing about programming, to compile. And just for fun, not telling them what language it actually is, but letting them see what happens with the compiler they use for all their other daily jobs.

We can only hope that standardized versions of these scripting languages of these will become widely supported. At least there is now a standard version of JavaScript, called ECMAScript-262. But, as before, both Microsoft and Netscape have added proprietary extensions to this language. So we are back to, when in doubt, use the lowest common denominator. I don't know about you, but I'm a best of the best programmer when it comes to tools. I really hate lowest common denominator stuff. But that's just me.

The Undefined Software Platform

Another important difference in platforms is the software that is installed or available on each system. We know that we can always use the Browser Capabilities component when writing ASP code, because we know that it's installed on our server. When we use objects in our HTML pages, we don't have any sort of assurance that this is the case. Just because I have a cool ActiveX control on my machine doesn't mean that you do too. We need to make sure that the code gets sent to the client machine so that it can be executed.

Both browsers that support objects, Navigator and Internet Explorer, have mechanisms to make sure that this happens, and we'll cover this in Chapter 12. Of course, if you're developing for the corporate intranet, you can control your whole environment. Selecting the correct browser software solves the problem as far as both the scripting language and object support are concerned. And you can also more closely control what software is installed on each client.

Summary

In this chapter, we've wandered across a lot of topics concerned with client/server applications, their design, and implementation. We've also talked about using the processing capabilities of modern browsers to spread the processing load, and minimize the network bandwidth our applications require.

In this part of the book, you're going to be seeing a lot more on these and other related topics. Our aim is to change your way of thinking from being *server*-centric to *application*-centric. After all, if you look at all the best sites out there on the Web at the moment, it soon becomes obvious that they are very cleverly designed and constructed client/server applications. And for the internal office network, as you develop your own intranet, this is the kind of technique that will offer you the fastest payback, and the optimum efficiency.

The main points of this chapter are:

- Developing applications with Active Server Pages is a very different task to the traditional static web sites we are used to seeing. We need to understand how **client/server theory and practice** are applied to our design and development efforts.

- By using **client-side programming techniques**, we can spread the processing load between the client and the server. We aim to place the **data capture** and **business rules** layers of the traditional client/server application model on the client wherever possible.

- To make client/server programming work on the Web, using HTTP, we take advantage of the **Application** and **Session** objects provided by ASP to preserve **state**. Unlike a traditional LAN-based application, this is the only way we can provide consistency over the network.

- Once we can maintain state in our application, we have ways of linking each phase of our application's environment to the appropriate client. The whole process is no longer **anonymous** like a traditional web site.

- We need to understand the importance of **good application design** before we can create professional and efficient client/server applications. To help us in our development goals we can take advantage of the many prewritten **components** available, or even create our own as required.

So now, we're ready to look in more detail at the specifics of creating client/server applications. First we'll look at the creation of on-line communities, then at how ASP interacts with IE4. Following that, we will look at an important old technology that's new again with IIS 4.0. The ability to write applications in a transaction-processing environment provides a number of advantages to the developer. IIS 4.0 now ships with Microsoft Transaction Server, which provides this kind of environment for developers. Then we will spend three chapters looking at an in-depth case study that uses all of the techniques for web-based application development that we have learned so far.

Creating Online Communities

CHAPTER 11

Over the past few years the Internet's population has exploded. This explosion has resulted in an equal explosion of great web sites offering tons of content. Two years ago the key to keeping users returning to your site and hitting the ad banners was keeping fresh, up-to-date content on the site, however today that no longer works as users expect dynamic, personalized content from good sites. Users are beginning to mark a good site by its associated **online community**, or lack thereof.

One of the problems with creating online communities is that the solution for each community is different and unique based on the type of content the site offers, the number of users, and the cross-section of the Internet users that use the site. In this chapter we will take a look at three different web site types in our investigation of online communities. The first type is a large online gaming site, where we expect to have 3,000 users connected to the system simultaneously. We can assume that the online gaming site will attract users who enjoy playing computer games online. The second type is a moderately sized online news site, with an expected simultaneous user load of 1,000 users. The news site attracts a broad spectrum of people. The final case will be a small commercial site with an expected simultaneous load of 100 users. This site has a history of attracting only users interested in that company's products or line of products.

In this chapter we will cover the various technologies that can be used to foster the development of an online community and how the web developer can leverage those technologies within their sites.

We will cover the following:

- Principles and theories that keep online communities communicating
- Describe the various technologies that foster online communities
- Show a small case study of a site that would promote an online community

First let's take a look at what it takes to create and foster the growth and development of an online community.

Online Community Theory

Creating online communities is probably the most difficult aspect of web development. Unlike working with complex database applications, online communities require equal effort and cooperation between the developers and the user. While the developer can create the infrastructure to encourage growth, without the user's cooperation and interaction the community will never establish itself.

Just as in real life, there are two important stages to the creation and development of online communities. The first is the emerging or developing period, and the second is the maintenance period. Each period requires different degrees of support and encouragement from the developer so we will take a look at the theory for each period independently.

Planning the Community

In physics you might have that an object at rest will remain at rest unless acted upon by another force. This principle applies to online communities as well as it does to suspended spheres. The process of starting an online community is very difficult, but possible, provided that you are patient and willing to adjust to the needs and wants of the community.

When starting an online community it is critical that the site already has a good layout, design, decent download times and updated content; ideally the site will already have a history and a consistent user load. A site that lacks a good design, updated content and decent download times probably will not develop the critical mass of users necessary to create a thriving community.

It is important to note that not all of the users on your site will participate in the community. Just as in real life, a majority of the users will not participate in community activities or they will participate occasionally. To make matters worse, on the Internet this participation is further fragmented by the media of the community. Some users prefer to participate in a community only through chat rooms, or only through newsgroups, and few users will participate equally in both forums. Unfortunately it is very difficult to guess what the majority of your users will participate in before you launch the community features. While a survey might give some indication, a large percentage of the users in your community will only participate after the community is somewhat stable.

Community Technologies

The first step of establishing the community is to decide what types of technologies you plan on using. We will discuss these technologies in depth later on in the chapter.

Technology	Minimum Simultaneous Users	Potential to build a community
Personalized Pages	Low	Supports a community but does not build
Newsgroups	Low	Good potential to build a community
Chat rooms	Medium to High	Highest potential to build a community

It is very important to decide these technologies early on and when to implementing more interactive technologies. For example, if chat rooms are implemented too early in the life of a small community (a site with a low number of simultaneous users) then there is the danger that users will enter chat rooms lacking people. If you've had any experience with IRC or Microsoft Chat, you know that an empty chat room is a very negative experience!

Ideally the technologies that the community uses should grow with the size and complexity of the community. A site that starts with a small number of users would probably start with newsgroups and then as the activity and the number of simultaneous users increase, the site would start to implement chat rooms. Whereas a site that already has a large number of simultaneous users would probably start with both newsgroups and chat rooms and then expand their scope as the community develops.

From Infancy to Stability

In the beginnings of the community, it is critical to ensure that the users know that the community features exist. This is a prime time to send out introductory email messages to your frequent users if you keep an email database. It is critical to tout that the community exists, and to encourage its growth.

During the first couple of months, it may be necessary to have staff members, and occasionally developers, reading the newsgroups or visiting the chat rooms to determine whether the community is working and to participate in its growth. Unlike building a set of web pages, building a community requires interaction between the developers (who act as the community leaders) and the users (who act as the townspeople).

Sysops

As the community develops you will start to notice key users that are trying hard to maintain the community. When these key users start to appear, it is typically a good idea to provide them with a title and some responsibilities. Several sites promote such individuals to 'sysops' or 'forum managers'. These users typically will be given rights to delete newsgroup messages that are out of context, kick or ban abusive users from a chat room, and accept complaints from other users. Often, users will assume these roles with a minimal amount of compensation; the bragging rights to be referred to and respected as a Sysop are quite strong within online communities. Sometimes just the additional usage rights, deleting and kicking/banning users will suffice, but you can also offer free services such as email accounts or web page space for Sysops.

As you promote more users to sysop positions, your staff doesn't have to spend as much time nudging the community's growth as it did during its infancy. This shouldn't however, be taken as a license to not cooperate with the community. As the community grows it will start to demand new features, and if the developers are participating in the newsgroups or chat rooms than they will be able to respond to these demands sooner.

Providing Feedback for Users

Throughout the life of the community it is very important to provide multiple methods for users and sysops to register complaints and ideas. Holding weekly or biweekly chat meetings with sysops or providing a sysop-only newsgroup is a good media to keep in contact with the sysops. You can also provide a comments and suggestions page and a bug reporting page (after new features are integrated into the site) in addition to the standard **webmaster@myserver.com** email alias.

Now that we have covered how online communities are started and maintained, we will take a detailed look at the various technologies which are available to foster community development.

Newsgroups

Newsgroups have been available on the Internet since the early 1970s, and they continue to support millions of online newsgroup communities. Newsgroups are akin to a bulletin board where users can post messages and reply to messages posted by other users. Collections of messages, i.e. messages and their replies, are referred to as threads.

Newsgroups as Community Elements

Because newsgroups do not require users to be logged into the system simultaneously in order to communicate with each other they are fantastic solutions for sites that lack a sufficient number of simultaneous users to support a chat forum. But their use should not be limited to just sites with a low number of simultaneous users. The popularity of Usenet (the public newsgroup network) illustrates how newsgroups can be used to support larger communities. Even Microsoft, whose web site spans several gigabytes, offer hundreds of public newsgroups for the support of its products and development tools.

Newsgroups also offer the unique advantage that long conversations and debates can be held over the course of days or months on a topic and other users can read the thread to determine where the conversation started and easily jump in. This is very difficult to achieve with chat rooms and forums.

Newsgroups are often chosen as the ideal forum for technical support, as users can easily post questions and the technical support staff can answer them at their convenience. Furthermore users can find answers to questions that might have already been posted, thereby helping multiple users with a single technical support response. This precludes the necessity of have a technical support person manning a chat forum twenty-four hours a day. By providing a series of newsgroups targeted to various aspects of your site or the corporation's products, you can easily provide a flexible technical support forum for users while reducing the number of calls placed into the technical support center.

When to use Newsgroups

No matter the size of the site and the community you are creating, newsgroups are a good element to always offer users. Newsgroups do have the unfortunate disadvantage that they require a separate client. While both Internet Explorer and Communicator offer newsgroup clients, they are separate applications and require the user to configure the client to access your newsgroup server.

Large Online Gaming Site

Since the online gaming site has such a large number of simultaneous users logged into the system its community would benefit from a large integration of the newsgroups into the community as other sites would. Considering that most of its users will be looking for trivial conversation or for opponents to play games against, newsgroups do not fit well into the site's context.

While newsgroups do not make much sense for the gaming site's primary means of community, they do make sense as a forum for technical support and to organize tournaments.

Moderate News Site

While the news site does have a large number of simultaneous users, unlike the gaming site its users would be more interested in discussing the issues of the news, etc. Given this user-base, it would make sense for the news site to offer its users newsgroups with topics that match the longer, more complicated issues in national or global news.

These newsgroups would automatically allow users to provide feedback, discuss the issues, and carefully read the replies and comments. It also allows users to read the previous threads to determine what the general consensus was two days or two months ago.

Small Commercial Site

The small commercial site is the type of site that would benefit most by a set of newsgroups. Unlike larger sites, the small commercial site lacks a sufficient number of simultaneous users to fully support chat rooms, and would have to rely on its newsgroups to foster the community until it builds to a level that would support the chat rooms.

Newsgroups would also give the small commercial site the ability to provide a comprehensive technical support and customer outreach program without the high costs of maintaining a technical support center and the toll-free (or toll) phone lines. Users can easily post their questions, and the technical support staff can reply during business hours.

Implementing Newsgroups in IIS 4.0

Implementing newsgroups into your web site is quite simple, especially since IIS 4.0 comes with a Network News Transfer Protocol (newsgroup) service. The only problem with newsgroups is that they can not easily be integrated into the web site. Unless you create a server-side object that acts like a newsgroup client and use ASP for the front-end, your users will have to configure their newsgroup clients independently. While the configuration process is quite simple, it is an extra step that will discourage some users.

Configuring the Newsgroup Server

Once the NNTP service is installed, configuring the server is quite simple. First you need to open the Internet Service Manager, and select the Default NNTP Site.

By right clicking the Default NNTP Site, you can get to the properties dialog box for the NNTP server.

This dialog allows you to fully customize how the NNTP server will operate. You can specify how many connections to permit, security settings, directory locations, etc. The Groups tab allows you to easily add, remove and modify the settings for the individual newsgroups running in your server. You can add a new newsgroup by clicking the Create new newsgroup button and providing the necessary information to the dialog box.

The newsgroup name, in this case public.widgets.announcements, acts as the address for the specific newsgroup. Newsgroup names typically describe whether they are public or private newsgroups, a general topic (in this case the company name widgets), and finally a brief description of the newsgroup.

The Description and Newsgroup prettyname specify a plain text description of the newsgroup. Newsgroup clients will display this description to the newsgroup clients.

The NNTP Service also allows you to establish moderated newsgroups. A moderated newsgroup only grants the newsgroup moderator permission to post messages. When a user 'posts' a message to the newsgroup that message is emailed to the newsgroups moderator who then decides whether or not the message should be posted. After clicking Ok the post is added and available on the NNTP server, ready for users to access it. However, there might just be one small catch, that needs to be sorted out.

Configuring the Newsgroup Server to work through Microsoft's Proxy Server

It's common for many enterprises today to receive their mail and news via a Proxy Server, which acts as a firewall and prevents outside users from getting onto their internal LAN. If you're setting up a news server together with a proxy server then the news server will need to be outside the firewall, to download the newsgroups. However, the catch is that the Proxy Server actually prevents users inside the firewall from downloading news and posting to newsgroups in the process. If you are using Microsoft's Proxy Server, then you will have to specifically enable newsgroup access through the Proxy Server, before you will be able to download newsgroups. This is a relative simple task and to do this, you need to start Proxy Server's Internet Service Manager.

If you right click on the WinSock Proxy computer and select Service Properties option from the menu that appears, then you will get to the Properties dialog. You need to set up Protocols and Permissions necessary before users can gain newsgroup access. From the Permissions dialog, you need to select the NNTP protocol and add all of the users that you wish to have newsgroup access to the list.

From the Protocols tab you need to select
NNTP, so that you can alter some of the
NNTP parameters in the Protocol Definition
dialog:

Typically the port will be 119, and you will need to ensure that the direction is Outbound (so that your
users can get from the proxy server to the news server.) However you will also have to add a Port under
the Port Ranges for Subsequent Connections so that news can be dragged off the news server by the
user and the direction for this needs to be Inbound. Once this is set up, you can then configure the
newsgroup client as normal.

Configuring the Newsgroup Client

Since newsgroups are not handled automatically by the browser, you will have to provide your users with
detailed instructions on how to configure their newsgroup client. The basic information that you need to
supply to the users is the following:

- The server name for your NNTP server
- Any usernames or passwords if you configured your server with security for the newsgroups
- Instructions for at least one of the more popular clients like Outlook Express or Netscape
  Communicator.

We have included instructions here for Microsoft's Outlook Express client to give you an idea of how to
setup newsgroup clients. Fortunately the configuration is similar for most of the clients.

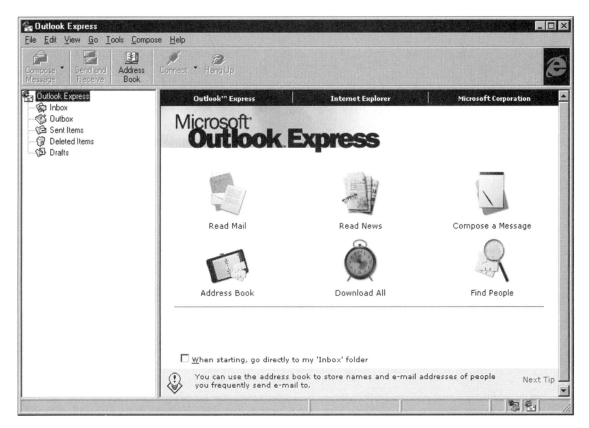

The first step is to open up Outlook Express and select the Accounts menu item from the Tools menu.

This will open the Internet accounts dialog box that allows users to add and modify all of their mail, directory services and newsgroup accounts. They then need to click the Add button and select News from the context menu.

This opens the new Account wizard that will guide them through the process of entering in their full names and email addresses. When they have completed that process, Outlook Express will present a dialog box asking whether it should download the list of newsgroups available on that server. At this point the user has configured and connected to your newsgroup server and can participate in all of the newsgroup threads.

Creating Web Interfaces for Newsgroups

While newsgroups are a good method of creating communities, they lack the seamless integration to the web that chat solutions can offer. As a result some companies have started offering web interfaces for newsgroups. These programs, whether CGI or ASP server-side objects, simply read the newsgroup information and parse the newsgroups into HTML pages. Through a series of image clicks and a lot of navigation the user can participate in the newsgroup with the same functionality as users connecting with a standard newsgroup client. These web interfaces offer the seamless integration at the price of performance. Whereas the newsgroup client only downloads clear text messages (similar to email), the web interface also has to send down the HTML formatting and layout that provides the navigation. The server also has to parse the information from the NNTP server into an HTML feed. This added computation requires additional server resources and additional bandwidth. Despite its shortcomings, web interfaces for newsgroups provide users with a valuable and seamless experience.

If your company already uses Microsoft's Exchange Server, than you can take advantage of a set of tools that Microsoft bundles with the server to easily create a web interface for not only NNTP newsgroups but also Exchange Public Folders. We're going to focus on the standard NNTP service that Microsoft ships with Internet Information Server 4.0, however if you are looking for an easy method to create a web interface you might consider using Exchange Server and its associated design-time controls.

Chat Rooms

Online chat rooms are the keystones of many online communities. These rooms allow users to interact on a personal, real time basis. Unlike newsgroups that allow the user to think and prepare their responses before posting them, chat rooms send messages as soon as the sentence is entered. This often results in conversations that mimic real conversations (include contextual humor, and of course misunderstandings). It is the similarity with real conversations that drives flocks of people into chat rooms for the purpose of chatting.

Chat rooms are basically text boxes where everyone reads the messages from other people sent in real time. An index of the currently connected users is often displayed, in addition to the message text box and a text box is provided so that the user can enter their contribution to the conversation.

Chat Rooms as Community Elements

The unique feature of chat rooms is that they allow instantaneous conversations to happen that mimic real conversations. When a chat room is full, the conversation typically does not die, and often is divided into multiple conversations within a single chat room. Whereas a full, or active, chat room inspires activity, an empty or sparsely populated chat room kills most conversations and can negatively affect the feeling of community.

Given chat rooms interactive nature they often foster the quick development of online communities provided that the chat rooms have people in them on a consistent basis. This does not necessarily mean that the chat rooms have to be in use twenty-four hours a day. Rather they could be heavily used during the peak usage hours of your site (based on your server logs) and then die off as your web hits decline. In judging the effectiveness of your chat rooms, you must correlate their usage with the overall usage of your web server.

While chat rooms are interactive, and foster quick growth, their abuse could quickly kill communities just as rapidly. For example, you don't want somebody harassing users or talking about crude, off topic issues within your site's chat rooms. While the community might force those members off of the chat, it is more likely that the community will dissolve unless steps are made to ensure that chat rooms are not abused. Ideally the communities sysops will provide the community policing however during the initial-growth-period someone will probably have to police and monitor the chat rooms. This policing has the side benefit in that at least one person is in all of the chat rooms at any point in time.

When To Use Chat Rooms

Because chat rooms require there to be at least two or more simultaneous users interested in chatting their use is typically reserved for sites that can maintain a simultaneous connection rate of at least 50 to 100 users.

One of the advantage of chat rooms over newsgroups is that individual users can create their own chat rooms in addition to the standard, **persistent** chat rooms offered on the system. These **dynamic** chat rooms are often great places for individuals to hold private conversations.

Large Online Gaming Site

The large online gaming site with its large numbers of simultaneous connections thrives on chat rooms. Typically these sites require users to log into a chat room in order to find other players, so naturally conversations start within these matchmaking rooms. Besides the matchmaking rooms, the large online gaming site has potential to offer both persistent chat rooms covering the various aspects of game play and the games offered for play on the site in addition to giving users the ability to create private chats amongst each other.

Since chat rooms are the keystones to the survival of a large gaming site, they must be carefully monitored and policed. During the initial community-building period, the developers will have to spend a significant amount of time developing the community and finding suitable users to become sysops. Without the support of sysops selected from the user community, large chat communities face the danger of channel abuse and anarchy. This lack of control is often the fate of large chat networks such as Undernet or Microsoft's Comicnet.

Provided that the chat rooms are well used, and policed by sysops, they have a great potential for developing the community and fostering tremendous growth.

Moderate News Site

The moderate news site can also benefit from chat rooms. Ideally these chat rooms would allow users to comment about the current article they are reading, thus extending their comprehension and understanding of the issues.

While the news site does not have as high a simultaneous user load as the gaming site, due to its broad user base and specific content (i.e. national or global news) it can easily support multiple chat rooms.

Like the online gaming site, the news site would need sysops monitoring the chat rooms to ensure that users did not abuse the rooms.

Small Commercial Site

Ironically the type of site that needs community building the most, can not effectively use chat rooms to build its community. For small commercial sites, chat rooms have the immediate danger of killing community development, however *if* the small commercial site can maintain at least a couple of people in its chat rooms than the community might grow. While creating any type of an online community involves risk, the smaller site involves the greatest amount of risk.

Provided that the small commercial site is willing to invest in developers strongly encouraging the growth of community development, then small commercial sites can become moderate to larger commercial sites with a strong community surrounding them.

Implementing Chat Rooms

Implementing chat rooms on a web site is a little more complicated than implementing newsgroups. Where newsgroups only required server configuration and some instructions to allow the users to configure their newsgroup readers, the implementation of chat rooms require a series of decisions to be made. The centerpiece of online communities based on chat rooms is the choice of chat clients.

Chosing a Chat Client

The choice of a chat client is the key decision that will determine the success or failure of the online community. If the chat client is difficult to use, or requires too much user intervention then users will refrain from using the chat client.

There are two different general types of clients available. The first is the stand-alone chat client that easily offers a platform-independent solution for online communities, but it lacks the ability to easily coordinate its actions with navigation in the web browser. The second type of client is either a plugin, Java applet, or ActiveX control that is placed within the context of a web page that can seamlessly fit into the site's design and interact with the web browser.

Stand-alone Chat Clients

Stand-alone chat clients are the easiest to deploy on a site, however they lack the seamless integration that embedded chat clients provide. The user typically downloads a stand-alone chat client, and similarly to newsgroups the user configures and navigates to the chat rooms within the chat client.

In exchange for the added hassle of making the user work with the client, stand-alone clients often provide more features than embedded chat clients. For example, most stand-alone chat clients allow the user to specify some sort of avatar, or personalized image, in addition to keeping address books and offering the capability to customize the user interface.

Embedded Chat Clients

Embedded chat clients are more difficult to deploy on a site as they require development time to integrate into the design and code of the web site, however they offer a seamless integration into the web site if designed properly. Typically these chat clients are either ActiveX controls or Java applets which tie into the Microsoft Internet Chat (MIC) or an Internet Relay Chat (IRC) chat server.

One of the advantages of embedded chat clients over stand-alone clients is that they are scriptable from the client-side code in web pages. This allows the chat clients to dynamically change chat rooms as the user navigates around the site, or around the page.

A chief drawback to embedded chat clients is that they often do not have the more advanced features of their stand-alone cousins.

Configuring the Chat Server

Similar to the newsgroup service, the Microsoft Chat Service is quite simple to set up and run. Unfortunately the chat service does not ship as a component of IIS 4.0. The Chat service can be obtained either by purchasing the Microsoft Exchange Server or the Microsoft Commercial Internet System (MCIS) Chat Server. Both applications offer the same chat service. One of the nicest features of the Microsoft Chat Service is its capability to communicate with both IRC and MIC chat clients. In this chapter we are going to go over the steps to set up the Microsoft Chat Service, however the majority of the available chat servers are also easily and similarly configured.

Once the chat service is installed, you need to open the Internet Service Manager and select the Chat service.

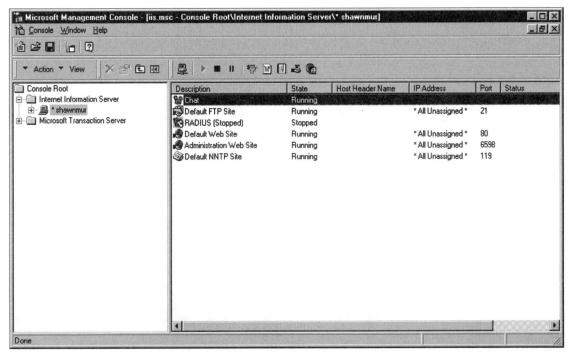

By right clicking on the chat service you can open the properties dialog box which will allow you to configure and set up the chat service. This dialog box allows you to easily add all of the **persistent** chat rooms (persistent chat rooms are always available on the server) as well as configure the security settings that will be used by the server. You can also modify the list of banned usernames and domains from within this dialog box. The chat service will refuse to allow users to log into a chat room running on your server from that domain or it will not allow them to log into a chat room using a specific username.

The Channels index tab allows you to configure the list of persistent chat rooms or channels. Clicking on the Add button will open the following dialog box that allows you to fully customize the chat room.

The following text describes the options in the above dialog and provides simple descriptions.

Field Name	Required	Description	# ANSI Characters
Name	Yes	Specifies the name of the persistent channel. If you are using an IRC chat client to connect to the chat server then the channel name can contain between 1 and 200 ANSI characters, but must begin with the number sign (#) or an ampersand (&). All characters except null, bell, CR, LF, space, comma, and backslash are permitted. If you are going to use a Microsoft Internet Chat (MIC) client such as the Microsoft chat ActiveX control then the channel can contain between 1 and 63 ANSI or Unicode characters. All characters except null, bell, CR, LF, space, comma, and backslash are permitted.	1 - 200 for IRC. 1 - 63 for MIC.
Member Keyword	No	Specifies a keyword with which users can join the channel.	< 31
Host Keyword	No	Specifies a password that members can use to join a channel with host permissions.	< 31
Owner Keyword	No	Specifies a keyword that members can use to join a channel with owner permissions.	< 31
Topic	Yes	Specifies the channel topic.	< 160
Subject	Yes	Specifies the channel subject. Channel subjects are used by Web-based searches.	< 31
Account	No	Specifies a security account, which is used to restrict or deny access to the channel.	< 31
Data	No	Specifies a text string that chat client developers can use to pass instructions or parameters to custom clients.	< 255
PICS	No	Specifies a Platform for Internet Content Selection (PICS) label that enables you to rate the channel based on its content. The server passes the PICS string to the chat client, which interprets it and allows (or prevents) access to the channel. The format of this string is defined by ratings organizations such as the Recreational Software Advisory Council (RSAC).	< 255
Language	No	Specifies the preferred language for a channel. Use the language codes specified by the Internet Engineering Task Force (IETF) in Request for Comments (RFC) 1766. These are the same codes used by Hypertext Transfer Protocol (HTTP).	< 31
On Join	No	Specifies a message that is automatically sent to users after they join a channel. The channel name is displayed as the sender of the message. Only the user who joins the channel can see the message.	< 255
On Part	No	Specifies a message that is automatically sent to users after they leave a channel. The channel name is displayed as the sender of the message. Only the user who leaves the channel can see the message.	< 255

Field Name	Required	Description	# ANSI Characters
Member Limit	Yes	Sets the maximum number of members who can be in the channel. You can set a value from 0 to 48000. If this limit is set to 0, the channel uses the default member limit on the Service property page. The default value is 0.	

After you have entered all of the required information into the dialog box and click Ok the persistent chat channel is added to your server and is ready for users to start accessing.

Using the Microsoft Chat ActiveX Control

Microsoft offers a simple ActiveX Control which allows web developer to easily connect to a MIC or IRC chat server, such as the Microsoft Chat service, from within a web page. We are going to first list all of the properties, methods and events that the chat control offers, and we will then demonstrate the creation of a simple page that uses the chat control to connect to a chat room. Using the control is quite simple as it requires no client-side code to initialize and allow users to start chatting, however the control can by easily extended into a very complex chat client as it exposes a plethora of properties, methods and events.

> You can get the Microsoft Chat Client SDK directly from Microsoft at
> http://www.microsoft.com/ie/chat/chat21sdk.htm

Microsoft Chat ActiveX Control Properties, Methods and Events

The following table lists all the properties of the Chat control, sorted into categories depending on the type of information that the property returns. We've included a brief description of what the property returns.

Chat Room Property	Description
history	Returns a string containing the contents of the history text pane.
lastMessageReceived	Returns a string containing the last message received from the chat server.
lastMessageSent	Returns a string containing that last message sent to the chat server.
maxMembers	Returns or sets a long value specifying the maximum number of users that can join the current chat room.
memberCount	Returns a long value specifying the number of users that are in the current chat room.
rating	Returns a string containing the chat room's rating using the Platform for Internet Content Selection.
roomPath	Returns a string containing the URL for the current chat room.
roomTopic	Returns or sets a string containing the current chat room's topic.

Chat User Property	Description
`thisParticipantAlias`	Returns a string containing the current user's alias.
`thisParticipantID`	Returns a string containing the current user's ID number.
`thisParticipantName`	Returns a string containing the current user's MS Windows user name.

Chat Control Property	Description
`Appearance`	Returns or sets a long value specifying the control's UI appearance.
`BackColor`	Returns or sets the background color for the text panes of the UI.
`BorderStyle`	Returns or sets a long value specifying how the borders between the panes of the UI are drawn.
`Height`	Returns or sets the height of the control in HiMetrics. 1 HiMetric = 0.01 millimeters.
`MaxHistoryLength`	Returns or sets a long value specifying the maximum length of the history pane in characters.
`maxMessageLength`	Returns or sets a long value specifying the maximum number of characters that are allowed in the Send text pane of the UI.
`state`	Returns a long value specifying the control's current state.
`UIOption`	Returns or sets a long value specifying the user interface options. Note: This property is a bitmask.
`width`	Returns or sets a long value specifying the width of the control in HiMetrics. 1 HiMetric = 0.01 millimeters

This section lists all the methods of the Chat control sorted alphabetically. We've included a brief description and a list of the parameters that each method supports.

Method	Description	Parameters
`aboutBox`	Displays the chat client about box.	None
`banParticipant`	Bans or allows a specified user from the current chat room.	**Name**: A string that specifies the username to be banned. **State**: Boolean value specifying whether to ban or unban the username.
`cancelEntering`	Cancels the entering of a chat room.	None
`clearHistory`	Empties the contents of the History pane.	None

Method	Description	Parameters
enterRoom	Connects the chat client to a specified chat room.	**RoomPath**: A string giving the path to access the chat room. **RoomPassword**: A string containing the chat room password. Use a null value if there is no password. **ThisParticipantAlias**: A string specifying the user's alias. **SecurityPackage**: A string set to null. **Flags**: A string set to 1 to join a standard chat room. **Type**: A string to set the parameters of the chat room if the room is being created.
exitRoom	Disconnects a user from a chat room.	None
GetParticipant_RealName	Gets the real name of a chat users from the server.	**ParticipantID**: A long integer indicating the **userId**. Use **−1** to specify the user selected in the participant list. **Alias**: A string specifying the alias of the user (**use either PartcipantID or Alias**). **Synchronous**: A Boolean value. Specify **FALSE** for web purposes, **RealName**: A string. Use an empty string for web purposes
InviteParticipant	Invites another chat user to the user's current chat room.	**Alias:** A string specifying the user alias to be invited to the chat room.
KickParticipant	Kicks a member from the current chat room.	**ParticipantID**: A long integer indicating the **userId.** Use **−1** to specify the user selected in the participant list. **KickMessage.** A string containing the text message the user will see when they are kicked.
moveSplitBar	Changes the cursor to a cross hair so that the chat control can be resized.	None
selectParticipants	Selects, deselects or inverts the current selection in the Participant pane.	**Value**: A small integer indicating what to select (deselect highlighted member **0**, select all **1**, or reverse selection **2**).

Method	Description	Parameters
sendMessage	Sends a message to the server or chat users.	**DestinationList**: A long integer indicating what **userID** to send the message to. **-1** sends to the whole room. **Count:** An integer determines the number of people who will receive the message 0 sends to the whole room. **Message:** A string.
setParticipant_ Status	Changes the status of a member in a chat room.	**ParticipantID**: A long integer **Mask:** A long integer indicating what type of status will be changed. **Status:** A long integer indicating the new status.

This section lists all the events of the Chat control sorted alphabetically. We've included a brief description of the event and its parameters.

Event	Description	Parameters
onBeginEnumeration	Fired when the control first joins a chat room, but before the Participants pane is populated with usernames.	None
onEndEnumeration	Fired when the Participants pane is fully populated with the list of users currently connected to the chat room.	None
onEnterParticipant	Fired when a new user joins the current chat room.	**ParticipantID**: A long integer. **Alias**: A string **Status:** An integer specifying whether they are host **1**, participant **2**, spectator **4**.
onError	Fired when an error occurs in the control.	**ErrorCode**: A long integer **Description:** A string
onExitParticipant	Fired when a user leaves the current chat room.	**ParticipantID**: A long integer
OnHistoryFull	Fired when the History pane is 90% of its maximum number of characters.	**Percent**: An integer specifying the exact percentage of the history box
onMessage	Fired when the user receives a messages from another chat user.	**SenderID**: A long integer. **Message**: A string. **MessageType**: An integer indicating whether it was whispered, etc.

Event	Description	Parameters
`OnParticipant_` `AliasChanged`	Fired when a chat user changes his alias.	`ParticipantID`: A long integer. `OldAlias`: A string. `NewAlias`: A string
`OnParticipant_` `Invited`	Fired when a chat user invites somebody to the current chat room.	`RoomName`: A string specifying the chat room you are invited to. `Alias`: A string specifying the user that invited you.
`onParticipant_` `Kicked`	Fired when a user is kicked from the current chat room.	`ParticipantID`: A long integer. `Reason`: A string specifying the kick message.
`onParticipant_` `RealName`	Fired when the `GetParticipantRealName` method completes successfully and the Synchronous parameter is set to **false**.	`Alias`: A string `RealName`: A string
`onParticipant_` `StatusChanged`	Fired when a member changes status.	`ParticipantID`: A long integer. `Status`: A long integer specifying the new status
`onRoomTopicChanged`	Fired when the chat room topic has been changed.	`NewRoomTopic`: A string
`onRoomTypeChanged`	Fired when the chat room type has been changed.	`NewRoomType`: An integer
`onStateChanged`	Fired when the current user's status has changed.	`NewState`: An integer indicating: (disconnected **0**, connecting **1**, connected **2**).
`onTextMessageSent`	Fired when the user sends a message to the server.	`TextMessage`: A string. `MessageType`: A short integer

A Simple Chat Control Page

To demonstrate how the Microsoft ActiveX Chat Control can be used in your pages to create an embedded chat room, we've created a simple page using the control's default user interface. This page should give you a starting point from which you can create more complex, graphically interesting web pages. This page allows the user to specify the **alias** or username that they will use to identify themselves. After specifying their username, the user clicks the Join the Chat button to enter a chat room running on our server.

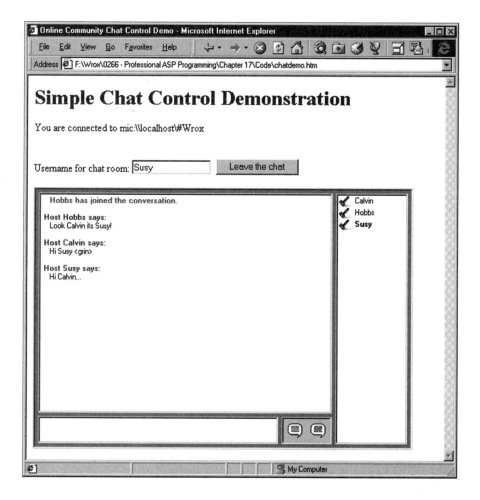

This example can be downloaded from the Wrox site at
http://rapid.wrox.co.uk/books/1266

As you can see this page is quite simple, and contains only a few lines of client-side code:

```
<HTML>
<HEAD>
<TITLE>Online Community Chat Control Demo</TITLE>
</HEAD>
<BODY BGCOLOR="white">
<H1>Simple Chat Control Demonstration</H1>
<P>You are connected to mic:\\localhost\#Wrox</P>
<BR>
<P>Username for chat room: <INPUT TYPE = "TEXT" NAME="Alias" VALUE="WroxVisit" SIZE =
"16">  <INPUT TYPE = "BUTTON" NAME="FluxBtn" VALUE = "Join the chat"><BR></
P>
<OBJECT
    STANDBY="Downloading the Microsoft MSChat ActiveX Control"
```

```
        CODETYPE="application/x-oleobject"
        CLASSID="clsid:D6526FE0-E651-11CF-99CB-00C04FD64497"
        CODEBASE="http://activex.microsoft.com/controls/mschat/mschatocx.cab#Version=4,71,
    730,0"
        WIDTH="600"
        HEIGHT="400"
        ID="Chat">
        <PARAM NAME="UIOption"    VALUE="2047">
        <PARAM NAME="Appearance"  VALUE="3">
        <PARAM NAME="BackColor"   VALUE="255">
    </OBJECT>
    <SCRIPT LANGUAGE="VBScript">
    SUB FluxBtn_OnClick()
        Select Case Chat.State
        Case 1
                If Alias.Value = "" then
                    'The user has not entered a username
                    msgbox "You need to specify an alias!"
                    Exit Sub
                Else
                    'Enter the chat room
                    Chat.EnterRoom "mic:\\localhost\#Wrox", "", Alias.Value, "", 1, 1
                End If
        Case 2
                'The user has pressed the cancel entering button so exit the chat room
                Chat.CancelEntering
                Chat.ClearHistory
        Case 3
                'The user has pressed the exit chat room button so exit the room
                Chat.ExitRoom
                Chat.ClearHistory
        End Select
    END SUB
    SUB Chat_OnStateChanged(ByVal NewState)
        Select Case NewState
        Case 1
                FluxBtn.Value = "Join the chat"
                Chat.BackColor = 255
        Case 2
                FluxBtn.Value = "Cancel Entering"
                Chat.BackColor = 33023
        Case 3
                FluxBtn.Value = "Leave the chat"
                Chat.BackColor = 49152
        End Select
    END SUB
    </SCRIPT>
    </BODY>
    </HTML>
```

The real work of the page is handled completely by the Chat Control that is inserted using the following
<OBJECT> tag. The control ships with both Exchange Server 5.5 and the MCIS Chat server, however
Microsoft has also made the control available from its ActiveX control server at the following URL:
http://activex.microsoft.com/controls/mschat/mschatocx.cab.

```
<OBJECT
   STANDBY="Downloading the Microsoft MSChat ActiveX Control"
   CODETYPE="application/x-oleobject"
   CLASSID="clsid:D6526FE0-E651-11CF-99CB-00C04FD64497"
   CODEBASE="http://activex.microsoft.com/controls/mschat/mschatocx.cab#Version=4,71,
730,0"
   WIDTH="600"
   HEIGHT="400"
   ID="Chat">
...
</OBJECT>
```

In order to initialize the chat control, we need to pass at least three parameters in the **<OBJECT>** tag; those parameters are the user interface **UIOption**, appearance of the control **Appearance**, and the initial background color **BackColor** of the control. In this example we are using the standard 'default' values. A **UIOption** of 2047 displays the control in its default configuration with all of the features enabled. An **Appearance** setting of 3 displays the control with a three dimensional appearance, and the value of 255 for the **BackColor** sets the color to red.

```
...
   <PARAM NAME="UIOption"    VALUE="2047">
   <PARAM NAME="Appearance"  VALUE="3">
   <PARAM NAME="BackColor"   VALUE="255">
</OBJECT>
```

Once the control is initialized and loaded into the page, we just need to have the user enter their username and click the Join the Chat button. This button changes its state depending on the state of the chat control so that when the control is not logged into a chat room the button will log the user into the chat room and visa-versa.

```
SUB FluxBtn_OnClick()
    Select Case Chat.State
    Case 1
        If Alias.Value = "" then
            'The user has not entered a username
            msgbox "You need to specify an alias!"
            Exit Sub
        Else
            'Enter the chat room
            Chat.EnterRoom "mic:\\localhost\#Wrox", "", Alias.Value, "", 1, 1
        End If
    Case 2
        'The user has pressed the cancel entering button so exit the chat room
        Chat.CancelEntering
        Chat.ClearHistory
    Case 3
        'The user has pressed the exit chat room button so exit the room
        Chat.ExitRoom
        Chat.ClearHistory
    End Select
END SUB
```

In creating your own pages, make sure that you change the following line to match your own chat server and chat rooms:

```
Chat.EnterRoom "mic:\\localhost\#Wrox", "",
```

One of the nicest features of the chat control is that it handles most of the errors that occur without requiring intervention by the web developer. The control will present the user with simple and easy to understand dialog boxes that explain if the server was unavailable, their alias was already in use, etc. Since the chat control intelligently handles error conditions, we can neglect error trapping, as our error messages would probably be displayed in addition to the error dialogs displayed by the chat control.

This simple demonstration of the chat control illustrates the raw potential of the control to create embedded chat rooms within web pages. While the control lacks an attractive design off the shelf, it does provide the functionality to connect to the chat server. Fortunately the chat control allows you to use it solely to connect to the chat server while the user interface is handled via client-side code and client-side ActiveX controls.

Using the Microsoft Chat Java Applet

In addition to the ActiveX control, Microsoft also offers a Java applet, which has similar functionality to the chat control. Unlike the chat ActiveX control, the Java applet doesn't allow you to create your own user interface, however the Java applet can be used on any platform or browser combination that supports Java whereas the ActiveX control can only be used in Windows platforms running Internet Explorer. Similar to the ActiveX control, we are going to detail the Java applet's parameters and public methods in addition to a simple web page that uses the Java applet.

In order to use the Microsoft Chat Java Applet you must first install all of the Java classes into the directory on your web server where the chat pages will be located. Microsoft has provided a self-extracting archive that will install all of the signed classes. The current installation files can be obtained in the updated copy of the Internet Client SDK from Microsoft at **http://www.microsoft.com/msdn/sdk/inetsdk**.

Microsoft Chat Java Applet Parameters and Public Methods

The following table lists the parameters that can be specified for the applet. We've included a brief description of the parameter and its default value. Since this is a Java applet, not all of these parameters are accessible from scripting via the public methods as an ActiveX control is.

Parameter	Default Value	Description
`Port`	`6667`	Sets a number containing the port the chat server is running on.
`Nickname`	`"Anonymous"`	Sets a string containing the user's username (alias or nickname)
`Room`	`Null`	Sets a string containing the chat room.
`Toolbar`	`True`	Sets a Boolean value specifying whether to display the toolbar in the chat applet. If the toolbar is displayed then the user has the capability to navigate between chat rooms, servers and change the display settings for the chat applet.
`Memberlist`	`True`	Sets a Boolean value specifying whether to display the member list in the chat applet.

Parameter	Default Value	Description
Observer	False	Sets a Boolean value specifying whether the user can participate in a chat conversation (False) or is only an observer (True).
Banner	Null	Sets a string containing the URL for an image that will be displayed while the applet loads.
Autoconnect	False	Sets a Boolean value specifying whether the applet will automatically connect to the chat room after it is fully loaded. If **autoconnect** is set to true then values must be specified for Nickname and Room.
Autodisconnect	False	Sets a Boolean value specifying whether the applet will automatically disconnect from the chat server when the page the control is placed on is unloaded from the browser.
Motd	True	Sets a Boolean value specifying whether the applet will display the chat server's Message Of The Day.
Stats	True	Sets a Boolean value specifying whether the applet will display statistics about the chat server after the applet has connected to it.
Id	Null	Sets a unique string to identify this chat control if multiple chat controls are located on the same page.
Font	Helvetica, 0 ,11	Sets a string containing the font-name, style code, and size for the chat text areas. Value font names are Helvetica, Dialog, TimesRoman and Courier. Valid values for the style code are 0 (plain style), 1 (bold style), 2 (italic style), or 3 (italicized bold style). Valid sizes for the font are 8 – 20 points.
bgcolor	C0C0C0	Sets a string containing the code for the background of the applet in hexadecimal RGB.

The following table lists all of the public methods that the applet supports in addition to the method's return value and a brief description.

Method	Return Value	Description
connect(string nickname,[string chat room])	void	Connects to the chat server using the username (alias or nickname) and logs into the chat room specified in the parameters of the method call. If the chat room is specified than the applet will log into the chat server without logging into the chat room. If the chat room is not specified (or it specified as a null string) then the applet logs into the chat room specified in the parameter for the applet.
disconnect()	void	Logs the user out of all of the chat rooms and disconnects from the chat server.
getNick()	string	Returns the user's current username (alias or nickname). If the user has not specified a username then the applet returns a null string.

Method	Return Value	Description
getRoom()	string	Returns the name of the chat room that the user is logged into. If the user is not logged into a chat room then the applet returns a null string.
join(string room, string password)	void	Logs out of the current chat room if the user was logged into a chat room and logs into the specified chat room using the specified password. If the chat room does not require a password, then set that parameter to a null string.
showRoomList()	void	Displays a dialog box listing all of the chat rooms on the chat server the applet is logged into and allows the user to log into any chat room from that list.
showEnterRoomDialog()	void	Displays a dialog box and prompts the user to type in the chat room name for a chat room to enter on the server.
showFontDialog()	void	Displays a dialog box that allows the user to select the font settings for the text areas.
showConnectDialog()	void	Displays a dialog box prompting the user for the URL to the chat server.
showAboutDialog()	void	Displays the About dialog box for the chat applet.

A Simple Chat Applet Page

Like our demonstration of the chat ActiveX control, our demonstration of the chat Java applet is quite simple and uses the default user interface. By default we have chosen to display the toolbar in the chat applet. This will allow the users to easily navigate between chat rooms and to modify the look and feel of the chat applet. If you decide to remove the toolbar, than you must provide the toolbar's functionality using you own custom images, buttons, etc.

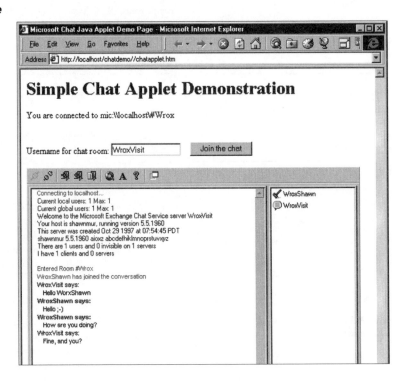

382

This example can be downloaded from the Wrox site at
http://rapid.wrox.co.uk/books/1266

One of the nice features of the Java applet is that the user can undock the applet from the web page using the docking button on the toolbar. The undocked version of the applet opens in a separate window and can be minimized, maximized or moved out of the way like any other window.

As you can see from the HTML code, the Java applet requires less code than the ActiveX control, however the Java applet lacks the customization capability that the ActiveX control offers.

```
<HTML>
<HEAD>
<TITLE>Microsoft Chat Java Applet Demo Page</TITLE>
</HEAD>
<BODY BGCOLOR="White">
<H1>Simple Chat Applet Demonstration</H1>
<P>You are connected to mic:\\localhost\#Wrox</P>
<BR>
<P>Username for chat room: <INPUT TYPE = "TEXT" NAME="Alias" VALUE="WroxVisit" SIZE =
"16">
  
<INPUT TYPE = "BUTTON" NAME="FluxBtn" VALUE = "Join the chat"
onClick="document.JavaChat.connect(Alias.value,'')">
<BR>
</P>
<APPLET CODE="MSChat" Name="JavaChat" ARCHIVE="mschat.jar" WIDTH="600" HEIGHT="450">
        <PARAM NAME="cabbase" VALUE="mschat.cab">
        <PARAM NAME="port" VALUE="6667">
    <PARAM NAME="room" VALUE="#Wrox">
    <PARAM NAME="autodisconnect" VALUE="TRUE">
```

```
    </APPLET>
    </BODY>
    </HTML>
```

The actual Java applet is inserted into the page using the following **<APPLET>** tag:

```
<APPLET CODE="MSChat" Name="JavaChat" ARCHIVE="mschat.jar" WIDTH="600" HEIGHT="450">
        <PARAM NAME="cabbase" VALUE="mschat.cab">
        <PARAM NAME="port" VALUE="6667">
    <PARAM NAME="room" VALUE="#Wrox">
    <PARAM NAME="autodisconnect" VALUE="TRUE">
</APPLET>
```

The **CODE** attribute indicates the name of the Java classes, in this case the MSChat classes. The **NAME** attribute, similar to the **ID** attribute for the **OBJECT** tag, indicates the object name that will refer to this applet in client-side code. The **ARCHIVE** attribute points the browser to the compiled Java classes located on the server for downloading.

```
<PARAM NAME="cabbase" VALUE="mschat.cab">
```

Internet Explorer supports placing Java applets into cabinet files, so the **CABBASE** parameter indicates where the compiled, compressed cabinet file is located on the web server. Providing a cabinet file for users to download will drastically reduce the download times necessary to install the control.

We have set the default port number that our chat server is currently running on using the **PORT** parameter, in addition to a default chat room "**#Wrox**" for users to enter. We have also enabled the **autodisconnect** feature of the chat control. This will ensure that when the user has unloaded the page, and can no longer participate in the chat, that they are logged off of the chat room. This will dramatically reduce the number of 'dead', non-responding users in the chat rooms and ensure that all of the users listed in the member list pane of the chat controls and applets are users that are capable of chatting.

The only line of client-side code that is required is to actually log into the chat room. Since we do not already know the user's preferred chat alias (nickname or username) we have decided to allow the user to enter their preferred username and then click the Join the Chat button to log into the chat room.

It is important to note that unlike the chat ActiveX control, we can not script off the applet. So unlike the control we can't change the color of the chat applet or the state of the Join the Chat button since we do not receive any events off the Java applet. Despite this limitation, the Java applet is an easy to use applet and offers a cross-platform, cross-browser, embedded chat client.

Personalized Pages

Personalized pages are one of the most unique aspects of an online community because they really don't encourage the growth of the community as well as newsgroups or chat rooms, yet they are required to provide the user with a sense of belonging. Personalized pages typically take the form of dynamically generated pages that display information that the user is interested in. Users typically provide this information when they register for the site, or through a special personalized page.

Personalized Pages as Community Elements

A key aspect to communities and community development in urban planning and architectural theory is that the users of a community must feel that they are connected to the community through some means. Typically architects will allocate a patch of land for a community park, garden or some other feature that is both for the community and a part of the community.

Since these physical features are absent in virtual online communities, the web developer, acting as the architect for the online community, has to use elements like personalized pages to allow the users to connect with the web site. If users feel that your site is customized to their needs, and allows them to grow and interact with other users and the information available within the site, than they will be more willing to participate in the community features.

In planning how a user will be able to customize their experience of the site, several key issues must be addressed. The primary issue is that regardless of the customization the user must be aware of the signage of the site and they must be aware of any and all ad banners. These elements are critical to the identity and profitability of the web site and can not be compromised. Another key issue is to ensure that the process of customizing the site is simple and painless for the user. If they have to navigate through a series of complex, complicated pages in order to customize their experience, then the user will probably never complete the process and find another community to participate in. Finally, the developer must determine which pages will be customizable. Typically the initial 'Start' page is the only page that can be fully customized, and the remaining pages are static and identical for every user.

When to Use Personalized Pages

Personalized pages are one of the few community elements that do not depend on the size or the number of simultaneous users logged into the system. Because of this, personalized pages can be used on any site without problems. Since each user's experience of the site is unique and doesn't have to correlate with other user's experience, personalized pages can be deployed on sites as small as personal web pages to sites as large as online gaming sites or major corporate sites.

When planning personalized pages, the developer has to take into account what the user base is. For example, if a site is designed primarily to offer users information about a product that they will not use frequently then it might not make a lot of sense to offer users the opportunity to personalize their experience.

Implementing Personalized Pages

Personalized pages are typically implemented in one of two methodologies.

The first methodology is to have all of the user's personalization settings stored in cookies on the client browser. The advantage to this methodology is that the server does not have to store and retrieve information from a database. This not only improves the responsiveness of the web server, by eliminating a call to a separate database server or service, but also reduces the cost of ownership for the server, as development time does not have to be allocated to database creation and maintenance. The problem with this implementation is that if the user deletes the cookie, moves between machines, or goes to the site with a different browser then their personalization settings are not available.

The second methodology places all of the personalization settings within a database that is located on the server or on a separate database server. This methodology eliminates the problems of user's settings being lost or not available if they move between computers or if their cookies are deleted. However every advantage always comes at a price, and by storing the personalization settings in a database the price is monetary. The database requires development time to create, maintain, and upgrade as the number of users increases over time. One disadvantage to the database methodology is that you will have to require users to enter in some sort of authentication information to access their stored settings. Of course one could always use cookies to authenticate users, and then fall back on a form-based login page if the cookie were destroyed.

In order to demonstrate personalized pages we are going to take a look at a fictitious online news site "TheNews.com". TheNews.com offers global news to its users, but more importantly it allows users to interact amongst each other using chat-rooms located at its servers. In addition to the chat rooms and newsgroups, TheNews.com also allows users to store their preferences in articles and their chat alias using cookies. Since TheNews.com expects a large number of both simultaneous users and of total users, they chose to place the personalization settings on the user's machine to reduce the database development and maintenance expenses. Keep in mind that this demonstration is for the community building features of this site and not an architecture demonstration for this site. If TheNews.com were a live site, it would need a server-side object to handle all of the story headlines and linking instead of the client-side scripting used in the example.

Tour of TheNews.com site

First we are going to take a brief tour of the site before and after the personalization settings have been made so that you already know what the page's output will be before we take a closer look at the code. When you first visit TheNews.com you are presented with **default.asp**. This is the front page of TheNews.com listing all of the feature articles, etc. Without having the personalization cookie your front page contains the standard headlines and features, and lets you know that this site can easily be personalized. The section pages and the article pages do not contain any personalized settings in this demonstration.

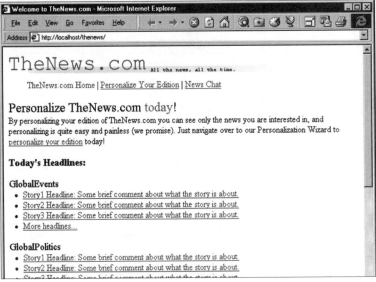

This example can be downloaded from the Wrox site at
`http://rapid.wrox.co.uk/books/1266`

If you click on the link to 'News Chat' it will open a second window containing `chat.asp`. Without the cookie, `chat.asp` requires to the user to enter their username into the textbox and click the Join the Chat button in order to join a chat room.

If the user wants to personalize their edition of TheNews.com they can simply click on any of the Personalize your Edition links on every page except for `chat.asp`. This takes the user to the personalization wizard that allows them to specify their name, preferred chat username, and which headline topic they want on their front page.

After the user has specified their personalized settings, they click the Save these Settings button which posts that information to the server to be saved as a cookie on the client and the server returns with a page specifying exactly what settings were set.

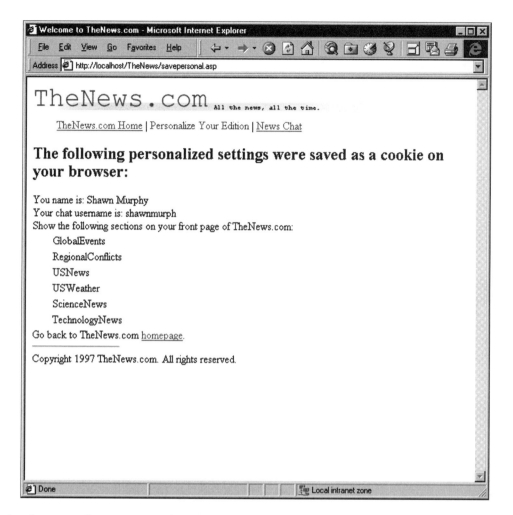

Now that the personalization settings have been saved, we will continue our tour to notice how the pages react differently.

TheNews.com front page, `default.asp`, now only displays the headlines for those topics that the user expressed interest in. In addition, the advertisement for the personalization features disappears in exchange for a personalized greeting.

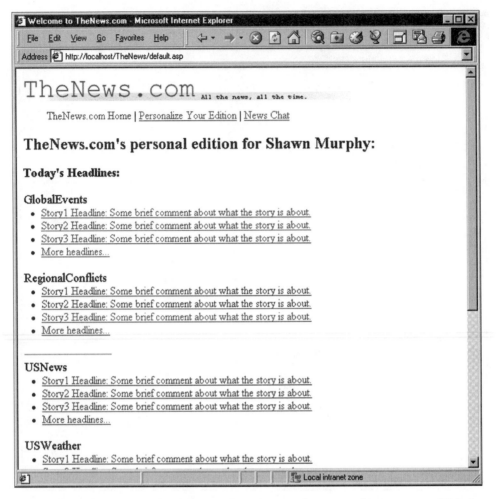

The behavior of the chat page is now different when a personalization cookie is present. With the cookie, **chat.asp** now automatically logs into the chat room using the stored chat alias.

When the user returns to the personalization wizard, **personal.asp**, to update their settings all of the settings from the cookie are automatically loaded into the form so the user can easily update the settings.

Now lets take a look at the code that does the work...

default.asp

Default.asp is the first page that users hit when they enter the site, and it is also the page with the most personalization settings. The code for this page is quite simple since all it is doing is modifying the output code based on the user's stored settings in their cookie.

```
<HTML>
<HEAD>
<TITLE>Welcome to TheNews.com</TITLE>

</HEAD>
<BODY BGCOLOR="White">
<TABLE WIDTH=500 CELLSPACING=0 CELLPADDING=0 BORDER=0>
<TR VALIGN="Top">
    <TD COLSPAN=4 HEIGHT="45"><IMG SRC="images/Banner.gif"></TD>
```

```
</TR>
<TR VALIGN="TOP">
    <TD WIDTH="35"></TD><TD><FONT COLOR="Maroon">TheNews.com Home</FONT> | <A
HREF="personal.asp">Personalize Your Edition</A> | <A HREF="chat.asp"
TARGET="_new">News Chat</A></TD>
</TR>
</TABLE>
<%  dim aryPerData(12)
    If NOT(Request.Cookies("TheNews")="") then
            aryPerData(0) = Request.Cookies("TheNews")("Name")
            aryPerData(1) = Request.Cookies("TheNews")("UserName")
            aryPerData(2) = Request.Cookies("TheNews")("GlobalEvents")
            aryPerData(3) = Request.Cookies("TheNews")("GlobalPolitics")
            aryPerData(4) = Request.Cookies("TheNews")("RegionalConflicts")
            aryPerData(5) = Request.Cookies("TheNews")("GlobalWeather")
            aryPerData(6) = Request.Cookies("TheNews")("USNews")
            aryPerData(7) = Request.Cookies("TheNews")("USWeather")
            aryPerData(8) = Request.Cookies("TheNews")("ScienceNews")
            aryPerData(9) = Request.Cookies("TheNews")("TechnologyNews")
            aryPerData(10) = Request.Cookies("TheNews")("EntertainmentIndustry")
            aryPerData(11) = Request.Cookies("TheNews")("EnvironmentalIssues")
            aryPerData(12) = Request.Cookies("TheNews")("Sports") %>
            <H2>TheNews.com's personal edition for <%= aryPerData(0) %>:</H2>
    <% Else
            aryPerData(0) = ""
            aryPerData(1) = ""
            aryPerData(2) = "1"
            aryPerData(3) = "1"
            aryPerData(4) = "1"
            aryPerData(5) = "1"
            aryPerData(6) = "0"
            aryPerData(7) = "0"
            aryPerData(8) = "1"
            aryPerData(9) = "1"
            aryPerData(10) = "1"
            aryPerData(11) = "1"
            aryPerData(12) = "1" %>
            <BR>
            <FONT Size="+2">Personalize TheNews.com <FONT COLOR="Red">today</FONT>!</
FONT>
            <BR>
            By personalizing your edition of TheNews.com you can see only the news you
are interested in, and personalizing is quite easy and painless (we promise). Just
navigate over to our Personalization Wizard to <A HREF="personal.asp">personalize your
edition</A> today!
    <% End If %>
            <H3>Today's Headlines:</H2>
            <% If aryPerData(2) = "1" then %>
                    <FONT SIZE="+1">GlobalEvents</FONT>
                    <TABLE BORDER=0 CELLSPACING=0 CELLPADDING=0>
                    <TR>
                    <TD WIDTH=10 ROWSPAN=10> </TD>
                    <TD><LI><A
HREF="article.asp?Section=GlobalEvents&Article=Story1">Story1 Headline: Some brief
comment about what the story is about.</A></TD></TR>
                    <TR><TD><LI><A
```

```
         HREF="article.asp?Section=GlobalEvents&Article=Story2">Story2 Headline: Some brief
         comment about what the story is about.</A></TD></TR>
                         <TR><TD><LI><A
         HREF="article.asp?Section=GlobalEvents&Article=Story3">Story3 Headline: Some brief
         comment about what the story is about.</A></TD></TR>
                         <TR><TD><LI><A HREF="section.asp?Section=GlobalEvents">More
         headlines...</A></TD></TR>
                         </TR>
                         </TABLE>
                         <BR>
                 <% End If %>


         ... ' More code similar to the about if then clause to direct output.

         <HR WIDTH="20%" ALIGN="Left" BGCOLOR="Yellow" NOSHADOW HEIGHT="5">
         Copyright 1997 TheNews.com. All rights reserved.
         </BODY>
         </HTML>
```

Checking the Cookie

The first thing that we need to do is to check whether the cookie is on the client computer and initialize all of the section variables depending on the cookie.

```
<%  dim aryPerData(12)
    If NOT(Request.Cookies("TheNews")="") then
```

First we have to check to see if the cookie exists. If the cookie exists then the client will send the cookie up in the HTML headers, if the cookie does not exist, than it will send a null string in the HTML header.

Loading the Cookie Values into an Array

If the cookie exists than we can simply read the stored keys in the cookie and write their values to an array.

```
            aryPerData(0) = Request.Cookies("TheNews")("Name")
            aryPerData(1) = Request.Cookies("TheNews")("UserName")
            aryPerData(2) = Request.Cookies("TheNews")("GlobalEvents")
            aryPerData(3) = Request.Cookies("TheNews")("GlobalPolitics")
            aryPerData(4) = Request.Cookies("TheNews")("RegionalConflicts")
            aryPerData(5) = Request.Cookies("TheNews")("GlobalWeather")
            aryPerData(6) = Request.Cookies("TheNews")("USNews")
            aryPerData(7) = Request.Cookies("TheNews")("USWeather")
            aryPerData(8) = Request.Cookies("TheNews")("ScienceNews")
            aryPerData(9) = Request.Cookies("TheNews")("TechnologyNews")
            aryPerData(10) = Request.Cookies("TheNews")("EntertainmentIndustry")
            aryPerData(11) = Request.Cookies("TheNews")("EnvironmentalIssues")
            aryPerData(12) = Request.Cookies("TheNews")("Sports") %>
```

Since this user has their personalization settings stored, we can now write to the client our customized greeting for them.

```
            <H2>TheNews.com's personal edition for <%= aryPerData(0) %>:</H2>
```

Loading Default Values if a Cookie does not exist

If the cookie does not exist on the client than we must load the array with the default values and display the personalization ad copy to the client.

```
<% Else
        aryPerData(0) = ""
        aryPerData(1) = ""
        aryPerData(2) = "1"
        aryPerData(3) = "1"
        aryPerData(4) = "1"
        aryPerData(5) = "1"
        aryPerData(6) = "0"
        aryPerData(7) = "0"
        aryPerData(8) = "1"
        aryPerData(9) = "1"
        aryPerData(10) = "1"
        aryPerData(11) = "1"
        aryPerData(12) = "1" %>
        <BR>
        <FONT Size="+2">Personalize TheNews.com <FONT COLOR="Red">today</FONT>!
        </FONT>
        <BR>
        By personalizing your edition of TheNews.com you can see only the news you
are interested in, and personalizing is quite easy and painless (we promise). Just
navigate over to our Personalization Wizard to <A HREF="personal.asp">personalize your
edition</A> today!
    <% End If %>
```

Parsing the Headlines

Now that **aryPerData** contains all of the personalized settings we can write the section headlines based on the users preferences. This is handled by a simple **if..then** clause surrounding the headlines.

```
<% If aryPerData(2) = "1" then %>
            <FONT SIZE="+1">GlobalEvents</FONT>
            <TABLE BORDER=0 CELLSPACING=0 CELLPADDING=0>
            <TR>
            <TD WIDTH=10 ROWSPAN=10> </TD>
            <TD><LI><A
HREF="article.asp?Section=GlobalEvents&Article=Story1">Story1 Headline: Some brief
comment about what the story is about.</A></TD></TR>
            <TR><TD><LI><A
HREF="article.asp?Section=GlobalEvents&Article=Story2">Story2 Headline: Some brief
comment about what the story is about.</A></TD></TR>
            <TR><TD><LI><A
HREF="article.asp?Section=GlobalEvents&Article=Story3">Story3 Headline: Some brief
comment about what the story is about.</A></TD></TR>
            <TR><TD><LI><A HREF="section.asp?Section=GlobalEvents">More
headlines...</A></TD></TR>
            </TR>
            </TABLE>
            <BR>
        <% End If %>
```

chat.asp

The chat page is slightly more complex than the front page as the chat page's functionality changes if the user has personalized settings stored or not. Unlike most ASP pages where the ASP code only modifies HTML content, this page modifies only client-side code to affect how the Java applet will behave.

```
<HTML>
<HEAD>
<TITLE>TheNews.com Chat</TITLE>
<SCRIPT LANGUAGE="JavaScript">
function changeroom()
{
    if (ChatPick.value == "other")
    {
            document.JavaChat.showRoomList();
            return true;
    }
    if (ChatPick.value == "new")
    {
            document.JavaChat.showEnterRoomDialog();
            return true;
    }
    document.JavaChat.join(ChatPick.value,"");
    return true;
}
</SCRIPT>
</HEAD>
<BODY BGCOLOR="White">
<TABLE WIDTH=500 CELLSPACING=0 CELLPADDING=0 BORDER=0>
<TR VALIGN="Top">
    <TD COLSPAN=2 HEIGHT="45"><IMG SRC="images/Banner.gif"></TD>

</TR>
</TABLE>
<BR>Username for chat room: <INPUT TYPE = "TEXT" NAME="Alias" VALUE="<%  dim
aryPerData(1)
    If Request.Cookies("TheNews").HasKeys then
            aryPerData(0) = Request.Cookies("TheNews")("Name")
            aryPerData(1) = Request.Cookies("TheNews")("UserName")
%><%= aryPerData(1) %><% Else %>MyUserName<% End If %> " SIZE = "16">
  
<INPUT TYPE = "BUTTON" NAME="FluxBtn" VALUE = "Join the chat"
onClick="document.JavaChat.connect(Alias.value,'')">
<BR><BR>
Log into chat room:
                    <SELECT NAME="ChatPick" onChange="changeroom();">
                        <OPTION Value="#Home">General Chat
                        <OPTION VALUE="#GlobalEvents">Global Events Chat
                        <OPTION VALUE="#GlobalPolitics">Global Politics Chat
                        <OPTION VALUE="#RegionalConflicts">Regional Conflicts Chat
                        <OPTION VALUE="#GlobalWeather">Global Weather Chat
                        <OPTION VALUE="#ScienceNews">Science News Chat
                        <OPTION VALUE="#TechnologyNews">Technology News Chat
                        <OPTION VALUE="#EntertainmentNews">Entertainment News Chat
                        <OPTION VALUE="#EnvironmentalIssues">Environmental Issues
                        Chat
                        <OPTION VALUE="#Sports">Sports Chat
```

```
                                <OPTION VALUE="other">Show all Chats
                                <OPTION VALUE="new">Start a Personal Chat Room
                        </SELECT>
<BR><BR>
<APPLET CODE="MSChat" Name="JavaChat" ARCHIVE="mschat.jar" WIDTH="550" HEIGHT="250">
        <PARAM NAME="cabbase" VALUE="mschat.cab">
        <PARAM NAME="port" VALUE="6667">
            <PARAM NAME="room" VALUE="#Home">
            <PARAM NAME="toolbar" VALUE="FALSE">
            <PARAM NAME="autodisconnect" VALUE="TRUE">
</APPLET>
<% If Request.Cookies("TheNews").HasKeys then %>
<SCRIPT LANGUAGE="JavaScript">
document.JavaChat.connect("<%= aryPerData(1) %>","#Home");
</SCRIPT>
<% End If %>
</BODY>
</HTML>
```

Placing the Username into the Textbox

If you remember from the tour, the chat page contains a text box which has the user's username or chat alias. The following code initializes all of the variables if the user has a personalization cookie stored and writes the user's preferred chat username into the textbox.

```
<BR>Username for chat room: <INPUT TYPE = "TEXT" NAME="Alias" VALUE="<%  dim
aryPerData(1)
    If Request.Cookies("TheNews").HasKeys then
            aryPerData(0) = Request.Cookies("TheNews")("Name")
            aryPerData(1) = Request.Cookies("TheNews")("UserName")
%><%= aryPerData(1) %><% Else %>MyUserName<% End If %> " SIZE = "16">
```

Notice that we have been very careful to place the server side code tags **<% %>** inline with the HTML. This will ensure that the code is parsed in a single line to the client.

```
<BR>Username for chat room: <INPUT TYPE = "TEXT" NAME="Alias" VALUE="shawnmur " SIZE =
"16">
```

The only other method to get the line to parse correctly is to include the entire **<INPUT>** tag in the **if..then** clause, but this increases the number of characters that the server must parse in order to deliver the page.

Parsing the Client-side Connection Code

If you remember, the chat page also automatically connects to the chat room if the user had a personalization cookie set. This is handled by checking to see if a cookie "TheNews" exists that has multiple keys, since our personalization cookie is stored as a cookie with multiple keys. If the personalization cookie does exist, then we simply write the entire script block to the client. We are also writing the user's preferred chat username from an array that we loaded in the previous server-side code block.

```
<% If Request.Cookies("TheNews").HasKeys then %>
<SCRIPT LANGUAGE="JavaScript">
document.JavaChat.connect("<%= aryPerData(1) %>","#Home");
</SCRIPT>
<% End If %>
```

personal.asp

The actual process of writing the cookie to the client happens across both **personal.asp** and
savepersonal.asp. **Personal.asp** displays the form for the user to specify their personalized settings
while **savepersonal.asp** writes those settings to the client computer as a cookie and then displays a
confirmation page indicating the settings that were saved.

```
<HTML>
<HEAD>
<TITLE>Welcome to TheNews.com</TITLE>

</HEAD>
<BODY BGCOLOR="White">
<TABLE WIDTH=500 CELLSPACING=0 CELLPADDING=0 BORDER=0>
<TR VALIGN="Top">
    <TD COLSPAN=4 HEIGHT="45"><IMG SRC="images/Banner.gif"></TD>

</TR>
<TR VALIGN="TOP">
    <TD WIDTH="35"></TD><TD><A HREF="default.asp">TheNews.com Home</A> | <FONT
COLOR="Maroon">Personalize Your Edition</FONT> | <A HREF="chat.asp" TARGET="_new">News
Chat</A></TD>
</TR>
</TABLE>
<H2>Welcome to the TheNews.com personalization wizard.</H2>
<P>After answering the following questions, we will save your personalization settings
in a cookie on your broswer so that whenever you return to TheNews.com those settings
will be available.
<BR><B>Note: You must have cookies enabled on your computer in order to use the
personalization feature of TheNews.com!</B></P>
<FORM NAME="PersonalData" ACTION="savepersonal.asp" METHOD="POST"
ENCTYPE="application/x-www-form-urlencoded">
What is your name: <INPUT TYPE="TEXT" NAME="TheName" VALUE="<% if
Request.Cookies("TheNews")("Name") = "" then %>Susan Doe<% Else %><%=
Request.Cookies("TheNews")("Name") %><% End If %>">
<BR>
What would you like your alias or username to be in TheNews.com chat rooms: <INPUT
TYPE="TEXT" NAME="UserName" VALUE="<% if Request.Cookies("TheNews")("UserName") = ""
then %> UserName<% Else %><%= Request.Cookies("TheNews")("UserName") %><% End If %>">
<BR>
Which of the following sections do you want headlines to appear on your front page of
TheNews.com?
<BR>
<TABLE BORDER=0>
<TR><TD><INPUT TYPE="CHECKBOX" VALUE="1" <% if
NOT(Request.Cookies("TheNews")("GlobalEvents") = "1") then %> <% Else %>CHECKED<% End
If %> NAME="GlobalEvents"></TD><TD>GlobalEvents</TD></TR>
<TR><TD><INPUT TYPE="CHECKBOX" VALUE="1" <% if
NOT(Request.Cookies("TheNews")("GlobalPolitics") = "1") then %> <% Else %>CHECKED<%
End If %> NAME="GlobalPolitics"></TD><TD>GlobalPolitics</TD></TR>
<TR><TD><INPUT TYPE="CHECKBOX" VALUE="1" <% if
NOT(Request.Cookies("TheNews")("RegionalConflicts") = "1") then %> <% Else %>CHECKED<%
End If %> NAME="RegionalConflicts"></TD><TD>RegionalConflicts</TD></TR>
<TR><TD><INPUT TYPE="CHECKBOX" VALUE="1" <% if
NOT(Request.Cookies("TheNews")("GlobalWeather") = "1") then %> <% Else %>CHECKED<% End
If %> NAME="GlobalWeather"></TD><TD>GlobalWeather</TD></TR>
<TR><TD><INPUT TYPE="CHECKBOX" VALUE="1" <% if Request.Cookies("TheNews")("USNews") =
```

```
"1" then %>CHECKED<% End If %> NAME="USNews"></TD><TD>USNews</TD></TR>
<TR><TD><INPUT TYPE="CHECKBOX" VALUE="1" <% if Request.Cookies("TheNews")("USWeather")
= "1" then %>CHECKED<% End If %> NAME="USWeather"></TD><TD>USWeather</TD></TR>
<TR><TD><INPUT TYPE="CHECKBOX" VALUE="1" <% if
NOT(Request.Cookies("TheNews")("ScienceNews") = "1") then %> <% Else %>CHECKED<% End
If %> NAME="ScienceNews"></TD><TD>ScienceNews</TD></TR>
<TR><TD><INPUT TYPE="CHECKBOX" VALUE="1" <% if
NOT(Request.Cookies("TheNews")("TechnologyNews") = "1") then %> <% Else %>CHECKED<%
End If %> NAME="TechnologyNews"></TD><TD>TechnologyNews</TD></TR>
<TR><TD><INPUT TYPE="CHECKBOX" VALUE="1" <% if
NOT(Request.Cookies("TheNews")("EntertainmentIndustry") = "1") then %> <% Else
%>CHECKED<% End If %> NAME="EntertainmentIndustry"></TD><TD>EntertainmentIndustry</
TD></TR>
<TR><TD><INPUT TYPE="CHECKBOX" VALUE="1" <% if
NOT(Request.Cookies("TheNews")("EnvironmentalIssues") = "1") then %> <% Else
%>CHECKED<% End If %> NAME="EnvironmentalIssues"></TD><TD>EnvironmentalIssues</TD></
TR>
<TR><TD><INPUT TYPE="CHECKBOX" VALUE="1" <% if
NOT(Request.Cookies("TheNews")("Sports") = "1") then %> <% Else %>CHECKED<% End If %>
NAME="Sports"></TD><TD>Sports</TD></TR>
</TABLE>
<BR>
<INPUT TYPE="Submit" Value="Save these settings!" Name="Submit">
</FORM>
<HR WIDTH="20%" ALIGN="Left" BGCOLOR="Yellow" NOSHADOW HEIGHT="5">
<INPUT TYPE="Button" NAME="Remove" VALUE="Remove my personalized settings"
onClick="document.location.href='removecookie.asp';">
<HR WIDTH="20%" ALIGN="Left" BGCOLOR="Yellow" NOSHADOW HEIGHT="5">
<BR>
<BR>
<BR>
<HR WIDTH="20%" ALIGN="Left" BGCOLOR="Yellow" NOSHADOW HEIGHT="5">
Copyright 1997 TheNews.com. All rights reserved.
</BODY>
</HTML>
```

If you remember from the tour, **personal.asp** pre-loads the form if you already have a personalization cookie, otherwise it presents the default values. The values are loaded in the same fashion as the values were loaded on the chat page using inline server-side code blocks.

For the textboxes, if the value stored in the cookie is a null string (indicating that the cookie does not exist or that the user specified a null string) then we write the default value to the client, otherwise we write the user's value.

```
What would you like your alias or username to be in TheNews.com chat rooms: <INPUT
TYPE="TEXT" NAME="UserName" VALUE="<% if Request.Cookies("TheNews")("UserName") = ""
then %> UserName<% Else %><%= Request.Cookies("TheNews")("UserName") %><% End If %>">
```

For the headline settings, we simply determine the state of the setting (either "**1**" or "**0**") and set the **CHECKED** attribute for the checkboxes if the value is "**1**".

```
<TR><TD><INPUT TYPE="CHECKBOX" VALUE="1" <% if
NOT(Request.Cookies("TheNews")("EnvironmentalIssues") = "1") then %> <% Else
%>CHECKED<% End If %> NAME="EnvironmentalIssues"></TD><TD>EnvironmentalIssues</TD></
TR>
```

After the user enters their personalized settings, they simply have to click the Save these settings button to submit the form to `savepersonal.asp`.

savepersonal.asp

Unlike most form submissions which are handled by a CGI script, we are using an ASP page to respond to the form post. Since form posts are submitted by placing all of the form data into the URL, we can use the `Request` object to retrieve these values.

```
<%
Response.Cookies("TheNews").Expires = "January 1, 1999"
Response.Cookies("TheNews")("Name") = Request("TheName")
Response.Cookies("TheNews")("UserName") = Request("UserName")
Response.Cookies("TheNews")("GlobalEvents") = Request("GlobalEvents")
Response.Cookies("TheNews")("GlobalPolitics") = Request("GlobalPolitics")
Response.Cookies("TheNews")("RegionalConflicts") = Request("RegionalConflicts")
Response.Cookies("TheNews")("GlobalWeather") = Request("GlobalWeather")
Response.Cookies("TheNews")("USNews") = Request("USNews")
Response.Cookies("TheNews")("USWeather") = Request("USWeather")
Response.Cookies("TheNews")("ScienceNews") = Request("ScienceNews")
Response.Cookies("TheNews")("TechnologyNews") = Request("TechnologyNews")
Response.Cookies("TheNews")("EntertainmentIndustry") =
Request("EntertainmentIndustry")
Response.Cookies("TheNews")("EnvironmentalIssues") = Request("EnvironmentalIssues")
Response.Cookies("TheNews")("Sports") = Request("Sports")
%>
<HTML>
<HEAD>
<TITLE>Welcome to TheNews.com</TITLE>

</HEAD>
<BODY BGCOLOR="White">
<TABLE WIDTH=500 CELLSPACING=0 CELLPADDING=0 BORDER=0>
<TR VALIGN="Top">
    <TD COLSPAN=4 HEIGHT="45"><IMG SRC="images/Banner.gif"></TD>

</TR>
<TR VALIGN="TOP">
    <TD WIDTH="35"></TD><TD><A HREF="default.asp">TheNews.com Home</A> | <FONT
COLOR="Maroon">Personalize Your Edition</FONT> | <A HREF="chat.asp" TARGET="_new">News
Chat</A></TD>
</TR>
</TABLE>
<H2>The following personalized settings were saved as a cookie on your browser:</H2>
You name is: <%= Request("TheName") %><BR>
Your chat username is: <%= Request("UserName") %><BR>
Show the following sections on your front page of TheNews.com:<BR>
<TABLE BORDER=0>
<% If Request("GlobalEvents") = "1" then %>
<TR><TD>      </TD><TD>GlobalEvents</TD></TR>
<% End If %>
<% If Request("GlobalPolitics") = "1" then %>
<TR><TD>      </TD><TD>GlobalPolitics</TD></TR>
<% End If %>
<% If Request("RegionalConflicts") = "1" then %>
```

```
<TR><TD>      </TD><TD>RegionalConflicts</TD></TR>
<% End If %>
<% If Request("GlobalWeather") = "1" then %>
<TR><TD>      </TD><TD>GlobalWeather</TD></TR>
<% End If %>
<% If Request("USNews") = "1" then %>
<TR><TD>      </TD><TD>USNews</TD></TR>
<% End If %>
<% If Request("USWeather") = "1" then %>
<TR><TD>      </TD><TD>USWeather</TD></TR>
<% End If %>
<% If Request("ScienceNews") = "1" then %>
<TR><TD>      </TD><TD>ScienceNews</TD></TR>
<% End If %>
<% If Request("TechnologyNews") = "1" then %>
<TR><TD>      </TD><TD>TechnologyNews</TD></TR>
<% End If %>
<% If Request("EntertainmentIndustry") = "1" then %>
<TR><TD>      </TD><TD>EntertainmentIndustry</TD></TR>
<% End If %>
<% If Request("EnvironmentalIssues") = "1" then %>
<TR><TD>      </TD><TD>EnvironmentalIssues</TD></TR>
<% End If %>
<% If Request("Sports") = "1" then %>
<TR><TD>      </TD><TD>Sports</TD></TR>
<% End If %>
</TABLE>
Go back to TheNews.com <A HREF="default.asp">homepage</A>.
<HR WIDTH="20%" ALIGN="Left" BGCOLOR="Yellow" NOSHADOW HEIGHT="5">
Copyright 1997 TheNews.com. All rights reserved.
</BODY>
</HTML>
```

Saving the cookie

Since the cookie is sent as a part of the HTML header, the cookie must be written to the client before any other information is written to the client. This requirement forces us to place the cookie code as the first line in our ASP file.

```
<%
Response.Cookies("TheNews").Expires = "January 1, 1999"
Response.Cookies("TheNews")("Name") = Request("TheName")
Response.Cookies("TheNews")("UserName") = Request("UserName")
Response.Cookies("TheNews")("GlobalEvents") = Request("GlobalEvents")
Response.Cookies("TheNews")("GlobalPolitics") = Request("GlobalPolitics")
Response.Cookies("TheNews")("RegionalConflicts") = Request("RegionalConflicts")
Response.Cookies("TheNews")("GlobalWeather") = Request("GlobalWeather")
Response.Cookies("TheNews")("USNews") = Request("USNews")
Response.Cookies("TheNews")("USWeather") = Request("USWeather")
Response.Cookies("TheNews")("ScienceNews") = Request("ScienceNews")
Response.Cookies("TheNews")("TechnologyNews") = Request("TechnologyNews")
Response.Cookies("TheNews")("EntertainmentIndustry") =
Request("EntertainmentIndustry")
Response.Cookies("TheNews")("EnvironmentalIssues") = Request("EnvironmentalIssues")
Response.Cookies("TheNews")("Sports") = Request("Sports")
%>
```

As you can see, we are simply setting the values of the individual keys in the cookie to the values of the form elements using the **Request** object to read the form element values from the URL. This allows a simple, elegant method to dealing with cookies.

The remainder of the **savepersonal.asp** page simply writes the personalization settings that were saved into the cookie to the client so that the user can verify that those are the settings they requested.

Summary

In this chapter we have covered the theory behind online communities and the various technologies that can be used to foster the development of an online community. We have looked at when to use chat rooms, newsgroups and personalized pages depending on the size of the web site and its number of simultaneous connections. We have also shown how to configure and setup the chat and newsgroup servers in addition to their respective clients. We have also looked at a small case study of a simple site that used personalized pages to customize the user's front page of a news site.

The most important points in this chapter are:

- The technologies used to foster development of an online community depend on the number of simultaneous users connected to the site.

- Newsgroups are good community builders for sites with a low number of simultaneous users and for sites with content that can be discussed over long periods of time.

- Chat rooms are excellent means to foster online communities, but require a high number of simultaneous connections

- Personalized pages do not directly build online communities, but they are a great method to capture users and make them feel connected to the site and the community that is building on the site.

In the next chapter we will take a look at ways to use ASP pages to customize the experience for users with the Internet Explorer 4 browser.

Interacting with Internet Explorer 4

In the previous chapter we covered how to create online communities using several different technologies and we also provided a small case study for a mythical online news site. In this chapter we are going to cover how to use Active Server Pages to provide an enhanced experience for users with Internet Explorer 4.x. We are going extend the TheNews.com case study in this chapter to show how an existing site can easily be upgraded to offer full support for Internet Explorer 4.x without requiring a lot of development time. This chapter will cover how to easily integrate Dynamic HTML into your pages for Internet Explorer 4.x users, and how to dynamically create channels.

In this chapter we will cover:

- ▲ Creating Dynamic HTML pages dynamically using ASP
- ▲ Creating CDF channels dynamically using ASP
- ▲ Using Enhanced Forms as an application interface for ASP

Lets first take a look at how TheNews.com site can dynamically provide users with Internet Explorer 4.x Dynamic HTML pages.

Dynamically Generating Dynamic HTML

ASP pages have always allowed developers to customize the output of HTML pages to suit the requesting browser, and this continues to hold true for Internet Explorer 4. Previously, there might only have been a moderate difference between an Internet Explorer 3.x page with ActiveX controls and a Netscape 3.x page without the ActiveX controls. However, unlike before, IE4 allows dramatically different capabilities with its full implementation of Dynamic HTML. We are going to take a look at a few easily ways that ASP allow you to customize and provide Dynamic HTML pages for Internet Explorer 4.0 users without requiring a lot of development time.

Browser Capabilities Component

Before we can start demonstrating how to dynamically add Dynamic HTML for users of Internet Explorer 4.x, we should explain how to detect for specific browsers. Once again we're going to use our old friend from Chapter 6, the Browser Capabilities Component. The Browser Capabilities component compares the user agent string transmitted to the server against a user-extendable table in the **browscap.ini** file located in the same directory as **browscap.dll** (typically this is in the **WinNTRoot/System32/ inetsrv** directory). The control then provides the set of properties and values defined in the browscap.ini file to your ASP pages.

Customizing The browscap.ini File

The **browscap.ini** file contains all of the browser configuration settings that will be used by the control. The file lists all of the variations of user agent strings and then the various settings for its properties.

The Browser Capabilities Component scans this file until it finds a label that matches the user agent string of the client browser. The text that follows the label defines the various properties and their respective values, with the exception of the parent property, which defines another label that contains additional properties.

Since all of the control's properties are read directly from this table, adding more properties is as easy as adding entries into the table. Since our demonstration site, TheNews.com, wants to customize the output for browsers that support Dynamic HTML (as implemented by Microsoft) we will add a property to the IE4 parent declaration that we can easily check for. We can then easily add this support for other browsers that support this implementation of Dynamic HTML by simply setting our new DHTML property to TRUE for those user agent strings in the **browscap.ini** file instead of manually updating all of the client detection scripts throughout the site.

```
;;;;;;;;;;;;;;;;;;;;;;;;;;;;;;;;;;;;;;;;;;; IE 4.x
[IE 4.0]
browser=IE
Version=4.0
majorver=4
minorver=0
dhtml = TRUE
frames=TRUE
tables=TRUE
cookies=TRUE
backgroundsounds=TRUE
vbscript=TRUE
javascript=TRUE
javaapplets=TRUE
ActiveXControls=TRUE
Win16=False
beta=False
AK=False
SK=False
AOL=False
crawler=False
cdf=True
```

Simple Demonstration

The following demonstration outputs the values for all of the properties defined in the **browscap.ini** file. You can see that the values it sends to the client depend on the client connected to the server. Here's an example of the responses generated by Netscape Communicator 4.01a.

```
<HTML>
<HEAD>
<TITLE>Browser Capabilities Control</TITLE>
</HEAD>
<BODY>
<%  Set bc = Server.CreateObject("MSWC.BrowserType") %>
<TABLE>
```

```
<TR><TD>UserAgent String</TD><TD>'<%= Request.ServerVariables ("HTTP_USER_AGENT")
%>'</TD></TR>
<TR><TD>Property</TD><TD>Value</TD></TR>
<TR><TD>browser</TD><TD><%= bc.browser %></TD></TR>
<TR><TD>Version</TD><TD><%= bc.Version %></TD></TR>
<TR><TD>majorver</TD><TD><%= bc.majorver %></TD></TR>
<TR><TD>minorver</TD><TD><%= bc.minorver %></TD></TR>
<TR><TD>dhtml</TD><TD><%= bc.dhtml %></TD></TR>
<TR><TD>frames</TD><TD><%= bc.frames %></TD></TR>
<TR><TD>tables</TD><TD><%= bc.tables %></TD></TR>
<TR><TD>cookies</TD><TD><%= bc.cookies %></TD></TR>
<TR><TD>backgroundsounds</TD><TD><%= bc.backgroundsounds %></TD></TR>
<TR><TD>vbscript</TD><TD><%= bc.vbscript %></TD></TR>
<TR><TD>javascript</TD><TD><%= bc.javascript %></TD></TR>
<TR><TD>javaapplets</TD><TD><%= bc.javaapplets %></TD></TR>
<TR><TD>ActiveXControls</TD><TD><%= bc.ActiveXControls %></TD></TR>
<TR><TD>Win16</TD><TD><%= bc.Win16 %></TD></TR>
<TR><TD>beta</TD><TD><%= bc.beta %></TD></TR>
<TR><TD>AK</TD><TD><%= bc.AK %></TD></TR>
<TR><TD>SK</TD><TD><%= bc.SK %></TD></TR>
<TR><TD>AOL</TD><TD><%= bc.AOL %></TD></TR>
<TR><TD>crawler</TD><TD><%= bc.crawler %></TD></TR>
<TR><TD>cdf</TD><TD><%= bc.cdf %></TD></TR>
<TR><TD>platform</TD><TD><%= bc.platform %></TD></TR>
</TABLE>
</BODY>
</HTML>
```

The control itself is loaded into the server using the server's **CreateObject** method and specifying the registered name for the control (in this case **MSWC.BrowserType**).

```
<% Set bc = Server.CreateObject("MSWC.BrowserType") %>
```

Once the control is loaded into memory and initialized, we can simply query the control using the properties defined in the browscap.ini file. For example:

```
<TR><TD>ActiveXControls</TD><TD><%= bc.ActiveXControls %></TD></TR>
```

The control will then output the value specified in the file or 'unknown' if that property did not have a specified value.

Stupid Font Tricks

One of the easiest methods of integrating Dynamic HTML into web pages is to provide simple rollover effects for anchors. Oftentimes manipulating fonts, i.e. providing rollover effects, are overused as demonstrations of Dynamic HTML and have been given the name 'Stupid Font Tricks'. Despite their overuse as technology demonstrations, manipulating fonts to provide a simple rollover effect is an easy way to provide positive feedback to your users.

Using the Browser Capabilities Component and our modified **browscap.ini** file, we can now easily add Dynamic HTML to TheNews.com. We have added Dynamic HTML coding to all of the TheNews.com pages so that as a user moves the mouse over an HTML anchor, the anchor text will change from navy colored text without an underline to maroon colored text with both an overline and an underline.

DHTML Code For The Rollover States

```
<STYLE>
.Normal            {
          color: Navy;
          font-style: normal;
          text-decoration: none;
          }
.Rollover     {
          color: Maroon;
          font-style: bold;
          text-decoration: underline overline;
          }
</STYLE>
```

To accomplish this we have assigned every anchor to a cascading style sheet class called '**Normal**'.

```
<A CLASS="Normal" HREF="personal.asp">Personalize Your Edition</A>
```

We can then simply assign Internet Explorer 4.x to call a custom JavaScript function whenever the user moves the mouse over or out of an object on the page.

```
<SCRIPT LANGUAGE="JavaScript" FOR="window" EVENT="onload">
document.onmouseover = rollover;
document.onmouseout = rollout;
</SCRIPT>
```

These custom functions will then change the CSS class on the text from normal to rollover when the user moves the mouse over the text and when the mouse moves out of the text.

```
<SCRIPT LANGUAGE="JavaScript">
function rollover()
    {
    if (window.event.srcElement.className == "Normal")
            {
            window.event.srcElement.className = "Rollover";
            }
    }
function rollout()
    {
    if (window.event.srcElement.className == "Rollover")
            {
            window.event.srcElement.className = "Normal";
            }
    }
</SCRIPT>
```

Implementing The DHTML Code For IE4

Since browsers will ignore all tags and attributes that it doesn't understand, we can place the **CLASS="normal"** attribute in every anchor tag within the site without worrying about errors. The problem is with the Dynamic HTML source code. If a scriptable client, like Internet Explorer 3.x or Netscape Navigator 4.x, tries to run the Dynamic HTML code it will generate errors. To solve this we can simply not write the script blocks to the client unless we've set the **dhtml** property in **browscap.ini** to **TRUE** for that client's user agent.

```
<% Set bc = Server.CreateObject("MSWC.BrowserType") %>
<% If bc.dhtml = "True" then %>
    <SCRIPT LANGUAGE="JavaScript" FOR="window" EVENT="onload">
    document.onmouseover = rollover;
    document.onmouseout = rollout;
    </SCRIPT>
    <SCRIPT LANGUAGE="JavaScript">
    function rollover()
            {
            if (window.event.srcElement.className == "Normal")
                    {
                    window.event.srcElement.className = "Rollover";
                    }
            }
    function rollout()
            {
            if (window.event.srcElement.className == "Rollover")
                    {
                    window.event.srcElement.className = "Normal";
                    }
            }
    </SCRIPT>
<% End If %>
```

This will ensure that only clients that we have acknowledged in the **browscap.ini** file will receive our Dynamic HTML code.

Customized Dynamic HTML

If you remember from Chapter 11, TheNews.com allowed users to store preferences on their preferred headlines using a client-side cookie. Using this cookie information we only sent the client down the information that they requested. While this improves their download times, and only delivers the content that they are interested in most, it does not allow them to easily browse the other headlines.

Refining TheNews.com Front Page

Instead of just limiting the content that the client receives, using Dynamic HTML we could place all of the content into a suede-tree control and then automatically expand the sections which the user expressed interest in. This still displays the information that the user wanted to view, however it also allows them the capability to easily browse the other headlines.

As you can see from the below images, the same page viewed in a browser that supports Dynamic HTML offers expandable headlines. However, the same page in a browser that we do not recognize as supporting Dynamic HTML (that is a user agent that does not have the `dhtml = TRUE` line in browscap.ini) displays the page identically as before.

The first image below is from Internet Explorer 4.0 as the page loads.

In the next image, we have clicked on the section title for Global Politics, and the corresponding headlines for that header will appear.

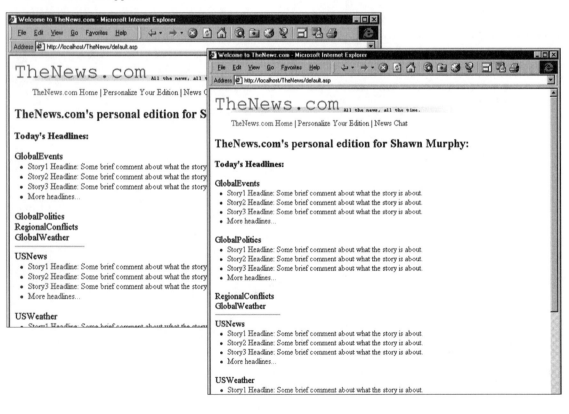

The same page viewed with a browser that does not support Dynamic HTML displays exactly like the older version of TheNews.com and completely lacks the option to read the non preferred sections.

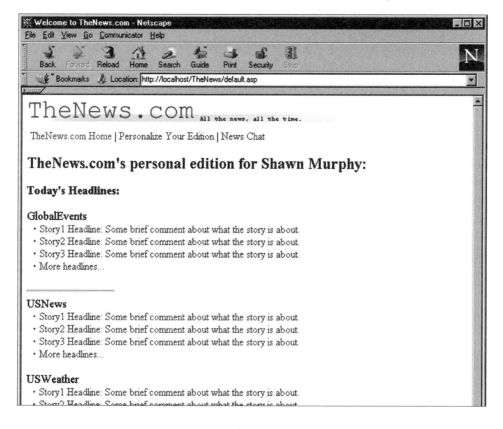

Coding The Refined TheNews.com Front Page

While it seems much more complex than the rollover states, the expanding directory is just as simple to implement as the rollover states.

Like the rollover states, we are once again allowing Cascading Style Sheets to control that appearance of the text, and we are allowing the CSS declarations to download for all of the browsers.

```
<STYLE>
.Normal            {
                   color: Navy;
                   font-style: normal;
                   text-decoration: none;
                   }
.Rollover   {
                   color: Maroon;
                   font-style: bold;
                   text-decoration: underline overline;
                   }
```

```
.Outline                    {
                     cursor: hand;
                     }
.OutlineItem                {
                     display: none;
                     }
.OutlineOpen                {

                     display: ;
                     }
</STYLE>
```

We have also added a new function to the event handling and script blocks. Whenever an object is clicked on the page, the **doOutline** function will check to make sure that the clicked object has been assigned to the CSS class **Outline** and it will then assign the child elements to the clicked object to the **OutlineOpen** or **OutlineItem** CSS class as appropriate.

```
<% Set bc = Server.CreateObject("MSWC.BrowserType") %>
<% If bc.dhtml = "True" then %>
   <SCRIPT LANGUAGE="JavaScript" FOR="window" EVENT="onload">
   document.onmouseover = rollover;
   document.onmouseout = rollout;
   document.onclick = doOutline;
   </SCRIPT>
   <SCRIPT LANGUAGE="JavaScript">
   function rollover()
          {
          if (window.event.srcElement.className == "Normal")
                 {
                 window.event.srcElement.className = "Rollover";
                 }
          }
   function rollout()
          {
          if (window.event.srcElement.className == "Rollover")
                 {
                 window.event.srcElement.className = "Normal";
                 }
          }
   function doOutline() {
     var targetId, srcElement, targetElement;
     srcElement = window.event.srcElement;
     if (srcElement.className == "Outline") {
            targetId = srcElement.id + "Child";
            targetElement = document.all(targetId);
            if (targetElement.className == "OutlineItem") {
                   targetElement.className = "OutlineOpen";
            } else {
                   targetElement.className = "OutlineItem";
            }
     }
   }
   </SCRIPT>
<% End If %>
```

The above changes will allow the outline to function. However, we still need to place the appropriate object **ID**s and class names into the page. As you can see, we have added some logic to the parsing of the headlines onto the front page.

```
<% If aryPerData(2) = "1" OR bc.dhtml = "True" then %>
    <FONT SIZE="+1" ID="GlobalEvents" CLASS="Outline">GlobalEvents</FONT>
    <TABLE ID="GlobalEventsChild" CLASS="<% If aryPerData(2) = "1" then
%>OutlineOpen<% Else %>OutlineItem<% End If %>" BORDER=0 CELLSPACING=0 CELLPADDING=0>
    <TR>
    <TD WIDTH=10 ROWSPAN=10> </TD>
    <TD><LI><A
CLASS="Normal"HREF="article.asp?Section=GlobalEvents&Article=Story1">Story1 Headline:
Some brief comment about what the story is about.</A></TD></TR>
    <TR><TD><LI><A
CLASS="Normal"HREF="article.asp?Section=GlobalEvents&Article=Story2">Story2 Headline:
Some brief comment about what the story is about.</A></TD></TR>
    <TR><TD><LI><A
CLASS="Normal"HREF="article.asp?Section=GlobalEvents&Article=Story3">Story3 Headline:
Some brief comment about what the story is about.</A></TD></TR>
    <TR><TD><LI><A CLASS="Normal"HREF="section.asp?Section=GlobalEvents">More
headlines...</A></TD></TR>
    </TR>
    </TABLE>
    <BR>
<% End If %>
```

With a few modifications we are able to enable this page for the IE4 version simply by assigning a few **ID**s and CSS class names to the objects.

```
<% If aryPerData(2) = "1" OR bc.dhtml = "True" then %>
```

Instead of simply blocking the HTML that contains the headlines for the unwanted sections, we are going to write them to the client if that client browser supports the **dhtml** property in **browscap.ini**.

```
<FONT SIZE="+1" ID="GlobalEvents" CLASS="Outline">GlobalEvents</FONT>
```

We need to assign the section name a unique **ID** and assign it to the CSS class **Outline** in order for it to work as the outline heading.

```
<TABLE ID="GlobalEventsChild" CLASS="<% If aryPerData(2) = "1" then %>OutlineOpen<%
Else %>OutlineItem<% End If %>"
```

We have assigned the table as the **Child** of the section heading and then assign it to the **OutlineOpen** or **OutlineItem** CSS class depending on whether we want that element displayed or hidden, respectively.

In Review - DHTML

As you can see, it is quite simple to add Dynamic HTML to your existing pages, especially when you use the Browser Capabilities Component. In adding Dynamic HTML to your pages, try to construct the pages so that the actual code is the only element that needs to have server-side logic determine whether the data should be sent to the client and allow the **ID**s and CSS declarations to be sent to every client. If implemented correctly, this philosophy will reduce development time and complexity, which in turn will reduce the number of bugs.

Dynamically Creating Channels

As you've probably already heard, Channels are the new smart-pull technology in Internet Explorer 4.x that allows web developers to specify which content is updated often so that the user can have their browser download those pages during off-peak hours and store that information in the browser's cache. This new technology has already redefined how some web sites operate, and a few sites have started to appear where the site is navigated completely within a channel. Since a full explanation of channels would extend well beyond a couple of chapters, we are going to briefly cover some of the channel basics and provide a brief example of how Active Server Pages can dynamically parse a channel definition file or CDF.

Channel Basics

CDF files are written in XML, or the eXtensible Markup Language, and are quite similar to HTML files in both syntax and usage. We are going to describe a simple demonstration channel to explain all of the CDF tags, values and uses.

CDF Header

Like HTML files, all XML files (which a CDF is) begin with a tag that defines the version and encoding this document use so that the parser, Internet Explorer 4.x, understands how to parse the file.

```
<?XML VERSION="1.0" ENCODING="UTF-8"?>
```

Defining the Parent Channel

A Channel is composed of several smaller "channels" and "items" arranged in a tree. The organization of a channel is similar to the organization of a hard drive, with "channels" acting as directories and "items" acting as files. Every CDF has a parent channel which all of the other "channels" and "items" are under.

Channel Tag

The **CHANNEL** tag has three required attributes that describe where the channel is located. The **HREF** attribute specifies the page that will be loaded from the cache when the user clicks on the channel name, icon or image. The **BASE** attribute works just like the **BASE** tag in an HTML file; it specifies the URL base for the remaining relative paths in all items and channels which are children to this channel. The **SELF** attribute provides the URL for the **CDF** itself and only needs to be specified in the parent channel.

```
<CHANNEL HREF="default.asp" BASE=" HYPERLINK "http://localhost/TheNews/"
SELF="NewsChannel.cdf">
<TITLE>Example Channel</TITLE>
<ABSTRACT>This is a text description of the channel</ABSTRACT>
<LOGO HREF="icon.gif" STYLE="ICON"/>
<LOGO HREF="image.gif" STYLE="IMAGE"/>
<LOGO HREF="imagewide.gif" STYLE="IMAGE-WIDE"/>
<SCHEDULE STARTDATE="1997.12.18" ENDDATE="1997.12.18">
    <INTERVALTIME DAY="1"/>
    <EARLIESTTIME HOUR="0"/>
    <LATESTTIME DAY="1" HOUR="4"/>
</SCHEDULE>
... Items go here
... Items go here
```

```
  ... Items go here
  </CHANNEL>
```

Defining the Custom Images

The parent channel may also provide information about the custom images and icons to distinguish this channel from other channels on the Channel Bar or the Channel menu.

The **LOGO** tag specifies the images used for the channel. The tag requires two attributes: **HREF** and **STYLE**. As to be expected **HREF** provides the URL for the image file. **STYLE** describes the type of image. A **Style** of **ICON** defines the image that will be placed adjacent to the channel title in the channels submenu of the Favorites menu in IE4.

```
  <LOGO HREF="icon.gif" STYLE="ICON"/>
```

A value of **IMAGE** for the **STYLE** attribute defines the image that will be placed on the channel bar. The image must be 80x32 pixels.

```
  <LOGO HREF="image.gif" STYLE="IMAGE"/>
```

A value of **IMAGE-WIDE** specifies the location of the wide channel bar image. The channel bar inside Internet Explorer displays this image instead of the smaller one. This image is 194x32 pixels.

```
  <LOGO HREF="imagewide.gif" STYLE="IMAGE-WIDE"/>
```

Defining the Download Schedule

A CDF allows the developer to exactly specify the range of times when the browser can update the information in the channel and download all of the content. This allows the developer to pick times when the servers are under the least load, yet the content on the site has been updated. The **SCHEDULE** tag handles the scheduling.

```
  <SCHEDULE STARTDATE="1997.12.18" ENDDATE="1998.12.18">
      <INTERVALTIME DAY="1"/>
      <EARLIESTTIME HOUR="0"/>
      <LATESTTIME DAY="1" HOUR="4"/>
  </SCHEDULE>
```

The **SCHEDULE** tag requires two attributes; **STARTDATE** and **ENDDATE**. These two attributes define the dates when the browser can start updating the CDF and when it can stop updating itself. If your site has information that is updated daily, then the **STARTDATE** and **ENDDATE** would probably be the same date (as shown above), however if your site is only updated biweekly or monthly, than the **STARTDATE** and **ENDDATE** would be 14 days or 30 days apart, respectively.

The **SCHEDULE** tag also has three required tags that must be within the **SCHEDULE** tag.

The **INTERVALTIME** specifies how often the updating and downloading interval is. In our case we specified one day. This will cause Internet Explorer 4.0 to update the CDF and the content in the cache everyday.

```
      <INTERVALTIME DAY="1"/>
```

The **EARLIESTTIME** tag defines the earliest time unit (day, hour, etc.) that Internet Explorer 4.x can begin downloading and updating the channel.

```
<EARLIESTTIME HOUR="0"/>
```

The **LATESTTIME** tag specifies that latest time that the browser may start the download time.

```
<LATESTTIME DAY="1" HOUR="4"/>
```

Based on the schedule that we have defined above. This demonstration channel will be downloaded from our server and all of the pages referred to in the CDF will be downloaded sometime between **0000 18 December 1997 GMT** and **0400 19 December 1997 GMT**. When Internet Explorer downloads the updated CDF, it will contain this information, only updated for the new time interval.

Defining the Channel Title

Every **CHANNEL** tag also has a **TITLE** tag within it. The **TITLE** tag specifies the title of the channel. This is the text that will appear in the channel menu, and this is the text that will appear next to the "book" icon in the Channel bar if this channel is a child of another channel.

```
<TITLE>Example Channel</TITLE>
```

Defining the Channel Abstract

The channel abstract is a simple text description of the channel. Internet Explorer 4.x displays the abstract text in a tool tip when the user moves the mouse over the channel icon or the channel image.

```
<ABSTRACT>This is a text description of the channel</ABSTRACT>
```

Defining Items

The items are the end nodes for the CDF. An item defines that actual HTML page the contains the information wanted by the user.

The item tag has four attributes: **HREF**, **LASTMOD**, **PRECACHE** and **LEVEL**.

The **HREF** attribute defines the location of the HTML page that will be loaded when the user clicks on the item. **LASTMOD** specifies the last time that the page was modified on the site. If Internet Explorer contains a version of the page that was modified at the same time or later than the time in the **ITEM** tag, it will not download the item again. **PRECACHE** defines whether the browser should download and cache the item. **LEVEL** defines how many levels the browser should download. If you specify "**0**" then the browser will only download the page that you specify. If you specify "**1**", than the browser will download the page you specify plus every page that is linked from the page you specify.

```
<ITEM HREF="page1.htm" LASTMOD="1997.12.18T08:00+0000" PRECACHE="Yes" LEVEL="0">
    <TITLE>This is page</TITLE>
    <ABSTRACT>A description of the page</ABSTRACT>
</ITEM>
```

The **TITLE** and **ABSTRACT** tags work as described above.

The **ITEM** tag also allows you to specify whether the page can be used as a screen saver by including a **USAGE** tag.

```
<USAGE VALUE='ScreenSaver"></USAGE>
```

Dynamic Channel Demonstration

Now that we have briefly explained how CDF files are created and what the basic tags are we can now describe how to create a CDF file dynamically using ASP.

Prior to the release of IIS4.0, developing dynamic channels was a difficult task as you had to manually change the MIME-type of the ASP file to the CDF MIME-type. If you give your dynamic channel file a **.cdx** extension IIS4.0 will automatically change the MIME-type to the CDF MIME-type after it has parsed the file using the ASP parsing engine. This allows you to easily create dynamic channel files as easily as creating Active Server Pages. We will first take a brief tour of the new TheNews.com dynamic channel, and then we will explain the code necessary to generate the channel

TheNews.com Dynamic Channel Tour

The TheNews.com channel allows users to specify which headline sections that they are interested in, and the main headlines from those sections will automatically download to their computer when new content is available.

From the user's perspective adding the dynamic channel is quite simple. They first navigate to the channel wizard page, **channelmake.asp**, by clicking on the 'TheNews.com Channel' links.

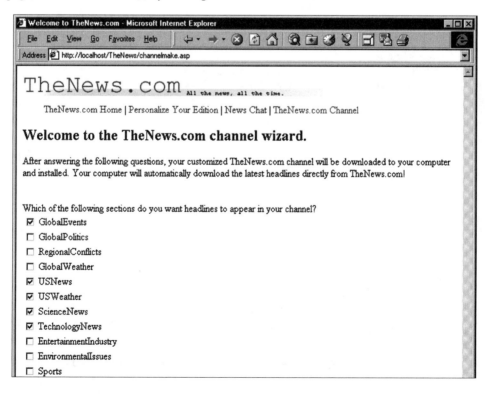

When the user is finished, they click the 'Add Active Channel' image to download the channel. After clicking the button, `channel.cdx` will parse the user's custom channel and then download it to the client. When Internet Explorer has downloaded the channel file, it will present the user with a dialog box confirming the download process and allowing them to customize when the channel will be updated.

Once the channel is downloaded, then the user can enjoy reading the news now that the files are automatically downloaded to the client. As you can see from the following image, the channel interface is actually quite pleasant for our news site.

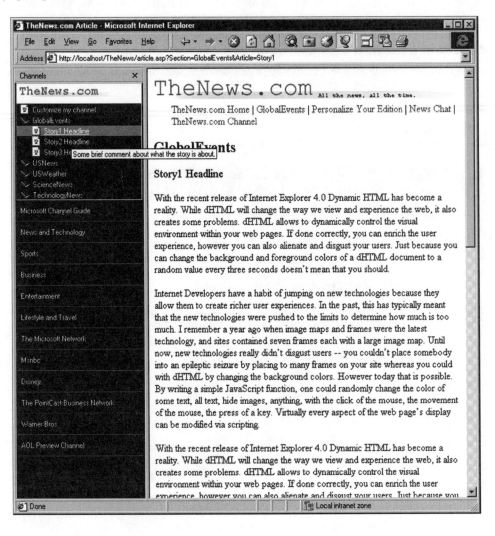

TheNews.com Dynamic Channel Code

The code to generate the dynamic channel is just as easy as the code to generate the front page based on the personalized settings.

Channel Settings Page (channelmake.asp)

If you remember from Chapter 11, the **channelmake.asp** code looks very familiar to the code on **personal.asp**.

```
<HTML>
<HEAD>
<TITLE>Welcome to TheNews.com</TITLE>
<STYLE>
.Normal                 {
                        color: Navy;
                        font-style: normal;
                        text-decoration: none;
                        }
.Rollover   {
                        color: Maroon;
                        font-style: bold;
                        text-decoration: underline overline;
                        }

</STYLE>
<%  Set bc = Server.CreateObject("MSWC.BrowserType") %>
<% If bc.dhtml = "True" then %>
<SCRIPT LANGUAGE="JavaScript" FOR="window" EVENT="onload">
document.onmouseover = rollover;
document.onmouseout = rollout;
</SCRIPT>
<SCRIPT LANGUAGE="JavaScript">
function rollover()
    {
    if (window.event.srcElement.className == "Normal")
            {
            window.event.srcElement.className = "Rollover";
            }
    }
function rollout()
    {
    if (window.event.srcElement.className == "Rollover")
            {
            window.event.srcElement.className = "Normal";
            }
    }
</SCRIPT>
<% End If %>
</HEAD>
<BODY BGCOLOR="White">
<TABLE CELLSPACING=0 CELLPADDING=0 BORDER=0>
<TR VALIGN="Top">
    <TD COLSPAN=4 HEIGHT="45"><IMG SRC="images/Banner.gif"></TD>

</TR>
<TR VALIGN="TOP">
```

```
        <TD WIDTH="35"></TD><TD><A HREF="default.asp" CLASS="Normal">TheNews.com Home</A>
| <A CLASS="Normal" HREF="personal.asp">Personalize Your Edition</A> | <A
CLASS="Normal" HREF="chat.asp" TARGET="_new">News Chat</A> | <FONT
COLOR="Maroon">TheNews.com Channel</A></TD>
</TR>
</TABLE>
<H2>Welcome to the TheNews.com channel wizard.</H2>
<P>After answering the following questions, your customized TheNews.com channel will
be downloaded to your computer and installed. Your computer will automatically
download the latest headlines directly from TheNews.com!</P>
<FORM NAME="Channel" ACTION="channel.cdx" METHOD="POST" ENCTYPE="application/x-www-
form-urlencoded">
<BR>
Which of the following sections do you want headlines to appear in your channel?
<BR>
<TABLE BORDER=0>
<TR><TD><INPUT TYPE="CHECKBOX" VALUE="1" <% if
NOT(Request.Cookies("TheNews")("GlobalEvents") = "1") then %> <% Else %>CHECKED<% End
If %> NAME="GlobalEvents"></TD><TD>GlobalEvents</TD></TR>
<TR><TD><INPUT TYPE="CHECKBOX" VALUE="1" <% if
NOT(Request.Cookies("TheNews")("GlobalPolitics") = "1") then %> <% Else %>CHECKED<%
End If %> NAME="GlobalPolitics"></TD><TD>GlobalPolitics</TD></TR>
<TR><TD><INPUT TYPE="CHECKBOX" VALUE="1" <% if
NOT(Request.Cookies("TheNews")("RegionalConflicts") = "1") then %> <% Else %>CHECKED<%
End If %> NAME="RegionalConflicts"></TD><TD>RegionalConflicts</TD></TR>
<TR><TD><INPUT TYPE="CHECKBOX" VALUE="1" <% if
NOT(Request.Cookies("TheNews")("GlobalWeather") = "1") then %> <% Else %>CHECKED<% End
If %> NAME="GlobalWeather"></TD><TD>GlobalWeather</TD></TR>
<TR><TD><INPUT TYPE="CHECKBOX" VALUE="1" <% if Request.Cookies("TheNews")("USNews") =
"1" then %>CHECKED<% End If %> NAME="USNews"></TD><TD>USNews</TD></TR>
<TR><TD><INPUT TYPE="CHECKBOX" VALUE="1" <% if Request.Cookies("TheNews")("USWeather")
= "1" then %>CHECKED<% End If %> NAME="USWeather"></TD><TD>USWeather</TD></TR>
<TR><TD><INPUT TYPE="CHECKBOX" VALUE="1" <% if
NOT(Request.Cookies("TheNews")("ScienceNews") = "1") then %> <% Else %>CHECKED<% End
If %> NAME="ScienceNews"></TD><TD>ScienceNews</TD></TR>
<TR><TD><INPUT TYPE="CHECKBOX" VALUE="1" <% if
NOT(Request.Cookies("TheNews")("TechnologyNews") = "1") then %> <% Else %>CHECKED<%
End If %> NAME="TechnologyNews"></TD><TD>TechnologyNews</TD></TR>
<TR><TD><INPUT TYPE="CHECKBOX" VALUE="1" <% if
NOT(Request.Cookies("TheNews")("EntertainmentIndustry") = "1") then %> <% Else
%>CHECKED<% End If %> NAME="EntertainmentIndustry"></TD><TD>EntertainmentIndustry</
TD></TR>
<TR><TD><INPUT TYPE="CHECKBOX" VALUE="1" <% if
NOT(Request.Cookies("TheNews")("EnvironmentalIssues") = "1") then %> <% Else
%>CHECKED<% End If %> NAME="EnvironmentalIssues"></TD><TD>EnvironmentalIssues</TD></
TR>
<TR><TD><INPUT TYPE="CHECKBOX" VALUE="1" <% if
NOT(Request.Cookies("TheNews")("Sports") = "1") then %> <% Else %>CHECKED<% End If %>
NAME="Sports"></TD><TD>Sports</TD></TR>
</TABLE>
<BR>
<INPUT TYPE="IMAGE" SRC="images/ieaddchannel.gif" Name="Submit">
</FORM>
<HR WIDTH="20%" ALIGN="Left" BGCOLOR="Yellow" NOSHADOW HEIGHT="5">
<P>Copyright 1997 TheNews.com. All rights reserved.</P>
</BODY>
</HTML>
```

In fact the only changes between the two pages are the removal of the usernames, the **FORM ACTION** attribute changing to point to **channel.asp** and the submit button has been replaced by a submit image. The page's similarities are an important feature. In order to set the personalization settings into a cookie, we had to load the values from the URL of the form submission. In the case of the dynamic channel, we want to be able to create the channel dynamically via a URL so that the channel can easily update itself. We can accomplish this task by initially loading the form values into the URL and pointing the form submission to a single page that only parses channel files, in this case **channel.cdx**.

Building the channel (channel.cdx)

As you can see from the code for **channel.cdx**, dynamically creating a channel on IIS4.0 is as easy as dynamically creating an HTML page.

```
<?XML VERSION="1.0" ENCODING="UTF-8"?>
<CHANNEL HREF="http://localhost/TheNews/default.asp"
    BASE="http://localhost/TheNews/"
    SELF="http://localhost/TheNews/channel.cdx?GlobalEvents=<%=
Request("GlobalEvents") %>&GlobalPolitics=<%= Request("GlobalPolitics")
%>&RegionalConflicts=<%= Request("RegionalConflicts") %>&GlobalWeather=<%=
Request("GlobalWeather") %>&USNews=<%= Request("USNews") %>&USWeather=<%=
Request("USWeather") %>&ScienceNews=<%= Request("ScienceNews") %>&TechnologyNews=<%=
Request("TechnologyNews") %>&EntertainmentIndustry=<%=
Request("EntertainmentIndustry") %>&EnvironmentalIssues<%=
Request("EnvironmentalIssues") %>&Sports=<%= Request("Sports") %>"
    >
    <TITLE>TheNews.com News Channel</TITLE>
    <ABSTRACT>All the news... all the time.</ABSTRACT>
    <LOGO HREF="http://localhost/TheNews/images/icon.gif" STYLE="ICON"/>
    <LOGO HREF="http://localhost/TheNews/images/image.gif" STYLE="IMAGE"/>
    <LOGO HREF="http://localhost/TheNews/images/imagewide.gif" STYLE="IMAGE-WIDE"/>
    <SCHEDULE STARTDATE="1997.12.18" ENDDATE="1998.12.18">
            <INTERVALTIME DAY="1"/>
            <EARLIESTTIME HOUR="0"/>
            <LATESTTIME DAY="1" HOUR="4"/>
    </SCHEDULE>
    <ITEM HREF="channelmake.asp" PRECACHE="Yes" LEVEL="0">
            <TITLE>Customize my channel</TITLE>
            <ABSTRACT>Customize your TheNews.com channel by following this link.</
ABSTRACT>
    </ITEM>
<% If Request("GlobalEvents") = "1" then %>
    <CHANNEL HREF="section.asp?Section=GlobalEvents">
            <TITLE>GlobalEvents</TITLE>
            <ABSTRACT>GlobalEvents Section Headlines</ABSTRACT>
            <ITEM HREF="article.asp?Section=GlobalEvents&Article=Story1"
PRECACHE="Yes" LEVEL="0">
                    <TITLE>Story1 Headline</TITLE>
                    <ABSTRACT>Some brief comment about what the story is about.</
ABSTRACT>
            </ITEM>
            <ITEM HREF="article.asp?Section=GlobalEvents&Article=Story2"
PRECACHE="Yes" LEVEL="0">
                    <TITLE>Story2 Headline</TITLE>
                    <ABSTRACT>Some brief comment about what the story is about.</
ABSTRACT>
            </ITEM>
```

```
                    <ITEM HREF="article.asp?Section=GlobalEvents&Article=Story3"
        PRECACHE="Yes" LEVEL="0">
                            <TITLE>Story3 Headline</TITLE>
                            <ABSTRACT>Some brief comment about what the story is about.</
        ABSTRACT>
                    </ITEM>
            </CHANNEL>
        <% End If %>
        ...
        ...
        ...
        </CHANNEL>
```

It is important to note how this document is updated. When the browser has determined, based on the schedule, that the channel needs to be updated it will go to the URL specified in the **SELF** attribute of the parent channel tag.

```
<CHANNEL HREF="http://localhost/TheNews/default.asp"
    BASE="http://localhost/TheNews/"
    SELF="http://localhost/TheNews/channel.cdx?GlobalEvents=<%=
Request("GlobalEvents") %>&GlobalPolitics=<%= Request("GlobalPolitics")
%>&RegionalConflicts=<%= Request("RegionalConflicts") %>&GlobalWeather=<%=
Request("GlobalWeather") %>&USNews=<%= Request("USNews") %>&USWeather=<%=
Request("USWeather") %>&ScienceNews=<%= Request("ScienceNews") %>&TechnologyNews=<%=
Request("TechnologyNews") %>&EntertainmentIndustry=<%=
Request("EntertainmentIndustry") %>&EnvironmentalIssues<%=
Request("EnvironmentalIssues") %>&Sports=<%= Request("Sports") %>"
    >
```

As you can see, the URL that we specified is the same URL from the form submission. All of the values are loaded into the URL so that the page can automatically be updated with the same channel information the user specified.

The actual CDF is generated with basic Boolean logic, similar to the logic found on **default.asp**.

```
<% If Request("GlobalEvents") = "1" then %>
    <CHANNEL HREF="section.asp?Section=GlobalEvents">
            <TITLE>GlobalEvents</TITLE>
            <ABSTRACT>GlobalEvents Section Headlines</ABSTRACT>
            <ITEM HREF="article.asp?Section=GlobalEvents&Article=Story1"
PRECACHE="Yes" LEVEL="0">
                    <TITLE>Story1 Headline</TITLE>
                    <ABSTRACT>Some brief comment about what the story is about.</
ABSTRACT>
            </ITEM>
            <ITEM HREF="article.asp?Section=GlobalEvents&Article=Story2"
PRECACHE="Yes" LEVEL="0">
                    <TITLE>Story2 Headline</TITLE>
                    <ABSTRACT>Some brief comment about what the story is about.</
ABSTRACT>
            </ITEM>
            <ITEM HREF="article.asp?Section=GlobalEvents&Article=Story3"
PRECACHE="Yes" LEVEL="0">
                    <TITLE>Story3 Headline</TITLE>
                    <ABSTRACT>Some brief comment about what the story is about.</
```

```
ABSTRACT>
            </ITEM>
       </CHANNEL>
   <% End If %>
```

In Review – Dynamic Channels

As you can see from our simple demonstration, creating dynamic channels for IE4 is as simple as dynamically creating HTML pages. While our example used hard-coded URLs for all of the stories, these URLs and headlines could also be loaded directly from a database using ADO. The important aspect to creating dynamic channels is to plan them carefully so that the channel can operate without user intervention. By allowing the channel to be created from values stored in the URL, we can eliminate the need to store custom CDF files on the server for every web customer and worry about creating unique filenames.

Using Enhanced Forms with ASP

The disadvantage to ASP applications is that they require every piece of information to be sent to the server via a form submission. This is not a major problem if the amount of information that needs to be collected is small. However, if the amount of information is large then the application requires massive forms that will intimidate users. Over the past several years, users have become accustomed to dialog box based 'wizards' that guide them through collecting large amounts of information or complex tasks. With the recent release of IE4.0 and IIS4.0, it is now possible to create these rich user interfaces that we are accustomed to. Through a combination of Dynamic HTML and a few tag additions, IE4.0 allows you to create rich web-based dialog boxes that you can use as a custom user interface for ASP applications.

A Tour of the Seismic Load Calculator

The seismic load calculator determines the seismic base shear, the force that an earthquake applies to a building, based on a series of building parameters that the user specifies. Since the number and complexity of the variables is quite large, it makes sense to offer the inputting of these values in a 'wizard' fashion.

The other advantage to using a 'wizard' is that validating the user's input is simplified. Within each pane of the wizard we can validate the user's input before proceeding. By validating along the way, the user can easily and quickly reference the form element that contains the error instead of having to scan twenty different form elements looking for the incorrect entry.

The seismic load calculator is actually composed of one HTML page and one ASP page. The dialog box user-interface is provided by **equakeget.htm** and the server-side calculations are provided by **seismic.asp**.

We are going to take a brief tour of the seismic load calculator and its various states so that you have a frame of reference when we dissect the code behind the pages.

When the user first connects to **seismic.asp** it determines whether or not the user has already specified the data to be processed by checked the URL. If there is not any data in the URL, then the page assumes that the user needs to input information about their building and it loads the wizard dialog box.

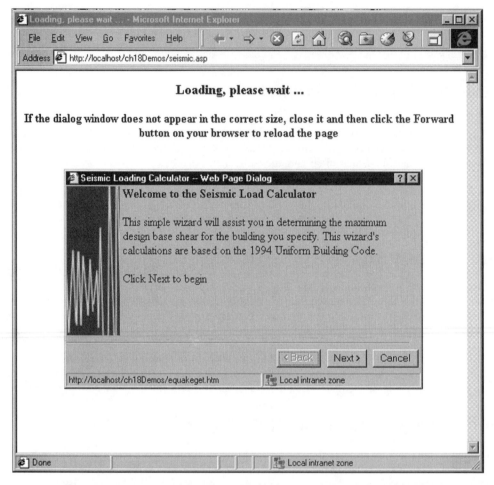

The user than clicks the Next button and navigates through the various panes of the wizard. Each of these panes are within the same HTML page and are displayed using Dynamic HTML.

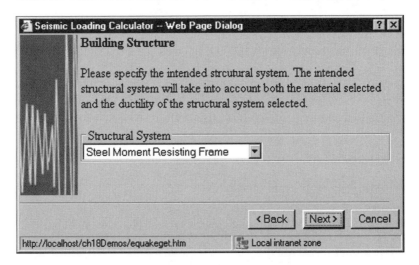

Seismic Loading Calculator -- Web Page Dialog [?][X]

Building Site

Please specify the following information as indicated by your soils engineer or soils report.

┌─ UBC Seismic Zone ──────────────────────────┐
│ Zone 4 (High Seismicity) [▼]   │
└───┘

┌─ UBC Soil Factor ───────────────────────────┐
│ 1.5 - Hard Soil   [▼]   │
└───┘

[< Back] [Next >] [Cancel]

http://localhost/ch18Demos/equakeget.htm   Local intranet zone

---

Seismic Loading Calculator -- Web Page Dialog [?][X]

Send Data to the Server

We have now collected all of the necissary information and we are ready to send that information to our server for processing.

Click 'Send' when you are ready to send the information to the server

[< Back] [Next >] [Send]

http://localhost/ch18Demos/equakeget.htm   Local intranet zone

---

After the user has specified all of the information about the building, the variables are collected and sent back to the page that called the dialog box. That page then sends the information to the server, which processes the request and returns the results.

Behind the scenes of the calculator

The entire calculator is a simple active server application, or a section of an application, but it illustrates how a developer can leverage Dynamic HTML and the new **FORM** tags to create these rich dialog box user interfaces.

Loading the dialog box

The dialog box itself is displayed and loaded by **seismic.asp**. When the file loads it determines whether any information is loaded into the URL by checking the value of the **Stuff** variable in the URL by using the Request object. If the value of **Stuff** does not equal **Yes**, the ASP writes to the client the code necessary to generate the web dialog box.

```
<%
If Request("Stuff") = "Yes" then
...
...
```

```
...
<% Else %>
    <HTML>
    <HEAD>
    <TITLE>Loading, please wait ...</TITLE>
    </HEAD>
    <BODY ONLOAD="OpenDlgPage()">
      <H3 ALIGN="CENTER">Loading, please wait ...</H3>
      <H4 ALIGN="CENTER">If the dialog window does not appear in the correct size,
      close it and then click the Forward buton on your browser to reload the page</
H4>
    </BODY>
    <SCRIPT LANGUAGE=JSCRIPT>
    function OpenDlgPage()
    {
      strholding = showModalDialog("equakeget.htm", "MyDialog",
"dialogWidth=500px;dialogHeight=295px; center=yes;border=thin;help=yes");
      if (strholding == "")
      {
      history.back(1)
      }
      location.href = strholding;
      event.cancelBubble = true;
    }
    </SCRIPT>
    </HTML>
<% End If %>
```

The dialog box is displayed using the **showModelDialog** method of the **window** object.

```
strholding = showModelDialog("equakeget.htm", "MyDialog",
        "dialogWidth=500px;dialogHeight=295px; center=yes;border=thin;help=yes");
```

This method requires two parameters and will accept a third parameter containing options for the display of the dialog. The first required parameter defines the URL to the HTML source of the web dialog box. The second parameter defines the name of the window object containing the modal dialog box.

Layout of the dialog box

As mentioned earlier, the dialog box is a single HTML page that updates itself using Dynamic HTML. The Image, Back, Front and Cancel buttons are located on every page and never move. The rest of the elements on the page are located within **DIV** tags that are positioned absolutely. By changing the **visibility** property of the **DIV** tags, we can control which pane of the wizard is displayed.

```
<HTML>
<HEAD>
<TITLE>Seismic Loading Calculator</TITLE>
</HEAD>
<BODY BGCOLOR="Silver">
<!-- Persistant Elements Begin -->
<IMG SRC="quake.gif" STYLE="position:absolute; top:1; left:1;">
<HR STYLE="position:absolute; top:210; left:0;">
<BUTTON DISABLED STYLE="position:absolute; top:220; left:295;" ID="Back" ACCESSKEY="N"
TITLE="Next" onClick="goBack();">
```

```
&lt; Back
</BUTTON>
<BUTTON STYLE="position:absolute; top:220; left:365;" ID="Next" ACCESSKEY="N"
TITLE="Next" onClick="goNext();">
Next &gt;
</BUTTON>
<BUTTON STYLE="position:absolute; top:220; left:428;" ID="Finish" ACCESSKEY="N"
TITLE="Cancel" onClick="closedialog();">
Cancel
</BUTTON>
<!-- Persistant Elements End -->
<DIV ID="Pane1" STYLE="position:absolute; top:1; left:80; height:200; width:400;
visibility: hidden;">
<H4>Welcome to the Seismic Load Calculator</H4>
<P>This simple wizard will assist you in determining the maximum design base shear for
the building you specify. This wizard's calculations are based on the 1994 Uniform
Building Code.</P>
<P>Click Next to begin</P>
</DIV>
<DIV ID="Pane2" STYLE="position:absolute; top:1; left:80; height:200; width:400;
visibility: hidden;">
<H4>Building Height</H4>
<P>What is the floor-to-floor height of the building in feet?  <INPUT
TYPE="TEXT" ID="dlgheight" SIZE="3" VALUE="15"> feet</P>
<P>How many floors are in the building?  <INPUT TYPE="TEXT" ID="dlgfloors"
SIZE="3" VALUE="10"> floors</P>
</DIV>
```

When the user clicks on the Next or Back buttons, they invoke a JavaScript routine that updates the dialog-box display provided that the user's input is valid.

```
function goNext()
    {
...
    if (currentpane == 2)
    {
            if (check2() == true)
            {
            document.all.Pane2.style.visibility = "hidden";
            document.all.Pane3.style.visibility = "";
            }
            else
            {
            return false;
            }
    }
...
...
...
    currentpane += 1
    }
```

If the user's input was not valid, then the **check2()** function displays a dialog box, and returns a **false** value, which prevents navigation to the next pane.

```
function check2()
    {
    if ((isNaN(dlgheight.value) == true) || (dlgheight.value == ""))
    {
            alert("You must specify a real number for the floor-to-floor height of the
building");
            return false;
    }
    if ((dlgheight.value > 15) || (dlgheight.value < 10))
    {
            alert("Please use a floor-to-floor height between 10 and 15 feet");
            return false;
    }
    if ((isNaN(dlgfloors.value) == true) || (dlgfloors.value == ""))
    {
            alert("You must specify a real number for the number of floors");
            return false;
    }
    if ((dlgfloors.value > 30) || (dlgfloors.value < 1))
    {
            alert("Our calculator is only approved for buildings under 30 stories");
            return false;
    }
    return true;
    }
```

Fieldset Tag

If you noticed from the tour, some of the HTML form elements are surrounded by borders that look quite similar to the borders found around radio buttons in typical applications. This border is provided by the new **FIELDSET** tag.

```
<FIELDSET>
    <LEGEND>Building Dimensions</LEGEND>
    What is length of the building?   <INPUT TYPE="TEXT"
        ID="dlglength" SIZE="3" VALUE="100"> feet<BR>
    What is width of the building?  <INPUT TYPE="TEXT"
        ID="dlgwidth" SIZE="3" VALUE="100"> feet
</FIELDSET>
```

The text descriptions that appear within the **FIELDSET** border are specified with the **LEGEND** tag within a **FIELDSET**.

```
    <LEGEND>Building Dimensions</LEGEND>
```

Unfortunately, and unlike their Visual Basic cousins, **FIELDSET**s are only visual elements in the current implementation of IE4.0. However, in later versions the **FIELDSET** tag will behave as a container for **FORM** controls, allowing the developer to manipulate sets of controls.

Button Tag

If you look carefully at the HTML source for the wizard panes, you will notice there is now a **BUTTON** tag. This tag defines a **FORM** button; however, where the **FORM** button's display name was specified with a **VALUE** attribute, the display content for the **BUTTON** tag is specified by the contained HTML.

```
<BUTTON DISABLED STYLE="position:absolute; top:220; left:295;" ID="Back" ACCESSKEY="N"
TITLE="Next" onClick="goBack();">
&lt; Back
</BUTTON>
```

In our example we used standard text for the button names. Alternatively we could have just as easily specified images, movies, or any other HTML element. This allows developers the capability to easily create descriptive buttons using graphics in a graphical format that is familiar to users.

Submitting the Data

When the user has specified all of the information, they simply click the Send button which fires the `closedialog()` function. If the user is on the last pane of the wizard, then the function places the values of all of the form elements in the wizard into the return string and closes the dialog box.

```
function closedialog()
    {
    if (currentpane == 7)
        {
        strpath="seismic.asp?Stuff=Yes&Height=" + dlgheight.value + "&Floors=" +
dlgfloors.value + "&Length=" + dlglength.value + "&Width=" + dlgwidth.value + "&Dead="
+ dlgdead.value + "&Live=" + dlglive.value + "&Import=" + dlgImport.value +
"&Stucture=" + dlgStructure.value + "&Zone=" + dlgZone.value + "&Soil=" +
dlgSoil.value
            window.returnValue = strpath;
            window.close();
            }
    else
        {
            if (confirm("Are you sure that you want to quit?"))
            {
                window.close();
            }
        }
    }
```

Once the dialog box is closed, **seismic.asp** reads the return string and if it contains data redirects the browser to itself so that the data can be loaded into the server.

```
function OpenDlgPage()
{
    strholding = showModalDialog("equakeget.htm", "MyDialog",
"dialogWidth=500px;dialogHeight=295px; center=yes;border=thin;help=yes");
    if (strholding == "")
    {
    history.back(1)
    }
    location.href = strholding;
    event.cancelBubble = true;
}
```

Creating the result

Once the data has been submitted to the server via the URL, the ASP page simply parses the variables, runs the calculations and returns the completed calculations to the user.

Summary

In this chapter we covered how to integrate Dynamic HTML into your pages and how to customize the output of your ASP pages depending on the browser with the help of the Browser Capabilities Control. We also covered how simple it is to create IE4 channels dynamically. In addition, we also covered how the new enhanced forms and Dynamic HTML can be combined to create rich dialog-box user interfaces for client-server ASP applications.

In this chapter we covered:

▲ Creating Dynamic HTML pages dynamically using ASP

▲ Creating CDF channels dynamically using ASP

▲ Using Enhanced Forms as an application interface for ASP

In the next chapter we will take a look at transactions.

Introducing Transactions

In Chapter 10, we began to look at the ways that IIS and ASP can be used to create a new type of client-server applications. By deploying applications in this manner we can help to alleviate some of the problems associated with traditional client-server applications. In the past, you were forced to install the client application logic onto each computer that would access the server. With the web-based model, the client is actually run on the server, with the user interface presentation usually being the only piece sent to the client. This provides for a much wider range of clients, as well as making it easy to update the clients when the application changes.

In the early days of web-based application development, the system was developed using either script-based or custom-written applications that ran on the web server and performed the application functionality. The advent of Active Server Pages from Microsoft allowed the development of script-based applications, which in turn accessed functionality from Component Object Model (COM) objects that ran on the server. This allows the business and data access logic to be encapsulated in high performance components. But at this stage, it was still left to the application developer to handle all of these components.

Now, with IIS 4.0 and Active Server Pages 2.0, we have access to a very powerful facility to perform the management of these server side components. Microsoft Transaction Server provides an environment in which the COM components of an application can be automatically managed by the system. This frees the developer from having to worry about the management of these objects. By putting the system in charge of handling the objects, the use of these components can be optimized to provide a much more scalable and robust solution. The system that will do this is called Microsoft Transaction Server, and we will become quite familiar with it in this chapter, and the case study that follows..

In this chapter, we will look at the features of Microsoft Transaction Server and see how it can be used to support applications developed with IIS and ASP. Specifically, we will examine:

- What is transaction processing?
- Why do we need transaction processing?
- The services offered by Microsoft Transaction Server (MTS)
- How MTS and IIS work together
- How to design components for use with MTS
- A simple case study that shows why transactions are useful

First of all, let's take a look at what transaction processing is.

What is Transaction Processing?

In Chapter 1, you were introduced to the concepts behind transaction processing. But you may still be wondering just what this is. Transaction processing has been around since the mainframe days of computing. You may have heard of, or have even used, products such as CICS, Tuxedo, or TopEnd. These are all examples of transaction processing systems, which provide transaction services to applications that use them. There are a number of attributes that make up transaction processing.

In order to discuss transaction processing, we must first agree on a definition of what a transaction is. A **transaction** is an atomic unit of work that either fails or succeeds. There is no such thing as a partial completion of a transaction. Since a transaction can be made up of many steps, each step in the transaction must succeed for the transaction to be successful. If any one part of the transaction fails, then the entire transaction fails. When a transaction fails, the system needs to return to the state that it was in before the transaction was started. This is known as **rollback**. When a transaction fails, then the changes that had been made are said to be "rolled back." In effect, this is acting similar to the way the Undo command works in most word processors. When you select undo, the change that you just may have made is reversed. The transaction processing system is responsible for carrying out this undo.

Applications Composed Of Components

An **application** that is used with a transaction processing system is composed of components. These components fall into two general categories. The first type is an application component. The job of this component is to perform some type of business rule processing for the application. An example of this could be an application component to compute the sales tax for an order.

A sales tax component would need to know each item that was being purchased. Each item would have a price associated with it. An item could also be taxable or non-taxable, or it could be taxed a rate that is different than other items. As we saw in Chapter 1, these are known as "business rules" for the application, as they provide information as to the business aspect of the application. The sales tax component would go through each item in the order and add up the total sales tax for the order. This value would then be returned to whatever system invoked the component.

The other general type of component is the **data access component**. The job of this component is to provide a method for the system to interact with the physical data itself. This physical data could be stored in a database, or in some other type of data storage mechanism. An example of a data access component could be a customer component.

The customer data component would be responsible for providing information about a selected customer based on that customer's unique identifier. The component would translate the information from the format that the data was stored in to the format that was used by the application. It could also be responsible for ensuring the integrity of the data. If there were two tables that held customer information, the data object would ensure that changes in one would be properly reflected in the other.

The application is built by connecting these application and data components together such that the system will perform the tasks that the user wishes to perform. They form the two middle tiers of the traditional four-tier client-server architecture, with the user interface and the database being the two remaining components. Each of the tasks the user wants to perform is called a transaction, as they represent a single instance of work that the application performs.

Components Are Single User

Each of the components that make up a transaction is developed as if it were a single-user component. In traditional multi-user application development, the developer needs to be aware of how multiple users are accessing a system. There are a number of areas where having multiple users accessing the same part of a system can cause problems. If two users are trying to update the same record at the same time, the system needs to arbitrate as to which user's updates are applied and which are ignored.

In a transaction processing system, the system deals with the intricacies of multiple users accessing a particular piece of data. The application and data objects appear to themselves to be the only ones interacting with the system. In reality, there could be tens, hundreds, or thousands of objects interacting with the exact same part of the system. The transaction server handles all of the interactions so that each component can assume that it is the only one interacting with the system at any one time.

Components Provide For Scalability

When a developer creates an application, a good deal of the design goes into defining what the capacities of the application are. How many records can the system hold? How many users can use the system at one time? How long will it take to retrieve a piece of data from the system? These are all questions about scalability. In other words, how well does the application grow? In a traditional application, it is up to the developer to provide answers to these questions when the system is being built. If the developer fails to address them, or does not address them properly, then the application will fail to scale. When this happens, as more users begin to access the system, and place a greater load on the system, things begin to fail. The system starts to buckle under the load of more users than it was designed for.

When working in a transaction-processing environment, those questions are answered for the developers without having to even think about them. The developer creates components that interact with the system as if they had exclusive access to the system, and had the full resources of the system available to it. The environment is responsible for efficiently managing the resources of the multiple objects that could be active at one time so that each one runs successfully. The environment can do things such as reusing objects, rather than creating new ones when they are needed and destroying them as their work is completed. By managing the lifetime of objects, the environment can ensure that as more and more objects are needed, which happens when more users are accessing the system, the system will be able to support them.

Maintaining Application Integrity

A critical part of any application is to ensure that any operations it performs are performed correctly. If an application were to only partially complete an operation, then the state of the application would not be correct. For example, look at the problem of a banking application that moved money from one account to another. If the money is taken out of one account and then something happens and the money can not be added to the other account, then the state of the application is not correct. It is said to have lost integrity.

There are two ways to combat this. In the traditional programming model, the developer must anticipate any way that the operation could fail. From any point of failure, the developer must then add support to return the application to the state it was in before the operation was started. In other words, the developer has to add the code to support a **rollback** of the operation from any point that it could fail.

The other, and much easier way to do this, is for the operation to take place within the environment of a transaction processing system. The job of the system is to ensure that the entire operation, the transaction, completes successfully. If it does, then the changes in the application state are **committed** to the system, and the user can proceed to their next task. If any part of the operation does not complete successfully, which would leave the system in an invalid state, then the system has to put the application back into its original state. The power of a transaction processing system is that the knowledge to perform these operations is inherent in the system itself. The developer does not have to explicitly support the rollback of any part of the transaction. In fact, all the developer has to do is have each component of the transaction let the system know if it was successful or not. The transaction processing system takes care of the rest.

Why Do We Need Transaction Processing?

Now that you have seen what transaction processing is, we need to look at why you would want to use it in developing your application. There were a number of reasons that became evident when looking at what transaction processing is. The ability to develop applications in a single-user mode, then use the transaction processing system to scale to hundreds or thousands of users is one reason. As a matter of course, the transaction processing system also provides the support for automatic rollback of transactions that did not complete successfully. There are other reasons for using transaction processing that become much more readily available to developers when working in a transaction processing system. These include the concepts of a three-tier application model, applications distributed across many systems, and the benefits of what is know as the ACID properties of transaction processing systems.

Three-tier Application Model

One of the key elements of any application design is the system architecture. The system architecture defines how pieces of the application interact with each other, and what functionality each piece is responsible for performing. There are three main classes of application architecture. They can be characterized by the number of layers between the user and the data. Each layer generally runs on a different system or in a different process space on the same system than the other layers. The three types of application architecture are single-tier (or monolithic), two-tier, and n-tier, where n can be three or more.

The monolithic application consists of a single application layer that supports the user interface, the business rules, and the manipulation of the data all in one. The data itself could be physically stored in a remote location, but the logic for accessing it is part of the application. Microsoft Word is an example of a monolithic application. The user interface is an integral part of the application. The business rules, such as how to paginate and hyphenate, are also part of the application. The file access routines, to manipulate the data of the document, are also part of the application. Even if there are multiple DLLs that handle the different functionality, it is still a monolithic application.

In a two-tier application, the business rules and user interface remain as part of the client application. The data retrieval and manipulation is performed by another separate application, usually found on a physically separate system. This separate application could be something like SQL Server or Oracle, which is functioning as a data storage device for the application. This type of application is widely used in the traditional client-server types of applications. PowerBuilder or Visual Basic both integrating with Oracle are two examples of tools that can be used to create client-server systems.

In another type of two-tier application, the business rules are executed on the data storage system. This is the case in applications that are using stored procedures to manipulate the database. A stored procedure is a database function that is stored at the database server. It can be executed one of two ways. A client application can explicitly call a stored procedure, which would then be run on the server. A trigger can also execute a stored procedure, which is the occurrence of a specific event in the data. For example, a trigger could be set to fire whenever the balance field in an account record reaches $50.00 or less. This trigger could execute a stored procedure that sent a notification to the account holder that their balance was low.

With three-tier applications, the business rules are removed from the client and are executed on a system in between the user interface and the data storage system. The client application provides user interface for the system. The business rules server ensures that all of the business processing is done correctly. It serves as an intermediary between the client and the data storage. In this type of application, the client would never access the data storage system directly. This type of system allows for any part of the system to be modified without having to change the other two parts. Since the parts of the application communicate through interfaces, then as long as the interface remains the same, the internal workings can be changed without affecting the rest of the system.

The transaction processing systems provide an environment in which the business and data objects of a system can operate. The system can manage these objects so that the system can operate at its highest efficiency, no matter what the load on the system.

Distributed Applications

Now that we have chosen to use a three-tier architecture, we have the system broken into three distinct segments. In a web-based application, the user interface segment is made up of one or more web pages. These pages can be statically created, and served up to the user when they request them. They could also be dynamically created using Active Server Pages and be customized for each user and session. The business logic is broken into a set of components that provide the support for all of the business rules of the system. These objects interact with the data storage system, either directly, or through another set of data components.

In looking at the system as a whole, it appears to be made up of a number of small components. Each component communicates with the other through the use of interfaces. Since these components are distinct, and have defined inputs and outputs, it becomes very easy to change the locations of these components. The functionality of the system can be distributed amongst many different systems. As long as there is a method for the components to communicate with the other components, the place of execution can vary.

A transaction processing system that is controlling these objects can also control where they execute. If there is a particular part of the application that is computationally intensive, then the transaction processing system can have that object execute on system that has sufficient resources to efficiently process the object. Likewise, if there are two components that need to pass a lot of data between each other, the transaction processing system can try to run the two components on the same machine, maybe even within the same process space.

ACID properties

When a transaction processing system creates a transaction, it will ensure that the transaction will have certain characteristics. The developers of the components that comprise the transaction are assured that these characteristics are in place. They do not need to manage these characteristics themselves. These characteristics are known as the ACID properties. ACID is an acronym for atomicity, consistency, isolation, and durability.

Atomicity

The atomicity property identifies that the transaction is atomic. An **atomic transaction** is either fully completed, or is not begun at all. Any updates that a transaction might affect on a system are completed in their entirety. If for any reason an error occurs and the transaction is unable to complete all of its steps, the then system is returned to the state it was in before the transaction was started. An example of an atomic transaction is an account transfer transaction. The money is removed from account A then placed into account B. If the system fails after removing the money from account A, then the transaction processing system will put the money back into account A, thus returning the system to its original state. This is known as a **rollback**, as we said at the beginning of this chapter..

Consistency

A transaction enforces **consistency** in the system state by ensuring that at the end of any transaction the system is in a valid state. If the transaction completes successfully, then all changes to the system will have been properly made, and the system will be in a valid state. If any error occurs in a transaction, then any changes already made will be automatically rolled back. This will return the system to its state before the transaction was started. Since the system was in a consistent state when the transaction was started, it will once again be in a consistent state.

Looking again at the account transfer system, the system is consistent if the total of all accounts is constant. If an error occurs and the money is removed from account A and not added to account B, then the total in all accounts would have changed. The system would no longer be consistent. By rolling back the removal from account A, the total will again be what it should be, and the system back in a consistent state.

Isolation

When a transaction runs in **isolation**, it appears to be the only action that the system is carrying out at one time. If there are two transactions that are both performing the same function and are running at the same time, transaction isolation will ensure that each transaction thinks it has exclusive use of the system. This is important in that as the transaction is being executed, the state of the system may not be consistent. The transaction ensures that the system remains consistent after the transaction ends, but during an individual transaction, this may not be the case. If a transaction was not running in isolation, it could access data from the system that may not be consistent. By providing transaction isolation, this is prevented from happening.

Durability

A transaction is **durable** in that once it has been successfully completed, all of the changes it made to the system are permanent. There are safeguards that will prevent the loss of information, even in the case of system failure. By logging the steps that the transaction performs, the state of the system can be recreated even if the hardware itself has failed. The concept of durability allows the developer to know that a completed transaction is a permanent part of the system, regardless of what happens to the system later on.

The Advantages Of Transaction Processing

We have now seen the reasons why we need transaction processing systems. The advantages of three-tier applications in creating scalable and robust applications are made feasible by transaction processing systems. The ability to distribute the components that make up applications amongst separate servers without explicitly having to develop for that architecture is another advantage of transaction server processing. Transaction processing systems also ensure that transactions are atomic, consistent, isolated, and durable. This alleviates the developer from having to support these characteristics explicitly.

With all of these excellent reasons for developing an application that uses a transaction processing system, we now need a system that provides these features. We will now turn our attention to a transaction processing system that is part of the standard IIS 4.0 installation: Microsoft Transaction Server.

Introducing Microsoft Transaction Server

Microsoft Transaction Server is a component-based transaction processing system that allows developers to build, deploy, and administer robust network applications. In being component based, Microsoft Transaction Server (MTS) uses standard COM components to encapsulate business logic that forms applications. MTS provides a development framework so that components can be easily created that can participate in transactions. MTS also provides the environment of execution for these objects, along with a set of administrator tools to manage the deployment of the objects that make up these applications.

Run-time Environment

The MTS run-time environment provides a number of services to components and applications that are executed within it. These services are controlled and managed by MTS, thus alleviating the programming from having to worry about these. This allows the developer to focus on solving the business problem at hand, rather than worrying about how to build all of the transactional plumbing.

Distributed Transactions

The MTS run-time environment automatically provides support for distributed transactions. As we described earlier, a transaction is an atomic unit of work that either succeeds or fails as a whole. By allowing a transaction to be distributed, the different components that make up the pieces of the transaction can be executed on physically separate systems. For example, a single transaction could consist of a component running on system A, performing database transaction with a SQL server on machine B. Then, another component in the transaction could be running on machine C, which performs database transactions on an Oracle server running on machine D. These four boxes, running four distinct pieces of code, can all participate in the same transaction.

Automatic management of processes and threads

The run-time environment will automatically manage all of the processes and threads for components executing within MTS. This frees the developer from having to worry about in what process or on what thread their components are executed.

> *Later in this chapter, we will look at what threads are and the different threading models that are available to components that will run within MTS.*

Object Instance Management

By providing object instance management for components executing within the run-time environment, MTS can efficiently use resources in the system. Though not fully supported in this release, MTS will be able to reuse objects, rather than having to create and initialize them every time they are used. All that developers need to do to support this is to provide a method for resetting any state within the object when its method is complete. This will be covered later in this chapter.

Resource Managers

A **resource manager** is a part of a database server that works with Transaction Server to manages durable data. **Durable data** is defined as data that will survive a system failure. Typically, a resource manager provides the database access functionality to the component running inside of MTS. SQL Server and Oracle are examples of database servers that also provide resource managers. The resource manager works with the transaction to support the ACID properties, as well as automating the process of rollback.

MTS Explorer

Not only does Microsoft Transaction Server provide an environment for executing transactional application, it provides a system to manage that environment. The MTS Explorer is a snap-in to the Microsoft Management Console that allows the developer to manage and deploy MTS applications.

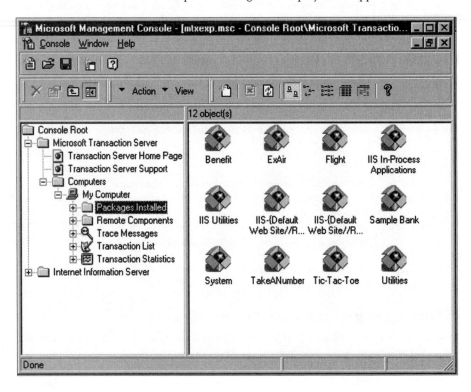

Components are grouped together inside of Transaction Server into what are known as **packages**. A package is generally made up of components that function together to create an application. Packages can be saved as redistributable components known as pre-built packages. These pre-built packages contain all of the files and information necessary to install the package on another system. This installation handles all the DCOM configuration allowing application on the remote system to be able to co-operate with the components in the package.

From the MTS Explorer, you can view information about each of the components within a package. The Explorer will display information about the methods and interfaces of the component. You can also use MTS Explorer to set some of the properties of a selected component, or group of components. One of these properties is the Transaction support flag for the component.

This flag determines how the selected component will support transactions within MTS. By allowing the MTS administrator to define how components will participate in transactions, MTS provides for consistent usage of the component. If this were left up to the developer, then they would be forced to choose the method of participation every time the component was accessed.

The four transaction participation states are:

▲ **Requires a transaction**–This indicates that the component must run within the context of a transaction. If this component is called from within an existing transaction, then it will execute within that transaction. If there is no current transaction, then MTS will automatically create a transaction in which to execute the component.

▲ **Requires a new transaction**–This indicates that this component must run within its own transaction. Even if this component was called from within an existing transaction, it is required that a new one is created for this component.

▲ **Supports transactions**–This indicates that the component can participate within a transaction, but a transaction is not required. If this component is called from within a transaction, it will run within the environment of that transaction. If there was no transaction currently executing, then this component would execute separately as well.

▲ **Does not support transactions**–This is used to indicate that the component does not support transactions. If this component were to be called from within a transaction, then it would be provided with an environment of execution outside of the current transaction. This is the default value for all components.

MTS Application Programming Interface

In addition to providing a run-time environment for execution and a user interface for management, MTS provides application programming interfaces (APIs) for creating MTS-aware components and applications. The APIs can be used to create clients that can access MTS components. They can also be used to create COM objects that can execute within the MTS run-time environment.

MTS makes every effort to be as transparent as possible to those applications that will utilize the services it provides. All that an application that wishes to use a transactional component needs to do is call the same COM function to create the object as it would for a normal, non-MTS component. This allows an application to be migrated from a standard environment to an MTS environment without any modification to the application itself. The underlying layers of COM will handle all of the support necessary.

For developing components that will execute within MTS, there is a set of COM Interfaces that the component can support. (COM interfaces were described in Chapter 1) These interfaces are used by the component to communicate with MTS. They allow the component to:

▲ Declare that an object's work is complete, if the component has completed its work successfully. The COM Interface allows the component to communicate with MTS to relay this information.

▲ Prevent a transaction from being committed if the component encountered an error or some other reason that prevented it from successfully completing.

▲ Create other objects that will execute within the Transaction Server environment.

▲ Include other objects' work within the scope of the current object's transaction

The final part of the MTS application programming interfaces supports the creation of applications that will automatically manage the packages and components inside of MTS. This API replicates the functionality provided by MTS Explorer. By taking advantage of these APIs in their applications, developers can ensure that MTS is properly configured to support their packages and components.

MTS and IIS

With the release of IIS4.0 and the Windows NT Option Pack, Microsoft has provided developers with a very powerful and integrated set of services from which to create robust and scalable applications. Two of the services that work very closely together in this new environment are IIS and Microsoft Transaction Server. Microsoft has tightly integrated the functions of IIS and MTS, which makes it very easy to take advantage of transaction processing applications from within traditional web page programming.

There are a number of different examples of the ways that MTS and IIS are closely integrated. These include:

- Transactional Active Server Pages
- Crash Protection for IIS Applications
- Transactional Events
- Object Context for IIS Built-In Objects
- Common Installation and Management

A developer can use one or more of these features in their applications that use both IIS and MTS. Because of their tight integration, the developer has little work to do to fully utilize these services.

Transactional Active Server Pages

In this chapter, we have looked at how you can group business functionality together inside of a transaction using MTS. With the integration of MTS and IIS, you can now include Active Server Pages scripts within a transaction. These scripts can include calls to server components that will also participate in the transaction. As with all transactions, if any one part of the transaction fails, then the entire transaction will be rolled back. The added advantage of transactional ASP scripts is that it makes it easy to tie multiple components together into one transaction.

There is one problem with using transactional scripts when dealing with a transaction that aborts. The changes that were made to databases accessed with the database's Resource Manager will be automatically rolled back. However, as of this release of MTS, the environment is unable to rollback changes made within the script itself. Any changes made using the script, such as changes to session or application variables, will not be automatically rolled back. However, you will see later how to use transactional events to be notified that a transaction has aborted. When you handle this event, you can manually rollback any changes that MTS cannot perform automatically.

You cannot have one transaction that spans multiple ASP script pages. If there is work from multiple components that you want to include in the same transaction, then you will need to call all of those components from the same ASP script. For example, there is an application that has one component to withdraw money from an account and one component to deposit money into an account. To transfer funds from one account to another, you would create an ASP script that used the withdrawal component to get the funds for transfer and the deposit component to put that money in the new account. All of this functionality would be put in a transaction ASP script, so that if any part failed, all of the account balances would be reset to their initial values.

To declare a script as transactional, you would use the following directive:

```
<%@ TRANSACTION = transParam %>
```

The **transParam** value can have the following values:

Requires_New	Starts a new transaction.
Required	Starts a new transaction.
Supported	Does not start a transaction.
Not_Supported	Does not start a transaction.

These values have the same effect as the settings for the transaction participation states that can be set for each component using the MTS Explorer.

This directive must be on the first line in the ASP script. If there is anything before this in the page, then a script error will be generated. There is no explicit indicator to show that a transaction has ended. The transaction ends when the script reaches the end of the current page. MTS will create a transaction context for the page. Each object that is called by the page can use this context to participate in the transaction. The transactional ASP script can do the same thing using the **ObjectContext** object.

The ASP ObjectContext Object

When you are dealing with transactional ASP scripts, you may want to be able to directly affect the outcome of the transaction that the script is encapsulating. As in the server components that support transactions, you will refer to the current transaction using the **ObjectContext** object. This object provides the encapsulation for all of the transaction-handling routines that a developer may need. This is exactly the same object that the server components participating in the transaction will be accessing. There are two methods that this component provides that can be accessed from ASP scripts.

SetComplete	The **SetComplete** method declares that the script is not aware of any reason for the transaction not to complete. If all components participating in the transaction also call **SetComplete**, the transaction will complete. The **SetComplete** method will be implicitly called when the ASP script reaches the end of the script, and **SetAbort** has not been called.
SetAbort	The **SetAbort** method declares that the transaction initiated by the script has not completed and the resources should not be updated.

Here is a step-by-step example of an ASP script that shows both the **@TRANSACTION** directive, and the use of the ASP **ObjectContext** object.

```
<%@ TRANSACTION = Required %>
```

This is the required first line of the script. It indicates that this script must be within the bounds of a transaction. Since a transaction cannot span multiple ASP scripts, there will be no active transaction when this page starts. This will force MTS to create a new transaction which will encompass this page and the two components referenced from it.

```
<%
    Set objOnHand = Server.CreateObject("BookComp.OnHand")
    Set objSales = Server.CreateObject("BookComp.Sales")
```

Even though this page is within a transaction, the usual **Server.CreateObject** method is used to create references to the **OnHand** and **Sales** components. Since MTS is providing the environment for this page, they will be created within the current object context of the transaction for this page. In this example, the values of **Quantity** and **ProductID** have been passed into this ASP file.

```
    iQuantity = Request("Quantity")
    ProductID = Request("ProductID")
    strStatus = objOnHand.CheckOnHand(iQuantity, ProductID)
```

```
    If strStatus = "INS"
       ObjectContext.SetAbort
       Response.Write "At this time, inventory levels are insufficient to complete your
    transaction"
```

When the value of **strStatus** is **INS**, the server component method indicated that there was insufficient inventory to process the request. The **SetAbort** method is explicitly called by the script to indicate that this transaction should not be completed. The script then outputs a message to the user indicating that the transaction was unable to complete. If the **CheckOnHand** method performed any database modifications, such as requesting that items be removed from inventory, then the act of aborting the transaction will cause any changes to the database to be rolled back.

By performing the return value check and calling **SetAbort** in the ASP script, some of the business rule processing is being handled at this level. But earlier in this chapter, we showed how business logic should be encapsulated within application components. Why wouldn't the **CheckOnHand** method call **SetAbort** itself when it determined insufficient inventory available?

This is an example of a business object that can be used for multiple purposes. There may be instances where a failure to have sufficient inventory is not reason enough to abort a transaction in progress. If the call to **SetAbort** had been in the method itself, then anytime this method was invoked within a transaction and there was insufficient inventory, the entire transaction would be aborted. There probably exists a case where a developer would not want this to happen. By putting the transaction decision logic in the ASP script, and not in the method itself, this decision can be made depending on the context of the application when the method is invoked.

```
   Else
       ObjectContext.SetComplete
       acctInfo = Request("AcctInfo")
       Update = objSales.ProcessSale(acctInfo)
    End If
  %>
```

If the inventory check was successful, then the sale transaction may continue. Since all of the processing that needs to be done by the script has completed successfully, the **SetComplete** method is called. It is not necessary to explicitly call this method, since it will be called once the script reaches the end. The final part of the script invokes the **ProcessSale** method to complete the sale. If for any reason this method fails, then the transaction can still be aborted. All that calling **SetComplete** did was indicate to MTS that the script processing completed successfully. It did not commit the transaction. The transaction is only committed when all components participating in the transaction provide the **SetComplete** indication.

If there were an error in the **ProcessSale** method then the transaction would be aborted. There are two ways that the script can be notified of this occurring. The script could check the return value from the **ProcessSale** method in the same manner it checked the return value from the **CheckOnHand** method. If the return value indicated an error, then the script could handle it accordingly. The other way that the script could handle a transaction abort is by handling a **transaction event**.

Transaction Events

There is no method for an ASP script to explicitly determine if a transaction that it is participating in has aborted or committed. As shown in the previous example, it can examine the return values of methods that it calls. But unless those methods provide indication in their return values that they have called **SetComplete** or **SetAbort**, there is no other indication of the transaction's state.

The ASP script can use transaction events to perform special processing if a transaction is being committed or being aborted and rolled back. The firing of the events cause methods of the **ObjectContext** object to be executed. The **ObjectContext** object provides two methods that the ASP script can handle. The **OnTransactionCommit** method is fired if the current transaction is successful. Since the transaction is not committed until after the script reaches the end, then this event will be not be fired until the entire page has been processed. The **OnTransactionAbort** method is called if the current transaction is being aborted. The method will be called immediately after any object participating in the transaction calls **SetAbort**.

Let's take a look at an example of how to use transactional events to provide a response if a transaction fails or succeeds.

```
<%@ TRANSACTION = Required %>
<HTML>
<BODY>
<H1>Completing your order...</H1>

<%
   dim iOrderNum
   Set objCredit = Server.CreateObject("BookComp.Credit")
   curOrderTotal = Request("OrderTotal")
   CustomerID = Request("CustID")
   iOrderNum = objCredit.ProcessCredit(curOrderTotal, CustomerID)
%>
```

The ASP script up to this point has basically the same structure as the one we looked at in the previous section. Values are passed into this script using a Form. A reference to a server component is created, and then a method of that server component is called. The value that the server component returns is the order number.

The difference comes about in that the ASP script does not immediately check for the return value. It merely gives the user an indication that the transaction is being processed. Since the **Buffer** property of the **Response** object is set to its default, which is false, this information will be displayed immediately on the client. The client is informed of the success or failure of the transaction through the use of transactional scripts.

```
<P>Thank you.  Your transaction is being processed.</P>
<%
Sub OnTransactionCommit()
    Response.Write("<P>Thank you for placing your order.</P>")
    Response.Write("<P>Your order number is "&   CStr(iOrderNum) & ".</P>")
    Response.Write("</BODY></HTML>")
End sub
```

If the transaction is successful, then the **OnTransactionCommit** method is called. This displays a message to the client indicating a successful order. The order number that is returned from the server component method is also displayed for the user.

If there is a failure somewhere in the transaction, the **OnTransactionAbort** method will be called. This message displays an indication on the client that the transaction was unsuccessful. Any changes to durable data that were made in the server component will be automatically rolled back. If there was any ASP session or application data that was changed in the transaction, those changes can be rolled back at this point. Since ASP does not provide for automatic rollback of changes made via ASP script, the code to support the rollback will need to be explicitly written, which is not shown in this example. The **OnTransactionAbort** method is the ideal place to reference that code from.

```
Sub OnTransactionAbort()
    Response.Write("<P>An error has occurred in processing your order</P>")
    Response.Write("<P>We are unable to complete it at this time.</P>")
    Response.Write("</BODY></HTML>")
End sub

%>
```

Now that we are able to handle transaction events, which give us the ability to determine if a transaction is successful or not, we can take a look at some of the other advantages that the integration of IIS and MTS provide. One of these is the "crash protection" that MTS provides for IIS and ASP applications.

Crash Protection for IIS Applications

As the web server moves beyond serving up pages, then through dynamic pages using ASP, up to providing applications using MTS, there are a number of changes that are occurring in the code that is being executed on the server. As the applications become more complex, there are more and more components that have to work together for the application to function successfully. These components are growing in complexity, and may be accessing multiple, disparate data sources. With all this added complexity comes a system that may be more prone to failure. Applications that fail are acceptable during development, but once deployed, failures should be handled as transparently as possible.

As more and more business critical applications are moved to web servers, the required availability of these systems becomes closer and closer to 100%. It is becoming quickly unacceptable for the entire web server to crash if an application crashes. And in the event of a crash, then the application needs to restart itself without operator intervention. It also becomes a problem if the application and its supporting files cannot be modified without taking the entire server offline.

With the merging of IIS and MTS, this problem is being alleviated. MTS provides a facility for each application that is running in IIS to be a part of a separate process space. Since this process space is separate from any other ASP applications running on the server, and separate from the IIS executable itself, it can be loaded and unloaded without affecting the rest of the system. It also prevents a crashing ASP application from affecting any other parts of the system.

To add crash protection to an ASP application, you will use the Microsoft Management Console (MMC). By viewing the properties of your ASP application, you can select to run the application in a separate process space. You can modify this property by selecting the Virtual Directory for your application from the MMC window. Once selected, you can right-click and select **Properties**. This will display the Application properties dialog box for your application.

To add crash protection to your application, make sure that the 'Run in separate memory space' check box is checked. This will cause any objects that the application uses to be created in an isolated process space. This will separate the execution of their code from the execution of the web server and other application's code. By running in a separate process space, an error will be confined to that process space, leaving all other processes on the machine running normally. While the term "crash protection" does not mean that it keeps *your* application from crashing, it prevents your application from crashing the rest of the system.

Component Design Issues

Up to this point, we have examined the features of transaction processing systems and how they can be used to create more robust applications. Microsoft Transaction Server is a transaction processing system that has been integrated with IIS and ASP to provide a complete application development platform for both Internet and intranet applications. Now what we have an understanding of what a transaction processing system can do, we need to look at how to create the components of the applications that will be part of the transactional application.

The components of the application will be straightforward COM components. They can be developed using any development tool that will create COM objects. These tools include Visual C++, Java, Delphi, and Visual Basic.

In a later section, we will cover the differences in the components created by these tools when we examine the differences in the threading model.

There are several areas that we will cover that make developing MTS-friendly components different from developing regular COM components. These areas include how to hold state in an object, issues surrounding the various threading models, and the scope at which objects are visible. In fact, every COM component can work in an MTS environment. It is just by adding a few bits of code that a COM component can become MTS-friendly, and thereby work much better.

Holding State

In developing objects, whether they are standard COM objects or COM objects enhanced to work better with MTS, an object can be one of two types. The two types are stateless and stateful. A **stateless object** does not retain any information from one method call to the next. A **stateful object** has some internal storage mechanism that allows it to retain information between two separate method calls.

An application designer can take advantage of either type of component in their applications. The two types of components can even be mixed in one application. There may be times that it is more efficient from a coding standpoint to develop a component that holds state within the object. However, there are tradeoffs in using stateful components within the context of MTS.

Activation and Deactivation

As we discussed earlier in this chapter, MTS can manage the creation and utilization of components automatically. This allows applications to scale much more efficiently than using other means. To look at the effect that state has on this mechanism, we need to look at the deactivation of objects.

An object has two modes inside of MTS. When it is first created, it is deactivated. A deactivated object looks to the client as a real object, but it consumes very few resources on the server. Through a process known as **just-in-time activation**, MTS will activate the component when the client actually calls a method on the object. This allows the clients to not have to worry about when it should create an instance of an object in relation to when it is used. The client can create the instance and hold it as long as it wants before using it, as MTS will not create and activate the object until it is needed. This is similar in the ASP world to using the **<OBJECT>** tag to create an object instance rather than **Server.CreateObject**.

There are three ways that an object, once activated, can be deactivated. Deactivating an object is different from destroying it. The object can request deactivation through the **ObjectContext** interface by calling either **SetComplete** or **SetAbort**. If the object is participating in a transaction, and that transaction is committed or aborted, then the object will be deactivated once all of the processing in the transaction is completed.. Finally, if all of the clients that are accessing the object release their references to that object, then it will be deactivated. When an object is deactivated, MTS can use the resources that were allocated to it for other objects. This means that any information that was stored inside of the object is lost. The recently deactivated object could also be recycled if MTS detects another client requesting the same object.

Stateful Objects

A **stateful object** is one that retains internal information from one method call to another. For an object to be able to do this, there are certain tradeoffs that must be made. MTS gains its efficiency from being able to automatically activate and then quickly deactivate objects. As we said earlier, when an object deactivates, it loses all information that is stored inside of it. In order for an object to be stateful, it must maintain internal information, which means it cannot be deactivated. If a stateful object were to be deactivated, it would lose all of its state, thus becoming a stateless object.

When an object decides to become stateful, MTS no longer has the ability to use its resources for any other objects. An object will become "stateful" if it does not call `SetComplete` or `SetAbort` when it finishes its processing. The stateful object has in effect locked a portion of the resources that MTS has to work with. MTS relies on its ability to dynamically manage resources in order to allow applications to effectively scale. Therefore, if a system is using a large number of stateful objects, then it will be much less efficient when scaling.

This does not mean to say that you should never use stateful objects when developing MTS applications. As we stated earlier, the use of stateful objects can make the development of client applications much easier. It is just important for the developer to understand the implications that using stateful objects will have on the scalability of their application.

Threading Model

An important issue that the developer of MTS applications needs to consider is the threading model that is used by the components of the application. The threading model of a component determines how the methods of the component are assigned to threads in order to be executed. The MTS environment itself manages all of the threads associated with its applications. A component should never create any threads on its own. This is primarily of concern to J++ and C++ developers, who have the ability to create threads directly. Developers creating objects in Visual Basic do not need to worry about this, as there is no way for them to explicitly create a thread.

A thread is simply defined as a single path of code that is being executed. There are four threading models that a component could have. The threading model for a component is determined at the compile time for the component. There is a registry attribute for each component in MTS called ThreadingModel, which indicates what threading model MTS should use for this component. The four threading models are single threaded, apartment-threaded, free-threaded, and both.

Single Threaded

If a component is marked as **Single Threaded**, then all methods of that component will execute on the main thread. There is one main thread for each MTS application. Since there is only one thread, it means that only one method can execute at any given time. If there are multiple single threaded components that are being accessed by multiple clients simultaneously, then it is easy to see why a bottleneck will occur. Since only one method can execute at a time, all of the other methods will be sitting around waiting their turn. This can essentially grind a system to a halt.

> *A good rule of thumb to remember is **Single Threading = BAD!***

Apartment Threaded

In a component that is marked as **Apartment Threaded**, each method of that component will execute on a thread that is associated with that component. Since each component running inside MTS has its own thread, this separates the methods into their own "Apartments", with each instance of a component corresponding to one apartment. While there is only one thread inside of a component, each instance of that component will have its own thread apartment. This will alleviate a great number of the problems that a single threaded component has. Since multiple components can be executing methods in their own apartments simultaneously, the scalability constraints that the single threaded components have are greatly relaxed.

Free Threaded

A **Free Threaded** object is also known as a multi-threaded or multi-threaded apartment object. An application in MTS can have only one multi-thread apartment (MTA) in it. This MTA can have zero or more threads within it. Any objects that are marked as free threaded will be created in the MTA, regardless of where they were created. Now, all of this may sound great. "Wow, multiple threads! Must mean great scalability!" This is not necessarily the case. To see the problem, we need to look at how calls are made from cone component to another.

When a call is made from one component to another component within the same the apartment, the call is a direct function call. In the Win32 environment, this is a very fast operation. If a call has to be made from one apartment to another, then a proxy needs to be created in order to make the call. What this does is add overhead to every function call, and slows down the system. Since a free threaded component will ALWAYS be created in the multi-threaded apartment, even if it was created from a single thread apartment, then all calls to access that component will have to be made by a proxy. And with proxy calls being slower than direct calls, the performance of this object will be reduced. This means that even though free-threaded components sound good, they will extract a performance penalty.

Both

There is another type of threading model called **Both**. This is a special type of threading model in that the object has the characteristics of an apartment-threaded object as well as a free-threaded object. The advantage that this threading model brings is that no matter where the component is created, it will always be created within the same apartment as the object that created it. If it is created by a component running in a single-thread apartment, then it will act like an apartment-threaded component, and be created in the apartment. This means that the calls between the components can be direct and not require a slower proxy.

Likewise, if the new component is created by a component running in the multi-thread apartment, it will act like a free-threaded component and be created in the MTA. This will allow the components direct access to each other, since they are running in the same apartment. In either case, to access this new component, proxy calls are not necessary. The access can be made using fast and efficient direct function calls.

Object Scope

An important issue when integrating your newly created server components with the ASP scripts themselves is the scope that these components will have. There are three possible levels of scope that are available in ASP. **Page-level** scope is where the object has a lifetime of a single page, and is only visible to that page. **Session-level** scope means that the object has the lifetime of an entire user session, and is visible to all pages that may be accessed during that session. **Application-level** scope means that the object is visible to all sessions accessing a particular application. The session and application-level scope object are created in the `global.asa` file, or by storing a reference to the object in an application-level or session-level variable.

Page Scope

A **page scope** object has the lifetime of a single ASP script page. The component is only visible from that single page. For components at this level, the best types of components to user are apartment-threaded and both-threaded. These components can be accessed directly, rather than by proxy. A free-threaded component is not nearly as good, since the calls must be via a proxy, and also a free threaded object cannot access the **ObjectContext**, which it needs to participate in the transaction. As in nearly every case, the single threaded object is bad, since all access is serialized across the application. This means that of all the users currently accessing the site, only once person can access the object at one time.

Session Scope

When an object is created with **session scope**, it will be available to all ASP script pages that are referenced during that user's session. Each session that is created in the application will also have its own instances of session-scope objects. To create a session scope object, you will add this entry to the **global.asa** file for the application.

```
<OBJECT RUNAT=Server SCOPE=Session ID=myID
  PROGID="objectID"><OBJECT>
```

This **<OBJECT>** tag must be outside of any **<SCRIPT>** blocks in the **global.asa** file. The **RUNAT=Server** parameter indicates that this object is a server side component. The **SCOPE=Session** indicates that this object will have session-level scope. It will be accessible to any ASP script that is part of the application, referenced through the **myID** object reference.

The choice of threading models for session-level objects is a bit different. As with the page-scope object, single threaded and free threaded are bad since access to them has to be through a proxy. An apartment threaded object is OK, but when the session-scope object is being accessed, then the session is locked down. This means that no other changes to any session-level variables can be made while the object is being accessed. For a session-level object, the optimal threading model is both.

Application Scope

An **application-scoped** object is one that can be accessed by any ASP script in the application. There is also only one instance of the object for the entire application. This object is inserted in the same way as the session scoped object, using the **<OBJECT>** tag. There is one change that needs to be made for an application-scoped object:

```
<OBJECT RUNAT=Server SCOPE=Application ID=myID
  PROGID="objectID"><OBJECT>
```

By changing the **SCOPE** parameter to **Application**, there will be one instance of this object available to all users of the application. This presents some interesting challenges when selecting a threading model for an application-scoped component. If this component is marked as using Apartment threading, then all access to this object will be serialized. That means that only one user out of all users accessing the site can use the object at any one time. All of the other users will have to wait until it is their turn. If a system is going to have very infrequent concurrent use, such as in an intranet that serves 25 people, maybe this is OK. If you are trying to run a production site that has thousands of simultaneous users, using an apartment threaded component would quickly bring the site to a grinding halt.

The best component to use is one that is marked both. A both-threaded component will be able to directly accessed through function calls, rather than having to use a slower proxy call. Most of all, the access to the component is not serialized, meaning that multiple users can access the component at one time. This will greatly enhance the scalability of the application over the user of apartment-model application scope components.

Component Creation Tools

There are three primary choices for languages with which to create server components. These choices are Visual Basic, C++, and Java. Each of these languages can produce COM objects that can be used as server components inside of MTS. They also have different levels of support when it comes to creating components using the various threading models that we just looked at.

Visual Basic is the quickest way to create application components. All of the examples in this chapter, as well as the case study that follows in the next few chapters, will be created using Visual Basic. However, with this ease of use comes a tradeoff. The default threading model for components created in Visual Basic is single-threaded. As you have probably gathered by now, single threading is bad. However, with the release of the Visual Studio Service Pack 2, Visual Basic can now create apartment threaded components. While these are not optimal in all uses, they will be sufficient for the majority of cases where application components are used.

C++ can also be used to create application components. Nearly all of the components that make up IIS and MTS and ASP are built using C++. A new feature of Visual C++, known as the Active Template Library, or ATL, has a wizard that lets you get a lot of the COM plumbing generated for you automatically. All that you will then need to write is your application specific code. C++ and ATL can generate components that use the both threading model. As we have seen, this is the most versatile threading model for all component uses.

Java, despite all of its hype, is an excellent programming language. With the COM-specific support that Microsoft has added to Visual J++, you can use Java to create server components. There are a set of Java classes that are provided with ASP that allow the developer to use standard Java to create the components. All of the COM-specific constructs, like variants, are mapped onto native Java types. By default, Java components are marked as both threaded, making them optimal for use in all parts of an ASP and MTS application.

Example: On-Line Banking with ASP and MTS

Now that we have examined the new features that the integration of ASP and Microsoft Transaction Server has given application developers, let's try out a simple example. We have seen how the use of MTS will make it simpler for developers to write applications that can be robust, yet easily scale to support vast numbers of users. Granted, it is probably difficult to show an example and definitively prove that it can support thousands of users simultaneously. That is, unless everyone reading this book decides to hit the example site at once. But, this example will use the concepts that we went over in this chapter to write scalable application components, and then in a leap of faith, we will rely on Transaction Server to come through and provide the scalability it promises. The example code shown in this section can be downloaded from **http://rapid.wrox.co.uk/books/1266**.

The Problem

One of the growing fields of internet electronic commerce is the area of on-line banking. Startup institutions like Security First Network Bank (**http://www.sfnb.com**) are providing banking throughout the US via the Internet. They offer all of their services electronically, without the need for traditional bank branches. Even at their one physical location in Atlanta, there are web terminals for customers to interact with the bank. Traditional financial institutions as well are beginning to offer banking over the Internet. There are a number of difficult problem areas that need to be solved to make Internet banking commonplace. In this example, we will look at just one small part of the total problem, and develop a solution that uses the power of transaction processing and Microsoft Transaction Server.

In our example, we will be assuming that a user has successfully passed through all the necessary security checkpoints that on-line banking will require. This user also has multiple accounts with our fictitious on-line bank. The task that our solution will allow the user to perform is to be able to transfer some amount of money from one account to another. The system will need to ensure that the user has sufficient funds in the account they are transferring the money from. The system must also provide an atomic operation that encompasses both the withdrawal of the money from the first account as well as the deposit of the same amount of money into the second account. First, we will design the components that will be used to manage the information in the accounts.

The Design

The first step in designing the components of this application is to look at the way that the permanent data for the application will be stored. For this example, our data will be stored in a SQL Server database. There will be three tables in this database. In a real banking application, the data would be much more complex. Since the example application is solving only one part of the problem, we will use a considerably less complex database.

Database Tables

The first table is the **CUSTOMER** table. This table will have information about each customer, including their name, address, and phone number. Each customer will have a unique **customerID**, which will be used to identify all of the customer's information stored throughout the system. The structure of the **CUSTOMER** table is:

Field Name	Type	Size
CustomerID	Int	
Name	Char	50
StreetAddr	Char	50
City	Char	40
State	Char	20
PostalCode	Char	20
PhoneNumber	Char	30

The next table that will be used in our example is the **ACCOUNT** table. This table will have information about each account that the bank has. This account information will be the account number, which will serve as the primary key of the table. The table will also have a field for the customer that owns the account. This field will have a foreign key from the **CUSTOMER** table. The table will also have the current balance of the account, as well as the date and time of the last transaction. The structure of the **ACCOUNT** table is:

Field Name	Type
AccountNumber	Int
CustomerID	Int
Balance	Money
LastTransaction	Datetime

The third table in the bank's database will be the **TRANSREC** table. This table will contain a record of all transactions that occur at the bank. There will be a unique **ID** field that will serve as the primary key for the table. The value of this field will be automatically generated when the record is created. There will be a field that identifies the transaction type. In the case that the example is covering, there is only one transaction type, account transfer. This will be indicated by a value of **TRANS** in this field. There will be fields that identify the detail data of the transaction, which includes the account numbers of the source and destination accounts, as well as the amount transferred. The record will also have a field that indicates the date and time that the transaction took place. The structure of the **TRANSREC** table is:

Field Name	Type	Size
TransactionID	Identity	
TransactionType	Char	5
SourceAccount	Int	
DestinationAccount	Int	
Amount	Money	
TransTime	Datetime	

Component Design

Now that we have designed the database tables that will hold the information, we need to create a set of application components that will have methods that let the application process the information to support the problem. If we review the steps that the application will follow to perform the transfer, we can begin to identify methods that will need to be created. Remember, in this example, the user has already been identified and verified.

Application Steps

- Select the customer's account to transfer the money **from.**
- Select the customer's account to transfer the money **to**.
- Enter the amount to transfer.
- Verify that the source account has sufficient funds for the transfer.
- Withdraw the transfer amount from the source account.
- Deposit the same amount into the destination account.
- Make a record of the transaction in the **TRANSREC** table.

By examining these steps, we can begin to identify the types of methods that our application components will need to perform.

Application Components

There will need to be a component that allows the user to select an account. We can divide our application logic between ASP script and the COM components that will run on the server. To allow the user to select an account, we need to present a list of all possible accounts. This implies that there is a method that returns a list of accounts for a given customer. The next method that we need will ensure that the source account has sufficient funds to transfer. This method will accept as input the source account number and the amount and return true if there is sufficient funds to transfer.

Next, we will need a method to withdraw money from an account. This method should take an account number and amount as parameters. Since this part of the application will be running inside of a transaction, the method should abort the transaction if it is unable to remove the money from the account. Once the money is withdrawn, we will need a method to deposit money into an account. This method will also take the account number and amount as parameters. As with the withdrawal method, this method should abort the transaction if it is unable to deposit the amount.

The final method that we will need is to log the transaction into the **TRANSREC** table. This method should accept as parameters all of the fields of the transaction table, except the timestamp, which it can generate internally. This method should return a true or false, depending on if it is able to successful update the database table

Component Development

Now, we will begin to develop the components that we outlined in the previous section. For this example, we will develop all of the server components using Visual Basic 5.0 with at least Service Pack 2 installed. This will allow us to develop components that use the Apartment threading model. While this is not as efficient as using the Both threading model, for the purposes of this example, it will suffice. We will be creating one application component that has multiple methods. This component will be called **Bank.**

Setting up the Project

The first step in developing the components for our application is to create a project in Visual Basic. The project type for all server components should be an ActiveX DLL. Usually, when VB starts up, it prompts you to create a project. You will select the ActiveX DLL icon from the dialog box.

For this example, we will name our project **BankExample**. To set the project name, you can use the dialog box that comes up when you select the Properties menu item from the Project menu. From this dialog, you can set the name of the project and also set the Threading model for the project. Since we will be creating a server component for use with MTS, you should select the Apartment threading model. If for some reason you do not see the Threading Model selection area in your dialog box, you need to check to make sure that you have installed the Visual Studio Service Pack 2 or 3. The original revision of Visual Basic 5.0 could only create single-threaded components. The capability to create apartment-threaded components was added with Service Pack 2.

Note, the Visual Studio Service Pack is different from the NT Service Packs, and needs to be installed separately.

To ensure that as you are developing this component you do not inadvertently add some type of visual output to your component, check the Unattended Execution box. When this is checked, any messages that might have been displayed with a dialog box are rerouted to an event log file.

The last step that you need to do to set up the project to create the server component is to add the references to the various COM Libraries that this component needs. All components that participate in MTS transactions and wish to have access to the current **ObjectContext** object will need to link in the Transaction Server type library. To add this to the project, you will use the Project...References... dialog box.

The three additional entries that you will need to add for this project are

- Microsoft Transaction Server Type Library
- Microsoft ActiveX Data Objects 1.5 Library
- Microsoft ActiveX Data Objects Recordset 1.5 Library

If you do not find these listed in the Available References listbox, then use the browse button to locate their DLLs. They are generally found in the following locations:

Type Library	DLL Location
MTS Library	`\WINDOWS\SYSTEM\MTS\MTXAS.DLL` or `\WINNT\SYSTEM32\MTS\MTXAS.DLL` *for Windows NT*
ADO Library	`\Program Files\Common Files\System\ADO\MSADO15.DLL`
ADO Recordset Library	`\Program Files\Common Files\System\ADO\MSADOR15.DLL`

Now that we have configured the project correctly, it is time to start developing the components.

Bank.ListAccounts

The **ListAccounts** method will take the **customerID** as a parameter and return a comma delimited list of account numbers. These account numbers can then be parsed and displayed by the client. This component will access the SQL Server database using ADO. Even though this method will not be participating in any transactions, it should make a call to **SetComplete** or **SetAbort** when it has finished processing. This will prevent the component from becoming stateful, as was mentioned earlier.

```
Option Explicit
Private oObjectContext As ObjectContext
Private oDb As ADODB.Connection
Private oRs As ADODB.Recordset
Private vSql As Variant

Const vDbConn As Variant = "DSN=Bank;UID=sa;PWD=;"
```

This initial section is creating some variables that will be used in every method that we will be creating. The **Option Explicit** statement will force Visual Basic to ensure that every variable that is used is declared. This is good programming practice, and should be in every application that you write. We have also created variables to hold references to the various objects that we will be using in the application. The database connection string is stored as a constant, making it easy to change without having to locate all instances of it in the source code.

```
Public Function ListAccounts(ByVal vCustID As Variant) As Variant
    Dim vAccounts As Variant

    On Error GoTo ListAccountsErrHandler
```

The **ListAccounts** method will accept a parameter of type **Variant**. The value of this parameter is the **customerID** number. The function will return a variant to the caller. This return value will be a string containing a comma delimited list of account numbers that the customer has.

If any errors occur during the processing of this method they will be intercepted by the **On Error** statement. This will allow the method to pass an error message back to the client, and also alleviate the need for error checking code throughout the method.

```
    Set oObjectContext = GetObjectContext()
    Set oDb = oObjectContext.CreateInstance("ADODB.Connection")
    oDb.Open vDbConn
```

The first step in the method is to obtain a reference to the current **ObjectContext** object. This reference will allow us to create other COM objects. These other objects will also be created inside of the environment that the **Bank** object is in, which is inside of Transaction Server. The other COM object that we will be using is the ADO Connection object. Normally, this object would be created with the standard Visual Basic **New** method. Since we want it to run in the current object's context, we will use the **CreateInstance** method of the **ObjectContext** object. This will return a reference to an ADO Connection object.

```
    vSql = "SELECT AccountNumber from ACCOUNT WHERE CustomerID = " & vCustID & ";"

    Set oRs = oDb.Execute(vSql)

    Do While Not oRs.EOF
        vAccounts = vAccounts + CStr(oRs("AccountNumber"))
        oRs.MoveNext
        If Not oRs.EOF Then
            vAccounts = vAccounts + ","
        End If
    Loop

    ListAccounts = vAccounts
    Exit Function
```

We will use a SQL statement to retrieve all of the account numbers from the database for the current customer. The **Execute** method of the ADO Connection object will return an ADO Recordset object. With this object, we can go through each record and add the account number to our return string, which is being built in the **vAccounts** variable.

We will be separating each account number with a comma. To determine if a comma should be added to the return string, we need to see if the number that was just added to the string was the last in the recordset. The previous statement, **oRs.MoveNext**, will move to the next record in the recordset. If there is a valid record, which is when the value of **EOF** is **false**, then a comma should be added to the return string. This check is made so that a comma is not put at the end of the string, which makes parsing the string easier.

Once we have added all of the accounts to the return string, we assign the value of the return string to the **ListAccounts** variable, which is the variable that will be returned to the caller. An explicit call to **Exit Function** is made so that the error handling code that follows will not be executed.

```
ListAccountsErrHandler:
    ListAccounts = "ERROR: " & Err.Description

End Function
```

The error handler will get executed if any error occurs during the processing of the method. The return value for the method is set to the string "**ERROR**" plus a description of the error from the Visual Basic **Error** object. By adding the upper case string to the return value, it acts as a flag to indicate that an error has occurred. The caller program can readily identify this flag and take appropriate action.

The next method that we need to add to our component is a method to check if an account has sufficient funds available.

Bank.FundsAvailable

This method will be used to determine if an account has at least a specified amount of funds available. It may seem that a method that just returns the balance in the account would be a more powerful method. In some instances it could be. But by encapsulating the business logic to determine if funds are available inside of the component, it frees the client from having to know about how the determination is made. It also provides a more secure environment, in that the actual balance is not passed back to the client. Only a boolean response to indicate if sufficient funds are available is returned.

```
Public Function FundsAvailable(ByVal vAcctNum As Variant, ByVal vAmount As Variant) As
Variant
Dim vRetVal As Variant

    On Error GoTo FundsAvailableErrHandler

    Set oObjectContext = GetObjectContext()
    Set oDb = oObjectContext.CreateInstance("ADODB.Connection")
    oDb.Open vDbConn
```

The calling application will pass in the account number using a variant data type. The other parameter will be the amount of funds that need to be available for this method to return a **True** response. The boolean return value will actually be returned as a variant data type.

The Visual Basic code to set up the method's error handler and open the connection to the database is the same as the **ListAccount** method's code. The SQL statement will retrieve the value of the **Balance** field from the record in the **ACCOUNT** table where **AccountNumber** matches the value passed into the method.

```
    vSql = "SELECT Balance from ACCOUNT WHERE AccountNumber = " & vAcctNum & ";"

    Set oRs = oDb.Execute(vSql)

    If oRs.EOF Then
        FundsAvailable = "ERROR: Invalid Account Number"
        Exit Function
    Else
        vRetVal = CCur(vAmount) <= CCur(oRs("Balance"))
    End If

    FundsAvailable = vRetVal
    Exit Function

FundsAvailableErrHandler:
    FundsAvailable = "ERROR: " & Err.Description

End Function
```

The **execute** method of the Connection object will return a recordset. If the recordset that is returned is empty, then the account number that the calling application supplied was wrong. This is indicated to the calling application by returning the same error flag as the **ListAccounts** method, with more description of the error included with the flag.

If there was a record found in the database, then the return value of the method will be set to the evaluation of the logical expression that will return **true** if the amount that was passed in to check is less than or equal to the balance in the account. At this point, additional business logic could be easily added. If there was a requirement to maintain a minimum $50 balance, then the logical expression could be written as: **vRetVal = CCur(vAmount)+ 50 <= CCur(oRs("Balance")).**   For this example, there are no extra business rules, so the logical expression just compares the parameter with the balance.

The error handler for this method also uses the Visual Basic **Err** object to return a detailed description of the error that caused the method to fail.

Now that we have determined that there are sufficient funds in the account, the next application component we need is one that will withdraw funds from a given account.

Bank.Withdrawal

This method will be used to decrease the balance of a specified account. The desired account number and the amount to withdraw will be supplied as parameters to the method. As a check, the method will return the amount withdrawn as its return value. The application can then double check to make sure this was the same amount desired.

```
Public Function Withdrawal(ByVal vAcctNum As Variant, ByVal vAmount As Variant) As
Variant
    Dim vRetVal As Variant

    On Error GoTo WithdrawalErrHandler
```

```
Set oObjectContext = GetObjectContext()
Set oDb = oObjectContext.CreateInstance("ADODB.Connection")
oDb.Open vDbConn

vSql = "SELECT * from ACCOUNT WHERE AccountNumber = " & vAcctNum & ";"
```

Up to this point, the **Withdrawal** method is identical to the **FundsAvailable** method that we described earlier. The error handler is installed, the reference to an ADO Connection object is created, and the database is opened using the global database connection string. The SQL statement is slightly different, in that the query in the **FundsAvailable** method only returned the **Balance** field from the **ACCOUNT** table. In this method, the SQL query will return all of the fields of the record that matches the account number passed into the method.

In the previous methods, we used the **Execute** method of the ADO Connection object. This created a recordset object, but it was a read-only recordset. Since this method will need to update the value in the **Balance** field, it will require a read-write recordset. We will need to explicitly create a Recordset object, and then open it using the SQL statement.

```
Set oRs = oObjectContext.CreateInstance("ADODB.Recordset")
oRs.Open vSql, oDb, adOpenDynamic, adLockOptimistic
```

The **Open** method accepts four parameters. The first parameter is the SQL query statement. The second is a reference to a valid Connection object. This is necessary so that ADO knows which database to open this recordset for. The third parameter identifies this recordset as a dynamic recordset. In a dynamic recordset, the information in the recordset will be updated automatically whenever any user, even on a separate client, changes any part of the recordset. This is essential, as there may be other applications that are affecting the balance in this account at the same time that funds are being withdrawn. The last parameter, **adLockOptimistic**, sets the lock type for the recordset. Since data will need to be updated, we need to have the ability to write to the database. This lock type will only lock the record for writing when the data is actually being updated, freeing it for other users to change while this recordset is still open.

```
If oRs.EOF Then
    Err.Raise vbObjectError + 500, "Withdrawal", "Invalid Account Number"
Else
    If CCur(vAmount) > CCur(oRs("Balance")) Then
        Err.Raise vbObjectError + 510, "Withdrawal", "Insufficient Funds"
```

In this method, we will be using the **Raise** method of the Visual Basic **error** object. Since this method will participate in a transaction, we want to centralize the transaction commit and transaction abort to one location in the method. The **Raise** method call will cause method's error handler to take over processing. All errors in Visual Basic are required to have an error number. These numbers should be unique across a single application. To ensure that user-created error numbers do not conflict with existing Visual Basic error numbers, the user numbers are generated by adding some unique number to the **vbObjectError** constant.The last parameter in the method will become the **Description** property of the **Error** object. It is this textual information that will be passed back to the calling application.

The previous function was used to check if an account had sufficient funds available. Since the balance in the account may have changed since that method was run, or if the client application chose not to call that method first, the **Withdrawal** method will generate an error, which will generate a transaction abort, if there are insufficient funds to make the withdrawal.

```
        Else
            Dim vNewBal As Variant
            vNewBal = CCur(oRs("Balance") - vAmount)
            oRs("Balance") = vNewBal
            oRs("LastTransaction") = Now
            oRs.Update
            vRetVal = vAmount
        End If
    End If
```

If there are sufficient funds for withdrawal, then first we will calculate the new balance by subtracting the withdrawal amount from the balance that was stored in the database. This new balance will be written back into the database, along with a timestamp of this transaction, and the database will be updated using the **Update** method of the Recordset object.

With the withdrawal successfully completed, the return value of the method is set to the amount of the withdrawal as a double check. To indicate that this method's processing was successful, the method calls the **SetComplete** method of the current object context. This indicates that this method's work in the transaction is complete and that the object can be released. Remember that the changes are not committed to durable data until ALL components participating in a transaction indicate completion.

```
    Withdrawal = vRetVal
        oObjectContext.SetComplete
        Exit Function

WithdrawalErrHandler:
  Withdrawal = "ERROR: " & Err.Description
        oObjectContext.SetAbort

End Function
```

When the error handler is fired, we know that an error has occurred and that the transaction should be aborted. By calling the **SetAbort** method of the current object context, the transaction will begin to rollback any changes that were made to durable data during the transaction. The type of error is indicated to the client through the use of the **error** flag along with a more detailed description. This description could either be one generated by Visual Basic, or one of the two errors that could be explicitly raised by this method.

Now that we have the money out of the account, we need to be able to put it in another account somewhere. This is the job for the **Deposit** method.

Bank.Deposit

This method will be used to increase the balance of a specified account. The desired account number and the amount to deposit will be supplied as parameters to the method. As a check, the method will return the amount deposited as its return value. The application can then double check to make sure this was the same amount desired. This method is nearly identical to the **Withdrawal** method. We are including the entire method here for completeness, but will only indicate those few areas that are different.

```
    Public Function Deposit(ByVal vAcctNum As Variant, ByVal vAmount As Variant) As
    Variant
        Dim vRetVal As Variant

        On Error GoTo DepositErrHandler
```

```
Set oObjectContext = GetObjectContext()
Set oDb = oObjectContext.CreateInstance("ADODB.Connection")
oDb.Open vDbConn

vSql = "SELECT * from ACCOUNT WHERE AccountNumber = " & vAcctNum & ";"

Set oRs = oObjectContext.CreateInstance("ADODB.Recordset")
oRs.Open vSql, oDb, adOpenDynamic, adLockOptimistic
```

Up to this point everything is nearly the same. The only difference is that the error information that is
generated if the account number is invalid has been changed.

The primary difference between the **Withdrawal** method and the **Deposit** method is the math used to
compute the new balance in the account. For a deposit, we are adding the deposit amount to the current
balance to arrive at the new balance.

```
If oRs.EOF Then
        Err.Raise vbObjectError + 600, "Deposit", "Invalid Account Number"
    Else
        Dim vNewBal As Variant
        vNewBal = CCur(oRs("Balance") + vAmount)
        oRs("Balance") = vNewBal
        oRs("LastTransaction") = Now
        oRs.Update
        vRetVal = vAmount
    End If

    Deposit = vRetVal
    oObjectContext.SetComplete
    Exit Function

DepositErrHandler:
    oObjectContext.SetAbort
    Deposit = "ERROR: " & Err.Description

End Function
```

We now have a complete component that can be used to transfer money from one account to another. But
these transfers should not take place without some checks and balances. By using MTS to manage the
transfer, we are ensuring that no money will be lost in the system. But to be prudent, we should keep a
record of each transaction. To accomplish this, we will create a **LogTransaction** method to write this
information to a database.

Bank.LogTransaction

When a funds transfer occurs, there should be a record kept so that the accounts can be audited at a later
date. Even though MTS ensures that funds will either be transferred successfully, or not at all, most
financial institutions have strict record keeping requirements. In our application, we will track the type of
transaction, the source and destination account numbers, the amount, and a timestamp indicating when the
transaction took place.

> *We are taking very big liberties with our transaction log format. Since our financial institution only
> support funds transfers, we can afford to be specific in our log format.*

The information that will be logged to the database is passed in as a series of parameters to the method. The failure return value for this method will be the same error flag plus descriptive information that was used in the previous messages. The success return value will be a string containing **'OK'**.

```
Public Function LogTransaction(ByVal vTransType As Variant, ByVal vSrcAcctNum As
Variant, vDestAcctNum As Variant, ByVal vAmount As Variant) As Variant
    Dim vRetVal As Variant

    On Error GoTo LogTransactionErrHandler

    Set oObjectContext = GetObjectContext()
    Set oDb = oObjectContext.CreateInstance("ADODB.Connection")
    oDb.Open vDbConn

    Set oRs = oObjectContext.CreateInstance("ADODB.Recordset")
    oRs.Open "TRANSREC", oDb, adOpenDynamic, adLockOptimistic
```

The **TRANSREC** table in the database will be explicitly opened. Since we are only adding information to the database, and not retrieving any, we do not need to limit the records using a SQL query.

> *The insertion of the transaction information in the database could be done using a SQL **INSERT** statement. If this was the case, then the bulk of this method would be used for building up the string that makes up the **INSERT** statement. Using the ADO Recordset object to add the information just makes for an easier explanation of the database manipulation that is taking place, even though its performance is less than using the SQL **INSERT** statement..*

```
    oRs.AddNew
    oRs("TransactionType") = vTransType
    oRs("SourceAccount") = vSrcAcctNum
    oRs("DestinationAccount") = vDestAcctNum
    oRs("Amount") = vAmount
    oRs("TransTime") = Now
    oRs.Update
    oRs.Close
```

The **AddNew** method of the Recordset object will create a blank record in the recordset. The values for the various fields in the record are then set to the values passed into the method as parameters. The **TransTime** field is a date/time stamp that indicates when the transaction took place. This is set to the current date and time of the server by using the Visual Basic **Now** function. Once all of the fields have been updated, the **Update** method writes the information to the database.

```
    LogTransaction = "OK"
    oObjectContext.SetComplete
    Exit Function

LogTransactionErrHandler:
  LogTransaction = "ERROR: " & Err.Description
    oObjectContext.SetAbort

End Function
```

The component is created using the Make command under the File menu in Visual Basic. This will create the **BankExample.DLL**, an ActiveX DLL that contains our application logic. We now have a complete application component that is ready to add to transaction server in anticipation of creating the application user interface using Active Server Pages.

Deploying the component

To deploy the BankExample component in Transaction Server, we will use the MTS Explorer. This application allows the user to manage the components that are already in MTS, as well as add new components to MTS. When you launch MTS Explorer, you will see a screen like this one:

To get ready to install the new application component, the first step is to create a new package. A package in MTS can hold one or more application components. Usually, a package is roughly associated with an application. You will need to navigate through the Microsoft Transaction Server part of the Console Root tree to the Packages Installed folder. When you get to this point, you will see a listing of all of the packages currently installed on this computer.

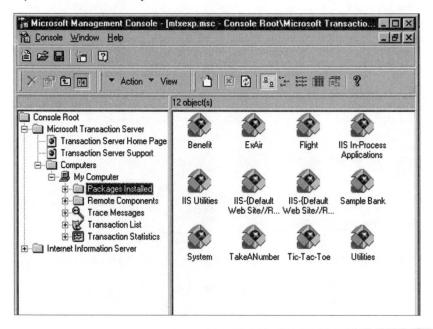

Since this is a new application, you will need to create a new package to hold it. To create a new package: Right-click on Packages Installed in the left pane and select New and then Package.

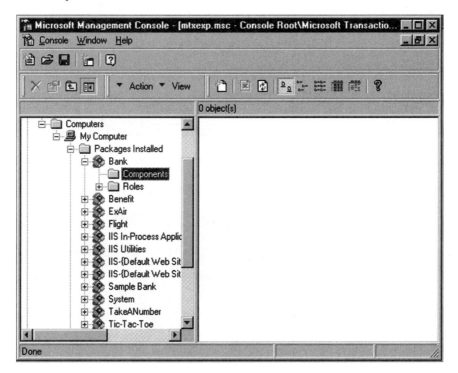

▲ You will be asked if you want to create a pre-built package or create an empty one. Since this is the first time that this application is being installed, choose to create an empty package.

▲ Enter a name for this new package. Call it **Bank**.

▲ Set the identity of the package to the Interactive User. Since this will be accessed from the web server, the **IUSR_ServerName** user will be the user that is accessing the package.

Your new package will now appear in the right hand pane of the MTS Explorer window. Now that you have a package created, you can add your application component to it. Expand the Packages Installed folder, and then expand the new Bank package. There are two folders under Bank: Components and Roles. Select the Components folder.

To add components to the Bank package, right click on the Components folder and select New then Component. The Component wizard will then run.

You can either install a new component, or select from a list of components that have already been registered. Since the **Bank** component has not been registered with MTS yet, choose to install a new component.

From the Install Components dialog box, press the Add files... button and navigate to where you created the **BankExample.DLL** file.

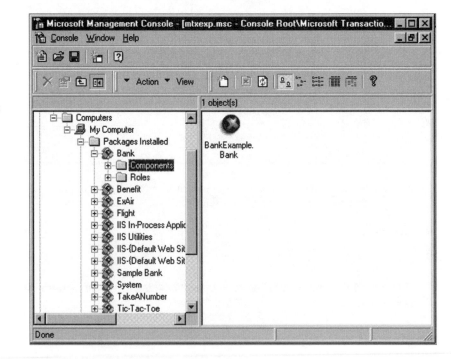

You will now see the file that you selected, along with a list of components contained in that file. Since our **BankExample.DLL** file only contains the **Bank** component, there is only one component listed in the component list. Click on Finish to complete the addition of the component.

You will now see the component in the right hand side of the MTS Explorer window.

The last step that you need to take to finish adding the component to MTS is to set its transaction attribute. If you remember earlier in this chapter, a component has a transaction attribute setting that identifies how it will participate in transactions. By default, a new component will not support transactions. However, we want the **Bank** component to be able to participate in a transaction.

To change this attribute, right-click on the component in the right-hand pane and select properties.

By setting the transaction attribute to Supports Transaction, this component can participate in existing transactions. It is not required to be inside of a transaction, and will not create one if one exists. This gives the component a great deal of flexibility.

Now that the component is successfully installed and configured inside of MTS, we can move on to the final part of our example. We will need a user interface to interact with the application components that we have developed here. This user interface will be web based, developed using Active Server Pages.

Developing the Server Pages

The last step in the development of this example application is to create the ASP scripts that will allow the user to interact with the application. These scripts will use the methods provided by the application object that we have just created. To determine the scripts that need to be created, we will use an approach similar to the one we used when determining the functionality of the application component. By analyzing the steps that the user has to go through to complete the task of transferring funds, we can identify the pieces of data that the user interface must supply at any given time and identify those pieces of data that the user must provide.

If you remember from the assumptions that were made at the beginning of the example, the user is currently logged into the system and has passed through all of the necessary security checkpoints. If we now trace through the steps the user must follow, we can begin to see the different ASP scripts that are needed for the application.

▲ Step 1: Select an account to transfer from. The user should be provided with a list of the accounts that they can transfer the money from.

▲ Step 2: Select an account to transfer to. The user can select from the same list of accounts. These two selections can actually appear on the same page. Since there is no concept of transferring funds between the same account, we should perform some client-side validation to ensure that the users did not select the same account for both.

▲ Step 3: Select the amount to transfer. The user should enter an amount. This could also appear on the same page as the account number selection. This amount needs to be validated at the server using the FundsAvailable method of our application object. If there are insufficient funds, then the user should be notified and asked to reduce the amount to transfer.

▲ Step 4: Transfer the funds. This needs to be carried out in a transaction. The funds should be withdrawn from the source account and deposited in the destination account.

▲ Step 5: Log the transfer. The information about the transfer needs to be logged into the database. Once this has complete successfully, the transaction can be committed and the user notified that everything was accomplished successfully.

From these steps, there looks to be 2 Active Server Pages script files that need to be created. One that will allow the user to select the accounts and the transfer amount. The second will be the script that actually performs the transaction, and then provides the response information to the user.

SelectAccounts.asp

This script will be used to allow the user to select the source account number, the destination account number, and the amount to transfer. To obtain the list of account numbers, it will use the **ListAccounts** method of the **application** object. Since this returns a comma-delimited string containing the list of accounts, the ASP script will need to parse this string to extract the individual account numbers. The user should be able to select the accounts for the transfer from a drop-down list. There will be some client-side validation code that will check to make sure that the account numbers for the source and destination are different. This will be called when the user attempts to submit the form.

The user will also be given a text box in which to type the amount for the transfer. This amount will be validated when the form is submitted to the server to ensure that the source has sufficient funds to make the transfer. If the funds are not sufficient, then the server will redirect the client back to this script.

```
<%
Option Explicit

dim custID
custID = 1
```

Since this is just an example, we are setting the customer **ID** to **1**. In a real application, this value could either come from a form value, a URL parameter, or from a session-level variable.

```
dim bNSF 'Set to TRUE if page is being displayed due to insufficient funds
bNSF = False
dim srcAcct, destAcct, xferAmt

if Request.QueryString("src") <> "" then
    bNSF = True
    srcAcct = Request.QueryString("src")
    destAcct = Request.QueryString("dest")
    xferAmt = Request.QueryString("xfer")
end if

dim objBank
Set objBank = Server.CreateObject("BankExample.Bank")
```

The **bNSF** flag is used to indicate if this page is being displayed as a result of the user's selected source account having insufficient funds to perform the transfer. You will see in the **Transfer.asp** file how this is determined. The values that the user had selected for source and destination accounts, as well as the amount of the transfer, are passed back to this script as part of the URL. These values will be displayed as the default values in the form on this page. For now, the values are stored in temporary variables.

Since we will be generating a list of accounts, we will first need a reference to the application object. The 'BankExample.Bank' string is the name of our component as it appears in the system registry.

```
dim strAccounts
strAccounts = objBank.ListAccounts(custID)

dim arAcct(), iArraySize, iAcctNums
iAcctNums = 0
iArraySize = 5
redim arAcct(iArraySize)
```

The **ListAccounts** method of the **Bank** object is called to return a list of accounts. The **customerID** is supplied as a parameter. The return value will be a comma-delimited list of accounts, which will be parsed in the next step.

```
dim iPos, iSrch, strAcct
iPos = 1
iSrch = Instr(iPos, strAccounts, ",")
do while not iSrch = 0
    strAcct = Mid(strAccounts, iPos, iSrch-iPos)
    arAcct(iAcctNums) = strAcct
    iAcctNums = iAcctNums + 1
    if iAcctNums = iArraySize then
            iArraySize = iArraySize + 5
            Redim preserve arAcct(iArraySize)
    end if
    iPos = iSrch + 1
    iSrch = Instr(iPos, strAccounts, ",")
loop
```

The value that is returned from the **ListAccounts** method will be a string that looks something like this: "**1234,6789,5432**". This will need to be parsed into an array, so that the array can be used to build a drop-down list box. The parsing routine will sequentially move through the string location each comma.

Each account number can then be extracted and stored in the **arAcct** array. This array is dynamically resized as needed. Rather than resizing the array every time a new entry is added, which would have a big cost in terms of performance, the array is increased in size by 5 each time it is resized.

```
strAcct = Mid(strAccounts, iPos, len(strAccounts))
arAcct(iAcctNums) = strAcct
iAcctNums = iAcctNums + 1

%>
<HTML>
<SCRIPT Language="JavaScript">
```

When we can find no more commas in the string, we still need to copy the final account number in the string. Since the end of the string, not a comma terminates this account number, it will not be caught by the parsing loop. This final account number needs to be added to the account number array.

We will be performing client-side validation of the form entry to ensure that three cases are not true.

- The Source Account number cannot be the same as the Destination Account number
- There must be a value in the Transfer Amount field
- The value in the Transfer Amount field must be greater than zero.

This validation is done using JavaScript, rather than VBScript, so that the client browser can be any browser that supports JavaScript, rather than just Internet Explorer.

```
<!--
function sendForm()
    {
            var xAmount;
        if (document.xfer.SourceAccount.value==document.xfer.DestAccount.value)
```

Examining the value property of the **SourceAccount** or **DestAccount** member of the **xfer** form collection, which is all part of the document object, retrieves the values that were selected for the Source Account and the Destination Account. If the values are the same, then a JavaScript alert is shown to the user.

```
    {
        alert("You cannot transfer to the same account.");
            return;
    }
        xAmount = parseFloat(document.xfer.xferAmt.value);
    if (xAmount == 0.0 || isNaN(xAmount))
```

The value contained in the Transfer Amount field is converted to a float value by using the JavaScript **parseFloat** method. To check to see if there is a value entered, we check to see if the float value is **0** or if it is set to **NaN**. NaN is a JavaScript constant that indicates that the value could not be converted to a numeric value. If this is the case, then we alert the user, again using the JavaScript alert.

```
    {
        alert("You must supply an amount to transfer.");
            return;
```

```
            }
        if (xAmount < 0.0 )
```

Finally, if the amount is less than **0**, we alert the user that they cannot transfer a negative amount. After each alert, this function returns to the caller. You will see when we get to the **<FORM>** tag how the form is prevented from being submitted. Finally, if all three validations are successful, then the form is explicitly submitted using the **submit** method of the form object.

```
        {
            alert("You cannot transfer a negative amount.");
                return;
        }
        document.xfer.submit();
    }
//-->
</SCRIPT>

<HEAD>
<TITLE>Account Transfer</TITLE>
</HEAD>
<BODY>
```

The **bNSF** flag indicates that the Source Account that the user selected does not have sufficient funds to complete the transfer. If this flag is set, then a message is displayed to the user that the transfer amount is too high and needs to be adjusted.

```
<% If bNSF then %>
<H2>Insufficient funds to complete transfer. Please adjust the amount.</h2>
<% End If %>
<FORM name="xfer" action="transfer.asp" method="POST"
onSubmit="sendForm();return(false);">
```

The **<FORM>** tag will submit the results of this form to the **Transfer.asp** script file for processing. When the user clicks the submit button, the **onSubmit** handler is called. The handler will first call the **sendForm** function that was declared earlier. If this function returns, which means that the values selected did not pass the validation routines, then the **onSubmit** handler returns false. This action will prevent the form from being submitted, and allow the user to make changes to their entries.

```
<H3>Select an account to transfer from: 
<SELECT name="SourceAccount">
<%
    dim iCnt
    for iCnt = 0 to iAcctNums - 1
            if arAcct(iCnt) = srcAcct then
%>
<option value="<%= arAcct(iCnt) %>" SELECTED><%= arAcct(iCnt) %>
<% Else  %>
<option value="<%= arAcct(iCnt) %>"><%= arAcct(iCnt) %>
<% End If %>
<% next %>
</SELECT>
```

The Source Account drop down list is created by going through each of the entries in the array of account numbers that was created earlier. If the account number is the same as the source account number then that value will be selected. This technique relies on the fact the VBScript initializes all variables to **0** or blank values. In the case where this page is being displayed without default values, then the value of **srcAcct** will always be blank, and therefore no option will be explicitly selected.

```
</H3>
<H3>Select an amount to transfer: 
<% If bNSF then %>
<input type="Text" name="xferAmt" value="<%= xferAmt %>" size="10">
<% Else %>
<input type="Text" name="xferAmt" size="10">
<% End If %>
</H3>
```

The text box for entering the amount of the transfer is displayed next. If the insufficient funds flag is set, then the value that the user had previously selected is entered as the default value for the text box. Otherwise, this box is initially left blank. Next, the destination account drop-down list is displayed. This code is identical to the code to display the source account list.

```
<H3>Select an account to transfer to: 
<SELECT name="DestAccount">
<%
    for iCnt = 0 to iAcctNums - 1
            if arAcct(iCnt) = destAcct then
%>
<option value="<%= arAcct(iCnt) %>" SELECTED><%= arAcct(iCnt) %>
<% Else  %>
<option value="<%= arAcct(iCnt) %>"><%= arAcct(iCnt) %>
<% End If %>
<% next %>
</SELECT>
</H3>
<input type="Submit" name="" value="Transfer Funds">
```

Finally a **Submit** button is displayed that allows the user to submit the form for processing. We could have also displayed a reset button that would have automatically cleared that values entered in the fields. For such a short form, this is probably unnecessary.

```
</FORM>
</BODY>
</HTML>
```

When this page is
displayed in the user's
browser, it will look like
this:

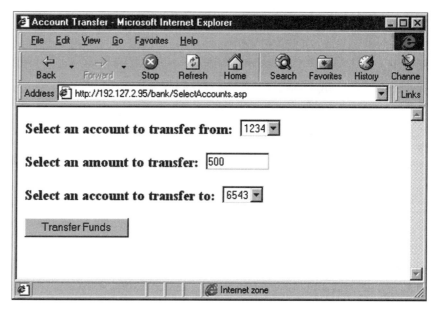

Now that we have the page to gather the information for the transfer from the user, we need to create the
Transfer.asp script. This script will perform the actual work to transfer the funds.

Transfer.asp

The **Transfer.asp** script is responsible for actually processing the funds transfer. The initial step that this
script must perform is to check to see if the source account has sufficient funds to perform the transfer. If it
does, then the script will withdraw the funds from the source account and then deposit the funds in the
destination account. When this is completed successfully, a record of the transfer is written to the
transaction log. When all of these steps have completed successfully, the transaction is committed. If any
one of these steps fail, then the entire transaction is rolled back.

```
<%@ TRANSACTION=Required %>
<%
Option Explicit

dim objBank
Set objBank = Server.CreateObject("BankExample.Bank")

dim srcAcct, destAcct, xferAmt
srcAcct = Request.Form("SourceAccount")
destAcct = Request.Form("DestAccount")
xferAmt = Request.Form("xferAmt")

dim bSufficientFunds
bSufficientFunds = objBank.FundsAvailable(srcAcct, xferAmt)
```

This page will be a single transaction. To identify this, the **TRANSACTION** parameter is set to **Required**.
This will force this page to participate in a transaction. Since a transaction cannot span multiple ASP script
pages, a new transaction will have to be created to encompass this page.

A reference to the application object is created. The values that were submitted on the form from the **SelectAccounts** page are stored in local variables. Since these values will have to be accessed multiple times on this page, storing their values in local variables will allow for faster access times than having to search the **Request.Form** collection. It also makes the code more readable and concise.

The **FundsAvailable** method is called to check that the amount of funds requested for transfer is available in the source account. If this method returns **False**, then the user will need to change the amount or select a different source account. In the **SelectAccounts.asp** script, there is code to support this. We need to redirect the browser to display this page with the user's values. This is done by using the **Response.redirect** method, and supplying the values from the form as URL parameters.

```
if not bSufficientFunds then
     Response.redirect "SelectAccounts.asp?src=" & srcAcct & "&dest=" & destAcct &
"&xfer=" & xferAmt
end if

%>
<HTML>
<HEAD>
<TITLE>Account Transfer</TITLE>
</HEAD>
<BODY>
<H3>Transfer in Progress</H3>
<HR>
<%
dim cWithdrawl, cDeposit, cTransRec, strError
cWithdrawl = objBank.Withdrawal(srcAcct,xferAmt)
```

The first step in performing the transaction is to withdraw the funds from the source account. The return value from this method will either be the amount that was withdrawn, or it will be an error. A string that begins with "**ERROR**" flags the error. We check to see if there was an error or if the amounts do not match. If neither of these are true, we can continue with processing.

The next step is to deposit the amount withdrawn into the destination account. At this point, if there were transaction fees that the bank wanted to apply, the amount of these fees could be deducted at this time.

Again, the return value of the **Deposit** method is checked to see if the amounts do not match or an error flag is encountered. If everything is successful, then the transfer is logged by using **LogTransaction** method.

```
if Left(CStr(cWithdrawl),5) <> "ERROR" or cWithdrawl = xferAmt then
    cDeposit = objBank.Deposit(destAcct,cWithdrawl)
    if Left(CStr(cDeposit),5) <> "ERROR"  or cDeposit = xferAmt then
          cTransRec = objBank.LogTransaction("TRANS", srcAcct, destAcct, xferAmt)
    else
```

This is the error handler for the **Deposit** method. If something happened that caused the method to fail, then the error message would be supplied in the return value. This is stored in a variable for later display to the user. The transaction is then explicitly aborted. While the **Deposit** method may have also aborted the transaction, there is no harm in having the script abort the transaction as well. All it takes is one part of a transaction signaling an abort to cause the entire transaction to be aborted.

```
                strError = cDeposit
                ObjectContext.SetAbort
        end if
   else
```

This is the error handler for the **Withdrawal** method. It is the same as the **Deposit** error handler, except it will store the result of the **Withdrawal** method for later display as an error.

```
        strError = cWithdrawl
        ObjectContext.SetAbort
   end if
```

The results of the transaction are displayed for the user by handling the transactional events that are generated. If the transaction completes successfully, then the **OnTransactionCommit** event will be fired. The handler for this event will display a message indicating successful completion of the transaction, as well as a statement documenting the details of the transfer.

```
sub OnTransactionCommit()
    response.write "<H4>Transaction Completed Successfully</H4>"
    Response.write "<H4>" & FormatCurrency(xferAmt) & " transferred from Account #" &
srcAcct & " to Account #" & destAcct & ".</H4>" & vbcrlf
    end sub
```

If the transaction is aborted, then the **OnTransactionAbort** event will be fired. The handler will display a message that the transaction was unable to complete. The error message that was generated by the component that failed will be displayed for the user.

```
sub OnTransactionAbort()
    response.write "Unable to complete the transaction<BR>"
    Response.Write strError
    end sub

%>
</BODY>
</HTML>
```

When the transaction completes successfully, you will see a page similar to this in your browser:

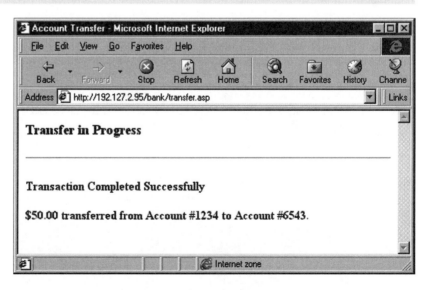

479

Next Steps

This example showed the basics of creating an application component that can participate in transaction server processing. It also showed how to create ASP scripts that used these components, and participate in transactions as well. There are a number of possible ways that this application could be extended and enhanced.

 Enhance the display of information to the user, by displaying account balances and past transaction history.

 Support user registration and login.

 Use Remote Scripting, as covered in Appendix F, to provide the funds availability validation without having to submit the entire form to the server.

Even with these extensions and enhancements, the basics about working with transactional components and MTS will remain the same.

Summary

This chapter has introduced you to the concept of transaction processing and how it is supported in Microsoft Transaction Server. As you come away from this chapter, the key points that you should remember are:

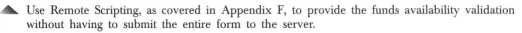 Transaction processing consists of applications composed of components, which are designed as single-user objects. These components are scalable to large numbers of users, with the system ensuring application integrity.

▲ Transaction processing provides support for the multi-tier application model. This model makes it easy to build distributed applications. The system ensures that transactions are atomic, consistent, isolated, and durable.

▲ Microsoft Transaction Server provides transaction processing services, consisting of a run-time environment, graphical user interface for management, and an application programming interface.

▲ The integration of Microsoft Transaction Server and Internet Information Server provide for services such as transactional Active Server Pages, crash protection for IIS applications, transactional events, object context for IIS objects, and common installation and management

▲ Issues relating to the design of transactional components included holding state in components, threading model selection, object scope, and tools for creating components

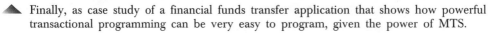 Finally, as case study of a financial funds transfer application that shows how powerful transactional programming can be very easy to program, given the power of MTS.

Now that we have introduced the concept of transactional processing, the next few chapters will be spent covering a detailed case study. This case study will use many of the concepts that were covered in this chapter, and will introduce a number of new concepts as well.

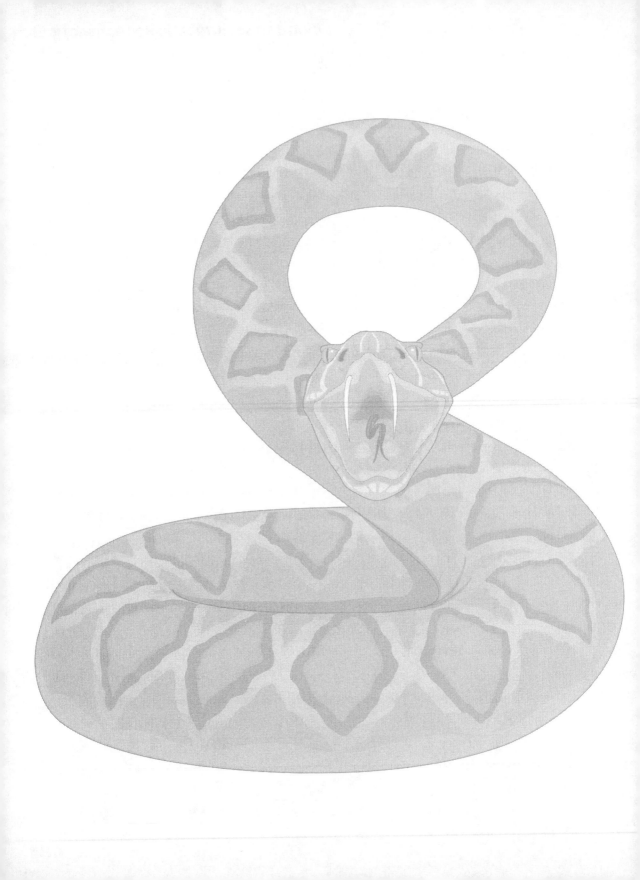

Implementing ASP Security

Many commercial organizations may regard the risks of doing business in cyberspace as unacceptable—but the rapid expansion of this powerful delivery channel means they make such decisions at their peril. The use of the Internet is no longer an option—any hesitation means that their rivals will gain a considerable head start in using this potent technology.

There is also a lot of unfortunate and ignorant hype over Internet security. Scare stories are often generated by the same people who are quite happy to hand over a credit card to complete strangers in a shop and allow them to swipe, and potentially copy, their credit card details. Like any commercial activity, the risks of using the Internet should be put in perspective. There now exists a comprehensive set of technologies enabling companies to build secure business applications for deployment over the Internet. To perform accurate risk analysis, it is important to understand what levels of protection each one provides.

In this chapter we shall address in depth the fundamental security technologies that are relevant to the Internet Information Server with Active Server Pages, and show how the Windows NT Web technologies provide the foundations of a bulletproof Internet solution. We will be covering security issues in four different but related areas:

- Understanding and assessing the risks we face on the Internet
- The security features available from the NT operating system and IIS
- How we can use Secure Channel Services for our transactions
- The effect Active Server Pages has on the security of our site

But first, a little history...

Stand and Deliver!

In days gone by, evil highwaymen, like the infamous Dick Turpin, patrolled the rough dirt tracks of Old England. They preyed on wayfarers and their possessions, thus causing fear throughout the land. Only when the protection of the travelers and their cargo could be assured were these rough tracks able to evolve into viable highways and therefore provide the essential communications infrastructure for modern business and human lifestyle.

Today's so-called information superhighways are now going through a similar inaugural phase. Only when business has confidence that the systems cannot be infiltrated, and network information can pass unimpeded will, electronic commerce—on a worldwide scale—intensify. We are on the way there, but there is still a long road lying out there in front of us.

Problems on the Internet

The security needs of Internet-based systems are very different from traditional networking. For example, there is no centralized infrastructure providing responsibility for network security. It is also on a huge global scale, with connected systems being open to a user base of potentially many millions. The initial conception and implementation of the Internet was to provide openness and robustness, and ensure the network was always available for all computers to connect to it. Even though the Internet was originally a network built for 'national defense', the security of confidential information was considered secondary, because only trusted users had access to it.

In order for a business to access the full potential of the Internet and the huge user base, it must open its network and provide a shop window to promote its affairs. While most visitors will be happy to look through this window, there will always be a few 'Peeping Toms' who will attempt to see things never intended for public scrutiny. Worse still, a small number of resourceful people will go one step further–and attempt to break the window, climb through, and undoubtedly cause concern and damage.

The bandits of today's superhighway can be classified into three groups:

- **The Charlatans**—those who impersonate either an existing or a false person/organization. For example, consider the purchase of a book from a web site. How can you be confident that the vendor is really a legitimate business? Could your credit details have been sent to some imposter? Alternatively, how can the vendor be confident they are dealing with a legitimate customer?

- **The Spies**—those who access confidential information. For example, consider the transfer of some business plans via electronic mail. How can you be confident that these details are not being intercepted? Could they get passed on to your direct competitors?

- **The Vandals**—those who tamper with data. For example, consider the payment of your electricity bill via an Internet home banking service. How can you be confident that the instructions have not been interfered with? Could the target account get altered, and the payment transaction redirected to someone else's account?

Of course, some of these loathsome rogues, or 'hackers', will be resident in more than one of these groups. As Internet technology expands, these people are always finding new and ingenious mechanisms for their attacks. Unfortunately, the severe damage they can cause is often not discovered until it is too late.

If Internet communications are to become a key component in an organization's IT strategy, a set of technologies and standards to outmanoeuver these bandits is required. The technologies that we will discuss in this chapter, in order to provide secure Active Server Pages solutions, are Windows NT Security and Secure Channel Services.

Windows NT Security Systems

The starting point for strong Internet security is the operating system of any machine connected to it. Fortunately for the organizations using IIS 4.0, strong levels of security were built into the core of Windows NT in order to meet and exceed certifiable security standards, i.e. the C2 security guidelines required by the U.S. Department of Defense's evaluation criteria. Windows NT security contrasts sharply with the thin and weak security layers that are bolted on to the top of some other operating systems.

Compliance with the C2 security standard was originally only required for government organizations. However, many commercial organizations are demanding the same level of security, and they recognize the value that such standards offer. The main requirements for C2 compliance are:

 User identification and authentication. Before gaining access to the systems, a user must prove their identity. This is typically done by providing a user-id / password combination, for example by entering the details via a keyboard or by the presentation of a device such as a smart card which stores such information.

 Discretionary access control. Each object within the system, for example files, printers and processes, must have an owner–who can grant or restrict access to the resources at various degrees of granularity.

▲ **Auditing Capabilities.** The system must provide the ability to log all user actions and object access, and include enough information to identify the user that performed any operation. Such information must only be accessible by system administrators.

▲ **Safe Object reuse.** The system must guarantee that any discarded or deleted object cannot be accessed, either accidentally or deliberately, by other entities.

▲ **System integrity.** The system must protect resources belonging to one entity, from being interfered with by another entity.

The C2 guidelines are applicable to standalone systems, and are specified in the document Trusted Computer System Evaluation Criteria (TCSEC). Fortunately, to make life simpler, this is often referred to as the **Orange Book**, thanks to the color of its cover. Other specifications that expand on the Orange Book include the Red Book for networking, and the Blue Book for subsystems.

Obtaining C2 certification is a long and complex task, and Microsoft are pushing hard for complete certification. Windows NT has passed the Orange Book certification process (for a standalone PC, not connected to a network) and is on the DOD's official list of evaluated products. At the time of writing, Windows NT 4.0 is undergoing Red and Blue book evaluations.

NT Directory Services

The following section is a crash course in **NT Directory Services** (NTDS). It is not intended to compete with the numerous books that are dedicated to NT administration, but is included to define various concepts that are used in the remainder of this chapter.

Directory Services is one of the services provided by NT. It enables a user to be identified, and provides access to the various resources throughout the systems and networks. In addition, it allows a system administrator to manage the users and the network, from any system on that network.

The reader should be aware that the future plans for Windows NT 5.0 include the **Active Directory**, which will be the next generation of NT Directory Services. This extends the previous Windows-based directory services and will provide a single administration point for locating and managing all system resources–the Active Directory will contain items such as: users, printers, email addresses, databases, fax servers, distributed components and so on. It is designed to scale to the largest of enterprises and contain millions of items that could be distributed over many thousands of computers. Wrox Press will be bringing a book out focussing on the Active Directory in the near future.

Understanding User Accounts

Everyone who has access to an NT system is identified by a **user account**, which comprises of a user name, a password, and a number of logon parameters that are applied to that user; for example, the location of a script file that is automatically invoked at logon. A special NT user account is that of the **administrator**. Initially it is actually called Administrator, but this really should be renamed: there is no point in giving a potential hacker half the account details for free!

The administrator has complete control over the system, including the ability to create, amend and delete user accounts. The management of user accounts is done using the User Manager utility that is usually found by selecting the Start | Programs | Administrative Tools menus.

Another special user account created during NT installation is the guest account–initially called Guest and is disabled. This is designed for people who require temporary access to the system.

Ideally, the administrators will assign meaningful names to the user accounts, however these names are only used externally. Internally, NT handles user account names by using a one-to-one mapping with a unique identifier called the **Security ID** (SID). Even if a user account is deleted and then recreated with identical name, password, and logon parameters, it will be assigned a new SID. The internal SID value is never exposed to any users–including administrators.

Understanding User Groups

A group is a collection of user accounts, and is a powerful mechanism for granting common capabilities to a number of accounts in one operation. This is extremely useful when administrating systems with a large number of accounts. Groups are created, and users added into the groups, with the same User Manager utility as manages user accounts.

There are a number of predefined groups, including:

Administrators	users having full system control.
Users	users that can perform tasks for which they have been granted rights.
Guests	users requiring temporary access to the system.
Server Operators	users that can manage server resources
Account Operators	users that can manage user accounts.
Backup Operators	users that can back up and restore files.
Print Operators	users that can manage printers.

Understanding Domains

A **domain** is a logical group of computers that share a set of common user accounts and security information–this is stored in a central Directory Services database. A version of the User Manager, called the User Manager for Domains, is used to maintain the users and users groups in a domain.

A domain includes one NT server designated as the **Primary Domain Controller** (PDC) that is responsible for storing the master users database. In addition, one or more **Backup Domain Controllers** (BDC's) may exist, which maintain a copy of the PDC's users database. The PDC and BDCs ensure that the various copies of the users databases are kept synchronized.

A user may logon to a domain, using any connected computer, and is validated by either a PDC or a BDC. The BDCs can share the workload in a heavily used network, and provide redundancy in case a PDC becomes unavailable. A PDC and BDC can also be an application server; for example, it can also host the Internet Information Server. In large enterprises, multiple domains may exist to reflect the business or territorial structure of the organization. It is possible to share resources across domains by setting up **Trust Relationships**.

However, the whole process of designing and setting up domains is outside the scope and concept of this book–we are assuming that you already have your internal network up and running, and you want to know more about how an Internet connection, and Active Server Pages, will affect it.

Understanding Access Rights

Once a user has successfully logged on to the domain, the NT security system dictates what resources that user may access. Different resources have different levels of access, and it is up to the users in the administrators and operators groups to define what level of access each user may have.

The User Rights Policy dialog within the User Manager utility can help to manage the rights granted to groups and user accounts. The security system will block any action by a user that does not have the appropriate rights.

User rights are applicable to the system functions and differ from permissions that regulate as to what level a user can access an individual object (such as a file or printer).

The following permissions can be assigned to a user for accessing a particular directory or file:

Read (R)	Allows viewing the names of files and subdirectories/file data.
Write (W)	Allows adding files and subdirectories/changing the file data.
Execute (X)	Allows running the file if it is a program file.
Delete (D)	Allows the deleting of a directory/file.
Change Permissions (P)	Allows changing the directory/file permissions.
Take Ownership (O)	Allows taking ownership of the directory/file.

Windows NT disks are either formatted as **FAT** (**File Allocation Table**) or **NTFS** (**NT File System**). Individual files resident on disks that are formatted as FAT do not have any security, and can only take the permissions of their parent directory. NTFS offers a greater level of security, since individual files can have their own specific permissions assigned.

Windows Explorer is used to apply or change the permissions of files and directories for individual users and groups. This is done by right-clicking on the appropriate directories, or files, and selecting the Properties option. In the Properties dialog, select the Security tab, followed by the Permissions button.

The security information of an object is stored in a **Security Descriptor**. This includes the name of the object owner and something called an **Access Control List** (ACL). The ACL is a list of user accounts and groups (i.e. SIDs), and their associated access permissions. Each entry in the ACL is called an **Access Control Entry** (ACE).

Once a user's logon has been successfully validated, the system produces a **Security Access Token** (SAT). This is attached to any process invoked by that user. The SAT identifies the user, and is applied during all interactions with secured objects to determine the level of access allowed. All these terms are clarified in this diagram:

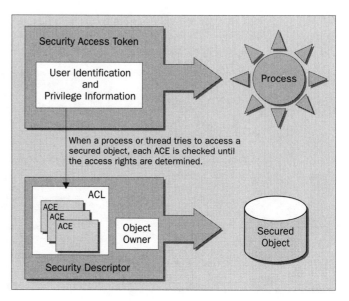

Internet Server Security

Having taken a brief tour of the security features of Windows NT Server, we shall now discuss how security is applied to users accessing our web site and see how we need to change our view of network security when we come to connect to the Internet.

In this section, we move on to see how security issues apply to Active Server Pages.

File Access Controls

The IIS 4.0, ISAPI and ASP facilities are built upon the NTDS security model. This means that all files and directories are protected by ACL permissions, applied as described above. All users accessing the IIS 4.0 **WWW** service are either given guest access or authenticated (as we will see shortly), and then given appropriate access to the various objects.

In Chapter 1 we saw that the **WWW** service restricts the files on the server that can be accessed to those that are resident in the home directory, any virtual directories and any subdirectories in the hierarchy beneath.

The Directory's **Access Permissions** allows **Read** and **Write** permissions to be applied to the contents of IIS 4.0 directories. Enabling these checkboxes allows:

- Read—when enabled, the Web users may read or download files located in the directory
- Write—when enabled, the Web users may upload files or change the content of files located in the directory

Furthermore, the Application Settings Permissions specify whether applications located in this directory may be executed. The options are:

▲ None—no items located in this directory may be invoked

▲ Script—only scripts, such as ASP documents, located in this directory may be invoked

▲ Execute—any application located in this directory may be invoked

IP Access Security Issues

This section describes some of the security options available for TCP/IP (Transmission Control Protocol/Internet Protocol). This is the communications protocol used by the Internet or an Intranet. Most of the protocol's configuration is complex, and well beyond the scope of this book. This chapter's focus is intended to highlight the security options available, and not get sucked into any of the low-level complexities of data communications—there are numerous books available dedicated exclusively to TCP/IP. What we are interested in is what we need to do to ensure secure operation.

All machines on the Internet (or an Intranet) are uniquely identified by four 8-bit numbers collectively known as an **IP address**. IIS 4.0 can be configured to either allow or deny access from any particular IP addresses. At first glance, you might think that this would provide a good mechanism for providing access control. However, the lack of available IP addresses has meant that many networks use techniques for randomly allocating IP addresses from an available pool, such as DHCP, when the client first starts—so in this case, you could not guarantee the identity of the user from the IP address.

The configuration of allowed/denied IP addresses is done using the IP Address and Domain Name Restrictions Manager section of the Directory Security property sheet.

In addition to IP addresses, all communication channels over the Internet / Intranet are identified by a number called a **port**. The value of the port number identifies the type of service operating on the channel. Some port numbers are reserved for common Internet services, for example:

21	**FTP**—File Transfer Protocol
23	**Telnet**—Terminal Emulation
25	**SMTP**—Simple Mail Transfer Protocol (email)
70	**Gopher**—navigation and file transfer of internet resources
80	**HTTP**—Hypertext Transfer Protocol (WWW)
119	**NNTP**—Network News Transfer Protocol (newsgroups)
194	**IRC**—Internet Relay Chat (conferencing)
443	**HTTPS**—Secure HTTP

Beginning with version 4.0, NT has the ability to filter IP protocol packets–allowing Internet services on particular ports to be either allowed or denied. Since you can use this to disable superfluous Internet services, NT can act in a similar way to a simple **firewall**. For example, you could configure NT with two network cards: one used to connect to the Internet, and the other to your LAN. Internet services on the Internet network card could be restricted to, for example, port **80** (HTTP) and port **21** (FTP). External access to any other services would be denied. To allow ASP full access to resources on the corporate LAN, all ports on the LAN network card would be enabled. This is shown here:

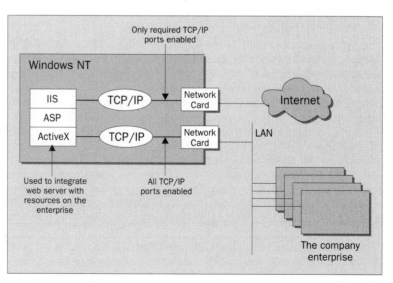

IP port filtering is enabled by means of the Network Control Panel. Select TCP/IP Properties on the Protocols tab. This provides an Advanced button, which displays a dialog including the Enable Security checkbox and a Configure button. This button finally produces another dialog where you can specify the filtering of ports.

To ensure that the TCP/IP stack does not transfer packets between the two network cards, the Enable IP Forwarding option on the TCP/IP properties must be unchecked.

If the clients accessing our site are within a known set of approved users, or a closed user group, we can make life awkward for casual surfers by changing the port number of our WWW service. The port number is configured using the Web Site property sheet. Users can access the HTTP service on a different port by specifying the port number as part of the URL. For example:

```
http://hornet.wrox.com:8080/
```

This would be a web HTTP request on port **8080**. Conventional requests, which did not include the port number, would fail.

User Authentication by the Web Server

In order to apply NT security to the access of HTML, Active Server Pages, and other files, every user accessing the web site must be associated with an NT user account. The process of determining the user's identity, and having confidence that it really is that person, is known as **authentication**.

Looking back at Authentication Methods dialog on the Directory Security property sheet, we can see that the WWW Properties page allows the following different authentication mechanisms to be configured:

Anonymous	A mechanism to allow access by a guest account user.
Basic Authentication	A mechanism to provide simple authentication as defined in the HTTP specifications by the World Wide Web Consortium (W3C), and the Organisation Européenne pour la Recherche Nucléaire (CERN–where the WWW was originally conceived).
Windows NT Challenge/Response	A mechanism developed by Microsoft to securely authenticate users.

The checkboxes for all of these methods work independently. This means that it is possible to enable multiple authentication mechanisms, and for the appropriate one to be automatically used for a request.

The IUSR Account – Anonymous Authentication

When IIS 4.0 is installed, it creates a user account called IUSR_*sysname,* where *sysname* is the computer name of the NT system, as specified in the Identification tab of the Network Control Panel. This account is assigned to the Guests account group, allocated a random password, and given the user right to Log On Locally—which is a prerequisite to access the IIS 4.0 WWW services. Provided that Anonymous authentication has been enabled, users accessing WWW services are allowed access to those resources with the permissions allocated to the IUSR_*sysname* account.

The Edit button on the Authentication Methods dialog allows the configuration of the Anonymous user.

> The IIS 4.0 installation also creates another user account called IWAM_*sysname.*
> When we create Web applications that use process isolation, IIS 4.0 creates an MTS package that is set to run under the IWAM_*sysname* identity. This is discussed in Chapter 1.

Basic and Challenge/Response Authentication

Both the Basic Authentication and the Windows NT Challenge / Response mechanism, work in a similar fashion. If the user requests a resource for which the IUSR_*sysname* user account does not have the appropriate permissions, the request is rejected with a 401 Access Denied message, and the browser is informed through HTTP what authentication methods the server *will* support.

Provided that a least one of these two authentication methods has been enabled, most modern browsers will then prompt the user for a user name and password, and submit these details with another request for the same resource. IIS 4.0 will then validate the user account details supplied and, if successful, invoke the request under the identity of this user rather than the IUSR_*sysname* account–thus having access to those resources for which the user account has permissions assigned. The difference between Basic Authentication and Windows NT Challenge/Response is that the latter provides encryption of the user name and password, whereas Basic Authentication sends this information as normal 'clear' text. At the time of writing, the only browser to support NT Challenge/Response is Microsoft's Internet Explorer.

> The undesirable transmission of user names and passwords as clear text can be overcome using Secure Channel Services encryption – which we will meet shortly.

Another big advantage of using NT Challenge/Response methods and Internet Explorer in an Intranet environment is that, should the user be currently logged on to an NT domain, their user account name and password will automatically be tried. This avoids the need to duplicate any logon process when retrieving files. Hence, access by different users to different sets of files and information can be secured–transparently and automatically in a normal LAN-like manner.

Authentication in Action

The following HTTP trace files show WWW authentication in action. Firstly, **Anonymous Authentication**, where IUSR_*sysname* has Read permission for the file **/rich/rhnav.htm**:

29/12/97 23:40:23 Sent GET /rich/rhnav.htm HTTP/1.0 Accept: image/gif, image/x-xbitmap, image/jpeg, image/pjpeg, application/vnd.ms-excel, application/msword, application/vnd.ms-powerpoint, */* Accept-Language: en UA-pixels: 800x600 UA-color: color8 UA-OS: Windows NT UA-CPU: x86 User-Agent: Mozilla/2.0 (compatible; MSIE 3.0B; Win32) Host: 194.1.1.32 Connection: Keep-Alive --	*This is the request message sent from the browser to the web server, to request the resource.*

29/12/97 23:40:23 Received HTTP/1.0 200 OK Server: Microsoft-IIS/4.0 Connection: keep-alive Date: Wed, 29 Dec 1997 23:40:23 GMT Content-Type: text/html Accept-Ranges: bytes Last-Modified: Sat, 11 Dec 1997 19:34:16 GMT Content-Length: 1653 <html> …. etc …. </html> --	*This is the response message, including the contents of the requested HTML file.*

Here, the request contains no account information about the user, just the usual HTTP Host IP address. The server logs on to NT using the IUSR_*sysname* account, and finds that it can access and retrieve the file–so it can return it to the requestor.

Next, we will see how **Basic Authentication** works. Both Anonymous Authentication and Basic Authentication have been enabled in the **WWW Properties** dialog. The difference this time is that the IUSR_*sysname* account does *not* have Read permission for the file:

30/12/97 14:52:49 Sent GET /rich/rhnav.htm HTTP/1.0 Accept: image/gif, image/x-xbitmap, image/jpeg, image/pjpeg, application/vnd.ms-excel, application/msword, application/vnd.ms-powerpoint, */* Accept-Language: en UA-pixels: 800x600 UA-color: color8	*This is the request message sent from the browser to the web server, to request the file. It is the same as the last time, of course, with no user account information.*

UA-OS: Windows NT
UA-CPU: x86
User-Agent: Mozilla/2.0 (compatible; MSIE 3.0B; Win32)
Host: 194.1.1.32
Connection: Keep-Alive

30/12/97 14:52:49 Received   HTTP/1.0 401 Access Denied
WWW-Authenticate: Basic realm="194.1.1.32"
Content-Length: 24
Content-Type: text/html
Error: Access is Denied.

30/12/97 14:53:23 Sent   GET /rich/rhnav.htm HTTP/1.0
Accept: image/gif, image/x-xbitmap, image/jpeg, image/pjpeg,
application/vnd.ms-excel, application/msword, application/vnd.ms-powerpoint, */*
Accept-Language: en
UA-pixels: 800x600
UA-color: color8
UA-OS: Windows NT
UA-CPU: x86
User-Agent: Mozilla/2.0 (compatible; MSIE 3.0B; Win32)
Host: 194.1.1.32
Connection: Keep-Alive
Authorization: Basic YWRtaW5pc3RyYXRvcjpob3JuZXXU=

  30/12/97 14:53:23 Received

      HTTP/1.0 200 OK
Server: Microsoft-IIS/4.0
Connection: keep-alive
Date: Thu, 30 Dec 1997 14:53:23 GMT
Content-Type: text/html
Accept-Ranges: bytes
Last-Modified: Wed, 22 Dec 1997 09:18:08 GMT
Content-Length: 909
<html>
...... etc ......
</html>

This is the response rejecting access, as the IUSR account does not have appropriate permissions. In the second line it informs the browser that Basic Authentication is enabled.

The browser then prompts for the user name and password.

This is the new request message (now including the account information) sent from the browser to the web server to request the resource.

Though the account information looks encrypted it is in fact only Base64 encoded. The account name and password can easily be identified.

The account details sent from the browser have been successfully validated. This is the response message including the contents of the file.

This process allows the web server to access files for which it does not have permissions, by simply passing on the user's ID and password. Providing that user has the correct permissions, NT then allows the web server to access the file, because it is acting on behalf of that user–this is called **impersonation**.

Lastly, let us look at the most complex of the three methods, **Windows NT Challenge/Response**. This time, all three types of authentication have been enabled in the WWW Properties dialog, and again the IUSR_*sysname* does not have Read permission for the file:

30/12/97 11:28:50 Sent   GET /rich/innav.htm HTTP/1.0
Accept: image/gif, image/x-xbitmap, image/jpeg, image/pjpeg,
application/vnd.ms-excel, application/msword, application/vnd.ms-powerpoint, */*
Accept-Language: en
UA-pixels: 800x600
UA-color: color8
UA-OS: Windows NT
UA-CPU: x86
User-Agent: Mozilla/2.0 (compatible; MSIE 3.0B; Win32)
Host: 194.1.1.32
Connection: Keep-Alive

This is the request message sent from the browser to the web server, to request the resource.

30/12/97 11:28:50 Received   HTTP/1.0 401 Access Denied
WWW-Authenticate: NTLM
WWW-Authenticate: Basic realm="194.1.1.32"
Content-Length: 24
Content-Type: text/html
Error: Access is Denied.

This is the response rejecting access, as the IUSR *account does not have appropriate permissions. This time it informs the browser that both* Basic Authentication *and* Challenge/ Response (NTLM) *are enabled.*

30/12/97 11:28:51 Sent
        GET /rich/innav.htm HTTP/1.0
Accept: image/gif, image/x-xbitmap, image/jpeg,
image/pjpeg, application/vnd.ms-excel, application/msword, application/vnd.ms-powerpoint, */*
Accept-Language: en
UA-pixels: 800x600
UA-color: color8
UA-OS: Windows NT
UA-CPU: x86
User-Agent: Mozilla/2.0 (compatible; MSIE 3.0B; Win32)
Host: 194.1.1.32
Connection: Keep-Alive
Authorization: NTLM TIRMTVNTUAABAAAAA7IAAAMAAwAnAAAABwAHAC
AAAABBMDIxMjgwQUNMAAAAQAAAAAAAAABAAAAAAcIAAA==

The browser will now attempt authentication using the same account information that the user is currently logged onto the network with.

This is the new request (now including the encrypted account information) sent from the browser to the web server to request the resource. The Microsoft IE browser will automatically choose Challenge/Response if this is available.

30/12/97 11:28:51 Received   HTTP/1.0 401 Access Denied
WWW-Authenticate: NTLM TIRMTVNTUAACAAAAAAA
AACgAAAABwgAAFoycWyKaYbMAAAAAkJMVAE==
Connection: keep-alive
Content-Length: 24
Content-Type: text/html
Error: Access is Denied.

This response message is sent back from the server. It is part of the NT Challenge/ Response negotiation, and contains further authentication details.

30/12/97 11:28:51 Sent   GET /rich/innav.htm HTTP/1.0
Accept: image/gif, image/x-xbitmap, image/jpeg,
image/pjpeg, application/vnd.ms-excel, application/msword, application/vnd.ms-powerpoint, */*
Accept-Language: en
UA-pixels: 800x600
UA-color: color8
UA-OS: Windows NT
UA-CPU: x86
User-Agent: Mozilla/2.0 (compatible; MSIE 3.0B; Win32)
Host: 194.1.1.32
Connection: Keep-Alive
Authorization: NTLM TIRMTVNTUAADAAAAAAAAAEAAAAAAAAAAQAAAAAA
AAABAAAAAAAAAAEAAAAAAAAAAQAAAAAAAAABAAAAAAcIAAA==

The browser automatically sends this request message back, again as part of the NT Challenge/Response negotiation.

At this point, the user ID and password that user logged into their workstation, LAN or domain with, is used by the web server to access the file, instead of the IUSR_*systemname* account information. If the user has permission for the file, it will now be returned—just like Basic Authentication. In our example, however, things are not that simple. Let us assume that the user does not have permission for the file with the details they logged on to the LAN with. NT, and therefore the web server, will again deny the request:

30/12/97 11:28:51 Received   HTTP/1.0 401 Access Denied
WWW-Authenticate: NTLM
WWW-Authenticate: Basic realm="194.1.1.32"
Content-Length: 24
Content-Type: text/html
Error: Access is Denied.

This is the response message that rejects access, because the user account currently logged on does not have the appropriate permissions. The browser automatically prompts for another user name and password.

30/12/97 11:29:38 Sent
        GET /rich/innav.htm HTTP/1.0
Accept: image/gif, image/x-xbitmap, image/jpeg,
image/pjpeg, application/vnd.ms-excel, application/msword,
application/vnd.ms-powerpoint, */*
Accept-Language: en
UA-pixels: 800x600
UA-color: color8
UA-OS: Windows NT
UA-CPU: x86
User-Agent: Mozilla/2.0 (compatible; MSIE 3.0B; Win32)
Host: 194.1.1.32
Connection: Keep-Alive
Authorization: NTLM TIRMTVNTUAABAAAAA5IAAAMAAwAgAAAAAAAAAAAA
ABBQ0wAAAAAAAAAAAAQAAAAAAAAABAAAAAAcIAAA==

This is the new request message, which now includes account information entered by the user for this particular request. It is sent from the browser to the web server to request the resource again.

30/12/97 11:29:38 Received
        HTTP/1.0 401 Access Denied
WWW-Authenticate: NTLM TIRMTVNTUAACAAAA
AAAAACgAAAABggAA5oKRq7FIM0QAAAAAAAAAA==
Connection: keep-alive

This response message is sent back from the server. It is part of the NT Challenge/Response negotiation.

Content-Length: 24
Content-Type: text/html
Error: Access is Denied.

30/12/97 11:29:38 Sent　GET /rich/innav.htm HTTP/1.0
Accept: image/gif, image/x-xbitmap, image/jpeg,
image/pjpeg, application/vnd.ms-excel, application/msword, application/vnd.ms-powerpoint, */*
Accept-Language: en
UA-pixels: 800x600
UA-color: color8
UA-OS: Windows NT
UA-CPU: x86
User-Agent: Mozilla/2.0 (compatible; MSIE 3.0B; Win32)
Host: 194.1.1.32
Connection: Keep-Alive
Authorization: NTLM TIRMTVNTUAADAAAAGAAYAHYAAAAYABgAjgAAAA4ADgB
AAAAAGgAaAE4AAAAOAA4AaAAAAAAAACmAAAAAYIAAEEAMAAyA
DEAMgA4ADAAYQBkAG0AaQBuAGkAcwB0AHlAYQB0AG8AcgBBADA
AMgAxADIAOAAwABYc4FDb+4fwflx6Qtntd5lrkgegMrMWjacvu349PYkEavY87CleD/lbMq4KSTedMg==

The browser automatically sends a further message back, this is part of the NT Challenge/Response negotiation.

30/12/97 11:29:38 Received　　　HTTP/1.0 200 OK
Server: Microsoft-IIS/4.0
Connection: keep-alive
Date: Thu, 30 Dec 1997 11:29:38 GMT
Content-Type: text/html
Accept-Ranges: bytes
Last-Modified: Wed, 22 Dec 1997 09:18:08 GMT
Content-Length: 909
<html>
..... etc .....
</html>

The entered account details have been successfully validated. This is the response message that includes the contents of the requested HTML file.

It is only after the user has entered details of a user account, that the web server is granted permission to retrieve the file and return the contents back to the browser. This allows the administrator to effectively divide up the resources on the site. Some can be available to individual users, who have to supply the relevant passwords before they can access them, while others will be freely available to everyone.

Delegation

We shall now highlight one security pitfall that IIS 4.0 Web site designers frequently encounter. When a Web user is authenticated using the NT Challenge/Response mechanism, IIS 4.0 does not actually receive a copy of the user's password in the clear. Instead IIS 4.0 receives an encrypted copy of the password which it passes onto the domain controller for verification.

The problem that this can cause is if there is any ASP logic that requires access to a resource on another Windows NT machine. The remote machine will initially challenge IIS 4.0 for proof of identification—however IIS 4.0 will be unable to participate in this authentication protocol because it does not have a copy of the users password and so cannot generate the appropriate messages. Microsoft claims that a solution to this will be available with Windows NT 5.0.

Secure Channel Services

We will now move on to look at a software technology that provides a higher level of security than those we have just seen. It enables additional endpoint authentication, message encryption, and message authentication to be used. In fact, all the weapons we need to defeat the charlatans, spies and vandals we met earlier. This software is called **Secure Channel Services** (SCS).

As we all know, the Internet or an Intranet is a network of many machines, all communicating using the **TCP/IP protocol** standards. A protocol is a set of rules and procedures that define how two entities communicate. A **protocol stack** is a combination of several protocols, where each layer is responsible for handling a specific function. The TCP/IP protocol stack is shown here:

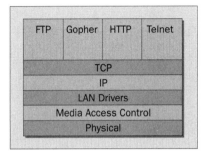

Transmission Control Protocol (the TCP part) is sometimes referred to as a transport protocol–it guarantees that packets of data are sent and received without error. It also ensures that received packets are ordered into the same sequence that they were transmitted.

Internet Protocol (the IP part) is sometimes referred to as a network protocol–it is responsible for addressing and routing packets over the network.

Application protocols (such as HTTP and FTP) provide the specific application data transfer logic using the lower levels for the actual delivery. Secure Channel Services transparently slots into the TCP/IP protocol stack, as shown here:

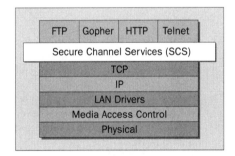

SCS is shipped with NT4.0 and IE4.0 as a dynamic-link library (**schannel.dll**) and provides the following features:

 Privacy—packets cannot be examined.

 Integrity—packets cannot be tampered with.

 Authentication—enables either the client or server to request identification of the other

SCS actually provides support for several standard security protocols:

SSL 2.0 / SSL 3.0	**Secure Socket Layer** developed by Netscape
PCT 1.0	**Private Communications Technology** developed by Microsoft
TLS	**Transport Layer Security** which is intended to provide a simpler and more robust solution by using the best parts of SSL and PCT

Before we can understand how SCS works, we need to investigate the cryptography it uses, and then see how to implement it on our systems.

Low-level discussions on cryptography are normally reserved for those with brains the size of a planet—since this book is supposed to be about Active Server Pages, we will keep things simple and dive in just deep enough to get a basic understanding of how it all works.

A Simple Guide to Cryptography

Cryptography is an ancient mathematical science that was originally used for military communications, and designed to conceal the contents of a message should it fall into the hands of the enemy. Recent developments in cryptography have added additional uses, including mechanisms for authenticating users on a network, ensuring the integrity of transmitted information and preventing users from repudiating (i.e. rejecting ownership of) their transmitted messages.

In today's world of electronic commerce on the Internet, the need for secure communications is obviously crucial. Cryptographic technologies provide enterprises with the best mechanisms of protecting their information, without putting the business at risk by exposing it on the Net.

What is Encryption?

Encryption is the name given to the process of applying an algorithm to a message, which scrambles the data in it—making it very difficult and time consuming, if not practically impossible, to deduce the original message. Inputs to the algorithm typically involve additional secret data called **keys**, which prevents the message from being decoded—even if the algorithm is publicly known.

The safekeeping of keys, in other words their generation, storage and exchange, is of paramount importance to ensure the security of the data. There is no point applying the strongest levels of cryptographic algorithms, if your keys are stored on a scrap of paper in your in-tray.

The strength of the encryption is dependent on two basic items: the nature of the mathematical algorithm and the size of the keys involved. Under US arms regulations, the length of the key that can be used in exported software is limited. However, there is no limitation on the level of encryption used *within* the US, or sold in Canada.

Unfortunately the 40-bit encryption limit, which has been in force up until recently, has been proven to provide little security from attack. Today's powerful processors, costing just a few hundred dollars, can crack such a message in a few hours by using brute force—that is, by trying every possible key until the decrypted message has been found. More expensive supercomputers can crack such messages in sub-second times! Each extra bit in the key doubles the time needed for the brute force attack, and most experts now claim that 128-bit keys are required to ensure complete confidence, and are vital for markets such as electronic commerce.

Many non-US companies have now developed add-on cryptographic products, using 128-bit key technology, to fill the vacuum left by the US software industry's inability to compete in this market. Naturally, there is a lot of discussion between concerned parties, and the future of these export restrictions is unclear.

Symmetric Cryptography – Secret Keys

In **symmetric cryptography**, the encryption algorithm requires the same secret key to be used for both encryption and decryption. Because of the type of key, this is sometimes called **secret key encryption**. This diagram shows how it works:

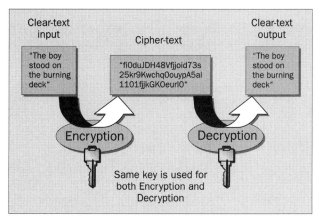

The advantage of these algorithms is that they are fast and efficient. However, the problem is that of key exchange–it is, the mechanism for safely ensuring both parties, the sender and the receiver, have the secret key. This is one of the weakest areas of symmetric cryptography. How do you send the key to your partners? You cannot just send it in an email message, because it could be intercepted and, possibly unknowingly, compromise your security. Furthermore, how can you be sure that your partners will keep your key secure?

Asymmetric Cryptography – Public/Private Keys

One solution to the problem of key security is **asymmetric cryptography**. This uses two keys that are mathematically related. One key is called the **private key** and is never revealed, and the other is called the **public key** and is freely given out to all potential corespondents. The complexity of the relationship between the public key and the private key means that, provided the keys are long enough, it is practically impossible to determine one from the other. The one problem with asymmetric cryptography is that the processing required is very CPU intensive and this can cause potential performance problems when many simultaneous sessions are required.

The almost universal public/private key algorithm is named **RSA** after its creators (Ron Rivest, Adi Shamir, and Len Adleman), and patented by RSA Data Security Inc. in 1977. A sender uses the receiver's public key to encrypt the message. Only the receiver has the related private key to decrypt the message. This is shown here:

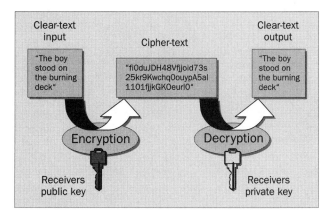

Digital Signature Encryption

An additional use of RSA is in **digital signatures**, which involves swapping the role of the private and public keys. If a sender encrypts a message using their private key, everyone can decrypt the message using the sender's public key. A successful decryption implies that the sender, who is the only person in possession of their private key, must have sent the message.

This also prevents **repudiation**, that is, the sender cannot claim that they did not actually send the message. A piece of data encrypted with a private key is called a digital signature. Common practice is to use a message digest as the item of data to be encrypted.

Using a Message Digest

A **message digest** is a digital fingerprint of a message, derived by applying a mathematical algorithm on a variable-length message. There are a number of suitable algorithms, called **hash functions**, each having the following special properties:

- The original message (the input) is of variable-length.
- The message digest (the output) is of a fixed-length.
- It is practically impossible to determine the original message (the input) from just the message digest (the output). This is known as being a **one-way hash function**.
- It is practically impossible to find two different messages (the inputs) that derive to the same message digest (the output)–this is known as being a **collision-free hash function**.
- The algorithm is relatively simple, so when computerized it is not CPU-intensive.
- The calculated digest is (often considerably) smaller than the item it represents.

You can use message digests to guarantee that no one has tampered with a message during its transit over a network. Any amendment to the message will mean that the message and digest will not correlate. Also, message digests can also be used to supply proof that an item of information, such as a password, is known–without actually sending the password or information in the clear.

The most common message digest algorithms designed for 32-bit computer systems are **MD4**, **MD5** and **Secure Hash Algorithm** (SHA), which offer–in that order–increasing levels of security, and therefore CPU usage. The next diagram illustrates how a message digest is used to digitally sign a document:

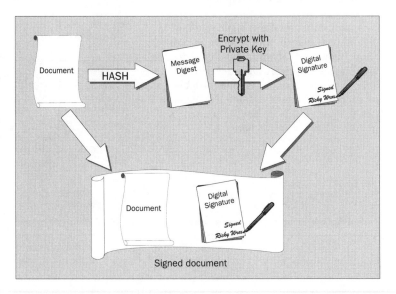

Note that this document is **signed** (its integrity and origin are assured) but it is not **encrypted** – anyone could look at the original document included with the signed digest. This does not imply that the document cannot be encrypted as well, however.

This diagram shows how the same document is validated:

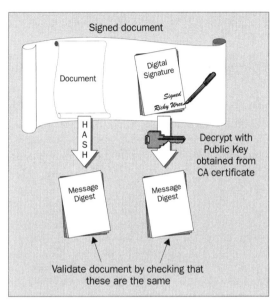

Digital Certificates and Certificate Authorities

A digital certificate is an item of information that binds the details of an individual or organization to their public key. The most widely accepted format for digital certificates is the X.509 standard, and is relevant to both clients and servers. If we can obtain access to someone's certificate we have their public key and can, therefore, get involved in the secure communications already discussed.

But what is there to stop anybody just creating a false certificate, and pretending that they are someone else? The solution is **Certificate Authorities** (CAs), who are responsible for the issuing of digital certificates. A CA is a commonly known **trusted third party**, responsible for verifying both the contents and ownership of a certificate.

There is an ever-increasing number of CAs. Different CAs will employ different amounts of effort in their verification processes, and they must publicly divulge what checks they perform. Then users can apply the appropriate levels of trust for each CA they encounter. Also, different classes of certificates are available, which reflect the level of assurance given by the CA–a certificate for users who just surf the web requires less verification than a certificate for a business server. If two entities trust the same CA, they can swap digital certificates to obtain access to each other's public key, and from then onwards they can undertake secure transmissions between themselves.

Digital certificates include the CA's digital signature (i.e. information encrypted with the CA's private key). This means that no one can create a false certificate. The public keys of trusted CA's are stored for use by applications like Internet Explorer as we will see in a while.

How Secure Channel Systems Work

Now that we have a good understanding of some basic cryptographic concepts, we will move on and see how they are actually put into practice. We learned earlier that SCS provides support for a number of security protocols. Each of these has their own specific low-level operation and complexities that we do not intend to cover. Instead, we will investigate how all such protocols solve the general problem of connection, negotiation, and key exchange; and how this software technology protects us against the spies, vandals and charlatans out there in the big wide world beyond our Internet connection.

Client-server Authentication with SCS

We will first look at how a client called **C** and a server called **S** negotiate a secure communications link. The following table shows the messages that pass between **C** and **S**. **S** has to prove that its certificate is valid by showing that it has the private key to encrypt a message digest:

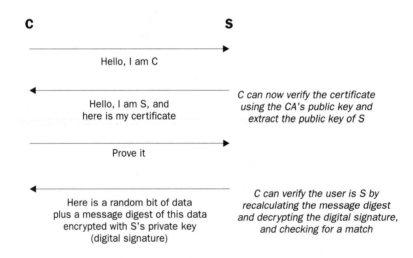

But what if there was an imposter called **I**, who was trying to impersonate **S**?

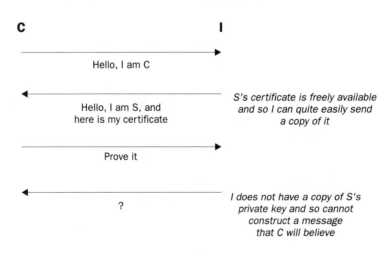

From this we can see how a user can be confident that remote server is who it claims to be. It also highlights the importance of the protection of private keys.

Encrypting and Sending Messages

Now that **c** has **s**'s public key, it can send a message to **s** that only **s** can decrypt, because this task requires **s**'s private key. However, we learned earlier that asymmetric cryptography is much more CPU-intensive than symmetric cryptography. Thus **c** generates a random secret key and informs **s** of its value using asymmetric cryptography. From then onwards, encryption is done by symmetric cryptography with only **c** and **s** knowing the secret key.

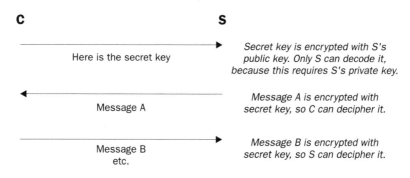

Authenticating Messages against Tampering

Now let us consider another bad guy called **E** who eavesdrops on the network, and could intercept and tamper with a messages en route to their destinations.

Because the message is encrypted, it is unlikely that tampering with it will create a valid message–but who knows, he might get lucky?

The solution is to attach a **message authentication code** (MAC) to each message. The MAC is a message digest value, calculated using a hash algorithm on the message contents and the secret key. The message receiver calculates the MAC value for the message and checks for a match with the attached MAC value. Since **E** does not know the secret key, it is unlikely that they could evaluate the correct MAC for his new tampered message.

Implementing Secure Channels

So now we know what Secure Channel Services are, and how they works in outline. The next step is to see how we configure IIS 4.0 Web services and Internet Explorer to use Secure Channels.

Configuring Internet Information Server

Enabling SSL security on IIS 4.0 requires us to first obtain a digital certificate that contains the details of our organization and is verified by a CA. The configuration of certificates with IIS 4.0 is handled by the Key Manager utility, which can be found by selecting the key manager tool button within the Internet Service Manager (MMC).

To create a new public/private key pair, click on the Web service and then select the Create New Key option from the Key menu; this invokes the Create New Key wizard.

The wizard will generate a key pair and a certificate request message that is sent to a CA to generate the digital certificate for our Web server. Over a series of wizard dialogs, we have to enter information about our organization and the key requirements.

The information we shall enter is:

- **Request File**—name of a file to be generated by the Key Manager, and used to store the information that is sent to the CA for the certificate to be generated.

- **Key Name**—name given to identify the key.

- **Password**—password used to protect the private key.

- **Bits**—key size: 512, 768, 1024 – large keys are more secure. Export versions are restricted to 512.

- **User Details**, comprising:

- **Organization**—company name *e.g. Wrox Press.*

- **Organization Unit**—unit name within company *e.g. Hornet.*

- **Common Name**—TCP/IP domain name of server *e.g. hornet.wrox.com.*

- **Country**—character ISO code *e.g. US.*

- **State/Province**—state name of address *e.g. Illinois.*

- **City/Locality**—city name of address *e.g. Chicago.*

- **Contact Details**, comprising:

- **Name**—contact name *e.g. Richard Harrison.*

- **Email Address**—email address of contact *e.g. rich@cyberdude.com.*

- **Phone Number**—phone number of contact *e.g. 1234567890.*

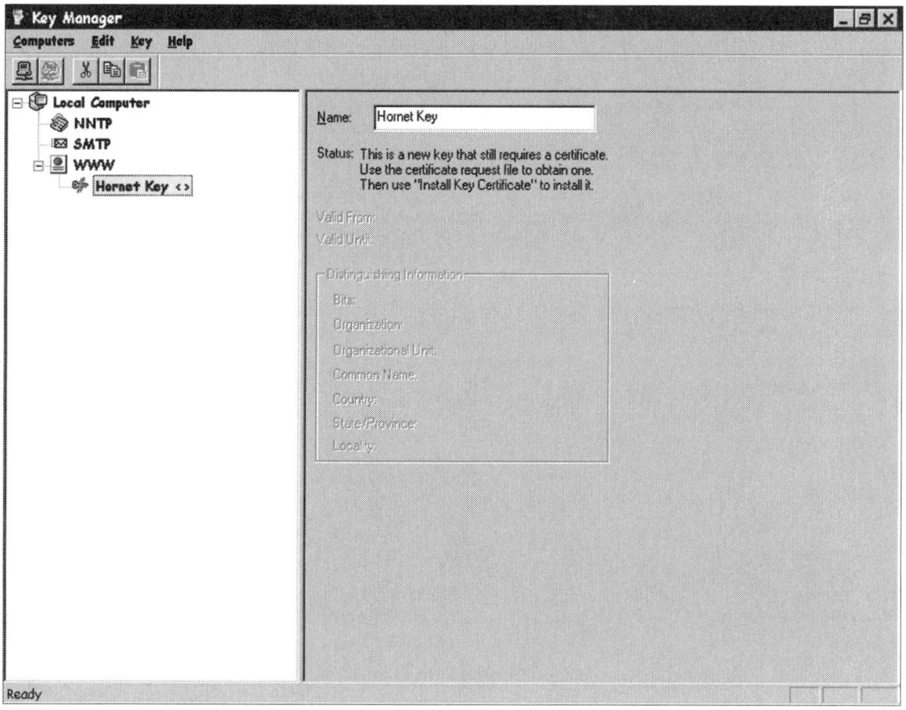

At this stage, we must enforce the changes by selecting the Commit Changes Now option from the Computers menu.

Sending the Certificate Request

Once the wizard has completed creating the key pair, we must send the generated Certificate Request details to our CA for the digital certificate to be generated. Here are the contents of a request file generated for some example details that we entered into the wizard:

```
Webmaster: rich@cyberdude.com
Phone: 1234567890
Server: Microsoft Key Manager for IIS Version 4.0

Common-name: hornet.wrox.com
Organization Unit: Hornet
Organization: Wrox Press
Locality: Chicago
State: Illinois
Country: US

-----BEGIN NEW CERTIFICATE REQUEST-----
MIIBMDCB2wIBADB2MQswCQYDVQQGEwJVUzERMA8GA1UECBMISWxsaW5vaXMxEDAO
BgNVBAcTB0NoaWNhZ28xEzARBgNVBAoTCldyb3ggUHJlc3MxDzANBgNVBAsTBkhv
cm51dEcMBoGA1UEAxMTd3d3Lmhvcm51dC53cm94LmNvbTCMA0GCSqGSIb3DQEB
AQUAA0sAMEgCQQCKMk2YPhZC10L4wAa5MdUHw85DgUGHExtIk/m43j1kuCfvlSa7
GkfBwG2X2FpJerhFrmHz1O81NhPr6WK9nhyNAgMBAAGgADANBgkqhkiG9w0BAQQF
AANBAFxwC8ST08adPnc5g/M1KW3DGcOhOpw8JAdiHuuFjAt46bQzg73JIIulAqZC
4FOHtTulelvgcUQ8MMtxK6D8Fgk=
-----END NEW CERTIFICATE REQUEST-----
```

A useful CA for the creation of certificates that can be used for demonstration and testing purposes is Entrust (`http://www.entrust.com/`) who, at the time of writing, provide the service free of charge. By navigating through the hyperlinks promoting demonstration certificates, we get to a screen where we can input our generated Certificate Request details.

Installing the New Certificate

The response screen generated from Entrust for the above request is as follows—selecting the Display Certificate button displays the CA generated X.509 digital certificate containing our details plus the CA's digital signature.

We just copy the section between, and including the `-----BEGIN CERTIFICATE-----` and `-----END CERTIFICATE-----` lines from the email message, paste it into a standard text file using, for example, NotePad, and save it on the server's hard disk.

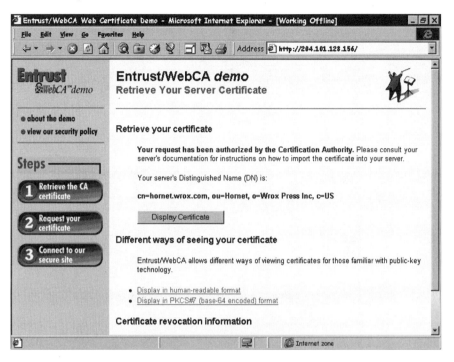

To install the digital certificate, right-click on it in Key Manager and select the Install Key Certificate menu option. A standard File Open dialog will now request the name of the file that we have just created and it will then request the key's password.

The next dialog allows us to specify which IP address the digital certificate is to be applied. Note that multiple IP addresses can be assigned to a certificate—but a maximum of one certificate can be applied to a single IP address. In our case, we shall keep things simple and assign all addresses to our digital certificate.

Finally, we must then enforce the changes by selecting the Commit Changes Now option from the Computers menu. If the key installation has completed successfully, Key Manager will show the key as being installed, and display the certificate details.

Once the certificate has been installed, we can enable SSL (one of the security protocols within SCS) on any directory using Internet Service Manager. This is done by selecting the Secure Communications option on the Directory Security property sheet within the WWW Properties dialog–on the Secure Communications dialog we must check Require Secure Channel. In addition, this dialog provides the Require Client Certificates check box. When this is checked, IIS 4.0 will instruct the browser to send a copy of its client certificate. We will see later how ASP can utilize the details in this certificate.

Configuring and Using Certificates in Internet Explorer

All we have done so far is install the Entrust generated digital certificate that contains our public details endorsed with the Entrust digital signature. We will next see how to install a **CA Certificate** on a browser that gives the Web user the Entrust public key. This is needed so that the browser can decode and verify digital certificates generated by Entrust. This also includes our own, which we have just created.

Then we will look at how we install a client certificate. A little earlier we set our server up so that it will require client browsers to supply a certificate–i.e. the details of the client browser user–when they request files from our server.

Installing Site Certificates from Entrust

The Entrust **site certificate** is installed on the browser by accessing their web site at `http://www.entrust.com/`, and following the instructions to the Client Certificate Demo page.

Once the process is complete, we get a confirmation message and can choose to accept and enable the site certificate.

We can also inspect the browser's currently installed site certificates by selecting Internet Options from the View menu, opening the Content tab, and clicking the Authorities button. Here, we can see that the Entrust demo CA certificate has been successfully installed. Now, when we log on to a site that uses the Entrust demo CA for their server's digital certificates, our browser will understand the contents of the certificates. In other words, we are telling the browser that we trust any sites that have this certificate.

> Since no verification of the server's credentials is done for the generation of Entrust demo certificates, we would suggest that you normally have the Entrust demo CA certificate disabled in your browser when surfing around the Internet. If you arrive at a site that claims it needs this CA certificate enabled then you must be fully aware that this is not really a secure site that you can trust!

Installing a VeriSign Client Certificate

The next task is to install a **client certificate** in our browser, which will be used when we access a site that requires them, i.e. has the Require Client Certificates checkbox set, like we did on our server earlier. At the time of writing, VeriSign are providing client certificates free of charge for Internet Explorer 4.0 users. These can be obtained from the VeriSign web site at:
`http://digitalid.verisign.com/class1MS.htm`.

To create a client certificate, we will be required to provide our:

- ▲ First Name
- ▲ Last Name
- ▲ Email address
- ▲ Option to include or omit our email address in the certificate
- ▲ Password, this can be later used to revoke the certificate

On submission, private key information is stored on our computer and any public information is sent to Verisign.

Once the details have been submitted, a confirmation screen is received informing us to expect an email message with further details for installing the digital certificate.

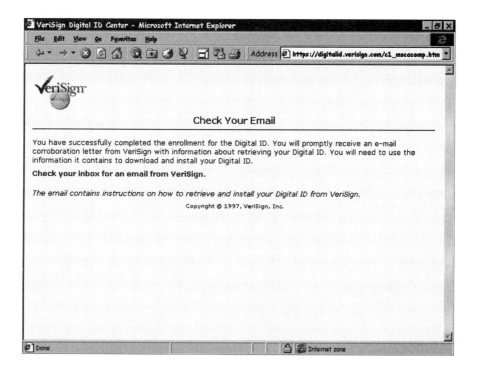

In our example, the following email message was received.

```
To: rich@cyberdude.com
From: VeriSign Digital ID Center <onlineca@verisign.com>
Subject: Trial Class 1 VeriSign Digital ID
Reply-To: ID-Center@verisign.com
Errors-To: onlineca-errors@verisign.com
Sender: ID-Center@verisign.com
MIME-Version: 1.0
Content-Type: text/plain; charset=us-ascii
Content-Transfer-Encoding: 7bit

QUICK INSTALLATION INSTRUCTIONS
-------------------------------


To assure that someone else cannot obtain a Digital ID that contains your
name and e-mail address, you must retrieve your Digital ID from
VeriSign's secure web site using a unique Personal Identification
Number (PIN).

Be sure to follow these steps using the same computer you used to
begin the process.

Step 1: Copy your Digital ID PIN number.
Your Digital ID PIN is: 99253a26b15a77dd2a9fd0346062cddf

Step 2: Go to VeriSign's secure Digital ID Center at
https://digitalid.verisign.com/mspickup.htm
```

```
Step 3: Paste (or enter) your Digital ID personal identification
number (PIN), then select the SUBMIT button to install
your Digital ID.
```

That's all there is to it!

So if we follow the instructions in the email message, our personal digital certificate is installed into our Internet Explorer configuration. This involves navigating to **https://digitalid.verisign.com/ mspickup.htm** and entering the Personal Identification Number (PIN) specified in the email message.

> **The digital certificate that is to be received is related to the private key information that was originally generated and stored on the computer – thus the certificate retrieval procedure must be undertaken on the same machine and with the same logged on user.**

Now we can inspect the browser's personal certificates by selecting Internet Options from the View menu, opening the Content tab, and clicking the Personal button. We can see then that the client certificate has been successfully installed. When we access a site that requires client certificates, Internet Explorer will present the user with a list of installed personal certificates–the user can then select the one that they wish to be submitted to the Web server.

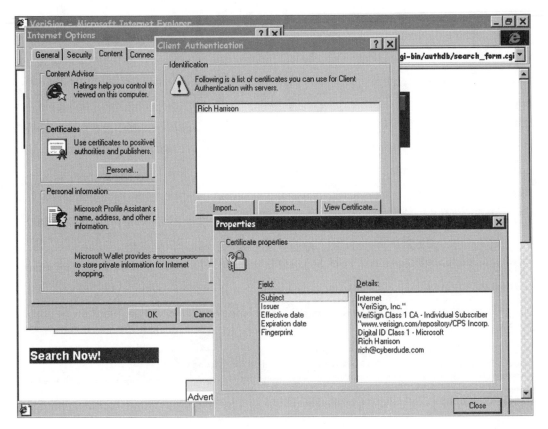

Security in Active Server Pages

Up to now, we have seen how to implement private information transfer and data integrity using Secure Channel Services, and how to enable access control by setting permissions on our server resources. All of this has been achieved by means of configuration of our NT system. There is one more area in which ASP scripting can add value.

Checking Client Certificates

In the previous section, we saw how to set up the server so that it would request a client certificate to be supplied by visitors. Active Server Pages code can help us to interrogate the contents of these client certificates, and act upon them accordingly. This might include additional verification, or personalization of page content.

We looked briefly at the **Request** object's **ClientCertificate** collection back in Chapter 3, without really letting on where the information in it actually came from. Well, now you know. The **ClientCertificate** collection contains the contents of the personal digital certificate that is released by the user.

The **Key** parameter to the collection is the name of the certification field to retrieve. A list of all possible values for the client certificate we created is shown in the example, and the corresponding screen dump given below. The following code simply iterates through the **ClientCertificate** collection, placing the contents into the page:

```
<HTML>
<HEAD>
</HEAD>
<BODY>
SECURED DOCUMENT<br><br>
<H3>Client certificate</H3>
<% For Each key in Request.ClientCertificate
    Response.Write(key & " = " &
    Request.ClientCertificate(key) & "<BR>")
  Next %>
</BODY>
</HTML>
```

When we access the page from the browser where we installed the VeriSign client certificate earlier, we get the following screen shot—notice that the URL in the Address box specifies a secure communications link using **https** rather than **http**.

We can also inspect the Web server's certificate credentials while we have the page displayed. This is done by right clicking on the Web page, selecting the Properties option, and opening the Certificates tab:

A list of the main key values for this collection is given in Chapter 3. Recapping, the most interesting ones include:

SUBJECT   A comma-separated list of fields within the certificate

SUBJECTCN   The Common name (i.e. users name)

SUBJECTOU   The Organization Unit (i.e. certificate authority)

VALIDUNTIL The expiry date of certificate

VALIDFROM The start date of certificate

So we could welcome someone to our site using the following code:

```
<HTML>
<BODY>
Hello <% = Request.ClientCertificate("SubjectCN") %>,
Welcome to our site <P>
</BODY>
</HTML>
```

If the browser does not present a certificate, all the members of the collection are **Empty**. The usual way to test for the presence of a certificate, as we saw in Chapter 3, is to check for a **Subject**. If all the collection fields are empty, we get an empty string:

```
<% If Len(Request.ClientCertificate("Subject")) = 0 %>
    You did not present a client certificate.
<% End if %>
```

Summary

That concludes our discussion on ASP security. We have seen how Windows NT, IIS 4.0 and ASP cooperate together to provide us with a comprehensive set of key software technologies enabling:

 Secure exchange of information over public networks

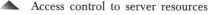 Access control to server resources

 Confident identification of client and server

The Microsoft Windows NT platform with IIS 4.0 forms a good secure foundation and a flexible architecture, allowing the new emerging security standards to be easily incorporated into our web sites later—with minimum investment impact. This is vital, as there are likely to be many future changes in this area. The following are known to be on the not so distant horizon:

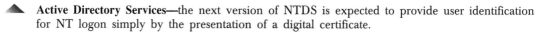 **Active Directory Services**—the next version of NTDS is expected to provide user identification for NT logon simply by the presentation of a digital certificate.

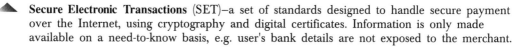 **Secure Electronic Transactions** (SET)—a set of standards designed to handle secure payment over the Internet, using cryptography and digital certificates. Information is only made available on a need-to-know basis, e.g. user's bank details are not exposed to the merchant.

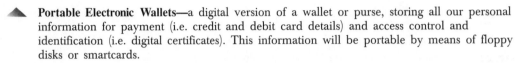

- **Portable Electronic Wallets**—a digital version of a wallet or purse, storing all our personal information for payment (i.e. credit and debit card details) and access control and identification (i.e. digital certificates). This information will be portable by means of floppy disks or smartcards.

- **Secure Channel Services**—support for a new protocol Transport Layer Security (TLS) that is the unification of Microsoft's PCT and Netscape's SSL.

Finally, remember that the weakest link is usually the administrator. These security technologies will only work if they have been configured correctly and *all* security holes are filled. If not there is always one smart person who will find a way to get through.

An Electronic Commerce Case Study

There are extra setup and installation notes at:

http://webdev.wrox.co.uk/books/1266/

We have progressed, piece by piece, through our studies of Active Server Pages, and all of the new features that IIS 4.0 has brought to us. You have seen how to use the ASP Object model to control what is displayed on a web page. Chapter 7, on ActiveX Data Objects showed how to access information from databases. The most recent chapters talked about creating transactional web pages through the integration of IIS and Microsoft Transaction Server.

Now, it is time to put ALL of these pieces together. The best way to do that is with a case study. We'll look at a real world problem, one that many people have had to solve in their businesses. The case of business boils down to trying to sell something to someone else. It can be cars, computers, or even books. The items may be drastically different, but the process is pretty much the same.

Our case study will involve how to sell books electronically, by using web-based technologies. In this chapter, and the next two as well, we will cover:

- ▲ A methodology for designing the application that has proven to provide an effective, efficient, and satisfying experience for the user.

- ▲ A data and application architecture that brings this design into reality.

- ▲ How to implement the design using the tools and technologies made available in IIS 4.0 and Active Server Pages.

- ▲ Ways to extend and enhance the application to make it fit your needs.

First off, it is important to know what we are talking about when we use the words *Electronic Commerce*. We will first set some expectations about what these words mean, then move into the design of the application.

What Is Electronic Commerce?

I'm sure that you have heard the term "Electronic Commerce". And I am also sure that you have some ideas as to what Electronic Commerce is. Trouble is, there are millions of other people out there who have their own definitions, most of which are probably different from yours.

An Electronic Commerce Definition

So how can we define what Electronic Commerce is? Taken literally, commerce is defined as:

> *The buying and selling of goods and services between two parties*

And electronic is defined as:

> *Involving the flow of electrons in a vacuum or through semiconductors*

So using these, we can build a definition of Electronic Commerce as:

> *The buying and selling of goods and services between two parties involving the flow of electrons through a vacuum or through semiconductors.*

Doesn't say much, does it? But it really gets across the point that there are many definitions of what Electronic Commerce is. In a nutshell, it is the use of electronic means to facilitate the buying and selling of goods. So what does that *really* mean?

Since the mid-1980's, Electronic Commerce had been synonymous with Electronic Data Interchange, or EDI, which is computer-to-computer interface that allows companies to conduct business electronically. EDI is a standards-based method for exchanging an electronic representation of standard business documents, such as Purchase Orders and Invoices. The exchange traditionally took place over store-and-forward private value-added networks, or VANs. At its ultimate form, EDI could be used so that the actual line-of-business applications, such as purchasing and accounting, of the two firms conducting business, could communicate with each other without human intervention.

And then the Web exploded. Now, the ability for buyers and sellers to communicate was available to everybody with an Internet connection. Electronic Commerce has grown to be much more than just the actual buying and selling. It has opened up the exchange of information, and the trading of information as a commodity itself. By using the low-cost public Internet instead of expensive private VANs, these new forms of electronic commerce have become much more accessible. With that increased accessibility has come increased interest and new ways for business to be conducted.

Companies such as Amazon.com have embraced this new paradigm of Electronic Commerce to create a business that wasn't possible only 5 years ago. They have no physical vending locations, only an electronic storefront on the web **http://www.amazon.com**. They coordinate their orders directly with the publishers, allowing them to only stock very high demand titles; every other title is shipped by the publishers themselves. Electronic Commerce has allowed very small companies, without any existing infrastructure, to do business on the web and appear the same as a huge organization. Not only has Electronic Commerce provided opportunities for new business, it has forced existing businesses to adapt to the way that business will be conducted in the future. For example, take a look at the efforts of the booksellers Barnes and Noble. Faced with the threat that Amazon.com posed to their business, they opened their own electronic storefront on the Web in response.

One of the advantages of Electronic Commerce over the Internet is that it alleviates the need for physical storefronts in order to conduct business. This also reveals a hidden advantage in that it removes a barrier to market for companies that traditionally relied on others to provide a physical location from which to sell their products. Now, these companies can offer their products directly to a consumer, through the use of an electronic storefront. You may have heard a term for this: **disintermediation**, or the removal of the "middle-men" between the manufacturer and the consumer. Direct telephone-based catalog sales was a first step towards disintermediation. Now, Electronic Commerce gives us another leap forwards in the process of disintermediation.

A Business for our Case Study

So let's take a look at a company that traditionally has relied on others to sell their products. A book publisher generally relies on a group of distributors to distribute their products to bookstores, which, in turn, sell the books to the customers. With these two layers of businesses between the publisher and the reader, there are a lot of costs that have to be recouped. When a person buys a book, not only is he paying for the publication of that book, plus some level of margin, he is also paying for its distribution, plus margin, as well as its selling, plus another margin.

What do these distribution methods mean for the publisher? It means one of two things. Either the publisher can make a comfortable margin, thus increasing the price of the book to the consumer, since each step along the way is still adding in their costs and margin. Or, the publisher can cut their margins to almost nothing, and hope to pass on a lower cost to the consumer. For most publishers, this second option is the way that they have proceeded.

But what if the two steps between the publisher and the consumer could be eliminated. What if the principles of disintermediation can be applied to the selling of books? Given the ability of the Internet to support Electronic Commerce between business and customers, a publisher now has the infrastructure available to sell their books directly to the consumer.

But an infrastructure is only part of the solution. There needs to be a system built on top of the infrastructure that provides the mechanisms to carry out the Electronic Commerce. In the next two chapters, we will take a look at a case study that builds this system to provide for the direct selling of books by a publisher. With a bit of insight, the examples presented here could be easily extended to support many different kinds of web-based electronic storefronts that both present and sell products.

To develop the Electronic Commerce system, we will follow this design methodology:

- Examine the business process
- Design and develop a data architecture
- Design application and security architecture
- Design objects to support the application
- Develop, test, and implement the application

First, we will take a look at the business problem that needs to be solved.

The Business Problem

In the definition of Electronic Commerce, we talked about the buying and selling of goods and services through electronic means. In looking at the business problem, we will use the first part of that definition: the buying and selling of goods and services. In other words, what is the interaction between the publisher and the consumer? Once we understand that interaction completely, we can move along in the design of our system.

There are many published methodologies for investigating and designing business systems. I have found that there isn't one particular method that is better than any other is. In effect, I tend to use a hybrid approach when analyzing a business problem and designing a system.

The User-Centered Approach

One methodology that I have used is based on the principles of User-Centered Design (UCD). In this approach, the problem is evaluated in three ways. By understanding the **users** of the system, the **tasks** that they are performing, and the **environment** of use, you can gain enough information to design a system that satisfies the needs of user.

The **users** of our system are more than just the people who connect to the web site to order books from the publisher. In UCD terms, any individual who has any contact with the system is a user of the system. Naturally, the end-user, accessing the system via the Web, is a user of the system. The operations people responsible for maintaining the catalog of books in the system are also users of the system. The marketing people who have to promote the site, and information technology people, who have to integrate the system into the other business applications, are users as well.

In examining the users, we can determine a number of requirements that the system must support in order for the users to be able to effectively use the system:

- System must be easy to use, as not all users will be technically savvy.

- System must support searching for titles by multiple means, as not all users know the exact title of the book.

- Multiple payment options need to be supported, as not all users are comfortable with giving credit card numbers over the web. Any payment option that the user chooses needs to be secure.

- The system must be easy to update so that new titles can be added quickly

- The system needs to be available whenever users wish to use it.

- System should be integrated with other business systems so that data and development efforts are not duplicated

The **environment** of use also drives a number of requirements for the system:

- Since the system is web-based, the system should support the majority of browsers

- Given that a majority of connections will be dial-up, with speeds under 33.6 Kbps, graphical content should be only used where necessary.

The final part of the user-centered design process is to understand the **tasks** that the users will be performing with the system. As with design methodologies, there are a number of methods that can be used to develop a task structure for a given system. The one that I have used most frequently is **task decomposition**.

In this method, the task is initially stated at a very high level, for example, "I want to buy a book." This high level task is then broken down into its component subtasks. These steps are repeated until such time as the task is fully decomposed. There is no hard-and-fast rule as to how decomposed a task needs to be.

Generally, the subtasks reach what are called "atomic" tasks. At this stage, each subtask is essentially an atomic, or freestanding, action that the user or the system performs.

These decomposed subtasks will be used in the next two stages of the design process. By examining the range of subtasks, we can determine what the data requirements for the system are, as well what the application flow will be. But first, we need to break down the stated task for our system: Purchase a book.

Tasks

The simple high-level task statement of "Purchase a book" can be broken down into all of the subtasks that are required to support the online purchasing of a book. To begin, let's break this task down into a set of high-level **subtasks**. A subtask can be thought of as an individual step that the user takes to accomplish the primary task. As you are breaking down the task into subtasks, you will go back and review the initial choices of subtasks to see if they themselves can be broken down even further. We will later find that these high-level subtasks also become the main parts of the application.

- Identify User
- Select A Book
- Select Quantity
- Add More Selections
- Make Purchase

These five subtasks encompass all of the high-level steps necessary to purchase a book electronically. At this point, it seems like there is data missing from the system. But remember we are still at a high level, and as we decompose each of these subtasks, we will begin to discover specific data requirements and application requirements too.

Identify a User

In order for a purchase to be made at our online store, we need to be able to identify the person making the purchase. This identification can be accomplished in two ways. If the customer has made prior purchases using the online system, then there should be a way to retrieve all of that user's information from a database, rather than having the user re-enter all of the information. If the user is new to the online store, then the system should request the required information from the user. Once this information has been gathered and verified, the user will select an ID and password that can be used for future visits.

In breaking down the subtasks of the identification task, we have:

- Request customer ID
- If existing customer:

    Display information for validation

    Allow user to make changes.
- If new customer:

    Query for required information

    Display gathered information for validation

Select a book

Once the user has been identified by the system, the next step is for the user to select the book that they are interested in. This selection process could be done in many ways, and the system should support multiple methods of selecting a book. By supporting multiple selection methods, the system is directly meeting a user requirement that was stated previously. The requirement was that the system support searching for titles by multiple means, as not all users know the exact title of the book.

While there are countless methods that can be used for searching for a particular book, this system will support those methods that would be commonly used by the target user population.

Search by Title

The user would be prompted to enter the title of the book and the system would display all books that had the same title. Additionally, the system could support the searching by partial title, or by keywords in a title.

Search by Author

The user would be prompted to enter the author of the book, and the system would display all books that were written by that author. The author's name could be entered in a number of different ways. The user could enter the complete christian and surname name of the author, just the surname of the author, or the first few letters of the author's surname, along with their first initial. Each of these methods could be considered as common search criteria for the system's target user group.

Search by Subject

The user would be prompted to select from a predefined list of subject classifications, and the system would display a list of all books that were in that classification. A domain expert, such as the publisher's editorial department, would determine the set of possible subjects. Each book in the system would be classified into one or more of these subjects. The user could select from a single subject, or from multiple subjects.

Search by ISBN

The user would be prompted to enter the exact ISBN number for the book. An ISBN number (International Standard Book Number) is a system of numerical identification for books. By assigning a unique, ten-digit number to each published title, the system provides that title with its own, unduplicated, internationally recognized "identity." Because of the nature of ISBN, the user would be required to enter the exact number for the book that they were interested in.

Predetermined Searches

The publisher could create a series of predetermined searches that would be displayed for the user. These searches would be displayed in the form of lists of books that the publisher wished to group together. For example, the publisher could create a list of "new releases," or "best sellers," or "recommended readings." These lists would be made easily accessible to the users.

Select Quantity

Once the user has selected the particular title that they are interested in, they then need to select the quantity of the book that they desire. At this point, the system should advise the user the number of the selected book that is currently in stock. If the number of books is below a certain threshold, then the user would be informed that the book is not in stock, and will need to be placed on back order. The choice for this threshold value should be based on the retailer's confidence in their inventory levels. If they are very confident that the number shown on hand is actually the number on hand, then this threshold can be very low. In many cases, the confidence in the inventory numbers is not this high, so the threshold number should reflect this. The aim is to ensure that if the system informs the customer that a book is available to be purchased, then there is actually one available. If there is a sufficient quantity available, then the user can select the number that they wish to purchase.

Add More Selections

At this point in the transaction, the user can select any additional books that they would like to purchase in exactly the same way as they selected the first book. Once a different title has been selected, and the number of that title required, the user can then add that book to their list of books to be purchased. In effect, they have added their subsequent selections to their electronic "shopping cart." At any time while viewing the shopping cart list, the user can choose to modify the number of a book selected, or they can remove any book from their shopping cart. Once they have selected all the books that they wish to purchase, they can move on to the final task of the process.

Make Purchase

At this point, the user can verify that their shopping cart contains all of the selections that they wish to purchase. The total amount of the order, along with calculated sales taxes and shipping costs, will be presented to the user for verification and acceptance. If the user accepts the order, then the system will submit the order, and the user will receive an indication that their order has been processed and an estimated shipment date.

Now that we have outlined the tasks that the user must perform to purchase a book, we need to take a look at the data structures that will be necessary to support these tasks. The data structures will need to support the presentation of all of the necessary information to the user, as well as tracking any information that the system needs to correctly process the order.

Data Architecture

To support the tasks of searching for a book electronically and then purchasing that book, there needs to be a data architecture that corresponds to the tasks. In reviewing the tasks, there are three main areas that need to be supported:

 The User/Shopper

 The Book Catalog

 The Electronic "Shopping Cart" / Order

Within these three areas, there are one or more supporting data tables that will contain the information necessary to support the user's tasks.

User Data

The user data is what is used to identify the particular user that is searching the book database and placing an order in the system. If we review the task list that was presented earlier and look for items of data that can be associated with a user, we come up with this following list:

▲ The **CustomerID** data item is relatively self-explanatory. The customer is assigned an ID that is unique to them. The ID is used to identify the customer's information within the system, so that the next time the user enters the system, the customer information can be retrieved from the database, rather than having to be re-entered by the user. In this application, we will be using the customer's e-mail address as their Customer ID.

▲ The Customer Information data is not explicitly defined in the tasks, but general business principles can be applied here. The Customer Information should include their name, address, contact information, such as phone number or e-mail address, as well as personal information that the online store could use for targeted marketing opportunities.

To support the user data needs in the application, the database will contain a **CUSTOMERS** table. This table will have the following data structure:

Field Name	Data Type
Email	Text
Firstname	Text
Surname	Text
Address	Text
City	Text
State	Text
ZipCode	Text
Country	Text
Phone	Text
Passcode	Text
UseCookie	Text
Interests	Text

Book Data

The data requirements for the titles in the book catalog are more extensive than the user data requirements. The database must support the information about the book, which includes:

▲ Title

▲ Author

▲ Subject

▲ Price

▲ ISBN

▲ Cover Picture file name

▲ Description

▲ Inventory

To support the book information in the database, the **CATALOG** table is used. This table has the following data structure:

Field Name	Data Type
CatalogID	Number
Code	Text
Name	Text
Description	Text
Author	Text
ImageURL	Text
Price	Text
PublicationDate	Date/Time
OnHand	Number

You may notice that one field, the author, is missing from this data definition. There are two business requirements regarding authors and their relationships to the catalog. First, one book can have multiple authors. Having multiple author fields within the **CATALOG** table could solve this. But, this would violate the normalization rules for relational databases. To effectively support this requirement, we have created a separate table that links multiple authors to a single book. This is the **AUTHORTITLE** table, which has the following structure:

Field Name	Data Type
ID	AutoNumber
CatalogID	Number
AuthorID	Text

The other business requirement for authors is that the same author can write multiple books. To support this, we created an **AUTHORS** table that assigns an **AuthorID** to each author in the catalog. It is this **AuthorID** value that is used in the **AUTHORTITLE** table instead of the author's name. The structure for the **AUTHORS** table is as follows:

Field Name	Data Type
AuthorID	Text
LastName	Text
FirstName	Text

There is also dynamic information about the book that the database must support. While the list price of the book is fixed at the time of printing, (since it is printed on the cover itself) special promotions can be offered which affect the price of the book. There needs to be support in the database for these promotions. Each particular book can have multiple promotions associated with it. For each promotion, the important information is the promotion type, the start date, and the end date.

A more sophisticated promotion model would allow for a single promotion to encompass multiple books. This would be a worthwhile extension to this case study.

The **PROMOTION** table has the following data structure:

Field Name	Data Type
ID	Text
CatalogID	Number
PromotionCdoe	Text
PromotionEndDate	Date/Time

Also, the user requirements call for the searching for a particular title in a number of ways. Some of the categories for searching, such as subject, title, and ISBN, can be directly supported by the fields in the title table. Another requirement is for the support of "predetermined searches," to support concepts such as a "top 10" or "best seller" lists. To support this requirement, the **CATEGORYDESC** and **CATEGORIES** tables are included in the database. The **CATEGORYDESC** table gives a textual description of each of the categorization methods.

The data structure for this table is:

Field Name	Data Type
CategoryID	Text
Description	Text

The **CATEGORIES** table assigns the **CatalogID** from the **CATALOG** table to the categories that match the particular title. The data structure for this table is as follows:

Field Name	Data Type
ID	AutoNumber
CategoryID	Text
CatalogID	Number

Order Data

The third major section of data is the order information. This data actually performs two functions. As the user proceeds through the system and adds selections to their electronic "shopping cart", that information is tracked by the system. The shopping cart data consists of the quantity of each book that the user has identified and its **CatalogID**. Once the user has selected all of the titles that they are interested in, the content of the shopping cart then becomes the order information.

There are two tables that support the order data. The first is the **ORDERBASKET** table. This table is used to hold the information about the shopping basket that the user adds items to. This information includes who the customer is as well as the order number for the current order. After the user decides to convert the contents of their shopping cart to an actual order, the **ORDERBASKET** table also holds information about the order, such as the shipping information, payment method and amount, as well as shipping dates. Those shopping carts that are not converted into orders will eventually be deleted from the database. The data structure for this table is as follows:

Field Name	Data Type
OrderID	AutoNumber
Email	Text
ShipAddress	Text
ShipCity	Text
ShipState	Text
ShipZipCode	Text
ShipCountry	Text
PaymentMethod	Text
OrderAmount	Currency
PromisedShipDate	Date/Time
ActualShipDate	Date/Time
Fulfilled	Number
BasketCreation	Date/Time

To store the contents of the shopping cart, the **BASKETCONTENTS** table is used. This table contains the ID of the **OrderBasket** that this item is part of, as well as the book's **CatalogID** and quantity. For each distinct book in a shopping basket, there will be one record in the **BASKETCONTENTS** table. The structure of this table is:

Field Name	Data Type
BasketID	AutoNumber
OrderID	Number
CatalogID	Number
NumItems	Number

Now that we have defined all of the data structures that will be used to support the application, we will develop the application architecture that will uses these data elements to present a functioning application for the user.

Application Architecture

In defining the application the login and registration part of architecture, we will combine the user tasks and the data architecture such that the system is able to present the appropriate information to the user when the user requires it and obtain information from the user when the user is best positioned to supply the information. The application architecture should closely parallel the user task flows. Here is a high-level diagram of the application architecture:

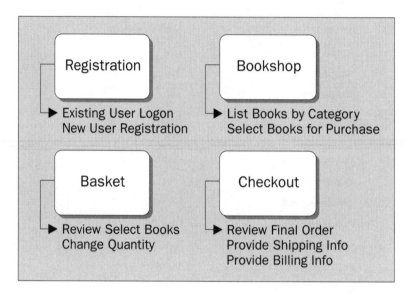

Login/Registration

The login and registration part of the application is responsible for allowing the user to identify themselves to the system. The application should ask the user if they are a new user to the system. If yes, then the system should ask the user to provide the information that will be held in the **CUSTOMERS** table. The system should give the user the option to store their login id as a cookie. This cookie would be placed on the user's system, and would automatically identify the user to the system next time the user visits. This is an optional feature, and would save the user from having to enter their user ID and password next time the user visits. In the case where the user selected to use the cookie, then for additional security, the system could query the user for their ID or password prior to finalizing any transaction and completing a purchase.

If the user is not new to the site, then the system should query the user for their user ID and password. Once the user's information has been retrieved from the database, it should be presented to the user for verification and/or modification.

Book Selection

Once the user has been successfully registered on the system, the next phase of the application will allow the user to select books from the catalog for purchase. The selection can be made in multiple ways. They will select from a list of books that match certain criteria. The user can select these criteria, such as subject, author, title, or ISBN, or the user can choose a predetermined criterion, such as a "bestsellers list."

Once the selection has been made, the system will return a listing of titles that match the criteria. These listings will contain detailed information about each title in the list, including title, author, description, cover image, retail price, and ISBN number. Along with each entry will be an option to purchase that entry. The purchase option will allow the user to select the quantity of the selected book to purchase, as well as advise the user on the selling price of the book. The selling price may differ from the retail price based on any promotions that are currently affecting that title. Once the user has determined that the wish to purchase a selected title, and selected the quantity for that title, the application moves to the next phase, which allows the user to view the contents of their electronic shopping basket.

Check Selections

After selecting a title for purchase, the user is presented with the current contents of their shopping basket. At this time, the user can modify the quantity of any previous selection. They also have the option to delete items from their shopping cart, add more items to their shopping cart by returning to the book selection phase of the application, or proceeding to the purchase phase of the application.

Purchase

Once the user has selected all of the titles that they wish to purchase, they can choose to move to the purchase phase of the application. In this phase, they are presented with detailed information about the items that they are purchasing, along with costs for taxes and shipping. After reviewing the information, the user can choose to amend their order, in which case they would be returned to the Check Selections phase of the application.

If the user chooses to continue with the purchase, they would then be prompted to select a payment method for the order. The system would then query they user for the detailed information for the selected payment method. The detailed information will vary based on the payment method selected. For example, if the user were paying by credit card, then the user would be asked to provide the credit card number along with the expiration date of the credit card.

After providing the payment information, the user will be asked to provide the shipping information for the order. This information will include the address that the order should be shipped to, as well as the shipment method. The system will default the shipment address to the user's address from their **CUSTOMER** table record. The user will then be able to accept the address, or enter a new one.

After the user has validated the shipping address, the system will calculate the ship date and the estimated arrival date, based on shipping method and destination, and present that information to the user. The user will also be given a unique order number so that if any questions arise the user can quickly reference the order with this number.

Breaking into Objects

Now that we have developed both an application architecture and a data architecture, we can design the objects that will be used by the system. There will be three main types of objects in the system: **User Interface Objects, Business Objects** and **Data Objects**. The User Interface Objects will actually be ASP pages, and we will develop these later. Here is a diagram that shows the Business and Data Access Objects that we will develop for this application:

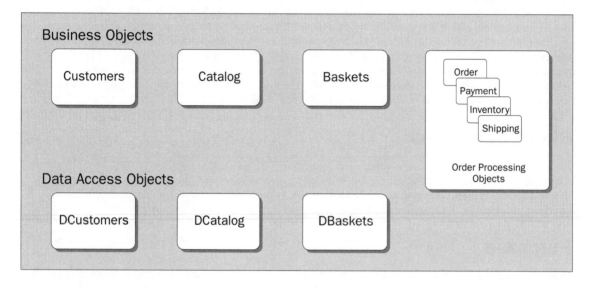

Business Objects

Business Objects are used to encapsulate the business logic of the system and will be called directly by the ASP source code. They will be responsible for manipulating the data in the system to provide the user with the proper information.

There are four application objects in our system. They roughly compare to the four primary sections of the application. There are application objects for **Customers**, **Catalog**, **Baskets**, and Order Processing.

The Customers Object

The **Customers** object will perform three functions:

▲ Authenticating existing customers. In doing this, it will query the customer database to see if a customer matching the supplied **customerID** and **password** exists.

▲ Registering new customers. The object will take the supplied customer information and insert it into the database.

▲ Updating of an existing customer's information.

The business logic behind authentication of existing customers and registering new customers will be encapsulated in this object. This will allow the ASP code to call one method, **RegisterCustomer**, which will then either validate that customer as an existing customer, or add that customer to the database and request the remaining information from the user.

The Catalog Object

The **Catalog** object is responsible for retrieving a list of titles from the system and for providing the ASP source with the data that it needs to display the list for the user. The object will support multiple methods for access based on the different available search categories. Each method will return the information to the server in the same format, so that one block of code can handle the multiple search types.

The **Catalog** object can also support the retrieval of possible values for each search category. This will allow the ASP source to display a list of possible values for a selected criterion to the user and allow the user to select from that list, rather than requiring the user to directly enter information. For example, the object could return a list of all possible entries in the **SUBJECT** field, which the ASP source could put into a selection list, that the user could choose from.

The Baskets Object

The **Baskets** object is responsible for maintaining the contents of the user's list of books currently selected for purchase. The object will have methods that provide for adding items to the basket, changing the desired quantity of an item in the basket, clearing all of the items from the basket, and returning the contents of the basket.

The Order Processing Objects

The Order Processing objects are collectively responsible for the final phase of the application. They are used to take the contents of the basket and turn them into a sale. These objects have four major pieces of functionality to support the order processing function.

 The **Order** object is used to compute the pricing information for the order. Its responsibilities include determining the selling price of each item in the basket. The selling price is determined by modifying the list price by any promotions that may be in effect at the time of purchase. It then calculates the total price of all items in the order. Next, it computes the shipping costs and the sales tax. Finally, all of these figures are added together by the object to arrive at the total cost for the order.

 The **Payment** object is responsible for validating the payment method that the user selects. This object can use multiple methods for validation, based on the method of payment being used.

 The **Inventory** object is responsible for maintaining the proper inventory information for all of the titles in the database. The object will deduct from the database the quantity of books ordered in each order. The object could also be responsible for sending notification if the inventory of an item drops below a certain threshold.

 The **Shipping** object is responsible for the processing of all of the shipping information for the order. This object will be used to transmit the shipment information to the shipping agent. It will also be responsible for determining the date that the order will ship and also estimated arrival date for the shipment.

Data Objects

Data Access Objects are used to encapsulate the database access of the system. Our newly created Business Objects will call these objects. In some instances, they can be directly called by the ASP source code. These objects will directly manipulate that information in the database as well as managing the connections to the database. There are three data objects in this system.

The DCustomers Object

The **DCustomers** object is responsible for managing the data connection between the **Customers** Application object and the database. This object supports the retrieval of customer information, the addition of new customers, the modification of existing customer information. This object interacts with the **CUSTOMERS** table in the database.

The DCatalog Object

The **DCatalog** object manages the data connection between the **Catalog** Application object and the database. This object supports the retrieval of items from the catalog based on criteria that is supplied to it. This criterion includes the field to search on, as well as the value for the search. The object returns the results of the search to the calling object, the **Catalog** object. This object interacts with the **CATALOG** table in the database, as well as the **AUTHORS** and **CATEGORIES** tables.

The DBaskets Object

The **DBaskets** object manages the data connection between the **Basket** and Order Processing Application objects. This object supports the basket manipulation methods of the **Baskets** Application object, such as adding items, retrieving basket contents, and modifying purchase quantities. The content retrieval method is also use by the Order Processing objects when converting the contents of the basket into a valid order.

Creating Data Objects in Visual Basic

Now that we have examined what the objects that make up the system are, let's move into the first steps of implementation. The architecture of this system is such that there is a close correlation between the Application Objects and the Data Objects. In many cases, the Application Object merely acts as an intermediary between the ASP source code and the Data Objects. This additional layer of abstraction may seem like overkill, but it is actually a very sound design decision.

By separating the business logic from the application logic, it allows us a number of advantages. Since the only knowledge that the Application layer code has of the database is through the methods of the Data objects, it is relatively painless to change the implementation of the data objects and the database itself without affecting the application objects.

This gets back to one of the primary tenets of object-oriented programming: **encapsulation**. By encapsulating the physical database information in an object, we have the ability to change its implementation without affecting the rest of the system.

In Chapter 13, you saw how you could use the transactional capabilities of Microsoft Transaction Server alongside of IIS 4.0. So now we will begin to put those ideas to good use. Our application will be built using components that take full advantage of transactions and all of the benefits that they bring. Since a good portion of our application deals with the manipulation of data in databases, the use of transactions to handle the data manipulations is a natural.

There are two steps that we will follow in putting together each of the data objects. We will separate these two steps to make the explanation clearer. As you become more comfortable with creating objects, the two steps will seamlessly meld into one.

The first step will be to write the database access code for each method that our object will support. Then we will add the necessary "plumbing" to make the application transaction aware and compliant. Once you have learned the steps to making your objects transactional, it will just become a natural part of your development process.

The objects that we will be developing make heavy use of collections. The use of collections makes it easy to modify the data that is being passed between the object and the caller. This is done for both cosmetic reasons, since a single collection passed as a parameter can encapsulate a large number of what were previously individual parameters, as well as for later modification and enhancement.

The Customer Data Object

The first object that we will be developing is the **CustomerData** object. This object is responsible for managing the interaction between the application and the customer information in the database. We will be developing this object, along with all of the other objects in this application, using Visual Basic 5.0.

> *At this point, we will assume that you are familiar with creating ActiveX components in Visual Basic. If you need to brush up on this, a good reference is Instant VB5 ActiveX Control Creation–ISBN 1-861000-23-5.*

There are three methods that the **CustomerData** Object supports for manipulating the data in the **CUSTOMERS** table of the database. These methods allow you to insert a new customer, select an existing customer, and update the information of an existing customer.

The SelectCustomer Method

The **SelectCustomer** method is used to retrieve information from the database and pass it back to the ASP source. The information that is passed back is a collection that is the contents of the desired record from the **CUSTOMERS** table in the database. To choose the particular record, the database is searched based on the supplied **customerID** and **password**. If a record is found that matches these criteria, then the data is passed back to the ASP source. If the record is not found, then the response back to the system is that the record does not exist. First, let's take a look at the method as it is implemented using Visual Basic.

```
Public Function SelectCustomer(ByVal vCustData As Variant) As Variant
On Error GoTo SelectCustomerErr
Dim vResponse As New Collection
    Dim vCustData2 As New Collection
Dim vInterests As Variant
    Dim vSql As Variant

    Let vSql = "SELECT * FROM CUSTOMERS " & _
               " WHERE CustomerID = '" & _
LCase(vCustData("CustomerID")) & "';"
Set oDb = oObjectContext.CreateInstance("ADODB.Connection")
oDb.Open vDbConn
```

```
Set oRs = oDb.Execute(vSql)
If Not oRs.EOF Then

        vCustData2.Add Trim(oRs.Fields("Password")), "password"
        vCustData2.Add CStr(oRs.Fields("CustomerId")), "customerid"
        vCustData2.Add Trim(oRs.Fields("Firstname")), "firstname"
        vCustData2.Add Trim(oRs.Fields("Surname")), "surname"
        vCustData2.Add Trim(oRs.Fields("Address")), "address"
        vCustData2.Add Trim(oRs.Fields("City")), "city"
        vCustData2.Add Trim(oRs.Fields("State")), "state"
        vCustData2.Add Trim(oRs.Fields("Zipcode")), "zipcode"
        vCustData2.Add Trim(oRs.Fields("Country")), "country"
        vCustData2.Add Trim(oRs.Fields("Phone")), "phone"
        vCustData2.Add Trim(oRs.Fields("UseCookie")), "usecookie"
        Set vInterests = BuildInterests(Trim(oRs.Fields("Interests")))
vCustData2.Add vInterests, "interests"

        vResponse.Add True, Key:="exists"
    vResponse.Add vCustData2, "custdata"
Else
        vResponse.Add False, Key:="exists"
End If

    oDb.Close
vResponse.Add False, Key:="error"
oObjectContext.SetComplete
Set SelectCustomer = vResponse

    Exit Function

SelectCustomerErr:
    oObjectContext.SetAbort
Set SelectCustomer = RaiseError("SelectCustomer")

End Function
```

Now, let's step through the source code of this method and take a look at how this database manipulation is accomplished.

```
Public Function SelectCustomer(ByVal vCustData As Variant) As Variant
```

The parameter that is passed in to the method is a collection, so it is passed as a **Variant** data type. This collection contains one data element, which is the **customerID**. The return value from the method will also be a collection, so the data type for the return is a **Variant** as well.

```
On Error GoTo SelectCustomerErr
```

There is a local error handling routine that will get called on any error that may occur in the method. This will be critical later on when we add support for transactions.

```
Dim vResponse As New Collection
Dim vCustData2 As New Collection
```

This method will use collections to pass the information back to the calling application. Some of the members of the collection will be collections themselves. These two statements are responsible for creating the new **vResponse** and **vCustData2** collections.

```
    Dim vInterests As Variant
    Dim vSql As Variant

    Let vSql = "SELECT * FROM CUSTOMERS " & _
               " WHERE Email = '" & _
    LCase(vCustData("CustomerID")) & "';"
```

The SQL statement will be used to extract the desired record from the database. The query will return all of the records in which the **CustomerID** field matches the value that is passed in to the method. Since the **CustomerID** field is a unique key for the table, at most one record will be returned.

```
    Set oDb = oObjectContext.CreateInstance("ADODB.Connection")
```

The database access in this method, along with all of the methods in all of the data components that we are creating, will be done using **ActiveX Data Objects**, or ADO. These are the same data access objects that are available directly from Active Server Pages. Being that they are the same objects, all of the methods and properties are the same as well.

For more information on ActiveX Data Objects, refer to Chapter 7.

The **oObjectContext** object is part of the Transaction server plumbing that we talked about in Chapter 13. We will go into greater detail about what this object represents in just a bit. For now, we will use its **CreateInstance** method to create a new ADO Connection object. This object will allow us to access information in the database.

```
    oDb.Open vDbConn
```

The database connection is opened with this method. The **vDbConn** parameter is an externally defined global variable that defines the connection string for all of the components. The current value of this parameter is **"DSN=Eshop;UID=sa;PWD=;"** This string will open the database that is referred to by the ODBC System DSN named **Eshop**. This DSN points to our MS Access database file, **ESHOP.MDB**. Remember, any errors that occur in opening the database will be handled via the **On Error Goto** statement at the beginning of this method.

> *We will be using Access as the database during the development of this case study. However, at this time, Access does not support the transactional capabilities of MTS. Having said that, the code we are writing can be used against a database such as SQL Server, which does support the transactional capabilities of MTS.*

```
    Set oRs = oDb.Execute(vSql)
```

We now create a recordset that contains the results of the SQL query by using the **Execute** method of the ADO Connection object. If the customer exists in the database, we then go through each of the fields in the record and add its contents to a collection that we will pass back to the calling application.

```
    If Not oRs.EOF Then

        vCustData2.Add Trim(oRs.Fields("Password")), "password"
        vCustData2.Add CStr(oRs.Fields("CustomerId")), "customerid"
        vCustData2.Add Trim(oRs.Fields("Firstname")), "firstname"
        vCustData2.Add Trim(oRs.Fields("Surname")), "surname"
        vCustData2.Add Trim(oRs.Fields("Address")), "address"
```

```
        vCustData2.Add Trim(oRs.Fields("City")), "city"
        vCustData2.Add Trim(oRs.Fields("State")), "state"
        vCustData2.Add Trim(oRs.Fields("Zipcode")), "zipcode"
        vCustData2.Add Trim(oRs.Fields("Country")), "country"
        vCustData2.Add Trim(oRs.Fields("Phone")), "phone"
        vCustData2.Add Trim(oRs.Fields("UseCookie")), "usecookie"
        Set vInterests = BuildInterests(Trim(oRs.Fields("Interests")))
```

The **BuildInterests** method is used to extract the information from the **Interests** field in the retrieved record. This information is placed into the **vInterests** collection, which is then added to the collection that contains all of retrieved customer information.

```
        vCustData2.Add vInterests, "interests"

        vResponse.Add True, Key:="exists"
        vResponse.Add vCustData2, "custdata"
```

Since the customer record that we were looking for was found, the **exists** element of the response collection is set to **True**. Then we add the customer data collection, which we just built, to the response collection as well.

```
    Else
        vResponse.Add False, Key:="exists"
```

This statement is called if the recordset that the initial query returned was empty. Since no data was found, there is no customer data collection. All we do is set the **exists** element of the collection to **False**.

```
    End If

    oDb.Close
```

Since we have now done all of the database access for this method, we close the connection to the database. Normally, this would automatically happen when the **oDb** object went out of scope. However, it is good practice to explicitly close all database objects that your method may have created.

```
        vResponse.Add False, Key:="error"
```

The **response** collection also has an element called **error** that indicates if an error occurred while processing the method. Since no error occurred, we will set this value to **False**.

```
        oObjectContext.SetComplete
```

This is another part of the Transaction Server plumbing that is in this method. This was covered in Chapter 13, but we will review what it does in just a little bit.

```
    Set SelectCustomer = vResponse

    Exit Function

SelectCustomerErr:
    oObjectContext.SetAbort
```

Again, here is some more of the Transaction Server plumbing. Don't worry, we are getting close to explaining what it is used for.

```
    Set SelectCustomer = RaiseError("SelectCustomer")

End Function
```

Transaction Server Plumbing

Now that we have created our first data object, let's take a look at the plumbing that we have added to this object to make it work with Microsoft Transaction Server. There is support that is added to each **.CLS** file that we create in Visual Basic, as well as support that is added to each method.

The first step that we need to take is to add the reference to the Microsoft Transaction Server Type Library to our project. In doing this, we can get access to those objects that we need to link our data object with Transaction Server. You will use the References command from the Project menu in Visual Basic.

From this dialog box, you can select the entry for Microsoft Transaction Server Type Library. If you do not see it listed here, the select the browse button and locate the file named **MTXAS.DLL**. Now you are ready to add the plumbing directly to your class module.

Adding Plumbing to your Class Module

Here is what we are adding to the **.CLS** module itself:

```
Implements ObjectControl
```

This statement tells Visual Basic that this class will support all of the methods of the **ObjectControl** interface. It is the responsibility of our data object to implement all of the methods though. This is the Visual Basic form of C++ inheritance, but only the interface is inherited. The implementation is left up to you. More information on interfaces is available in the Visual Basic documentation.

```
Private oDb As ADODB.Connection
Private oRs As ADODB.Recordset

Private oObjectContext As ObjectContext
```

We create a few class level variables that will be used throughout this module. The **ObjectContext** variable will be used in this module to provide access to the current object's context. The context of an object is information specifically about that object. It includes information about the environment the object is executing in and also about the transaction that the object is a part of. Earlier in this section, you saw how this object reference was used in three places in our **SelectCustomer** method. We will examine that in detail in just a bit.

The CanBePooled Method

This is the first of the three methods that we are required to implement since we set this class to also implement the **ObjectControl** class.

```
Private Function ObjectControl_CanBePooled() As Boolean
    ObjectControl_CanBePooled = True
End Function
```

This method is used to identify if this particular object can be recycled. When an object is pooled for reuse, it is not destroyed after it is deactivated. Rather, the object is restored to its initial and returned to a pool. When a new instance of this object is needed, it can be drawn from the pool rather than being created.

Just because we set this value to **True** does not mean that the object will ALWAYS be pooled. In fact, only objects that have a threading model of **Both** will be pooled. Back in Chapter 13, we looked at the threading models associated with MTS components. Visual Basic can only create objects that are Single Threaded or Apartment Threaded. Since only both threaded model objects can be pooled, our object can never be pooled. But, since we are required to implement this function, we might as well be optimistic and allow MTS to pool it if in a future version of MTS allows for pooling of objects created in VB.

The Deactivate Method

The **Deactivate** method is called when the current instance of the object is no longer needed.

```
Private Sub ObjectControl_Deactivate()
    Set oObjectContext = Nothing
    Set oDb = Nothing
    Set oRs = Nothing
End Sub
```

This method should be used to clean up any objects that may have been created during the lifetime of the class. By setting the object references to **Nothing**, their resources will be freed.

The Activate Method

The final **ObjectControl** method that we need to implement is the **Activate** method.

```
Private Sub ObjectControl_Activate()
    On Error GoTo OCActivateErr

    Set oObjectContext = GetObjectContext()

    Exit Sub

OCActivateErr:
    Call RaiseError("OCActivate")

End Sub
```

This method is called when the object is activated for use. Transaction Server uses a process called "just-in-time activation." This means that an object will only be activated when it is needed to process requests from a client. This allows for a more effective utilization of server resources.

In our implementation of the **Activate** method, we will be grabbing a reference to the current object context and storing it in a module level variable. This will save us the overhead of having to call **GetObjectContext** every time we need a reference to the current object context. We will use the reference to this object in our data manipulation methods.

Transaction Server Plumbing in the SelectCustomer Method

Now, let's take a look inside the **SelectCustomer** method of the **DCustomers** object at those places where the Transaction Server plumbing has been included.

In the CreateInstance Method

The first use of the **ObjectContext** is in this statement:

```
Set oDb = oObjectContext.CreateInstance("ADODB.Connection")
```

Normally, you would simply use the Visual Basic **New** operation to create an instance of the **ADODB.Connection** object. But since we are running this object inside of a Transaction Server context, we want to create any new object inside this context as well. The **CreateInstance** method of the current object context has the same parameters as the **CreateObject** method, but it creates the new object inside Transaction Server. The **Connection** object will be running on the same thread of execution as the **DCustomers** object is running. Now that we have this reference to a **Connection** object inside of Transaction Server, we can go on and do our database processing.

In the SetComplete and SetAbort Methods

The next time we encounter the Transaction Server plumbing is once we have completed all of the database manipulations in the method. When you start a transaction, it can have two outcomes. It can complete successfully, or it can't complete successfully. A successfully completed transaction is one that successfully completes all of the steps that make up the transaction. It is the responsibility of each object in the transaction to tell the Transaction Server if it completed successfully or not. If the component completes successfully, then it calls this method:

545

```
oObjectContext.SetComplete
```

When this method is called, Transaction Server notes that this step in the transaction completed successfully. When all objects in a transaction have all called their **SetComplete** method, Transaction Server will then commit the transaction. By calling this method, you are also telling Transaction Server that it is OK to deactivate this object.

If during the processing of the method an error occurs that does not permit the successful completion of that method, then it is the responsibility of the object to notify the transaction that it did not complete successfully. To do this, the object should call this method:

```
oObjectContext.SetAbort
```

When Transaction Server sees that one of the objects that made up the transaction did not complete successfully, it will abort the entire transaction. It will also deactivate any objects that made up the transaction.

Now that you have seen how easy it is to add Transaction Server support to our objects, let's move forward with the other two methods in the **Customers** data object.

The InsertCustomer Method

Now that we are able to determine if a particular user is in the database, we need to be able to add a new user to the database.

In this method, the information for the new customer is passed in as a parameter. This parameter is a collection of information that the system has gathered from the user. At this point in the application, the user has entered their **customerID** and **password**. This information has been passed to the **SelectCustomer** method, which was unable to locate the matching customer record, and so returned **False** to the application. The application can then call the **InsertCustomer** method to create a new customer record in the database.

```
Public Function InsertCustomer(ByVal vCustData As Variant) As Variant
```

This method is very similar to the **SelectCustomer** method we defined previously. The parameter that is passed to the method is a collection, as is the value returned by the method.

```
On Error GoTo InsertCustomerErr

Dim vResponse As New Collection
Dim vCustData2 As New Collection

Set oRs = oObjectContext.CreateInstance("ADODB.Recordset")
```

In this method, we will be using the ADO **Recordset** object, instead of the ADO connection object. Since we will be manipulating the database directly, rather than through the use of SQL, the **Recordset** object is all that we need to use.

```
oRs.Open "customers", vDbConn, adOpenKeyset, adLockPessimistic, adCmdTable
```

We will initialize the **Recordset** by using its **Open** method. Since we have not defined a database connection, we pass the **vDbConn** variable, which as we saw before, is a global variable that holds the database connection string. Since you will be adding information to the database, and don't need to access new information from other users, the **adOpenKeyset** flag will update the recordset only with new records that you add. The **adLockPessimistic** flag will cause the record that the recordset is currently working to be locked at all times. Since the first parameter, "customers," represents the name of a table in the database, the **adCmdTable** flag is included to identify this as such.

```
oRs.AddNew
oRs.Fields("Email") = LCase(vCustData("email"))
oRs.Fields("Password") = LTrim(vCustData("password"))
oRs.Fields("Firstname") = ""
oRs.Fields("Surname") = ""
oRs.Fields("Address") = ""
oRs.Fields("City") = ""
oRs.Fields("State") = ""
oRs.Fields("Zipcode") = ""
oRs.Fields("Country") = ""
oRs.Fields("Phone") = ""
oRs.Fields("UseCookie") = "N"
oRs.Fields("Interests") = ""
oRs.Update
```

With the recordset now open, we will create a new record with the **AddNew** method. Then we set the fields in that record with the values passed into the method. Since the only fields that have data in them are the user's email address and password, all of the other fields will be initialized to their default values. The ASP user interface will use another method, **UpdateCustomer**, to set the remaining fields in the record.

```
vCustData2.Add Trim(oRs.Fields("Email")), "email"
vCustData2.Add Trim(oRs.Fields("Password")), "password"
vCustData2.Add CStr(oRs.Fields("CustomerId")), "customerid"
```

Once we call the **Update** method of the recordset, the new record is added to the database. Since the **CustomerID** field is automatically generated after a new record is added, we can get its value from the recordset and pass it back to the application in the **response** collection.

```
vCustData2.Add "", "firstname"
vCustData2.Add "", "surname"
vCustData2.Add "", "address"
vCustData2.Add "", "city"
vCustData2.Add "", "state"
vCustData2.Add "", "zipcode"
vCustData2.Add "", "country"
vCustData2.Add "", "phone"
vCustData2.Add "N", "usecookie"
vCustData2.Add BuildInterests(""), "interests"

vResponse.Add False, Key:="error"
vResponse.Add True, Key:="exists"
vResponse.Add vCustData2, "custdata"
```

Next, we create the **response** collection in the exact same way that we did in the **SelectCustomer** method. Since the majority of the fields have no data, we just add blank strings for those entries in the collection.

```
        oRs.Close

    oObjectContext.SetComplete
    Set InsertCustomer = vResponse

    Exit Function

InsertCustomerErr:
    oObjectContext.SetAbort
    Set InsertCustomer = RaiseError("InsertCustomer")

End Function
```

Now that we have seen how to search for a customer in the database and add a new customer to the database, let's take a look at how to update an existing customer in the database.

The UpdateCustomer Method

In this method, we will pass in a collection that includes all of the fields of information about a particular customer. The collection will include the value that uniquely identifies this customer. This value will be used to look up the existing record in the database. Then the new values will be written into the database from the passed-in collection.

```
Public Function UpdateCustomer(ByVal vCustData As Variant) As Variant
    On Error GoTo UpdateCustomerErr

    Dim vResponse As New Collection
    Dim vSql As Variant

    Let vSql = "SELECT * FROM CUSTOMERS " & _
               " WHERE email = '" & LCase(vCustData("email")) & "';"
```

This is the same SQL statement that was used in the **SelectCustomer** method. Since the email field is a unique key in the table, at most one record will be returned. In our application logic, we will ensure that the customer has been validated before their information can be updated. Therefore, we can assume that only one record will be returned by this SQL query.

```
    Set oRs = oObjectContext.CreateInstance("ADODB.Recordset")
    oRs.CursorType = adOpenKeyset
    oRs.LockType = adLockPessimistic
    oRs.Open vSql, vDbConn
```

In this method, we will again be using a recordset directly. We have changed the **CursorType** of the recordset to be an **adOpenKeyset** recordset. This will allow the recordset to reflect any changes made by anyone accessing the database. Since we have ensured through application logic that only validated users can call this method, we do not check to see if the recordset has valid data in it. If any errors occur, the error handling that was set up at the beginning of the method will catch them.

```
    oRs.Fields("Email") = Trim(LCase(vCustData("email")))
    oRs.Fields("Password") = Trim(vCustData("password"))
    oRs.Fields("Firstname") = Left(Trim(vCustData("firstname")), 25)
    oRs.Fields("Surname") = Left(Trim(vCustData("surname")), 25)
    oRs.Fields("Address") = Left(Trim(vCustData("address")), 40)
```

```
        oRs.Fields("City") = Left(Trim(vCustData("city")), 20)
        oRs.Fields("State") = Left(Trim(vCustData("state")), 20)
        oRs.Fields("Zipcode") = Left(Trim(vCustData("zipcode")), 10)
        oRs.Fields("Country") = Left(Trim(vCustData("country")), 20)
        oRs.Fields("Phone") = Left(Trim(vCustData("phone")), 20)
        oRs.Fields("UseCookie") = Left(Trim(vCustData("UseCookie")), 1)
        oRs.Fields("Interests") = ExtractInterestCodes(vCustData("interests"))
        oRs.Update
```

After setting all of the fields in the recordset to the data passed in via the collection, we call the **Update** method of the recordset. This method writes all of the changes out to the database.

```
        oRs.Close

    vResponse.Add False, Key:="error"

    oObjectContext.SetComplete
    Set UpdateCustomer = vResponse
```

Since the method completed successfully, and all of the data has been written to the database, we flag this method as successful by calling **SetComplete**.

```
    Exit Function

UpdateCustomerErr:
    oObjectContext.SetAbort
    Set UpdateCustomer = RaiseError("UpdateCustomer")

End Function
```

In our error handling routine, we call the **SetAbort** method of the object context. This will cause the current transaction to be aborted. Now that we have created the data objects that allow us to interface with the physical database, we will create the application objects that encapsulate the business logic of the system.

Implementing Application Objects

Now that we have created our data objects, we will need to create the application object that provides the link between the Active Server Pages-generated user interface and the database objects. The **Customers** application object will expose methods to Active Server Pages and these methods will encapsulate the business logic as well as work with the **Customers** data object to manipulate the database. There are three methods that the **Customers** application object has. These methods allow you to authenticate a customer, register a new customer, and update an existing customer. Since this component is also going to participate in transactions, it needs virtually the same Transaction Server plumbing that the data objects has.

Transaction Server Plumbing

This object will use the same basic mechanism to support transactions as the **Customers** data object used. The application object will:

▲ Add a reference to the Microsoft Transaction Server Type Library

▲ Implement **ObjectControl** to support all of the methods of the Object Control class

▲ Implement the **ObjectControl_CanBePooled** and **ObjectControl_Deactivate** methods using the same code as before

The object will also implement the **ObjectControl_Activate** method. This method is slightly different from the same method in the **Customers** data object.

```
Private Sub ObjectControl_Activate()
    On Error GoTo OCActivateErr

    Set oObjectContext = GetObjectContext()
    Set oDCustomers = oObjectContext.CreateInstance("DpkgCustomers.DCustomers")
```

We will grab a reference to the current object context and store it in a variable for later use. We will also create an instance of the **Customers** data object, using the **CreateInstance** method of the current object context. The reference to this instance will be stored in a global variable for use in the methods of this class.

```
    Exit Sub

OCActivateErr:
    Call RaiseError("OCActivate")

End Sub
```

The AuthenticateCustomer Method

The role of the **AuthenticateCustomer** method is to check to see if the email and password that a user has entered into the system matches an existing customer. If no matching email address can be found in the system, then the method responds that the user does not exist. If the email address is found, but the password does not match, then the method responds by indicating an invalid password. Finally, if the email address is in the database and the password matches, then the method responds by indicating this is a valid customer.

```
Public Function AuthenticateCustomer(ByVal vCustData As Variant) As Variant
    On Error GoTo AuthenticateCustomerErr

    Dim vPassword2 As Variant
    Dim vResponse As Variant
    Dim vCustData2 As Variant
    Dim vResponse2 As Variant

    vPassword2 = vCustData("password")
```

The customer data is passed in via a collection. The collection currently has two entries in it. One corresponding to the email address that the customer supplied. The other is the password that the customer supplied as well. The password that the customer entered is stored in a local variable for later verification.

```
    Set vResponse = oDCustomers.SelectCustomer(vCustData)
```

The **SelectCustomer** method of the **Customers** data object is called. This object will fill the **vResponse** collection with all of the customer information if there is a matching customer.

```
If Not vResponse("error") Then
    If vResponse("exists") Then
        Set vCustData2 = vResponse("CustData")
        Set vResponse2 = New Collection
        vResponse2.Add False, Key:="error"
        vResponse2.Add True, Key:="exists"
```

The **vResponse2** collection will be the information that is passed back to the caller of the **AuthenticateCustomer** method. Since we know that the customer exists at this point, the "exists" key in the collection is set to True.

```
        vResponse2.Add vCustData2, Key:="custdata"
        If (Trim(vCustData2("password")) Like Trim(vPassword2)) Then
            vResponse2.Add True, Key:="passwordvalid"
        Else
            vResponse2.Add False, Key:="passwordvalid"
        End If
```

We then check to see if the password that was entered by the user matches the one that was stored with the customer record in the database. This is an example of the separation of business rules from database access. The validation of a password is considered a business rule in this case. Therefore, the logic of checking the entered password against the one from the database is performed here, rather than in the data object, or in the ASP source.

One reason for doing this is that in this example the passwords are merely clear text that is validated character for character. If business rules changed and the passwords needed to become formatted differently, or passed through some sort of encryption algorithm, the only place that changes would need to be made would be in this method. No other code in any other module would have to be changed.

```
        Set vResponse = vResponse2
    End If
End If

oObjectContext.SetComplete
Set AuthenticateCustomer = vResponse

Exit Function

AuthenticateCustomerErr:
    oObjectContext.SetAbort
    Set AuthenticateCustomer = RaiseError("AuthenticateCustomer")

End Function
```

As with the data object, if the method completes successfully, then we indicate this to the Transaction Server with the **SetComplete** method. Conversely, if the method does not complete successfully, we call the **SetAbort** method of the object context to tell Transaction Server that a problem happened, and not to carry out the current transaction.

The RegisterCustomer Method

The **RegisterCustomer** method handles the registration of customers into the system. This method performs two actions. First, it checks to see if the customer information is in the database and that the passwords match. Second, if the customer is not in the database, it adds that customer information to the database. By doing this, it ensures that every person who uses the system has information in the **Customers** database. Even if all that information consists of is email and password, the entry is still made to the database.

```
Public Function RegisterCustomer(ByVal vCustData As Variant) As Variant
    On Error GoTo RegisterCustomerErr

    Dim vResponse As Variant

    Set vResponse = AuthenticateCustomer(vCustData)
```

The **AuthenticateCustomer** method that we defined above is used to validate that the email address entered by the user matches an email address in the database. It also performs the password validation on the password that the user enters into the system.

```
    If Not vResponse("error") And _
        Not vResponse("exists") Then
```

If the email address does not match any address in the database, then the **vResponse** collection has its "exists" element set to False. When this method detects this, it then knows to add that customer information to the system.

```
        Set vResponse = oDCustomers.InsertCustomer(vCustData)
        vResponse.Add True, Key:="passwordvalid"
```

The customer information is added to the database by using the **InsertCustomer** method of the **Customers** data object. Since this is a new customer, we can assume that the password that they entered is the one they want, so we will make that password valid by setting the proper key in the response collection to **True**.

```
    End If

    oObjectContext.SetComplete
    Set RegisterCustomer = vResponse

    Exit Function

RegisterCustomerErr:
    oObjectContext.SetAbort
    Set RegisterCustomer = RaiseError("RegisterCustomer")

End Function
```

As with all methods that participate in transactions, if the method is successful, then you need to call **SetComplete**. If the method failed for any reason, you call **SetAbort** and the entire transaction that invoked this method is rolled back.

The UpdateCustomer Method

The **UpdateCustomer** method is used to write any changes in the customer's information back to the database. Since there are no business rules that are being applied here, the application object's method is very straightforward.

```
Public Function UpdateCustomer(ByVal vCustData As Variant) As Variant
On Error GoTo UpdateCustomerErr

    Dim vResponse As Variant

    Set vResponse = oDCustomers.UpdateCustomer(vCustData)
```

The revised customer data is passed into the function in the **vCustData** collection. This collection is passed in its entirety to the **UpdateCustomer** method of the **Customers** data object. The error handler that was defined catches any errors that occur in the data object's **UpdateCustomer** method at the beginning of the method.

```
    oObjectContext.SetComplete
    Set UpdateCustomer = vResponse

    Exit Function

UpdateCustomerErr:
    oObjectContext.SetAbort
    Set UpdateCustomer = RaiseError("UpdateCustomer")

    End Function
```

Now that we have defined the business object to handle the customer information, let's move on to the "user interface" for this object. The user interface in our system is actually a web page. The HTML pages that will be displayed on the user's browser are created using Active Server Pages. Our next step will be to integrate these pages with the components that we have just created.

Using Custom Objects in ASP

The initial task that the user must perform when using our system is to identify themselves to the system. This is the registration step and we will be using one ASP source file to handle all of the registration details. To have one ASP source file handle multiple functions, we will be including a "**state**" variable in the page. Based on the value of this variable, the page will perform different functions. We could have just as easily created multiple pages so that each served its own function, but by using one file, we have all of the ASP source related in customer registration in one place.

Global Stuff

We will start off this ASP file with most of the normal stuff that you find at the top of any ASP source file. Later, we will come back and add some more code at the top here.

```
<%@ LANGUAGE="VBSCRIPT" %>
<% Option Explicit %>
<% Response.Expires = 0 %>
```

We want this page to be regenerated every time the browser loads it, so we set the **Expires** property of the ASP **Response** object to **0**.

```
<HTML>
<HEAD>

<TITLE>Home</TITLE>
<LINK REL="stylesheet" TYPE="text/css" HREF="main.css">
</HEAD>
<BODY BGCOLOR=Cyan>

<% Dim state %>
<% Dim objCustomers %>
<% Dim objUtility %>
<% Dim objCustData %>
<% Dim objResponse %>
<% Dim objInterest %>
<% Dim vData %>

<TABLE WIDTH=100% CELLSPACING=0 CELLPADDING=0 BORDER=0>
<TR CLASS="pageheader">
<TH ALIGN=left> Register with WROX
</TH>
</TR>
</TABLE>
```

Now that we have dispatched with the variable declarations and header information we will get to the part that handles the **state** for this particular request. The **state** for the page should be passed in as part of the URL that references this page. We can query for its value by examining the **Request** object's **QueryString** collection.

```
<% if not Request.QueryString("state") = "" then %>
<%     state = Request.QueryString("state")  %>
<% else %>
```

If there is no **state** parameter in the URL string, then we will try to figure out what the state is in another way. Later in this section, you will see that once a user is successfully registered in the system, we set a Session-level variable called **auth** to **true**. By checking for this value, we can determine if we need to query for the customer's email and password.

```
<%     if Session("auth") = true then %>
<%         state = 2 %>
<%     else %>
<%         state = 1 %>
<%     end if %>
<% end if %>
```

Step 1 – Obtain Email and password

When the "**state**" is set to **1**, we need to query the user for the email and password. To do this, we will just use a simple fill-in form and prompt the user as to why they are entering this information.

```
<% if state = 1 then %>

<P>To use the Wrox bookshop you must be registered with us.
    You are identified by your email address and a password

    <FORM ACTION="m4register.asp?state=2" METHOD="POST">
```

We will be using a **POST** type of Form. The destination page for this Form will be the page we are currently on, **m4register.asp**, but with a **URL** parameter of **state = 2**. This will cause the next step in the registration process to occur.

```
    <TABLE BORDER="0">
    <TR>
        <TD>Email</TD>
        <TD><INPUT TYPE="text" SIZE="20" NAME="email"
          VALUE="<% =Session("email") %>"></TD>
    </TR>
    <TR>
        <TD>Password</TD>
        <TD><INPUT TYPE="password" SIZE="20" NAME="password"
          VALUE="<% =Session("password") %>"></TD>
```

When we query the user for the email address and password, we would like to give them default values, if they exist. You will see in a later state, that once the user is registered, their email and password will be stored in Session-level variables. The values in these variables will be displayed to the user as the default value.

```
    </TR>
    </TABLE>
    <INPUT TYPE="hidden" NAME="register1" VALUE="1">
```

We are also including a hidden field that will identify that this request came from the form when the **state** value was **1**. You will see when we go over **state 2** how this value is used. Basically, it is the flag to indicate that the email and password submitted needs to be validated by the **application** object.

```
    <HR>
    <INPUT TYPE="submit" NAME="submit" VALUE="Submit">
    </FORM>

<% end if %>
```

This ASP code will generate a page that looks something like this:

Step 2 – Validate and obtain information for update

Once the user has entered their email and password, we can now try to validate that information against the information in the database. To handle this processing, we will again be using the same **m4register.asp** file, but this time there will be a URL parameter that sets the **state** to a value of 2.

Validate supplied information

The first thing we need to do is validate the information supplied by the user and determine if they are a registered user or not.

```
<% if state = 2 then %>

   <% if Request.Form("register1") = "1" then %>
```

If you remember from the previous step, there was an invisible field that was passed in the form along with the email and password. The value in this field indicated that there was information being passed from the form. We then grab that information from the **Request.Form** collection and store it in Session-level variables.

```
<%     Session("email") = Request.Form("email") %>
<%     Session("password") = Request.Form("password") %>
<%     if Session("email") = "" or Session("password") = "" then %>
<%         state = 1 %>
           <p class=errmsg>Both fields are mandatory</p>
```

If the user fails to enter their email or password before submitting the form, then we cannot continue our processing. There are two steps that are taken to handle this. The state variable is reset to 1, which will cause the form prompting for the email and password to be redisplayed. If you remember from the previous section, the default values for the two fields are taken from the Session-level variables, which we have just set here. The other step is to add a prompt to the user that both fields are mandatory for registration.

```
<%    else %>
<%          set objUtility = Server.CreateObject("BpkgUtility.NewCollection") %>
<%        set objCustData = objUtility.NewCollection() %>
```

Since we are using collections inside of our application and data objects, we are going to fill up those collections using VBScript inside of our ASP source. To create the collection, we have a Utility class package that has a **NewCollection** class in it. This class has a method to create a new Visual Basic 5.0 collection and pass a reference to it back to ASP. With this reference, we can use VBScript to add new elements to the collection.

```
<%        objCustData.Add Session("email"),"email" %>
<%        objCustData.Add Session("password"),"password" %>
```

The email and password that the user entered are added to the collection. These are the two pieces of data that will be passed to the **Customers** application, which in turn will register this user as a new customer.

```
<%        set objCustomers = Server.CreateObject("BpkgCustomers.Customers") %>
<%       set objResponse = objCustomers.RegisterCustomer(objCustData) %>
```

After creating a reference to the **Customers** application object, we use its **RegisterCustomer** method to add this new user to the system. The **RegisterCustomer** method returns its information in the **objResponse** collection. First, we should check to see if any error occurred in the method.

```
<%          if objResponse("error") then %>
<!--#include file=error.inc-->
```

If the **error** element of the collection returned by the **RegisterCustomer** method is set to **True**, then we know that an error occurred. To handle this error, we will use a server-side include file that centralizes all of the error handling for this application in one place. The ASP source contained in this include file outputs the error message to the browser, and then presents the user with a link to **Abandon** the current session and start over.

```
<%        else %>
<%          if objResponse("exists") then %>
<%            if objResponse("passwordvalid") = false then %>
                <p class=errmsg>Email exists / password mismatch</p>
<%            state = 1 %>
<%          end if %>
<%        end if %>
```

If there are no errors in the processing of the method, but the password that the user entered was not validated against the system, then we must ask the user to enter their information again. By setting the **state** to **1**, the form that requests the email and password will be displayed again. This time, the form will be preceded by a prompt that the password was not valid.

```
<%            if state = 2 then %>
<%                  set objCustData = objResponse("custdata") %>
<%                  Session("auth") = True %>
```

If we reach this point in the ASP source, then we know that we have a valid user, and that their password has been validated as well. The next step is to transfer all of the customer information from the collection returned by the **RegisterCustomer** method. We will also set the session-level variable **auth** to **True**, indicating that the user of the current session has been validated.

```
<%                  Session("email") = objCustData("email") %>
<%                  Session("firstname") = objCustData("firstname") %>
<%                  Session("surname") = objCustData("surname") %>
<%              Session("address") = objCustData("address") %>
<%                  Session("city") = objCustData("city") %>
<%                  Session("state") = objCustData("state") %>
<%                  Session("zipcode") = objCustData("zipcode") %>
<%                  Session("country") = objCustData("country") %>
<%              Session("phone") = objCustData("phone") %>
<%              Session("usecookie") = objCustData("usecookie") %>
<%                  set Session("interests") = objCustData("interests") %>
```

Since the **interests** element of the **CustomerData** collection is itself a collection, we need to use the **Set** command to assign a reference to this collection to a session-level variable.

```
<%            end if %>
<%        end if %>

<%        set objCustomers = Nothing %>
<%        set objResponse = Nothing %>
<%        set objCustData = Nothing %>
<%    end if %>
<% end if %>
```

Finally, we free all of the collections that we have used up to this point by setting their references to **Nothing**. This will release all of the resources that have been used by these collections.

```
<% if state = 2 then %>

<P>Please enter your details</P>
<FORM ACTION="m4register.asp?state=3" METHOD="POST">
```

Next, we will display a form that shows all of the user's information. The user will be able to modify any of the information that is displayed. In the case of a new user, the only information that will be already in the system will be the email and password. At this time, this new user can fill out the rest of their information.

```
<table border="0">
<TR>
    <TD ALIGN=right>Email:</TD>
    <TD><% =Session("email") %></TD>
</TR>
<TR>
    <TD ALIGN=right>First name:</TD>
    <TD><INPUT TYPE="text" SIZE="20" NAME="firstname"
```

```
          VALUE="<% = Session("firstname") %>" ></TD>
        <TD ALIGN=right>  Surname:</TD>
        <TD><INPUT TYPE="text" SIZE="20" NAME="surname"
          VALUE="<% = Session("surname") %>" ></TD>
    </TR>
    <TR>
        <TD ALIGN=right>Address:</TD>
        <TD><INPUT TYPE="text" SIZE="20" NAME="address"
          VALUE="<% = Session("address") %>" ></TD>
        <TD ALIGN=right>City:</TD>
        <TD><INPUT TYPE="text" SIZE="20" NAME="city"
          VALUE="<% = Session("city") %>" ></TD>
    </TR>
    <TR>
        <TD ALIGN=right>State:</td>
        <TD><INPUT TYPE="text" SIZE="20" NAME="state"
          VALUE="<% = Session("state") %>" ></TD>
        <TD ALIGN=right>Zip code:</TD>
        <TD><INPUT TYPE="text" SIZE="20" NAME="zipcode"
          VALUE="<% = Session("zipcode") %>" ></TD>
    </TR>
    <TR>
        <TD ALIGN=right>Country:</TD>
        <TD><INPUT TYPE="text" SIZE="20" NAME="country"
          VALUE="<% = Session("country") %>" ></TD>
        <TD ALIGN=right>Phone:</TD>
        <TD><INPUT TYPE="text" SIZE="20" NAME="phone"
          VALUE="<% = Session("phone") %>" ></TD>
    </TR>
    <TR>
        <TD ALIGN=right>Password:</TD>
        <TD><INPUT TYPE="password" SIZE="20" NAME="password"
          VALUE="<% = Session("password") %>" ></TD>
    </TR>
    </TABLE>
    <P>Store logon details as cookie?
    <INPUT TYPE="checkbox" SIZE="20" NAME="usecookie"
<%    if Session("usecookie") = "Y" then %>
        checked
<%    end if %>
 VALUE="Y">
    <P>Which of the following are your main interests?</BR>
<% vData = "" %>
<% for each objInterest in Session("interests") %>
```

The session-level variable **interests** contains a collection that identifies all of the available interests, and whether or not the current user has that as one of their interests. In fact, each member of the **interests** collection is in itself a collection. The **for...each** method allows us to go through each element in the **interests** collection one at a time.

```
<%    vData = vData & "<input type=" & chr(34) & "checkbox" & chr(34) %>
<%    if objInterest("enabled") then %>
<%      vData = vData & " checked " %>
<%    end if %>
<%    vData = vData & " name = " & chr(34) & objInterest("name") & chr(34) %>
<%    vData = vData & " value = ""Y"" > " %>
<%    vData = vData & objInterest("name") & "  "  %>
      <% next %>
```

This will build a list of check boxes, each one corresponding to a particular interest. Each checkbox will be followed by a caption. If the user has a particular interest as one of their own, then the checkbox will be checked.

```
<% Response.Write vData %>
    <HR>
<INPUT TYPE="submit" NAME="Update" VALUE="Update">
```

If the user wishes to update the information, then they can click the Update button. This will submit the form, which will be processed by the **m4register.asp** file, this time with a state value of **3**. We will cover this case in just a minute.

```
<INPUT TYPE="button" VALUE="Enter shop"
onclick="window.document.location.href='m4bookshop.asp?state=3'">
```

If the user is satisfied with the information that is displayed, then they can choose to enter the bookshop. The **onclick** handler will redirect the browser to the **m4bookshop.asp** page. We will cover what this page does in the next chapter.

```
    </form>
  <% end if %>

<% end if %>
```

The user will see a page that looks like this:

Step 3 – Update and proceed

If in the previous step, the user wishes to update the information that is displayed in the form, then we need to have some ASP code to pass that information to the system for update. This will occur when the **m4register.asp** file is called with a state value of **3**.

```
<% if state = 3 then %>
```

First, we will update all of the session-level variables with the information that was entered on the form from the previous step.

```
<% Session("firstname") = Request.Form("firstname") %>
<% Session("surname") = Request.Form("surname") %>
<% Session("address") = Request.Form("address") %>
<% Session("city") = Request.Form("city") %>
<% Session("state") = Request.Form("state") %>
<% Session("zipcode") = Request.Form("zipcode") %>
<% Session("country") = Request.Form("country") %>
<% Session("phone") = Request.Form("phone") %>
<% Session("password") = Request.Form("password") %>
<% If Request.Form("usecookie") = "" then %>
<%     Session("usecookie") = "N" %>
<% else %>
<%     Session("usecookie") = "Y" %>
<% end if %>
<% for each objInterest in Session("interests") %>
<%     objInterest.Remove "enabled" %>
<%     if Request.Form(objInterest("name")) = "" then %>
<%         objInterest.Add false, "enabled" %>
<%     else %>
<%         objInterest.Add true, "enabled" %>
<%     end if %>
```

To rebuild the interest collection, we will go through each element, which is also a collection, in the existing collection. First, we remove the **enabled** element from the element's collection. Then we check to see if there is an entry in the **Request.Form** collection in the name of the particular interest. If there is, then we know that the user checked this item, so we set its enabled property to **True**.

```
<% next %>

<% set objUtility = Server.CreateObject("BpkgUtility.NewCollection") %>
<% set objCustData = objUtility.NewCollection() %>
```

Next we create a new collection and add all of the user information to that collection. This code is identical to the code used in step 2 when we are registering a customer with the system.

```
<% objCustData.Add Session("email"),"email" %>
<% objCustData.Add Session("password"),"password" %>
<% objCustData.Add Session("firstname"),"firstname" %>
<% objCustData.Add Session("surname"),"surname" %>
<% objCustData.Add Session("address"),"address" %>
<% objCustData.Add Session("city"),"city" %>
<% objCustData.Add Session("state"),"state" %>
<% objCustData.Add Session("zipcode"),"zipcode" %>
<% objCustData.Add Session("country"),"country" %>
```

```
<% objCustData.Add Session("phone"),"phone" %>
<% objCustData.Add Session("usecookie"),"usecookie" %>
<% objCustData.Add Session("interests"),"interests" %>

<% set objCustomers = Server.CreateObject("BpkgCustomers.Customers") %>
<% set objResponse = objCustomers.UpdateCustomer(objCustData) %>
```

The only difference between this step and step 2 is that we are calling the **UpdateCustomers** method of the **Customers** application object instead of the **RegisterCustomers** method.

```
<% if objResponse("error") then %>
<!--#include file=error.inc-->
```

If there is a problem in updating the data, then we display the standard error information for the user. You can see that by including the error display code in server-side include file, it allows us to easily add it anywhere with little effort. It also makes it easier to change the code later on if we need to.

```
<% else %>
      <P>Details for <% = Session("firstname")%> <% = Session("surname")%>
updated</P>
   <HR>
      <INPUT TYPE="button" VALUE="Enter shop"
          onclick="window.document.location.href='m4bookshop.asp?state=3'">
```

Since the information was updated successfully, then we display a message to the user indicating the success, and then give them a link to the bookshop. This is the same link that was available at the end of step 2.

```
<% end if %>

<% Set objCustomers = Nothing %>
<% Set objUtility = Nothing %>
<% Set objCustData = Nothing %>
```

Now, just to be good citizens, we will set all of the object references that we used to **Nothing**. This will free up any resources that may have been allocated to them.

```
<% end if %>
```

When the user sees this page, it will look like this:

So now we have successfully identified and registered a customer into the system. We are now ready to move into the shop and display the books for the user to choose from, and then process their order. This is the task for the next chapter.

Summary

We have now reached the end of the first part of our Electronic Commerce Case Study. In the next chapter, we will look at the other two parts of the applications. The validated user will be able to browse the collection of books, select books to purchase, and then complete their order transaction.

In this chapter we have:

- 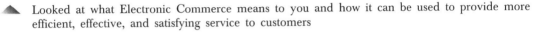 Looked at what Electronic Commerce means to you and how it can be used to provide more efficient, effective, and satisfying service to customers

- Examined the Business problem of selling books electronically. This was done using the User-Centered Design methodology, based on examining users, task, and environment

- Developed a data model that supported the business problem. The data model consisted of customer, book, and order information

- Developed a business model to encapsulate the business rules of the system. The design encompassed four basic steps to the application: Login/Registration, Book Selections, Check Selections, and Purchase.

- Created application and data objects to support the data model and the business model

- Created the **Customers** data object using Visual Basic 5.0. The data object was designed to participate in Microsoft Transaction Server transactions.

- Created the **Customers** application using VB 5.0 as well. This object encapsulated the business logic necessary to provide for the login and registration of customers into the system.

- Developed the Active Server Pages code to present the login and registration task to the user.

Next, we will look at developing the rest of the application.

Creating Components in the Electronic Commerce Case Study

In the previous chapter, we looked at two parts of the application. We created the design of the application using the principles of User Centered Design. We then expanded the design to a three-tier application architecture, which consisted of a user interface layer, a set of business objects, and a set of data objects. Finally, we began the construction of the application by focusing on the pieces needed to allow the user to register with the system. Based on our design, this was the first task that the user needed to complete before continuing with the application.

Now that there is a registered user interacting with the system, the next step is to allow them to browse the catalog and select items for purchase. In this chapter we will cover:

- ▲ Creation of the data access objects to manage the information to support the book catalog and the electronic "shopping basket."
- ▲ Creation of the business objects to apply the business rules associated with the book catalog and shopping basket.
- ▲ Implementation of the Active Server Pages necessary to support the user interaction with the electronic store.

Before we begin looking at the case study again, lets take a look at a few issues surrounding the use of components and Microsoft Transaction Server in conjunction with Active Server Pages.

Design for Scalability

One of the important issues that we need to keep in mind when building this electronic store in our case study is how we will handle success. The goal behind almost every business is to be successful and profitable and have more orders than you can handle. As we are designing and implementing the system, we should keep in mind that one day there may be lots and lots of people using this system. The application that we develop should be built in a way that will allow it to scale easily to handle this increased load.

One of the features of IIS 4.0 and ASP that makes it so easy to scale is the integration of Microsoft Transaction Server. In Chapter 13, you learned about what transaction server does and how it is integrated with IIS 4.0. In the last chapter, we showed how to make the user registration components participate in transactions hosted by Transaction Server. There are a few additional issues to review about components and how they interact with Transaction Sever. By keeping these issues in mind when developing your components, you will have built-in the necessary scalability needed to make your application support your wildly successful business.

Threading Review

In Chapter 13, where we introduced Microsoft Transaction Server, we had a detailed discussion of threads and threading models. Let's just take a moment here to review what we covered there. A thread is the basic entity to which the operating system allocates CPU time. A thread is used to execute a part of the applications code. A single application occupies an area called a "process." Within this process, there can be one or more threads executing code for your application.

The Microsoft Transaction Server run-time environment manages threads for you. Microsoft Transaction Server components do not need to create their own threads. Actually, they *shouldn't* create their own threads. Every Transaction Server/COM component has a `ThreadingModel` attribute stored in the registry. This is specified when you create the component. This attribute determines how the component's objects are assigned to threads for method execution. There are four types of Threading Model that Transaction Server, and Windows in general, supports. These models are Single-Threaded, Apartment-Threaded, Free-Threaded, and Both.

Single-Threaded Components

A single-threaded component executes all of its objects on the main thread. The main thread is the initial thread that was created when the process was created. All objects of a single-threaded component execute on the main thread. If a component does not explicitly have it `ThreadingModel` attribute set, it will be a single-threaded component.

Since a component of this type can only execute on the main thread, only one object in the component can execute at one time. In fact, since all single-threaded components in a process operate on the main thread, one and only one can be executing at one time. If you think about how this would impact performance, especially if there were a number of components trying to execute at once, you can see how a single-threaded component is very bad for scalability.

Apartment-Threaded Components

An apartment-threaded component executes on a separate thread from the main thread in the process. The entire lifetime of the component occurs within this thread. In other words, the component lives in its "apartment" its entire life. Since each component has its own thread, it can better coexist with other components in the application. The apartment-threaded component model is significantly better than single-threaded, especially where multiple components are trying participate in the application at one time.

Free-Threaded Components

A free threaded component is also known as a multi-threaded or multi-threaded apartment object. An application in MTS can have only one multi-thread apartment (MTA) in it. This MTA can have zero or more threads within it. Any components that are marked as free threaded will be created in the MTA, regardless of where they were created. Since this new component is not in the same apartment as the component that created it, a proxy needs to be created in order to make the call. What this does is add overhead to every function call, and slows down the system. This means that free-threaded component will extract a performance penalty.

Both-Threaded Components

The final type of component uses the both threading model. This is a special type of threading model in that the component has the characteristics of an apartment-threaded object as well as a free-threaded object. The advantage that this threading model brings is that no matter where the component is created, it will always be created within the same apartment as the object that created it. This means that the calls between the components can be direct and not require a slower proxy call.

Component Granularity

When you create a component, either for Transaction Server or in general, you can determine the number of tasks that the particular component will perform. This is known as the granularity of the component. This will affect the performance, debugging, and reusability of the components that you create. A fine-grained component performs a single task. For example, creating a component that calculates the tax given the total amount of the order and the customer's zip code. Fine-grained components allocate resources and quickly release them after completing a task. These components are generally easier to test, since there is not a number of tasks being performed by the same component. Also, they are usually easier to reuse in other applications since their functionality is very focused on the task they are performing.

When you create a component that processes multiple tasks, you have a coarse-grained component. While these components are nice in that they encapsulate all of the functionality for a complicated business process in one place, they are generally harder to debug and reuse in other applications. For example, an `OrderProcessing` component may calculate final totals generate merchandise pick lists, create shipping labels, and transfer data to accounts receivable. This `OrderProcessing` component is a more coarsely grained component because it performs multiple tasks, even though each task is related to a single business process.

In our case study, we will have some components, like the Catalog and Baskets components, which are more finely grained. Other components, like the Customer, support multiple tasks, and therefore could be considered more coarsely grained. In this case, we have selected the granularity to match the business process and the design of the application.

Filling Your Shopping Basket

In the previous chapter, we developed the objects and ASP code to register a user with the system. Now that the user is logged on to the bookseller system, they can browse through the catalog of books. When they find a book that they are interested in purchasing, they can add it to their electronic shopping basket.

In this section, we will be developing the data and application components to support the browsing and selection of titles from the catalog. There will be a data object that gives us access to the listing of books. Another data object will be responsible for providing access to the list of books that the user has chosen to purchase. There will be two application objects, one that is responsible for retrieving the list of books desired by the user and calculating the current price for those books. The other application object is responsible for maintaining the list of books selected for purchase by providing methods to add and remove items from the list.

Data Components

First, we will examine the two data components of this part of the application. The Catalog data component provides access to the data that is stored in the database. The catalog information is stored in the **CATALOG** table in our database. There is also information about the categorization of the titles that is stored in the **CATEGORIES** and **CATEGORYDESC** tables. The Baskets data component provides access to the data stored in the **ORDERBASKET** table in the database.

Catalog Data Component

There is one method in the Catalog data component. The **GetCatalogItemsByTypes** method will accept as a parameter a comma-delimited list of Book categories that will define the list of book categories to retrieve from the database. The possible values for the category parameter that can be passed will be found in the **CATEGORYDESC** table. The object will then perform a database query to retrieve the desired list of books. The entire list will be returned by the method in a collection.

All of the components that we will develop in the rest of this case study will be Microsoft Transaction Server components. The Transaction Server plumbing that was described in the previous chapter will be a part of each object that we develop here. Since the code is pretty much the same for each component, we will not show examples of it from now on. However, in the example files themselves, each component will have the proper plumbing already installed. The entire case study can be found on the Wrox web site at **http://rapid.wrox.co.uk/books/1266**

GetCatalogItemsByTypes

This method is the only way that the application can retrieve titles from the database. It will need to return a list of books that match the criteria of possible categories that is supplied by the caller. The list of books will be returned to the caller as a collection. All of the information that is stored in the database that could be relevant to the application will be passed in this collection.

```
Public Function GetCatalogItemsByTypes(ByVal vTypeCodes As Variant) As Variant
    On Error GoTo GetCatalogItemsByTypesErr

    Dim vResponse As New Collection
...Define a bunch of variables here...
    Dim bOr As Boolean

    Let vSql = "SELECT DISTINCTROW Catalog.*, Promotion.PromotionCode,
Promotion.PromotionEndDate FROM (Catalog INNER JOIN Categories ON Catalog.CatalogId =
Categories.CatalogID) LEFT JOIN Promotion ON Catalog.CatalogId = Promotion.CatalogID
WHERE"
```

This SQL Query is used to extract all of the titles that match a certain set of interests that the user has selected. The query also returns any promotion information that may be associated with a title. The relationship between the three tables is shown by this diagram:

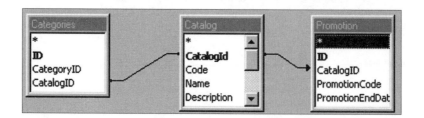

This query is designed such that we will get all of the catalog records that are in a certain category. Then, for each of these catalog records, we will retrieve any promotion records that may be associated with the catalog records. However, if there are no promotions, we still want to get the catalog record back.

The **join** type between Categories and Catalog is an **inner** join. This will cause only the records that match in both tables to be returned. The join between Catalog and Promotion is a **left** join. A left join will return all of the records in the Catalog table, granted they match other criteria, and will return those records from Promotion that are related to the ones returned from Catalog. This is different from an inner join in that there does not have to be a matching Promotion record in order for a record from Catalog to be returned.

Once we have defined the data that will come back from the query, we need to select the records that we want. To do this, we will dynamically build a **WHERE** clause. The list of categories that the user is interested in is passed into this method in a comma-delimited string. Our next step is to parse this string into a series of entries for the **WHERE** clause of the SQL query.

```
vTypeCodesLen = Len(vTypeCodes)

If vTypeCodesLen > 0 Then
    iStartPos = 1
    Do
        iCommaPos = InStr(iStartPos, vTypeCodes, ",")
        If iCommaPos = 0 Then
            vID = Mid(vTypeCodes, iStartPos, vTypeCodesLen)
            bOr = False
        Else
            vID = Mid(vTypeCodes, iStartPos, iCommaPos - iStartPos)
            bOr = True
        End If
        iStartPos = iCommaPos + 1
```

We will use a simple parsing algorithm to iteratively extract each entry from the comma-delimited list. As each entry is returned, we create a relation that will be added to the **WHERE** clause for the query.

```
        vSql = vSql & "(Categories.CategoryID = '" & vID & "')"
        If bOr Then vSql = vSql & " OR "
    Loop Until iCommaPos = 0

    vSql = vSql & " ORDER BY PublicationDate DESC;"
```

Finally, we set the sorting order that we wish the records to be returned in. In this case, the records will be sorted in reverse order of publication date. This will cause the newest book published to be at the head of the list.

```
        Trace (vSql)
```

The **Trace** method is a global helper method that allows the object to write debug-type information out to a file on the server. Since there is no easy interactive way to debug your components, using this method can be invaluable in tracking down problems. Naturally, it isn't the kind of thing you would want a production object to do, but while in development, it works out great. This **Trace** method call writes a line of text to the trace file that looks similar to this:

```
  10:29:52 PM SELECT DISTINCTROW Catalog.*, Promotion.PromotionCode,
Promotion.PromotionEndDate FROM (Catalog INNER JOIN Categories ON
Catalog.CatalogId = Categories.CatalogID) LEFT JOIN Promotion ON
Catalog.CatalogId = Promotion.CatalogID WHERE(Categories.CategoryID =
'B') OR (Categories.CategoryID = 'I') OR (Categories.CategoryID =
'O') ORDER BY PublicationDate DESC;
```

We will be using the ActiveX Data Objects Connection object to create a recordset based on this SQL query. As in the Customers data object, we will use the global connection string stored in the **vDbConn** variable.

```
    Set oDb = oObjectContext.CreateInstance("ADODB.Connection")
    oDb.Open vDbConn
    Set oRs = oDb.Execute(vSql)

    While Not oRs.EOF
        Dim CatalogItem As New Collection
```

We will create a collection that holds each of the fields from the recordset. To make the code a bit clearer, first we will assign each of the fields from the recordset to a temporary variable.

```
        vCode = oRs.Fields("code")
        vName = oRs.Fields("name")
        vPrice = Format(oRs.Fields("price"), "#,##0.00")
        vCatalogId = oRs.Fields("catalogid")
        vDescription = oRs.Fields("description")
        vImageURL = oRs.Fields("imageurl")
        vPromotionCode = oRs.Fields("promotioncode")
        vPromotionEndDate = oRs.Fields("promotionenddate")
        vPublicationDate = oRs.Fields("publicationdate")
```

Next, we will add each field to the collection that we are building. Each entry to the collection will have a key associated with it, to allow for easier retrieval later on.

```
        CatalogItem.Add vCode, Key:="code"
        CatalogItem.Add vName, Key:="name"
        CatalogItem.Add vPrice, Key:="price"
        CatalogItem.Add vCatalogId, Key:="catalogid"
        CatalogItem.Add vDescription, Key:="description"
        CatalogItem.Add vImageURL, Key:="imageurl"
        CatalogItem.Add vPromotionCode, Key:="promotioncode"
        CatalogItem.Add vPromotionEndDate, Key:="promotionenddate"
        CatalogItem.Add vPublicationDate, Key:="publicationdate"
```

Finally, this collection that contains the information from a single record in the recordset is added to a collection that will hold all of the records from the recordset. This is the information that will eventually be passed back to the method's caller.

```
        vItems.Add CatalogItem

        Set CatalogItem = Nothing
        oRs.MoveNext
```

Having completed all of our work with this record, we will release the collection that we built that contains all of the fields of the current records. By setting the reference to this collection to **Nothing**, all of the elements of the collection will be deleted. Then, we will move to the next record in the recordset.

```
        Wend

        oRs.Close

    End If

    vResponse.Add False, Key:="error"
    vResponse.Add vItems, Key:="items"

    oObjectContext.SetComplete
    Set GetCatalogItemsByTypes = vResponse
```

Having successfully completed processing all of the records in the recordset, we will add the entire collection to another collection, which will serve as this method's response. If everything was completed successfully, the **error** element in this response collection will be set to **False**. Finally, with all steps in this method completing successfully, we call the **SetComplete** method of the current object context to indicate this object's success to the transaction.

```
        Exit Function

    GetCatalogItemsByTypesErr:
        oObjectContext.SetAbort
        Set GetCatalogItemsByTypes = RaiseError("GetCatalogItemsByTypes")

    End Function
```

If any errors do occur while processing this function, they will be handled by this code here. When an error occurs, the transaction cannot continue. To notify Transaction Server of this, we use the **SetAbort** method of the current object context.

Next, we will create the data access component that will let our application work with the items that the user has selected for purchase by placing in their shopping basket.

Baskets Data Component

There are four methods in the Baskets data access component that allow the application to talk to the database tables that comprise the electronic "shopping basket." There are methods that determine the order number for the current customer, either existing or new. Another method is responsible for returning the contents of the customer's basket. The other methods support the addition of new items to the basket, the updating of quantity information in the basket, as well as clearing the contents of the basket.

GetOrder

This method is used to determine the order number for the current user. There are two possible outcomes when this method is called. The current user's email address is supplied as a parameter. The method determines if there is an existing shopping basket for this customer. An existing basket is one that has not been converted to an order or explicitly cancelled. Even if the user leaves the site before completing their order, their basket information will be retained and available the next time they visit. If an order can be found, then its ID is returned to the caller. If no open order matches the customer's information, then a new entry will be created and its ID returned to the caller.

As before, all components and methods are Transaction Server compliant, so we will dispense with covering those portions of the code.

```
Public Function GetOrder(ByVal vEmail As Variant) As Variant
    On Error GoTo GetOrderErr

    Dim vResponse As New Collection
    Dim vSql As Variant
    Dim vOrderID As Variant

    Let vSql = "SELECT * FROM ORDERBASKET WHERE (Email = '" & Trim(vEmail) & "')" & _
        "AND (Fulfilled = 0);"
```

We will determine if there is an existing order for the current user through this SQL query. The **ORDERBASKET** table holds all of the shopping basket/order information except the contents of the basket. We will see this table in just a bit. We need to select all of the records that match the customer's email and do not have the **Fulfilled** flag set. This flag indicates if a basket contains a pending order, a completed order, or a cancelled order. A value of 0 indicates a pending order, and this is the one we are interested in.

```
    Set oRs = oObjectContext.CreateInstance("ADODB.Recordset")

    oRs.CursorType = adOpenDynamic
    oRs.LockType = adLockPessimistic
    oRs.Open vSql, vDbConn
```

After executing the query, we check to see if any records were returned. Since a customer can have at most only one pending order, the recordset that is returned could either be empty or have at most one record. If no records are returned, then we will create a new record.

```
    If oRs.EOF Then
        Dim vNow As Variant
        vNow = Now
```

One of the fields in the **ORDERBASKET** table is an auto-generated field. The value for this field is randomly generated by the system when a new record is created. There is no facility through ActiveX Data Objects to directly retrieve the value that is placed in this field. We have to perform a workaround to retrieve this value, which will become our Order ID. The steps for this work around are:

 Ensure that the record has another field with a value that has a good chance of being unique for a particular customer. For example, a date-time stamp indicating the time of creation of the record is a good choice.

 Store the current date/time value, give through the **Now** function, in a temporary variable. We will be using this value to query the database later, so we can't expect the **Now** function to return the same value later on in the code.

```
        oRs.AddNew
        oRs.Fields("Email") = vEmail
        oRs.Fields("BasketCreation") = vNow
        oRs.Update
```

Add a new record and set the values for the fields that you have. For the creation timestamp, **BasketCreation**, use the temporary variable for the time that you created.

```
oRs.Close
vSql = "SELECT * FROM ORDERBASKET WHERE (Email = '" & Trim(vEmail) & "')" & _
" AND (Fulfilled = 0) and BasketCreation = #" & vNow & "#;"
oRs.Open vSql, vDbConn
```

Issue a SQL query that looks for the record that matches both the customer's email address with the one you just added and also that has a **BasketCreation** value that is equal to the timestamp that is held by the temporary variable.

This will now return a recordset that contains only the new record that was added. From this recordset, you can obtain the value of the auto-number field, which becomes your Order ID.

```
End If
vOrderID = oRs("OrderID")
oRs.Close

vResponse.Add vOrderID, "OrderID"
vResponse.Add False, Key:="error"
```

Now that we have retrieved the value of the OrderID for the record we just added, we can add this value for the Order ID to the response collection of this method. Remember to put in your Transaction Server plumbing for the object to participate in transactions correctly.

We will use this Order ID on all other calls to the data object for this customer. It will be the responsibility of the business rules to ensure that every method call into the data object has a valid Order ID passed with it.

AddItem

Now that a valid shopping basket has been created, we can begin to add items to that basket. To successfully add an item to a shopping basket, we need to know three things. First, we need the Order ID, so that the item can be associated with the proper basket. Second, we need the catalog ID number of the item that we are adding. Lastly, we need the quantity of the item we are placing in the basket.

```
Public Function AddItem(ByVal vOrderID As Variant, ByVal vCatalogId As Variant, ByVal
vNumItems As Variant) As Variant
    On Error GoTo AddItemErr

    Dim vResponse As New Collection
    Dim vSql As Variant

    Let vSql = "SELECT * FROM BasketContents " & _
        "WHERE (OrderID = " & vOrderID & ")" & _
        " AND (CatalogId = " & vCatalogId & ") ;"
```

The first thing we need to do in this method to see if the shopping basket already contains one of the items that we are trying to add to it. This SQL Query will retrieve the record, if one exists, from the basket that matches the catalog ID of the item we are trying to insert. We also need to select only those records from the current order, by matching the OrderID numbers.

```
        Set oRs = oObjectContext.CreateInstance("ADODB.Recordset")
        oRs.CursorType = adOpenDynamic
        oRs.LockType = adLockPessimistic
        oRs.Open vSql, vDbConn

        If oRs.EOF Then
```

If the query returns no records, then we need to add a new record to the database for this new entry in the shopping basket.

```
            oRs.Close
            oRs.Open "BasketContents", vDbConn, adOpenKeyset, adLockPessimistic,
    adCmdTable
```

To add the record, we will use a recordset that is comprised of the entire **BasketContents** table. First, we will create the new record, and then add the information about the particular entry to the fields in the new record.

```
            oRs.AddNew
            oRs.Fields("OrderID") = vOrderID
            oRs.Fields("CatalogId") = CLng(vCatalogId)
            oRs.Fields("NumItems") = CLng(vNumItems)
        Else
```

If the item that we are trying to add to the basket is already in there, we will simply increment the quantity of that item by the number that was passed in as a parameter.

```
            oRs.Fields("NumItems") = oRs.Fields("NumItems") + CLng(vNumItems)
        End If

        oRs.Update
        oRs.Close
```

Once all of our database modifications have been completed, we will update and close the recordset. Notice that even though we are manipulating the database in two different ways, we can still call the same **Update** method. Finally, add the requisite Transaction Server compliant code to the end of the method.

At this point, we can add as many items to our shopping basket as we want to. The next thing we would probably want to do is see what are all the items we have put in there. This is done with the **GetBasketItems** method.

GetBasketItems

The **GetBasketItems** method is used to examine the contents of the shopping basket. The actual **BasketContents** table contains just the catalog ID and quantity of each entry. While this is proper and concise for the database, it doesn't really provide all of the information we need to effectively display the data. This method provides detailed information about each catalog entry in the basket as well. As with all of the other methods in this application that provide a list of information, the results from this method will be returned in the form of a collection.

```
    Public Function GetBasketItems(ByVal vOrderID As Variant) As Variant
        On Error GoTo GetBasketItemsErr
```

```
    Dim vResponse As New Collection
… Define a bunch of local variables…
    Dim vNumItems As Variant

    Let vSql = "SELECT BasketContents.*, Catalog.*, Promotion.PromotionCode,
Promotion.PromotionEndDate" & _
        " FROM (BasketContents INNER JOIN Catalog ON BasketContents.CatalogId =
Catalog.CatalogId) LEFT JOIN Promotion ON Catalog.CatalogId = Promotion.CatalogID" & _
        " WHERE BasketContents.OrderID = " & vOrderID & ";"
```

We will be using a SQL query to join together information from three tables to return from this method.
The **BasketContents** table provides the quantity of each item in the basket, as well as the catalog ID of
each item. Rather than just return a meaningless ID, we will join the Catalog table with this ID. This will
allow us to return more descriptive information about the item, such as its title or price.

Since we are also interested in returning pricing information about the item, we need to take into account
any promotions that may be in effect on the item as well. Since not every item will have a promotion in
place on it, we will use what is called a left join. This will return all of the Catalog records that match the
search criteria. For those records that have information in the Promotion table as well, that information will
be returned as well. In the case where there is no promotion information, those fields in the resulting
recordset will just be left empty.

```
    Set oDb = oObjectContext.CreateInstance("ADODB.Connection")
    oDb.Open vDbConn
    Set oRs = oDb.Execute(vSql)

    While Not oRs.EOF
        Dim BasketItem As New Collection
```

Now that the recordset containing detailed information about the basket has been created, we will iterate
through the results. Each record will be first added to the **BasketItem** collection.

```
        vBasketId = oRs.Fields("basketid")
        vCode = oRs.Fields("code")
        vName = oRs.Fields("name")
        vPrice = oRs.Fields("price")
        vNumItems = oRs.Fields("numitems")
        vPromotionCode = oRs.Fields("promotioncode")
        vPromotionEndDate = oRs.Fields("promotionenddate")

        BasketItem.Add vBasketId, Key:="basketid"
        BasketItem.Add vCode, Key:="code"
        BasketItem.Add vName, Key:="name"
        BasketItem.Add vPrice, Key:="price"
        BasketItem.Add vNumItems, Key:="numitems"
        BasketItem.Add vPromotionCode, Key:="promotioncode"
        BasketItem.Add vPromotionEndDate, Key:="promotionenddate"
```

As we did in the **GetCatalogItemsByTypes** method that we looked at earlier, we will first store the
fields that we are interested in from the current record into temporary variables. Then the values in the
temporary variables will be added to the **BasketItem** collection. This is done merely to make the code
more readable and understandable.

```
        vItems.Add BasketItem
```

The **BasketItem** collection, containing all of the fields that we are interested in, will be added to the **vItems** collection. This collection will contain a set of **BasketItem** collections, one for each record in the result recordset. Then we will move on to the next record in the recordset, until we have reached the end of the data.

```
        Set BasketItem = Nothing
        oRs.MoveNext
    Wend

    oRs.Close

    vResponse.Add False, Key:="error"
    vResponse.Add vItems, Key:="items"
```

The **vItems** collection of collections with then be added to the **vResponse** collection, which will be passed back to the caller. This may seem like a lot of indirection to get to the data we are interested in, what with a collection containing a collection of collections containing field information. But when one variable can return all of that information, it makes the parameters for the method very succinct. It also allows us to change the information that is passed back to the caller without having to redefine the interface completely. Finally comes the Transaction Server plumbing that goes at the end of every method we write.

So now that we can see the items that are in the shopping basket, we may want to go in and modify some of the data. One way to do this is with the **UpdateNumItems** method.

UpdateNumItems

Once you have added an item to the shopping basket, you may want to change the quantity of that item in the basket. There are two ways you can do this. We have already seen that the **AddItem** method will check to see if the item is already in the shopping basket. If it is, then it will just add the new quantity to the existing quantity. This is fine for when we are interacting with the catalog in the system. But we also have a user requirement that the system will allow the user to review their selections, and modify quantity. To accomplish this, we will need a method that allows the user update the quantity of a particular item that they desire

```
Public Function UpdateNumItems(ByVal vBasketId As Variant, ByVal vNumItems As Variant)
As Variant
    On Error GoTo UpdateNumItemsErr

    Dim vResponse As New Collection
    Dim bRet As Boolean
    Dim vSql As Variant

    Let vSql = "SELECT * FROM BasketContents " & _
               " WHERE BasketId = " & vBasketId & ";"
```

To select the particular entry from the **BasketContents** table that you want to modify, we will query based on the **BasketID** field. This is the primary key for the field, so this will only return one record.

```
    Set oRs = oObjectContext.CreateInstance("ADODB.Recordset")
    oRs.CursorType = adOpenDynamic
```

```
    oRs.LockType = adLockPessimistic
    oRs.Open vSql, vDbConn

    If oRs.EOF Then
        bRet = False
```

If for some reason this particular **BasketID** cannot be found, then this method will notify the caller that the record was not updated.

```
    Else
        oRs.Fields("NumItems") = CLng(vNumItems)
        oRs.Update
```

If the query is able to locate the record, then we will update the quantity variable with the new value that the user selected. This is different to what happens in the **AddItem** method, where we are adding the new quantity to the existing quantity. In this method, we will be replacing the quantity with the new quantity.

```
        bRet = True
    End If

    oRs.Close

    vResponse.Add False, Key:="error"

    oObjectContext.SetComplete
    Set UpdateNumItems = vResponse

    Exit Function

UpdateNumItemsErr:
    oObjectContext.SetAbort
    Set UpdateNumItems = RaiseError("UpdateNumItems")

End Function
```

Now that we are able to update the quantity of items in our shopping basket, the last thing that the user should be able to do is to empty their basket and start over. This will be done using the **EmptyBasket** method.

EmptyBasket

This method simply removes all of the items from the user's shopping basket. Since the SQL **DELETE** command will accomplish this automatically, there is very little actual code in this function. In fact, you will see that the majority of the code is the support for the Transaction Server, and for passing notification of success or failure back to the caller.

```
Public Function EmptyBasket(ByVal vOrderID As Variant) As Variant
```

The only parameter that is needed to identify which basket that we are emptying is the **OrderID**. This is a foreign key of the **BasketContents** table, and identifies which actual basket the record belongs to.

```
    On Error GoTo EmptyBasketErr

    Dim vResponse As New Collection
    Dim vSql As Variant
```

```
        Let vSql = "DELETE FROM BasketContents" & _
                   " WHERE OrderID = " & vOrderID & ";"
```

This SQL **DELETE** command is used to delete all of the records from **BasketContents** table that match the criteria that we have set. In this case, it will be all records that have an **OrderID** value that matches the parameter that was passed into this method.

```
        Set oDb = oObjectContext.CreateInstance("ADODB.Connection")
        oDb.Open vDbConn
        Call oDb.Execute(vSql)
```

Since there will be no data returned by the query, we do not need to have a recordset or other type of object to perform the query. The ADO Connection object allows us to issue SQL commands against a database without the use of a recordset. The last block of code we use is again the standard method completion code that we have used in every method up to this point, we won't bother reproducing it again.

Now that we have developed methods for accessing the database in the way we need, let's take a look at the methods that will be calling these database methods. Since we are encapsulating all of our business logic inside of objects, it is these objects that will be responsible for calling the data object methods.

Application Components

In this part of the system, there are two application components that are responsible for providing the interface between the ASP source and the data components, which in turn access the database. The Catalog application component is responsible for returning the list of titles that match the user's search criteria. The Baskets component is responsible for manipulating the contents of the electronic shopping basket.

Catalog Component

The Catalog component serves as the interface between the display of the list of books on the screen and the database containing the list of books. It is responsible for accepting the user's selection criteria and returning the list of books that match the supplied criteria. In addition to that, the component must apply the application rules of the system. Namely, it is responsible for computing the price of the book and setting the "new title" flag as well.

GetCatalogListByInterests

The **GetCatalogListByInterests** method is the only method of the catalog component. It is responsible for performing all of the business functionality related to the catalog of books. The **CATALOG** table in the database contains the list price for the book. However, a book is not always sold for list price. There could be a promotion in place that would reduce the price of the book. This information about the existence of a promotion is returned by the Catalog data component. It is the responsibility of the Catalog application to compute the new price based on the type of promotion. In the next chapter, when we cover order completion, we will see how the actual selling price is recomputed at the actual time of purchase.

Another business requirement is for the user to receive some type of indication if a title is a new publication. The business rules define a new publication as a title that has a publication date within three months of the current date. Rather than storing a flag in the database itself to indicate if a title is new, the Catalog application component will dynamically determine if a title is new. This is done by having the publication date as a field in the **CATALOG** table.

```
Public Function GetCatalogListByInterests(ByVal vInterests As Variant) As Variant
    On Error GoTo GetCatalogListByInterestsErr

    Dim vResponse As Variant
... Define a bunch of local variables
    Dim vInterestCodes As Variant
    vInterestCodes = ExtractInterestCodes(vInterests)
```

The parameter that is passed to this method is a collection of all of the possible interests that the system supports. Each interest is itself a collection with two elements. The first element indicates the database code that corresponds to that element. The second indicates if the user has selected that interest. The **ExtractInterestCodes** method will turn that collection into a comma-delimited string that can be passed to the data object.

```
    Set vResponse = oDCatalog.GetCatalogItemsByTypes(vInterestCodes)
    If Not vResponse("error") Then

        Set vCatalog = vResponse("items")
```

Once the database object method returns successfully, we will extract the **vCatalog** collection from the method's response. This is a collection of all book records that match the search criteria.

```
        For Each vCatalogItem In vCatalog

            vPublicationDate = CDate(vCatalogItem("publicationdate"))
            vPrice = vCatalogItem("price")
            vPromotionCode = vCatalogItem("promotioncode")
            vPromotionEndDate = vCatalogItem("promotionenddate")
```

First, we will extract those values from the catalog record collection that we need to perform the pricing and date calculation in the method. By extracting these values from a collection and storing them in local variables, this will increase the performance of the object. In order to extract an element by key from a collection, the collection must be iterated item by item. If the server has to do this many times, it tends to slow the system down.

```
            If DateDiff("d", Now, DateAdd("m", 3, vPublicationDate)) > 0 Then
                vNewFlag = True
            Else
                vNewFlag = False
            End If
            vCatalogItem.Add vNewFlag, Key:="newflag"
```

To determine if the catalog item should be considered a "new item" we will use the VB **DateDiff** function. This will calculate the date three months after the date of publication. If this calculated date is prior to today's date, then it means the book is more than three months old. If the calculated date is after today's date, then the book should be flagged as new.

```
            vTodaysPrice = AdjustTodaysPrice(vPrice, vPromotionCode,
        vPromotionEndDate)

            If vTodaysPrice = vPrice Then
                vPromotionFlag = False
            Else
                vPromotionFlag = True
            End If
```

The **AdjustTodaysPrice** method is a utility method that will compute the promotion price of an item. The method uses the retail price of the item, the type of promotion, and the ending date of the promotion to compute the promotion price. If the ending date of the promotion has passed, then no promotion will be applied and the method will return the retail price. In our application, the pricing calculations are simple, since there can be at most one promotion associated with a catalog item. The application object then checks to see if the promotional price is different from the retail price. If there is a difference, then a flag is set to indicate that a promotion is in effect.

```
vTodaysPrice = Format(vTodaysPrice, "$#,##0.00")

vCatalogItem.Add vTodaysPrice, Key:="todaysprice"
vCatalogItem.Add vPromotionFlag, Key:="promotionflag"
```

The new price is formatted for display as currency using the **Format** function of Visual Basic. This will convert the currency value to a string that displays the proper format and decimal place for a currency display. This information is then added to the collection that contains all of the information about the particular catalog item.

```
        Next

    End If

    oObjectContext.SetComplete
    Set GetCatalogListByInterests = vResponse

    Exit Function

GetCatalogListByInterestsErr:
    oObjectContext.SetAbort
    Set GetCatalogListByInterests = RaiseError("GetCatalogListByInterests")

End Function
```

Once we have finished iterating through all of the members of the collection, we have successfully completed this method. At this point, we perform the standard Transaction Server method of **SetComplete** to indicate the successful completion. With this method completed successfully, the ASP source can then go about displaying the information to the user. With this information, the user can select the book that they wish to purchase. At that point, the application will use the Baskets application object to process the user's request.

Baskets Component

The Baskets application component is responsible for managing the contents of the user's shopping basket. There are methods that support adding items to the basket, listing the contents of the basket, changing the quantity of an item, and emptying the basket. Since there is very little application logic involved in interacting with the shopping basket, the methods in this component are primarily just thin wrappers around the Baskets data components.

GetBasketItems

The **GetBasketItems** method is responsible for retrieving the contents of a shopping basket from the database object. The particular shopping basket is identified by its **OrderID**, which is supplied to this method by the caller.

```
Public Function GetBasketItems(ByVal vOrderID As Variant) As Variant
    On Error GoTo GetBasketItemsErr

    Dim vResponse As Variant
    Dim vBasket As Variant
    Dim vBasketItem As Variant
    Dim vPrice As Variant
    Dim vPromotionCode As Variant
    Dim vPromotionEndDate As Variant
    Dim vTodaysPrice As Variant

    Set vResponse = oDBaskets.GetBasketItems(vOrderID)
```

This method passes the **OrderID** that was passed in as a parameter to the Baskets data object's
GetBasketItems method. If you remember from the previous section, this method will return a
collection containing information about each item in the user's basket.

```
If Not vResponse("error") Then

    Set vBasket = vResponse("items")

    For Each vBasketItem In vBasket
```

Since the price of each item that is return from the data object is the retail price of the object, we will
need to apply the promotional pricing algorithms that were shown in the Catalog data object's
GetCatalogListByInterests method. The actual selling price will be computed by using the
AdjustTodaysPrice utility function, and this new price will be part of the collection that is returned to
the caller of the **GetBasketItems** method.

```
        vPrice = vBasketItem("price")
            vPromotionCode = vBasketItem("promotioncode")
            vPromotionEndDate = vBasketItem("promotionenddate")

            vTodaysPrice = AdjustTodaysPrice(vPrice, vPromotionCode,
vPromotionEndDate)
            vTodaysPrice = Format(vTodaysPrice, "$#,##0.00")
            vBasketItem.Add vTodaysPrice, Key:="todaysprice"

        Next

    End If
```

After computing the selling price for each item in the shopping basket, the method is complete. So, as with
all the other methods in our application, we will finish with the Transaction Server code to indicate a
successful completion.

```
    oObjectContext.SetComplete
    Set GetBasketItems = vResponse

    Exit Function

GetBasketItemsErr:
    oObjectContext.SetAbort
    Set GetBasketItems = RaiseError("GetBasketItems")

End Function
```

This method provides for the viewing of items that are already in the shopping basket. To insert those items into the shopping basket, we will need a method that calls the **AddItem** method of the Baskets data object.

AddItem

The **AddItem** method is responsible for adding new catalog items to the shopping basket. In order for an item to be added, there first needs to be a valid shopping basket that the item can be added to. Once this has been done, then the item can be added to the shopping basket.

```
Public Function AddItem(ByVal vOrderID As Variant, ByVal vCustomerId As Variant, ByVal
    vCatalogId As Variant, ByVal vNumItems As Variant) As Variant
```

In order to call the **AddItem** method, the calling application must supply some information about both the item and the destination of the item. The caller must supply the **OrderID** that corresponds to the desired basket. The caller must also supply the **CustomerID**, which is their email address, along with the **CatalogID** and quantity of the item that is being added.

```
    On Error GoTo AddItemErr

    Dim vResponse As Variant

    If vOrderID = "" Then
```

If the caller is unable to supply the **OrderID**, then this method needs to determine one. The **CustomerID** parameter is passed to the **GetOrder** method of the Baskets data object. As was shown in the last section, this method will either locate an existing basket or create a new one. This **OrderID** number is stored in a local variable for use later in the method.

```
        Set vResponse = oDBaskets.GetOrder(vCustomerId)
        vOrderID = vResponse("OrderID")
    End If
```

Once a valid **OrderID** number is known, the **AddItem** method of the Baskets data object can be called to add the desired item to the shopping basket. To supply the caller with the **OrderID** for the current user, the valid **OrderID** number is included in the collection that is passed back to the calling application.

```
    Set vResponse = oDBaskets.AddItem(vOrderID, vCatalogId, vNumItems)

    vResponse.Add vOrderID, "OrderID"
    oObjectContext.SetComplete
    Set AddItem = vResponse

    Exit Function

AddItemErr:
    oObjectContext.SetAbort
    Set AddItem = RaiseError("AddItem")
End Function
```

At this point, the method has either successfully completed, or the error handler at the beginning of the method has trapped an error. If an error has occurred, then the transaction needs to fail, so this method calls the **SetAbort** method of the current object context. If everything was successful, then **SetComplete** will indicate the success to the current transaction.

UpdateNumItems & EmptyBasket

These two methods act as very thin wrappers around the corresponding Baskets data object's methods. The **UpdateNumItems** will change the quantity selected of a particular item in the shopping basket. While the **EmptyBasket** method will remove all of the items from the current basket. There is no application logic that needs to be applied to these two methods. Because of this, these two methods are very similar and very simple, so we won't bother discussing the code here.

Now that we have completed the two application objects that will handle this phase of the application, we need to create the user interface for this phase. As with the first phase, the user interface will be a set of Active Server Pages that will both display the information to the user, as well as allow the user to select items for purchase.

Creating the Active Server Pages

To support this phase of the application, there are a set of 6 Active Server Pages source files that allow the user to interact with the catalog and shopping basket. These pages are responsible for both presenting information to the user; such as the list of books or the contents of the shopping basket, and for obtaining information from the user; such as the criteria for book selection and the title that the user is interested in ordering.

CheckReg.asp

This page is responsible permitting access to the catalog portion of the application. It ensures that the current user is properly registered in the system. If the user has not registered, then they are redirected to the proper registration page. If the user has been properly registered, then they are directed to select the criteria they wish to see. Since this page relies on information that is present in the current user's session information, there is no user interface portion for this page.

```
<%@ LANGUAGE="VBSCRIPT" %>
<% Option Explicit %>
<% Response.Expires = 0 %>

<%    if Session("auth") = True then %>
<%        Response.redirect " SelectBookCriteria.asp" %>
<%    else %>
<%        Response.redirect "m4register.asp?state=1" %>
<%    end if %>
```

The session-level variable "**auth**" is set to True when the user is properly authenticated in the system. If this is the case, then the user is redirected to the **SelectBookCriteria.asp** file, which we will cover next. If the user has not been properly registered, then they will be redirected to the **m4register.asp** page, with the state variable set to 1. If you remember from the previous chapter, this will bring up the login screen, therefore taking the user through the login and registration process.

SelectBookCriteria.asp

At this point, a registered user is ready to display a list of books. In the registration phase, they selected a set of interests corresponding to the different categories of books. The user is presented with a list of categories, from which they can choose the ones that they want to see. This list is initially set so that the user's interests from the database form the default set of criteria for the search.

From this page, the user can choose to see the list of books that match their criteria, view the contents of their shopping basket, or proceed to order checkout.

```
<%@ LANGUAGE="VBSCRIPT" %>
<% Option Explicit %>
<% Response.Expires = 0 %>
```

Since the display of this page requires that the current user be registered with the system, we want to prevent this page from being displayed from the browser's cache. By setting the **Expires** property of the **Response** object to 0, the browser will be instructed not to store this page in its cache.

```
<HTML>
<HEAD>
<META HTTP-EQUIV="Pragma" CONTENT="no-cache">
```

This **<META>** tag serves the same purpose as the **Response.Expires** property. This is done as a backup in case the browser that is viewing the page does not properly handle the **Response.Expires** method of controlling the caching of the page. Hopefully, the browser will properly interpret at least one of these commands.

```
<TITLE></TITLE>
<LINK REL="stylesheet" TYPE="text/css" HREF="main.css">
</HEAD>
<BODY>
```

```
<% dim objInterest %>
<% dim vData %>
```

We will be creating two temporary variables to be used during the processing of the page. Because of the **Option Explicit** statement at the top of the page, every variable used in this page must be explicitly declared. This will eliminate the problems associated with misspelled variable names, which can be very hard to track down. This is excellent programming practice, and should be done on every page, regardless of the **Option Explicit** command.

```
<TABLE WIDTH=100% CELLSPACING=0 CELLPADDING=0 CORDER=0>
<TR CLASS="pageheader">
<TH ALIGN=left> WROX Bookshop
</TH>
</TR>
</TABLE>
```

This table will display the standard format header, with the title of the page displayed inside a black border, as seen in the picture above.

```
<FORM ACTION="ShowBookList.asp" METHOD="POST">
  <P>Which categories would you like to see listed?</P>
```

Since this page will be accepting user input, we will need to handle the **FORM** processing with another ASP page. The **ShowBookList.asp** file will be covered next. It is responsible for taking the criteria set in this page, and displaying a list that matches that criteria.

```
<% vData = "" %>
<% for each objInterest in Session("interests") %>
```

When the user registered in the system, all of their information was loaded into session-level variables. The information we are interested in is the user's interests. These are stored in a collection. The collection actually contains one collection for each possible interest that the system supports. Each of these collections have both the database ID for the particular interest, as well as a flag indicating if the user has selected that interest.

This page will iterate through each element in the interests collection. A series of checkboxes will be created in a string variable. Each checkbox corresponds to a single interest. If the user has indicated that interest as one of their own, then the checkbox will be initially selected.

```
<%    vData = vData & "<input type=" & chr(34) & "checkbox" & chr(34) %>
<%    if objInterest("enabled") then %>
<%       vData = vData & " checked " %>
<%    end if %>
<%    vData = vData & " name = " & chr(34) & objInterest("name") & chr(34) %>
<%    vData = vData & " value = ""y"" > " %>
<%    vData = vData & objInterest("name") & "  " %>
<% next %>
<% Response.Write vData %>
<P>
<HR>
<INPUT TYPE="submit" NAME="List" VALUE="List items">
<INPUT TYPE="button" VALUE="Basket"
onclick="window.document.location.href='m4basket.asp'">
```

```
   <INPUT TYPE="button" VALUE="Checkout"
onclick="window.document.location.href='m4checkout.asp'">
   </FORM>
</BODY>
</HTML>
```

From this page, the user has the option of viewing a list of books, viewing the contents of their basket, or proceeding to checkout. If the user has chosen to display a list of books that match their criteria, then the processing of that request is handled by the **ShowBookList.asp** file.

ShowBookList.asp

When the user has requested a list of books that match a certain criteria, it is the responsibility of this file to both process the request and display the list of books for the user. First, the information that was submitted by the previous page must be parsed and put into a form that the application object is expecting. Once the application object generates the list of books matching the criteria, this file is responsible for properly displaying that data to the user.

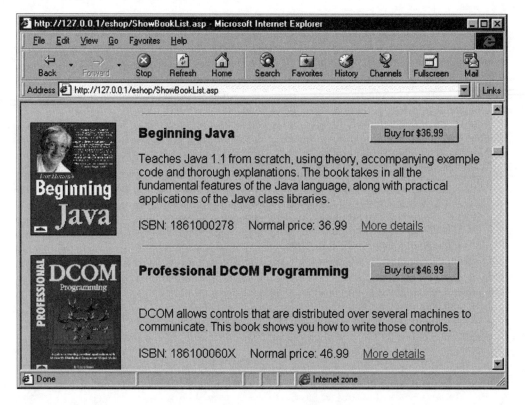

The first part of the file will be used to declare the variable that will be used in the page, as well as setting some initial parameters. As with all of the pages in this case study, the use of **Option Explicit** will ensure that every variable that is used is properly declared. This will ensure that any typos in variable names will be caught, therefore, avoiding anomalous errors.

```
<%@ LANGUAGE="VBSCRIPT" %>
<% Option Explicit %>
<% Response.Expires = 0 %>
<% dim objUtility %>
<% dim objInterest %>
<% dim objInterestItem %>
<% dim objInterestList %>
<% dim objCatalog %>
<% dim objResponse %>
<% dim objItems %>
<% dim objBook %>


<HTML>
<HEAD>
<META HTTP-EQUIV="Pragma" CONTENT="no-cache">
<LINK REL="stylesheet" TYPE="text/css" HREF="main.css">
</HEAD>
```

The style of the text displayed in this file will be consistent with the rest of the application since they all share a common external style sheet. The no-cache setting and setting **Response.Expires** to 0 will ensure that this page will be reloaded by the browser each time it is accessed. The standard application header will also be displayed at the top of the page.

```
<BODY>
<TABLE width=100% CELLSPACING=0 CELLPADDING=0 BORDER=0>
<TR CLASS="pageheader">
<TH ALIGN=left> WROX Bookshop
</TH>
</TR>
</TABLE>

<%    set objUtility = Server.CreateObject("BpkgUtility.NewCollection") %>
<%    set objInterestList = objUtility.NewCollection() %>
```

Since the Catalog application component expects the interest parameter in the form of a collection, we will need to create one using the **NewCollection** method of the **Utility** object. This will return a reference to a collection that can be used to transfer data to the application object. The **InterestList** collection will be made up a set of collections, each one containing information about a particular interest. The Session-level collection "interests" contains information about each interest.

```
<%    for each objInterest in Session("interests") %>
<%        set objInterestItem = objUtility.NewCollection() %>
<%            objInterestItem.Add objInterest("name"),"name" %>
<%            objInterestItem.Add objInterest("code"),"code" %>
```

With each interest that is supported by the system, a new collection will be created using the same **Utility** method as before. The name and code of the interest will be added to this new collection.

The form on the previous page consisted of a series of checkboxes. Each checkbox corresponding to and sharing the same name as one interest. If the checkbox was checked when the form was submitted, then its name would be found in the **Request.Form** collection in this file. If there is a value, then we know that the user clicked the checkbox and, therefore, set the "enabled" element of the collection to True. If the value is empty, then the "enabled" element should be set to false.

```
<%        if Request.Form(objInterest("name")) = "" then %>
<%            objInterestItem.Add false,"enabled" %>
<%        else %>
<%            objInterestItem.Add true,"enabled" %>
<%        end if %>
<%        objInterestList.Add objInterestItem %>
```

This particular **InterestItem** collection is then added to the **InterestList** collection, which will eventually be passed to the application object. This **InterestItem** is released by setting it to nothing, before the file moves on to process the next interest.

```
<%        set objInterestItem = nothing %>
<%    next %>
<%    set objCatalog = Server.CreateObject("BpkgCatalog.Catalog") %>
<%    set objResponse = objCatalog.GetCatalogListByInterests( objInterestList ) %>
```

With the collection of interests successfully constructed, it is then time to pass the information off to the application object. This will take these interests and return a list of books that match any of the interests.

```
<%    if objResponse("error") then %>
<!--#include file=error.inc-->
<%    else %>
```

If an error occurs in the application object, then we will be unable to display the list to the user. The **error.inc** server-side include file will display the common error information, and then allow the user to continue with the application.

```
<%        set objItems = objResponse("items") %>
        <TABLE>
<%        for each objBook in objItems %>
```

The successful output from the application object will be a collection that contains information about each book that matches the user's criteria. This information will be displayed in a table on the final page. The page will iterate through each item in the collection to build this table.

```
        <TR>
        <TD rowspan=2>
<%            Response.Write "<img border=1 src=images/" & objBook.item("imageurl") &
">" %>
        </TD>
```

The URL of the image is one of the items contained in the response collection. The location of the image file is stored in the database as a relative directory reference. In our case, all of the images will be stored in the images directory below the directory containing the ASP file.

> *If you wanted to store your images in another location, or make it easy to move the images from location to location, you could store just the file name of the image without the directory information in the database. You could then use either the ASP file or the application object to add the appropriate directory reference at run-time.*

```
            <TD>
            <FONT SIZE=4>
<%          Response.Write "<B>" & objBook.item("name") & "</B>"  %>
<%          if objBook.item("newflag") = true then %>
<%              Response.Write "<img src=images/new.gif>" %>
```

If the book is a new title, as determined by the application object, then we will display an image that will
visually identify the item as new. Here is an example of how a new item is identified.

To allow the user to purchase a book, the page will present a button that they can press. The caption of
this button will be the price that they will have to pay for the book. The price is calculated by the
application object, and is based on the list price takeing into account any promotion that may be in effect
at the time. In addition to displaying the price, if there is a promotion in effect, then a image will be
displayed to show the user that are to receive a discount if they decide to purchase this book.

```
<%          end if %>
            </FONT>
            </TD>
            <TD>
            </TD>
            <TD>
<%          Response.Write "<INPUT TYPE=""button"" VALUE=""Buy for " & _
            objBook.item("todaysprice") & """ " & _
```

```
               "onclick=window.document.location.href='" & _
               "addBook.asp?catalogid=" & objBook.item("catalogid") & _
               "' > " %>

<%        if objBook.item("promotionflag") = true then %>
<%           Response.Write "<img src=images/promotion.gif>" %>
<%             end if %>
          </TD>
          </TR>
          <TR>
          <TD colspan=3>
<%           Response.Write objBook.item("description")  %>
             <BR><BR>
          ISBN:
<%        Response.Write objBook.item("code")%>
             
          Normal price:
<%        Response.Write objBook.item("price")%>
             
```

The remaining information about the book will also be displayed to the user. This information includes a brief description of the book, its ISBN number, and normal price. There is also a link that the user can select if they wish to view more detailed information about any specific title.

```
<%        Response.Write "<a href=bookDetails.asp?catalogid=" & _
                  objBook.item("catalogid") & ">" & _
                  "More details</a><br>"  %>
          </TD>
          </TR>
          <TR>
          <TD colspan=4>
          <HR width=50%>
          </TD>
          </TR>
<%   next %>
          </TABLE>
<%     end if %>
<CENTER>End of list</CENTER>
```

Once the page has displayed all of the titles that the application object returned, the end of the list will be indicated to the user viewing the page. The collections that were used in this page are then set to *nothing*, freeing any resources that were allocated to them. While this will automatically happen when the page exits, it is good programming practice to explicitly carry the action out.

```
<%     set objCatalog = nothing %>
<%     set objInterestList = nothing %>

</BODY>
</HTML>
```

Now that the list of books has been displayed for the user, they are able to peruse the list. While they are looking at the different titles on the list, they can choose to purchase any of the books. Also, if they are interested in learning more about a particular book, then they can select the More Details link.

BookDetails.asp

In this system, there is certain information about each book that is displayed to the user when looking at a list of books. This includes a short synopsis, the author, ISBN number, and price. To keep the listing concise, not all the information about a book is displayed in the list format. For additional information, the user can select to view an entire page dedicated to information about one book.

In this application, we have provided the link to get to more detail about a book, but have not provided the additional detail itself. There is a wide range of additional information that could be displayed about a book. For example, a biography of the author, a few reviews; possibly in the form of links to on-line book review sites. There may even be an area for the reader to provide their own feedback about the book, and also view other reader's comments.

To support this part of the application, the additional information could be extracted from the database by using a method of the Catalog data object. This information could be modified by the Catalog application object, then passed back to the ASP page for display to the user. Our example application has not included this page, but it can be easily developed extending the business and application objects that have already been created.

AddBook.asp

Once the user has decided to purchase a book, then they need to add it to their shopping basket. By placing it in the basket, the user can then go back and select more books to order. This allows them to purchase multiple books without having to provide all of the order information for every book. To initiate the selection process, the user simply presses the button that is associated with the title that they desire.

As the system is processing the request to add the item to the shopping basket, the user is presented with the message that the Transaction is being processed. When the item is successfully added to the basket, the user will be notified that this action has taken place.

```
<%@ TRANSACTION=Required %>
<% Option Explicit %>
<% Response.Expires = 0
   Response.Buffer = True
%>
```

Since this page will be making changes to the database when it adds an item to the user's basket, it should operate within the scope of a transaction. By setting the **TRANSACTION** directive to **Required**, a new transaction will be created that will encompass this page and all of the objects referenced by it. Since we want this page to be read from the database each time it is accessed, setting **Response.Expires** to 0 will prevent the browser from caching this document.

In this page, we will be using what are known as Transactional Scripts (introduced in Chapter 13). These scripts are called when the transaction is complete. As we stated earlier, a transaction can have two completion states. It can either complete successfully or not complete successfully. When using transactional scripts, an event will be fired that can be handled in the ASP file. This process will be dealt with later. Since we may want to change the **Response** information when handling these scripts, we want to have the ASP output held in a buffer and only sent to the client when the program sends it. This will allow us to take actions based on the success or failure of the transaction. Setting the **Response.Buffer** to **True**, will cause the response information to be held on the server until it is sent using the **Flush** method.

```
<HTML>
<HEAD>
<META HTTP-EQUIV="Pragma" CONTENT="no-cache">

<TITLE></TITLE>
<LINK REL="stylesheet" TYPE="text/css" HREF="main.css">
</HEAD>

<BODY>

<% dim objResponse %>
<% dim objBaskets %>

<TABLE WIDTH=100% CELLSPACING=0 CELLPADDING=0 BORDER=0>
<TR CLASS="pageheader">
<TH ALIGN=left> WROX Bookshop
</TH>
</TR>
</TABLE>
```

This page will have the standard header that all of the other pages had. It will also use the same style sheet as all of the other pages in the system.

```
<%    set objBaskets = Server.CreateObject("BpkgBaskets.Baskets") %>
<%    set objResponse = objBaskets.AddItem(Session("orderID"), Session("email"), _
                        Request.QueryString("catalogid"), 1) %>
```

We will be using the **AddItem** method of the Baskets application object. This method takes an Order ID, the customer's email address, and the catalog ID of the item to add. The last parameter indicates that the user is wishing to order one of these books. Since there was not application requirement to order multiple books at one time, this is a hardcoded value, rather than data that is sent by the user to the server.

```
<P>Thank you.  Your transaction is being processed.</P>
<%  Response.Flush()%>
</BODY>
</HTML>
```

Once the **AddItem** method is called, the confirmation message to the user that the transaction is in process is sent to the user. To have this display in the user's browser immediately, we will use the **Flush** method of the **Response** object to immediately send that information to the client.

Next, we will add the two transaction event handling scripts to the page. The **OnTransactionCommit** event is fired when a transaction completes successfully. The piece of information that we are interested in capturing from the **AddItem** method is the **OrderID** for this user. If you remember from the application object, if the user does not supply the **OrderID**, then it will be either retrieved from the database or generated by the data object. In either case, the **OrderID** will be stored in a session-level variable for later use.

```
<%' Display this page if the transaction succeeds.
Sub OnTransactionCommit()
    Session("orderID") = objResponse("orderID")
    Response.Write("<p>Item added to basket</p>")
    Response.Write("<hr>")
    Response.Write("<input type=BUTTON value='Shop'
onclick='window.history.back(1)'>")
    Response.Write("<input type=BUTTON value='Basket'
onclick=""window.document.location.href='m4basket.asp'"">")
    Response.Write("<input type=BUTTON value='Checkout'
onclick=""window.document.location.href='m4checkout.asp'"">")
    Response.Flush()
end sub
```

The user is provided with a textual indication that the transaction completed successfully, and their book has been added to the shopping basket. The user is also given a set of navigation controls that will allow them to move to other parts of the application. These are **FORM** type buttons, but instead of being processed by another ASP page, they are processed in client side scripting. When they are pressed, they fire an **onclick** event, which is handled by the client-side code. Depending on which button the user presses, the browser will load a different page.

```
' Display this page if the transaction fails.
Sub OnTransactionAbort()
    Response.Write "<p class=errmsg>" & objResponse("errorinfo") & "</p>"
    Response.Write "<a href=abort.asp>Abandon</a>"
    Response.Flush()
End sub
%>
```

If for some reason the transaction does not complete successfully, the **OnTransactionAbort** method will be fired. This will display error information for the user to indicate what caused the problem in the transaction. From that point the user can abandon their current session and start a new one.

One of the options after the successful addition of a book to the shopping basket is for the user to view the contents of the said basket.

ViewBasket.asp

As the user progresses through the application, they can add books that they want to purchase to their shopping basket. One of the tasks that the user might well like to perform is the, aforementioned, viewing of the basket. In viewing the contents, they should be able to see the name of each book, along with its price and quantity. While viewing the quantity is important, it would make the interface more efficient if the user were able to adjust the quantity of the book from the list.

From this page, the user is able to change the quantity of each book and then select the Update button to update the information. They can choose to clear all of the contents of the shopping basket, return to the bookshop to select more books, or they can choose to proceed to checkout.

```
<%@ LANGUAGE="VBSCRIPT" %>
<% Option Explicit %>
<% Response.Expires = 0 %>
```

To ensure that the latest contents are displayed for the user, the **Response.Expires** parameter will be set to 0. This will tell the browser not to cache this document. Just for backup, the no-cache **<META>** tag; which tells the browser the same thing, is included as well.

```
<HTML>
<HEAD>
<TITLE></TITLE>
<LINK REL="stylesheet" TYPE="text/css" HREF="main.css">
</HEAD>
<META HTTP-EQUIV="Pragma" CONTENT="no-cache">
```

```
<BODY>
<% dim objBaskets %>
<% dim objItems %>
<% dim objBook %>
<% dim objResponse %>

<TABLE WIDTH=100% CELLSPACING=0 CELLPADDING=0 BORDER=0>
<TR CLASS="pageheader">
<TH ALIGN=left> Basket Contents
</TH>
</TR>
</TABLE>

<%    set objBaskets = Server.CreateObject("BpkgBaskets.Baskets") %>
<%    set objResponse = objBaskets.GetBasketItems(Session("orderID"),
Session("email")) %>
```

The contents of the basket are retrieved by the **GetBasketItems** method of Baskets application object.
The user's current order ID and email address are supplied as parameters to the method. The method will
return a collection that contains all of the information about the contents of the basket.

```
<%    if objResponse("error") then %>
<!--#include file=error.inc-->
<%    else %>
<%       set objItems = objResponse("items") %>
         <p>Basket contents for
<%       Response.Write Session("firstname") & " " & Session("surname") %>
         </p>
```

If there is an error in retrieving the basket contents, the standard error screen will be displayed for the
user. If the application object was successful in retrieving the contents of the basket, then the browser will
display the list. The list will be personalized as the user name is stored in session-level variables.

If the collection of basket items that is returned by the application object is empty, then we know that the
user has not yet added any items to the basket. Since there are no books to display, the system will display
a message that the basket is empty.

```
<%       if objItems.count = 0 then %>
         <P>Your basket is currently empty</P>
         <HR>
<%        else %>
             <FORM ACTION="updateBasket.asp" METHOD="POST">
             <TABLE CELLSPACING=0 CELLPADDING=0 BORDER=0>
```

The contents of the basket will be displayed in a table, which will organize that data for easy viewing by
the user. Since there are fields in the display that the user will be able to modify; namely the quantity of
each book, the entire table will be enclosed in a **<FORM>** processing block. This will pass the information
about the quantities of each item to the **UpdateBasket.asp** file to update the database.

```
             <TR class="tableheader">
             <TH>Item</TH>
             <TH width=15> </TH>
             <TH>Unit price</TH>
```

```
                <TH WIDTH=15> </TH>
                <TH>No.</TH>
                </TR>
<%              for each objBook in objItems %>
```

Each entry in the Items collection will be displayed on a new row in the table. The name and price will each be output to their own cells in the table. Since the application object takes care of formatting the price, there is no need to use the VBScript FormatCurrency method to correctly display this information.

```
                <TR CLASS="tabledata">
                <TD>
<%              Response.Write objBook.item("name")  %>
                </TD>
                <TD> </TD>
                <TD ALIGN=right>
<%              Response.Write objBook.item("todaysprice") %>
                </TD>
                <TD> </TD>
```

To allow the user to change the quantity of each item, the initial quantity is placed inside of a form **TEXT** field. This will allow the user to change that quantity, and then have that new value passed to the page that is handling the form request. To identify which book the particular quantity is for, the **basketid** value is used as the name of the **TEXT** field. You will see in the next section how this is processed.

```
                <TD ALIGN=right>
            <INPUT TYPE=text SIZE=3 NAME=
<%              Response.Write objBook.item("basketid") %>
            VALUE=
<%              Response.Write objBook.item("numitems") %>
                >
                </TD>
                </TR>
<%          next %>
            </TABLE>
            <HR>
```

The user has four choices of actions to take from this page. These choices are displayed as buttons at the bottom of the list. The first two buttons actually submit the **FORM** that contains the quantity information. The button that the user selects to clear the contents of the basket has a name property of "clear." The button to update the quantity has a name of "update." This will be very important in the next section when we look at the code to handle these buttons. The second two buttons will redirect the browser to different pages to allow the user to check out or to select more books.

```
                <INPUT TYPE="submit" NAME="clear" VALUE="Clear All">
                <INPUT TYPE="submit" NAME="update" VALUE="Update">
            <INPUT TYPE="button" VALUE="Select More Books"
                onclick=window.document.location.href='SelectBookCriteria.asp'>
            <INPUT TYPE="button" VALUE="Checkout"
                onclick=window.document.location.href='m4checkout.asp'>

                </FORM>
<%          end if %>
```

```
<%    end if %>
<%    set objBaskets = nothing %>

</BODY>
</HTML>
```

After viewing the list of books in the shopping basket, and either deciding to empty the basket, or change the quantity of one or more items, the user has to request that the system process their request. This is done by selecting one of the first two buttons at the bottom of the page. This button will submit the form that will be processed by the **UpdateBasket.asp** file.

UpdateBasket.asp

There are two actions that the user can take while viewing the contents of the shopping basket. They can adjust the quantity of one or more items and request that the system processes those updates. The user can also decide to empty all of the items from their shopping basket. These two functions are initiated by buttons that are found on the **ViewBasket.asp** screen. Both functions are handled by **UpdateBasket.asp** file. The file will process the request, and display a message to the user indicating that the update was successful.

```
…Standard Page Stuff Left out here…
<%    set objBaskets = Server.CreateObject("BpkgBaskets.Baskets") %>
```

The first thing that we will do is create a reference to the Baskets application object, which will be used to modify the contents of the basket in this page. Since there are two possible functions for this page, we need to determine which function this particular instance is requesting. The **Form** collection contains both the quantities from the text fields, as well as from the button that was used to submit the form. By checking for the value of the Update button, we can determine if it was the Update button or the Clear All button that was pressed. The first case that is handled is for the Update button.

```
<%    if Request.Form("UPDATE") = "Update" then %>
<%        bErr = false %>
<%        for each objBook in Request.Form %>
```

To check each quantity for each book, we will iterate through the entire **Form** collection. This will allow us to check each entry in this collection individually. One of the entries in the collection represents the update button. Since this has nothing to do with the quantity of an item, we need to skip over it when it comes up.

```
<%            if not objBook = "update" then %>
<%                if isnumeric(Request.Form(objBook)) then %>
<%                if Request.Form(objBook) >= 0 then %>
<%    set objResponse = objBaskets.UpdateNumItems(objBook, Request.Form(objBook)) %>
```

For each **TEXT** field in the collection, we will first check to see if the value is a number. If it is, then we check to make sure that it is not a negative number. There is no way for a user to buy a negative number of books. The quantity is then sent to the **UpdateNumItems** method of the Baskets application object. The application object is responsible checking to see if the new number is the same as the old before updating the database. This eases the burden for the ASP developer as this business rule is automatically checked.

```
<%                        if objResponse("error") then %>
<!--#include file=error.inc-->
<%    end if %>
```

If an error occurs in the processing of the update, the standard error message is displayed to the user. If the quantity that the user entered is less than 0, or they entered a non-numeric character, then this is flagged as a user error, and a different error message is displayed.

```
<%                      else %>
<%                            bErr = true %>
<%                      end if %>
<%                else %>
<%                            bErr = true %>
<%                end if %>
<%           end if %>
<%       next %>
<%       if bErr then %>
    <p class=errmsg>Invalid 'Number of Items' detected</p>
<%       end if %>
```

The other function that this ASP file handles is for clearing the contents of the basket. Since there are only two buttons that can submit the form, and we checked for the first, then if the user pressed the second, this next block of code will be executed.

```
<%    else %>
<%       set objResponse = objBaskets.EmptyBasket(Session("orderID")) %>
```

The method to empty the basket is very straightforward. The current user's order ID is passed in as a parameter, and the application object uses the data object to remove all of the contents from the shopping basket. If an error occurs, then the standard error message is displayed. If it method is successful, then user is notified that the details have been updated. At this point, the user can return to viewing the contents of the basket by clicking on the button.

```
<%        if objResponse("error") then %>
<!--#include file=error.inc-->
<%        end if %>
<%    end if %>
    <P>Details updated</P>
    <INPUT TYPE="button" VALUE="View Basket"
      onclick=window.document.location.href='viewBasket.asp'>
</BODY>
</HTML>
```

In our application tour, therefore, we have looked at registration, browsing, and selection. All that is left to do now is to complete the order for the book. This will be covered in the next chapter when we conclude our electronic commerce case study with the introduction of the Microsoft Message Queue Server and how it can be used to support the order processing portion of our application.

Summary

We have now reached the end of the second part of our Electronic Commerce Case Study. In the next chapter, we will look at the final part of the application. The user will be able to take the contents of their shopping basket and use them to complete an order. That chapter will introduce the topic of the Microsoft Message Queue Server (MSMQ) and how it can be used to support both on-line and off-line applications.

In this chapter we have:

- Reviewed the parts of the application that were developed in Chapter 15

- Examined some of the issues relating to the scalability of server components when working with Internet Information Server, Active Server Pages, and Microsoft Transaction Server.

- Created the Catalog and Baskets data objects using Visual Basic 5.0. These data objects were designed to participate in Microsoft Transaction Server Transactions.

- Created the Catalog and Baskets application objects using VB 5. These objects encapsulated the business logic necessary to provide for the display of the catalog as well as the selection of items for purchase in the application.

- Developed the Active Server Page code to present the catalog and shopping basket displays to the user, as well as providing a method for the user to place items into their shopping basket.

Next, we will look at developing the final part of the application, and how IIS, ASP, & Microsoft Transaction Server can be enhanced with the addition of MSMQ.

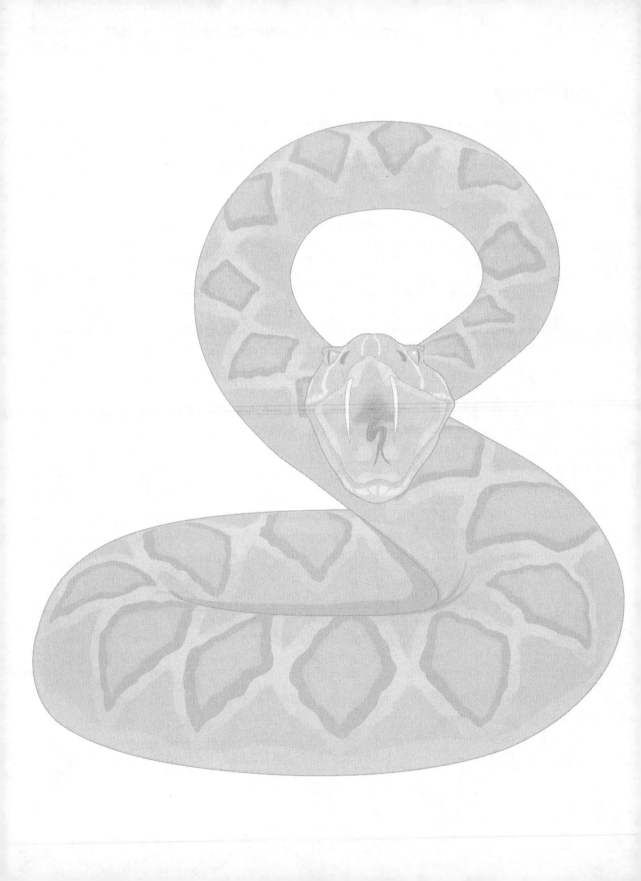

Message Queueing in the Electronic Commerce Case Study

In the previous two chapters, we have looked at how to build an Electronic Commerce application using IIS 4.0, Active Server Pages, and Microsoft Transaction Server. In Chapter 15, we introduced a design methodology known as **User-Centered Design**, and then designed and built the part of the application that allowed a user to log into the system. Chapter 16 showed how to build the parts of the application that allowed the user to browse the content of the electronic store and select items for purchase.

The last step in the application is to take the contents of the user's "shopping basket" and handle the fulfillment processing to complete the order. In this chapter, we will develop that part of the application. To provide a more robust solution for this part of the application, we will introduce a technology known as Message Queues. This technology will allow the application to support different interfaces to multiple users and other systems, some of which may be connected via unreliable communication networks, and may all not be connected at the same time.

What is Message Queuing?

Message queuing is a system that allows different applications to communicate with each other. These applications can be on the same or different physical platforms. The platforms can be located in the same room, on the same LAN, or at any locations that are electronically connected, maybe even distributed around the world. The connection does not even need to be permanent. The platforms can even be running different operating systems, as we will see later in the chapter.

This sounds like a very heterogeneous system. Different applications, wide geographic locations, different connection types, and different operating systems are all characteristics of the Internet-connected world that we are living in today. Being able to move data between these systems has always been a goal of those who preach about connectivity.

Technologies such as SQL, ODBC, FTP, and HTTP all provide different mechanisms for data to be moved between systems in this heterogeneous environment. The only drawback is that the applications on each end have to both understand the exact same protocol for the way the data is formatted and the two systems communicating must both be participating in the communication at the same time. To maintain this communication, the network connecting the two systems needs to be reliable. While large numbers of systems have been created using these systems, that doesn't mean that a more efficient method of communication can't be found.

The next step is to let different applications exchange application information, which can be characterized as a richer set of information than just plain data. There are some competing technologies that are available today that perform these functions. You probably have heard the discussions between the proponents of COM, the Component Object Model of the Windows platform, and CORBA, the Common Object Request Broker Architecture of the ABM (anybody but Microsoft) group. These technologies both provide mechanisms for applications and their components to communicate with one another. But, for this communication to take place, both applications must be running and the connection between the two of them intact.

For many applications, this constraint is not a problem. But what happens if one of the systems is not available, or the connection between the two of them is not active? Neither COM nor CORBA can handle this situation. There needs to be something between the two applications that can manage the communications and deal with these problems. One type of software that can overcome these issues is called a message queuing system. The message queuing system that is a companion to IIS 4.0 is called the Microsoft Message Queue System (MSMQ).

Types of Communication

When two applications are trying to exchange information with each other, this is a form of communication. When two components of an application are working together, calling methods and passing data between them, this is another form of communication. There are basically two methods of communication. These methods are defined by what the initiator of the conversation does once it stops sending. These two methods are **synchronous** and **asynchronous** communication.

Synchronous

In a synchronous communication, when the initiator of the conversation stops sending their information to the receiver, it goes into a waiting mode. It will remain in that waiting mode until it receives a response back from the receiver with the information that the receiver is sending. Only once it receives this information will the initiator continue on with its processing.

Synchronous communication is like making a function call. When you make a function call in an application, you package up the information that you are sending to the receiver and call the function. Then you wait. Your program will not continue to execute until the function returns the results of the function call to you.

Asynchronous

In an asynchronous communication, the sender in the conversation will send its information and then go on its merry way. It will not wait for any response from the receiver in the conversation. In many cases, there is no response that is ever sent back to the sender. If there is a response that is sent back, then the original sender can decide for itself when and even if to process the response.

Asynchronous communication is similar to event handling in Visual Basic. In Visual Basic, you can cause something to happen that will fire an event. But while you are waiting for that event to fire, you are free to go off and do whatever other processing that you want to do. When that event is fired, you can choose to handle the event using an event handling routine, or just ignore the event and continue processing.

Why use Asynchronous?

There are three primary reasons that you would want to use asynchronous communication over synchronous communication in your applications. If your sender always has to wait for a response then the system will spend a lot of time waiting for something else to happen, rather than on running the application. Asynchronous communications will make the system seem faster to the user, since it can devote the majority of its time to processing rather than waiting.

There may be instances where the sender really doesn't care when the receiver will deal with the message. It's like delegating a task to someone. An efficient manager will not wait for that task to complete before going on to other tasks. This is being asynchronous. If a manager has to wait for the task to complete before doing anything else, first of all they are not an efficient delegator, and second, they are performing synchronously.

If your application is running in an environment where the connection between the two applications is not reliable, or if one of the applications is running on a disconnected computer, like a laptop, then asynchronous communications can be a real benefit. Also, if one of the applications only ran during off-hours, then without asynchronous communications, the sender would have to wait until the next day to complete its processing.

Message Queues

There are two primary components that make a message queuing system. One of these is, of course, a message. A message is a piece of information or data that is sent between two computers. The data can either be text or binary. The other component of the system is the queue. A queue is a container that can hold messages. Applications can then either put messages into a queue or read messages from a queue.

Message Content

A message is made up of a number of different components. The main part of the message is its content. As stated before, the message can either be text or binary data. The format of the content is determined by the two applications that are passing the message between themselves. There is no standard method for formatting the content of a message. This means that, unlike an e-mail system, where parts of the body of the message can be interpreted by the system, the only applications that can read the contents of the message are those that know exactly what the content consists of.

A message also consists of information about who the sender and the receiver are. It will also include a timestamp as to when it was sent. Some messages can include an expiration date, after which if they are not read, they will be deleted.

Message Queue

A message queue is where a message is sent until it is picked up by the destination application. In this case, the message queue is similar to a set of office mail slots. In an office mail slot, everyone has a slot, and to get a document to someone else, you put it in their slot. Later, they can come by and pick up all of their messages. In a message queuing system, messages will be placed in a queue until the destination application explicitly asks for the message. If there is a failure on the system that is holding the queues, then when the system restarts the queues will automatically be restored to their state before the crash. If there is a failure during the transmission of the message, the last server to have a valid copy of the message before the crash will be able to send it on its way once the system is restored.

There can be one or more queues in a system. The Microsoft Message Queue System actually supports vast hierarchies of systems that are connected together. This is beyond the scope of this chapter. However, on a single machine, the queue manager application manages all of the queues on that machine. It is up to the queue manager to determine if the destination of a message is local or not. If it is local, it simply drops the message in its destination queue, which it is also managing. If it is not local, then it locates the machine where the destination queue is by using a directory server. It then negotiates the transfer of that message with the destination machine's queue manager. Once the destination queue manager receives the message, it then deposits it in the destination queue.

Message Queuing vs. E-Mail

Doesn't this sound a lot like e-mail? Both e-mail and message queue systems have messages, with senders and receivers. An e-mail system has mailboxes and a message queue system has queues, but they generally are similar. And the queue manager is a lot like an e-mail server in that it will forward messages to their proper destinations. So what is the difference?

You can think of e-mail as person to person communications. The information that is sent has to be readable and interpreted by humans. Message queue messages are for application to application communications. The applications have to be able to programmatically interpret the results of the message. This is more than just interpreting the body of the message. If a message cannot be delivered, then the human can generally figure out why from the text in the response. A message queue message has to provide this type of information in a standard way that the application reading the message can understand.

In the body of an e-mail message, the content is understandable by anyone who can understand the language it is written in. That is, unless the message body is encrypted. In a message queue message, the content is only understood by the sending application and the receiving application. This means that intercepting a message between two systems is useless unless you know exactly how to interpret the message. Another by-product of this is that the message can be made very concise. The information can be in shorthand known by the two applications, rather than in verbose text that has to be understood by humans.

A message queue system also has more safeguards in place to ensure that a message arrives at its destination. With e-mail, especially over the Internet, reliable delivery is not something one can always count on. Message queuing systems have the capability to ensure that a message arrives at its destination. There are two types of delivery methods that are supported MSMQ: Express and Recoverable. An Express message is one that resides only in memory, thereby consuming fewer resources and being able to move through the message queuing system faster. The other type of message, a recoverable message, is written to permanent storage at every step from the sender to the destination.

This means that if you have two messages, one Express and one Recoverable, that are in a queue server waiting to be routed to another queue server, and that queue server dies, the express message will die with it. Since there is no copy of the message written to permanent storage, it will be lost. The recoverable message, having been stored by the server, will be restored once the server is restarted. It is up to the sender of the message, based on the performance vs. reliability tradeoff, to determine the message type for each message being sent.

Why use Message Queuing?

Now that we have a better understanding of what message queuing is, we need to look at why systems of today require their use. We need to examine if there are other technologies available that can play the same role as message queuing. We also need to look at when should message queuing be used over other technologies? To do this, we need to look at the changing architectures of systems today. We also need to look at the tradeoffs that selecting message queuing over another technology will present to us.

Distributed Systems

As we've seen in Chapter 1, with the evolution of ever cheaper and more powerful computers, the ability to run a system with applications distributed over a number of machines has turned from a pipe dream into a reality. Correspondingly, the need for system users to access the system from a single machine has developed into each user having his own computer and accessing the required application over a network.

However, as you distribute the processing and the data in a system, you then have to start worrying about how the systems are connected together. In many instances, the connection may not be permanent. You may have to dial-up or dock your machine in order to connect and exchange information. It is these types of distributed systems where message queuing can provide great advantages.

A disconnected user can perform local tasks with their application. That application can queue messages for delivery to other applications until the computer is connected to the network again. When the computer is connected to the network, the queued messages can be sent, and messages bound for this computer can be received and processed automatically. This support for distributed applications makes message queuing technology an important technology in creating tomorrow's business applications.

What about speed?

But what about speed? Isn't it faster just to open up a TCP socket on another machine and let my applications exchange information that way? Or maybe using a named pipe, or some other communication method? Well, in a narrow view of things, yes that is faster. But why should you as an application developer worry about these low-level issues when you should be worrying about how to solve your business problems. Even for the case of message delivery speed, if you are in a connected environment that supports these connected communication methods, then express delivery of message queue messages gives nearly similar performance. But what happens if the system is not connected using a high-speed, inexpensive link?

If your application is relying on communication protocols that require a permanent connection, then in order for that application to work, the connection has to be in place. This means having your system connected to the network at all times, via LAN or by phone, or by some other means. Even these types of connections are not always reliable. Communication protocols such as TCP require a reliable communication link, and writing code to handle breaks in the network can become very complex. Another problem with these types of links is that they can become rather expensive. When the means of connection is not inexpensive, this method of communication ceases to be an effective means of distributing an application. If the application supports queuing, then all that needs to happen during a connected state is an exchange of messages. All of the other work can take place off-line, when connect charges are not being incurred.

What about COM?

So then, should you always use message queuing for communication between applications? This isn't the case either. If your business environment requires some activities be carried out synchronously, then a communication method such as DCOM or CORBA is better suited to perform this type of processing. If everybody using the application is always connected to the LAN, and all of the application servers are connected over fast, local, reliable links, then messaging may not necessarily be the best answer either. And for many developers, message queuing is a new and unfamiliar technology that they may not be willing to make an investment in.

A few short guidelines on when to use message queuing can help to clarify the decision to use it or not:

▲ If the application you are communicating with is not running at the same time as your application, use message queuing.

▲ If the message is important and will cause problems if it is lost, use message queuing

▲ If your application is not always connected to receiver application, but still needs to be functional, use message queuing.

▲ If your application cannot maintain a reliable network connection to the receiver application, use message queuing.

▲ And if you perform many communication tasks with other applications asynchronously, and may or may not care about their response, use message queuing

Message Queuing In Practice

It may be helpful to look at a few business examples of where message queuing can be used to provide a more effective application. Remember, not every application is suitable for message queuing. In fact, used in the wrong place for the wrong application, message queuing can sometimes cause more harm than good. Based on the guidelines that were outlined in the last section, let's look at some business cases and see how message queuing can be applied there.

Let's say you have an organization that relies on a group of mobile sales personnel. These sales personnel both present the products of the company to prospective buyers and generate orders based on what the buyer wants. In this business, it is critical for the sales person to have up-to-date information about the products that are available to sell. It is also critical for them to be able to show the products and generate orders without having to connect their laptop to a phone line. By now, you should see at least two applications for message queuing.

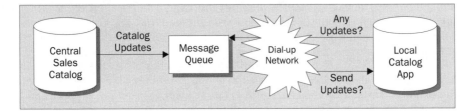

For the first application, the home office can produce updates and additions to the sales catalog application. These changes can then be routed to the individual sales personnel through a message queue. The message queuing system will hold these messages until the user connects their computer to the network. At that time the message queuing manager on the salesperson's computer will receive those messages that are waiting for it on the central queuing manager. The messages will then be delivered to the catalog application on the user's computer, which will process the updates contained in the messages.

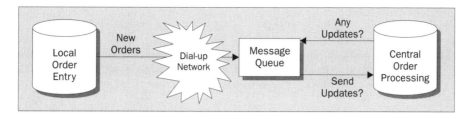

A similar scenario, yet flowing in reverse, will allow the salesman to write orders on their laptop. The sales orders will be packaged as messages and held by the local machine's queue manager. When the queue manager can again communicate with the other queues in the company, it can send these messages on their way to the order-processing queue. By marking these messages as **recoverable**, they are guaranteed to be delivered even if one of the systems in between has a failure. The message queuing system can automatically provide the acknowledgment that the message successfully arrived at the destination.

Another example, which we will look at in greater detail at the end of the chapter, is the use of message queuing in a web application. If you think about each web page or set of web pages that a user may access as an application, then an easy way to pass information from one application to another is through queuing. ASP currently has technologies that permit communication between pages in the same web application, through the use of the **Session** object. But what if the communication needs to be between two separate web applications? In the case study that we have been looking at for the past few chapters, we have shown the client end of a bookstore application. But what happens after the consumer decides they want to buy? Well, an order has to be generated. There are people who need to know about the order so they can pull the books in the order from inventory. Others who will need to package the books for shipment. There may also be a way for the author to be notified that someone has purchased one of his or her books.

Since we are working in the web world, there is no concept of a continually running shipping or author-notification application. Each of these applications will be run when the interested party accesses the web page that corresponds to that application. So what is the best way to connect applications that may not be running at the same time? Yes, this is another example of where message queuing can be used. At the end of the chapter, we will look at how the placing of the order will generate an order list that can be created when the stock clerk runs his application. We will also look at how the author can find out which books were purchased, and by whom. But first, lets spend a little time looking at the system that will actually run all of this: Microsoft Message Queue Server.

Introduction to MSMQ

Microsoft Message Queue Server (MSMQ) is part of the Microsoft NT Server set of products. It was first made widely available in the Windows NT 4 Option Pack. MSMQ is also included as part of Windows NT Server Enterprise Edition in a complete implementation. A more limited implementation is available on the regular Windows NT Server. There are clients available for every Windows platform, as well as for other platforms, such as IBM CICS and MQSeries. MSMQ provides the technologies that allow the transmission of messages over network connections, management of these messages as they are grouped into queues, and a programmatic API that allows developers to access all of the functionality of this technology.

MSMQ also provides ActiveX support for working with messages and queues. It is this ActiveX support that provides the close integration between MSMQ and IIS, ASP, and MTS. MSMQ can be enabled to understand the relative costs of connections, and thereby choose the most efficient routing method for messages within a network infrastructure. As with many of the other tools that are part of the BackOffice family, MSMQ provides graphical management through the Microsoft Management Console (MMC) which provides centralized management facilities for even the most widely distributed systems.

System Architecture

The primary parts of the MSMQ system architecture are the messages, the queues, the queue managers, and the set of COM interfaces that allows programs to access the information. The system operates transparently with respect to physical location. This means that an application can be sending a message to another application without having to worry about how the message actually gets there. MSMQ provides a facility for programmatically searching the set of queues available throughout a system. Once the application finds the queue it is interested in, it can send messages to it without worrying about how the message will actually get there. This happens transparently to the client, regardless if the destination queue is on the same machine or on a machine halfway around the world. MSMQ will get the message there, and will guarantee that it gets there.

Working with Queues and Messages

It is surprising how easy it is to support message queues in your application, given the power and flexibility that MSMQ provides. By making the implementation of message queuing so easy, Microsoft hopes that more and more developers will take advantage of it. There are two primary operations that you can do with a message queue. You can open or close the queue and you can send or receive a message. There are other methods that allow you to search for a queue, create or delete queues, and manage the properties of existing queues.

> *Since this is a book about ASP, and ASP works best with ActiveX objects, all of the code snippets that we will be showing will be using the MSMQ ActiveX objects, as opposed to the native COM interfaces.*

There are a series of ActiveX objects that encapsulate the functionality of MSMQ. These can be created in ASP pages, using the **Server.CreateObject** method. They can also be created in VB Active Server Components running inside the MTS environment by using the **ObjectContext.CreateInstance** method.

Step 1: Get a Queue

The first thing that you will need to do is get your hands on a queue to send your messages to. There are two ways to get a queue. If the queue exists, then you can locate it. If it doesn't exist then you can create it. The **MSMQQueueInfo** object allows you to manipulate properties and methods that describe a queue. To create a new queue, you will use this object's **Create** method. Prior to calling create, you will need to set some information about the queue. This information at least has to include the location of the queue.

The location of a queue is called its **path name**. This path name indicates three things about the queue:

- ▲ The machine it is located on
- ▲ Whether it is public or private
- ▲ The name of the queue

The format of the queue name is **machinename\queuename** for a public queue or,
.\PRIVATE$\queuename for a private queue. In the syntax for creating a private queue, the '**.**' is used
to indicate the local machine. Private queues can only be created on the local machine, so a machine name
is not needed. To set the **pathname** you would use this code:

```
Dim qinfo as New MSMQQueueInfo
qinfo.PathName = "myserver\TestQueue"
```

Once the queue has been named, other properties can be set. The **pathname** parameter is the only
required parameter. The other parameters are documented in the MSMQ documentation. To create the
queue, all you now need to do is call its **create** method:

```
qinfo.Create
```

We now have a reference to a valid queue that can be used in step 2: opening the queue.

If you know that the queue you are interested in already exists, but do not know the exact name of it, you
can look up a reference to the queue. Using the **LookupQueue** method of the **MSMQQuery** object does
this. This is the only method of this object, and will return a **MSMQQueueInfos** object, which is a
collection of queues based on criteria that you set. For the criteria, you can choose from one or more of
the following properties of the queue:

Parameter–*Optional*	Value
QueueGuid (String)	Identifier of queue.
ServiceTypeGuid (String)	Type of service provided by the queue.
Label (String)	Label of queue.
CreateTime (Variant Date)	Time when queue was created.
ModifyTime (Variant Date)	Time when queue properties were last set (both when the queue was created and the last time **Update** was called).

Since these parameters only allow you to set a single value for the parameter, to make the query more
effective, you can also set a Boolean operation for each parameter. In other words, when you enter a
parameter value, say for **Label**, the method will only return those queues that exactly match the value
you entered. By setting the *relationship parameter*, you can specify that the value you are entering is some
boolean relation to the search value. These possible boolean operators are:

Boolean Operator	Value	Boolean Operator	Value
REL_EQ	Equals	**REL_LE**	Less Than or Equal To
REL_NEQ	Not Equal to	**REL_GE**	Greater Than or Equal To
REL_LT	Less Than	**REL_NOP**	Ignore the Parameter
REL_GT	Greater Than		

The relationship parameters are:

Relationship Parameter	Criteria Parameter
RelServiceType	ServiceTypeGuid
RelLabel	Label
RelCreateTime	CreateTime
RelModifyTime	ModifyTime

To call the **LookupQueue** method using Visual Basic, you would do something like the following:

```
Dim query As New MSMQQuery
Dim qinfos As MSMQQueueInfos
Dim qinfo As MSMQQueueInfo
Set qinfos = query.LookupQueue(Label:="Bill")
```

This will return a collection of queues, all of which have a **Label** value of '**Bill**.' While this return value is a collection, it is not navigable using the same methods as other collections. To navigate, there is a **Reset** method to move in front of the beginning of the collection, and a **Next** method to get the next entry in the collection. To navigate through each entry in the collection, you can use this:

```
qinfos.Reset  ' This ensures we are at the beginning of the collection
Set qinfo = qinfos.Next
Do While Not qinfo Is Nothing
'    Do something with this queue
   Set qinfo = qinfos.Next
Loop
```

This gives you two methods to retrieve a queue. The next step is to open the queue.

Step 2: Open a Queue

The **MSMQQueueInfo** object that was returned when you created a queue or found one using **LookupQueue** is merely information about a queue. To actually work with a queue, that is use it to send and receive messages, you have to open it. When you open a queue, you call a method on the **MSMQQueueInfo** object and are returned an **MSMQQueue** object. It is this object that you will subsequently use in working with the queue. To open a queue, you first need to set two parameters. The first parameter will determine what you are doing with the queue and the second will determine what others can do with it while you have it open.

When you have an open queue in your application, there are three operations that you can perform on it. You can:

 Send messages to the queue,

 Retrieve messages from the queue,

 Peek at messages in the queue.

Reading and writing messages are self-explanatory. Peeking at a message in the queue means to look at the contents of a message in the queue without removing it from the queue.

You also need to decide how other people can interact with the queue when you have it open. If you have opened the queue for sending or peeking, then the only valid choice is to allow others to fully interact with the queue. If you have opened the queue for receiving, then you can either allow others full access to the queue, or you can prevent others from receiving messages from the queue as well. Even if you choose this option, other applications can still send messages to the queue and peek at messages in the queue. These choices are determined by setting two values when opening the queue: the **queue access mode**, which governs how you will be able to access the queue, and the **queue sharing mode**, which governs how others can access the queue.

The set of possible values for the queue access and queue sharing modes are:

Queue Access Mode	Queue Sharing Mode
MQ_PEEK_ACCESS	MQ_DENY_NONE
MQ_SEND_ACCESS	MQ_DENY_RECEIVE_SHARE
MQ_RECEIVE_ACCESS	

Once you have determined the parameter settings for your queue, you can issue the **open** call. The format for this call is:

```
Open(accessmode, sharemode)
```

To open a queue for sending messages to it, you would:

```
qInfo.Open(MQ_SEND_ACCESS, MQ_DENY_NONE)
```

Now that you have a queue open for writing, the next step that you need to follow is to create a message that can be sent to that queue.

Step 3: Create a Message

To send a message, you will need to create an instance of the **MSMQMessage** object. This object encapsulates all of the data and methods that you need to create and send a message. There are a number of properties that you can set when sending a message. Some of these parameters are considered core properties, such as the body of the message. Others allow you to modify certain characteristics about how the message is delivered, or other characteristics. This table shows the characteristic properties of an **MSMQMessage** object:

Property	Description
`Ack`	MSMQ can acknowledge when certain events happen to this message after it is sent. Acknowledgements can be positive or negative. This parameter is used to set what actions this message will acknowledge. Possible values are: **MQMSG_ACKNOWLEDGMENT_FULL_REACH_QUEUE** Positive if the message reaches its destination queue, negative if it fails to arrive within the timeout. **MQMSG_ACKNOWLEDGMENT_FULL_RECEIVE** Positive if the message is retrieved from its queue before it expires. Negative if it expires. **MQMSG_ACKNOWLEDGMENT_NACK_REACH_QUEUE** Negative if the message fails to arrive at the queue. No positive acknowledgement sent. **MQMSG_ACKNOWLEDGMENT_NACK_RECEIVE** Negative if the message is not retrieved from its queue before it expires. No positive acknowledgement is sent. **MQMSG_ACKNOWLEDGMENT_NONE** This is the default value – no acknowledgements sent.
`AdminQueueInfo`	If the message is going to send acknowledgements, this is the queue that it will be sent to.
`Body`	The contents of the message
`CorrelationId`	If you are responding to a message, you can put the ID of the incoming message in this field, so that the other application can correlate the two messages.
`Delivery`	**MSMQ_DELIVERY_EXPRESS**—for Express Delivery **MSMQ_DELIVERY_RECOVERABLE**—for Recoverable Delivery
`Label`	A description of the message
`MaxTimeToReachQueue`	Timeout value in seconds after which the message will be deleted if it does not reach its destination queue
`MaxTimeToReceive`	Timeout value in seconds after which the message will be deleted if it is not retrieved from its destination queue.
`Priority`	Sets how quickly a message will be routed and where it is placed in the destination queue. Higher values are routed faster and placed in front of lower priority messages. Messages with the same priority are in the queue in chronological order.
`ResponseQueueInfo`	If the sending application wants a response to this message, in can include the queue it wants the response sent to in this parameter.

The primary parameter for the **MSMQMessage** object is the **Body** parameter. This holds the actual contents of the message. This value can be a string, or any type of binary information that both the sending and receiving application know how to handle.

Lets take a look at an example that will create a message, set its properties, and set its content. This will
be everything that needs to be done to get the message ready to send.

```
Dim msgSent As New MSMQMessage
msgSent.Label = "My Message"
msgSent.Body = "Test message with acknowledgment."
msgSent.Ack = QMSG_ACKNOWLEDGMENT_FULL_RECEIVE
msgSent.MaxTimeToReceive = 60
Set msgSent.AdminQueueInfo = qinfoAdmin
```

This will create a new **MSMQMessage** object and set its **Label** and **Body**. This message will send an
acknowledgment when it is retrieved from its destination queue. This acknowledgment will be send to the
qinfoAdmin queue. If the message is not retrieved within 60 seconds, it will be deleted from the
destination queue, and a negative acknowledgment will be sent.

The last step in the process of creating and sending the message is to send it to its destination queue.

Step 4: Send a Message

To send a message, you will need both a **queue** that is open for sending and an **MSMQMessage** object
that has been properly configured. The **Send** method is actually a method of the message object, not the
queue. The destination queue is passed as a parameter to the **Send** method. To send this message to the
queue that we have already opened, you would type:

```
msgSent.Send qInfo
```

The message is now on its way to its destination queue. Once it arrives there, it will wait for 60 seconds. If
no application retrieves it within that time, it will delete itself from the queue. If an application retrieves
the message before the 60 seconds are up, then a positive acknowledgement message will be sent to the
queue defined by **qinfoAdmin**. If the message times out and deletes itself, then a negative
acknowledgement will be sent to the **qinfoAdmin** queue.

Step 5: Retrieving a Message

Now that there is a message sitting in this queue, we need to be able to retrieve it and use its contents in
another application. There are two methods that can be used to retrieve messages from a queue. A queue
can be read synchronously, wherein all program execution will be blocked until a message is available in
the queue, or a timeout value is reached. A queue can also be read asynchronously, where a queue will
fire events as messages arrive, and these events can be handled by the application. In the web-based
application world, the majority of message retrieval will be done using synchronous reads. We are using the
synchronous message since there really is no concept of a "running application" that can receive the
message arrival events that an asynchronous read would generate. In a web-based application, the system
will check for a waiting message when the user tries to load a specific page in the application. While a
synchronous message retrieval on a web application sounds like it may adversely impact system
performance, we can first check to see if there is a message waiting before we actually do the read.

In the previous examples, we sent the message to the queue with the label of 'Bill.' We can now use
exactly the same steps as were used in steps 1 through 3 above, except now we will open the queue for
read.

```
Dim query As New MSMQQuery
Dim qinfos As MSMQQueueInfos
Dim qinfo As MSMQQueueInfo
Set qinfos = query.LookupQueue(Label:="Bill")
qinfos.Reset
Set qinfo = qinfos.Next
qInfo.Open(MQ_RECEIVE_ACCESS, MQ_DENY_NONE)
```

In the **Open** method, we specified that this queue will be used to retrieve messages. This mode will also allow us to peek at messages that may be waiting in the queue. To peek at a message in the queue, you would:

```
Set msgDest = qInfo.Peek(ReceiveTimeout:=100)
```

This will check to see if there are any messages in the queue. If after 100 milliseconds, or $1/10^{th}$ of a second, there are no messages, then this method will return. To check to see if a message was found, you will check to see if **msgDest** properly references an object. If it is set to **Nothing**, then no message was waiting in the queue.

If a message is found in the queue, then it can be retrieved. There could be more than one message waiting in the queue. If there is, then the message that will be retrieved will be the first one in the queue. This is the message with the highest priority, or if more than one message has the same priority, then the one that has been in the queue the longest will be retrieved. To retrieve this message, you would:

```
Set msgDest = qDest.Receive(ReceiveTimeout:=10)
```

This will put the contents of the message that was in the queue into the **msgDest** object. You can then get the information that this message contained by examining the contents of its body. Once you have read this message from the queue, you can close the queue. This will free up the resources used by the **queue** object. The **MSMQMessage** object that you retrieved will still be valid, even after you close the queue. To close the queue, you would:

```
qInfo.Close()
```

Now that we have looked at the steps to work with messages and queues, let's step back a bit from the specific implementation and look at how MSMQ and other key pieces of Microsoft technology can work together.

Features and Benefits of MSMQ

Microsoft Message Queue Server provides a number of key benefits to developers because of its close integration with other Microsoft technologies. We have already touched on one key benefit, which is the integration of MSMQ and ActiveX. The use of the MSMQ ActiveX components allows **any** application development environment that supports ActiveX to use the features of message queuing in their applications. These development environments include Visual C++, Visual Basic, Visual J++, and ActiveX Scripting Hosts. It is this ability to use MSMQ from VBScript that allows for integration with Active Server Pages.

Integration with ASP

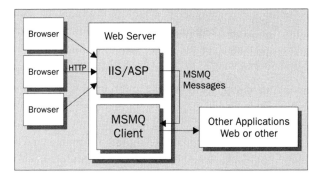

By using the ActiveX controls for accessing MSMQ, you can have your Active Server Pages applications use all of the features of message queuing. This is actually a very efficient way to deploy message queuing applications. Each of the clients that are accessing the application needs only to have a browser on their system. They do not need a copy of the MSMQ client, as the true MSMQ client is the ASP script itself.

The steps that an ASP application goes through to use MSMQ are pretty straightforward. As with any ASP application, the browser client makes a request to an Active Server Pages script file. Within this script file, there are calls to the MSMQ ActiveX objects. These objects can then be used to send or receive messages, manage queues, or monitor the status of queues. The information that these objects provide can then be displayed back on the client with a dynamically created HTML page.

Delivery Options

Microsoft Message Queue Server supports three options for the delivery of messages. Each of these delivery options provides different advantages to the transmission of messages. Likewise, they each have tradeoffs associated with each one. The three types of delivery options are:

- 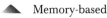 Memory-based
- Disk-based
- 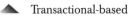 Transactional-based

Memory-based delivery means that the message remains in the system memory as it moves from queue manager to queue manager through the message queue system. If there is a problem in the network and the queue manager that is currently processing the message cannot contact the next queue manager in the network, then the message will be held until the connection can be restored. Memory-based delivery is very fast, since the message is never transferred from system memory to disk storage. While this type of message will survive a failure in the network connection between two queue managers, it will not survive a failure of the machine that it is currently on. Since the message is held in memory, if the machine it is currently on fails, then the message will be lost. This is the tradeoff that you must pay to get the speed advantage of memory-based delivery.

Disk-based delivery means that as the message moves from queue manager to queue manager, it is written to permanent disk storage on each machine. When the message is transferred off to the next machine, it will be removed from the previous machine's disk storage. Since this message has to be written to disk on every machine that it passes through, this means that it will take the message much longer to reach its destination. This method of delivery is slower than memory-based delivery. But here, the tradeoff is in terms of recoverability. Since each queue manager it passes through writes every message sent with this delivery method to disk, a system failure would not destroy the message. This relies on the use of a recoverable file system, such as NTFS or a RAID partition, to recover the messages in the case of a disk corruption.

With **transactional delivery**, the progress of each message from sender to receiver is considered a transaction. If you recall from the introduction, transactions have the ACID characteristics. This means that a transactional delivered message will be atomic, consistent, independent, and durable. To be durable, a transactional message uses the disk-based delivery method of writing every message to permanent storage as it moves through the system. The atomic characteristic means that the message will be delivered **exactly** one time, and in the same order it was sent. Transactional messages use the functionality that is available in Microsoft Transaction Server to provide the transactional characteristics of the messages delivery.

Dynamic Routing

In a large enterprise, a message queuing network is made of three primary types of systems:

- Primary Enterprise Controller
- Site Controller
- Message Router

The **Primary Enterprise Controller**, or PEC, is responsible for maintaining the configuration of the entire enterprise system. There is only one PEC within an enterprise-wide installation. This system is responsible for holding the certification keys, which are used to validate messages in the system. Even if a message queuing network consists of only one computer, that computer must be configured as the Primary Enterprise Controller.

A **Site Controller** has information about the computers and queues that are at one site where a site is regarded as a number of computers that are connected together via a fast network. Fast in this definition means 10Mbit Ethernet speeds and faster. In the site where the PEC is located, the PEC also functions as a site controller.

A **Message Router** supports the routing of message from one site to another. The Message Routing server is the system that holds the messages as they are moving from sender to receiver. If using memory-based delivery, the messages will be in the Message Router's system memory. For disk and transactional-based delivery, the messages will be stored on this systems disk. Site Controllers and Enterprise Controllers function as Message Routers as well. Since every site has at least a PEC or Site Controller, then every site will by default have a Message Router. Additional Message Routers can be added to a site if a particular site generates a great deal of traffic.

Dynamic routing means that there does not have to be a single defined path between the sender and the receiver of messages. In static types of routing, as in the Internet, the routing tables along the way define a single path between two points. Techniques such as a spanning-tree algorithm to resolve multiple paths are used to ensure this. In dynamic routing, there can be multiple paths between a sender and a receiver. Each machine in this path is a message router (or a PEC or Site Controller).

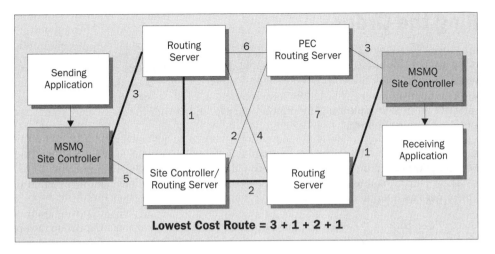

When configuring an enterprise installation of MSMQ, you determine the "cost" of the links between two message routers. This cost can be based on any factors that you determine as relevant. Things such as speed of link, available bandwidth on link, and actual financial cost of the link can go into computing the "cost" for a link. When performing dynamic routing, MSMQ will compute the lowest cost link between the sender and the receiver and send the message that way. This makes the configuration of an MSMQ enterprise much simpler, as static routes do not need to be explicitly created.

Platforms

If you have been following the press recently, you would be led to believe that Microsoft is forcing the entire industry to submit to using Windows and its technologies everywhere. With MSMQ, this is completely false. MSMQ is designed to be both platform and protocol independent. This will mean that any system that can be reached via a network, and understands the messaging protocol of MSMQ, can participate as a client or a message router. While the initial release of MSMQ is for Windows NT and Windows 95, third parties are already working on developing support for non-Windows clients. One of these third parties, Level 8 Systems (`http://www.level8.com`), will have support for many platforms including IBM MVS and CICS, Sun Solaris, HP-UNIX, and AIX UNIX platforms, as well as OS/2, VMS, and AS/400 platforms. Their product also supports the mapping of native IBM MQSeries API (MQI) calls and CICS Transient Data API calls to the MSMQ API calls. With this support, it is apparent that no matter what type of application or what platform it is running, developers can take advantage of the features of message queuing and the support offered by Microsoft Message Queue Server.

Next, we will take a look at the last step in the case study that we have examined over the past two chapters. In this final step, we will look at how to use MSMQ to help us fulfill the book order.

Fulfilling the Order

In the two previous chapters, we have developed an electronic commerce case study application. This application allows users to browse the contents of an on-line book publisher's database. While viewing these contents, the users can choose to select books for purchase. Each book that they choose goes into their "electronic shopping basket." Once they have selected all of the books that they wish to purchase, they can proceed to order completion. The previous chapter ended with the user being able to browse the contents of their shopping basket.

In this chapter, we will look at the steps the user has to follow to fulfill their order. When the user entered their registration information, they were asked to enter their name and address information. To complete the order, all that remains is to gather the payment information. Once this payment information is gathered, the order can then be processed.

We will look at three parts of the order fulfillment process. One part will display the invoice information to the user then request and obtain the payment information. This will be developed using the similar 3-tier techniques used in the previous two chapters. The next part will show the transmission of the credit card information for processing by the credit card issuer. This will be developed using the techniques looked at in this chapter. Namely, we will be creating a server component that works with Message Queue Server to transmit the information to an acquirer bank who then routes it onto the card issuer. There are many issuers of cards—you wouldn't have a link with each. Instead you have an agreement with one bank that acquires your transactions. It's their problem interfacing with all the card issuers. The last part will show how to create the receiving end of this message. This part will show how to use MSMQ functionality directly from an ASP page. While it will not be realistic in terms of how credit processing really occurs, it will show integration of ASP and MSMQ. There are several commercial solutions available for integrating ASP with banks, such as Verifone and Trintech.

Order Fulfillment

The order fulfillment part of the application will display the order based on the contents of the user's shopping basket. This order includes the price and quantity of each book, along with additional charges for taxes and for shipping. Once the user views the order, they can choose to go back and modify the contents of their basket, or they can proceed to providing payment information.

Application Component

The application component is responsible for creating what is called the **TransactionDetails**. The **TransactionDetails** basically represent the line items in the final order. Each line in the order corresponds to either a book that was purchased, with its quantity and price, or a charge for shipping or for taxes. The information that the application component builds can then be displayed for the user for verification before proceeding to payment.

```
Public Function BuildTransactionDetails(ByVal vOrderID As Variant) As Variant
    On Error GoTo BuildTransactionDetailsErr

    Dim vResponse As Variant
...Declare a bunch of variables here...
    Dim vOrderItem As Collection
```

The **BuildTransactionDetails** method will take a valid **OrderID** as its input parameter and return a variant that contains the **TransactionDetails** in a collection of information. The next step is to declare all of the variables that will be used in the method. Since there are a lot of them, we will omit most of them to save space. So if later in the method you see a variable that wasn't declared, we omitted it on purpose.

The variable that will hold the total amount of the order will be initialized to 0. The shipping cost for the order is initialized to $4. This is an implementation of one of the business rules. The business rule for computing shipping costs is $4 per order, plus an additional $1.50 per book. We are hard-coding this amount for simplicity, but storing this value externally so that it can be changed without modifying the application component would make more sense in a production application. The next step is to retrieve the contents of the shopping basket by using the **Baskets** data component. This component, which was introduced in the previous chapter, has a method that returns a collection containing all of the items in the user's shopping basket.

```
vOrderTotalPrice = 0
vShippingPrice = 4
Set vResponse = oDBaskets.GetBasketItems(vOrderID)
If Not vResponse("error") Then

    Set vBasket = vResponse("items")
```

The next step is to iterate through each item in the basket. To make the code a bit more readable, the elements of the **BasketItem** collection will be read into local variables. These four variables will be used to calculate the selling price of a single item, as well as the total line item price.

```
For Each vBasketItem In vBasket
    vPrice = vBasketItem("price")
    vPromotionCode = vBasketItem("promotioncode")
    vPromotionEndDate = vBasketItem("promotionenddate")
    vNumItems = vBasketItem("numitems")
```

To calculate the selling price of an item, we will use the same method we used in the previous chapter. The **AdjustTodaysPrice** method will calculate the actual selling price of the item based on any promotions that may be in effect. This calculated price would then be formatted for display using the VB method **FormatCurrency**. This information will be added to the collection that holds all of the information about the line item.

```
    vTodaysPrice = AdjustTodaysPrice(vPrice, vPromotionCode, vPromotionEndDate)
    vTodaysPrice = Format(vTodaysPrice, "$###,##0.00")
    vBasketItem.Add vTodaysPrice, Key:="todaysprice"

    vTotalPrice = vNumItems * vPrice
    vTotalPrice = Format(vTotalPrice, "$###,##0.00")
    vBasketItem.Add vTotalPrice, Key:="totalprice"
```

Once we have calculated the actual selling price for one item, we need to then calculate the price for this line in the sale. This is determined by multiplying the selling price for one item by the quantity of that item ordered. This amount is calculated then formatted into a currency format. The formatted amount is added to the basket item collection as the **totalprice** key.

As we are iterating through each item in the basket, we will also be calculating a running total for the entire order. The total amount for each line is added to this running total. We are also calculating the total shipping cost as we iterate through each item. The shipping cost for each line is computed to be $1.50 per book. Again, this is stored here for simplicity, and would probably come from an external source in a production application. For example, if the line item included three copies of the book, then the shipping charge for that line item would be $4.50.

```
      vOrderTotalPrice = vOrderTotalPrice + vTotalPrice
      vShippingPrice = vShippingPrice + (1.5 * CDec(vNumItems))

   Next
```

After we have iterated through each item in the basket, we are ready to add the summary information to the collection that will be returned to the client. This collection that is returned, **vOrder**, will be a collection of collections. Each collection that it contains will contain information about a particular part of the order. The reason that a collection of collections is used is so that each part of the order can contain different informational details. There will be entries in the **vOrder** collection for:

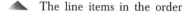 The line items in the order

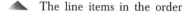 The shipping total

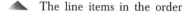 The tax on the order

 The entire total of the order

```
   Set vOrder = New Collection

   Set vOrderItem = New Collection
   vOrderItem.Add vBasket, Key:="basketitems"
   vOrder.Add vOrderItem, "basket"
   Set vOrderItem = Nothing
```

The collection containing information about the line items in the order will be stored in the **vOrder** collection using the key "**basket**." This collection will simply contain the collection of line items with the information that was calculated earlier in the method.

```
   Set vOrderItem = New Collection
   vTotalPrice = Format(vShippingPrice, "$###,##0.00")
   vOrderItem.Add vTotalPrice, Key:="totalprice"
   vOrderItem.Add "$4.00 and $1.50 per item", "details"
   vOrder.Add vOrderItem, "shipping"
   vOrderTotalPrice = vOrderTotalPrice + vShippingPrice
   Set vOrderItem = Nothing
```

The shipping information and the tax information will both contain their amount as well as detail information about how the amount is calculated. The price for each is stored using the same key, "**totalprice**," so that the same piece of code in the ASP script can be used to display both of these items in the order. This also makes it very easy to extend the application to support other kinds of charges, without having to change the display code, or the method for returning information to the client.

```
    Set vOrderItem = New Collection
    vTaxPrice = vOrderTotalPrice * 0.125
    vTotalPrice = Format(vTaxPrice, "$###,##0.00")
    vOrderItem.Add vTotalPrice, Key:="totalprice"
    vOrderItem.Add "12.5%", "details" ' Tax % hardcoded in this example - would be
stored externally in a production application
    vOrder.Add vOrderItem, "tax"
    vOrderTotalPrice = vOrderTotalPrice + vTaxPrice
    Set vOrderItem = Nothing
```

The total price for the order has been calculated as we have moved through this method. This total amount is added to the **vOrder** collection so that it can be returned to the client. Once we have added all of the information to the response collection, we indicate a successful completion of this method by setting the **error** element to false.

```
    Set vOrderItem = New Collection
    vTotalPrice = Format(vOrderTotalPrice, "$###,##0.00")
    vOrderItem.Add vTotalPrice, Key:="totalprice"
    vOrder.Add vOrderItem, "ordertotal"
    Set vOrderItem = Nothing

    vOrder.Add False, Key:="error"

    Set vResponse = vOrder
End If
```

Finally, we add the standard Transaction Server plumbing. When the method has completed successfully, the **SetComplete** method of the current object context is called. This indicates that this method is casting its vote in favor of completing the transaction it may be in. If there is an error, then the method-level error handler routes it to the error-handling routine. This aborts the current transaction, using the **SetAbort** method. It then uses the global **RaiseError** method to generate an error collection and causes an error message to be written to the error log.

```
    oObjectContext.SetComplete
    Set BuildTransactionDetails = vResponse

    Exit Function

BuildTransactionDetailsErr:
    oObjectContext.SetAbort
    Set BuildTransactionDetails = RaiseError("BuildTransactionDetails")

End Function
```

Now that we have our application logic complete, we can take a look at how the user interface that displays this information to the user is made up.

Building the Active Server Pages

The **BuildTransactionDetails** method computes the detailed information about the order that is created from the contents of the user's shopping basket. This information is then displayed for the user to review. They can choose to move forward with the purchase process, revise the contents of the order, or abort the transaction completely. If the user chooses to revise the contents of the shopping basket, they are returned to the screen showing the contents of the basket that was examined in the previous chapter.

```
<%@ LANGUAGE="VBSCRIPT" %>
<% Option Explicit %>
<% Response.Expires = 0 %>
<% if not Session("Auth") = true then %>
  <% Response.Redirect "checkreg.asp"%>
<% End If %>
```

The ASP script will check to make sure that the user has already registered with the system. If they have not properly registered, they will be redirected to the login page. This will prevent users from typing in this URL directly and accessing this page without passing the proper information to the server. This part of the case study was described in Chapter 15. As with the other ASP scripts in this case study, we will set the page to expire immediately. This will cause it to be regenerated by the server every time it is accessed.

```
<HTML>
<HEAD>
<META HTTP-EQUIV="Pragma" CONTENT="no-cache">

<TITLE>Review Order</TITLE>
<LINK REL="stylesheet" TYPE="text/css" HREF="main.css">
</HEAD>
<BODY>
```

Since we have elected to use **Option Explicit**, which you should use in all but the simplest of ASP scripts, we will need to declare all of the variables that this page will use.

```
<% dim state %>
<% dim objDB %>
<% dim objOrder %>
<% dim objResponse %>
<% dim objOrderItems %>
<% dim objBasketItems %>
<% dim objItem %>

<TABLE WIDTH=100% CELLSPACING=0 CELLPADDING=0 BORDER=0>
<TR CLASS="pageheader">
<TH ALIGN=left> Shop Checkout
</TH>
</TR>
</TABLE>
```

We need to check to make sure that the current logged in user has a valid **orderID**. This **orderID** can be retrieved from the database using the **GetOrder** method of the **Baskets** data object. In all of the previous pages, we have only accessed the Application objects. This example shows that we can bypass the application objects if we want, and use the **Data** object to get the information that we want. Just because the system is set up as a three tier system, it does not mean that ALL access has to go through all tiers. In this instance, it is more efficient to retrieve information directly from the **Data** object.

```
<%   if Session("OrderID") = "" then %>
<%   set objDB = Server.CreateObject("DpkgBaskets.DBaskets") %>
<%   set objResponse = objDB.GetOrder(Session("email")) %>
<%   Session("OrderID") = objResponse("OrderID") %>
<%   End If %>
```

```
<% set objOrder = Server.CreateObject("BpkgOrderProcessing.Order") %>
<% set objResponse = objOrder.BuildTransactionDetails(Session("OrderID")) %>
```

We will then call the **BuildTransactionDetails** method that we have just created. This will return a
collection of the line items in the order. We first need to check to make sure that no errors occurred. If
there were errors in the method, then we will notify the user via the standard error display method
included in a server-side include file. If the method was successful, we will store the information returned
in a session-level variable for later use.

```
<% if objResponse("error") then %>
<!--#include file=error.inc-->
<% else %>
<% set Session("OrderItems") = objResponse %>
<% set objOrder = nothing %>

 <p>Order details for
<% Response.Write Session("firstname") & " " & Session("surname") %>
 </P>

<% set objOrderItems = Session("OrderItems") %>
```

We will first retrieve the items that were in the shopping basket. These items are stored as a collection of a
collection. The **basket** item in the **OrderItems** collection is a collection of information about the
contents of the basket. The **basketitems** item of this collection is a collection of the information about
each item in the basket itself.

```
<% set objBasketItems = objOrderItems("basket")("basketitems") %>

<% if objBasketItems.count = 0 then %>
   <P>Your basket is currently empty</P>
```

If there are no items in the basket, then there is nothing to display. We output a message to the user
indicating that their basket is empty. If there are items, then we set up a table to display the information in
a structured format. The next step is to iterate through all of the items in the **BasketItems** collection.
This will give us each item in the order, which we can display for the user.

```
<% else %>
   <TABLE CELLSPACING=0 CELLPADDING=0 BORDER=0>
   <TR CLASS="tableheader">
   <TH>Item</TH>
   <TH width=15> </TH>
   <TH>Unit price</TH>
   <TH width=15> </TH>
   <TH>No.</TH>
   <TH WIDTH=15> </TH>
   <TH>Total</TH>
   </TR>
<%    for each objItem in objBasketItems %>
```

There may be items in the basket that have a quantity of 0. This may have happened if the user reduced
the number desired to 0. Since these items really aren't part of the order, we will check to see if the
quantity is greater than 0 before displaying a particular item. The information displayed for each item
includes the name, the unit price, the quantity, and the total price for the line item.

623

```
<%      if objItem("numitems") > 0 then %>
        <TR CLASS="tabledata">
          <TD>
<%         Response.Write objItem("name") %>
          </TD>
          <TD> </TD>
          <TD ALIGN=right>
<%          Response.Write objItem("todaysprice") %>
          </TD>
          <TD> </TD>
          <TD align=right>
<%          Response.Write objItem("numitems") %>
          </TD>
          <TD> </TD>
          <TD align=right>
<%          Response.Write objItem("totalprice") %>
          </TD>
          </TR>
<%      END IF %>
<%      NEXT %>
```

After iterating through all of the items in the order, we will then display the additional charges. These charges include the shipping cost and the taxes. The totals for the entire order are stored in the same manner in the collection returned from the application object. This allows us to use very similar code to retrieve and display this data for the user. Each piece of information is stored as an element of a collection of a collection. For example, to retrieve the shipping price, we want the `totalprice` element of the `shipping` collection, which is an element of the `OrderItems` collection.

```
        <TR CLASS="tabledata">
        <TD COLSPAN= 6>
        <I>plus</I> Shipping:
<%      Response.Write objOrderItems("shipping")("details") %>
        </TD>
        <TD ALIGN=right>
<%      Response.Write objOrderItems("shipping")("totalprice") %>
        </TD>
        </TR>
        <TR CLASS="tabledata">
        <TD COLSPAN=6>
        <I>plus</I> Tax:
<%      Response.Write objOrderItems("tax")("details") %>
        </TD>
        <TD ALIGN=right>
<%      Response.Write objOrderItems("tax")("totalprice") %>
        </TD>
        </TR>
        <TR CLASS="tabledata">
        <TD COLSPAN=6>
        <B>Order total</B>
        </TD>
        <TD ALIGN=right>
        <HR><B>
<%      Response.Write objOrderItems("ordertotal")("totalprice") %>
<%      Session("totalprice") = objOrderItems("ordertotal")("totalprice") %>
        <B>
```

```
            </TD>
            </TR>
          </TABLE>
     <%  END IF %>
        <HR>
```

Once all of the order details have been displayed for the user, we will present them with a list of options to take from this page. The user can choose to continue with the purchase, which will take them to the payments area. Or, they can choose to amend the order, which will return them to the page where they can view the contents of the basket.

```
    <%  if objBasketItems.count > 0 then %>
        <INPUT TYPE=button VALUE="Purchase"
               onclick=window.document.location.href='GetCreditInfo.asp'>
        <INPUT TYPE=button VALUE="Amend order"
               onclick=window.document.location.href='viewBasket.asp'>

      <% end if %>
    <%  end if %>
    </BODY>
    </HTML>
```

When the user displays this page in the browser, they will see:

Now that we have seen how the user can review the details about their order, including the additional charges, we can move on to the final phase of the order process. The final phase requires the user to provide payment information before the order can be completed.

Posting Payments

In this part of the application, the user's payment information will be packaged and forwarded to the credit card processor for payment. The user will enter the information into the system. A feature that could be added would be for the credit card information to be instantly validated. There are a number of 3rd party tools and code examples that show how to perform card validation. This is not shown in the case study, but the source code indicates where this type of feature could be easily added. The validation action is different from the processing action. In validation, a third party is merely verifying that this is a valid credit card for this particular customer. The validation could either check against a list of stolen cards, or do an online check against the account, to see if there is sufficient credit available. The customer's credit card account is actually charged for the amount of the order during the processing of a payment.

We will be looking at the method of transmitting this information to the credit card processor. In reality, there are many systems in place on the Internet that will handle credit card processing for on-line transactions. In this example, we will create our own system for processing payments. In the first part, we will create the system that will transmit the payment information to the credit card processor. This will be done using a message queuing system. The information will be packaged into a message and sent to a queue. In the second part, we will create a method for the credit processor to retrieve the message from the queue, examine its contents, and then proceed using their own internal methods for payment.

This may not be a realistic system in the way that actual on-line transactions are handled. But, it is a good example of how message queuing can be used to reliably transmit information between two applications, even when the applications are not running simultaneously. Whenever money is changing hands, a reliable system is absolutely critical to the business. In this case, our two applications are the book purchasing application, and the credit payment verification application.

We will be showing two methods for integrating Active Server Pages with Microsoft Message Queues Server. The first part of the application will show an ASP script interacting with a server component written in Visual Basic. This server component will interact with MSMQ using the ActiveX interface that we covered earlier in this chapter. The second part of the application will use the MSMQ ActiveX API directly from an ASP script.

Post Payment Component

This active server component will be used to post the order payment information to the credit card processor. The payment information will be transmitted in an MSMQ message. This message will contain the following information:

- Credit Card number
- Credit Card holder's name
- Credit Card expiration date
- Order ID number—for the processor to print on the customer's statement
- Order Amount

This message will be sent to a queue on an MSMQ server. The message will also contain a request for response, and include the queue that the response should be sent to. This method will be called from an Active Server Page script that will supply the method with the information that it needs from the current session-level variables.

```
Public Function PostPayment(vOrderID As Variant, vCardNumber As Variant, vCardName As
Variant, vCardAmount As Variant, vCardExpireDate As Variant) As Variant
```

The parameters that will compose the message are passed as variants. This makes the use of this method more flexible. If, for example, the **CardExpireDate** had been declared as a date type, then we would need to ensure that the value passed from the ASP script was a valid Visual Basic date. Since the information is not being processed by this method, rather it is just being packaged and sent on, the validation of the data in the method itself is not critical.

```
On Error GoTo PostPaymentErr

Dim strBody
  strBody = "OrderID=" & vOrderID & "&"
  strBody = strBody & "CardNumber=" & vCardNumber & "&"
  strBody = strBody & "CardName=" & vCardName & "&"
  strBody = strBody & "CardAmount=" & vCardAmount & "&"
  strBody = strBody & "CardExpireDate=" & vCardExpireDate
```

We will be using an encoded string to package the information that will be passed in the message. The format of the string will be similar to the way that parameters are passed in an HTTP **GET** method, with name/value pairs separated by the ampersand (&) character. Since the body of a message can contain only one binary object, this encoding method will package up distinct pieces of information for later retrieval. You will see in the next section how easy this makes it to retrieve the information.

Next, we need to define some variables that we will use to locate and manipulate the message queues that this method will send the message to. The first step is to locate the queue to send the message to. We will use the **LookupQueue** method to attempt to locate a queue with a specific label. This label identifies the queue as one that will accept pending credit processing messages.

The **LookupQueue** method returns a collection of queues that match the search criteria. Since this list of queues maintains its own internal pointer, we need to reset the pointer to the beginning of the list. Then, we can ask the list to give us its first element.

```
Dim query As New MSMQQuery, respQuery As New MSMQQuery
  Dim qinfos As MSMQQueueInfos, qRespInfos As MSMQQueueInfos
  Dim qinfo As MSMQQueueInfo
  Dim q As MSMQQueue
  Dim msg As New MSMQMessage

'Find the queue to send the credit request to and open it
  Set qinfos = query.LookupQueue(Label:="Credit Processing Pending")
  qinfos.Reset
  Set qinfo = qinfos.Next
```

If the object that this element refers to is undefined, we know that the search was unsuccessful. This could mean that this was the first time the application was run. It could also mean that the destination queue was inadvertently deleted. To give our message a destination, we will create a queue to send the message to.

```
If qinfo Is Nothing Then
    Set qinfo = New MSMQQueueInfo
  qinfo.PathName = "BOFFIN\CreditProcessingPending"
  qinfo.Label = "Credit Processing Pending"
  qinfo.Create False, True
  End If
```

627

The queue will be created on a machine named **BOFFIN**. This machine should have MSMQ running on it, and should be accessible from our web server.

> *In your installation, you will need to change the name of the server to match the name of the MSMQ server that you wish to create the queue on.*

The **Label** of the new queue will be set to "**Credit Processing Pending**". This is the same value that we searched for earlier and were unable to find. Creating the queue using this label will allow it to be found in the future.

The next step is open the queue. We will be setting the parameters to allow send access to the queue. We set the share flag to **DENY_NONE**, which means that other applications will be able to write messages to this queue and retrieve messages from it. This is the only valid option when opening a queue for sending.

```
Set q = qinfo.Open(MQ_SEND_ACCESS, MQ_DENY_NONE)

    Dim qResponse As MSMQQueueInfo
'Create a queue to send the response to
    Dim strLabel
    strLabel = CStr(vOrderID)
    Set qResponse = New MSMQQueueInfo
    qResponse.PathName = "BOFFIN\CreditResult" & strLabel
    qResponse.Label = "CreditResult" & strLabel
    qResponse.Create False, True
```

Next, we need to create a response queue. The message that we are sending to the credit processor will contain a pointer to a response queue. It is the responsibility of the receiving application to recognize this in the message, and send a response to this queue. This is different from an acknowledgment. In an acknowledgment, MSMQ is responsible for sending the message automatically, depending on what conditions are met. A response message needs to be explicitly sent by the receiving application. The format of this response message is mutually determined by the two applications.

The response queue will be created with the value of the **OrderID** appended to it. Since this **OrderID** is a unique value, this means that every order will have its own response queue. It will be created and will wait to accept the response message from the credit processor. While we will not show it here, when the message is retrieved from the queue, the queue should be deleted to free up resources in the MSMQ server.

```
    msg.Label = "Credit Processing - Order Num:" & strLabel

    msg.Body = strBody

    Set msg.ResponseQueueInfo = qResponse

    msg.Send q
```

Finally, we will create the message and then send it. The message is given a label that both describes what the message is, "**Credit Processing**", it also identifies the order. Even though the **orderID** is stored in the body of the message, by including it in the label it allows administrators to see which orders are pending by using the MSMQ management tools. The body of the message is set to the encoded string that contains all of the order information. To indicate that the receiver should respond to the message, and to show where to respond to, the **ResponseQueueInfo** property is set to the response queue that we created earlier. Finally, the message is sent to the queue that was located and then opened. Notice that we do not need to open the response queue, as we are merely passing a reference to it. It will be the responsibility of the credit processing application to open this queue and send the response to it.

```
    Dim vResponse As New Collection
    vResponse.Add False, Key:="error"

    oObjectContext.SetComplete
    Set PostPayment = vResponse

    Exit Function
PostPaymentErr:
    oObjectContext.SetAbort
    Set PostPayment = RaiseError("PostPayment")
End Function
```

This method has basically the same ending code as all of the other application and data components that we have created in the case study. For this method to participate in transactions, we allow it to add its vote to the success or failure of the transaction it is participating in.

Next, we will take a look at the ASP script code that will call this method to generate the message to the credit processor.

Building the Active Server Pages

In this script file, we will take an order that has been validated by the user, along with the payment information supplied by the user, and transmit that information to the credit processor. At this point, the user has already entered their credit card number and expiration date. While we did not show this, it is a relatively straightforward HTML FORM and ASP script to put the values into session-level variables.

This script file will take the information stored in the session-level variables and call the **PostPayment** method that was defined above. Based on the response from the **PostPayment** method, this script file will either display an error message for the user, or will indicate successful transmission of the payment information.

```
<%@ LANGUAGE="VBSCRIPT" %>
<% Option Explicit %>
<% Response.Expires = 0 %>
<% if not Session("Auth") = true then %>
<%   Response.Redirect "checkreg.asp"%>
<% End If %>
<% if Session("CardValidated") <> true then %>
<%   Response.Redirect "GetCreditInfo.asp" %>
<% End If %>
```

Before this script begins its application processing, it needs to ensure two things about the user accessing this page. First, the user has to be properly logged into the application. If they are not, then the client is redirected to the login page. Second, the user must have submitted valid credit card information. This is indicated by a session-level variable that is called **CardValidated**. If this variable is not set to true, then we know that the user has not submitted valid credit card information. The script will then redirect the browser to the page where the credit card information can be submitted.

```
<HTML>
<HEAD>
<META HTTP-EQUIV="Pragma" CONTENT="no-cache">

<TITLE></TITLE>
<LINK REL="stylesheet" TYPE="text/css" HREF="main.css">
</HEAD>
<BODY>


<TABLE WIDTH=100% CELLSPACING=0 CELLPADDING=0 BORDER=0>
<TR CLASS="pageheader">
<TH ALIGN=left> Processing Payment
</TH>
</TR>
</TABLE>
```

The next part of the script file is the standard header information that appears in all of the script files in this application. We will also need some local variables to interact with the application object. A message is presented to the user that the data is being transmitted to the credit card processor. Since we have not set the **Buffer** property of the **Response** object to true, the client will output this text before the application object is called. This will give the user some indication that the server is processing the request.

```
<%   dim objOrder %>
<%   dim objResponse %>
     <P>Transmitting data to Credit Card Processor...

<%    set objOrder = Server.CreateObject("BpkgOrderProcessing.Payment") %>
<%        dim strCardName %>
<%        strCardName = Session("firstname") & " " & Session("surname") %>
<%    set objResponse = objOrder.PostPayment(Session("OrderID"),
Session("cardnumber"), strCardName, Session("totalprice"), Session("expirydate")) %>
```

The five parameters that the **PostPayment** method requires are extracted from the current session. Concatenating the first name and the surname creates the credit card holder's name. Since all of the parameters that the **PostPayment** method expects are variants, we do not need to worry about explicitly setting the datatypes of the parameters.

```
<%    if objResponse("error") then %>
<!--#include file=error.inc-->
<%    else %>
<P>Information Sent Successfully...
<P>Your order has been completed. Thanks for shopping at WROX.
<% End If %>
</BODY>
</HTML>
```

All of the work of the payment transmission is done in the **application** object. All that the client needs to do is show the user the results. If the method was not able to complete successfully, the standard error handling code will be used to output an error message to the client. If there were no errors, then the client will indicate a successful completion of the order.

The browser would display this page as:

```
http://localhost/eshop/ConfirmPurchase.asp - Microsoft Internet Expl... [_][□][X]

 File   Edit   View   Go   Favorites   Help                              (e)

  ↵  ,    ➡  ,     (X)      [↻]       🏠        (Q)       [*]         (🕐)
 Back     Forward      Stop     Refresh    Home      Search    Favorites    History

 Address  [e] http://localhost/eshop/ConfirmPurchase.asp            [▼]  Links

 ┌──────────────────────────────────────────────────────────────────────┐
 │ Processing Payment                                                      │
 │                                                                         │
 │ Transmitting data to Credit Card Processor.                             │
 │                                                                         │
 │ Information Sent Successfully...                                        │
 │                                                                         │
 │ Your order has been completed. Thanks for shopping at WROX.             │
 │                                                                         │
 └──────────────────────────────────────────────────────────────────────┘

                               Local intranet zone
```

Since there are more steps to actually fulfilling an order than we have shown in this case study, there would probably be more information displayed to the user at this point. Some of these additional pieces of information could be:

 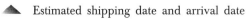 URL to check on the status of the order

 Estimated shipping date and arrival date

 Credit Card Confirmation number

 Tracking number of the courier

We'll leave the creation of these other pieces of information up to you. This case study has shown you the basics of how to perform electronic commerce. You should be able to build on these pieces to create the rest of the application.

One of the pieces that we will create is the application used by the credit card processor to check for the pending credit card orders that need to be processed. This is the example that will be covered in the next section.

Credit Payment

The credit payment application will be used by the credit card processor to obtain the information about the credit card payment and pass a response back to the customer that the payment has been processed. As we have stated before, this is probably not an exact representation of how a credit card processor operates in real life. What it does show is an example of how information can be read from message queues and messages can be sent just using Active Server Pages.

The credit payment processing application will consist of two Active Server Pages scripts. The first one will retrieve a message from the queue, display the information contained in the message, and then allow the user to either accept or reject the charge. The second script will process the acceptance or rejection of the charge by sending a response message to the customer. It will then inform the user if there are additional payments pending, in which case it will give them an option to retrieve them.

Building the Active Server Pages

The first Active Server Page will locate the message queue. If it is found, it will see if there are any messages there. If there is a message, it will retrieve the first one. The information contained in the message will be displayed for the user and the user will be given the options to approve or deny this payment.

Let's start with the standard header stuff that is at the top of each of our ASP script files.

```
<%@ LANGUAGE="VBSCRIPT" %>
<% Option Explicit %>
<% Response.Expires = 0 %>
<HTML>
<HEAD>
<META HTTP-EQUIV="Pragma" CONTENT="no-cache">

<TITLE></TITLE>
<LINK REL="stylesheet" TYPE="text/css" HREF="main.css">
</HEAD>
<BODY>

<TABLE WIDTH=100% CELLSPACING=0 CELLPADDING=0 BORDER=0>
<TR CLASS="pageheader">
<TH ALIGN=left> Verify Credit Payment
</TH>
</TR>
</TABLE>
<%
    Dim objquery
    Dim objqinfos
    Dim objqinfo
    Dim objq
    Dim objMsg

    set objquery = Server.CreateObject("MSMQ.MSMQQuery")
```

The first step we need to take is to create an instance of the **MSMQQuery** object. This object will be used to look for a queue that matches a set of criteria. The **LookupQueue** method of this object will look for all queues that have a label set to "Credit Processing Pending." The **LookupQueue** method consists of all optional parameters. Since there is no way in VBScript to use named parameters as we did in Visual Basic, we must place the parameter that we are supplying at the correct position in the parameter list. The **Label** parameter is the third parameter; therefore we have to preface it with two commas, to indicate the optional parameters.

If a queue with this label cannot be found, then we know that there are no messages pending. We will then output a message to the user indicating that there is nothing to process.

```
    Set objqinfos = objquery.LookupQueue (,,"Credit Processing Pending")
    objqinfos.Reset
    Set objqinfo = objqinfos.Next
    If objqinfo Is Nothing Then
%>
    <P>No pending payments could be located</P>
<%
    else
```

If a valid queue matching the criteria can be found, then we will open that queue. Since we will be reading messages out of it, we will open it with **RECEIVE** access, by setting the first parameter of the **Open** method to 1. To allow other applications to deposit messages into the queue, we will set the share flag to **DENY_NONE**, which is indicated by a 0 for the second parameter. This will also allow multiple users of the credit processing application to retrieve messages at the same time. Since the **LookupQueue** method only checks for the existence of a queue, we do not know if there are actually any messages in the queue. The **Receive** method also consists of optional parameters. We will be supplying the timeout value, which is the fourth parameter. This makes it necessary for us to precede the parameter with 3 commas, to indicate the three leading optional parameters.

```
        Set objq = objqinfo.Open(1, 0)
        Set objMsg = objq.Receive(,,,10)
        objq.Close
        if objMsg is Nothing then
```

If the **Receive** method times out, or is unable to retrieve a message from the queue, then the **objMsg** variable will not have a value. If this is the case, then we will need to output a message to the user that no messages could be found. If we do find a valid message, then we will need to read the encoded string that was used to send the order information to the message queue. The encoded string will look like this:

**OrderID=884537142&CardNumber=4444333322221111&CardName=Nigel
Reader&CardAmount=$379.07&CardExpireDate=09/99**

We will be using a simple parsing routine that will look for each name/value pair. Once the routine has located the next name/value pair, it will break it into separate variables for name and value. A **Scripting.Dictionary** object will be used to store the names and values. The key will be set to the parameter name, and the item value will be set to the value of the parameter.

```
%>
                <P>No pending payments could be located</P>
<%
        else
                dim strBody
                dim objqResponse

                strBody = objMsg.Body

                Dim dBody
                Set dBody = CreateObject("Scripting.Dictionary")

                dim iAmpersand, iPos, strItem, iEquals
                dim strVar, strVal
                iAmpersand = -1
                iPos = 1
```

```
                        do while not iAmpersand = 0
                                dim iEnd
                                iAmpersand = InStr (iPos, strBody, "&")
                                if iAmpersand = 0 then
                                        iEnd = len(strBody)
                                else
                                        iEnd = iAmpersand - 1
                                end if
                                strItem = Mid(strBody, iPos, iEnd-iPos+1)
                                iEquals = Instr(strItem, "=")
                                strVar = Left(strItem, iEquals-1)
                                strVal = Mid(strItem, iEquals+1, len(strItem))
                                dBody.Add strVar, strVal
                                iPos = iAmpersand + 1
                        loop
```

The **Dictionary** object that contains the **Body** of the message and the pointer to the Response queue will be saved into local and session-level variables. The pointer to the incoming message queue is also saved. This will be used in the other script of this application. We could have used the same method in that script to locate the queue, but since we have the reference, we might as well save it. The information that was contained in the body of the message is then displayed for the user.

```
                        set objqResponse = objMsg.ResponseQueueInfo
                        set Session("objResponseQ") = objqResponse
                        set Session("dMsgBody") = dBody

                        dim keys, items, i
                        keys = dBody.Keys
                        items = dBody.Items
                        for i = 0 to dBody.count - 1
                                Response.Write "<P>" & keys(i) & ": " & items(i) & "</P>" &
        vbcrlf
                        next
        %>
```

Finally, we present the user with two choices. They can choose to approve the payment of this order, or they can choose to decline the payment. They make their selection by choosing from one of the two links that are displayed. These two links will launch the second ASP script. The parameter named **approve** is used to indicate to this second script whether the payment has been approved or not.

```
                        <HR>
                        <P><A HREF="CreditResponse.asp?approve=true">Approve this
        transaction</a>
                        <P><A HREF="CreditResponse.asp?approve=false">Deny this
        transaction</a>

        <%              end if
            end if
        %>
        </BODY>
        </HTML>
```

When this server page is viewed in a browser, it will look like:

The second part of this application will be to process the approval or denial of this payment. This script file will be responsible for creating the response message and sending it to the response queue. After sending the message, the script will then check to see if there are any more messages in the queue. If there are, it will ask the user if they wish to process the remaining messages.

```
<%@ LANGUAGE="VBSCRIPT" %>
<% Option Explicit %>
<% Response.Expires = 0 %>
<HTML>
<HEAD>
<META HTTP-EQUIV="Pragma" CONTENT="no-cache">

<TITLE></TITLE>
<LINK REL="stylesheet" TYPE="text/css" HREF="main.css">
</HEAD>
<BODY>

<TABLE WIDTH=100% CELLSPACING=0 CELLPADDING=0 BORDER=0>
<TR CLASS="pageheader">
<TH ALIGN=left> Verify Credit Payment
</TH>
</TR>
</TABLE>
<%
```

```
     Dim objquery
     Dim objqinfos
     Dim objqinfo
     Dim objq
       Dim objMsg

       set objMsg = Server.CreateObject("MSMQ.MSMQMessage")
       set objqinfo = Session("objResponseQ")
       Set objq = objqinfo.Open(2, 0)
```

Since we will be generating a new message to send, we will need to create an instance of an
MSMQMessage object. This message object can then be sent to the response queue that was determined by
the incoming message. The reference to the response queue is stored in a session-level variable, and we
will store it in a local variable for use in the script. This queue will be opened with **SEND** permissions,
which is indicated by the value of 2 for the first parameter of the **Open** method.

The next step is to create the contents of the message that will be sent as the response. All that this
message needs to do is indicate to the client whether or not the payment was approved or denied. Since
the response queue was created solely to receive this one message, we do not need to pass a great deal of
data in it.

```
     dim strLabel
     if Request.QueryString("approve") = "true" then
             objMsg.Body = "APPROVED"
             strLabel =     "Credit Card Approved for Order #"
     else
             objMsg.Body = "DENIED"
             strLabel =     "Credit Card Denied for Order #"
     end if
     strLabel = strLabel & Session("dMsgBody").Item("OrderID")

     objMsg.Label = strLabel
```

If the payment has been approved, then we will send "**APPROVED**" in the body of the message. The label
for the message will state that the payment for the specified order number was approved.

If the payment is denied, then the body of the response message will contain "**DENIED**." The label for the
denial message will state that the payment was denied, and again state the order number.

This message is then sent to the response queue. After the message is sent, the user is notified that the
response message has been processed. The next step is to determine if there are any messages remaining in
the incoming queue. We stored the reference to this queue in the previous script. We can use this reference
to open the incoming queue. This time, we will be opening for peek access. Peek access allows us to look
at the messages in the queue, but not retrieve them. If we peek at the queue and find a message, then we
will ask the user if they wish to process this next payment.

```
     objMsg.Send objq

%>

     <P>Response Processed.....

<%
```

```
        Set objqinfo = Session("objIncomingQ")
    Set objq = objqinfo.Open(32, 0)
        Set objMsg = objq.Peek(100)
        objq.Close
        if not objMsg is Nothing then
%>
    <P>No further payments to process</P>

<%
else
%>
        <P><A HREF="CreditAuthorization.asp">Click here to process the next payment</A>


<% End If %>
</BODY>
</HTML>
```

When this page is displayed in the browser, it will look like this:

We now have an application that can be used to retrieve messages from a queue, process the body of the message, and then respond to that message with another message. While this was a simple example, this is pretty much all there is to using message queuing systems. The information can be much more complex, and the routing of messages much more involved, but the simple elements of messages and queues stay the same.

Summary

In this chapter, we have concluded our look at the electronic commerce case study. This case study has shown how a book publisher can sell their books electronically. In the examination of this case study, we have seen how to use some of the technologies that Microsoft has introduced in the NT4 Option Pack. The previous two chapters dealt with how to use Microsoft Transaction Server to create three-tier applications in a web environment. In this chapter, we were introduced to Microsoft Message Queue Server, and looked at how to add the finishing pieces to the electronic commerce case study.

Specifically, we looked at:

- What is message queuing technology and how can it be used to communicate between applications

- What are some of the reasons to use message queuing and when not to use it

- An introduction to the Microsoft implementation of message queues, and how to use the ActiveX components to work with it

- Some of the features that are provided in Microsoft Message Queue Server

- How to implement the payment processing section of the electronic case study application using messages and queues

This concludes our look at how to build client-server applications using the technologies that are part of IIS 4.0. We introduced two powerful systems that offload a great deal of the work in creating powerful, scalable systems. By integrating Transaction Server and MSMQ with ASP and IIS, Microsoft has produced a world-class enterprise-level application development and deployment platform. And in this section of the book, we have shown you real-world examples of how to implement these kinds of systems.

ASP and Internet Mail

One of the new components that is packaged with Internet Information Server 4.0 is an SMTP (Simple Mail Transfer Protocol) server. There's also an interface called Collaboration Data Objects for NT Server (CDO for NTS) which can be used for manipulating the SMTP server from Active Server Pages.

You might say "Excellent!". Or, like a great many other people, you might just say "Huh?". Internet messaging, to the uninitiated, often seems like a big, scary jungle. Except instead of tigers, the jungle is full of three- and (worse still) four-letter acronyms just waiting to pounce on the unsuspecting. I'll be honest, just thinking about acronyms like SMTP, POP3, IMAP4, MIME and RFCs makes me feel like I'm sprouting a pony-tail and the kind of anti-social behavior patterns that only a mother can love. (If you come from a messaging background, I'm only joking... well, sort of...).

In all seriousness, however, you just have to take a look at some of the questions that appeared in the public newsgroups when IIS 4.0 was in beta and then released to know that an awful lot of people don't really know how Internet messaging works. And why should they? I drive to work every day and I don't know how my car's alternator works. (Most of my passengers also say that I don't know how to drive, but that's a different matter). The same goes for messaging. You can use it every day, but that doesn't mean you know how it works.

So before we look at what you can and can't do with messaging from Active Server Pages, we'll look at some of the basics of Internet mail. Once we've done that we can look at **what** the CDO for NTS interface allows us to do from our Active Server Pages and then we'll look at **how** we can do it. This chapter covers:

- Standards and Protocols
- The SMTP Service
- CDO Messaging for NTS
- Future Directions

Standards and Protocols

Given the number and diversity of the mail systems and computer types that communicate with each other across the Internet, the formulation and adoption of standards is vital. The primary vehicle for the definition of such standards is the **RFC** or **Request for Comments**. As its name suggests, the idea behind an RFC is that someone writes up a proposed solution to a problem, publishes the proposal and requests comments on it. After a period of time, if the proposal is successful it is accepted as a standard solution. Full details of all Requests for Comments and their current status can be found at `http://ds.internic.net/ds/rfc-index.html`.

One of the most important of these standards as far as Internet Mail is concerned is the Simple Mail Transfer Protocol.

Simple Mail Transfer Protocol

RFC 821 and RFC 822, published in August 1982, define the Simple Mail Transfer Protocol, more commonly abbreviated to SMTP. The opening words of RFC 821 summarize the purpose of this protocol quite succinctly... *"The objective of the Simple Mail Transfer Protocol (SMTP) is to transfer mail reliably and efficiently."* (RFC 821)

There are three main areas of messaging which SMTP standardizes. These are address format, message content and message delivery.

Address format has changed little since the original RFC which specified that senders and receivers should be identified by a user name and domain name in the format **username@domainname**, as in **rob.smith@ivory.co.uk**.

As for content, the original specification stated that messages should contain no more than 1000 characters and that these should all be 7-bit ASCII characters (i.e. the letters, numbers and punctuation that form the American English character set). The increasing need to transmit messages to users who did not use American English caused e-mail vendors to supplement the specification by providing support for additional character sets. At the same time, the desire to send longer messages – and to send attachments with the message – meant that vendors added support for programs such as UUENCODE which is able to convert binary data such as bitmaps or executable files into and out of text format for transmission.

One of the major problems with this solution was the fact that attachments encoded in a format such as UUENCODE could not pass through gateways to X.400 systems. The X.400 standard stated that attachments should be converted to (**not** encoded in) a text format or else be discarded. To address this and other limitations with existing 7-bit encoding methods, a newer technique, called Multipurpose Internet Mail Extensions (MIME), was developed in 1992. Defined by RFC 1521, this standard has now been adopted by many vendors.

To understand the delivery mechanism employed by SMTP, have a look at the diagram below which illustrates the SMTP model.

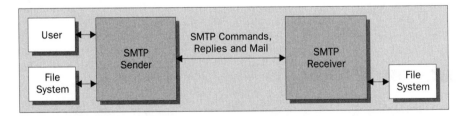

A user makes a mail request and this causes an SMTP sender to initiate a two-way transmission channel to an SMTP receiver on TCP Port 25. The SMTP sender sends a number of commands to the SMTP receiver and this in turn sends back replies in response to these commands. The sequence of commands and responses is described below:

▲ The first command sent by the SMTP sender is a HELO command, indicating the sender's domain. The receiver acknowledges this with an OK.

▲ Next, a MAIL command is sent to indicate the sender of the mail message. If the receiver can accept mail it returns an OK reply.

▲ Then, the SMTP sender issues one or more RCPT commands indicating the recipients of the message. The SMTP receiver responds to each of these commands in turn indicating whether or not it can accept messages for each of the recipients.

▲ The next stage is the transmission of the message data which ends with a special closure sequence. If the SMTP receiver was able to process the data successfully it responds with another OK reply.

▲ Finally, the sender terminates the connection with a QUIT command. That's all there is to it!

The sequence below shows the commands and responses sent between the sender and receiver for a typical SMTP message. (Bold text indicates commands sent from the sender).

```
<connection made on port 25>

220 exserver.microsoft.com ESMTP Server (Microsoft Exchange Internet Mail Servic
e 5.5.1960.3) ready
HELO test.com
250 OK
MAIL FROM: testuser@test.com
250 OK - mail from <testuser@test.com>
RCPT TO: administrator@exserver.microsoft.com
250 OK - Recipient <administrator@exserver.microsoft.com>
DATA
354 Send data.  End with CRLF.CRLF
You owe me $50


250 OK
QUIT
221 closing connection
```

The SMTP model works well for transferring messages between servers and also for transferring messages between servers and clients on a local area network. However, it is not very good for transferring messages to clients connecting to the Internet by modem. There are several reasons for this, but one of the most significant is that SMTP, by itself, does not provide for any storage mechanism. Consequently, the recipient of the mail message must be connected when the SMTP sender sends the mail for the mail to be delivered correctly. In order to solve this problem, **Post Office Protocol version 3** was developed.

Post Office Protocol, v.3 (POP3)

Post Office Protocol version 3, usually abbreviated to POP3, is defined in RFC 1939 and was designed… *"to permit a workstation to dynamically access a maildrop on a server host in a useful fashion. Usually this means that the POP3 protocol is used to allow a workstation to retrieve mail that the server is holding for it."* *(RFC 1939)*

The process employed by POP3 is quite straightforward. A server starts the POP3 service by listening on TCP port 110. When a client wishes to use the POP3 service it establishes a connection with the server using that port. The POP3 server replies with a greeting and the client and server then exchange commands and responses until the connection is closed. The POP3 protocol has less than a dozen commands and its purpose is simply to allow for the retrieval of messages from a maildrop server.

The most important thing to remember about POP3 and SMTP is that SMTP is a mechanism used for sending and receiving messages and that POP3 is used for storing and retrieving messages. It should also be noted that an SMTP receiver receives all mail for a domain, whereas POP3 clients retrieve only mail from the user's individual mailbox.

Internet Message Access Protocol, v.4 (IMAP4)

Internet Message Access Protocol, version 4 is a more complex protocol, which provides more extensive functionality than is available through POP3. With IMAP4, clients can not only retrieve messages from a server, but they can also manipulate the remote message folders (or mailboxes) in which the messages are stored. Whereas POP3 simply allows messages to be downloaded to a local mailbox, IMAP4 includes operations for creating, deleting and removing remote mailboxes as well as for checking for new messages and selective fetching of message attributes. Of particular appeal to many users is the fact that it also provides facilities for offline support and synchronization.

The formal definition of the IMAP4 protocol can be found in RFC 1730.

Network News Transfer Protocol (NNTP)

So far, we have looked at three of the protocols used in sending and retrieving Internet Mail. However, mail is not the only method used for the dissemination of information across the Internet. Instances often arise where a particular message is of interest to a wide number of users. As the appeal of the message grows, so the inefficiencies of using a mail-based mechanism for transporting that message increase also, as the practice of sending a separate copy of the message to each of the interested parties consumes large quantities of bandwidth, CPU resources and disk space among the many destinations.

Significant economies can be achieved if these popular messages are hosted in a single database instead of in each subscriber's mailbox. This single database is a news server and the messages on such a server are called news items or articles. NNTP (the Network News Transfer Protocol) defines a protocol for the distribution, inquiry, posting and retrieval of such news items between a news server and clients and is designed to allow messages to be stored on a central host server with clients connecting via a connection stream such as TCP. (News distribution between servers typically uses another protocol called Unix-to-Unix Copy or UUCP).

The NNTP protocol also allows for the introduction of intermediate or 'slave' servers that accept newsfeeds from central master news servers and in turn provide service of these cached news articles to local clients.

Standards support in IIS 4.0

Internet Information Server 4.0 provides both SMTP and NNTP servers. The SMTP server component provides a new method for a web application built using Active Server Pages on IIS 4.0 to dynamically send Internet mail, while the NNTP server allows for the hosting of newsgroups.

We will be looking at the SMTP service and – more particularly – at the interface that is provided through the Collaboration Data Objects for Windows NT Server (there is no corresponding interface for the NNTP service). That should help us to determine just what we can and cannot do with it. However, it is worth pointing out from the outset that one of the things that IIS 4.0 does not give you is a POP3 server. What this means is that although you will be able to use IIS 4.0 to send Internet Mail, you might struggle to use it as a full mail server. The lack of POP3 functionality means that although there is a mechanism for storing incoming messages, there is no method for the automatic delivery of incoming mail messages to the desktop of individual users.

In fact, the SMTP service does provide a universal inbox into which all incoming messages are placed. Later on in this chapter we will look at how you can read the inbound messages addressed to specific users from an Active Server Page. However, for more comprehensive functionality, many users will feel tempted to implement a product such as Microsoft Exchange Server, which provides both SMTP and POP3 support. In essence, the SMTP server component of IIS 4.0 has been designed to make the process of creating and sending Internet Mail messages as easy as possible. It's quick and it's easy, it may well be all you need for mail-enabling your web site, but it probably won't be the answer to all your messaging problems.

The SMTP Service

The SMTP Server component installed with Microsoft Internet Information Server 4.0 is designed to allow for the easy transmission of Internet Mail. We will start by looking briefly at the SMTP service and then we will look at how it can be used to send messages from Active Server Pages using the interface provided by CDO for NTS.

Installing the SMTP Service

The SMTP service is a component of Internet Information Server 4.0 and can only be installed on Windows NT Server. In other words, the SMTP service cannot be installed as part of Peer Web Services for Windows NT Workstation or the Personal Web Server for Windows 95.

Both the SMTP service and the SMTP documentation are installed as part of the minimum and typical installations.

How the SMTP Service works

When the SMTP service is installed, it creates a directory called **MailRoot** with a number of subdirectories which are used for the processing of SMTP Mail. The names and purposes of these subdirectories are described below.

Mailroot\Pickup

The **Pickup** directory is used as the primary location for outgoing mail messages. Whenever a mail message is placed in this directory, the SMTP service will pick up the message and process it. This means that you can copy a text file into this directory and, if it is in the correct format, it will be sent as a mail message.

Mailroot\Queue

After a message has been retrieved from the **Pickup** directory, SMTP attempts to send it immediately. If the message cannot be sent immediately, it is placed in the **Queue** directory and the SMTP service attempts to re-send the message at regular intervals. The number and frequency of retries can be configured via the Delivery tab of the property sheet for the SMTP site in the Microsoft Management Console.

The **Queue** directory also contains transcript files. These are text files and have either an **LTR** (local transcript) or **RTR** (remote transcript) extension and can be used to determine the reason for the non-delivery of a particular mail message.

Mailroot\BadMail

If a message cannot be delivered (and the maximum number of retries has been exceeded) and the message cannot be returned to the sender as undeliverable, it is placed in the **BadMail** directory. After installation, the location of the **BadMail** directory can be altered via the Messages tab of the tab of the property sheet for the SMTP site in the Microsoft Management Console.

Mailroot\Drop

This is the location for incoming messages for all of the local domains that make up a particular site. Note that there is only a single **Drop** directory for all users on all local domains. The SMTP service within IIS 4.0 has no concept of local mailboxes and so delivery of incoming mail messages to individual mailboxes is not supported. However, inbound messages in the **Drop** directory can be read from an Active Server Page, and this is illustrated with a code sample towards the end of this chapter.

As you can see, the SMTP service in IIS 4.0 is all directory-based and it is really fairly simple to follow. Hopefully, this has given you a good high-level understanding of how it works. If you feel that you need more information on the installation and configuration of the SMTP server component, you should consult the Microsoft SMTP Service documentation that is installed when you install IIS 4.0. Otherwise, we probably have enough information under our hats to get into what is the main thrust of this chapter.

Messaging with CDO for NTS

So far, we have looked at the basics of Internet messaging and the SMTP service that comes with Internet Information Server 4.0. We shall now take a detailed look at the methods by which we can interface with the SMTP service from Active Server Pages. The primary component that provides this interface is called the Collaboration Data Objects for Windows NT Server (CDO for NTS).

Evolution of CDO for NTS

CDO for NTS is the latest of a number of incarnations of ActiveX messaging components made available by Microsoft to web developers. The first of these was the OLE Messaging component which had a makeover after Microsoft's image police got hold of it and re-emerged as the Active Messaging component. This was simply a library (**OLEMSG.DLL**) whose fairly rudimentary object hierarchy was exposed by the type libraries **MSDISP.TLB** and **MSDISP32.TLB**. One of the problems with OLE Messaging was that in order to send even a simple mail message, the developer had to have a fairly clear understanding of MAPI (the Messaging API which formed part of Microsoft's open systems architecture model.)

The following portion of code illustrates the amount of code required to create a simple message using the OLE Messaging from Visual Basic.

```
Dim objSession As Object
Dim objMessage As Object
Dim objRecipient As Object

Set objSession = CreateObject("mapi.session")
objSession.Logon ProfileName:="My Profile"
Set objMessage = objSession.Outbox.Messages.Add
objMessage.Subject = "Bad News."
objMessage.Text = "I owe you £50."
Set objRecipient = objMessage.Recipients.Add
objRecipient.Name = "John de Robeck"
objRecipient.Type = mapiTo
objRecipient.Resolve
objMessage.Send showDialog:=False
MsgBox "Message sent successfully!"
objSession.Logoff
```

After the initial dimensioning of the variables, the first statement creates a **Session** object.

```
Set objSession = CreateObject("mapi.session")
```

The **Logon** method of this object is then invoked and the name of the user's profile is supplied as the named **ProfileName** argument.

```
objSession.Logon ProfileName:="My Profile"
```

The next step is to create a new **Message** object and append this to the **Messages** collection of the **Outbox** object for the current **Session**.

```
Set objMessage = objSession.Outbox.Messages.Add
```

The subject text and body text for this message are then set.

```
objMessage.Subject = "Bad News."
objMessage.Text = "I owe you £50."
```

The next stage is to build the recipient list. This is done by creating a **Recipient** object, specifying the name of the recipient and then stating that the recipient is a 'To' recipient (as opposed to a CC or BCC recipient).

```
Set objRecipient = objMessage.Recipients.Add
objRecipient.Name = "John de Robeck"
objRecipient.Type = mapiTo
```

The next statement causes the recipient's name to be resolved to the name of a user designated in the appropriate address book. If the name cannot be resolved directly, a dialog will be displayed to allow the user to select an appropriate name.

```
objRecipient.Resolve
```

After silently sending the message, a dialog is displayed to indicate that the message has been sent and the session is closed.

```
objMessage.Send showDialog:=False
MsgBox "Message sent successfully!"
objSession.Logoff
```

When we step through the code like this, it is easy enough to see how it all works. Having said that, it is not very intuitive to newcomers.

Active Messaging

With Microsoft Exchange Server version 5.0, Active Messaging 1.1 was unleashed into the developer community. In fact, Active Messaging 1.1 consisted of two components. The Active Messaging Component was used to log on to a mail server in similar fashion to the previous OLE Messaging component. Once a connection had been made, the other component - the HTML Rendering Component - allowed web developers to easily convert MAPI elements such as mailboxes and messages into HTML text which could be used in conjunction with Active Server Pages. The Exchange Web Client, which shipped with Exchange Server 5.0 and provided the capability to connect to an Exchange Server and access one's mailbox via the Internet, was probably the most obvious demonstration of the capabilities of the use of these components.

The next version of Active Messaging to be released accompanied the launch of Exchange Server version 5.5. Again, the Microsoft marketing people got into the act and Active Messaging was granted the ultimate seal of approval – a TLA (three letter acronym) – and it was renamed as Collaboration Data Objects or CDO 1.2.

Collaboration Data Objects 1.2

CDO 1.2 does actually represent a significant step forward from Active Messaging 1.1. Whereas Active Messaging was designed to allow developers to have programmatic access to simple messaging functionality, CDO 1.2 provides support for more advanced features such as calendaring, collaboration and workflow. CDO 1.2 can be used to design complex messaging applications on both the client and server sides and can be accessed from a variety of languages such as VBScript, Java, C, C++ and Visual Basic. CDO 1.2 has been designed for use with Exchange 5.5 and it doesn't have any user interface elements such as logon boxes or dialogs. However, as with its predecessor, CDO 1.2 contains a set of rendering objects which allow the automatic rendering of content to HTML for display in web browsers. We will look very briefly at CDO 1.2 later on in this chapter, but first we will look at the most recent incarnation of messaging libraries made available by Microsoft.

CDO for NTS

Collaboration Data Objects for NT Server (CDO for NTS) is a subset of CDO 1.2 and is designed for use by developers who want the ability to incorporate fast large-scale messaging into their applications without the need for advanced functionality such as calendaring, scheduling or workflow. It is shipped with Internet Information Server 4 and can be run against either the SMTP Server component of IIS4 or against Exchange Server 5.5 itself. The limited functionality of the SMTP Server in IIS4 is mirrored in the reduced complexity of CDO for NTS when compared to the full-blown CDO 1.2 implementation. CDO for NTS is basically an interface to allow developers to easily add simple mailing capabilities to their web sites.

The emphasis on ease of use at the expense of sophistication is best illustrated by the **NewMail** object in CDO for NTS. Using this new object, it is now possible to send a message in as few as three lines of code.

```
Set objMail = CreateObject("CDONTS.Newmail")
objMail.Send ("rob@here.com", "jdr@there.com", "Bad news", "I owe you £50")
Set objMail = Nothing
```

When deciding whether to use CDO 1.2 or CDO for NTS, you should bear in mind that CDO 1.2 is best at what Microsoft Exchange is good at. So if your application requires calendaring functionality, threaded conversations, complex messaging or workflow, you would be better off with CDO 1.2. However, if all you want is a lightweight component for sending out messages without the need for individual mailboxes, then CDO for NTS probably fits the bill.

Applications which use CDO for NTS can be run against Exchange Server 5.5 but, if this is to be done, then IIS 4.0 must also be installed on the Exchange server. The typical installation of IIS 4.0 is sufficient to install the relevant library (**CDONTS.DLL**). You should note that once IIS 4.0 has been installed on the Exchange server, you will need to run the IMS Wizard, which is part of Exchange Server 5.5. If you don't run this wizard, then applications using CDO for NTS will use the SMTP service provided by IIS 4.0 rather than running against the Exchange server.

Using CDO for NTS

As with any of the other components that can be accessed from Active Server Pages, one of the keys to getting the best out of CDO for NTS is to understand the object model that underlies it. As you can see from the diagram below, the CDO for NTS object model is actually fairly simple.

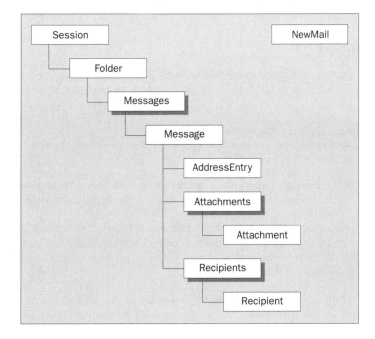

The CDO for NTS object model is chiefly comprised of a hierarchy of objects headed by the **Session** object. In addition to this, however, there is another discrete object, which is quite separate from the hierarchy. We'll start by looking at this object, the **NewMail** object, and then move on to the other, hierarchical objects.

Using Constants

As an aside, it is worth noting that the CDO for NTS library (**CDONTS.DLL**) includes declarations for constants which can be used in place of explicit values in certain expressions. The constants which are identifiable by the prefix **cdo** (such as **cdoEncodingBase64** which has a value of **1**) are available from Visual Basic, but are NOT available from within VBScript. If you want use these values, however, you can create a separate file containing these declarations and include it in your script with a set of statements at the head of the page like this:

```
<% @ LANGUAGE="VBSCRIPT" %>
<% Option Explicit %>
<!--#include file="cdovbs.inc"-->
```

The **Option Explicit** is particularly useful here as it will cause an error to be generated if a particular constant declaration cannot be found. Without the **Option Explicit**, if a constant such as **cdoEncodingBase64** were used later in the code without having been previously declared, VBScript would interpret the undeclared constant a variable with a value of **0** and continue execution without raising an error. The problems that result from this type of error can be very, very hard to debug.

Unlike **adovbs.inc** which contains the type library declarations for ADO, Microsoft does not provide a **cdovbs.inc** file when CDO for NTS is installed.

> You can download a sample **cdovbs.inc** which you can use, from the Wrox web site
> **http://rapid.wrox.co.uk/books/1266**.

The NewMail Object

The **NewMail** object provides the quickest method of mail-enabling a web page and allows us to send a message in just three or four lines of code. In its simplest format we can send a message using the **NewMail** object like this:

```
Set objMail = CreateObject("CDONTS.Newmail")
objMail.Send ("rob@here.com", "jdr@there.com", "Bad news", "I owe you £50")
Set objMail = Nothing
```

This would cause an SMTP message to be sent to **jdr@there.com** with a subject of "Bad News", a body text reading "I owe you £50". The message will appear to have been sent from **rob@here.com**.

The first line of code creates an instance of the **NewMail** object. The second causes the message to be sent and the last line clears up by reclaiming the resources that had been allocated to the **NewMail** object when it was instantiated. There is no need to deal with folder or message collections and, interestingly, there is no need to log on either.

As you can see, most of the key information about the message is provided in the form of parameters to the **Send** method. If we wanted to, however, we could explicitly set the properties of the **NewMail** object like this:

```
Set objMail = CreateObject("CDONTS.Newmail")
objMail.From = "rob@here.com"
objMail.To = "jdr@there.com"
objMail.Subject = "Bad News"
```

```
objMail.Body = "I owe you £50"
objMail.Send
Set objMail = Nothing
```

This achieves exactly the same result as the three previous lines of code, but has the advantage of making the code easier to read (and therefore to debug if it doesn't produce the desired results).

> **Because there is no logon authentication and it is up to you to specify who the message is from, you can send anonymous mail from CDO for NTS by simply omitting to specify the** From **property!**

Specifying Recipients

You may have noticed from the example above that the intended recipient of the mail message was referenced using a full SMTP address (i.e. **jdr@there.com**). When specifying recipients in CDO for NTS you always have to use the full SMTP address as there is no concept of address books or address resolution.

Recipients are specified using the **To**, **Cc** and **Bcc** properties, like this:

```
objMail.To = "jdr@there.com"
objMail.Cc = "stephen@there.com"
objMail.Bcc ="margaret@here.com"
```

In this case, the message would be sent to **jdr@there.com**; a copy would be sent to **stephen@there.com**; and a blind copy would be sent to **margaret@here.com**.

> *When a person is specified as the BCC (Blind Carbon Copy) recipient of a mail message, it means that they are sent a copy of the mail message, but that neither the original recipient nor anyone who was specified as a copy recipient knows that the BCC recipient has been sent a copy.*

In order to specify multiple recipients for a message, simply separate the recipients' names with a semicolon:

```
objMail.To = "jdr@there.com;stephen@there.com;margaret@here.com"
```

Multiple recipients can be specified for the **To**, **Cc** and **Bcc** properties. However, messages can only have one sender, so the **From** property of the **NewMail** object should always be a single SMTP address.

The Message Body

To specify the text that will appear as the body of the message, simply set the **Body** property of the **NewMail** object.

```
objMail.Body = "I owe you £50"
```

Although plain text is the default, the **NewMail** object also supports HTML as a format for the body of the mail message. To send a message which contains HTML in its body, we need to change the **BodyFormat** of the **NewMail** object to **cdoBodyFormatHTML** and then set the **Body** property to a string containing HTML.

```
Set objMail = CreateObject("CDONTS.Newmail")
sHTML = "<HTML>"
sHTML = sHTML & "<HEAD>"
sHTML = sHTML & "<TITLE>Bad News!</TITLE>"
sHTML = sHTML & "</HEAD>"
sHTML = sHTML & "<BODY>"
sHTML = sHTML & "<P>I owe you <FONT COLOR="#FF0000"><STRONG>"
sHTML = sHTML & "£50</STRONG></FONT>!</P>"
sHTML = sHTML & "</BODY></HTML>"
objMail.From = "rob@here.com"
objMail.To = "jdr@there.com"
objMail.BodyFormat = cdoBodyFormatHTML
objMail.Body = sHTML
objMail.Send
Set objMail = Nothing
```

If the body of our message is in HTML and it contains a number of URLs, we can streamline things somewhat by taking advantage of the **ContentBase** and **ContentLocation** properties of the **NewMail** object. If the **ContentLocation** property has been specified for a **NewMail** object, then any URLs in the message body are deemed to be relative to the path specified in the **ContentLocation** property. If the **ContentBase** property has also been set, then the path in the **ContentLocation** property is deemed to be relative to the path in the **ContentBase** property.

To make this a little clearer, have a look at the following code:

```
Set objMail = CreateObject("CDONTS.Newmail")
sHTML = "<HTML>"
sHTML = sHTML & "<HEAD>"
sHTML = sHTML & "<TITLE>Bad News!</TITLE>"
sHTML = sHTML & "</HEAD>"
sHTML = sHTML & "<BODY>"
sHTML = sHTML & "<P><IMG SRC="ouch.gif" WIDTH="28" HEIGHT="28"></P>"
sHTML = sHTML & "<P>I owe you <FONT COLOR="#FF0000"><STRONG>"
sHTML = sHTML & "£50</STRONG></FONT>!</P>"
sHTML = sHTML & "</BODY></HTML>"
objMail.From = "rob@here.com"
objMail.To = "margaret@here.com"
objMail.BodyFormat = cdoBodyFormatHTML
objMail.ContentBase = "http://www.here.com/"
objMail.ContentLocation = "miscellaneous/"
objMail.Body = sHTML
objMail.Send
Set objMail = Nothing
```

When this message is displayed, the browser will prefix the image source **ouch.gif** with the values read from the **ContentBase** and **ContentLocation** properties and attempt to retrieve the image file from **http://www.here.com/miscellaneous/ouch.gif**.

If you prefer, you can specify the **ContentBase** and **ContentLocation** in UNC format:

```
objMail.ContentBase = "\\our_server\"
objMail.ContentLocation = "miscellaneous\"
```

Sending Attachments

It is easy to attach files to mail messages using the **AttachFile** method of the **NewMail** object. So if we wanted to attach a bitmap to the mail message we could do so like this:

```
objMail.AttachFile ("c:\images\logo.bmp", "Our logo")
```

This would attach the file **logo.bmp** with the caption "Our logo". By default, the attachment is encoded using the UUENCODE format, but we can override this default and send the attachment using Base 64 format by supplying the optional *encodingmethod* parameter to the **AttachFile** method.

```
objMail.AttachFile ("c:\images\logo.bmp", "Our logo", cdoEncodingBase64)
```

To set the encoding method for this attachment back to UUENCODE we would use the constant **cdoEncodingUUEncode** instead. Bear in mind that changing the encoding method for a **NewMail** object only affects that object. It does not alter the default method used for encoding new **NewMail** objects.

Changing the Message Format

By default, messages sent with the **NewMail** object are sent as plain text. If we want, however, we can send a message in MIME format by changing the **NewMail** object's **MailFormat** property like this.

```
objMail.MailFormat = cdoMailFormatMIME
```

If we wanted to explicitly set the format of the message back to plain text, we would use the constant **cdoMailFormatText**. Again, bear in mind that changing the **MailFormat** property affects only the current **NewMail** object. It has no effect on the default format used in **NewMail** objects that are created in the future.

Changing the **MailFormat** property of a message also affects the default method used for encoding any attachments that the message might have. If the message is to be sent as plain text, the default encoding method for any new attachments is to use the UUENCODE format. If the message is to be sent in MIME format, then the default for any new attachments is to use Base 64 encoding. Finally, it should be noted that if we explicitly specify that an attachment is to use the Base 64 encoding method, the **MailFormat** property of the message to which it is attached is automatically changed to **cdoMailFormatMIME**.

With the wide variety of encoding and formatting options available how do you select the best one to use? Well, that really depends on two things; what is the purpose of your message and who is it being sent to? Here are some suggestions for you to bear in mind.

If you are using CDO for NTS simply to provide you with notification you of some exceptional event which has occurred – a form of administrative alert – then you will probably not be too concerned about how pretty the message appears. You won't want to go through the hassle of formatting the message in HTML when plain text will do just as well.

However, if you are using CDO for NTS to allow you to dispatch promotional material such as an electronic marketing brochure to subscribers to your web site, then you might want to spend some time formatting the message in HTML to make it look as eye-catching and slick as possible. (In this situation, you could use a tool such as Microsoft FrontPage 98 to generate the HTML and then paste it into the ASP code).

Bear in mind, however, that the presence of all those tags means that HTML documents are larger than plain text documents. Larger documents, and especially ones which contain images, mean longer download times and bigger phone bills for recipients who are downloading your message over a dial-up connection.

You should also think about the capabilities of the mail clients that will be used by recipients of your messages. Most modern mail clients can cope with messages which use the MIME format, but there may be some who do not. So if you are not sure about the capabilities of your target audience, you might want to go for the safer option and send the message as plain text instead.

Changing the Message Priority

It is also possible to change the importance, or priority, of a mail message generated by using the **NewMail** object. This is done by setting the object's **Importance** property. By default, messages are assigned an importance of Normal, which is represented by the constant **cdoNormal**. To change the importance of the message to high, simply use the constant **cdoHigh**, and to make it a low importance message, use **cdoLow**.

```
objMail.Importance = cdoLow
```

You can also change the importance of the message by supplying a value for the optional **Importance** parameter of the **Send** method of the **NewMail** object, like this:

```
objMail.Send ("rob@here.com", "jdr@there.com", "Bad news", "I owe you £50", cdoHigh)
```

You should be aware that changing the importance of a mail message will not necessarily have any effect on the speed with which the message is actually delivered to the recipient, as the implementation of this feature may vary among the various servers in the path from your server to the destination mail server. You should also note that although some mail clients visually differentiate high, normal and low importance messages through some type of icon, you might not be in a position to guarantee that this functionality is available to all of the message's recipients.

Adding Custom Headers

It was stated earlier in this chapter that the **NewMail** object was designed to allow for the quick and easy generation of mail messages from a web page and we looked at an example of sending a message in three lines of code.

```
Set objMail = CreateObject("CDONTS.Newmail")
objMail.Send ("rob@here.com", "jdr@there.com", "Bad news", "I owe you £50")
Set objMail = Nothing
```

The screenshot below shows how such a message would appear to the recipient if viewed in Microsoft Outlook Express.

Now let's have a look at the source of the actual message that was sent. Different mail clients provide different methods for viewing the message source, but in Outlook Express you do this by opening the message and then selecting the Properties item from the File menu. On the Details tab of the dialog which then appears, click the Message Source... button. This will display the native source code for the message you are looking at and it will probably look something like this.

```
x-sender: rob@here.com
x-receiver: jdr@there.com
Received: from mail pickup service by asti.ivory.co.uk with Microsoft SMTPSVC;
        Sun, 14 Dec 1997 12:01:31 +0000
From: <rob@here.com>
To: <jdr@there.com>
Subject: Bad News
Date: Sun, 14 Dec 1997 12:01:31 -0000
X-MimeOLE: Produced By Microsoft MimeOLE V4.71.1712.3
Message-ID: <002dd3101120ec7ASTI@asti.ivory.co.uk>

I owe you £50
```

You will notice that as well as the body text, there is a lot of extra information contained in the message source which is not displayed when the mail message is viewed. This header information is automatically generated based on the values that were specified either as explicit property settings for the **NewMail** object or as parameters to the **Send** method. It also includes details such as the time-stamp line below which are generated by the SMTP server itself.

```
Received: from mail pickup service by asti.ivory.co.uk with Microsoft SMTPSVC;
        Sun, 14 Dec 1997 12:01:31 +0000
```

If we want, however, we can add our own headers to the message we are sending. The reason for doing this is that many messaging systems are able to interpret certain other headers which are not automatically added by the **NewMail** object. Details of these headers, such as the **Keywords**, **References** and **Reply-To** headers, can be found in the document entitled Standard for the Format of ARPA Internet Text Messages (STD011) located at **http://ds1.internic.net/std/std11.txt**.

To add a custom header to the message we use the **Value** property of the **NewMail** object. So if we want to add a **Reply-To** header, we would do so like this.

```
Set objMail = CreateObject("CDONTS.Newmail")
objMail.Value("Reply-To") = "stephen@ivory.co.uk"
objMail.Send ("rob@here.com", "jdr@there.com", "Bad news", "I owe you £50")
Set objMail = Nothing
```

If we then look at the message source of the message that this creates, we can see that it now has an appropriate line added to the headers indicating the reply address:

```
x-sender: rob@here.com
x-receiver: jdr@there.com
Received: from mail pickup service by asti.ivory.co.uk with Microsoft SMTPSVC;
        Sun, 14 Dec 1997 12:01:31 +0000
Reply-To: <stephen@ivory.co.uk>
From: <rob@here.com>
```

To: <jdr@there.com>
Subject: Bad News
Date: Sun, 14 Dec 1997 12:01:31 -0000
X-MimeOLE: Produced By Microsoft MimeOLE V4.71.1712.3
Message-ID: <002dd3101120ec7ASTI@asti.ivory.co.uk>

I owe you £50

And when we open the resulting message and attempt to reply to the sender, the reply is correctly addressed to the person specified in the **Reply-To** header.

The **Value** property is actually the default property of the **NewMail** object, which means that we could achieve the same effect by using this code instead:

```
Set objMail = CreateObject("CDONTS.Newmail")
objMail("Reply-To") = "stephen@ivory.co.uk"
objMail.Send ("rob@here.com", "jdr@there.com", "Bad news", "I owe you £50")
Set objMail = Nothing
```

You can set the **Value** property of a **NewMail** object as many times as you want. Every time you set the property it adds a new header to the message, so you can add a number of custom headers to the same message.

```
Set objMail = CreateObject("CDONTS.Newmail")
objMail("Reply-To") = "stephen@ivory.co.uk"
objMail("Keywords") = "Bet,England,Rugby,Lose"
objMail.Send ("rob@here.com", "jdr@there.com", "Bad news", "I owe you £50")
Set objMail = Nothing
```

Other Considerations

We have spent a good deal of time looking at the **NewMail** object and how it can be used. Before we leave this and go on to investigate the hierarchy of other objects in the CDO for NTS hierarchy, there are a few other observations that are worth making.

The first point to make is that with the exception of the **Version** property (which returns the version of the CDO for NTS library), none of the properties of the **NewMail** object are readable. The reason for this is that the **NewMail** object is designed to be operated without user-intervention and there is therefore no need to provide either a user interface or a mechanism for reading properties. A further implication of this is that recipients, attachments and headers, once added, cannot be removed from a **NewMail** object.

Secondly, you should be aware that once the **Send** method has been invoked against the **NewMail** object, the **NewMail** object is invalidated and cannot be reused. Attempting to access the object after it has been invalidated will lead to a run-time error in the ASP script. To send another message you will need to create a new **NewMail** object.

Finally, it is worth reiterating that the **NewMail** object is completely distinct from the other objects that form the hierarchy of Collaboration Data Objects for NT Server. These other objects provide a greater granularity of control and are more suited when you want to do something a little more complex than can be achieved through the limited functionality of the **NewMail** object. We'll have a look at those other objects now.

The CDO for NTS Hierarchy

We saw earlier that the majority of the objects within the CDO for NTS library form a hierarchy topped by the **Session** object.

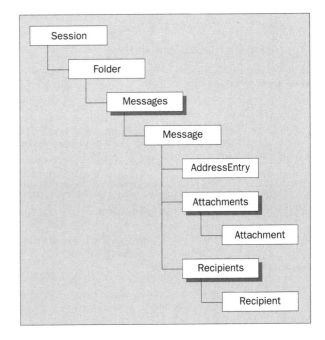

Clearly, using the object hierarchy to send mail messages is going to be a more long-winded process than using the **NewMail** object, but the corollary is that the degree of control that the object hierarchy provides to the programmer is significantly increased.

Sessions and Logging On

The top-level object of the CDO for NTS hierarchy is the **Session** object, which is used to store settings and options that apply throughout a user's session. Once we have created a **Session** object, the first thing we should do is to invoke the object's **LogonSMTP** method to indicate the context for the **Session** object.

```
Set objSession = CreateObject("CDONTS.Session")
objSession.LogonSMTP ("Rob Smith", "rob@ivory.co.uk")
```

This creates a **Session** for a user, sets the user's SMTP address to **rob@ivory.co.uk** and sets the user's friendly name to **Rob Smith**.

> Note that the user's identity is not validated by the **LogonSMTP** method. In other words, any SMTP address and friendly name can be provided as parameters to the **LogonSMTP** method and CDO for NTS will use them without complaint. However, if the SMTP address is incorrect the message will not be deliverable.

Once a session has been established, we can then access the Inbox and Outbox folders for that particular session.

When we have finished with the **Session** object, we should log off by invoking the **LogOff** method and then set the **Session** object to **Nothing**.

```
objSession.Logoff
Set objSession = Nothing
```

Accessing the Inbox and Outbox

A folder is any location in which messages can be stored. These include the Inbox, in which incoming messages are stored; the Outbox in which outgoing messages are held before they are sent; and any personal folders that might have been set up when using other servers such as Exchange Server.

In order to manipulate the messages in a folder, we must first set a reference to the folder itself. The easiest way to do this in CDO for NTS is to use the **Inbox** and **Outbox** properties of the **Session** object which each return a folder object.

```
Set objSession = CreateObject("CDONTS.Session")
objSession.LogonSMTP ("Rob Smith", "rob@ivory.co.uk")
Set objInbox = objSession.Inbox
```

Once we have a folder object, we can then go on to inspect any messages that are stored within that folder, by using the **Messages** property of the folder. This returns a **Messages** collection which contains all of the messages in the folder.

```
Set objSession = CreateObject("CDONTS.Session")
objSession.LogonSMTP ("Rob Smith", "rob@ivory.co.uk")
Set objInbox = objSession.Inbox
Set colMessages = objInbox.Messages
Response.Write objInbox.Name & " - " & colMessages.Count & " messages"
```

The actual folders returned by the **Inbox** and **Outbox** properties of a **Session** object depend on whether CDO for NTS is being run against the SMTP service of IIS 4.0 or against Exchange Server.

> If CDO for NTS is being run against Exchange Server, the **Inbox** property will return the user's regular mailbox and the **Outbox** property will be the user's outbox.

▲ If CDO for NTS is being run against IIS 4.0, the **Inbox** property will return the **Drop** directory. Although this contains all of the messages for recipients on the server, only those messages addressed to the user who was bound to the **Session** object by the **LogonSMTP** method will be available.

Once we have created a reference to a folder representing an Inbox we can view and delete the messages in that Inbox, through the **Messages** collection and the **Message** object. By contrast, the Outbox folder is where we will create any **Message** objects that we want to send out.

The **GetDefaultFolder** method of the **Session** object can also be used against an IIS 4.0 SMTP server to return the Inbox or Outbox folder. However, the **GetDefaultFolder** method is more useful against an Exchange Server where it can be used to retrieve other types of folders such as Outlook calendar or contacts folders.

Viewing Messages in the Inbox

You will have noticed by now that using the CDO for NTS object hierarchy is considerably more involved than simply using the **NewMail** object. But it is when we see what can be done with the **Messages** collection and **Message** object that we begin to realize how much more powerful the object hierarchy is. So far, we have looked at how to create a session and set a reference to an Inbox or Outbox folder. Now we will look at what we can do with the messages inside those folders.

The following code demonstrates how it is possible to display a summary of all messages received for a particular user, which contain a given string in their body text.

```
<%@ LANGUAGE="VBSCRIPT"%>
<%Option Explicit%>
<% Response.Buffer=True %>


<%
'Dim all the variables here
...
%>
```

```
<HTML>
<HEAD>
<TITLE>Search Results</TITLE>
</HEAD>
<BODY>

<H1>Search Results</H1>
<TABLE>
    <TR>
       <TD>User:</TD>
       <TD><I><%=Request.QueryString("Name")%></I> </TD></TR>
    <TR>
        <TD>Address:</TD>
        <TD><I><%=Request.QueryString("Address")%></I> </TD></TR>
    <TR>
        <TD>Search String:</TD>
        <TD><I><%=Request.QueryString("Text")%></I> </TD></TR>
</TABLE>
<p>
<%
```

```
sName = Request.QueryString("Name")
sAddress = Request.QueryString("Address")

Set objSession = CreateObject("CDONTS.Session")
objSession.LogonSMTP sName, sAddress

Set objInbox = objSession.Inbox

If objInbox.Messages.Count = 0 Then
    Response.Write "There are no messages in the Inbox"
    Set objInbox = Nothing
    objSession.Logoff
    Set objSession = Nothing
    Response.End
Else
%>
<P>

    <TABLE BORDER="0" BGCOLOR="#C0C0C0" CELLSPACING="2">
        <TR>
            <TD BGCOLOR="#E0E0E0" WIDTH="200"><B>Subject</B></TD>
            <TD BGCOLOR="#E0E0E0" WIDTH="150"><B>Sent By</B></TD>
            <TD BGCOLOR="#E0E0E0" WIDTH="200"><B>Time Sent</B></TD></TR>
<%
    Set colMessages = objInbox.Messages
    iHits = 0
    For iLoop = 1 to colMessages.Count
            Set objMessage = colMessages(iLoop)
            If Instr(objMessage.Text, Request.QueryString("Text")) Then
                iHits = iHits + 1
%>
    <TR>
        <TD BGCOLOR="#E0E0E0" WIDTH="200"><%=objMessage.Subject%></TD>
        <TD BGCOLOR="#E0E0E0" WIDTH="100"><%=objMessage.Sender%></TD>
        <TD BGCOLOR="#E0E0E0" WIDTH="200"><%=objMessage.TimeSent%></TD>
    </TR>
<%
            End If
    Next
%>
</TABLE>
<%
    If iHits = 0 Then
            Response.Clear
            Response.Write "No messages contained the specified text"
    End If
End If

Set objMessage = Nothing
Set colMessages = Nothing
Set objInbox = Nothing
objSession.Logoff
Set objSession = Nothing
%>
</BODY>
</HTML>
```

When this script is run and the appropriate arguments are passed in as `QueryString` parameters, a page similar to this one will be displayed.

The first few lines of code are responsible for displaying the parameters which are passed in as `QueryString` parameters:

```
<TABLE>
    <TR>
        <TD>User:</TD>
        <TD><I><%=Request.QueryString("Name")%></I> </TD></TR>
    <TR>
        <TD>Address:</TD>
        <TD><I><%=Request.QueryString("Address")%></I> </TD></TR>
    <TR>
        <TD>Search String:</TD>
        <TD><I><%=Request.QueryString("Text")%></I> </TD></TR>
</TABLE>
```

The `Name` argument (`John.de.Robeck`)is the friendly name of the recipient of the messages which we want to search through. The `Address` argument (`jdr@here.com`) corresponds to the person's SMTP address. And the `Text` argument supplies the text which we will be search for in the body of that person's messages. Note that we use the encoded value `%20` to represent a space in the `Text` argument.

The next step is to create a `Session` object and log on using the name and SMTP address supplied as arguments.

```
sName = Request.QueryString("Name")
sAddress = Request.QueryString("Address")

Set objSession = CreateObject("CDONTS.Session")
objSession.LogonSMTP sName, sAddress
```

Next, we create a reference to the Inbox by using the **Inbox** property of the **Session** object. Because we will be executing this code against an IIS 4.0 SMTP server, this will give us access to all of the messages in the Drop directory which were addressed to the person whose address we used when we performed the **LogonSMTP** method.

```
Set objInbox = objSession.Inbox
```

The **Messages** property of the Inbox object **objInbox** returns a collection containing all of the messages in the Inbox. We can then inspect the **Count** property of this collection to determine whether or not there are any messages addressed to this person.

```
If objInbox.Messages.Count = 0 Then
    Response.Write "There are no messages in the Inbox"
    Set objInbox = Nothing
    objSession.Logoff
    Set objSession = Nothing
    Response.End
```

If the **Count** property returns **0**, we display a message saying that there are no messages and after reclaiming the memory allocated to the various objects we have instantiated so far, we end our script.

However, if the Inbox does contain messages, we must inspect them each to determine whether they contain the text which was supplied in the **Text** argument to this page. We start by caching the **Messages** collection of the Inbox in an object variable for performance purposes and then initialize a counter.

```
Set colMessages = objInbox.Messages
iHits = 0
```

We then loop through each of the **Message** objects in the **Messages** collection and assign each one to a variable (**objMessage**) in turn. Note that the collection is not zero-based. In other words, the first item in the collection has an index of **1** rather than **0**.

```
For iLoop = 1 to colMessages.Count
    Set objMessage = colMessages(iLoop)
```

In order to determine whether the message we have cached contains the selected string, we use the **Instr** function. This searches one string for occurrences of a substring and, if it is found, returns the starting position of the substring. We are only concerned that the substring should be located and are not bothered about its position, so we simply need to check that the **Instr** function returns a non-zero value.

```
If Instr(objMessage.Text, Request.QueryString("Text")) Then
```

If the text for which we are searching is found, we increment our hit counter and then add a row to the table displaying the results.

```
iHits = iHits + 1
%>
    <TR>
        <TD BGCOLOR="#E0E0E0" WIDTH="200"><%=objMessage.Subject%></TD>
        <TD BGCOLOR="#E0E0E0" WIDTH="100"><%=objMessage.Sender%></TD>
        <TD BGCOLOR="#E0E0E0" WIDTH="200"><%=objMessage.TimeSent%></TD>
    </TR>
```

We then continue our loop until we have searched through all of the messages in the Inbox. If none of the messages were found to contain the selected text, the hit counter (**iHits**) will still be at zero. If this is the case, we clear the contents of the Response buffer (which would have contained the headings for the result table) and display a message indicating that the text could not be found in any of the messages.

```
If iHits = 0 Then
    Response.Clear
    Response.Write "No messages contained the specified text"
End If
```

All that remains is to reclaim all the resources which was allocated to our object variables and end the script.

```
Set objMessage = Nothing
Set colMessages = Nothing
Set objInbox = Nothing
objSession.Logoff
Set objSession = Nothing
```

This is just one example of the way that you can manipulate messages in the Inbox. Most of the time you will only be able to inspect the messages and their properties in the Inbox. The key exception to this role is when you use the **Delete** method of the **Messages** collection to delete a message. By way of contrast, messages that you create in the Outbox can be modified and this is what we do when we want to send a message using the CDO for NTS object hierarchy.

Sending Messages

The principle behind sending a message using CDO for NTS objects is straightforward, although clearly not as simple as if we were just to use the **NewMail** object. Here is an example of how it works.

```
Set objSession = CreateObject("CDONTS.Session")
objSession.LogonSMTP "John", "jdr@there.com"

Set objOutbox = objSession.Outbox
Set objMessage = objOutbox.Messages.Add

objMessage.Subject = "Where are my books?"
objMessage.Text = "I can't find them anywhere and I need them now!"
objMessage.Importance = cdoHigh

objMessage.Attachments.Add "BookList.txt", cdoFileData, "c:\pressies.txt"
objMessage.Recipients.Add "Rob", "rob@ivory.co.uk", cdoTo
objMessage.Recipients.Add "Jim", "jim@ivory.co.uk", cdoCC
objMessage.Send

Set objMessage= Nothing
Set objOutbox = Nothing
objSession.Logoff
Set objSession = Nothing
```

Executing this script should cause the following message to be sent. The message is displayed in Outlook Express. It may look different when viewed in other mail clients.

Note the image of a stamp in the upper right corner bearing an exclamation mark. This is how Outlook indicates that the message has a high priority.

If you have managed to follow this chapter so far, there shouldn't be anything in this code fragment that will throw you. We start of with the now familiar process of creating a **Session** object and logging on as **John**, with an SMTP address of **jdr@there.com**.

```
Set objSession = CreateObject("CDONTS.Session")
objSession.LogonSMTP "John", "jdr@there.com"
```

This time, however, we are not going to be looking in John's Inbox. Rather, we want to send a message and for that we need access to his Outbox. So we set a reference to the Outbox and then create a new message in the Outbox.

```
Set objOutbox = objSession.Outbox
Set objMessage = objOutbox.Messages.Add
```

Next, we need to set the properties of the message. We fill in the subject line and body text of the message and then set its importance as high.

```
objMessage.Subject = "Where are my books?"
objMessage.Text = "I can't find them anywhere and I need them now!"
objMessage.Importance = cdoHigh
```

Next, we add an attachment to the message. There are two types of attachment that we can add to messages. The first type, which is denoted by the constant **cdoFileData,** are operating system files, such as Word documents or Excel spreadsheets. To attach these we use the syntax we have used here:

```
objMessage.Attachments.Add "BookList.txt", cdoFileData, "c:\pressies.txt"
```

This line adds a new **Attachment** object to the collection of **Attachments** for the current message. When adding a file attachment, we pass three parameters to the **Add** method of the **Message** object:

- ▲ The first parameter (**"BookList.txt"**) specifies the caption which will appear against the attachment when viewed by a client.

- ▲ The second parameter (**cdoFileData**) signifies that the attachment is a file.

- ▲ The third parameter (**"c:\pressies.txt"**) indicates the location of the file which is to be attached.

The second type of attachment, denoted by the constant **cdoEmbeddedMessage**, is an embedded message. This would be used if you wanted to embed another mail message in the message you were sending. To embed a message we would have used this syntax:

```
objMessage.Attachments.Add "", cdoEmbeddedMessage, objOldMessage
```

When embedding a message, the three parameters to the **Add** method have the following meanings:

- ▲ The first parameter (**""**) specifying the name of the attachment is always ignored when embedding a message.

- ▲ The second parameter (**cdoEmbeddedMessage**) signifies that the attachment is an embedded message.

- ▲ The third parameter (**objOldMessage**) is a **Message** object representing the message which is to be embedded.

The penultimate step is to specify the two recipients of the message.

```
objMessage.Recipients.Add "Rob", "rob@ivory.co.uk", cdoTo
objMessage.Recipients.Add "Jim", "jim@ivory.co.uk", cdoCC
```

The first recipient has a display name of **Rob**, an SMTP address of **rob@ivory.co.uk** and is the primary recipient of the message. The second recipient has a display name of **Jim**, an SMTP address of **jim@ivory.co.uk** and will receive a copy of the message.

All that remains now is to send the message.

```
objMessage.Send
```

As with the **NewMail** object, the **Send** method causes the **Message** object to be sent and then invalidates it. This means that any subsequent reference to the **Message** object will generate an error. All that remains is to log off and free up the resources that had been allocated to the objects we used in this code.

The AddressEntry object

There is one object in the CDO for NTS hierarchy at which we have not yet looked and that is the **AddressEntry** object. Although displayed in the hierarchy as if it were a child of the **Message** object, this is not strictly true. In fact, the **AddressEntry** object is accessed through the **Sender** property of the **Message** object, like this:

```
Dim objAddressEntry
Set objAddressEntry = objMessage.Sender
sAddressName = objAddressEntry.Name
sAddressType = objAddressEntry.Type
sAddress = objAddressEntry.Address
```

As you may have guessed from this, the purpose of the **AddressEntry** is to provide more information about the sender of a message. So far we have concerned ourselves solely with the use of CDO for NTS as a method for manipulating mail within a purely SMTP environment. However, as we noted earlier, CDO for NTS can be used against Exchange Server 5.5. In Exchange, with the appropriate connectors installed, one can receive messages from senders on a variety of other messaging systems, such as MS Mail or cc:Mail.

We saw earlier that the format of an SMTP address is always in the format **username@domainname**, as in **rob.smith@ivory.co.uk**. However, different messaging systems use different formats for their addresses. Consequently, in an environment such as Exchange 5.5, where messages may be received from heterogeneous messaging systems, we need a mechanism for determining both the messaging system and the address of the sender of a message if we are to reply to that message.

The **AddressEntry** object provides this mechanism and has three specific properties (**Name**, **Type** and **Address**) in addition to the properties which are common to all objects in the CDO for NTS hierarchy.

- The **Name** property returns the friendly name. This is the name that is typically displayed by the mail client in its From: box.

- The **Type** property returns the messaging system used by the sender of the message.

- The **Address** property returns the true messaging system-specific address of the sender of the message.

To see how this works, let's consider the message that we created in the previous example. In this example, the **Name** property of the **AddressEntry** object representing the sender of the message would be **John**. Why? Because that was the display name that we used when we logged on to the session from which we sent the message.

```
objSession.LogonSMTP "John", "jdr@there.com"
```

Similarly, the **Address** property would return **jdr@there.com** because that was the address we used to log on with.

And finally, the **Type** property would return **SMTP**. In fact, when using CDO for NTS with the SMTP server that comes with IIS 4.0, the **Type** property of all **AddressEntry** objects will be **SMTP**. When running CDO for NTS against Exchange Server 5.5, however, the **Type** might vary and the table below gives a few examples of the values that one might encounter in such a heterogeneous environment.

Name	Type	Address
John	SMTP	jdr@there.com
John2	CCMAIL	John de Robeck at There
John3	MS	THERE/EDINBURGH/JOHND
John4	X400	c=UK;a= p=There; o=Edinburgh; s=deRobeck; g=John

The primary use for the **AddressEntry** object is in constructing a valid **Recipient** object for use in replies to messages. By concatenating the **Type** property and the **Address** property of the **AddressEntry** object in the form *type: address* one can form a return address which is acceptable to Exchange Server as in the example below:

```
Set objAddressEntry = objOldMessage.Sender
sReturnAddress = objAddressEntry.Type & ": " & objAddressEntry.Address
objNewMessage.Recipients.Add objAddressEntry.Name, sReturnAddress, cdoTo
```

Common Properties

There are four properties common to all objects in the CDO for NTS object hierarchy. These are the **Application**, **Class**, **Parent** and **Session** properties. The following table details what each of these objects returns together with notes on their use.

Property	Returns	Note
Application	String	The string indicates the version of CDO for NTS. For the version of CDO for NTS released with IIS 4.0 the application object returns: **Collaboration Data Objects for NTS version 1.2**
Class	Long Integer	The integer indicates the type of object of which this is a property. The objects indicated by each of the return values are as follows: 0 **Session** object 2 **Folder** object 3 **Message** object 4 **Recipient** object 5 **Attachment** object 8 **AddressEntry** object 16 **Messages** collection 17 **Recipients** collection 18 **Attachments** collection
Parent	Object or **Nothing**	The object returned is the immediate parent of the specified object in the CDO for NTS hierarchy (see diagram above). Two cases worthy of note are: the **AddressEntry** object, which returns as its parent the **Message** object from whose **Sender** property it is derived; and the **Session** object which returns **Nothing**.
Session	**Session** object	This returns the **Session** object at the top of the CDO for NTS hierarchy.

Where Now?

The purpose of this chapter has been to introduce you to CDO for NTS, the messaging library that is packaged with Internet information Server 4.0. CDO for NTS is suitable for providing quick and easy access to SMTP messaging from a web page, but it really begins to show up its limitations when you try to use it for anything more complex than routine tasks such as sending out acknowledgement messages, producing bulk mailings or sending marketing literature to subscribers to your web site.

If you want to build a web site which relies on messaging and workflow or which requires access to advanced messaging capabilities such as calendaring and scheduling, then you need something altogether more heavy-duty, like CDO 1.2. The full CDO 1.2 library is vast compared to its kid brother CDO for NTS and it really is beyond the scope of this book to take a detailed look at all the functionality that it opens up to you. Plus, CDO 1.2 is primarily designed for use with Exchange 5.5 and Outlook 8.03 (or higher) although it will provide limited functionality against any MAPI-compliant mail system. Probably the best place to find information on developing applications with Exchange 5.5, Outlook 8.03 and CDO 1.2 is the Exchange AppFarm. This is a cool site, packed with heaps of sample code, and can be found at:

`http://www.microsoft.com/technet/appfarm`

But to give you a taster, here are just three of the things that you can do if you get round to installing Exchange Server 5.5 and Outlook 8.03.

Calendaring

Apart from being a truly revolting word, calendaring is the word that Microsoft uses to describe the ability to programmatically manage calendars and schedules. So whereas the key messaging element in CDO for NTS is the **Message** object, the full-blown implementation of CDO 1.2 also includes objects such as the **AppointmentItem** object and the **MeetingItem** object. These allow developers to build web pages which can interact with either Schedule+ or Outlook calendars (a single interface provides access to both) and so produce web-based applications which can be used for tasks such as sophisticated resource scheduling.

Message Filtering

The **MessageFilter** object provides developers with the ability to simply filter all of the messages in a particular folder to select only those which meet certain criteria. The criteria on which the filter can be applied are exposed as properties. The following code fragment illustrates how easy the **MessageFilter** object is to use.

```
Set objMsgFilt = objSession.Inbox.Messages.Filter
objMsgFilt.Unread = True    ' Allow only unread messages
objMsgFilt.Subject = "Cow" ' Allow only messages with "Cow" in the Subject
```

HTML Rendering

A key component of CDO 1.2 is a set of HTML rendering objects which allow Exchange data to be converted automatically into HTML. These rendering objects are written in C and provide a much quicker method of generating HTML than could be achieved by looping through the various collections in VBScript code. In fact, using these rendering objects it is possible to render an entire page in HTML in as few as five lines of code. Because these rendering objects take advantage of the **Response** object, pages are rendered using the code page of the browser as opposed to that of the server and so will display appropriate characters in international environments. This means that developers are relieved of a significant burden when developing Web applications for international distribution.

Summary

In this chapter, we have dealt with the question of messaging with CDO for NTS in quite a lot of detail. Although CDO for NTS is one in what is now a fairly long line of messaging libraries released by Microsoft, I think it is evident that there is still a long way to go. As has been mentioned more than once in this chapter, the messaging support it provides is fairly meager, given that it only supports SMTP mail and there is no real provision for delivering inbound mail to the desktop.

But it's a question of horses for courses. Although the SMTP Server that IIS 4.0 provides is of limited use, it is a lot cheaper, a lot thinner and a lot easier to maintain than a full-blown Exchange implementation.

One of the really useful features however, is the fact that applications that use CDO for NTS against the IIS 4.0 SMTP server will run against Exchange Server and CDO 1.2 without the need for extensive rewriting.

CDO 1.2 looks set to expand as well. The current release can render calendars into HTML in a daily and weekly view, but there is no support yet for monthly views. Also, there is no explicit support for either contacts or tasks, both of which will need to be implemented if contact management or workflow applications are to be developed without the need for awkward workarounds.

So the message is, if all you need is the capability to send out e-mail acknowledgements from your web site or are looking for a cheap method of implementing bulk mailing via web subscription, then get your teeth into CDO for NTS. But if you want anything more than that, then think carefully whether your time might be better spent developing with full-blown CDO 1.2 and Exchange 5.5.

Integrating Microsoft Index Server

As with a book, indexing serves a crucial purpose in a Web environment. If your web site contains more than a handful of pages, it can be difficult for visitors to quickly find information about a particular topic. For example, on a software support title, visitors may need help installing a particular component. Instead of coursing through a labyrinth of menu hyperlinks to locate the relevant support page, many users would probably find it easier to specify what they're looking for, and to get a list of matching pages.

The need to provide this support increases as the manageability of the desired information decreases. Imagine, for example, a situation in which a newspaper wants to provide users with the ability to retrieve stories from archive. Because it's impossible to anticipate the course of a user's interest, you simply can't use a menu of hyperlinks to lead a visitor through this exercise. You have to build in search capabilities, and the less the user is required to know about the mechanics of the search, the better.

The Microsoft Index Server allows you to make your site's content available to web searches. Using a background application that maintains one or more on-disk catalogs, the Index Server makes it possible for you to present your clients with sophisticated query options, and to determine in detail how the results of a search are presented to your clients.

In this chapter, we'll review the architecture of the Index Server, and examine each of these querying approaches in turn. Specifically, we'll look at:

- An overview of the Index Server, to see its architecture and capabilities, including the kinds of documents it stores, the kinds of information it indexes, and the kinds of queries we can perform.

- An introduction to static querying, to see how we can combine Internet Data Query (IDQ), HTML, and HTX files to perform fast and easily configured searches without writing ASP code.

- An introduction to the new **Query** and **Utility** objects, which provide us with the ability to describe and execute a query, and get back an ADO **Recordset** that contains the query's results.

- A brief look at how we can use ActiveX Data Objects (first introduced in Chapter 7) to query Index Server just as we would query any other database.

Before we do, however, we should be precise regarding what this chapter is intended to achieve. This chapter is not intended to be an exhaustive treatment of the Index Server. Indeed, the more you learn about the Index Server, the more you realize that it's a universe of its own, justifying its own book-length treatment. The treatment you'll get here is intended simply to introduce you to the key concepts defined by the Index Server, and to provide a survey of the various ways in which you can query the Index Server and present query results.

Overview of Index Server

Undoubtedly, this has happened to you: You wrestle tirelessly with a complex subject, and having mastered it at last, you immediately think of concrete measures the subject's teacher could have taken to frame the subject more simply, and to make mastering the subject more pleasant.

The Index Server is a complex subject. Although remarkably powerful, it consists of an initially bewildering array of pieces. First, there's the notion of catalogs and scope (we'll get to this soon enough). Then there's the query language. Then there's the process of hiding the details of this language from your users through the use of intuitive search forms. Finally, add to this the fact that there are three quite distinct approaches you can take to querying the Index Server.

- **Static searching**. You can use a combination of HTM, IDQ and HTX files to build indexing into your site. Although this process is less amenable to customization than are other approaches to Index Server searching, it comes with the advantage of enabling you to provide search capabilities in your site without having to write code.

- **Active Server Pages** (ASP) **searching**. The newest version of the Index Server defines the **Query** and **Utility** objects, two scriptable objects specifically designed to support searching from within ASP code. When you execute a query using these objects, you get back an ActiveX Data Objects (ADO) **Recordset**. This **Recordset** object, like any other, contains fields of information through which you can iterate, just as you would through a **Recordset** retrieved from a database table.

- **ActiveX Data Objects** (ADO) **searching** using a SQL statement rather than the **Query** and **Utility** objects. The Index Server is an OLE DB provider. That's a fancy way of saying that you can use the ADO to query an Index Server catalog, submitting SQL queries to the catalog transparently as if it were just another database.

Object-Based Searching

At first, it's tempting to confuse the Active Server Pages approach with the ADO approach; both approaches result in the creation of an ADO **Recordset**. However, the two approaches differ in two regards. With the ASP approach, the **Recordset** is created using the **Query** and **Utility** objects. With the ADO approach, the **Recordset** is created using some combination of the **Connection** and **Command** objects. More importantly, the query that you use to perform an ASP search consists of some combination of Index Server query language statements. The searches that you execute using ADO consist of SQL statements, which usually incorporates several of the unique features of the Index Server.

Having now messed around with the Index Server at some length, here's the conceptual shortcut I've found most useful: Think of the Index Server as a database, such as SQL Server or DBASE, a powerful engine that can process complex queries and return what amounts to a result set. Throughout this chapter, as we examine each feature of the Index Server, we'll do so with reference to this analogy. A database consists of tables of data, and these tables consist of discrete fields in which various types of information are stored.

To get at this information from within a program, you generally have to be acquainted with a query language designed to identify the information in which you are interested. After you execute this query against the database, you get back rows of data that (hopefully) mirror what you were hoping to find.

The Index Server is intentionally modeled after the *ODBC* approach to data retrieval. Within this model, a common language (SQL) can be used to retrieve data from any number of databases, provided that an ODBC driver for the target database is installed on the client system. To the user, the actual source of the data, whether SQL Server, MS Access, or an Excel spread sheet, is transparent. This transparency enables the user to focus on the *data*, instead of on the proprietary format in which the data is stored or on the functional peculiarities of any particular database.

How Index Server Works

Before we go on to look at how we can integrate Index Server into our Active Server Pages sites, or at how we can exploit its new capabilities, let's look at what the Index Server is, and how it actually works. It's a surprisingly powerful search engine package, and can quite easily perform the most complex kinds of query and search tasks.

Once installed, Index Server is, to a large extent, self-maintaining. During periods of little or no system activity, it trawls the folders in the selected areas of your system, building and maintaining **catalogs** of information about each document stored there. When you perform a search in the catalog, it uses the contents of the index to perform the search and, optionally, to build an HTML results page and return it to the client. The cataloging and indexing system is practically transparent as far as the user is concerned. It is also very fast, because only the index file needs to be searched each time.

Searches that you perform in a catalog are expressed in terms of the Index Server query language, which, like the familiar SQL, combines field names and comparison and logical operators to identify the documents you want to retrieve. For more information on this language, see "The Index Server Query Language" later in this chapter.

Using Catalogs

A catalog is a collection of directories that make up a discrete unit within an Index Server search. You can think of a catalog like you would think of a database. It is a collection of virtual tables (directories) that contain data indexed by the Index Server. When you execute queries against the Index Server, you specify the catalog that you want to query.

If you do not specify a catalog, the default catalog is used. This catalog contains a number of default directories, including (most importantly) the **\Inetpub\wwwroot** directory, which you typically use to store your server's Web sites.

To add or delete catalogs to and from the Index Server, to add directories to an existing catalog, or to perform routine Index Server maintenance (such as directory re-scans), use the Index Server Manager. This is a snap-in for the Microsoft Management Console application, and is installed with Index Server.

Note that the index file can be up to 40% of the total size of the documents on your system, if you have full indexing features in use.

Using Scope

If a catalog is analogous to a database, the concept of **scope** encompasses one or more tables in that database. As mentioned in the section on Catalogs, a catalog can consist of any number of directories. However, it is often not in your interest to search every single directory in a catalog. This is where scope comes into play. The scope of a search defines the sub-directories within a catalog that are included in the search.

Consider most web hosting facilities host scores of sites, commercial and personal. Chances are, if your server hosts the Acme Service Corporation, and if the virtual directory for Acme appears as a sub-directory of `\Inetpub\wwwroot`, Acme's directory is part of the default catalog of directories.

However, if Acme sports a search form in their pages, they'll only want to return information about Acme to users, and want specifically to exclude information about any other of the sites you happen to be hosting.

Each of the search types that the Index Server supports provides a means by which you can limit the query's scope to a specific directory or directories. Within an ASP search, for example, you use the `Utility` object's `AddScopeToQuery` method to specify the scope. With an ADO search, you specify the query's scope within the SQL text of the command that you execute.

Within the directory to which you limit your search, you can also limit the **traversal level**, which defines the depth to which a search extends. If the scope of a search specifies the **shallow traversal** of a directory, only the files in that directory are searched. If **deep traversal** is specified, all the sub-directories of a given directory are included in the search.

The Types of Information Index Server Stores

Index server doesn't just keep a list of file names (if we wanted to do this, we could activate the Windows Find dialog from the Start menu, and use this dialog to perform the search). It also stores a multitude of document details. These include many of the stored document's properties, the time and date it was created and last updated, the size, the file attribute status, etc. Plus—and here's the clever bit—it keeps an **abstract** of the contents.

This abstract is a selection of the text in the document, irrespective of what type of document it actually is. And Index Server contains natural language processing systems, dedicated to your own particular spoken language, so that it really "understands" (as far as computers can understand) the file contents.

This means that you can search for a word, or group of words, as well as specifying the type of the file and other properties such as the author. The language engine can match words literally, so that `catch*` will include `catcher` and `catching`, and also grammatically where `catch**` will include `catching` and `caught`. No doubt you're aware that in a typical file search (from the Windows command line, for example) an asterisk is a wildcard character for which any combination of characters will be substituted to perform the search. In the second example provided here, the double asterisk is also a wildcard character, but one that encompasses all grammatical variations on the word `catch`.

The Index Server also includes a **noise list** file. This is an editable file that prevents words such as **and**, **or**, **the**, etc., from being included in the index. This makes the Index Server a very powerful and precise way of finding information stored anywhere on your system.

The Types of Documents that Can Be Cataloged

Index Server will catalog, by default, all the documents stored in the virtual paths set up in Internet Information Server. These can be HTML files, documents created in Microsoft Word, Excel or PowerPoint, or plain text files. Index Server even maintains a list of non-document files in the catalog, such as executables (although such files seldom contain meaningful, human-readable information).

You'll find that there are many document types that are not directly supported by Index Server. At the moment, only the Microsoft formats are supported. However, Index Server has a filter interface, which enables third party software vendors to provide the logic to enable Index Server to support their own application file formats. This means that other suppliers can, potentially, allow any file type to be fully cataloged; and hence the types of files Index Server can search is expected to increase.

Index Server in Action

To show you what Index Server can do with very little effort on our behalf, here is an example of Index Server in action from the end-user's point of view. As you read through this section, keep in mind that this sample illustrates the **static** approach to Index Server searching. We'll look at code samples of both static and object-based searching a little later.

All we need is a **<FORM>** section in a page, with a single text box and a **Submit** button. Here, we've also included the standard **Reset** button to clear the text box as well. We use the text box to enter a search criterion for which matching files will be listed. In this case, we've entered the criterion **zip*** to find any documents containing words that start with **zip**:

Enter the contents of a document to find:

| zip* | Search Now | Clear |

Clicking Search Now sends Index Server off to look in its catalog, and after a short while, a list of matching documents appears. Here, we've found fifteen that match, and the list shows details of the first 10 of these:

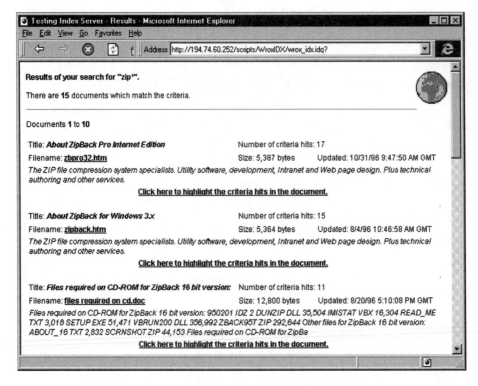

For each one there's the document title, filename, and some of the abstract information. The page also shows the number of 'criteria hits'–the number of times the keyword is found in the document. However, the documents are actually listed in descending order based on their ranking by the search engine, and not just the number of keyword hits.

> *The ranking is generated automatically and reflects how well the document matches the query, so that the most appropriate search results can be listed first; for example, when doing a NEAR search (a search in which you specify that one search term must be found within so many words of another), the ranking is affected by the proximity of the keywords, and not just by their frequency.*
>
> *The role of rank in search results can also be affected by how you initialize the objects that you use to perform the search. For example, if you use the* **Query** *object, which is examined later in this chapter, you can specify how documents are sorted, in which case the rank of a document within the search is not relevant to the document's position in the list of documents resulting from the search.*

There's also the size, in bytes, of the document, and the date and time it was last updated. At the bottom of the page is a button where we can show the next page of results. Notice that it "knows" that there are only five more to look at. Clicking it displays the next page with the title 'Documents 11 to 15':

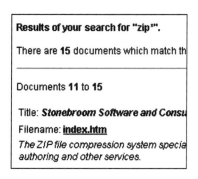

At the bottom of this page is a message confirming that there are no more matches, and some controls that allow us to perform a new search. One of the strengths of Index Server is that there are several ways we can specify the documents we want to find. The default, which we've been using here, is to search for the text in the content of the document.

For the code that drives the search illustrated here, see the section 'How to Perform Static Queries' later in this chapter.

The Index Server Query Language

When composing a query, we need to keep in mind a few simple rules:

Words separated by spaces or ordinary punctuation (which is not listed as a special character in the tables later in this section) are treated as a **phrase**. The search will only return documents that contain this phrase. However, words within the phrase which are listed in the **noise list** (such as a, as, and, but, for, etc.) are ignored completely. Matching is also case-insensitive. So searching for **the State; and the County** will also match **the state of a county**.

To search for a phrase that contains quotation marks, or one of the special characters such as an exclamation mark, we have to enclose the whole phrase in quotation marks, and then place double quotation marks where we want a quotation mark to appear. For example, **"he yelled ""Hello!"" from across the street"**. To search for several individual words in a document, we separate the words with a comma. The result will be documents that contain all, or only some, of the words listed. The more that match, however, the better the ranking of the result.

Other than that, we can use the normal wildcard and Boolean operators. An asterisk matches any number of characters, and a question mark matches any single character. There's also the option of a **fuzzy search**. Adding two asterisks to the end of a word will match 'stem words' with the same meaning. A search for **catch****, for instance, will include catching and caught.

To combine words in the search string, we use Boolean operators like this:

Boolean Keywords	Shorthand	Meaning
`Apples AND Pears`	`Apples & Pears`	Both must exist in the document.
`Apples OR Pears`	`Apples	Pears`	Either must exist in the document.
`Apples AND NOT Pears`	`Apples & !Pears`	The first word must exist in the document, but the second must not.
`Apples NEAR Pears`	`Apples ~ Pears`	Both must exist in the document, and be within 50 words of each other. The closer they are, the higher the ranking in the search result.
`NOT @size < 2049`	`! @size < 2049`	Document must be larger than 2 KB.

Catalog Properties and Attributes

As you can see from the last entry in the previous table, we can also search by any other of the attributes or properties of the documents that Index Server stores in its catalog, for example:

Attribute or Property	Meaning
`Contents`	Words or phrases in the document. This is the default if no other attribute or property is specified.
`Filename`	The name of the file.
`Size`	The size of the file in bytes.
`Path`	The actual path and file name of the document.
`Vpath`	The server's virtual path and file name for the document.
`HitCount`	The number of hits for the content search in the document.
`Rank`	The relative matching score for the query, from 0 to 1000.
`Create`	The date and time that the file was originally created.
`Write`	The date and time that the file was last updated.
`DocTitle`	The **Title** property for the document.
`DocSubject`	The **Subject** property for that document.
`DocPageCount`	The number of pages in the document.
`DocAuthor`	The **Author** property for the document.
`DocKeywords`	The keywords specified for that document.
`DocComments`	The value of the **Comments** property for that document.

The properties starting with DOC are only available for documents created by applications which can store these document properties in their files. In the case of an executable file, for example, there will be no **DocPageCount** *or* **DocKeywords** *properties available.*

We can search for the value of a property, or the attributes of a file, using the **@** or **#** prefixes. In a relational expression, like the expression **! @size < 2049** that we used in the table above, the prefix is **@**. For a normal expression-based search, we use **#**. For example **#filename *.xlw** will only match Microsoft Excel workbook files.

There's one other prefix that you'll find useful: **$contents**. The use of this keyword takes advantages of the Index Server's capabilities as a natural language processor. By pre-pending the **$** to **contents**, you tell the Index Server to treat what follows **$contents** as 'free text'. When you execute a free text query, the Index Server extracts nouns and phrases from the text you supply to construct a query for you. For example, if you specify **$contents tell me how to create a query**, the Index Server returns any document that covers creating queries even though the precise text 'tell me how to create a query' appears in none of those documents.

One final note: The information presented in this section is included for you, the search developer. As we'll see in the samples presented in this chapter, the trick of designing effective searches is to design intuitive search forms that do not require the end user to know anything about the Index Server query language.

How to Perform Static Queries

A static query involves the interaction of a HTML file, an Internet Data Query (IDQ) script, and an Extended HTML Template (HTX) file. The following figure illustrates the interaction among these components.

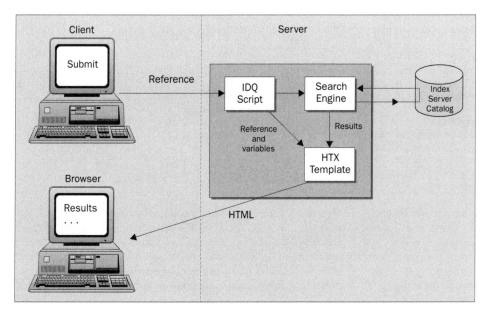

The substance of this interaction is quite simple. An HTML form posts a query to an IDQ file. The query is executed by the IDQ file, which pipes the results of the query to an HTX file identified in the IDQ file. And that's that. In fact, this process was graphically illustrated in the section "Index Server in Action," which appears earlier in this chapter. In this section, let's take a look at the details of how this output is produced.

Referencing the IDQ Script

To post the contents of a form field to an IDQ file, you reference the IDQ file in the **<FORM>** section of an HTML page. Optionally, you can supply the contents of a form's controls in the **HREF** argument of an **<A>** tag. In the illustration that appears in the section "Index Server in Action", the following code is used to create the text box and buttons (we've omitted the server address from the **ACTION** tag for clarity).

```
<FORM ACTION="wrox_idx.idq" METHOD="POST">
Enter the contents of a document to find:<P>
<INPUT TYPE="TEXT" SIZE="70" MAXLENGTH="70" NAME="CiRestriction">
<INPUT TYPE="SUBMIT" VALUE="Search Now">
<INPUT TYPE="RESET" VALUE="CLEAR">
</FORM>
```

Two things in this code are worthy of note. First, the HTML form defined here does not post to a CGI or ASP script. It posts to an IDQ file, which defines the elements of the query that will be built around the user-supplied text. Second, note that the **CiRestriction** name we assign our text form field identifies for the IDQ file the field that contains the text that we're looking for.

Inside the IDQ Script

So what essentially is the IDQ script to which the HTML form posts its data? The IDQ file is a script that defines every element of the query's execution, including the columns to be returned, the form field that contains the text to be retrieved, and the sort order of the result set.

Here's an excerpt from the **wrox_idx.idq** file, the file referenced in the HTML file that we defined in the preceding section. Note that the **CiColumns** entry is actually all on one line:

```
[Query]
CiColumns=filename,size,characterization,rank,path,hitcount,
          vpath,DocTitle,write
CiCatalog=c:\IndexServer
CiScope=/
CiFlags=DEEP
CiRestriction=%CiRestriction%
CiMaxRecordsInResultSet=1000
CiMaxRecordsPerPage
CiTemplate=/wrox_idx.htx
CiSort=rank[d]
```

Hearkening back to the database analogy that I promised would dominate our examination of Index Server, you'll realize that the **CiColumns** parameter in the IDQ file acts rather like the **SELECT** clause in an SQL statement. It defines which properties and attributes of the indexed files are returned from the catalog. With the exception of **characterization**, we've already looked at the selection above—when we talked about the query language of Index Server. The **characterization** property is the abstract that Index Server automatically builds from the document, and is intended to indicate its broad contents.

Having specified which properties we want, we have to tell Index Server where to search for the documents. **CiCatalog** is the location of the catalog storing the document details (it's possible to create different ones), and **CiScope** is the virtual root from where we want to include documents. We can select any physical or mapped virtual folder here. In our case, we're starting at the main Internet Server root. To include all the subfolders below it, we've included **CiFlags=DEEP**.

The **CiRestriction** line in the script defines the query we want to use, and because it's sent from the browser as the value of the text box named **CiRestriction**, we use this value in our script by enclosing it in percent signs, as **%CiRestriction%**. We can either send the values of these variables from the controls on the form like this, or preset them directly as text values within the IDQ file.

The next two lines set the maximum number of documents to return, and the number we want to display in each page of the resulting HTML code that is sent back to the browser. Lastly, we specify the location of the HTX template file, and how the matching document details are to be sorted. In this case, we've chosen the usual: descending order by rank.

IDQ File Variables Summary

As a summary, the next table shows a list of common variables that are set in an IDQ script—either directly, or as a variable from a control in the **<FORM>** section of a page:

Variable	Meaning
CiCatalog	Location of the catalog, if not using the default.
CiForceUseCi	**TRUE** to use the current index, even if out of date.
CiScope	Start directory for the search.
CiFlags	**DEEP** to include all subdirectories below **CiScope**, or **SHALLOW** for only the directory in **CiScope**.
CiColumns	List of all the indexed values to be returned, i.e. the columns for the results set, separated by commas.
CiRestriction	The query to be executed, i.e. what to search for.
CiMaxRecordsInResultsSet	Maximum number of documents to be retrieved.
CiMaxRecordsPerPage	Maximum number of documents to be returned on each page.
CiSort	Order of the returned records, using the column names separated by commas. **[d]** indicates descending order. For example: **State, Size [d], Name**
CiTemplate	Full virtual path to the **HTX** template file.

Inside the HTX Template

All the work of formatting the information that is to be returned to the browser is done in the HTX template. Like Active Server Pages, it uses the **<%...%>** tags to delineate code or values. However, we don't have to include an equals sign, as we do in ASP, when placing the value of a variable in the page. The two special tags **<%BeginDetail%>** and **<%EndDetail%>** denote a section that is repeated for each 'record' returned by the Index Server engine. We also have options for displaying the information as separate pages, rather than a single long page. The IDQ variable **CiMaxRecordsPerPage** tells Index Server how many records to retrieve each time.

Index Server HTX templates also support **<%If** *condition*%**>...<%Else%>...<%EndIf%>**, and in a template we can retrieve the value of any of the controls on the form which originally referenced the IDQ script, or which are listed in the **CiColumns** line of the script. We can also use the regular HTTP variables, such as **SCRIPT_NAME** or **SERVER_NAME**, as we did with ASP in earlier chapters.

IDQ Return Variables Summary

After running the IDQ script, Index Server sets the values of various built-in variables, which indicate the results of the query:

Variable	Meaning
CiMatchedRecordCount	Total number of documents which match the query.
CiTotalNumberPages	Total number of pages used to contain query results.
CiCurrentRecordNumber	Number of current document in the total matched.
CiCurrentPageNumber	Current page number of query results.
CiFirstRecordNumber	Number of the first document on the current page.
CiLastRecordNumber	Number of the last document on the current page. May not be correct until after the **<%EndDetail%>** section.
CiContainsFirstRecord	Set to **1** if the current page contains the first document in the query results, or **0** otherwise.
CiContainsLastRecord	Set to **1** if the current page contains the last document in the query results, or **0** otherwise. May not be correct until after the **<%EndDetail%>** section.
CiBookmark	Reference to the first document on the current page.
CiOutOfDate	Set to **1** if the content index out of date, or **0** if OK.
CiQueryIncomplete	Set to **1** if the query could not be completed using the current content index, or **0** if completed.
CiQueryTimedOut	Set to **1** if the query exceeded the time limit for query execution, or **0** if completed.
CiRecordsNextPage	Number of records on the next page for a paged query.

Here are the 'working parts' of the template file we used to create the query results pages you saw earlier. We've omitted the code that just creates the header and footer:

```
...
<B>Results of your search for "<%CiRestriction%>".</B><P>
There are <%CiMatchedRecordCount%> documents which match the criteria.
<HR>
<%If CiMatchedRecordCount NE 0%>
  Documents <%CiFirstRecordNumber%> to <%CiLastRecordNumber%><P>
<%EndIf%>
<TABLE WIDTH=100%>
  <%BeginDetail%>
    <TR>
     <%If DocTitle ISEMPTY%>
      <TD>Untitled document</TD>
     <%Else%>
      <TD>Title: <I><B><%DocTitle%></B></I></TD>
     <%EndIf%>
```

```
        <TD COLSPAN="2">Number of criteria hits: <%HitCount%></TD>
      </TR>
      <TR>
      <TD>Filename:<A HREF="<%EscapeURL vpath%>"><%filename%></A>
       </TD>
      <TD>Size: <%size%> bytes</TD>
      <TD>Updated: <%write%> GMT</TD>
      </TR>
      <TR>
      <TD COLSPAN="3"><I><%characterization%></I></TD>
      </TR>
      <TR>
      <TD COLSPAN="3" ALIGN="CENTER">
       <!-- following must be all on one line -->
       <A HREF="http://<%SERVER_NAME%>/scripts/srchadm/webhits.exe
          <%EscapeURL vpath%>?CiRestriction=
          <%EscapeURL CiRestriction%>&CiBold=YES">
       Click to highlight the criteria hits in the document.</A>
       </TD>
      </TR>
      <TR>
      <TD COLSPAN="3" ALIGN="RIGHT">.</TD>
      </TR>
    <%EndDetail%>
  </TABLE>
  <FORM ACTION="<%EscapeURL SCRIPT_NAME%>?" METHOD="POST">
   <%If CiMatchedRecordCount EQ 0%>
   Enter the criteria for a new search:<P>
   <INPUT TYPE="TEXT" SIZE="70" MAXLENGTH="70"
          NAME="CiRestriction">
   <INPUT TYPE="SUBMIT" VALUE="New Search">
   <INPUT TYPE="RESET" VALUE="Clear">
   <%Else%>
   <%If CiRecordsNextPage EQ 0%>
    <HR><B>No more matches.</B>
    Edit the criteria for a new search:<P>
    <INPUT TYPE="TEXT" SIZE="70" MAXLENGTH="70"
           NAME="CiRestriction" VALUE="<%CiRestriction%>">
    <INPUT TYPE="SUBMIT" VALUE="New Search">
   <%Else%>
    <INPUT TYPE="HIDDEN" NAME="CiBookmark"
           VALUE="<%CiBookmark%>">
    <INPUT TYPE="HIDDEN" NAME="CiBookmarkSkipCount"
            VALUE="<%CiMaxRecordsPerPage%>">
    <INPUT TYPE="HIDDEN" NAME="CiMaxRecordsPerPage"
           VALUE="<%CiMaxRecordsPerPage%>">
    <INPUT TYPE="HIDDEN" NAME="CiRestriction"
           VALUE="<%CiRestriction%>">
    <INPUT TYPE="HIDDEN" NAME="CiScope" VALUE="<%CiScope%>">
    <INPUT TYPE="SUBMIT"
           VALUE="Next <%CiRecordsNextPage%> Documents">
   <%EndIf%>
   <%EndIf%>
  </FORM>
  ...
```

683

From your knowledge of Active Server Pages, it should be obvious how the IDQ variables (such as `<%CiRestriction%>`) and the values obtained from the search (such as `<%DocTitle%>`) are used. We create a table to hold the results and, within the `<%BeginDetail%>` `<%EndDetail%>` section, create a table row containing the document title, size, last update time, filename, hit count and abstract. Because some documents do not have a title, we use an `<%If...%>` `<%Else%>` `<%EndIf%>` construct to display 'Untitled document' in this case:

```
...
<%If DocTitle ISEMPTY%>
  <TD>Untitled document</TD>
<%Else%>
  <TD>Title: <I><B><%DocTitle%></B></I></TD>
<%EndIf%>
...
```

> *Note that we can't put a `<%BeginDetail%>` `<%EndDetail%>` section inside an `<%If...%>` `<%Else%>` `<%EndIf%>` construct. If we do, we get an error message saying that an `<%Else%>` or `<%EndIf%>` can't be found.*

How to Perform Queries in ASP

The previous section of this chapter illustrated how we can use a combination of HTML, IDQ and HTX files to add search capabilities to our sites. The selling point of this approach is that it is efficient and very fast, and that it does not require us to write ASP code. Additionally, the ability to easily separate the search results into multiple pages is built into the environment itself—a feature that you sorely miss when you move from static to object-based searching.

The Limitations of Static Searches

Think, however, about the things that you cannot do using the approach we've just illustrated. Suppose that a situation arises in which you want to send back to the client browser only a subset of the information that your search locates. Or suppose that, for whatever reason, you want to process the data without sending it back to the client browser at all.

There is no way to do this using the static HTM/IDX/HTX trio. The data entered into the HTML form gets posted to the IDX file. What gets posted to the IDX file gets piped to the HTX file and sent back to the client browser. Period. Clearly, for all the simplicity and power of static querying, there are trade-offs.

Object-Based Searches

In the initial release of the Index Server, the HTM/IDQ/HTX approach to content searching was the only one supported. In the current release, the limitations of static querying have been addressed by the introduction of two new scriptable objects, the **Query** and the **Utility** objects. Using these objects, we can define and execute queries within ASP code. Instead of piping the results of a query back to the client browser, the **Query** object stores the query's results in an ActiveX Data Objects (ADO) **Recordset**. We can do anything we like with the contents of this **Recordset**—we can send all the contents back to the client browser, send a subset of the contents, or perform our own processing on the contents and send back the results of this processing.

The **Utility** object supports methods that enable us to perform various tasks in conjunction with a **Query** object. The most important of these tasks involves defining the query's scope, which we accomplish using the **Utility** object's **AddScopeToQuery** method.

The Query Object

The ASP **Query** object encapsulates an Index Server search. It supports the properties that you use to describe the information you're looking for, the columns to return, and the order in which to sort the query's results.

We create a **Query** object in an Active Server Page as we create most other ASP objects: by using the **Server** object's **CreateObject** method to store a reference to the object in a variable. The *ProgID* for this object is **ixsso.Query**.

```
Set objQuery = Server.CreateObject("ixsso.Query")
```

Having created our **Query** object, let's look at some of the new object's capabilities.

Query Object Methods and Properties

The methods and properties supported by the **Query** object fall roughly into two categories: those that we use to describe our query, as well as the results we want to get, and those that help us initialize the query from a URL instead of building it up piece by piece. Here's a list of the **Query** object's methods:

Method	Description
CreateRecordset	Executes the query stored in the **Query** property, and returns the query's results as an ADO **Recordset**.
DefineColumn	Associates a new friendly name with a column.
QueryToURL	Builds a URL out of the **Query** object's current state.
Reset	Clears the settings of the **Query** object, rendering it stateless.
SetQueryFromURL	Initializes the **Query** property from the contents of a URL.

Here's a list of the **Query** object's properties:

Property	Description
AllowEnumeration	Allows the query to use enumeration (as opposed to an index).
Catalog	A string that specifies the name of the catalog to search.
Columns	A string that contains a comma-delimited list of the columns to return in the **Recordset**.
LocaleID	Specifies the query's locale.
MaxRecords	Specifies the maximum number of records to return.
OptimizeFor	Allows you to set performance priorities on the query.

Property	Description
`Query`	A string that contains the query to execute. This string consists of some combination of Index Server query language properties and operators. Functionally analogous to an SQL **WHERE** clause.
`SortBy`	A comma-delimited string that specifies the columns on which the search results should be sorted.

Here's a shortcut for quickly mastering the use of the **Query** object, particularly if you've tinkered around with the static querying that we described earlier: every single property supported by the **Query** object maps conceptually to some setting in an IDQ file. For example, the **Query** object's **Query** property serves precisely the same purpose that the **CiRestriction** setting does. The **Columns** property serves a function identical to that served by **CiColumns**. You get the idea.

Initializing the Query Object

Of all the properties that we listed in the previous section, the most essential are the **Query** and **Columns** properties, which specify the query to execute and the columns to return, respectively. These properties are indispensable; no query makes sense without them, so you have to initialize them before calling the object's **CreateRecordset** method. (Generally, however, you'll also want to initialize the **SortBy** property, to determine the order in which your search results should be listed.)

Setting Query Properties Explicitly

You can initialize the properties of the **Query** object in one of two ways. In the first scenario, you parse the contents of a posted request, manually build a query string, and then explicitly initialize the **Query** object's **Query** property to reference this query string.

For example, if you wanted to retrieve the filename and document author for all the server-based documents that contain the word "Tolstoy", and that are less than 100 bytes in size, here's the initialization code you would use.

```
objQuery.Query = "CONTAINS Tolstoy AND @size < 100"
ObjQuery.Columns = "DocAuthor,filename"
```

Setting Query Properties Implicitly

In the second approach, you create a **<FORM>** that uses a group of conventional names for its form fields, and you use the **Query** object's **SetQueryFromURL** method to initialize the **Query** object for you. If you use this approach, keep the following in mind:

The form fields in your form must be named in accordance with a particular set of conventions. For example, the field that contains the text of your query should be named **qu**. The form field that identifies the catalog you want to search should be named **ct**. When you post this form to an ASP page, and then call the **Query** object's **SetQueryFromURL** method, the method automatically maps the contents of the **qu** form field to the **Query** object's **Query** property. Similarly, the contents of the **ct** form field are automatically mapped to the object's **Catalog** property. Other implicit property mappings are **mh** (**MaxRecords**), **sd** (**SortBy**), and **ae** (**AllowEnumeration**). The full list is enumerated and explained in the Index Server online documentation.

An Implicit Query Object Properties Example

In the meantime, let's take a look at this approach to query-building in action. First, we're going to create an HTML form that adheres to the naming conventions expected by the **SetQueryFromURL** method. Then, we're going to post the form to an ASP that creates a **Query** object, and calls **SetQueryFromURL** on that object. Finally, we're going to enumerate the values stored in the object's properties to demonstrate that **SetQueryFromURL** did its job—that is, that it initialized our **Query** object for us.

Here's the HTML form, **query_url.htm**, that we'll use:

The code that creates it looks like this:

```
<HTML>
<HEAD>
<TITLE>Setting Queries from URLs</TITLE>
</HEAD>
<BODY>
<H2>Setting Queries from URLs</H2>
<P>The following form illustrates the CGI naming
conventions for setting queries from URLs.</P>

<FORM method="GET" action="query_url.asp">
<TABLE border="0" width="100%">
 <TR>
  <TD width="28%">Search Text</TD>
  <TD width="72%">
   <P><INPUT type="text" name="qu" size="34"></P>
  </TD>
 </TR>
 <TR>
```

```
      <TD width="28%">Maximum Hits</TD>
      <TD width="72%"><P>
       <INPUT type="text" name="mh" size="20"></P>
      </TD>
     </TR>
     <TR>
      <TD width="28%">Sort By:</TD>
      <TD width="72%"><p>
       <SELECT name="sd" size="1">
        <OPTION value="DocAuthor">Document Author</OPTION>
        <OPTION value="Filename">Filename</OPTION>
        <OPTION value="size">Size</OPTION>
       </SELECT></P>
      </TD>
     </TR>
     <TR>
      <TD width="28%">Allow Enumeration:</TD>
      <TD width="72%"><P>
       <SELECT name="ae" size="1">
        <OPTION value="1">True</OPTION>
        <OPTION value="0">False</OPTION>
       </SELECT></P>
      </TD>
     </TR>
     <TR>
      <TD width="28%">Catalog:</TD>
      <TD width="72%"><P>
       <INPUT type="text" name="ct" value="Web" size="20"></P>
      </TD>
     </TR>
     <TR>
      <TD width="28%"></TD>
      <TD width="72%"><P>
       <INPUT type="submit" value="Show Object" name="Action"></P>
      </TD>
     </TR>
    </TABLE>
   </FORM>
  </BODY>
</HTML>
```

In this form, we've included the form fields for the **Query** property (**qu**), the **MaxRecords** property (**mh**), The **SortBy** property (**sd**), the **AllowEnumeration** property (**ae**), and the **Catalog** property (**ct**). Note: the names that you assign your form fields should match exactly the ones I've used here.

Now, here's the **query_url.asp** file, the ASP to which this HTML file posts its contents.

```
<%
'Create a Query object, initialize it using
'SetQueryFromURL, and dump the object state
Set objQuery = Server.CreateObject("ixsso.Query")
objQuery.SetQueryFromURL(Request.QueryString)
%>
```

```
<HTML>
<HEAD><TITLE>QueryFromURL Results</TITLE></HEAD>
<BODY>
<P>The following reflects the property settings
on the Query object.</P>

<TABLE border="0" width="100%">
 <TR>
  <TD width="30%">Query.Query</TD>
  <TD width="70%"><%= objQuery.Query%></TD>
 </TR>
 <TR>
  <TD width="30%">Query.MaxRecords</TD>
  <TD width="70%"><%= objQuery.MaxRecords%></TD>
 </TR>
 <TR>
  <TD width="30%">Query.SortBy</TD>
  <TD width="70%"><%= objQuery.SortBy %></TD>
 </TR>
 <TR>
  <TD width="30%">Query.AllowEnumeration</TD>
  <TD width="70%"><%= objQuery.AllowEnumeration%></TD>
 </TR>
 <TR>
  <TD width="30%">Query.Catalog</TD>
  <TD width="70%"><%= objQuery.Catalog%></TD>
 </TR>
</TABLE>
</BODY>
</HTML>
```

And here's the result it produces:

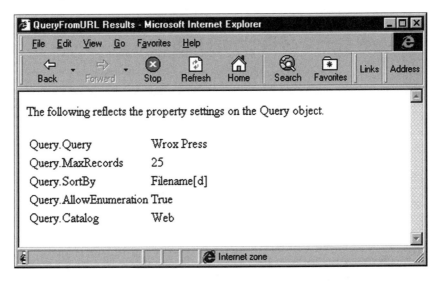

A last word before we go on to look at what the other object, the **Utility** object, brings to the picture. Here, our objective was simply to do a **Query** object property dump. To make this example a working search, we would have needed to make only minor modifications to **query_url.asp**. Such modifications would include initializing the **Query** object's **Columns** property, eliminating the HTML text that dumps the **Query** object's settings, and finally, using the **CreateRecordset** method to return a **Recordset** containing the query's results. Shortly, we'll take a look at an example that illustrates this whole process.

The Utility Object

You can use the **Query** and **Utility** objects independently (as in our previous example), but you probably won't. These objects are designed to coordinate. The most important feature of the **Utility** object is that it supports a method called **AddScopeToQuery**, which enables you to add scope to a query defined in the **Query** object. In addition, this object makes it possible to do other interesting things, such as retrieving **Recordset** elements by index, and truncating strings to a specified white space.

To create a **Utility** object, use the Server object's **CreateObject** method, specifying **"isxxo.Util"** as the *ProgID*.

```
Set objUtility = Server.CreateObject("isxxo.Util")
```

Utility Object Methods Summary

The **Utility** object contains no properties. The following table lists and briefly describes the methods that the object supports:

Method	Description
AddScopeToQuery	Associates a **Utility** object with a **Query** object, defining the physical scope of the query.
GetArrayElement	Returns an element in an array. Usually, you'll use this method to access specific elements of a **Recordset** by index.
ISOToLocaleID	Returns the Win32 locale ID for a specified ISO 639 language code.
LocaleIDToISO	Returns the ISO 639 language code for the specified Win32 locale ID.
TruncateWhiteSpace	Truncates a string at the specified white space. This method is particularly useful when you want to limit how much of a large piece of text will be displayed.

How to Add Scope to a Query

We've addressed query scope previously in this chapter. Limiting a query's scope can enhance significantly the speed with which a search executes. The **Utility** object's **AddScopeToQuery** method accomplishes this, identifying which directories are to be searched, and specifying the depth of the search within the specified directory tree. This method is functionally equivalent to the **CiScope** setting in a static query's IDQ file.

The following code fragment demonstrates the use of the **Utility** object's **AddScopeToQuery** method. This call to **AddScopeToQuery** identifies the **Query** object on which to set the scope, the directory to be searched, and the depth to which the search should extend. The use of the **"shallow"** parameter indicates that only the named directory (rather than its sub-directories) will be searched. The specification of scope in this fashion replaces the default scope, which encompasses a deep search of the default catalog:

```
Set objUtil = Server.CreateObject("ixsso.util")
objUtil.AddScopeToQuery objQuery, _
        "d:\Inetpub\wwwroot\IndexSample", "shallow"
```

A Query and Utility Object Sample

Imagine a situation in which you want to retrieve documents that contain a specified text string, and that have been modified within a specified number of days or hours. Here's how you might represent such information graphically in an HTML form:

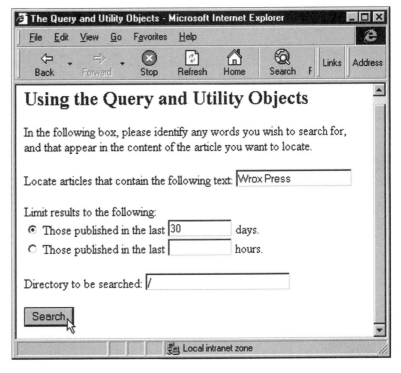

This page can be run or downloaded from our web site at
http://rapid.wrox.co.uk/books/1266/ *and is named* **query_sample.htm**.

In one text box the user can type any identifying content. Using the radio buttons, they can specify that they want to locate only those documents written in a given period of time. Finally, the user fills in a text box with a path that identifies the scope of the search. Note that this directory can be either a fully qualified or relative path.

The HTML Form Code

Here's the text of the HTML file, **query_sample.htm**, which creates the form displayed above:

```
<HTML>
<HEAD><TITLE>The Query and Utility Objects</TITLE></HEAD>
<BODY>
<H2>Using the Query and Utility Objects</H2>
<P>In the following box, please identify any
```

```
words you wish to search for, and that appear
in the content of the article you want to locate.</P>

<FORM method="post" action="query_sample.asp">
 Locate articles that contain the following text:
 <INPUT type="text" name="SearchString" size="20"><P>
 Limit results to the following:<BR>
 <INPUT type="radio" value="Days" checked name="Limit">
 Those published in the last
 <INPUT type="text" name="Days" size="10"> days.<BR>
 <INPUT type="radio" name="Limit" value="Hours">
 Those published in the last
 <INPUT type="text" name="Hours" size="10"> hours.<P>
 Directory to be searched:
 <INPUT type="text" name="Scope" size="25"><P>
 <INPUT type="submit" value="Search" name="Action">
 </FORM>
 </BODY>
 </HTML>
```

The Active Server Pages File

In the ASP file that processes this form, we first read the values stored in our form fields so that we can build up a query from these values. If the **SearchString** form field is empty, we assume the user is interested only in documents modified within a specified number of hours or days. If **SearchString** is not empty, we assume that the user is looking for the search string in the contents of the document itself:

```
<%
'Create the query based on user input
If Request("SearchString") <> "" Then
  Query = "@contents " & Request("SearchString") & " and "
End If
If Request("Limit") = "Days" Then
  Query = Query & " @write > " & "-" & Request("Days") & "d"
Else
  Query = Query & " @write > " & "-" & Request("Hours") & "h"
End If
...
```

Having built up our query, we create a **Query** object and initialize its properties, specifying that the maximum number of records returned should be 5, that the results should be sorted in descending order by filename, and indicating the columns of information we want to return:

```
...
Set objQuery = Server.CreateObject("ixsso.Query")
objQuery.Query = Query
objQuery.MaxRecords = 5
objQuery.SortBy = "filename[d]"
objQuery.Columns = "vpath,path,filename,size,write,characterization"
...
```

Next, we determine the scope for the query. Remember, if the scope is not explicitly defined (using the **AddScopeToQuery** method), then the **Query** object will perform a deep (or recursive) search of the entire default catalog. For illustrative purposes that's not necessary, so here we specify that we want to perform a shallow search of whatever directory the user specified:

```
...
If Request("Scope") <> "" Then
  Set objUtil = Server.CreateObject("ixsso.util")
  objUtil.AddScopeToQuery objQuery, Request("Scope"), "shallow"
End If
...
```

Now we call the **Query** object's **CreateRecordset** method to create an ADO recordset, and iterate through it putting the values into the page. Note that each column that we specified in the **Columns** property maps to a field in the returned recordset. If there are no records, we output an error message:

```
...
Set objRS = objQuery.CreateRecordset("nonsequential")
If objRS.EOF Then
  Response.Write("No records found!")
  Response.End
End If
%>
...
```

Finally, we can add the HTML that creates the return page that the user sees:

```
...
<HTML><HEAD><TITLE>Search Results</TITLE></HEAD>
<BODY>
<H1>Search Results</H1>
<TABLE border="0" width="100%">
<% do while not objRS.EOF %>
 <TR>
  <TD width="20%" align="right"><b>Virtual Path:</B></TD>
  <TD width="80%"><%= objRS("vPath")%></TD>
 </TR>
 <TR>
  <TD width="20%" align="right"><b>Physical Path:</B></TD>
  <TD width="80%"><%= objRS("Path")%></TD>
 </TR>
 <TR>
  <TD width="20%" align="right"><b>Filename:</B></TD>
  <TD width="80%"><%= objRS("Filename")%></TD>
 </TR>
 <TR>
  <TD width="20%" align="right"><B>Size:</B></TD>
  <TD width="80%"><%= objRS("Size")%></TD>
 </TR>
 <TR>
  <TD width="20%" align="right"><B>Last Modified:</B></TD>
  <TD width="80%"><%= objRS("Write")%></TD>
 </TR>
 <TR>
  <TD width="20%" align="right"><B>Exceprt:</B></TD>
  <TD width="80%"><%= objRS("Characterization")%></TD>
 </TR>
<% objRS.MoveNext %>
<% Loop %>
</TABLE>
</BODY>
</HTML>
```

And here's the result of our code—a page containing some of the properties of the matching documents:

For the sake of simplicity, this sample does not demonstrate how to separate search results across multiple pages (usually called **paging**). We've seen how it's done in static searches earlier, and we'll have a brief look at how we can do it in an object-based search at the end of this chapter. There are also examples included with the Index Server documentation. For instructions on how to access these samples, see the Summary at the end of this chapter.

How to Perform Queries using ADO

In Chapter 7, we looked at ActiveX Data Objects (ADO), a powerful and straightforward collection of Component Object Model (COM) objects that make it possible for you to programmatically access and manipulate data in a database from within Active Server Pages.

As that chapter demonstrated, one of the features that makes ADO powerful is that it **abstracts** the data source. For example, to open a database connection you create a **Connection** object and call its **Open** method, specifying a data source name (DSN) as the method's parameter. Whether the database that the DSN represents is an Access, SQL Server, dBase or any other database, you connect to it in precisely the same way.

OLE DB Providers

The same principle applies to the Index Server. The Index Server is an **OLE DB provider**. We use this term to indicate that a driver exists on the system that exposes a particular database's capabilities through a common programmatic interface. Regardless of the way in which a database stores its data internally, those that are OLE DB providers present a common face to the world.

Because the Index Server is an OLE DB provider, we can use the Active Data objects to submit SQL queries to the Index Server, just as we used them in Chapter 7 to submit queries to a Microsoft Access database. In this section, we'll have a look at how to do this.

If you haven't read this book's chapter on ADO, you may wish to do that before proceeding.

The Index Server SQL Extensions

To make it possible to access all of the capabilities of the Index Server with ADO, Microsoft has added a few extensions to the SQL language specification. For the most part, these extensions simply take into account those features of querying that exist in the Index Server, but that have no parallel in the database world.

For example, in an SQL **SELECT** statement, you usually reference the rows that you want to retrieve from a database table. With the Index Server, you're dealing with a *virtual* table, a collection of predefined "column names" that you identify by their friendly names (for example, **DocAuthor**, **Characterization**, **Directory**, and so on).

Whereas the **FROM** clause for a query generally references the table or tables you want to search, an Index Server query references the catalog you want to query and the query's scope. The **WHERE** clause, like the **SELECT** clause, specifies which rows in the virtual table will make up the resulting **Recordset**.

In this section, we'll identify the Index Server's SQL extensions as we encounter them. For an exhaustive treatment of these extensions, see the Index Server reference documentation.

Connecting to Index Server

The ActiveX Data Objects **Connection** object encapsulates a live connection to a data source. To connect to a data source, we use the object's **Open** method, specifying as a parameter the DSN to which we want to connect:

```
Set objConnection = Server.CreateObject("ADODB.Connection")
objConnection.Open "MyDSN"
```

Connecting to an Index Server is very similar, with one crucial difference: The Index Server catalog is not represented by a DSN. This means that there's nothing for us to configure in the Control Panel's ODBC32 applet. This also means that we have to specifically identify the Index Server as our data provider when we initialize our **Connection** object. The following statements illustrate how to do this:

```
Set objConnection = Server.CreateObject("ADODB.Connection")
objConnection.ConnectionString = "provider=msidxs;"
objConnection.Open
```

We now have a live connection to the Index Server. It's time to execute a command against this connection, and create a recordset from it.

Packaging the Command

Because we've messed around with the ADO before, we do have some experience to fall back on. We know that we can package up an SQL command in any number of ways, depending largely on the level of efficiency we want to achieve in the query's execution. For example, we can build up an SQL command based on user form input, and then pass the command string to the **Connection** object's **Execute** method to retrieve a navigable **Recordset**. Or we can associate a **Command** object with an active **Connection**, and then initialize the **Command** object's **CommandText** property to the SQL string.

But regardless of the approach we take to the command's execution, it all begins with the command itself; a string that consists of an SQL query. Since it's also a given fact that we'll build this command based on a site visitor's form input, let's start with a simple form. You can copy this HTML page, which is named **sql_sample.htm**, from the web site for this book at **http://rapid.wrox.co.uk/books/1266/**.

```
<HTML><HEAD><TITLE>Simple SQL Search Form</TITLE></HEAD>
<BODY>
<FORM METHOD="POST" ACTION="sql_sample.asp">
<INPUT TYPE="TEXT" SIZE="20" NAME="SearchString">
<INPUT TYPE="SUBMIT" NAME="ACTION" VALUE="Submit">
</FORM>
</BODY>
</HTML>
```

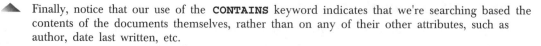

This form consists of just a text box named **SearchString** and a Submit button. When the user clicks the Submit button to post the contents of **SearchString**, our **sql_sample.asp** file retrieves the contents of this form field from the **Request** object, and builds it into an SQL command:

```
SQL = "SELECT filename, size FROM SCOPE() WHERE CONTAINS "
SQL = SQL & "('" & Request("SearchString") & "'" & ") > 0"
```

Despite the apparent simplicity of this SQL string, it takes into account no less than three of the SQL extensions included with the Index Server. Let's review them.

- The field names that follow the **SELECT** keyword identify the friendly names of Index Server fields that we want to retrieve.

- The **FROM** clause in this query identifies **SCOPE()** as the source of the data we want to retrieve. Used like this, the **SCOPE** of this query is open. In the parentheses that follow the **SCOPE** keyword, we could specify both a catalog and a scope within that catalog. We don't do this (yet), so the catalog used by this query is the system default, and the scope of this query extends to all the directories that are included in the default system catalog.

- Finally, notice that our use of the **CONTAINS** keyword indicates that we're searching based the contents of the documents themselves, rather than on any of their other attributes, such as author, date last written, etc.

We'll develop these concepts further in an integrated example that appears later in this chapter. First, though, let's look at how we execute this command.

Executing the Command

Remember that we mentioned that there were any number of ways to package an SQL command, depending on the efficiency level you want to achieve in the query's execution? Well, the same generalization applies to a **Command**'s execution. However, in executing the command, it's not just efficiency we're after. The idea is to retrieve a **Recordset** that contains only the capabilities that we need.

For simplicity's sake, we're going to assume here that we're creating a forward-scrolling read-only **Recordset**. In that case, here's how we execute the command we packaged in the previous section:

```
Set objRecordset = objConnection.Execute(SQL)
```

What follows now is the complete source code of the page that our HTML form posts its data to. It's named **sql_sample.asp**:

```
<%
'Make sure the user entered something
If Request("SearchString") = "" Then
   Response.Write("No search text entered!")
   Response.End
End If

'create the SQL query string
strSQL = "SELECT Filename, size from SCOPE() WHERE CONTAINS "
strSQL = strSQL & "('" & Request("SearchString") & "') > 0"

'create and open a connection
Set objConnection = Server.CreateObject("ADODB.Connection")
objConnection.ConnectionString = "provider=msidxs;"
objConnection.Open

'fill a recordset with the results
Set objRS = objConnection.Execute(strSQL)
If Not objRS.EOF Then
%>

<HTML><HEAD><TITLE>A Simple ADO Search</TITLE></HEAD>
<H3>Here are the results of your search:</H3>
SQL Query is: <%= strSQL %><P>
<TABLE BORDER="0">
 <TR>
  <TH ALIGN="LEFT">Filename</TH><TH ALIGN="RIGHT">Size</TH>
 </TR>

<% Do While Not objRS.EOF %>

 <TR>
  <TD><%= objRS("Filename") %>  </TD>
  <TD ALIGN="RIGHT"><%= objRS("size") %></TD>
 </TR>

<% objRS.MoveNext %>
<% Loop %>
```

```
      </TABLE>
      </BODY>
      </HTML>

      <% End If %>
      <% Set objRS = Nothing %>
      <% objConnection.Close %>
      <% set objConnection = Nothing %>
```

And here's the result it produces with our search for 'wrox':

A Paged Result Set Example

So far we've looked at the discrete pieces of an ADO query, including how to create a **Connection** object, how to use the **Connection** to execute a query, and how to iterate through the records in a **Recordset**. As yet, though, we haven't looked at an integrated sample.

The sample that follows is intended to illustrate how to use the **Connection** and **Recordset** objects to execute a query and produce a result set that spans across multiple pages. For an example that illustrates the same effect using the **Query** and **Utility** objects, see the samples that accompany the IIS.

The HTML Form for the Pages Exaple

Here's the HTML page for our example, **ado_sample.htm**:

Here's the HTML source of the Paged ADO search page, containing a **<FORM>** on which the query will be based:

```
<HTML>
<HEAD><TITLE>Paged ADO Search Sample</TITLE></HEAD>
<BODY>
<H2>Paged ADO Search Sample</H2>
<P>This sample illustrates how to execute a query against
Index Server using ADO and return the results as separate pages.</P>

<FORM method="POST" action="ado_sample.asp">
 <TABLE border="0" width="100%">
  <TR>
   <TD width="15%">Field:</TD>
   <TD width="85%"><P>
    <SELECT name="Where" size="1">
     <OPTION selected value="Content">Characterization</OPTION>
     <OPTION value="Create">Created</OPTION>
     <OPTION value="DocAuthor">Document Author</OPTION>
     <OPTION value="Directory">Directory</OPTION>
     <OPTION value="FileName">Filename</OPTION>
     <OPTION value="Path">Filepath</OPTION>
     <OPTION value="Size">Size</OPTION>
     <OPTION value="vPath">Virtual Path</OPTION>
    </SELECT></P>
   </TD>
  </TR>
  <TR>
```

```
   <TD width="15%">Operator</TD>
   <TD width="85%">
    <SELECT name="Operator" size="1">
     <OPTION value="=">=</OPTION>
     <OPTION value="&gt;">&gt;</OPTION>
     <OPTION value="&lt;">&lt;</OPTION>
     <OPTION value="!=">!=</OPTION>
     <OPTION value="&lt;=">&lt;=</OPTION>
     <option value="&gt;=">&gt;=</OPTION>
    </SELECT>
   </TD>
  </TR>
  <TR>
   <TD width="15%">Value:</TD>
   <TD width="85%"><input type="text" name="Criteria" size="41"></TD>
  </TR>
 </TABLE>

 <TABLE border="0" width="100%">
  <TR>
   <TD width="21%">Scope:</TD>
   <TD width="79%"><input type="text" name="Scope" size="37"></TD>
  </TR>
  <TR>
   <TD width="21%">Search Type:</TD>
   <TD width="79%"><input type="radio" value="Shallow" checked name="Depth">Shallow</
TD>
  </TR>
  <TR>
   <TD width="21%"></TD>
   <TD width="79%"><input type="radio" value="Deep" name="Depth">Deep</TD>
  </TR>
 </TABLE>

 <TABLE border="0">
  <TR>
   <TD align="center"><input type="submit" value="Execute Query" name="Action"></TD>
   <TD align="center"><input type="reset" value="Reset" name="Action"></TD>
  </TR>
 </TABLE>
 </FORM>
 </BODY>
 </HTML>
```

The ASP File for the Paged Example

The page to which the **<FORM>** in the HTML file we just looked at is posted is somewhat complex. We'll go through it step by step. The first part of the target page defines a few ADO constants required by our code that will call the **Recordset** object's **Open** method later in the page:

```
<%
Const adOpenKeyset = 1
Const adLockReadOnly = 1
Dim strQuery    'to hold our query string
...
```

Next, we determine whether the user clicked the "New Query" button. You won't find this button anywhere in the HTML page we looked at earlier. That's because we define it later within *this* page. After the HTML page above posts its data to this page, the user will get back a page that contains a "New Query" button. A click of this button will cause this page to post to *itself*. And when they do finally get here from clicking the "New Query" button, we simply redirect them to the original HTML page:

```
...
If Request("Action") = "New Query" Then
   Response.Redirect("ado_sample.htm")
   Response.End
End If
...
```

Building the SQL Query

Otherwise, we can proceed to build a query that reflects what the user entered into the HTML file. This input can come from one of two places: the .HTM file, or this file itself. This file takes the form fields in the .HTM file and reproduces them as a group of hidden fields. This ensures that, regardless of whether we're on the first or last page of our result set, we'll always be able to reconstitute the query with which the search originated. We've included a function called **BuildQuery()** (defined at the end of our ASP), which parses user input into an SQL query. Here's the code of that function:

```
<SCRIPT LANGUAGE=VBScript RUNAT=Server>
Function BuildQuery()
  SQL = "SELECT Filename, Size, Vpath, Path, Write, Characterization FROM "
  If Request("Scope") = "" Then
    SQL = SQL & "SCOPE() "
  Else
    SQL = SQL & "SCOPE('"
    If Request("Depth") = "Shallow" Then
      SQL = SQL & "SHALLOW TRAVERSAL OF " & """" & Request("Scope")
      SQL = SQL & """" & "'" & ")"
    Else
      SQL = SQL & "DEEP TRAVERSAL OF " & """" & Request("Scope")
      SQL = SQL & """" & "'" & ")"
    End If
  End if
  If Request("WHERE") = "Content" Then
    SQL = SQL & " WHERE CONTAINS(" & "'" & Request("Criteria") & "'" & ") > 0"
    BuildQuery = SQL
  ElseIf Request("WHERE") = "Size" Then
    SQL = SQL & " WHERE " & Request("Where") & Request("Operator")
    SQL = SQL & Request("Criteria")
    BuildQuery = SQL
  Else
    SQL = SQL & " WHERE " & Request("Where") & Request("Operator")
    SQL = SQL & " '" & Request("Criteria") & "'"
    BuildQuery = SQL
  End If
End Function
</SCRIPT>
```

Back in the main body of the page, our code can use this function, and check whether it was successful:

```
...
'Build up the query string
strQuery = BuildQuery()
If strQuery = "" Then
  Response.Redirect("ado_sample.htm")
  Response.End
End If
...
```

Opening the Connection to Index Server

If we successfully built a query, it's time to create a **Connection** object, and to execute the query against that **Connection** using the **Recordset** object's **Open** method:

```
...
'Create a connection object to execute the query
Set objConn = Server.CreateObject("ADODB.Connection")
objConn.ConnectionString = "provider=msidxs"
objConn.Open
Set objRS = Server.CreateObject("ADODB.RecordSet")
objRS.Open Query, objConn, adOpenKeyset,adLockReadOnly
If objRS.EOF Then
  Response.Write("No records found!")
  Set objRS = Nothing
  objConn.Close
  Set objConn = Nothing
  Response.End
End If
...
```

If the **Recordset** we get back is not empty, the next step is to initialize the **Recordset** object's **PageSize** property. This essentially dictates that only five records from this **Recordset** can be examined at a time. When you reach the fifth record, the **Recordset**'s **EOF** property will evaluate to **True**.

The Paging Mechanism

And here's where things get tricky, because this is where the paging mechanism comes into play. In the ASP, we determine whether there exists, in the page that posted to this one, a **Request** field named **Scroll**. If it does not exist, we can safely conclude that the user posted to this page from our HTML file, and that we should begin with Page 1 of our query. If such a field does exist, however, it means that this page posted to itself—and that we're in the middle of our search results. You'll see where it is defined later in our page.

So we use the value of **Scroll** to keep track of our position in the query results set. Later in the page we'll define buttons named **Scroll**, which we'll initialize to contain the word "Page" followed by a number that indicates which page we're on. Identifying that page is just a matter of using the **Mid** function to parse the value of **Scroll**:

```
...
'Set the page number - each page holds five records
objRS.PageSize = 5
Scroll = Request("Scroll")
If Scroll <> "" Then
  Page = mid(Scroll, 5)
  If Page < 1 Then Page = 1
```

```
  Else
    Page = 1
  End If
  objRS.AbsolutePage = Page
  %>
  ...
```

Having determined what page we're on, the last line of the code above sets the **Recordset** object's **AbsolutePage** property to contain that page number value. When we set this property, we're effectively instructing the **Recordset** as to where to begin counting records in the **Recordset**. It does this by multiplying the value of **AbsolutePage** by the value of **PageSize** was previously set.

The HTML Part of the Page

Now, it's time to fire a page at the user. This is the HTML that creates the visible part, which consists primarily of a table displaying the search results:

```
  ...
  <HTML>
  <HEAD><TITLE>Paged ADO Example</TITLE></HEAD>
  <BODY>
  <H3>Your query returned the following results:</H3>
  <TABLE border="0" width="100%" height="66">

  <% RowCount = objRS.PageSize %>
  <% Do While Not objRS.EOF And RowCount > 0 %>

   <TR>
    <TD width="20%" align="right"><B>Virtual Path:</B></TD>
    <TD width="80%"><%= objRS("vPath")%></TD>
   </TR>
   <TR>
    <TD width="20%" align="right"><b><strong>Physical Path:</B></TD>
    <TD width="80%"><%= objRS("Path")%></TD>
   </TR>
   <TR>
    <TD width="20%" align="right"><B><strong>Filename:</B></TD>
    <TD width="80%"><%= objRS("Filename")%></TD>
   </TR>
   <TR>
    <TD width="20%" align="right"><B><strong>Size:</B></TD>
    <TD width="80%"><%= objRS("Size") & " bytes"%></TD>
   </TR>
   <TR>
    <TD width="20%" align="right"><B><strong>Last Modified:</B></tD>
    <TD width="80%"><%= objRS("Write")%></TD>
   </TR>
   <TR>
    <TD width="20%" align="right"><B><strong>Excerpt:</B></TD>
    <TD width="80%"><%= objRS("Characterization")%></TD>
   </TR>

  <% RowCount = RowCount - 1 %>
  <% objRS.MoveNext %>
  <% Loop %>
```

```
    </TABLE>

    <% Set objRS = Nothing %>
    <% objConn.Close %>
    <% Set objConn = Nothing %>
```

Before we go on, let's just reinforce what you just read. First, within a **Do While** loop, we initialized a **RowCount** variable to the **Recordset**'s **PageSize** property, and with each iteration through the **Recordset**, we decremented this variable. The sole purpose of doing this is so that we know whether we've reached the end of our scrolling results. Think of it this way: given that **RowCount** is originally initialized to the **Recordset**'s **PageSize**, if we run out of data before **RowCount** reaches **0** that means we've reached the end, not just of one of the **Recordset**'s pages, but the end of the entire **Recordset** itself.

Inserting Next and Previous Page Buttons

Now, notice how we use the value of **RowCount** below. If the **Page** variable is greater than **1**, we conclude we need a "previous page" button. If **RowCount** is equal to zero, we conclude that we haven't reached the end of our **Recordset**, and that we need a "next page" button. Whether there's a "next page" button, a "previous page" button or both, we give these buttons the name **Scroll**, and we assign a value to them. The value consists of the word "Page", followed by the number that designates the previous or next page, respectively. When the user clicks one of these buttons to post this page to itself we parse the value of **Scroll** (as we saw above) to determine where we are in the **Recordset**, and to determine what the new value of these buttons should be:

```
...
<FORM METHOD="POST" ACTION="ADO_SAMPLE.ASP">
<INPUT TYPE="SUBMIT" NAME="ACTION" VALUE="New Query">
<INPUT TYPE="HIDDEN" NAME="Scope" VALUE="<%=Request("Scope")%>">
<INPUT TYPE="HIDDEN" NAME="Depth" VALUE="<%=Request("Depth")%>">
<INPUT TYPE="HIDDEN" NAME="Criteria" VALUE="<%=Request("Criteria")%>">
<INPUT TYPE="HIDDEN" NAME="Operator" VALUE="<%=Request("Operator")%>">
<INPUT TYPE="HIDDEN" NAME="Where" VALUE="<%=Request("Where")%>">

<% If Page > 1 Then %>
  <INPUT TYPE="SUBMIT" NAME="Scroll" VALUE="<%="Page " & Page - 1 %>">
<% End If %>
<% If RowCount = 0 Then %>
  <INPUT TYPE="SUBMIT" NAME="Scroll" VALUE="<%="Page " & Page + 1 %>">
<% End If %>

</FORM>
</BODY>
</HTML>
```

The Result—Paging In Action

Here's the results of the page you see above in action. With the values for the query we entered into the HTML form page earlier in this section, we get the following results:

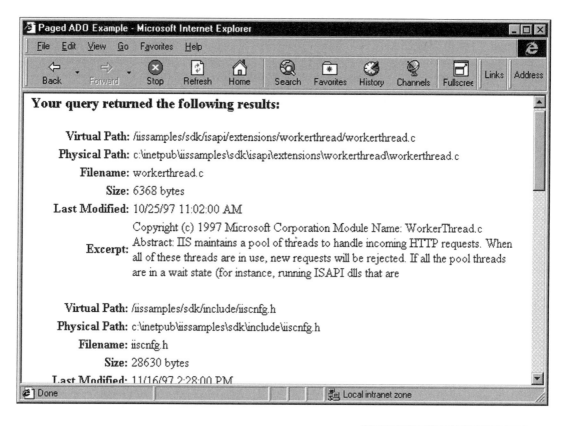

At the bottom of this page are two buttons—the "New Query" button we mentioned earlier, and the "next page" button:

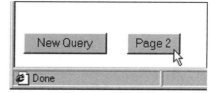

Clicking the "Page 2" button displays the next five matching records, then adds both "next page" and "previous page" buttons:

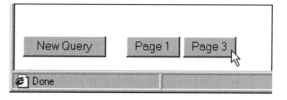

Finally, clicking the "Page 3" button takes us to the end of the recordset, and only the "New Query" and "Page 2" buttons are shown. Clicking the "New Query" page button at any point simply takes us back to the original HTML query page:

Passing Query Strings Via HTML Controls

One final note: You may wonder why we store the elements of our query as distinct hidden HTML field controls in the page, instead of generating the appropriate SQL statement once and then passing the entire SQL statement in a hidden field from page to page. The answer lies in the nature of HTML and SQL.

When you design SQL queries to be executed against Index Server, they're likely to contain a large and varied combination of single and double quotation marks, as well as parameters. When you store such a statement in a hidden field, the browser often doesn't know what to make of the use of quotation marks in the statement. Consequently, you're likely to end up with a stray bracket or quotation mark displayed on your page.

Summary

In this chapter, we've briefly examined Index Server, a powerful component of Internet Information Server on Windows NT Server. We've reviewed the various ways in which we can use Index Server to incorporate sophisticated search capabilities into our web sites.

The main things we've covered in this chapter are:

 An overview of Index Server. In this section, we examined the Index Server architecture and reviewed some of its major capabilities, including the kinds of documents it stores, the kinds of information it indexes, and the kinds of queries we can perform.

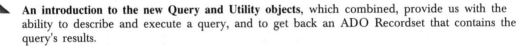 **An introduction to static querying.** In this section, we looked at how we can combine Internet Data Query (IDQ), HTML, and HTX files to perform fast and easily configured searches without writing code.

An introduction to the new Query and Utility objects, which combined, provide us with the ability to describe and execute a query, and to get back an ADO Recordset that contains the query's results.

An overview of how to use the Active Data Objects (first introduced in Chapter 7) to query the Index Server just as we would query any other database.

The code samples in this chapter are designed to accomplish two objectives. First, they're intended to illustrate concepts (such as **scope**) that are not covered intensively in the samples included with the Index Server. Second, they're intended to be simpler that those included with the Index Server. Sometimes, this simplicity is achieved at the expense of capabilities you're likely to want to build into your site. These capabilities include the following:

 The ability to define your own searchable document properties. In addition to using the **write**, **content**, **filename**, and other document properties that we've discussed, you can define new properties. We purposely ignored this subject in view of the small number of developers that are likely to need to do this.

The ability to build 'paging' into search pages that use the **Query** and **Utility** objects. We intentionally used a non-paging sample here. Building multi-page capabilities into these samples is a project of its own, though the samples included with the Index Server do illustrate this capability in more detail.

You can access the Index Server samples from the Windows NT Option Pack option on the Start menu, or by opening them directly in your browser. If you accepted the default directories when installing the Option Pack, you can get to the Index Server samples from: `http://localhost/IISamples/` `ISSamples/Default.htm`.

This chapter finishes our discussion of new topics. In the final two chapters we'll be looking at two topics that it's easy to forget about in the flush of new development that occurs with an exciting language like Active Server Pages. In the final chapter we look at how we can use existing 'legacy' components and sub-components to build Active Server Components that we can use in ASP. In the next chapter, however, we tackle the more mundane task of browser compatibility. This is addessed through a case study that attempts to provide the best results on all kinds of different browsers.

A Case Study in Compatibility

We've covered a lot of techniques and a lot of technology so far in this book. It's very easy by now to think that the whole world revolves around the amazing things that you can achieve server-side with Active Server Pages. However, as you'll be only too aware, things are not getting any easier on the client-side. The recent release of HTML 4.0 and the two version 4.0 browsers from Netscape and Microsoft have resulted in a complete mess of compatibility issues. This adds to the problems that already existed between different browser types and versions.

In fact you might think of server-side programming as being a 'positive' activity. You should know that your version of Active Server Pages supports the **Response.Flush** method, and that your server has a component called **Acme.DoSomethingUseful** installed that provides a **SoDoItNow()** method. As long as your scripts contain no errors, everything will work fine.

On the client, programming can best be regarded as an optimistic activity. If you are serving pages anonymously over the Web, you've got no idea what browser or other application is going to request a document. You've got even less idea of what features that browser or application might support–or even which version of HTML it is compatible with.

In this chapter, we're going to look at a Web-based information application that is designed to offer optimal performance on all kinds of client systems. The issues we'll cover are:

- ▲ Considering what minimum features our application will demand
- ▲ Knowing what features the client can support
- ▲ Using client-side HTML elements to optimize performance and compatibility
- ▲ Recognizing the formatting issues between different browsers
- ▲ Accessing data, and providing it in the best format for all clients

We've chosen an actual live application on the Wrox web site, the Wrox Ultimate HTML Reference Database to demonstrate the problems of compatibility. This provides comprehensive information on the elements and attributes supported by a range of browsers and HTML versions.

Why Worry About Compatibility?

As an example of how the techniques of programming on the server and the client differ, consider the situation where your company is in the business of manufacturing car tires. The phone rings and a customer simply says 'Hi, send me a set of tires for my sports car please', then puts the phone down. OK, so you can probably assume that they'll need four tires, but what size, which tread pattern, and what about the speed rating?

When your Web server receives a request for a page from somewhere out there on the 'Net, this is very much the situation you have to cope with. The browser says to your server 'Hey, I've got this user who wants to see the page **wonderful.html** that's on your site, and by the way I'm **AcmeBrowse/ 7(compatible; MSIE3.0)**'. Then it, too, effectively puts the phone down.

The Information Provided by the Browser

So, the browser doesn't really say much about what kind of capabilities it has. It may provide the client's screen resolution, and will probably tell your server the IP address it's using. The only really useful item of information here, however, is the browser version string. This is referred to as the **User Agent** property, and is made available to ASP through the **Request.ServerVariables** collection:

```
strUserAgent = Request.ServerVariables("HTTP_USER_AGENT")
```

The Browser Capabilities Component

You may recognize the value of this property from the discussion in Chapter 6 of the Browser Capabilities component that is supplied with Active Server Pages. Basically, this component looks up the value of the **HTTP_USER_AGENT** sent from the browser in a special text file on the server, and from that exposes a range of properties that tell you whether the browser supports client-side scripting, frames, ActiveX controls, Java applets, etc.

This is an ideal way to cope with the common browsers (and many of the less common ones), but does require some effort on your behalf. It's not foolproof either, but depends on you keeping the text file that describes each browser up to date. On top of that, it means that the server has to instantiate the control and use it each time.

Using Browser-Specific Pages

Once we know exactly what features a browser supports, we can build pages aimed directly at that particular mix of features. This is a great trick where you want to offer interactive pages using Dynamic HTML, or take advantage of the special features of a particular browser or application. You can redirect users to a page designed to get the most out of their browser. Of course, this makes the job of building and maintaining your site a lot more time consuming.

Letting the Client Decide

An alternative is to actually let the *client* application decide what to display to the user. This means that we have a much simpler task in preparing the pages at our end, because we don't have to supply different versions of them to different browsers. In some ways, we're looking to provide the lowest common denominator, and add a little spice where possible without making the pages browser-version specific.

While this may appear to be very limiting, take a look at the final application. You can run it yourself from **http://rapid.wrox.co.uk/html4db**

This application provides plenty of user control, and is widely compatible across a range of browsers. It's driven by Active Server Pages, but includes extra features such as client-side scripting, which allow the newer browsers to provide the user with a more interactive environment.

The main thing is that it still works, and is usable, on older browsers. Those that don't support scripting at all will display extra controls for the user to carry out the tasks that a script-enabled browser does automatically. We'll look at this application in detail throughout the chapter as we consider the issues involved in maximizing compatibility for our pages.

Designing for Compatibility

Building applications to run 'out in the wild' on the Web means making sacrifices. As you've already seen, we can't expect anything except the simplest page to work properly on all the browsers or applications that might load it. There will be occasions where our page is requested by one of the specialist user agents that are designed for people with disabilities, such as those that convert the content into spoken output. There will also be times when it's displayed on a visual browser that has no graphical abilities at all.

This means that we need to decide early on about what minimum level features we'll expect the browser to support in order for our application to meet its purpose, and also think about how we provide graceful fallback to other browsers.

The Minimum Features We'll Expect

In most cases, decisions on which features to exploit in the browser fall into four categories:

- Scripting
- Frames
- Tables
- Formatting

These four categories are listed in 'reverse' order. In general, if a browser supports, say, frames–it will also support tables and the formatting techniques we'll be describing in this chapter. If it doesn't support tables, there's not much chance of it supporting scripting or frames either.

A Little History

To give you some broad basis for making a decision on each feature in the list above, the following sums up where each one was introduced into the major browsers and HTML versions:

	HTML	Navigator	Internet Explorer
Client-side scripting	Since version 3.2	Since version 2	Since version 3
Frames support	New in 4.0	Since version 2	Since version 3
Tables support	Since version 3.2	Since version 2	Since version 2
Direct formatting	New in 4.0	Since version 2	Since version 2

As you'll see from the table, the features tend to be widely supported in browsers before their adoption into the HTML standards. But it's the browser that reads your page, not the HTML standard, so you can reasonably safely assume that it's OK to use tables and direct formatting (such as with the **<FONT>** element) in all your pages. Older browsers may not recognize the more esoteric attributes, but will create tables and the majority of the formatting you require.

> *The one possible discrepancy is that Navigator 2 will not recognize the* **FACE** *attribute for the* **<FONT>** *element–you can control the size and color but not the font face itself.*

Frames have less overall support, they were late appearing in Internet Explorer. However, the wide adoption of Internet Explorer 3 over the rather poor version 2 means that, in general, frames are a safe bet. However, they *are* new in HTML 4.0. Frames have never been part of the HTML standards up until 1997, and so the older and non-graphical browsers are less likely to support them.

Scripting is even more difficult, because of the different languages available. Internet Explorer supports VBScript, but little else does (without a proprietary plugin). However, both Internet Explorer and Navigator support JavaScript-syntax languages–Microsoft's version is called JScript. Scripting support is less common in the non-graphical browsers and specialist applications.

Using Client-side Scripting

So, which features will we assume to be present on the client for our application? We really need to do some work in script code to provide the maximum usability for our application, but we *must* ensure that it will work as well as possible on non-script enabled browsers as well. Through some careful design and planning, this is quite possible to achieve. For example, we can use script to automatically submit a form in response to an event such as selecting a value in a list. At the same time, we can display a normal **SUBMIT** button so that the user can click this to submit the form if their browser doesn't support scripting. You'll see this done later on.

Of course, as we build more complex applications, the requirements for client-side scripting tend to increase. It provides a huge advantage over repeatedly submitting the form to the server for minor functions, such as checking that an email address is properly formatted. It may be that some functions just have to be allowed to gracefully degrade on older browsers. You'll see an example in our application, where direct navigation from one particular page to another can only be done on a JavaScript-enabled browser.

Using Frames

The use of frames prompts another difficult decision. Although the HTML standards have only just recognized them, the two most popular browsers have supported them for some time. They also tend to be popular (at least with HTML authors) because they can provide such a huge boost in both appearance and usability. The 'navigation bar' frame down the left-hand side of the window is becoming ubiquitous with modern Web page design techniques.

In our case, we chose to use frames because we want to implement a 'control panel' for users. We know that our pages may be quite long when viewers select and display information about an element with a lot of attributes. If we placed the controls at the bottom of the page they would have to keep scrolling down. At the top of the page, our application just looks like a Web search engine.

Lack of support for frames is most likely to be a problem on non-graphical browsers and specialist applications. Unlike script code, which is invisible to the user, frames are at the core of the page design. Your decision on whether to use them might be different to ours, but–if you do use them–be sure to provide graceful fallback for users whose browsers don't support them. Again, you'll see more later.

Using Tables

Having decided to use frames, we can reasonably safely assume that tables will be OK. HTML recognized them first in version 3.2, but both mainline graphical browsers already supported them in previous versions.

Tables provide a quick, easy, and quite controllable environment for laying out structured information such as we intend to provide. Managing without them would be less easy, probably involving use of list elements like **<UL>** and **<DL>**. One thing you might like to be sure of, however, is that you avoid the short-hand technique of omitting the closing tags in table cells and rows. This can cause formatting problems in, for example, Navigator:

```
<TABLE>
  <TR>
    <TD>
      cell content here
    </TD> <!-- optional, but safer if always included -->
  </TR>   <!-- optional, but safer if always included -->
</TABLE>
```

Formatting Issues

HTML as a language was designed to avoid direct formatting of page content. The original plan was that you would use just text (and possibly images) to convey technical information. Formatting was limited to the use of tags like **<EM>** for emphasizing a point, or **<DL>** to create a definition list. As the language developed, browser manufacturers added lots of new tags that control formatting and presentation of information, such as **<FONT>**, **<SMALL>**, **<BLINK>**, **<MARQUEE>**, etc.

We're aiming to achieve maximum compatibility from a single set of pages, so we use the **<FONT>** element to provide all the basic formatting we need, plus the standard and almost universally supported **<B>** and **<I>** elements. If the browser doesn't recognize **<FONT>**, the worst that will happen is that all the text will appear in the same default font and size. Not ideal, but acceptable.

In HTML 4.0, however, the move is towards a more structured approach to page design—using absolute positioning and style sheets to provide a standardized way to control layout and presentation. Only the most recent browsers support this approach, and if we are looking for the broadest levels of compatibility we need to avoid most of the exciting new techniques such as Dynamic HTML. Because of the major changes between the most recent browsers and early ones, and even between different manufacturer's versions of Dynamic HTML, we have no option but to create different pages for each browser if we want to make the best of all of them.

And it's not the tags that each browser supports which are important. Different browsers can treat the same tag in different ways. For example, the **<PRE>** element produces text in a mono-spaced font and preserves formatting, so that carriage returns and multiple spaces are not lost as they are in normal HTML rendering. But, as we discovered in the building of this application, using **<PRE>** within a table produces unpredictable results. You'll see more of this later.

Client-side Decision Making

We can allow the browser itself to make decisions on how our pages appear. We want them to gracefully degrade on browsers that don't support all the features we assume to be present. To achieve this successfully, the browser needs a little help from us. For example, we can use the **<NOSCRIPT>** element to provide alternative content for browsers that don't support scripting, and the **<NOFRAMES>** element for those that don't support frames.

Using the <NOSCRIPT> Element

Of these two, we've made particular use of **<NOSCRIPT>** to control the appearance of a **SUBMIT** button. The theory is simple enough:

```
<FORM ACTION="http://myserver.com/scripts/doit.asp" METHOD="POST">
 <INPUT TYPE=CHECKBOX NAME="MyCheck" ONCLICK="someScriptCode()">
 <NOSCRIPT>
  <INPUT TYPE=SUBMIT VALUE="Do It Now">
 </NOSCRIPT>
 </FORM>
```

Browsers that support scripting should also support the **<NOSCRIPT>** element, and ignore its content. This means that they won't display the **SUBMIT** button, but will run the code specified in the **ONCLICK** attribute of the checkbox **<INPUT>** tag when the user clicks on the checkbox. This code can carry out any tasks required, then submit the form for processing by calling its **submit()** method.

Browsers that don't support scripting won't know about **<NOSCRIPT>** either, so they will ignore the tags and display the content. The user gets a **SUBMIT** button, which is handy because clicking the checkbox will have no effect (other than changing its value). Their browser won't recognize the **ONCLICK** attribute either, so will ignore the script code it contains.

Using Images and Colors

On a more basic level, we also need to cover ourselves for browsers that don't display images for any reason, or don't recognize standard color names. Every image should have an **ALT** attribute included in its tag, and this should impart at least the minimum level of information about what the image contains. For example, we use graphics in our application to indicate which browser versions support each element and attribute. For each one, the **ALT** text provides both text information while the image loads (or if it fails to load), and a description for use in non-visual applications:

```
<IMG SRC="db_images/h4.gif" ALT="HTML 4.0">
<IMG SRC="db_images/h4d.gif" ALT="HTML 4.0 DEPRECATED">
```

Some older browsers will not recognize color names either, or at least not the less popular ones. Rather than using:

```
<BODY BGCOLOR="lavenderblush">
```

you'll get a more universal level of support with:

```
<BODY BGCOLOR="#FFF0F5">
```

You can find the equivalent color values using a graphics program such as PaintShop Pro or Windows own Paint application. Define a custom color then read off the values in the Custom Color dialog, and convert them into hexadecimal—you can use the Windows Calculator applet for this.

General Support for Esoteric Elements

Because browsers will ignore any elements or element attributes that they don't recognize, your pages should still work *reasonably* well in most browsers. For example, if you use the **<BLINK>** element, you'll only annoy Navigator users. Internet Explorer users will just see the content as normal static text. Of course, Navigator users will be spared the effort of reading the oscillating text in your **<MARQUEE>** elements, as it scrolls from side to side in Internet Explorer only.

The situation is the same with inserted objects, or inclusions. You've more chance of a browser recognizing an **<APPLET>** element and a Java applet, than an ActiveX control in an **<OBJECT>** element. Again, you can tell the user what went wrong with the page by including alternative content within the **<APPLET>** or **<OBJECT>** element, but outside any **<PARAM>** elements:

```
<OBJECT NAME="MyControl" CLASSID="...">
 <PARAM NAME="param1" VALUE="value1">
 There should be an ActiveX control here. If you see this text
 instead, your browser can't display the object. Sorry...
</OBJECT>
```

Even though a browser may support a particular element, it might not recognize all the attributes of that element that you presume it will. For example, the **<TABLE>** element provides a **WIDTH** attribute, to let you specify the overall width of the table. This is supported as far back as version 2 by Navigator, but only from version 3 onwards in Internet Explorer.

Also, try not to depend on the use of the more esoteric attributes (such as **BORDERCOLORDARK** in Internet Explorer to change the inner border of a 3D table). Instead, look to find other ways of achieving the same end. You'll see some more examples of this in the rest of the chapter.

The Ultimate HTML Database

The Wrox Ultimate HTML Reference Database arose from the problems we've been discussing so far in this chapter. It can be very time consuming trying to find precise and comprehensive information on which browsers support which elements and attributes. We put together a database of compatibility for the book Instant HTML Programmer's Reference HTML 4.0 Edition ISBN 1-861001-56-8, and a limited version of this (containing only a few elements) is available for use by anyone interested in authoring for the Web. The full version can be run directly from our Web site at **http://rapid.wrox.co.uk/html4db/**.

The online application provides the following basic features:

- ▲ A listing of all elements used in HTML, with a brief description of each one.

- ▲ A listing of all the possible attributes for a selected element with descriptions, plus–where appropriate–a list of the possible values and the equivalent Cascading Style Sheets property.

- ▲ The ability to filter the list to show only elements and/or attributes for a particular make of browser, or the various W3C standards.

- ▲ The ability to display the results as a compact list, without the descriptions and values.

- ▲ A series of pages showing the relationships between the elements, and the way they can be used.

This is quite a task list, but is well within the capabilities of Active Server Pages. Using ASP, we can collect the data from our database on the server, and format it in various ways to present it to the end user. Here's the result, and in the rest of the chapter we'll show you (in outline) how it's achieved.

The Wrox Ultimate HTML Database - Microsoft Internet Explorer

File   Edit   View   Go   Favorites   Help

Back   Forward   Stop   Refresh   Home   Search   Favorites   Print   Font   Mail   Address   Links

WROX
WROX PRESS
The Ultimate HTML Reference Database

<TD> 4.0 3.2 N4 N3 N2 IE4 IE3   See: Tables

Specifies a cell in a table.

<event-name> 4.0 IE4

Description: Inline script code or the name of a script routine, executed when the specified event occurs.

Values: <event_name>=script_code

ABBR 4.0

Description: A shortened or abbreviated version of the contents for use where space is limited.

Values: ABBR=string

ALIGN 4.0 3.2 N4 N3 N2 IE4 IE3 IE2

Description: Specifies how the cell contents are to be aligned.

Values: ALIGN=CENTER | LEFT | RIGHT | JUSTIFY | CHAR

CSS Equiv: { text-align: left | right | center | justify}

AXIS 4.0

Description: Defines the abbreviated name for a header cell. The default if omitted is its content.

HTML Element: <TD>

Listing style:
◉ Detailed
○ Compact

☑ Include HTML
☑ Include Navigator
☑ Include MSIE

Designing the Application

One of the neat tricks with ASP is to create a single page that displays entirely different content depending on the values passed to the server with the page request. This is how our main 'results' page (`result.asp`) works. Each time the user makes a selection in the 'control panel' frame, the page is referenced with the values of all the controls in that frame. The main one we're interested in is the selection made in the list of element names. Here's the 'control panel', with an element being selected:

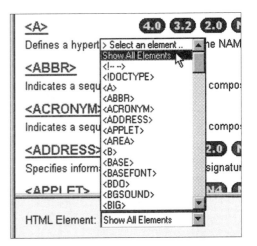

The value of the user's selection is taken from the **VALUE** attribute of the chosen **<OPTION>** tag. In the case of the first option, this is **"none"** and the second is **"showall"**. Otherwise it's the name of the element–excluding the '**<**' and '**>**' characters. This value is passed to **result.asp**:

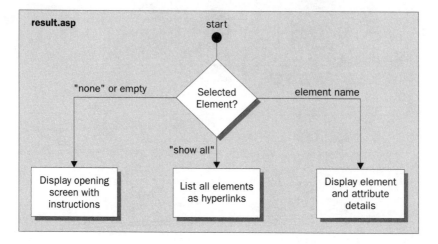

This means that when the page is first loaded as part of the frameset, rather than by the **ACTION** attribute of the **<FORM>** in the 'control panel' frame, it will display just the opening screen–because there are no values sent to it.

Listing All The Elements

If the user selects the Show All Elements option, we provide a listing of all the elements from the database, filtering it to meet the criteria they select for the browser or HTML version they are interested in.

The initial filtering of the element list is done by the ASP code that creates the recordset, using an appropriate SQL statement. You'll see this in more detail later. For the meantime this is the outline plan–notice how, for each element, we have to check which browser type options the user selected so that we only display the compatibility images for that browser type:

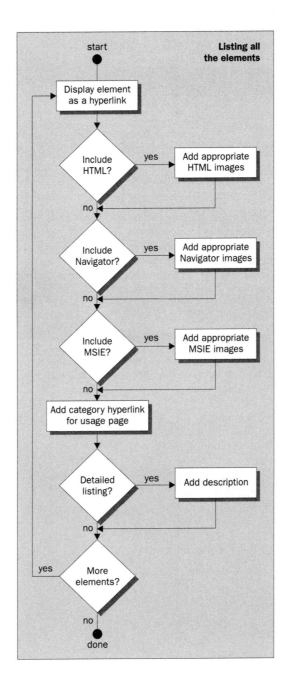

The Data Source

The database itself consists of just two tables, the **Elements** and **Attributes** tables. Each attribute record in the **Attributes** table holds a reference to a single element in the **Elements** table that supports it:

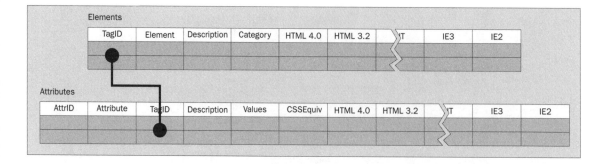

You'll notice that this design means there are multiple entries in the **Attributes** table for each attribute, where it is supported by more than one element. This isn't the most efficient way of storing all the information—it would be more efficient to have just one entry in the **Attributes** table for each attribute, and provide an intermediate table to link that attribute record to all the elements which support it. However, this would make the design of the application more complex, and make it impossible to individually tailor each attribute's values or description for a particular element.

Displaying an Element and its Attributes

When the user selects an individual element, we go through a similar process to that we did for all the elements earlier. This time, however, we do it once for the selected element, then repeatedly for each attribute it supports. This is the outline plan:

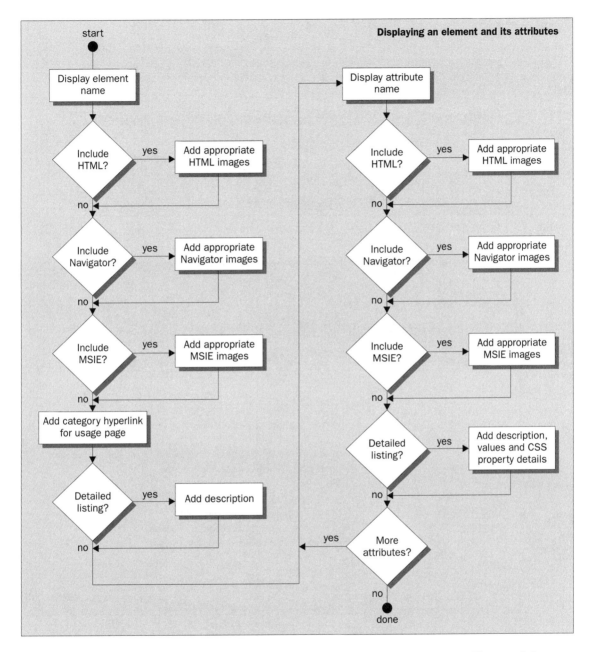

So you can see that there is quite of lot of decision-making going on in the ASP page. The joy of this is that the final output passed back to the client is just a list of the results as plain HTML. This will display correctly on any browser that meets our minimum feature requirement of supporting frames. As you'll see when we come to look at the code, we are insisting on frames as the minimum feature level for browsers that we will support with our application.

Displaying the Element Usage Pages

Displaying the 'usage' pages is probably the easiest part of the job. Each element in our database has an entry for the Category it belongs to. This category name is also the filename of the appropriate 'usage' page, excluding the `.asp` extension. Therefore, we only need to turn this into a hyperlink, and provide the 'usage' pages as separate files:

Implementing the Application

In this section of the chapter, we'll look at the various pages that make up the application in turn. We won't be going into full details about how each one works, because you'll have learned the techniques from the earlier chapters in this book. What interests us here is how we ensure that our design turns into reality, and how we maximize compatibility with as wide a range of browsers as possible along the way.

The Main Frameset Page

Our application consists of a frameset containing three frames, and this is the first page to be loaded, being named **Default.htm**. The top frame is a simple title page, the bottom one the 'control panel', and the main central one is where the results are displayed. The code for the frameset uses a **<NOFRAMES>** element to catch the browsers that don't support frames. If it made sense to display the 'results' page without a frameset, we could provide the user with a link here to load it. In our case it doesn't, because the whole application (as you'll see) depends on the 'control panel' being present.

```
<HTML>
<HEAD>
<TITLE>The Wrox Ultimate HTML Database</TITLE>
</HEAD>

<FRAMESET ROWS="60,*,70">
  <FRAME SCROLLING=NO SRC="title.htm" MARGINWIDTH=10 MARGINHEIGHT=0>
  <FRAME SRC="result.asp" NAME="winResult">
  <FRAME SCROLLING=NO SRC="select.asp" NAME="winSelect"
         MARGINWIDTH=10 MARGINHEIGHT=0>
</FRAMESET>

<NOFRAMES>
  Sorry, this application requires a browser that supports frames.
  You can download a suitable browser from various sources, including:<P>
  <A HREF="http://www.microsoft.com">http://www.microsoft.com</A><BR>
  <A HREF="http://www.netscape.com">http://www.netscape.com</A><BR>
  <A HREF="http://lynx.browser.org">http://lynx.browser.org</A>
</NOFRAMES>
</HTML>
```

Notice that we turn off scrolling for the top and bottom frames, but omit the customary **NORESIZE** attribute. If the user is displaying the page in a large font size, they might need to enlarge a frame to see all the content. This is particularly important for the lower 'control panel' frame. On the other hand, if they are short of screen real-estate, they might like to shrink the top 'title' frame to make more room for the results.

We also assign names to the 'title' and 'results' frames, because we're going to be using some client-side code to refer to them in our pages. In the **<NOFRAMES>** section, we make it clear that we expect frames support, and provide links to sites that suitable browsers can be obtained from.

Controlling Margin Width and Height

By default, the browser provides a margin of some 10 to 20 pixels around the actual content of a page when it renders it. For a 'busy' application like ours, this is wasted space. If you're a confirmed Internet Explorer user, you'll probably avoid this by setting the **TOPMARGIN** and **LEFTMARGIN** attributes in the opening **<BODY>** tag.

This isn't going to do much good in any other browser, however. Only Internet Explorer supports these attributes. Instead, in Navigator and now in version 4.0 of HTML, we can use the **MARGINWIDTH** and **MARGINHEIGHT** attributes of the **<FRAME>** tag to do the same. Internet Explorer supports only this from version 3 onwards, however. The easy answer, as we've done in our application, is to use both. We're covered then for browsers that support either method. We defined the **MARGINWIDTH** and **MARGINHEIGHT** in the frameset, and we add the **TOPMARGIN** attribute to the opening **<BODY>** tag:

```
<BODY BGCOLOR="#FFFFFF" TOPMARGIN=3>
```

The 'Control Panel' Page

Now we're getting into the core of the application. The lower frame page, **select.asp**, displays controls that allow the user to interact with our application. These are placed within a table to provide neat formatting. In this code segment, we've omitted some of the detail for the **<SELECT>** element contents:

```
<%@LANGUAGE="VBScript"%>
<% Response.Buffer = True %>
<HTML>
<HEAD>
</HEAD>
<BODY BGCOLOR="#FFFFC0" TOPMARGIN=8>
<% Response.Flush %>

<FORM ACTION="result.asp" NAME="frmSelect"
      TARGET="winResult" METHOD="POST">
<TABLE WIDTH=100%>
 <TR>
  <TD>
   <FONT FACE="Arial" SIZE=2>HTML Element:</FONT>
   <SELECT NAME=lstTagName
ONCHANGE="parent.status='Searching...';document.frmSelect.submit();">
    <OPTION VALUE="none">> Select an element ..
    <OPTION VALUE="showall">Show All Elements

    ... code for creating rest of options list goes here ...

    <OPTION VALUE="none">> More Information ..
   </SELECT>
  </TD>
  <TD>
   <NOSCRIPT>
   <INPUT TYPE="SUBMIT" VALUE="Go">
   </NOSCRIPT>
  </TD>
  <TD NOWRAP>
   <FONT FACE="Arial" SIZE=2> Listing style:<BR>
   <INPUT TYPE="RADIO" NAME=optDetail VALUE=0 CHECKED
ONCLICK="parent.status='Searching...';document.frmSelect.submit();">
    Detailed<BR>
   <INPUT TYPE="RADIO" NAME=optDetail VALUE=1
ONCLICK="parent.status='Searching...';document.frmSelect.submit();">
    Compact</B>
   </FONT>
  </TD>
  <TD NOWRAP>
```

```
        <FONT FACE="Arial" SIZE=2>
        <INPUT TYPE="CHECKBOX" NAME=chkHTML CHECKED
    ONCLICK="parent.status='Searching...';document.frmSelect.submit();">
        Include HTML<BR>
        <INPUT TYPE="CHECKBOX" NAME=chkNN CHECKED
    ONCLICK="parent.status='Searching...';document.frmSelect.submit();">
        Include Navigator<BR>
        <INPUT TYPE="CHECKBOX" NAME=chkMSIE CHECKED
    ONCLICK="parent.status='Searching...';document.frmSelect.submit();">
        Include MSIE
        </FONT>
      </TD>
    </TR>
  </TABLE>
  </FORM>
  </BODY>
  </HTML>
  <% Response.End %>
```

You'll see that we have placed the individual groups of controls into separate cells of the table, and used the **NOWRAP** attribute in some of the opening **<TD>** tags to provide finer control of the layout. If the browser has only minimal width available to display the page (such as on a VGA resolution screen), we force it to keep the cells containing the option buttons and checkboxes at the minimum width required–without wrapping the text under the controls, which looks untidy. However, we're happy for it to wrap the **<SELECT>** list underneath its caption if required. The browser will add a horizontal scroll bar to the window if the table is still too wide to be fully visible.

> *The **NOWRAP** attribute is supported in Navigator from version 2, Internet Explorer from version 3, and HTML from version 3.2–although it's deprecated in favor of style sheets for the future.*

We've also used the **<NOSCRIPT>** element to add a **SUBMIT** button that will only be visible in browsers that don't support scripting, as we described earlier.

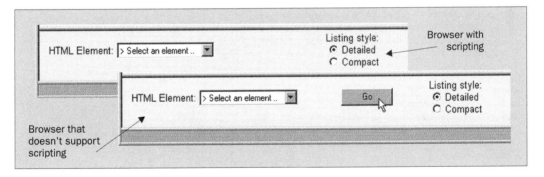

Client-side Script in the Control Panel Page

If our client can support script, they won't see the **SUBMIT** button. In order to submit the form when they make a selection, we use some 'vanilla' JavaScript code (which is supported by almost every script-enabled browser). JavaScript is available in various versions, and an organization called ECMA are working on a standardized version called ECMAScript for future release as part of the HTML standards. In the meantime, using the plainest syntax will ensure maximum compatibility.

To learn more about programming with JavaScript, look out for Instant JavaScript from Wrox Press, ISBN 1-861001-27-4

When a user makes *any* selection on the control panel, including the option buttons or check boxes, we want to submit the form to the server for processing. So, in all the controls on our page, we've added the **ONCLICK** or **ONCHANGE** attribute with the value:

```
ONCLICK="parent.status='Searching...';document.frmSelect.submit();">
```

This displays the message Searching... in the browser's status bar (to show something is happening) and submits the form to the address in the **ACTION** attribute of the **<FORM>** element–just as though a **SUBMIT** button had been clicked.

Creating the List of Elements

The missing part of the code above is concerned with creating the list of available elements. We added the first two entries and the last one to the list using normal HTML. The remainder are created using Active Server Pages code, by pulling the list of all elements directly from the **Elements** table in the database. Here's the code that achieves it:

```
...
<OPTION VALUE="none">> Select an element ..
<OPTION VALUE="showall">Show All Elements
<! get list of tags>
<%
On Error Resume Next
QUOT = Chr(34)
CRLF = Chr(13) & Chr(10)
Set oConn = Server.CreateObject("ADODB.Connection")
oConn.Open "data_source"
strSQL="SELECT Element FROM Elements ORDER BY Element;"
Set oRs = oConn.Execute(strSQL, lngRecs, 1) 'adCmdText
If (oRs.EOF) Or (Err.Number > 0) Then
  Response.Clear
  Response.Write "<FONT FACE=" & QUOT & "Arial" & QUOT _
    & "SIZE=3><B>Sorry, the database cannot be accessed " _
    & "at present.</B></FONT></BODY></HTML>"
  Response.Flush
  Response.End
End If
oRs.MoveFirst
Do While Not oRs.EOF
  txtElement = oRs.Fields("Element")
  Response.Write "<OPTION VALUE=" & QUOT & txtElement _
    & QUOT & ">&lt;" & txtElement & "&gt;" & CRLF
  oRs.MoveNext
Loop
oRs.Close
%>
<OPTION VALUE="none">> More Information ..
...
```

When the server processes this, it inserts the list of options we want into the output HTML stream. We added a carriage return to each one to make it look tidy in case our user decides to view the source of the page, but it's not actually necessary. Here's what the list looks like when it gets to the client:

```
...
<OPTION VALUE="none">> Select an element ..
<OPTION VALUE="showall">Show All Elements

<! get list of tags>
<OPTION VALUE="!-- -->&lt;!-- --&gt;
<OPTION VALUE="!DOCTYPE">&lt;!DOCTYPE&gt;
<OPTION VALUE="A">&lt;A&gt;
<OPTION VALUE="ABBR">&lt;ABBR&gt;
... etc ...
```

Coping with Database Errors

Like most things in life, computers (and especially databases) are not always 100% reliable. There may be times when we can't read data from our database due to server load or other problems. To take care of this, we've used a common technique in all our pages that access it. We also provide progressive rendering of the pages at the same time.

We turn on page buffering at the beginning of the page with:

```
<% Response.Buffer = True %>
```

This prevents the server sending any of the content to the client until we're ready. Then, once we've created a section of the page (such as the **<HEAD>** and opening **<BODY>**) we send it to the client with:

```
<% Response.Flush %>
```

Next, we turn off the default error handling, which prevents an error message being sent to the client if anything goes wrong:

```
<%
On Error Resume Next
...
```

Now, we create our connection to the database, and open it. If any part fails, the code continues running without producing an error. Before we start to use the data that we think we've got, we check to see if anything went wrong. If the value of **Err.Number** is greater that zero, or there are no records in our recordset, we need to stop here. Because we've buffered the page, we can clear any content that hasn't already been flushed, and create a message of our own. This is flushed to the client, and we prevent any further execution or delivery of the rest of the page:

```
...
If (oRs.EOF) Or (Err.Number > 0) Then
  Response.Clear
  Response.Write "<FONT FACE=" & QUOT & "Arial" & QUOT _
    & "SIZE=3><B>Sorry, the database cannot be accessed " _
    & "at present.</B></FONT></BODY></HTML>"
  Response.Flush
  Response.End
End If
...
```

The 'Results' Page

This is the page that really does all of the work in our application. We saw during the design stage how it provides three different formats, depending on the selection made in the control panel page. The first of these is a plain set of instructions about the application, the second is a listing of all the elements, and the third the listing of a single selected element with all its attributes.

This is achieved with a main code construct that looks in outline like this:

```
<HTML>
...
<%
txtTagName = Request("lstTagName")  'from <SELECT> list
If txtTagName = "none" Or txtTagName = "" Then
   'no element selected, display 'welcome' page
Else
  If txtTagName = "showall" Then
     'show list of all elements from database
  Else
     'show a single element and its attributes
  End If
End If
%>
...
<! display copyright and contact information >
...
</BODY>
</HTML>
```

The 'Welcome and Instructions' Page

The first part of the script creates the 'welcome' page. This is all basic HTML, with one exception. We want to promote our products to visitors (someone's got to pay the bills, after all), so we open a separate small browser window when they first hit our application, showing a few appropriate books. To prevent it appearing every time they load the page during one visit, we use a cookie to indicate that we've opened it once already. This is stored on their machine until they close their browser down.

This is the first section of the HTML that our application generates when the user displays the 'welcome and instructions' page:

```
<BODY BGCOLOR="#FFFFFF" TOPMARGIN=5 ONLOAD="CookieStuff()">
<SCRIPT LANGUAGE="JAVASCRIPT">
<!--
function CookieStuff()
{
  strCookie = document.cookie;
  if (strCookie.indexOf("SeenBooksPage=True") < 0)
  {
    document.cookie = "SeenBooksPage=True";
    window.open("bookinfo.htm","new_win",
                "resizable=yes,scrollbars=no,toolbar=no," +
                "location=no,directories=no,status=no," +
                "menubar=no,width=520,height=200,top=5,left=5")
  }
}
```

```
// -->
</SCRIPT>
...
```

This is client-side code (there's no **RUNAT=SERVER** attribute in the opening **<SCRIPT>** tag), so it is sent to the browser as it stands. It runs when the page is loaded, and checks for a cookie named **SeenBooksPage**. Only if it *isn't* present is the new window opened. While we can use ASP code and the **Request.Cookies** collection to examine cookies, we still need to run the **window.open** code on the client to create the new window. This way, the client does all the work instead.

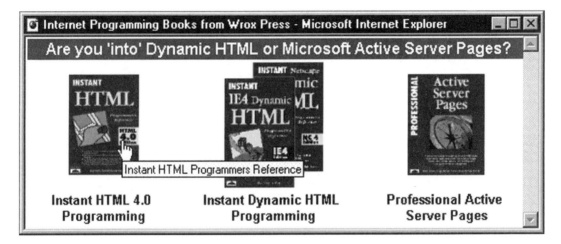

Processing the User's Input Choices

When the user selects either Show All Elements or a particular element, we need to fetch the details of that element or elements and present them within the 'results' page. The first step is to collect the values they submitted from the **<FORM>** in the 'control panel' page. In this case the **METHOD** is **"POST"**, so the values will appear in the **Request.Form** collection.

However, there is another situation that arises when the values are submitted on the URL, as part of the query string. This happens when they select an element within the list on the results page–as you'll see in a while–and in this case the values will appear in the **Request.QueryString** collection.

So, instead of examining the **Form** collection for values directly, we use the short-cut syntax of specifying just the **Request** object. This will search through its collection until a value is found. Because we know we'll only have values in *either* the **Form** or **QueryString** collection, there is no risk of confusion. The first line of this code also sets a Boolean variable named **blnElementList** to **True** if we are going to show all the elements–the **txtTagName** variable was set at the top of the page to the selection they made in the drop-down list:

```
...
If txtTagName = "showall" Then blnElementList = True
If Request("optDetail") = 0 Then blnDetailed = True
If Request("chkHTML") = "on" Then blnHTValues = True
If Request("chkNN") = "on" Then blnNNValues = True
If Request("chkMSIE") = "on" Then blnIEValues = True
```

```
If Not(blnHTValues OR blnNNValues OR blnIEValues) Then
    Response.Write "<FONT FACE=" & QUOT & "Arial" & QUOT _
      & "SIZE=3><B>You must select at least one compatibility " _
      & "type (W3C, Navigator or MSIE).</B></FONT></BODY></HTML>"
    Response.Flush
    Response.End
End If
...
```

The second section of the code above makes sure we have at least one browser version selected. If not there's no point in continuing because no records will match the criteria. As you can see, we've used the same technique to abort execution of the page as we did with the database connection earlier on.

Building an SQL Query String

Once we've got the values from the 'control panel' safely stored in variables, we can build up the SQL query that will extract the appropriate elements from the database. This is done with three strings— **strLimit** holds the **OR** clauses that will include only particular browser types, **strWhere** is the final criteria part of the SQL query, and **strSQL** is the complete query:

```
...
If (blnHTValues) Then
    strLimit = "(HTML20<>'N') OR (HTML32<>'N') OR (HTML40<>'N')"
End If

If (blnNNValues) Then
    If Len(strLimit) Then strLimit = strLimit & " OR "
    strLimit = strLimit & "(NAV2<>'N') OR (NAV3<>'N') OR (NAV4<>'N')"
End If

If (blnIEValues) Then
    If Len(strLimit) Then strLimit = strLimit & " OR "
    strLimit = strLimit & "(IE2<>'N') OR (IE3<>'N') OR (IE4<>'N')"
End If

If (blnElementList) Then
    strWhere = "WHERE (" & strLimit & ") ORDER By Element"
Else
    strWhere = "WHERE (Element='" & txtTagName & "')"
End If

strSQL="SELECT * FROM Elements " & strWhere & ";"
...
```

The result, when the user selects Show All Elements and only Internet Explorer (Include MSIE) is checked, is:

```
SELECT * FROM Elements WHERE ((IE2<>'N') OR (IE3<>'N') OR (IE4<>'N')) ORDER By
Element;
```

> *The nine fields in database that indicate whether a browser supports a particular element or attribute hold either 'N' (no), 'Y' (yes), or 'D' (deprecated).*

However, if the user selected the **<FONT>** element for example, **blnElementList** will be **False**, so the final query string will specify just this one element:

```
SELECT * FROM Elements WHERE (Element='FONT');
```

Fetching the Element Records

Now we can create our database connection, open the recordset with just the appropriate element(s) in it, check for errors, and get ready to loop through them. We save the **TagID** of the first element for use if this is a display of one particular element–ready for when we come to retrieve a list of its attributes:

```
...
Set oConn = Server.CreateObject("ADODB.Connection")
oConn.Open "data_source"
strSQL="SELECT * FROM Elements " & strWhere & ";"
Set oRs = oConn.Execute(strSQL, lngRecs, 1) 'adCmdText
If (oRs.EOF) Or (Err.Number > 0) Then
   Response.Write "<FONT FACE=" & QUOT & "Arial" & QUOT _
     & "SIZE=3><B>Sorry, the database cannot be accessed " _
     & "at present.</B></FONT></BODY></HTML>"
   Response.Flush
   Response.End
End If
oRs.MoveFirst
keyTagID = oRs.Fields("TagID") 'used in Attributes SQL query later
%>
...
```

Displaying the Elements

Now we can create a table and loop through the recordset. However, to make it easy for users to select an element in the case where we're listing all elements, we make each one a hyperlink. This is where our **QueryString** comes in, because we add all the current values we collected from the 'control panel' **<FORM>** to the **HREF** attribute, so that they're passed back to the page when it is loaded again. We also include an extra name/value pair: **Reset=Yes**. You'll see why in a while:

```
...
<TABLE BORDER=0>
<% Do While Not oRs.EOF %>
<TR>
<TD VALIGN="TOP">
<FONT FACE="Arial" SIZE=3><B>
<% If blnElementList Then
   strHRef = Request.ServerVariables("SCRIPT_NAME") _
           & "?1stTagName=" & oRs.Fields("Element") _
           & "&Reset=Yes" & "&optDetail=" & Request("optDetail")
   If blnHTValues Then strHRef=strHRef & "&chkHTML=" & Request("chkHTML")
   If blnNNValues Then strHRef=strHRef & "&chkNN=" & Request("chkNN")
   If blnIEValues Then strHRef=strHRef & "&chkMSIE=" & Request("chkMSIE")
%>
   <A HREF="<% = strHRef %>">
<% End If %>
&lt;<% = oRs.Fields("Element") %>&gt;
<% If blnElementList Then %></A><% End If %>
</B></FONT>
</TD>
...
```

So, if the user has specified only the Include MSIE option, and set the list style to Detailed, the code above produces this HTML result for the **FONT** element entry:

```
<A HREF="result.asp?lstTagName=FONT&Reset=Yes&optDetail=0&chkMSIE=on>
&lt;ACRONYM&gt;</A>
```

Of course, if **blnElementList** is **False**, we just get the element name as text instead. This is repeated for each element in the recordset, and when one is then clicked it simulates effect of the user submitting the form via the 'control panel' page:

Adding the Compatibility Images and 'Usage' Link

The next step is to add the compatibility images:

```
...
<TD VALIGN="TOP">
<%
If blnHTValues Then
   Select Case oRs.Fields("HTML40")
   Case "Y" %>
   <IMG SRC="db_images/h4.gif" ALT="4.0" ALIGN="MIDDLE">
<% Case "D" %>
   <IMG SRC="db_images/h4d.gif" ALT="4.0 DEP" ALIGN="MIDDLE">
```

```
<% End Select
   Select Case oRs.Fields("HTML32")
   Case "Y" %>
   <IMG SRC="db_images/h3.gif" ALT="3.2" ALIGN="MIDDLE">
<% Case "D" %>
   <IMG SRC="db_images/h3d.gif" ALT="3.2 DEP" ALIGN="MIDDLE">
<% End Select
   Select Case oRs.Fields("HTML20")
   Case "Y" %>
   <IMG SRC="db_images/h2.gif" ALT="2.0" ALIGN="MIDDLE">
<% Case "D" %>
   <IMG SRC="db_images/h2d.gif" ALT="2.0 DEP" ALIGN="MIDDLE">
<% End Select
End If 'blnHTValues

If blnNNValues Then
... as above, but for Navigator ...
End If 'blnNNValues

If blnIEValues Then
... as above, but for Internet Explorer ...
End If 'blnIEValues %>
</TD>
...
```

Next, we add a space between the last image and the Category hyperlink. This uses the old trick of providing a single pixel transparent GIF file, and specifying the appropriate **HSPACE** and/or **VSPACE** attributes to create white space around it. It's followed by the hyperlink, which uses the element category stored in the database for that element, plus the **.asp** file extension, to create the **HREF** attribute:

```
...
  <TD VALIGN="TOP">
   <IMG SRC="db_images/spacer.gif" ALT="-space-" HSPACE=7>
   <FONT FACE="Arial" SIZE=2>See:
   <A HREF="<% = oRs.Fields("Category") %>.asp">
   <% = oRs.Fields("Category") %></A>
   </FONT>
  </TD>
 </TR>
...
```

In the case of the **FONT** element, this produces:

```
<FONT FACE="Arial" SIZE=2>See:
<A HREF="Text-Styles.asp">Text-Styles</A>
</FONT>
```

Adding the Description

The last action is to add the description of the element to the next line if this is required. At the start of the process, we stored the value of the Compact or Detailed option button setting in the variable **blnDetailed**. If it's **True**, we can add the description retrieved from the database. Notice that we first pass the description to the **Server.HTMLEncode** method in case it contains any non-legal HTML content:

```
. . .
<!only include following if Detailed listing>
<% If blnDetailed Then %>
 <TR>
  <TD COLSPAN=3 VALIGN="TOP">
   <FONT FACE="Arial" SIZE=2>
     <% = Server.HTMLEncode(oRs.Fields("Description")) %>
   </FONT>
  </TD>
 </TR>
<% If blnElementList Then %>
 <TR>
  <TD COLSPAN=3>
   <IMG SRC="db_images/spacer.gif" ALT="-space-" VSPACE=1>
  </TD>
 </TR>
<% End If 'blnElementList
  End If 'blnDetailed
 oRs.MoveNext
 Response.Flush
Loop
oRs.Close %>

</TABLE>
. . .
```

You'll see that we include our invisible spacer GIF if this is a listing of just elements with descriptions (rather that a list showing the attributes as well), so as to separate them into a more readable format.

Displaying The Attributes

If we aren't displaying a list of elements, i.e. **blnElementList** is **False**, we now need to add the attributes for this element. The process is almost identical to that we used to display the element and the appropriate compatibility images. However, this time we don't need to worry about making the attributes hyperlinks or providing a link to a 'usage' page. We also make use of the **TagID** we saved when we opened the recordset for the elements earlier, to get a list of the appropriate attributes:

```
. . .
<% If blnElementList = False Then
   strSQL = "SELECT * FROM Attributes WHERE (TagID=" & keyTagID _
        & ") AND (" & strLimit & ") ORDER BY AttributeName;"
   'create connection and open recordset

<TABLE BORDER=0>
<% Do While Not oRs.EOF %>
<TR>
  'write the attribute name as plain text
</TR>
. . .
```

Again, we only include the description if the **blnDetailed** variable is **True**. This time, however, we also need to insert the values and (if available, i.e. not equal to **Null**) the CSS equivalent:

```
. . .
<!only include following if Detailed listing>
<% If blnDetailed Then %>
```

```
 <TR>
  <TD> </TD>
  <TD ALIGN="RIGHT" VALIGN="TOP">
   <FONT FACE="Arial" SIZE=2>Description:</FONT>
  </TD>
  <TD ALIGN="LEFT"><FONT FACE="Arial" SIZE=2>
   <% = Server.HTMLEncode(oRs.Fields("Description")) %></FONT>
  </TD>
 </TR>
 <TR>
  <TD> </TD>
  <TD ALIGN="RIGHT" VALIGN="TOP">
   <FONT FACE="Arial" SIZE=2>Values:</FONT>
  </TD>
  <TD ALIGN="LEFT"><FONT FACE="Arial" SIZE=2>
   <% = Server.HTMLEncode(oRs.Fields("AttributeValues")) %></FONT>
  </TD>
 </TR>

<% txtCSS = oRs.Fields("CSSValues")
If Not IsNull(txtCSS) Then %>
 <TR>
  <TD> </TD>
  <TD ALIGN="RIGHT" VALIGN="TOP">
   <FONT FACE="Arial" SIZE=2>CSS Equiv:</FONT>
  </TD>
  <TD ALIGN="LEFT"><FONT FACE="Arial" SIZE=2>
    <% = Server.HTMLEncode(txtCSS) %></FONT>
  </TD>
 </TR>
<% End If 'for txtCSS %>
 . . .
```

Finally, we can move to the next attribute, and flush the output so far to the browser to provide progressive rendering. Once complete, we close the recordset and add the closing copyright and contact information:

```
 . . .
   oRs.MoveNext
   Response.Flush
Loop
oRs.Close
%>

</TABLE>
<HR>

<% End If 'for blnDetailed %>
<% End If 'for blnElementList %>

<FONT FACE="Arial" SIZE=2><I>
&copy;1997 Wrox Press Limited, USA and UK. No parts of ... etc.
. . .
</I></FONT><HR>
</BODY>
</HTML>
<% Response.End %>
```

Notice that always add the **Response.End** statement to the end of the page. This should not be necessary, because ASP will flush the rest of the page when it finished processing it. However, we've discovered that this can provide faster response, and is generally good practice when you use buffering in the page.

Jumping to an Element from the All Elements List

When we provide a listing of all the elements, each one (as we've seen earlier) is a hyperlink that displays details of that element by calling the same 'results' page again. It also sends it the other values that it collected from the 'control panel' form in the first place, such as the selected browser types and the setting of the Compact/Detailed option. This is great except for one small problem. Because we don't reload the 'control panel' page, the values in its controls will still be the same as when the list of elements was first displayed.

The **<SELECT>** list will still contain the value Show All Elements, so if the user clicks any of the other controls (for example, to change from Compact to Detailed or to see the values for a different browser type), they'll go back to a listing of all the elements again.

To prevent this, we need to change the selection in the list box to match the element they clicked on, and this is where the extra name/value pair, **Reset=Yes**, comes in. At the start of the 'results' page, we set a variable named **blnReset** to **True** if this name/value pair is present:

```
...
If Request.QueryString("Reset") = "Yes" Then blnReset = True
...
```

Then (if **blnReset** is **True**), when we create the opening **<BODY>** tag we include an **ONLOAD** attribute that will run some client-side script when the page has loaded:

```
...
<BODY BGCOLOR="#FFFFFF" TOPMARGIN=5
  <% If blnReset Then %> ONLOAD="ResetStuff()"<% End If %>
>
...
```

Further down the 'results' page, we include the script itself—again only if **blnReset** is **True**:

```
...
<% If blnReset Then %>
<SCRIPT LANGUAGE="JAVASCRIPT">
<!--
function ResetStuff()
{
  theList = parent.frames['winSelect'].document.forms[0]
                          .elements['lstTagName'];
  for (i = 0; i < theList.options.length; i++)
    if (theList.options[i].value == '<% = txtTagName %>')
      theList.selectedIndex = i
}
// -->
</SCRIPT>
<% End If %>
```

This code will run as soon as the 'results' page is loaded, and it creates a reference **theList** pointing to the **<SELECT>** list in the 'control panel' page. Then it loops through all the options in this list until it finds the one that matches the name of the element the user clicked, and selects it. Now, when they click any other control in the 'control panel' page, the correct element will still be displayed.

Of course, this will only work in a browser that supports client-side script. However, the user without a suitably equipped browser will still be able to use the links to individual elements, they'll just have to change the setting in the **<SELECT>** list themselves.

The Element 'Usage' Pages

The final part of the application is concerned with displaying the pages that show how each element is related to others, and how it can be used. Each page follows a standard format, using a table to show the order of the element tags and which ones can enclose other elements. We indent them to provide a clear view of the structure:

Laying Out Pre-Formatted Text

In the left column of the table we use a mono-pitch font, for which the obvious choice is the **<PRE>** element. This would allow us to use spaces to indent each line as appropriate. However, because **<PRE>** is a block-level element, the next element should be placed on a new line below it. In Netscape Navigator, this means that there is a blank line below the text in each row of the table, producing unsightly results. The same happens in Internet Explorer 4, but *not* in Internet Explorer 3! This provides a timely lesson– always test your pages in as many different browsers as you can get your hands on.

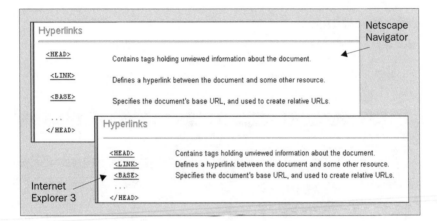

Instead, we use the **<CODE>** tag, which produces an in-line, rather than block-level, element. However, because it's in-line, we lose the ability to precede the text with spaces to provide the appropriate indentation of the elements. The way we get round this is to use the non-breaking space character ** **. Most browsers recognize this, and it gives us the ability to indent lines as required. Where a browser doesn't recognize it, the text will just appear flush to the left margin. It's not exactly what we want, but it doesn't stop the page performing its task.

But we're still not finished. The **<CODE>** element displays text in a smaller font than the surrounding text. So, to balance it out, we have to specify a larger font size as well. The 'normal' font size for our page is 2, but the text in the **<CODE>** element needs to have a font size of 3.

The Code for the 'Usage' Pages

Because the 'usage' pages are all very similar, we'll examine just one. This is the entire ASP code and HTML for the Hyperlinks page you saw earlier:

```
<%@LANGUAGE="VBScript"%>
<% Response.Buffer = True %>
<HTML>
<HEAD>
<TITLE>Hyperlinks</TITLE>
<!-- #include file="seltag.inc" -->
</HEAD>
```

```
<BODY BGCOLOR="#FFFFFF" LINK="#000000" VLINK="#000000">
<FONT FACE="Arial" SIZE=4 COLOR="#A9A9A9">Hyperlinks</FONT>
<!-- #include file="writetag.inc" -->
<TABLE>
<%
OpenTag 1, "HEAD"
OpenTag 2, "LINK"
OpenTag 2, "BASE"
Content 2, "..."
ClosTag 1, "HEAD"
OpenTag 1, "BODY"
Content 2, "..."
OpenTag 2, "A"
Content 3, "link content   "
ClosTag 2, "A"
OpenTag 2, "MAP"
OpenTag 3, "AREA"
OpenTag 3, "AREA"
Content 3, ".. areas .."
ClosTag 2, "MAP"
Content 2, "..."
ClosTag 1, "BODY"
%>
</TABLE>
<HR>
<FORM ACTION="result.asp" METHOD="POST" ONSUBMIT="return goback()">
<INPUT TYPE=SUBMIT VALUE="Return to Details Page ..">
</FORM>
</BODY>
</HTML>
<% Response.End %>
```

Using Server-side Include (SSI) Files

You'll notice that the code above uses two server-side **include files**:

```
<!-- #include file="seltag.inc" -->
```

and

```
<!-- #include file="writetag.inc" -->
```

This technique means that the common parts of the page only need to be stored once on the server, allowing easier maintenance. When we change edit an SSI file, perhaps to update it or correct an error, all the 'usage' pages (there are ten of them in all) will automatically use the new version.

The file **seltag.inc** contains two client-side script routines, which we'll look at in a while. The other file, **writetag.inc**, contains some ASP code that is common to all the pages. The first section of this code fetches a list of all the elements and their corresponding descriptions from the database when the page first opens. It uses the same techniques we've seen earlier in the chapter to trap errors and flush the page progressively to the client:

```
<%
Response.Flush
QUOT = Chr(34)
```

```
CR = Chr(13) & Chr(10)
Set oConn = Server.CreateObject("ADODB.Connection")
oConn.Open "data_source"
strSQL="SELECT Element, Description FROM Elements;"
Set oRs = oConn.Execute(strSQL, lngRecs, 1) 'adCmdText
If (oRs.EOF) Or (Err.Number > 0) Then
  Response.Write "<FONT FACE=" & QUOT & "Arial" & QUOT _
    & "SIZE=3><B>Sorry, the database cannot be accessed " _
    & "at present.</B></FONT></BODY></HTML>"
  Response.Flush
  Response.End
End If
arResult = oRs.GetRows()
oRs.Close
Set oRs = Nothing
%>
```

It stores these values in an array named **arResult** using the **GetRows()** method of the **Recordset** object named **oRs**, then closes the recordset. We can access this array in our code to get the descriptions of each element as we build the page. This is more efficient than searching the recordset every time.

> *We need to collect descriptions of all the elements, not just the ones that belong to the selected 'usage' category, because we'll be including elements from other categories in the pages as well.*

Next is a server-side **<SCRIPT>** section (using **RUNAT=SERVER**) which provides three subroutines.

```
<SCRIPT RUNAT="SERVER" LANGUAGE="VBSCRIPT">
Sub OpenTag(intSpaces, strTagName)
  strResult = "<TR><TD NOWRAP><FONT SIZE=3><CODE>"
  For i = 1 To intSpaces
    strResult = strResult & " "
  Next
  strResult = strResult & "<A HREF=" & QUOT _
            & "javascript:selectTag('" _
            & strTagName & "');" & QUOT & ">&lt;" _
            & strTagName & "&gt;</A>" _
            & "</CODE></FONT></TD><TD NOWRAP><FONT FACE=" _
            & QUOT & "Arial" & QUOT & " SIZE=2>"
  For i = 0 To UBound(arResult, 2)
    If arResult(0, i) = strTagName Then
      strResult = strResult & arResult(1, i)
    End If
  Next
  strResult = strResult & "</FONT></TD></TR>"
  Response.Write strResult & CR
  Response.Flush
End Sub

Sub ClosTag(intSpaces, strTagName)
  strResult = "<TR><TD NOWRAP><FONT SIZE=3><CODE>"
  For i = 1 To intSpaces
    strResult = strResult & " "
  Next
  strResult = strResult & "&lt;/" & strTagName _
            & "&gt;</CODE></FONT></TD><TD></TD></TR>"
```

```
      Response.Write strResult & CR
   End Sub

   Sub Content(intSpaces, strContent)
      strResult = "<TR><TD NOWRAP><FONT SIZE=3 COLOR=" _
                 & QUOT & "#A9A9A9" & QUOT & "><CODE>"
      For i = 1 To intSpaces
         strResult = strResult & " "
      Next
      strResult = strResult & strContent _
                 & "</CODE></FONT></TD><TD></TD></TR>"
      Response.Write strResult & CR
   End Sub

   </SCRIPT>
```

These are the routines that build up the rows of the table, one for each opening tag, closing tag or text content row in the page. This is why we only need to supply a list of calls to the individual routines to create the page that we want:

```
   ...
   OpenTag 2, "A"
   Content 3, "link content  "
   ClosTag 2, "A"
   ...
```

The routine for the opening tag is more complex that the others, because we place this tag in the page as a hyperlink. We'll look at how this is done, and why, next.

Providing a Link Back to the Results Page

The 'usage' pages provide two ways for the user to get back to the 'results' page and display details of individual elements. The first is a button at the foot of the page. The second way is through the fact that we display each opening tag in the page as a hyperlink–users can select a different element and display its details and attributes directly.

Both involve reloading the 'results' page, and we achieve this by re-submitting the form in the 'control panel' page. To do this, the button at the foot of the 'usage' page is a **SUBMIT** type, and it is on a **<FORM>** whose **ACTION** is the 'results' page. When this form is submitted, it will (normally) display the original opening screen in our application, because there are no parameters sent with the request:

```
   <FORM ACTION="result.asp" METHOD="POST" ONSUBMIT="return goback()">
   <INPUT TYPE=SUBMIT VALUE="Return to Details Page ..">
   </FORM>
```

However, the opening **<FORM>** element also contains the **ONSUBMIT** attribute, pointing to a client-side script function named **goback()**. This function is one of the two in the **seltag.inc** SSI file, and this is how it appears in the 'usage' pages:

```
   <SCRIPT LANGUAGE=JAVASCRIPT>
   <!--
   function goback()
   {
     parent.frames['winSelect'].document.forms[0].submit();
```

```
      return false;
   }
   ...
```

This submits the form in the 'control panel' page (*not* the current 'usage' page), which then reloads the 'results' page and displays details of the element selected last time. In other words, they go back to where they were before they opened this 'usage' page. To prevent the form in the 'usage' page being submitted as well, the function returns the value **false**.

Note that we have to use **ONSUBMIT="return goback()"** in the **<FORM>** tag to return the false value to the browser's internal mechanism, and prevent the form being submitted.

So, if the browser supports scripting the user will be returned to the element they selected previously. If it doesn't, they'll go back to the main 'welcome' page instead. However, from the 'usage' page they can click the Back button on their browser to go back to the previous page as well, and we'll let them know what's going to happen by displaying a message in browsers that don't support scripting:

```
<NOSCRIPT>
   Note that, because your browser doesn't support scripting, the
   button at the foot of this page will return you to the opening
   screen. Instead, you can return to the previous page by clicking
   the 'Back' button in your browser. Also note that the links to
   individual elements will not work in your browser.
</NOSCRIPT>
```

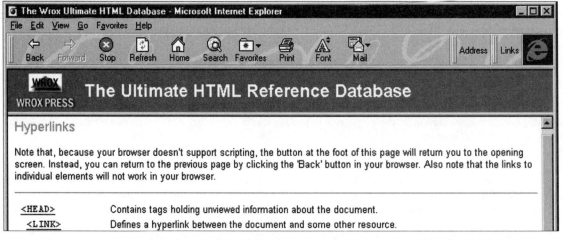

Providing a Link to a Different Element

The second way that a user can get back to the 'results' page (providing their browser supports scripting) is by clicking on an opening tag displayed on the 'usage' page. This allows them to display a different element to the one they last selected, perhaps to find one more suited to the task in hand. To achieve this, we face the same problem as we did earlier of changing the selection in the 'control panel' **<SELECT>** list to the required element before submitting its form.

We employ a clever trick that JavaScript allows for hyperlinks. Earlier in this part of the chapter, we saw the code that creates the opening tags in the 'usage' pages. The core of it looked like this:

```
...
strResult = strResult & "<A HREF=" & QUOT _
            & "javascript:selectTag('" _
            & strTagName & "');" & QUOT & ">&lt;" _
            & strTagName & "&gt;</A>" _
            & "</CODE></FONT></TD><TD NOWRAP><FONT FACE=" _
            & QUOT & "Arial" & QUOT & " SIZE=2>"
...
Response.Write strResult & CR
...
```

If we call this code with, for example, **OpenTag 2, "A"** it produces HTML output that contains this hyperlink code:

```
<A HREF="javascript:selectTag('A');">&lt;A&gt;</A>
```

The syntax **javascript:**_function_name_ causes the browser to execute the named function instead of jumping to another page. We've specified the function **selectTag()**, which is also contained in our **seltag.inc** SSI file and so is placed in the 'usage' page. It does the same as the function we saw when we looked at the 'results' page code earlier on. It changes the setting of the **<SELECT>** list to point to the element named in its parameter, then finishes up by calling the **goback()** function–which submits the 'control panel' page form:

```
...
function selectTag(strTagName)
{
  theList = parent.frames['winSelect'].document.forms[0]
                          .elements['lstTagName'];
  for (i = 0; i < theList.options.length; i++)
    if (theList.options[i].value == strTagName)
      theList.selectedIndex = i;
  window.status = 'Searching..';
  goback();
}

// -->
</SCRIPT>
```

This works just the same as if the user had made the selection in the **<SELECT>** list in the 'control panel' themselves, loading the 'results' page with the chosen element displayed. Again, this only works on browsers that support client-side scripting, but our note at the top of the page in non script-enabled browsers informs users that this is the case.

Summary

And that's it. What might seem to be a fairly simple application from the outside turns out to be quite complex once you get under the hood. We had to make a lot of decisions about what level of features we would expect our visitor's browsers to support in order to achieve optimum performance and usability, but we have also managed to provide an application that is usable with browsers that fall short of this level.

In this chapter, we've attempted to step back from the leading edge approach to Active Server Pages to consider how we interface with the client—especially in areas where the client could be any one of many different types of application. In particular we've looked at the issues of compatibility between different browsers, and how we can get the best from all of them.

ASP can provide information about the browser that accesses the page through the Browser Capabilities component, or directly through the **HTTP_USER_AGENT** value that is sent to the server. However, to really take advantage of this information, we should be providing physically different pages to each browser type. In many cases, the extra work involved is out of the question, and we can often achieve quite respectable results by just appreciating what the different browsers can do, and how we can let them choose the best way to display our pages.

In fact, this technique, commonly known as **fallback**, is a major issue in HTML 4.0. As browsers and client-side applications become ever more complex, there has to be ways of displaying alternative content in older browsers that may access a page designed for the newer ones. Taking advantage of this where possible, and adding some carefully designed 'extras' to the page, means that we can achieve maximum compatibility with minimum effort.

A Case Study in Legacy Component Reuse

This the final case study of this book is a little more complex than some of the previous case studies. However, it's when a task becomes ever more difficult that the real computer nerds show their mettle–like famous mountaineers–we "do it because it's there". With enough effort, any problem can be worked around. In any case, having it all fall over is a lot less painful in computing than in mountaineering.

Basically, in this chapter, we're going to take an existing application and cleave it viciously into two separate parts–so that we can use it over the Web in conjunction with Active Server Pages. The 'reasons why' might seem to make less sense than the 'how it's done', but if you are implementing an Intranet, Extranet or Web-based application in the real world, this is a situation that you will come across at some stage.

In fact, before we get our hands dirty with keyboard and code, we'll take a brief look at the way that designing for the Intranet or the Web changes the whole structure of our applications. This generally means either a complete new application, or the adaptation of an existing one to work in this new environment. It's this last situation in which we find ourselves in this chapter.

So, we'll be looking at:

- How the nature of the network changes our application design philosophy
- How we can reuse existing components in a Web-based application
- How Active Server Pages acts as the glue to hold it all together
- How we adapted our zip file components to work over the Web
- How you can use the finished component in your own pages

We start with a look at the nature of the network.

Distributed Applications and Users

The core of what we do with computers is their ability to exchange information. This might be a document in any of a million different types or formats: from e-mail to accounts data; from pictures to personal information. What all these kinds of information share is the network that connects the computers together.

The Need for Network Speed

Imagine the situation where you're sitting in front of your PC on the 40th floor of a tower block in Somewhere City. The phone rings, and a colleague on the other side of the world asks you to send him the latest version of a particular document, because he needs to refer to the content urgently. You flip the document open in your word processor to check it's the right one, drop it into your zip file manager to compress it, and insert the result into an email message to send to your colleague.

The fact that you've got a local network connection to your office server means that you don't have to think about the way the process works—you just do it. On a simple 10-base-T network, you've got around 10Mbs to play with, or as much as 100Mbs if it's a reasonably up-to-date network.

Now imagine the situation where the cost of office space in Somewhere City has soared yet again, and anyway you're fed up with an hour a day spent sitting in rush-hour traffic. So, the boss's suggestion to telework from home using the Internet is welcome. However, now—as you lounge in the armchair with your new laptop—you're probably hanging off the end of a piece of wire that can only reliably manage 28.8kbs or so. Even on a good day, with a 56kbs modem or an ISDN connection, you don't get anywhere near the kind of speed you're used to on the office network—and we're talking about factors of 10, 100, or even 1,000 times less.

The process you followed in the office is now out of the question. When you casually opened the document in your word processor, you probably dragged a few megabytes across the network from the server to your machine. Then, when you zipped it up, you dragged the same few megabytes across the same network again, then sent the compressed file back to the server along the same path. The only efficient part of the whole process, as far as the network is concerned, is when your e-mail server software sent the compressed file out onto the Net for delivery.

Fat Clients, Thin Clients and Dumb Clients

The model we've been looking at here is the now infamous **fat client**. (No, this isn't an insult instituted by a rebellious customer service department.) In Chapter 9 we examined the different network strategies in more detail, so it suffices here to say that the system of placing all the application on the client, and dragging whole data files across the network, is not the most efficient way of working when network bandwidth is limited.

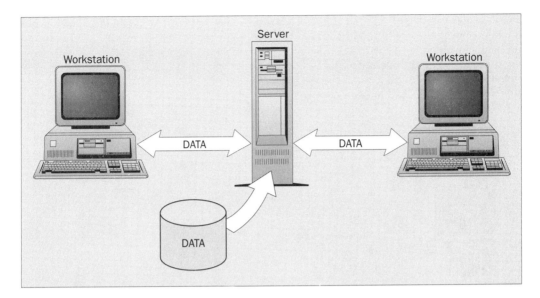

A better way, as you've seen earlier in this book, is to place the interface code that the user sees on the client and the code that does all the file handling and real processing on the server, then simply send instructions and results between the two. Instead of opening the word processor document on our machine to see if it's the right one, we just ask the system to tell us if it is. Instead of transporting the file across the network to our computer to compress it, we simply tell the server to compress it for us.

This approach is usually referred to as a **dumb terminal**, named after the original terminals used when computing power was so incredibly expensive that you only ever had a bit, and kept it all in one place. Users had a terminal that simply sent instructions to the central computer, and then displayed the results it sent back.

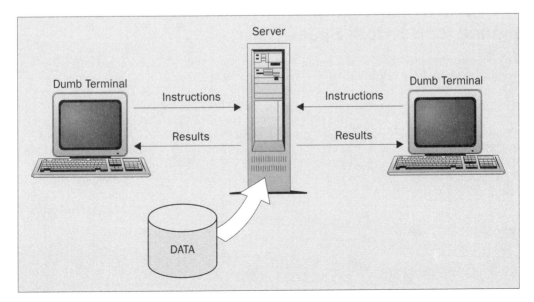

In fact, in most database applications we use, the processing is separated from the interface in exactly this way. In ASP, we tend to use a SQL query string with our ADO component, or execute a procedure stored in the database on the server, so that we only get back the information we want. Rather than transport the whole Product table across the Web, it's far more efficient to just retrieve the technical specification for Type 17 Widget Springs—if that's all we want to know.

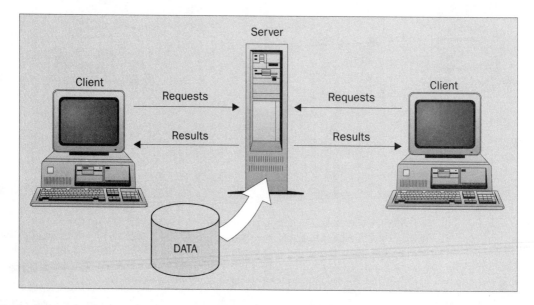

Rather than a dumb terminal, we tend to use the term **thin client** for a PC connected to the Web. Therefore, because computing power is cheap, we allow the client to act intelligently with the data, and manipulate and present it in different ways. In fact, this is all down to the **browser** that we're so used to seeing running on our desktop. It's this browser that is acting as the client.

Designing for Network Speed

So, it's obvious that to make the switch from local network to the Web, be it an Intranet, Extranet, or the wide world outside, we have to prevent our application from dragging whole files across the network. Instead, to make it work with a browser or other thin-client technology, we need to partition it into separate sections and position these sections at opposite ends of the network.

In effect, we need to run our application on the server, but control it from the client. There are many remote access technologies available that allow users to run applications as though they were working locally. However, these are not Web applications in the full sense of the word. What we would like is to be able to design our own Web pages that can use the services of our own custom applications, running on the server.

Remote Application Control

If you are adapting your own custom applications to work in this new environment, you first have to find ways to separate the interface and the working parts. Then, you need to have a way to connect them back together—across the Web or your corporate Intranet. While it's possible to create custom formats for control information, and tunnel it via HTTP, this isn't the easiest of solutions.

Instead, Active Server Pages provides a universal glue that can do all the work. To see this, you only need to look at the configuration utilities included with Windows NT4 Option Pack and Windows NT5. Many are available as HTML pages that allow easy use from a remote location. Basically, this is what we are aiming to achieve with our custom applications.

Working With Components

Whether it's possible to convert your applications to work well over the Web depends on the application itself. If you have followed current trends, and created (or purchased) components to use in the application, you have a fighting chance of success. In fact, the rewards to be gained from designing applications themselves as components, and using existing components (something that everybody always said was the 'proper' way to do it) may only now appear, as you start to restructure it for the Web.

This is even more so the case if, as in the example in this chapter, the 'grunt-work' of manipulating the files is done by components and our custom code provides only the interface. The split that we need to find between interface and back-end then becomes more obvious, and the adaptation to the Web should be easily achievable.

Once we've achieved the separation, we can use ordinary HTML pages to collect information on the client and send it back to Active Server Pages scripts on the server. These scripts can then manipulate the back-end component to carry out the task and pass the results back to the client as plain HTML.

We'll move on to see how all this came together with our next example.

The ServerZip Active Server Component

Unlike many examples you see, this chapter is about developing a component to meet a real-life purpose, rather than a sample that was carefully designed to accentuate the techniques and avoid the pitfalls. This means that you'll see the rough edges which adjusting the requirements and the design would have hidden, but would have failed to provide the functionality actually required.

It also means that you'll see a situation that could well be closer to your own requirements. The nice neat model that we follow when developing an application from scratch isn't always an option in the confines of the corporate "why isn't it working yet?" environment.

The Requirements

One of the ways that we create compressed zip files on our local networks is with a simple VB-based utility that combines the tasks of selecting files, compressing them and e-mailing them to colleagues. It's firmly based in the fat client world, with the entire application running on the client and the files being fetched and returned across the network.

ZipBack Pro - Internet Edition

Source Files

. {All Files}   ▼   Browse..   Zip

d: [DATA]   ▼

02661901.bmp   Search
d:\   02661902.bmp
1266 proasp2   02661903.bmp
ch19   02661904.bmp   Sets
figs   02661904a.bmp
02661904b.bmp   Help
02661905.bmp
02661905a.bmp   Exit
02661905b.bmp
02661906.bmp
02661907.bmp

Target File and Folder   **Options Set:**

figs   .zip   Zip   UnZip   About

c: [SYSTEM]   ▼   Browse..   □ Store Full Path to Files in Zip
c:\   □ Store Sub-folder Names Only
temp   □ Include Sub-folder Contents
vbe   □ Update or Add New Files Only
word8.0   □ Span Zip Across Floppy Disks
wwwroot   ☑ Insert in New Mail Message
Free Space:
247 MB   ☑ Set Advanced Options Active
24 %

Welcome to ZipBack Pro   Press F1 for Help

Underneath the visible front-end is a set of Windows OCX (OLE Control Extension) components that are embedded on the forms that make up the interface. These components talk directly to a set of DLL (Dynamic Link Library) files, which actually carry out the compression.

You can immediately see how this provides us with what appears to be an ideal opportunity to practice our surgery techniques, and split it into two separate parts. The interface can talk to the OCX controls across the Web and can tell the DLLs running on the server what needs to be done.

In order to demonstrate what we are aiming for, here is a page we prepared earlier. It uses standard HTML code and HTML controls to collect information, rather than the Visual Basic form in the original application.

Of course, if we are only aiming our application at a limited audience, we can use more of the client browser's features to make the page more appealing. For example, in Internet Explorer 4, we could create a Web dialog containing controls (complete with the standard 'chrome' appearance) that are interactive, and even context-sensitive help.

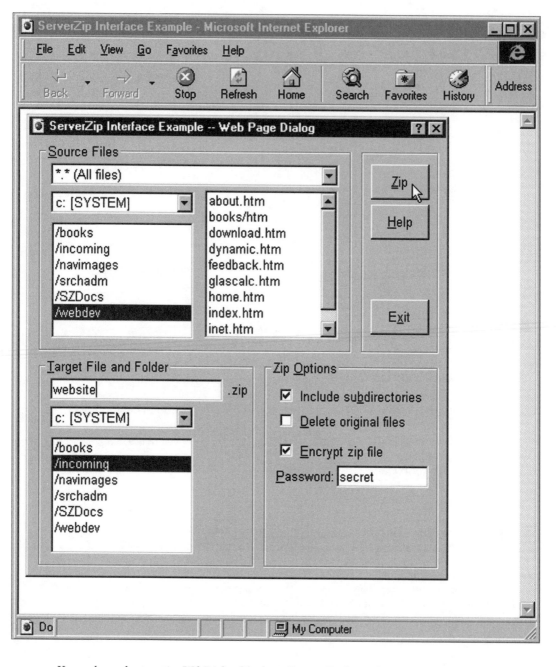

You can learn about creating Web Dialogs like this in Internet Explorer 4 from the book Professional IE4 Programming, published by Wrox Press, ISBN 1-861000-70-7.

The point is that the real work is now being done by a 'component' on the server, rather than by our application. All we are doing is finding different methods of providing the instructions and displaying the results. This division of the application into separate client and server-based sections also provides an added bonus–it can be used in an environment such as the Web where the client application is not as standardized as would be required for a traditional local network-based application.

In other words, as long as the client's browser application can display HTML pages created by Active Server Pages and send instructions back that ASP can decipher, it doesn't matter what the client actually is. The type of machine and operating system, and to a large extent the make and version of the browser, are irrelevant. If required, we can always use the abilities of ASP to explicitly tailor the pages we send to that particular browser anyway.

The Design

So, having conceptually identified the site of the split we need to make in our application, it's time to start sharpening the axe. This is how the original application looks under the hood:

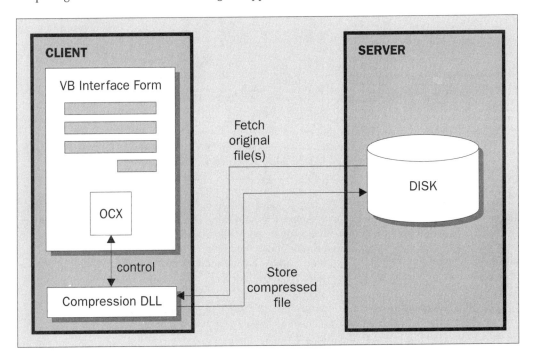

What we want to do is create two sections that are joined by the network:

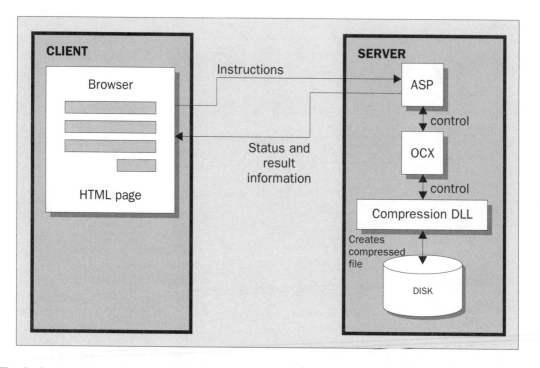

This looks very tidy, and currently there's no sign of problems that might appear later on. In fact, a couple of hours should see it all put to bed. We are only going to offer compression (i.e. zipping) and not unzipping for the time being. This means that we only need one OCX control and one 'action' DLL–plus the support files that the OCX and our component require. As we're working with Visual Basic this includes the VB run-time library. Of course, components can also be created using other languages, such as C++, Java, Delphi, etc.

The first step is to consider how we are going to connect our OCX control to Active Server Pages. In fact, it should be possible to do away with the OCX altogether, and talk directly to the DLL from VB code. Unfortunately, we need to be able to handle several callback functions–as well as some pretty complex function calls–in order to drive the DLL. Even with its new **AddressOf** statement, Visual Basic just can't manage these so we are stuck with the OCX control in our example.

> **Callback functions** *are used by a DLL to communicate with the application code that called it, rather like events do from objects. In our case, the DLL throws up message boxes if we don't handle all the callbacks–not a situation we really want to arise on the server.*

Components and Classes

We'll implement the server end of our application as an **Active Server Component**, which can be used with Active Server Pages. In Chapter 6 we looked at the basics for creating Active Server Components, including the way that we connect them to ASP itself.

Active Server Components are generally implemented as ActiveX DLLs, allowing them to provide multiple instances of the component to the Web server each time a page that uses the component is loaded and interpreted by ASP. To create an ActiveX DLL using Visual Basic, we have to provide at least one **class module** within the component. The name of this class is appended to the component name to identify the component, and the code in it provides the properties and methods that ASP will use.

Unattended Execution

Inside the component, we can implement other classes as required–plus code modules and other objects. For a component that is designed to run on the server, we can also use the Unattended Execution option in the Properties dialog to suppress any dialogs or messages:

This also changes the threading model of the component to allow it to handle multiple concurrent requests from the applications that use it. Finally, it's useful to prevent us including forms, or code that would cause messages to be displayed, in the component.

Unfortunately, in our case, we can't use the Unattended Execution option. The DLL we are using expects a response to its own dialogs (that indicate errors have occurred), and this response depends on the reason the dialog was displayed. If we simply suppress the dialogs, the DLL will not work correctly. In our example, we have to explicitly handle the callbacks individually.

Including a Form in a Server Component

In fact, the situation is more difficult than that anyway. The particular OCX control we want to use doesn't appear to work correctly if we create an instance of it in code using the **WithEvents** keyword. It was never designed to be used this way. For the callback functions to operate we need to place it on a form. This means that we must include a form, with its **Visible** property set to **False**, in our component. Now, the Unattended Execution option is grayed out and no longer available.

We've added a form named **ocxform** to the component, placed the OCX control we need to use on it, and added the code that manipulates the OCX interface and actually creates the zip file. This interface is proprietary and only available to registered users of the control, so we can't show you all the code detail in this book.

However, the form provides a **Public** function in its code that we can call from the component class code when we're ready to create the zip file. This function takes as arguments the values required for the compression process:

```
Public Function createZip(strSource As String, _
                          strTarget As String, _
                          intCompress As Integer, _
                          blnRecurse As Boolean, _
                          strEncrypt As String, _
                          blnDelete As Boolean) _
                          As Integer
```

The arguments are effectively the properties that we will expose to our ASP pages from the **ServerZip** class. The script in the page can set the properties for a particular zip file, and then call the **createZip** function to start the process off.

Bear in mind that the function you see in the code above is in the **ocxform** object, not the **ServerZip** class—we will set the properties and call this function using **Public** members of the **ServerZip** component. These members will, in turn, call the **createZip** function in the **ocxform** object and pass on the arguments. Look at the schematic diagram at the end of this section if you're not sure how this all fits together.

Including a Module in a Server Component

So, our component is already looking a bit of a mess, with a form we didn't really want. To make matters worse, we also need to be able to read values from Windows Registry within the component, to allow administrators to limit the use of some of the methods it provides. We have to use Windows API (Application Programming Interface) calls to access the Registry, and the declaration of these must be in a Code module and not a Class module. This means we need to add a new code module to our component as well.

This screenshot shows the project window for the complete component, including our OCX form, the **Globals** module with the Registry access code, and the **ServerZip** class module:

When the component is used in ASP, a new instance of the **ServerZip** class is created for each page that references it. The code in the **Globals** module, however, is available to all instances of the class. This means that we have to be very careful if we declare any variables here. For example, if we save the IP address of the client in a variable declared in the **Globals** module, each ASP page that creates a reference to our component will update a single instance of this variable. It will only ever contain one IP value–the address of the last client that accessed an ASP page containing the component.

> *In fact, we experimented by declaring the* **ScriptingContext** *object here, to see the effect. As each client accessed a page containing the component, they received the output that was already being generated for the previous client–which never received the rest of their page. (You'll see more about the* **ScriptingContext** *object later on.)*

Creating Instances of the Objects

When ASP references our component it will automatically create an instance of the **ServerZip** object. This is only the **ServerZip** *class* itself, not any other objects within the component. We need to create our own new instance of the **ocxform** object when an instance of our **ServerZip** object is created, as well as capturing a reference to the **ScriptingContext** of this ASP page.

We can create the new **ocxform** object, here named **objOCXForm**, by declaring it in our **ServerZip** class module code. As we're only going to use it within our class, we make it **Private**:

```
Private objOCXForm As New ocxform
```

The **ScriptingContext** object provides the link between our code and Active Server Pages. To get VB to recognize the object, and to be able to use it easily in our code, we only need to add a reference to the file **asp.dll** in the Visual Basic Project | References dialog. The DLL will probably be in the **Winnt\System32\inetsrv** directory on your server.

If you are creating the component on a normal PC, rather than the one that hosts the Web server, you can copy the DLL into a directory on the PC and create the reference from there, as we've done in the screenshot here.

```
References - Stonebroom.vbp                                    [X]

Available References:                                         [ OK ]

☑ Visual Basic For Applications                 ▲           [ Cancel ]
☑ Visual Basic runtime objects and procedures
☑ Visual Basic objects and procedures                       [ Browse... ]
☑ OLE Automation
☑ DynaZIP ZIP Control
☑ Microsoft Active Server Pages Object Library   ▓        [ ↑ ]
☐ Active Setup Control Library
☐ API Declaration Loader                                    Priority
☐ Application Performance Explorer Client                             [ Help ]
☐ Application Performance Explorer Expediter
☐ Application Performance Explorer Instancer    [ ↓ ]
☐ Application Performance Explorer Logger
☐ Application Performance Explorer Manager
☐ Application Performance Explorer Pool Manager  ▼

┌─ Microsoft Active Server Pages Object Library ──────────┐
│      Location:    E:\VB5\asp.dll                        │
│      Language:    Standard                              │
└─────────────────────────────────────────────────────────┘
```

Moving Components to Another Machine

VB5 automatically registers components it creates in the local machine's Registry. When you move a component to another machine–such as in this case when you copy the DLL to your server–you need to register it in that machine's Registry yourself. This is done with the **RegSvr32.exe** utility that is found in your **System** (or **System32**) folder:

```
regsvr32 <path and component name>
```

Once you have compiled the component the first time, it's worth going into the Component tab of the Project Properties page, and setting the Binary Compatibility option. This forces the component to use the same Class ID, so you won't have to register it each time:

The other issue is that, in the case of Active Server Components, you also have to stop the server and restart it if the component is already running, to allow it to be replaced by the new one. More detailed instructions are included in the documentation supplied with the sample ServerZip component.

The ScriptingContext Object

When ASP interprets a page containing an Active Server Component (as we saw in Chapter 12) it raises the **onStartPage** event to each component in the page. We need to react to this by adding a **Public** method to our **ServerZip** component:

```
Public Sub onStartPage(SContext As ScriptingContext)   'in ServerZip class
    Set objOCXForm.objScript = SContext
End Sub
```

Notice that we have defined the object reference as a **Public** variable in the **ocxform** code, and *not* in the main **ServerZip** class:

```
Public objScript As ScriptingContext                    'in ocxform code
```

This is because we need to be able to use the **ScriptingContext** object within the code in **ocxform** to provide status messages from the OCX to the user. We can refer to the **ocxform** object, and any of its **Public** members, using the **objOCXForm** reference variable, because we created it in our **ServerZip** component. So the **ScriptingContext** object, when seen from the **ServerZip** class, is **objOCXForm.objScript**. When we come to use the **createZip** function we met briefly earlier on, which is also in the **ocxform** object, we'll call it with **objOCXForm.createZip(***arguments***)**.

The Final Gotcha

After all this, there is one final problem. Our OCX talks to a DLL and this DLL carries out the actual file compression. The OCX is a 'proper' ActiveX control, and so we can create separate instances of it on each **ocxform** object we create. The values we pass through it to the DLL can be different for each instance of the OCX.

Unfortunately, the DLL is not an ActiveX control, or even an object of any kind. It is well designed, robust, reliable, and almost fully bulletproofed against errors. But it's still just a plain lump of executable code, and to make matters worse it is not **re-entrant**. In other words, if we attempt to start a second compression operation while one is still running, both the new and currently executing processes return an error.

Shared Address Space

In normal situations, different instances of a Win32 application have their own separate and protected address spaces. They load into local memory their own copy of a DLL when they use it. Internet Information Server normally runs components in its own address space, and loads only one instance of a DLL which it shares among all processes running in its address space. Hence, we are well and truly stuffed when it comes to allowing concurrent compression operations.

> *Internet Information Server 4 allows you to specify that components can run in separate address space from the Web server for any particular virtual directory. This is recommended, where the bulk of the processing is in the component, rather than in communication between the component and the ASP page (which is less efficient in this mode). However, IIS still shares this separate address space between all instances of the component, so the problem remains.*

With our component, each compression operation places a lot more load on your server that the more usual "Web-serving" tasks, so this limitation is probably not as serious as it could be in other less specialist situations. It just means that you may need to add code to the ASP **Application** object (via **global.asa**) to limit users of the page to one at a time.

Semaphore Flag Variables

In order to prevent errors in the component if there is a concurrent access, we've added code that stops a new instance of the **ServerZip** object from accessing the DLL while another process is using it. To achieve this, we take advantage of the effect we came across earlier when including a global Module in a component. A Boolean 'flag' variable defined in the **Globals** module is available to all instances of the **ServerZip** object, and starts off as **False** when the component is first loaded by the server.

Each **ServerZip** object instance then checks the value of this flag, and can only call the DLL if it is still **False** at the point when they are ready to start compressing a file. When they do enter the DLL, they set the flag to **True**, and then back to **False** when complete. This technique is often referred to as a **semaphore flag variable**, and it used in Windows own operating system code where DLLs are not re-entrant.

A Schematic View of the ServerZip Component

To finish this section, here's a schematic view of the completed design for the component. What looked like a couple of hours work when we started has grown to become something of a monster. However, we now have a good idea of how it will be implemented, and can move on to the detailed topics–such as deciding what properties and methods we will make available outside the component. It's these properties and methods that Active Server Pages will use to manipulate the component and compress files.

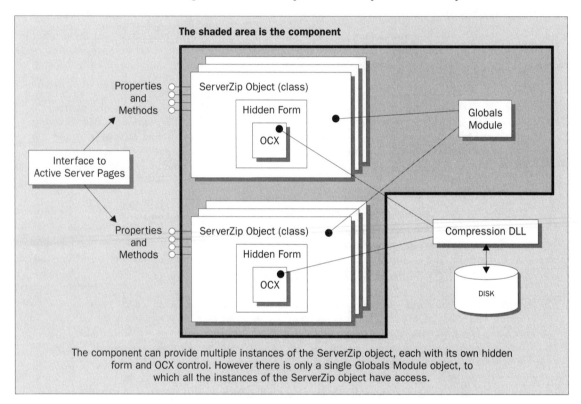

The component can provide multiple instances of the ServerZip object, each with its own hidden form and OCX control. However there is only a single Globals Module object, to which all the instances of the ServerZip object have access.

The Interface

Having seen how the component fits together, we'll now look briefly at the interface it exposes to Active Server Pages. The component actually carries out three different tasks:

- Listing files in a given directory on the server
- Compressing one or more files into a single zip file
- Removing zip files that have been collected by users

One thing we have to consider when we carry out operations like this on the server is that we have to allow for the possibility of different users creating files with the same name in the same directory. We're allowing the component to be used to create zip files in any virtual directory on the server, and with any name. To prevent clashes we place each file in a separate subdirectory within the specified virtual directory, and give each new subdirectory a unique name.

This also achieves another purpose. By coding the current date into the directory name, we can easily identify old ones and remove them after a specified number of days. So, after five zip operations have taken place, the directory on the server might look like this:

Here's the full list of properties and methods for the **ServerZip** component, broken down into the three functional categories.

Listing Files

To list the names of files that are stored on the server in the user's browser, you must provide the directory name. You can also specify text and HTML that is placed before and/or after each file in the list. To create the listing, you then call the **fileListing()** method, with an optional parameter that is a file specification which limits the files included in the list to those that match the specification.

Property	Description
`fileListRoot`	String. Either the full physical path or the virtual path of the directory where the files that are to be listed reside.
`beforeFileHTML`	Optional String. The text and HTML that is placed before each file in the listing. Allows you, for example, to create `<OPTION>` lists, `<A>` hyperlinks, or format file names as required. The default if omitted is an empty string.
`afterFileHTML`	Optional String. The text and HTML that is placed after each file in the listing. Allows you to add closing element tags, or format file names as required. The default if omitted is a carriage return.

Method	Parameters	Description
`fileListing`	`fileSpecification` (optional) String containing the specification, including wildcards if required, of the files to include - i.e. `"sz*.doc"`. The default if omitted is `"*.*"` (all files).	Starts the file listing, using the property values previously set, or the defaults where not specified. Returns a count of the number of files listed.

Compressing Files

To compress files, you set the appropriate properties then call the `doZip()` method. An error occurs if a required property is not set correctly.

Property	Description
`sourceFileList`	String. Either a full physical file path and name or a virtual directory path and name. For a physical path, the standard DOS wildcards can be included if required. To specify more that one file just separate the individual file names with spaces. If a virtual path is used only one file can be specified, and it cannot include wildcards. Note that ALL filenames that include spaces must be enclosed in double quotes, for example: `c:\documents\mydoc.doc` `"c:\My Documents\another.doc"` `c:\uploads\*.txt`
`zipFileName`	String. The file name only for the target zip file. This will be placed within a uniquely named directory ready for the user to collect.
`virtualTargetRoot`	String. The base virtual directory within which the unique download directory will be created. Must be a virtual, not a physical, directory specification.
`compressionRate`	Optional Integer. Specifies the compression rate for the file, values from 1 to 9. 1 is fast speed but low compression rate, 9 is slow speed but gives the highest compression rate. The default if not specified is 5.

Property	Description
recurseDirs	Optional Boolean. If **True**, specifies that files in the subdirectories below the source file directory, and which match the source file specification, will be included in the zip file. The default is **False**.
deleteOriginalFiles	Optional Boolean. If **True**, specifies that all the original files which are included in the zip file will be deleted once the compression has competed successfully. The default is **False**.
encryptCode	Optional String. A code string of up to 65 characters that is used to securely encrypt the contents of the zip file. An empty string (the default) means that the file is not encrypted.
zipIsBusy	Returns **True** if the component is currently executing a zip process, or **False** if not. Only one concurrent zip process is allowed, although you can list and delete files while a zip is in progress.
zipfileDownloadHref	Read-Only String. Returns the full virtual path and filename of the zip file as a string once compression is complete—otherwise it is undefined.

Method	Parameters	Description
doZip	*none*	Starts the compression process, using the property values previously set, or the defaults where not specified. Returns **True** if the process completes successfully, or **False** otherwise.

Removing Old Files

Each **doZip()** process creates a new unique directory within an existing virtual directory on the server, and places the zip file that is to be downloaded within it. To remove the old directories, you use the **deleteOldFiles()** method. You can specify how many days old the directory must be before it is deleted.

Property	Description
virtualTargetRoot	String. The base virtual directory from which the unique download directories will be deleted. Must be a virtual, not a physical, directory specification.
daysOldToDelete	Optional Integer. Specifies the number of days that the download directories must be older than in order to be deleted. The default if omitted is 2.

Method	Parameters	Description
deleteOldFiles	*none*	Starts the delete process using the property values previously set, or the defaults where not specified. Returns a count of the number of directories successfully deleted.

Security and Configuration

The `ServerZip` component provides wide-ranging access to all the drives and directories of your server, and could possibly be used by unwelcome visitors to cause damage to the server installation. To prevent this, you can set options that control how much freedom the component has to access files and directories. These setting are stored in Windows Registry under a key named:

`HKEY_LOCAL_MACHINE\SOFTWARE\Stonebroom\ServerZip\`

The settings are:

Key	Description
`AllowVirtualSourceOnly`	A value of `"1"` prevents the `sourceFileList` property from being set to a physical path. Only virtual directories can be specified as the source of files to compress. The default value of `"0"` allows either physical or virtual directories to be specified.
`AllowVirtualFileListOnly`	A value of `"1"` prevents the `fileListRoot` property from being set to a physical path. Only virtual directories can be specified as the source of files to list. The default value of `"0"` allows either physical or virtual directories to be specified.
`DisableDeleteOriginalFiles`	A value of `"1"` prevents the `deleteOriginalFiles` property from being set to `True`, and so the original files cannot be deleted. The default value of `"0"` allows the original files to be deleted.
`DisableIncludeSubdirectoryFiles`	A value of `"1"` prevents the `recurseDirs` property from being set to `True`, and so files in subdirectories cannot be included in the compressed file. The default value of `"0"` allows the subdirectory contents to be included.

The easiest way to change the settings is to run the Security Manager utility, named `SZConfig.exe`, which is installed with the component. This provides a checkbox for each Registry setting, allowing you to change it easily. The required Registry keys and values are created automatically.

The Implementation

It's time now to take a look at how the component works. This isn't a book about Visual Basic programming, so we aren't going to provide full listings of all the routines—or explain them all in great detail. What we will show you is the important techniques that are involved in using VB to create out ServerZip Active Server Component, together with a few items of interest along the way.

The Component Files

The component consists of three Visual Basic files. These are in the samples you can download from our Web site at **http://rapid.wrox.co.uk/books/1266**:

 ServerZip.cls is the main interface class that ASP uses to create each instance of the **ServerZip** object. It contains the interface code that provides the public properties and methods you've just seen, and some ancillary routines to provide the extra features such as listing and deleting files.

 ocxform.frm is the hidden form that the component uses to hold the OCX control. The code in this form implements the **createZip()** function, which is called by the **ServerZip** class when it wants to create a zip file. It also holds the reference to the **ScriptingContext** object, and handles the writing of status information and results back to the browser.

 servzipg.bas is the **Globals** module file, which contains a couple of global variable declarations, the Windows Registry API function declarations, and the routine that reads values from the Registry using these API functions.

We've supplied these files with the other samples that you can download from our Web site at **http://rapid.wrox.co.uk**. You can also download the complete component and experiment with it on your own server.

> *Note that, because of the restrictions placed on distribution of the DynaZIP© compression code by the manufacturers, parts of the* **ocxform.frm** *file have been removed. Details of the proprietary interface to the compression code is only available to registered users of the code. For more information, contact Inner Media Inc, NH, USA. Their Web site is at* **http://www.innermedia.com**

The ServerZip.cls Class File

The **ServerZip.cls** file defines the interface for the component, and it's this class that is used to create the **ServerZip** object within Active Server Pages. It creates its own instance of the **ocxform** object–the hidden form containing the OCX control. Remember, it's the OCX control that actually interacts with the DLL to carry out the compression.

The Variable Declarations

Here's the definition of the **ocxform** object, and the local member variables that will store the property values. We also define an array that will hold the error messages:

```
Private objOCXForm As New ocxform

'the local member variables for the properties
Private m_sourceFileList As String
Private m_zipFileName As String
Private m_virtualTargetRoot As String
Private m_compressionRate As Integer
Private m_recurseDirs As Boolean
Private m_encryptCode As String
Private m_deleteOriginalFiles As Boolean
Private m_daysOldToDelete As Integer
```

```
       Private m_fileListRoot As String
       Private m_beforeFileHTML As String
       Private m_afterFileHTML As String
       Private m_zipfileDownloadHref As String

       'an array of error messages
       Private m_errors(33) As String
       ...
```

Initializing the ServerZip Object

When ASP creates an instance of the **ServerZip** class, three things need to occur. We need to create the
ocxform object for this class instance. This is done automatically because we defined a reference variable
to it using the **New** keyword in the previous code. We then need to initialize the variables inside our class
to suitable default values, including filling in the error message array:

```
    ...
    'set the initial values of the properties, etc.
    Private Sub Class_Initialize()
       m_sourceFileList = ""
       m_zipFileName = ""
       m_virtualTargetRoot = ""
       m_compressionRate = 5
       m_recurseDirs = False
       m_encryptCode = ""
       m_deleteOriginalFiles = False
       m_daysOldToDelete = 2
       m_fileListRoot = ""
       m_beforeFileHTML = ""
       m_afterFileHTML = "<BR>" & CRLF
       m_zipfileDownloadHref = ""
       m_errors(0) = "Operation complete, no errors."
       m_errors(1) = "Undefined error."
       m_errors(2) = "Unexpected end of zip file."
       '... etc ...
    End Sub
    ...
```

Finally, we need to store a reference to the **ScriptingContent** object that ASP passes to us when it
calls the **onStartPage** method in our component. It's through this object that we'll be able to write into
the returned HTML stream using the **Response.Write** method, and take advantage of the ASP **Server**
object's **MapPath** method to translate virtual paths to physical paths in our code:

```
    ...
    'set the reference to the ASP page
    Public Sub onStartPage(SContext As ScriptingContext)
       Set objOCXForm.objScript = SContext
    End Sub
    ...
```

The Property Let and Get Routines

To expose properties from an Active Server Component, we create **Property Let** and **Property Get**
subroutines, just as we would when creating any other ActiveX control. We've listed a few here to show
you how we can validate the user's proposed values before accepting them. For example, in the code

below, we're only going to accept a physical path for the **sourceFileList** property if the appropriate Registry setting is not set to **"1"**:

```
...
Public Property Let sourceFileList(ByVal vData As String)
    If (GetKeyValue("AllowVirtualSourceOnly") = "1") _
    And ((InStr(vData, ":")) Or (InStr(vData, "\"))) Then
      WriteToResponse "<P><B>Error:</B> Permission to use " _
                  & "physical source directory paths denied.</P>"
      m_sourceFileList = ""      'don't accept value from user
    Else
      m_sourceFileList = vData  'accept value proposed by user
    End If
End Property
...
```

The **GetKeyValue()** function is in the **Globals** module, and simply returns the current setting of the Registry sub-key value passed to it–in this example **AllowVirtualSourceOnly**. You'll see this code later on.

Providing a **Property Let** routine makes it a Write property and allows the user to set the value. To return the value of a property, making it Read and Write, we also have to provide the appropriate **Property Get** routine. This routine just returns the current value of the private internal member variable:

```
...
Public Property Get sourceFileList() As String
    sourceFileList = m_sourceFileList
End Property
...
```

The same process is used for the other properties. We make life easier for users by automatically adding the **.zip** extension to the **zipFileName** property if they omit it, and only accept values for the **compressionRate** property between **1** and **9**. Other properties apply limits in much the same way, you can view the source code in the **ServerZip.cls** file to see them all:

```
...
Public Property Let zipFileName(ByVal vData As String)
    m_zipFileName = vData
    If (Len(m_zipFileName) > 0) And (InStr(m_zipFileName, ".") = 0) Then
        m_zipFileName = m_zipFileName & ".zip"
    End If
End Property

Public Property Get zipFileName() As String
    zipFileName = m_zipFileName
End Property

Public Property Let compressionRate(ByVal vData As Integer)
    If IsNumeric(vData) Then
        If vData > 0 And vData < 10 Then m_compressionRate = vData
    End If
End Property
```

```
Public Property Get compressionRate() As Integer
    compressionRate = m_compressionRate
End Property
...
'routines for other properties
...
```

For two of the components properties, **zipfileDownloadHref** and **zipIsBusy**, we've only provided **Property Get** routines. We want these to be a Read Only properties, and this is achieved by not providing a **Property Let** routine for them. You'll come across the **blnBusy** variable, which is used to provide the **zipIsBusy** property, later in this section of the chapter:

```
...
Public Property Get zipfileDownloadHref() As String
    zipfileDownloadHref = m_zipfileDownloadHref
End Property

Public Property Get zipIsBusy() As Boolean
    zipIsBusy = blnBusy    'global variable referenced in Module
End Property
...
```

Outputting Information in the Page

Next come some general routines that we call from various places in our class. One thing we regularly need to do is write into the HTML stream being returned to the user as our component runs. We can provide status information as the compression process executes, and the results when it is complete. To do this, we created a general-purpose **WriteToResponse** subroutine:

```
...
Private Sub WriteToResponse(strText As String)
    #If DebugVer Then            'not running under NT and ASP
        Debug.Print strText
    #Else
        objOCXForm.objScript.Response.Write strText & CRLF
        If objOCXForm.objScript.Response.Buffer Then
            objOCXForm.objScript.Response.Flush
        End If
    #End If
End Sub
...
```

Recall that we saved a reference to the ASP **ScriptingContext** object in the **objScript** variable in our **ocxform** code, when the **ServerZip** object was created by ASP in the current page. We can therefore use the **Response.Write** method to insert text and HTML into the page as our component runs. We also expect our user to have turned on buffering for the page before they created the object (using **<% Response.Buffer = True %>** before the opening **<HTML>** tag). We can flush our text and HTML to the page in this case, instead of waiting until the component has finished running.

Using Conditional Compilation

Notice in the previous code that we use **conditional compilation** to decide which code to include in our component when it's compiled. While we're developing it, we can set the value of a compiler argument named **DebugVer** to **True** (**-1**) in the Project Properties dialog. Then, the component will write the output to the VB Immediate (or Debug) window instead of to the HTML stream:

This technique is useful if you are developing the component on a machine that doesn't have NT and IIS installed. You can create a Project Group in Visual Basic 5, add a form with buttons that set the properties and call the methods in the component, then test away to your heart's content.

Starting the doZip() Method

The major method our component provides is the **doZip()** method. This is implemented by a **Public** subroutine within the **ServerZip** class file. Here's the first part of the code. It checks each of the properties to make sure that valid values are available. If any error is found, an appropriate error number is stored in the variable **intResult**. These numbers correspond to the error message we placed in the **m_errors** array earlier on:

```
...
Public Function doZip() As Integer
    'returns True on success, or False otherwise
    '... declare local variables here ...
    On Error GoTo FDZI_Err
    m_zipfileDownloadHref = ""
    intResult = 0
    WriteToResponse "<P><B>Stonebroom ServerZip&copy;</B> v1.0<BR>"
    If Len(m_sourceFileList) = 0 Then intResult = 22
    If intResult = 0 Then
      If InStr(m_sourceFileList, ":") = 0 Then  'physical path
        Set objASPServer = objOCXForm.objScript.Server
        m_sourceFileList = objASPServer.MapPath(m_sourceFileList)
      End If
```

```
         If Len(m_sourceFileList) = 0 Then intResult = 22
      End If
      If intResult = 0 Then
         If Len(m_zipFileName) = 0 Then intResult = 23
         If Len(m_virtualTargetRoot) = 0 Then intResult = 24
      End If
      If intResult = 0 Then       'don't allow physical target root
         If InStr(m_virtualTargetRoot, ":") _
         Or InStr(m_virtualTargetRoot, "\") Then intResult = 25
      End If
      ...
```

Notice how we use the ASP **Server** object's **MapPath** method to convert a virtual path into a physical one. Remember, the **ScriptingContext** object is referenced in our **ocxform** object. To make the code simpler, we create a temporary variable **objASPServer** and assign the actual ASP **Server** object to it, then use the variable to access the object:

```
   Set objASPServer = objOCXForm.objScript.Server
   m_sourceFileList = objASPServer.MapPath(m_sourceFileList)
```

Calling the createZip Function

At this point we will have either zero in **intResult**, indicating everything is OK to proceed, or an error number if "all is not well". If we have got zero we can get ready to create the zip file. The function **CreateUniqueDirectory()** used here is one of our own custom functions—you'll see it listed later on. After that, we check that the DLL is not currently in use by examining the **blnBusy** variable that is declared in the **Globals** module. If no other process is using the DLL it will be **False**, and we can go ahead:

```
      ...
      If intResult = 0 Then
         If Right(strPhysicalRoot, 1) <> "\" Then
            strPhysicalRoot = strPhysicalRoot & "\"
         End If
         strUniqueDir = CreateUniqueDirectory(strPhysicalRoot)
         If Len(strUniqueDir) = 0 Then intResult = 27
      End If
      strPhysicalRoot = strPhysicalRoot & strUniqueDir _
                     & "\" & m_zipFileName
      If intResult = 0 Then
         'ready to do the zip
         If blnBusy Then
            WriteToResponse "<P><B>Busy at present, " _
                        & "please try again later.</B></P>"
            doZip = 0
            Exit Function
         End If
         blnBusy = True  'prevent other accesses
         WriteToResponse "Creating " & m_zipFileName & " please wait<BR>"
         'run the createZip() function in the ocxform code
         intResult = objOCXForm.createZip(m_sourceFileList, _
                                    strPhysicalRoot, _
                                    m_compressionRate, _
                                    m_recurseDirs, _
                                    m_encryptCode, _
                                    m_deleteOriginalFiles)
```

```
        blnBusy = False
    End If
    ...
```

The **createZip()** function returns an error code if anything went wrong, or zero on success. After setting the **blnBusy** flag back to **False**, so that other processes can use the DLL, we can insert the results into the page–the message in **m_errors(0)** is Operation complete, no errors:

```
    ...
    If intResult > 0 Then strMesg = "<B>ERROR:</B> "
    strMesg = strMesg & m_errors(intResult)
    WriteToResponse "<BR>" & CRLF & strMesg & "<P>"
    If intResult = 0 Then    'zip process succeeded
        If m_virtualTargetRoot <> "/" Then
            m_zipfileDownloadHref = m_virtualTargetRoot
        End If
        m_zipfileDownloadHref = m_zipfileDownloadHref & "/" _
                            & strUniqueDir & "/" & m_zipFileName
        WriteToResponse "The file <B><A HREF=" & Chr(34) _
                        & m_zipfileDownloadHref & Chr(34) _
                        & ">" & m_zipFileName _
                        & "</A></B> is ready to collect.<P>"
    End If
    doZip = (intResult = 0)
    Exit Function
FDZI_Err:
    doZip = 0             'general error
    WriteToResponse "<P><B>Error:</B> " & m_errors(28) & "<P>"
    blnBusy = False
    Exit Function
End Function
...
```

You'll see how this code sets the complete **HREF** (HTTP address) of the file it created into the internal m_**zipfileDownloadHref** member variable, then uses it to create a hyperlink to the file in the page. This allows the user to download the file immediately, but also makes the address available to ASP via the Read Only **zipfileDownloadHref** property, as we saw earlier. This screenshot shows the result:

Source file list is **d:\wwwroot\website*.***

Stonebroom ServerZip© v1.0

Creating website.zip, please wait ..

Operation complete, no errors.

The file website.zip is ready to collect.

Creating the Unique Directory

To prevent name clashes between zip files, we place each one in a uniquely named subdirectory within the **virtualTargetRoot** directory specified by the user. This is one of the reasons that we provide the full **HREF** as a property of the component, because the Web author cannot know beforehand what it will be. Creating a unique directory is easy enough–the two functions listed here do all the work:

```
...
Private Function CanMakeDir(strDirName As String)
   On Error GoTo FCMD_Err
   MkDir strDirName
   CanMakeDir = True
   Exit Function
FCMD_Err:
   CanMakeDir = False
   Exit Function
End Function

Private Function CreateUniqueDirectory(strRoot As String) As String
   Dim strDirName As String
   Dim intRand As Integer
   Randomize
   strDirName = "SZ" & Format(Now(), "yyyyMMdd-hhmmss") & "-"
   intRand = CInt((Rnd * 10000) - 1)
   strDirName = strDirName & CStr(intRand)
   If CanMakeDir(strRoot & strDirName) Then
      CreateUniqueDirectory = strDirName
   Else
      CreateUniqueDirectory = ""
   End If
End Function
...
```

The deleteOldFiles() Method

The **ServerZip** component provides two other methods, **deleteOldFiles()** and **fileListing()**.
Both are VB-only code routines in the **ServerZip** class code. They make no use of the **ocxform** or the
compression DLL. We've listed the **deleteOldFiles()** method code below, followed by the two
functions it calls. Notice how the general format is very similar to the **doZip()** function:

```
...
Public Function deleteOldFiles() As Integer
   'returns number of deleted unique directories
   '... declare local variables here ...
   On Error GoTo FDOF_Err
   intResult = 0
   intCount = 0
   If Len(m_virtualTargetRoot) = 0 Then intResult = 24
   If intResult = 0 Then
      Set objASPServer = objOCXForm.objScript.Server
      strPhysicalRoot = objASPServer.MapPath(m_virtualTargetRoot)
    If Len(strPhysicalRoot) = 0 Then intResult = 26
   End If
   If intResult = 0 Then
      If Right(strPhysicalRoot, 1) <> "\" Then
         strPhysicalRoot = strPhysicalRoot & "\"
      End If
      lngCurrent = CLng(Format(Now(), "yyyyMMdd")) 'today as a number
      strFoundDir = Dir(strPhysicalRoot & "SZ*", vbDirectory)
      Do While Len(strFoundDir)
         If (Len(strFoundDir)>10) And (Left(strFoundDir, 2)="SZ") Then
            'get the date of the found directory as a number
            lngFound = CLng(Val(Mid(strFoundDir, 3, 8)))
```

```
            If lngCurrent >= lngFound + m_daysOldToDelete Then
               If DeleteThisDir(strPhysicalRoot & strFoundDir) Then
                  intCount = intCount + 1
               End If
            End If
         End If
         strFoundDir = Dir
      Loop
   Else
      WriteToResponse "<P><B>Error:</B> " & m_errors(intResult) & "<P>"
   End If
   deleteOldFiles = intCount
   Exit Function
FDOF_Err:
   deleteOldFiles = 0     'general error
   WriteToResponse "<P><B>Error:</B> " & m_errors(29) & "<P>"
   Exit Function
End Function


Private Sub DeleteTheseFiles(strFileSpec)
   On Error GoTo SDTF_Err
   Kill strFileSpec
SDTF_Err:
   Exit Sub
End Sub


Private Function DeleteThisDir(strDirName As String) As Boolean
   On Error GoTo FDTD_Err
   ChDir strDirName
   DeleteTheseFiles (strDirName & "\*.*")
   ChDir ".."
   RmDir strDirName
   DeleteThisDir = True
   Exit Function
FDTD_Err:
   DeleteThisDir = False
   Exit Function
End Function
...
```

The fileListing() Method

The **fileListing()** method allows the Web author using our component to generate lists of files that the remote user can compress and download. Again, the way it works is similar in outline to the previous methods. It checks that the required property values are available and converts virtual to physical paths with the **Server.MapPath** method.

Notice that our **fileListing()** method has an optional parameter, **fileSpec**. Alternatively, we could have implemented this as a property of the class, but doing it this way shows how we can use it in code, and how we cope with it being optional. These are all standard Visual Basic techniques.

You can also see how the two properties **beforeFileHTML** and **beforeFileHTML** are used to enclose the file name when it's written into the page:

```
...
Public Function fileListing(Optional fileSpec As String) As Integer
   'returns number of files listed
   '... declare local variables here ...
   On Error GoTo FFLI_Err
   intResult = 0
   intCount = 0
   If IsMissing(fileSpecification) Then
      strFileSpec = "*.*"
   Else
      strFileSpec = fileSpec
   End If
   If Len(m_fileListRoot) = 0 Then intResult = 32
   If intResult = 0 Then
      If InStr(m_fileListRoot, ":") = 0 Then
         Set objASPServer = objOCXForm.objScript.Server
         strPhysicalRoot = objASPServer.MapPath(m_fileListRoot)
      Else
         strPhysicalRoot = m_fileListRoot
      End If
      If Len(strPhysicalRoot) = 0 Then intResult = 33
   End If
   If intResult = 0 Then
      If Right(strPhysicalRoot, 1) <> "\" Then
         strPhysicalRoot = strPhysicalRoot & "\"
      End If
      strFoundFile = Dir(strPhysicalRoot & strFileSpec, _
                       vbArchive + vbNormal + vbReadOnly)
      Do While Len(strFoundFile)
         If Left(strFoundFile, 1) <> "." Then
            WriteToResponse m_beforeFileHTML & strFoundFile _
                          & m_afterFileHTML
            intCount = intCount + 1
         End If
         strFoundFile = Dir
      Loop
   Else
      WriteToResponse "<P><B>Error:</B> " & m_errors(intResult) & "<P>"
   End If
   fileListing = intCount
   Exit Function
FFLI_Err:
   fileListing = 0      'general error
   WriteToResponse "<P><B>Error:</B> " & m_errors(31) & "<P>"
   Exit Function
End Function
```

The servzipg.bas Module File

The **Globals** module, **servzipg.bas**, provides two global variables and a function, which are available to all instances of our **ServerZip** class. The function is used to retrieve the **(Default)** value from a particular Registry key:

```
Public CRLF As String
Public blnBusy As Boolean
```

```
Const OUR_SUBKEY = "SOFTWARE\Stonebroom\ServerZip\"
Const HKEY_LOCAL_MACHINE = &H80000002
Const ERROR_SUCCESS = 0&

Declare Function RegCloseKey Lib "advapi32.dll" (ByVal hKey As Long) As Long

Declare Function RegOpenKey Lib "advapi32.dll" Alias "RegOpenKeyA" (ByVal hKey As
Long, ByVal lpSubKey As String, phkResult As Long) As Long

Declare Function RegQueryValue Lib "advapi32.dll" Alias "RegQueryValueA" (ByVal hKey
As Long, ByVal lpSubKey As String, ByVal lpValue As String, lpcbValue As Long) As Long

Function GetKeyValue(strKeyName As String) As String
   Dim lngResult As Integer
   Dim lngThisKey As Long
   Dim lngLength As Long
   Dim strValue As String
   strValue = String(1024, "0")
   lngLength = 1023
   lngResult = RegOpenKey(HKEY_LOCAL_MACHINE, OUR_SUBKEY _
                          & strKeyName, lngThisKey)
   If lngResult = ERROR_SUCCESS Then
      lngResult = RegQueryValue(lngThisKey, vbNullString, _
                                strValue, lngLength)
   End If
   If lngResult = ERROR_SUCCESS Then
      GetKeyValue = Left(strValue, lngLength - 1)
   Else
      GetKeyValue = ""
   End If
   lngResult = RegCloseKey(lngThisKey)
End Function
```

Which Registry Section?

You might be tempted to use the built-in Visual Basic **GetSetting** and **SaveSetting** routines to access and store Registry values. This is fine for normal applications, but no good for server components. The VB functions can only be used to place values in the **HKEY_CURRENT_USER** section of the Registry. Because the Web server runs as a service under Windows, there is no concept of a current user here. Only when someone is logged into the machine locally do they become the current user, and it could be *any* user. The setting for the server's services are generally stored in the **HKEY_LOCAL_MACHINE** section of the Registry, and that's where our code looks for its values.

Setting Registry Values

The **ServerZip** component is supplied with a simple single-form application named **SZConfig.exe** that can be used to change the value of these Registry settings.

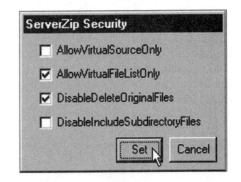

It uses the same code as that shown above to read the four Registry settings when it loads and displays these settings in check boxes. When the Set button is clicked, it uses the following code to store the values back in the Registry. By using the **RegCreateKey** API function, we create a new key if it does not already exist, or open an existing one:

```
Const OUR_SUBKEY = "SOFTWARE\Stonebroom\ServerZip\"
Const HKEY_LOCAL_MACHINE = &H80000002
Const ERROR_SUCCESS = 0&
Public Const REG_SZ = 1

Declare Function RegCloseKey Lib "advapi32.dll" (ByVal hKey As Long) As Long

Declare Function RegCreateKey Lib "advapi32.dll" Alias "RegCreateKeyA" (ByVal hKey As
Long, ByVal lpSubKey As String, phkResult As Long) As Long

Declare Function RegSetValue Lib "advapi32.dll" Alias "RegSetValueA" (ByVal hKey As
Long, ByVal lpSubKey As String, ByVal dwType As Long, ByVal lpData As String, ByVal
cbData As Long) As Long

Function SetKeyValue(strKeyName As String, strValue As String) As Boolean
   Dim lngResult As Integer
   Dim lngThisKey As Long
   lngResult = RegCreateKey(HKEY_LOCAL_MACHINE, OUR_SUBKEY _
                            & strKeyName, lngThisKey)
   If lngResult = ERROR_SUCCESS Then
      lngResult = RegSetValue(lngThisKey, vbNullString, REG_SZ, _
                              strValue, Len(strValue))
   Else
      MsgBox "Cannot set Registry value", vbExclamation, "Error"
   End If
   lngResult = RegCloseKey(lngThisKey)
End Function
```

The ocxform.frm Form File

The final part of the component code is the **ocxform** object code, stored in the **ocxform** form. We've removed the parts that are proprietary, but essentially you can see that all it really consists of is the **createZip()** function that we call from the **doZip()** code in the **ServerZip** class module, and several callback functions that the DLL and OCX use to provide status information. It also holds the reference to the **ScriptingContext** object (as we've discussed earlier), and the **blnCancel** variable that can be used to cancel the zip process when the component goes out of scope:

```
Public objScript As ScriptingContext
Public blnCancel As Boolean
...
```

The main part of interest is how we can write this status information into the page as the DLL is creating the zip file. This can prevent connection time-outs when large files are being compressed or the server is very busy, and may help to stop the user drifting off to sleep while they wait for their file. Again, we use the **DebugVer** conditional compilation argument to print the output into the Visual Basic Immediate window if we are in 'test' mode:

```
...
Public Function createZip(strSource As String, _
                          strTarget As String, _
                          intCompress As Integer, _
                          blnRecurse As Boolean, _
                          strEncrypt As String, _
                          blnDelete As Boolean) As Integer
'.......................................
'code to interface with OCX goes here
'.......................................
End Function


'.......................................
'other OCX interface callback code goes here
'.......................................

Private Sub Callback1(ItemName As String, Cancel As Integer)
    #If DebugVer Then
        Debug.Print "<BR>" & CRLF & ItemName & " ";
    #Else
        objScript.Response.Write "<BR>" & ItemName & "   "
        If objScript.Response.Buffer Then objScript.Response.Flush
    #End If
    Cancel = blnCancel
End Sub

Private Sub Callback2(Cancel As Integer)
    #If DebugVer Then
        Debug.Print ".";
    #Else
        objScript.Response.Write "."
        If objScript.Response.Buffer Then objScript.Response.Flush
    #End If
    Cancel = blnCancel
End Sub
```

Wasted Status Information

Finally, just to prove that you can never rely on anything, we were quite put out to discover that—despite going to all this effort to provide status information at each stage of the compression process—the browser itself does its best to ruin the effect. Our code writes the Item number on a new line in the page, then places a full stop for each segment of the file as it's being compressed. It should work like a crude status gauge, with dots progressing across the screen (just like in the Windows NT start-up screen). Unfortunately, all the browsers we tested tend to cache the output until a **
** or **<P>** is reached, so the effect is somewhat lost.

Using the ServerZip Component

In the remainder of this chapter, we'll be putting the ServerZip component to work. You can download the finished component from **http://rapid.wrox.co.uk** or **http://www.rapid.wrox.com**. Included with it are a series of sample pages that demonstrate the features it provides. These are designed to allow you full freedom to experiment with all the properties and methods that the component provides.

> Allowing anonymous remote users free access to all the properties and methods is probably not a good idea. In your ASP applications, you'll want to expose only a selected set of properties and methods over the Web, and verify and set the others within your ASP script code. You can also limit the available options using the SZConfig utility that is provided with the component.

Even though you may not have built the component yourself, there's nothing to stop you using it in your own pages. In fact, there are now so many Active Server Components available that you may never have to build your own.

For some idea of the range of Active Server Components that are available, visit **http://www.15seconds.com**, **http://www.asphole.com**, **http://www.activeserverpages.com**, **http://www.swynk.com**, *and of course* **http://www.microsoft.com/iis/**

The ServerZip Sample Pages

In the section about the component interface, earlier in this chapter, we listed all the available properties and methods of the component. Here, we'll be using all these in a series of four sample pages:

- **Step 1** - Setting the file listing properties to display files on the server.
- **Step 2** - Displaying the files list and setting options for the **doZip()** method.
- **Step 3** - Creating a zip file, and setting the options which will delete old files.
- **Step 4** - Deleting old download directories and returning to Step 1.

To run these pages, you must first have installed the ServerZip *component (instructions are provided in the download file). Copy the sample pages from the installation directory into a directory somewhere below the* **WWWRoot** *directory on your server (or create a virtual directory pointing to the directory they are installed in), and make sure that this directory has* Script Execute *access permission.*

Setting the fileListing Properties

The first page, **szexamp.htm**, is not an ASP page at all, it just contains the controls where the user can set the values to be used for listing files:

The controls are on a **<FORM>**, whose **ACTION** is the file **szfiles.asp**. We use **METHOD="POST"** (as recommended by HTML 4.0), and so we'll be able to collect the values in the next page using the ASP **Forms** collection:

```
<FORM ACTION=szfiles.asp METHOD="POST">
<TABLE WIDTH=100% CELLPADDING=5>
 ...
 <TR>
  <TD>Directory name (physical or virtual):</TD>
  <TD><INPUT TYPE="TEXT" NAME=txtFileRoot SIZE=25></TD>
  <TD><B>= fileListRoot</B></TD>
 </TR>
 <TR>
  <TDText/HTML to go before filename: </TD>
  <TD><INPUT TYPE="TEXT" NAME=txtBeforeHTML SIZE=25
      VALUE="&lt;OPTION&gt;">
  </TD>
  <TD ALIGN="LEFT"><B>= beforeFileHTML</B></TD>
 </TR>
 <TR>
  <TD>Text/HTML to go after filename: </TD>
  <TD><INPUT TYPE="TEXT" NAME=txtAfterHTML SIZE=25></TD>
  <TD><B>= afterFileHTML</B></TD>
 </TR>
 <TR>
```

```
 <TD>File type specification:</TD>
 <TD><B>fileListing(
   <INPUT TYPE="TEXT" NAME=txtFileType SIZE=8 VALUE="*.*"> )</B>
 </TD>
 <TD><B>Method parameter</B></TD>
 </TR>
 <TR>
 <TD COLSPAN=3 ALIGN="RIGHT">
   <INPUT TYPE="SUBMIT" VALUE="Next &gt;">
 </TD>
 </TR>
</TABLE>
</FORM>
```

The last row of the table is the **SUBMIT** button, which sends the values of all the controls to the file
szfiles.asp.

Listing files and Setting the doZip() Options

The remaining three pages are all Active Server Pages **.asp** files. Because the ServerZip component works
best with buffering turned on, we've included the following line at the beginning of each page:

```
<% Response.Buffer = True %>
```

In the page **szfiles.asp**, we use the component to create a list of files in a **<SELECT>** control–this is
why the default value of the **beforeFileHTML** property control in the previous page was set to
<OPTION>. Here's the code that creates the new instance of our component, sets its properties, and calls
the **fileListing()** method–again, all the controls are on a **<FORM>**, whose **ACTION** this time is the file
szdozip.asp:

```
<FORM ACTION=szdozip.asp METHOD="POST">
...
<SELECT MULTIPLE SIZE=10 NAME=selSourceList>
<%
Set objSZ = Server.CreateObject("Stonebroom.ServerZip")
objSZ.fileListRoot = Request.Form("txtFileRoot")
objSZ.beforeFileHTML = Request.Form("txtBeforeHTML")
objSZ.afterFileHTML = Request.Form("txtAfterHTML")
intFiles = objSZ.fileListing(Request.Form("txtFileType"))
Set objSZ = Nothing
%>
</SELECT>
...
```

We also use the return value of the **fileListing()** method to show how many files were listed:

```
...
Listed <% = intFiles %> files.
...
```

Finally, we store the value of the **fileListRoot** property in a **HIDDEN** control, so that we can pass it on
to the next page where we'll need it again:

```
...
<INPUT TYPE="HIDDEN" NAME="hidListPath"
VALUE="<% = Request.Form("txtFileRoot") %>">
...
```

And here's the result. You can see we found three files:

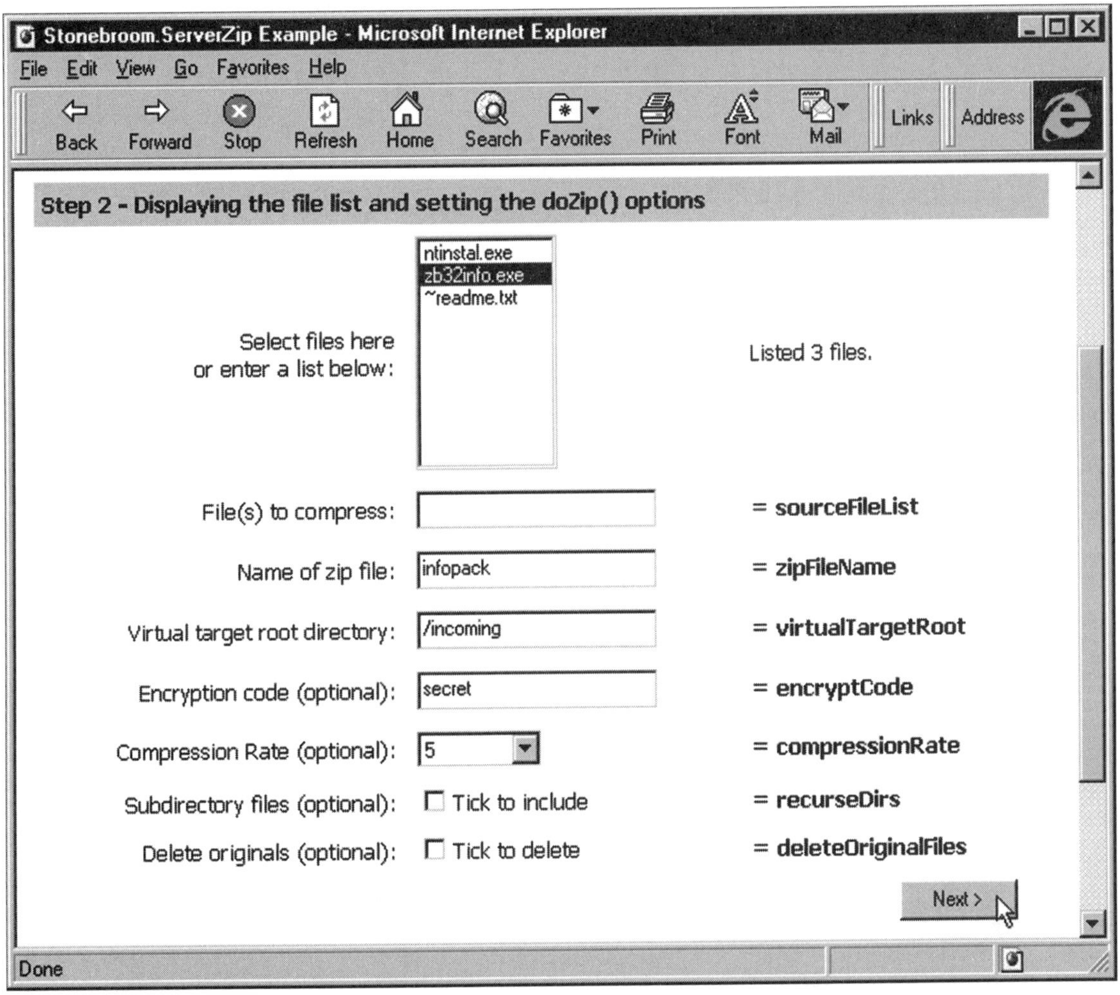

The remainder of this page is just more HTML controls on the same `<FORM>` as the `<SELECT>` list. When the user clicks the Next button, the values of these controls will be passed on to the next page, `szdozip.htm`.

Creating a Zip File

Now we come to the most complicated page. This page has to collect all the values sent from the previous page, and execute the `doZip()` method of the component. However, things are made more complex by the fact that we're allowing the user to select files using the list we provided. Alternatively, they can type a physical or virtual file specification into the text box below the list. So the first thing our code has to do in the **szdozip.asp** page is figure out what the **sourceFileList** property should be.

The value sent from the **txtSourceList** control contains the text typed into the **sourceFileList** text box. If there was a value there, we simply use it as the **sourceFileList** property. However if it was empty, we know that we have to use the items selected in the list instead. This is a multiple-select list (it includes the **MULTIPLE** attribute in its opening HTML tag), so the value could be more that one filename. In this case, the browser returns all the selected entries as a single string with each one separated from the rest by a comma.

Handling Multiple-Select Lists

Our ASP code has to break this list up into a format suitable for the component's **sourceFileList** property, and add the path that the user provided for the file listing to each one. This is why we carried it forward in the hidden control from the previous page. If the path is a virtual one we can only use one file, and this will be the first one selected. However if it's a physical path, we have to collect all the files from the list. The first part of our code decides which type of values we're dealing with:

```
<%
strSourceList = Request.Form("txtSourceList") 'value from text box
If Len(strSourceList) = 0 Then              'use files selected in list

  'the file list directory they used to get the list of files
  'is carried forward from a hidden control in the form:
  strListPath = Request.Form("hidListPath")
  If InStr(strListPath, ":") Or InStr(strListPath, "\") Then
    blnPhysical = True    'its a physical path
    If Right(strListPath, 1) <> "\" Then
      strListPath = strListPath & "\"
    End If
  Else  'its a virtual path
    blnPhysical = False
    If Right(strListPath, 1) <> "/" Then
      strListPath = strListPath & "/"
    End If
  End If

  'All the items selected in the list box are comma-delimited
  'in a single string from the form. We get this string with:
  strFileList = Request.Form("selSourceList")
  If Instr(strFileList, ",") Then 'several files selected
    'get the first one into strSourceList
    strSourceList = strListPath _
                  & Left(strFileList, Instr(strFileList, ",") - 1)
  Else   'a single file selected
    strSourceList = strListPath & strFileList
    strFileList = ""
  End If
  ...
```

Our component expects any files whose names include a space to be enclosed in double quotes (ASCII character **34**). We'll add these for the one file we've already got in **strSourceList** now, if they're required:

```
...
If InStr(strSourceList, " ") Then
   strSourceList = Chr(34) & strSourceList & Chr(34)
End If
...
```

If we're dealing with a physical path and have a list of files, we can carry on splitting each one off the original string, wrapping them up in double quotes where necessary, and adding them to the **strSourceList** string. Each entry in **strSourceList** needs to be the full path and name of a file we want to include in the zip file, separated from its neighbors by a single space character:

```
...
If (blnPhysical) And (Len(strFileList)) Then
   'physical directory, so we can get the rest of the files
   strFileList = Trim(Mid(strFileList, Instr(strFileList, ",") + 1))
   strNextFile = strListPath _
                  & Left(strFileList, Instr(strFileList, ",") - 1)
   If InStr(strNextFile, " ") Then
      strNextFile = Chr(34) & strNextFile & Chr(34)
   End If
   'component expects a source file list delimited with spaces
   strSourceList = strSourceList & " " & strNextFile
   Do While Instr(strFileList, ",")
      strFileList = Trim(Mid(strFileList, Instr(strFileList, ",") + 1))
      If Instr(strFileList, ",") Then   'more files to come
         strNextFile = strListPath _
                     & Left(strFileList, Instr(strFileList, ",") - 1)
      Else   'this is the last one in the list
         strNextFile = strListPath & strFileList
      End If
      If InStr(strNextFile, " ") Then
         strNextFile = Chr(34) & strNextFile & Chr(34)
      End If
      strSourceList = strSourceList & " " & strNextFile
   Loop
   End If
End If
Response.Write "Source file list is <B>" & strSourceList & "</B><P>"
...
```

Setting the Script Time-Out Value

The last step in the code above is to write the value of the **strSourceList** into the page, so that the user can see what we think they selected. Before we actually start zipping the files, however, there is one other task. Because the operation may take a while to complete, we'll change the script execution timeout from the default 20 seconds to a higher value–here we've allowed up to 10 minutes for the creation of very large zip files:

```
...
Server.ScriptTimeOut = 600
...
```

Setting the Component Properties

Finally, we're ready to create the component object and set the properties. Notice how we use the value of the checkboxes (which return **"on"** if checked or nothing if not checked) to set the Boolean properties of the component. We also need to convert the compression rate value into a number before we try and apply it to the component:

```
...
Set objSZ = Server.CreateObject("Stonebroom.ServerZip")
objSZ.sourceFileList = strSourceList
objSZ.zipFileName = Request.Form("txtZipFile")
objSZ.virtualTargetRoot = Request.Form("txtTargetRoot")
objSZ.encryptCode = Request.Form("txtEncryptCode")
objSZ.compressionRate = CInt(Request.Form("selCompressRate"))
objSZ.recurseDirs = (Request.Form("chkRecurseDirs") = "on")
objSZ.deleteOriginalFiles = (Request.Form("chkDeleteOriginals") = "on")
...
```

Checking if the Component is Busy

Everything is now ready to start the zip process, but before we go leaping headlong into it we need to remember that the component does not allow concurrent operations. To get round this, we use the **zipIsBusy** property that it exposes, and wait up to a couple of minutes for it to become available:

```
...
If objSZ.zipIsBusy Then
  Response.Write "Waiting to access the component ...<P>"
  Response.Flush
  'force display by the browser with 2 Write/Flush operations
  Response.Write ""
  Response.Flush
  'then wait up to two mins for component to become available
  intWaitUntil = Minute(Now) + 2
  Do While (objSZ.zipIsBusy) And (Minute(Now) < intWaitUntil)
  Loop
End If
If objSZ.zipIsBusy Then
  Response.Write "Sorry, the component is too busy at present.<P>"
  Response.Flush
Else    'OK to do the zip
  blnWorked = objSZ.doZip()
End If
Set objSZ = Nothing
%>
```

And here's the result. Notice that the file is placed in a hyperlink ready to collect. The status bar shows the path to it, complete with the unique subdirectory within the target directory where it was placed:

The remaining section of this page provides the controls for deleting old files and directories that should have already been collected. You can see that the Virtual target root text box already contains the path that we used for this zip file. This saves having to type it in if you want to clear old directories from the same virtual root. It's achieved with the value of the **virtualTargetRoot** property that we used earlier in the page:

```
<INPUT TYPE="TEXT" NAME="txtTargetRoot" SIZE=25
       VALUE="<% = Request.Form("txtTargetRoot") %>">
```

Using Other Zip Properties

In the previous example we only typed in values for the required properties of the component, in the controls on the page, leaving the others at their defaults. However, we can also provide an encryption code, include any subdirectory contents, and delete the original files:

You can see here that we've entered a physical path to the source files, and included the wildcard file specification ***.*** (all files). We've also turned on the 'Subdirectory files' and 'Delete originals' options. To prevent the deletion of files by accident, a warning dialog pops up when you turn on the Delete originals option. This is done by some client-side JavaScript code written in the page:

```
<INPUT TYPE="CHECKBOX" NAME=chkDelete onClick="deleteConfirm()">
...
<SCRIPT LANGUAGE="JAVASCRIPT">
<!--
function deleteConfirm() {
if (document.forms[0].elements["chkDeleteOriginals"].checked)
  { var strMesg = 'WARNING: You have elected to delete the '
               + 'original files once compression is complete. '
               + 'Make sure that you do not include files that '
               + 'you do not want to delete.';
   alert(strMesg);
  }
}
//-->
</SCRIPT>
```

However, we've also set the Registry value DisableDeleteOriginalFiles to **"1"** on our server using the supplied SZConfig utility, so when the zip operation takes place an error message is inserted into the page and the originals are not deleted:

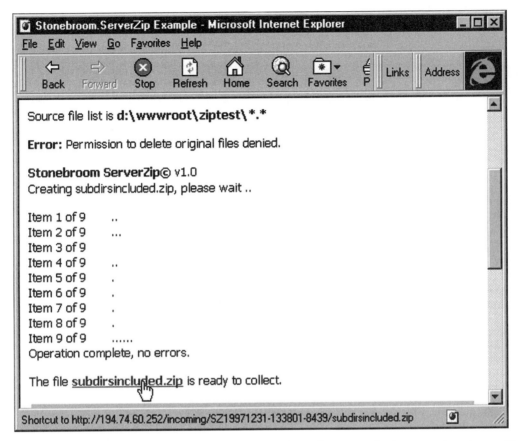

This time, you see the nine source files being compressed one by one, and when complete the resulting zip file can be collected. When viewed in a zip file manager, you can see the single subdirectory and its contents that were within the source directory:

And because we provided an encryption key for the **encryptCode** property, we can't unzip the files without it:

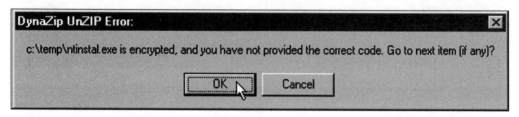

Deleting Old Unique Download Directories

The final page in our examples, **szdelete.asp**, is used to remove old downloaded zip files and the uniquely-named directories that they reside in. We only need to worry about two properties for this, one of which defaults to a sensible value if not specified.

The bottom section of the page **szdozip.asp** that we've just been working with contains the two controls for the **virtualTargetRoot** and **daysOldToDelete** properties. These values are passed to the page **szdelete.asp** when the Next button is clicked, and we use these to set the properties of the component:

```
<%
Set objSZ = Server.CreateObject("Stonebroom.ServerZip")
objSZ.virtualTargetRoot = Request.Form("txtTargetRoot")
objSZ.daysOldToDelete = Cint(Request.Form("txtDaysOld"))
intFiles = objSZ.deleteOldFiles()
Set objSZ = Nothing
%>
```

This removes the old directories and files, and places a confirmation message in the page. We use the value returned by the **deleteOldFiles** method to show how many directories were deleted:

```
...
<B>ServerZip</B> reports that it deleted<B> <% = intFiles %> </B>
unique directories and their contents within the virtual root<B>
<% = Request.Form("txtTargetRoot") %>
...
```

Here's how it looks in the browser:

At the bottom of the page is a button that returns us to the original `szexamp.htm` page, so that we can go round again. Rather than use client-side script to load the page, we've made the button a **SUBMIT** button, and placed it on a form whose **ACTION** is the ordinary HTML page we want to load. In order for this to work, we have to break with the recommendations of HTML 4 and use **METHOD="GET"**. If we use **"POST"**, the server will report an error:

```
...
<FORM ACTION="szexamp.htm" METHOD="GET">
<TABLE WIDTH=100%>
 <TR>
  <TD ALIGN="RIGHT"><INPUT TYPE="SUBMIT" VALUE="Next &gt;"></TD>
 </TR>
</TABLE>
</FORM>
...
```

Summary

And that's it, both for this chapter and the book as a whole. In this chapter, we've explored the background, requirements, techniques and implementation of a custom Active Server Component, and seen how it can be used with ASP script in our applications. Developing components is not really an Active Server Pages topic, but if you understand how they are built, how they work and interact with ASP, and the limitations that they have to work under, it makes it easier to decide when a component is a good solution to your requirements.

We've used Visual Basic in this chapter to build our component, with the intention of making it easy to follow how it works, and what it's doing behind the scenes. Of course, any other language that can create COM-enabled objects, such as C++, Java, Delphi, etc. can be used instead. In our case, where all the real processing is done by a legacy DLL, Visual Basic proves plenty fast enough to act as the interface and the glue that links Active Server Pages with the internal objects inside our component.

We've covered most aspects of building and using components here, coming from the direction of a real-life problem based on an existing application. As we converted it to work over the Web, you saw:

▲ How the nature of the network changes our application design philosophy

▲ How we can reuse existing components in a Web-based application

▲ How Active Server Pages acts as the glue to hold it all together

▲ How we adapted our zip file components to work over the Web

▲ How you can use the finished component in your own pages

And having worked through this book, you're ready to set to work designing and building your own Web sites and Intranet applications, using all the advanced features and techniques that Active Server Pages provides.

The VBScript Language

Array Handling

Dim—declares an array variable. This can be static with a defined number of elements or dynamic and can have up to 60 dimensions.

ReDim—used to change the size of an array variable which has been declared as dynamic.

Preserve—keyword used to preserve the contents of an array being resized. If you need to use this then you can only re–dimension the rightmost index of the array.

```
Dim strEmployees ()
ReDim strEmployees (9,1)

strEmployees (9,1) = "Phil"

ReDim strEmployees (9,2)              'loses the contents of element (9,1)
strEmployees (9,2) = "Paul"

ReDim Preserve strEmployees (9,3)    'preserves the contents of (9,2)
strEmployees (9,3) = "Smith"
```

LBound— returns the smallest subscript for the dimension of an array. Note that arrays always start from the subscript zero so this function will always return the value zero.

UBound—used to determine the size of an array.

```
Dim strCustomers (10, 5)
intSizeFirst = UBound (strCustomers, 1)      'returns SizeFirst = 10
intSizeSecond = UBound (strCustomers, 2)     'returns SizeSecond = 5
```

> The actual number of elements is always one greater than the value returned by UBound because the array starts from zero.

Assignments

Let—used to assign values to variables (optional).
Set—used to assign an object reference to a variable.

```
Let intNumberOfDays = 365

Set txtMyTextBox = txtcontrol
txtMyTextBox.Value = "Hello World"
```

Constants

Empty—an empty variable is one that has been created but not yet assigned a value.
Nothing—used to remove an object reference.

```
Set txtMyTextBox = txtATextBox        'assigns object reference
Set txtMyTextBox = Nothing            'removes object reference
```

Null—indicates that a variable is not valid. Note that this isn't the same as **Empty**.
True—indicates that an expression is true. Has numerical value −1.
False—indicates that an expression is false. Has numerical value 0.

Error constant:

Constant	Value
vbObjectError	&h80040000

System Color constants:

Constant	Value	Description
vbBlack	&h00	Black
vbRed	&hFF	Red
vbGreen	&hFF00	Green
vbYellow	&hFFFF	Yellow
vbBlue	&hFF0000	Blue
vbMagenta	&hFF00FF	Magenta
vbCyan	&hFFFF00	Cyan
vbWhite	&hFFFFFF	White

Comparison constants:

Constant	Value	Description
vbBinaryCompare	0	Perform a binary comparison.
vbTextCompare	1	Perform a textual comparison.
vbDatabaseCompare	2	Perform a comparison based upon information in the database where the comparison is to be performed.

Date and Time constants:

Constant	Value	Description
VbSunday	1	Sunday
vbMonday	2	Monday
vbTuesday	3	Tuesday
vbWednesday	4	Wednesday
vbThursday	5	Thursday
vbFriday	6	Friday
vbSaturday	7	Saturday
vbFirstJan1	1	Use the week in which January 1 occurs (default).
vbFirstFourDays	2	Use the first week that has at least four days in the new year.
vbFirstFullWeek	3	Use the first full week of the year.
vbUseSystem	0	Use the format in the regional settings for the computer.
vbUseSystemDayOfWeek	0	Use the day in the system settings for the first weekday.

Date Format constants:

Constant	Value	Description
vbGeneralDate	0	Display a date and/or time in the format set in the system settings. For real numbers display a date and time. For integer numbers display only a date. For numbers less than 1, display time only.
vbLongDate	1	Display a date using the long date format specified in the computers regional settings.
vbShortDate	2	Display a date using the short date format specified in the computers regional settings.

Table Continued on Following Page

Constant	Value	Description
vbLongTime	3	Display a time using the long time format specified in the computers regional settings.
vbShortTime	4	Display a time using the short time format specified in the computers regional settings.

File Input/Output constants:

Constant	Value	Description
ForReading	1	Open a file for reading only.
ForWriting	2	Open a file for writing. If a file with the same name exists, its previous one is overwritten.
ForAppending	8	Open a file and write at the end of the file.

String constants:

Constant	Value	Description
vbCr	Chr(13)	Carriage return only
vbCrLf	Chr(13) & Chr(10)	Carriage return and linefeed (Newline)
vbLf	Chr(10)	Line feed only
vbNewLine	–	Newline character as appropriate to a specific platform
vbNullChar	Chr(0)	Character having the value 0
vbNullString	–	String having the value zero (not just an empty string)
vbTab	Chr(9)	Horizontal tab

Tristate constants:

Constant	Value	Description
TristateTrue	−1	True
TristateFalse	0	False
TristateUseDefault	−2	Use default setting

VarType constants:

Constant	Value	Description
vbEmpty	0	Un–initialized (default)
vbNull	1	Contains no valid data
vbInteger	2	Integer subtype
vbLong	3	Long subtype
vbSingle	4	Single subtype
vbDouble	5	Double subtype
vbCurrency	6	Currency subtype
vbDate	7	Date subtype
vbString	8	String subtype
vbObject	9	Object
vbError	10	Error subtype
vbBoolean	11	Boolean subtype
vbVariant	12	Variant (used only for arrays of variants)
vbDataObject	13	Data access object
vbDecimal	14	Decimal subtype
vbByte	17	Byte subtype
vbArray	8192	Array

Control Flow

For...Next—executes a block of code a specified number of times.

```
Dim intSalary (10)
For intCounter = 0 to 10
   intSalary (intCounter) = 20000
Next
```

For Each...Next Statement—repeats a block of code for each element in an array or collection.

```
For Each Item In Request.QueryString("MyControl")
  Response.Write Item & "<BR>"
Next
```

Do...Loop—executes a block of code while a condition is true or until a condition becomes true.

```
Do While strDayOfWeek <> "Saturday" And strDayOfWeek <> "Sunday"
   MsgBox ("Get Up! Time for work")
   ...
Loop

Do
   MsgBox ("Get Up! Time for work")
   ...
Loop Until strDayOfWeek = "Saturday" Or strDayOfWeek = "Sunday"
```

If...Then...Else—used to run various blocks of code depending on conditions.

```
If intAge < 20 Then
   MsgBox ("You're just a slip of a thing!")
ElseIf intAge < 40 Then
   MsgBox ("You're in your prime!")
Else
   MsgBox ("You're older and wiser")
End If
```

Select Case—used to replace **If...Then...Else** statements where there are many conditions.

```
Select Case intAge
Case 21,22,23,24,25,26
   MsgBox ("You're in your prime")
Case 40
   MsgBox ("You're fulfilling your dreams")
Case 65
   MsgBox ("Time for a new challenge")
End Select
```

Note that **Select Case** can only be used with precise conditions and not with a range of conditions.

While...Wend—executes a block of code while a condition is true.

```
While strDayOfWeek <> "Saturday" AND strDayOfWeek <> "Sunday"
   MsgBox ("Get Up! Time for work")
   ...
Wend
```

Functions

VBScript contains several functions that can be used to manipulate and examine variables. These have been subdivided into the general categories of:

 Conversion Functions

 Date/Time Functions

▲ Math Functions

- ▲ Object Management Functions
- ▲ Script Engine Identification Functions
- ▲ String Functions
- ▲ Variable Testing Functions

For a full description of each function, and the parameters it requires, see the VBScript Help file. This is installed by default in your **Docs/ASPDocs/VBS/VBScript** subfolder of your IIS installation directory.

Conversion Functions

These functions are used to convert values in variables between different types:

Function	Description
Asc	Returns the numeric ANSI code number of the first character in a string.
AscB	As above, but provided for use with byte data contained in a string. Returns result from the first byte only.
AscW	As above, but provided for Unicode characters. Returns the **Wide** character code, avoiding the conversion from Unicode to ANSI.
Chr	Returns a string made up of the ANSI character matching the number supplied.
ChrB	As above, but provided for use with byte data contained in a string. Always returns a single byte.
ChrW	As above, but provided for Unicode characters. Its argument is a **Wide** character code, thereby avoiding the conversion from ANSI to Unicode.
CBool	Returns the argument value converted to a **Variant** of subtype **Boolean**.
CByte	Returns the argument value converted to a **Variant** of subtype **Byte**.
CDate	Returns the argument value converted to a **Variant** of subtype **Date**.
CDbl	Returns the argument value converted to a **Variant** of subtype **Double**.
CInt	Returns the argument value converted to a **Variant** of subtype **Integer**.
CLng	Returns the argument value converted to a **Variant** of subtype **Long**.
CSng	Returns the argument value converted to a **Variant** of subtype **Single**.
CStr	Returns the argument value converted to a **Variant** of subtype **String**.
Fix	Returns the integer (whole) part of a number.
Hex	Returns a string representing the hexadecimal value of a number.
Int	Returns the integer (whole) portion of a number.
Oct	Returns a string representing the octal value of a number.
Round	Returns a number rounded to a specified number of decimal places.
Sgn	Returns an integer indicating the sign of a number.

Date/Time Functions

These functions return date or time values from the computer's system clock, or manipulate existing values:

Function	Description
Date	Returns the current system date.
DateAdd	Returns a date to which a specified time interval has been added.
DateDiff	Returns the number of days, weeks, or years between two dates.
DatePart	Returns just the day, month or year of a given date.
DateSerial	Returns a **Variant** of subtype **Date** for a specified year, month, and day.
DateValue	Returns a **Variant** of subtype **Date**.
Day	Returns a number between **1** and **31** representing the day of the month.
Hour	Returns a number between **0** and **23** representing the hour of the day.
Minute	Returns a number between **0** and **59** representing the minute of the hour.
Month	Returns a number between **1** and **12** representing the month of the year.
MonthName	Returns the name of the specified month as a string.
Now	Returns the current date and time.
Second	Returns a number between **0** and **59** representing the second of the minute.
Time	Returns a **Variant** of subtype **Date** indicating the current system time.
TimeSerial	Returns a **Variant** of subtype **Date** for a specific hour, minute, and second.
TimeValue	Returns a **Variant** of subtype **Date** containing the time.
Weekday	Returns a number representing the day of the week.
WeekdayName	Returns the name of the specified day of the week as a string.
Year	Returns a number representing the year.

Math Functions

These functions perform mathematical operations on variables containing numerical values:

Function	Description
Atn	Returns the arctangent of a number.
Cos	Returns the cosine of an angle.
Exp	Returns **e** (the base of natural logarithms) raised to a power.
Log	Returns the natural logarithm of a number.

Function	Description
`Randomize`	Initializes the random–number generator.
`Rnd`	Returns a random number.
`Sin`	Returns the sine of an angle.
`Sqr`	Returns the square root of a number.
`Tan`	Returns the tangent of an angle.

Object Management Functions

These functions are used to manipulate objects, where applicable:

Function	Description
`CreateObject`	Creates and returns a reference to an ActiveX or OLE Automation object.
`GetObject`	Returns a reference to an ActiveX or OLE Automation object.
`LoadPicture`	Returns a picture object.

Script Engine Identification

These functions return the version of the scripting engine:

Function	Description
`ScriptEngine`	A string containing the major, minor, and build version numbers of the scripting engine.
`ScriptEngineMajorVersion`	The major version of the scripting engine, as a number.
`ScriptEngineMinorVersion`	The minor version of the scripting engine, as a number.
`ScriptEngineBuildVersion`	The build version of the scripting engine, as a number.

String Functions

These functions are used to manipulate string values in variables:

Function	Description
`Filter`	Returns an array from a string array, based on specified filter criteria.
`FormatCurrency`	Returns a string formatted as currency value.
`FormatDateTime`	Returns a string formatted as a date or time.

Table Continued on Following Page

Function	Description
FormatNumber	Returns a string formatted as a number.
FormatPercent	Returns a string formatted as a percentage.
InStr	Returns the position of the first occurrence of one string within another.
InStrB	As above, but provided for use with byte data contained in a string. Returns the byte position instead of the character position.
InstrRev	As InStr, but starts from the end of the string.
Join	Returns a string created by joining the strings contained in an array.
LCase	Returns a string that has been converted to lowercase.
Left	Returns a specified number of characters from the left end of a string.
LeftB	As above, but provided for use with byte data contained in a string. Uses that number of bytes instead of that number of characters.
Len	Returns the length of a string or the number of bytes needed for a variable.
LenB	As above, but is provided for use with byte data contained in a string. Returns the number of bytes in the string instead of characters.
LTrim	Returns a copy of a string without leading spaces.
Mid	Returns a specified number of characters from a string.
MidB	As above, but provided for use with byte data contained in a string. Uses that numbers of bytes instead of that number of characters.
Replace	Returns a string in which a specified substring has been replaced with another substring a specified number of times.
Right	Returns a specified number of characters from the right end of a string.
RightB	As above, but provided for use with byte data contained in a string. Uses that number of bytes instead of that number of characters.
RTrim	Returns a copy of a string without trailing spaces.
Space	Returns a string consisting of the specified number of spaces.
Split	Returns a one-dimensional array of a specified number of substrings.
StrComp	Returns a value indicating the result of a string comparison.
String	Returns a string of the length specified made up of a repeating character.
StrReverse	Returns a string in which the character order of a string is reversed.
Trim	Returns a copy of a string without leading or trailing spaces.
UCase	Returns a string that has been converted to uppercase.

Variable Testing Functions

These functions are used to determine the type of information stored in a variable:

Function	Description
IsArray	Returns a **Boolean** value indicating whether a variable is an array.
IsDate	Returns a **Boolean** value indicating whether an expression can be converted to a date.
IsEmpty	Returns a **Boolean** value indicating whether a variable has been initialized.
IsNull	Returns a **Boolean** value indicating whether an expression contains no valid data.
IsNumeric	Returns a **Boolean** value indicating whether an expression can be evaluated as a number.
IsObject	Returns a **Boolean** value indicating whether an expression references a valid ActiveX or OLE Automation object.
VarType	Returns a number indicating the subtype of a variable.

Variable Declarations

Dim–declares a variable.

Error Handling

On Error Resume Next–indicates that if an error occurs, control should continue at the next statement. **Err**–this is the error object that provides information about run–time errors.

Error handling is very limited in VBScript and the **Err** object must be tested explicitly to determine if an error has occurred.

Input/Output

This consists of **Msgbox** for output and **InputBox** for input:

MsgBox

This displays a message, and can return a value indicating which button was clicked.

```
MsgBox "Hello There",4116,"Hello Message","c:\windows\MyHelp.hlp",123
```

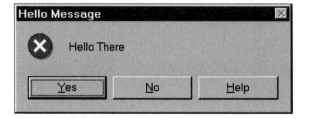

The parameters are:

"Hello There"—this contains the text of the message and is obligatory.

4116—this determines which icon and buttons appear on the message box.

"Hello Message"—this contains the text that will appear as the title of the message box.

"c:\windows\MyHelp.hlp"—this adds a Help button to the message box and determines the help file that is opened if the button is clicked.

123—this is a reference to the particular help topic that will be displayed if the Help button is clicked.

The value of the icon and buttons parameter is determined using the following tables:

Constant	Value	Buttons
vbOKOnly	0	OK
vbOKCancel	1	OK Cancel
vbAbortRetryIngnore	2	Abort Retry Ignore
vbYesNoCancel	3	Yes No Cancel
vbYesNo	4	Yes No
vbRetryCancel	5	Retry Cancel
vbDefaultButton1	0	The first button from the left is the default.
vbDefaultButton2	256	The second button from the left is the default.
vbDefaultButton3	512	The third button from the left is the default.
vbDefaultButton4	768	The fourth button from the left is the default.

Constant	Value	Description	Icon
`vbCritical`	16	Critical Message	
`vbQuestion`	32	Questioning Message	
`vbExclamation`	48	Warning Message	
`vbInformation`	64	Informational Message	

Constant	Value	Description
`vbApplicationModal`	0	Just the application stops until user clicks a button.
`vbSystemModal`	4096	Whole system stops until user clicks a button.

To specify which buttons and icon are displayed you simply add the relevant values. So, in our example we add together **4 + 16 + 4096** to display the Yes and No buttons, with Yes as the default, with the **Critical** icon, and the user being unable to use any application, besides this one, when the message box is displayed.

You can determine which button the user clicked by assigning the return code of the **MsgBox** function to a variable:

```
intButtonClicked = MsgBox ("Hello There",35,"Hello Message")
```

Notice that brackets enclose the **MsgBox** parameters when used in this format. The following table determines the value assigned to the variable **intButtonClicked**:

Constant	Value	Button Clicked
`vbOK`	1	OK
`vbCancel`	2	Cancel
`vbAbort`	3	Abort
`vbRetry`	4	Retry
`vbIgnore`	5	Ignore
`vbYes`	6	Yes
`vbNo`	7	No

InputBox

This accepts text entry from the user and returns it as a string.

```
strTextEntered = InputBox ("Please enter your name","Login","John Smith",500,500)
```

"Please enter your name"–this is the prompt displayed in the input box.
"Login"– this is the text displayed as the title of the input box.
"John Smith"– this is the default value displayed in the input box.
500–specifies the x position of the input box.
500–specifies the y position of the input box.

As with the **MsgBox** function, you can also specify a help file and topic to add a Help button to the input box.

Procedures

Call–optional method of calling a subroutine.
Function–used to declare a function.
Sub–used to declare a subroutine.

Other Keywords

Rem–old style method of adding comments to code.
Option Explicit–forces you to declare a variable before it can be used.

Visual Basic Run—time Error Codes

The following error codes also apply to VBA code and many will not be appropriate to an application built completely around VBScript. However, if you have built your own components then these error codes may well be brought up when such components are used.

Code	Description	Code	Description
3	Return without GoSub	71	Disk not ready
5	Invalid procedure call	74	Can't rename with different drive
6	Overflow	75	Path/File access error
7	Out of memory	76	Path not found
9	Subscript out of range	322	Can't create necessary temporary file
10	This array is fixed or temporarily locked	325	Invalid format in resource file
11	Division by zero	380	Invalid property value
13	Type mismatch	423	Property or method not found
14	Out of string space	424	Object required
16	Expression too complex	429	OLE Automation server can't create object
17	Can't perform requested operation	430	Class doesn't support OLE Automation
18	User interrupt occurred	432	File name or class name not found during OLE Automation operation
20	Resume without error		
28	Out of stack space	438	Object doesn't support this property or method
35	Sub or Function not defined		
47	Too many DLL application clients	440	OLE Automation error
48	Error in loading DLL	442	Connection to type library or object library for remote process has been lost. Press OK for dialog to remove reference.
49	Bad DLL calling convention		
51	Internal error		
52	Bad file name or number	443	OLE Automation object does not have a default value
53	File not found		
54	Bad file mode	445	Object doesn't support this action
55	File already open	446	Object doesn't support named arguments
57	Device I/O error		
58	File already exists	447	Object doesn't support current locale setting
59	Bad record length		
61	Disk full	448	Named argument not found
62	Input past end of file	449	Argument not optional
63	Bad record number	450	Wrong number of arguments or invalid property assignment
67	Too many files		
68	Device unavailable	451	Object not a collection
70	Permission denied	452	Invalid ordinal
		453	Specified DLL function not found

Table Continued on Following Page

Code	Description	Code	Description
454	Code resource not found	1025	Expected end of statement
455	Code resource lock error	1026	Expected integer constant
457	This key is already associated with an element of this collection	1027	Expected 'While' or 'Until'
458	Variable uses an OLE Automation type not supported in Visual Basic	1028	Expected 'While', 'Until' or end of statement
481	Invalid picture	1029	Too many locals or arguments
500	Variable is undefined	1030	Identifier too long
501	Cannot assign to variable	1031	Invalid number
1001	Out of memory	1032	Invalid character
1002	Syntax error	1033	Un–terminated string constant
1003	Expected ':'	1034	Un–terminated comment
1004	Expected ';'	1035	Nested comment
1005	Expected '('	1036	'Me' cannot be used outside of a procedure
1006	Expected ')'	1037	Invalid use of 'Me' keyword
1007	Expected ']'	1038	'loop' without 'do'
1008	Expected '{'	1039	Invalid 'exit' statement
1009	Expected '}'	1040	Invalid 'for' loop control variable
1010	Expected identifier	1041	Variable redefinition
1011	Expected '='	1042	Must be first statement on the line
1012	Expected 'If'	1043	Cannot assign to non–ByVal argument
1013	Expected 'To'		
1014	Expected 'End'		
1015	Expected 'Function'		
1016	Expected 'Sub'		
1017	Expected 'Then'		
1018	Expected 'Wend'		
1019	Expected 'Loop'		
1020	Expected 'Next'		
1021	Expected 'Case'		
1022	Expected 'Select'		
1023	Expected expression		
1024	Expected statement		

For more information about VBScript, visit Microsoft's VBScript site at:

`http://www.microsoft.com/vbscript/us/techinfo/vbsdocs.htm`

JScript
Reference

JScript is a scripting language which can be used on both the client (inside HTML pages) and the server— in Active Server Pages. JScript is the Microsoft implementation of the scripting language, which is specified by ECMA (European Standards Organization) as the standard scripting language (see **ECMA-262** specification). This specification can be obtained from **http://www.ecma.ch/stand/ecma-262.htm.**

Below is a reference for the Microsoft version of the language, which includes some enhancements that take advantage of the capabilities of Microsoft Internet Explorer. Note that one can also access the browser/ASP object model using JScript, so all the objects, properties and methods are detailed in the following appendices are also available using Jscript. For a thorough, no nonsense guide to JScript and the wider compatibility issues surrounding Javascript and Jscript, you can't do better than Instant JavaScript, *ISBN 1-861001-27-4,* by Nigel McFarlane and published by Wrox Press.

Script Formatting and Comments

▲ **Unicode 2.0** characters may be used to write a script. Only ASCII characters can appear outside string literals and comment text.

▲ **Whitespace** separates language elements not otherwise separated by punctuation characters, it also improves readibility and consists of one or more of these characters:

Character name	Unicode value	ASCII decimal code
Tab	\u0009	9
Vertical Tab	\u000B	11
Form Feed	\u000C	13
Space	\u0020	32

▲ **Line terminators** also separate language elements, but cannot appear directly inside a string literal:

Character name	Unicode value	ASCII decimal code
Line Feed	\u000A	10
Carriage Return	\u000D	14

▲ **Comments** are non-functional text. Single line comments can appear inside multi-line comments but no other combination is possible.

```
// single line comment
```

```
/* multi-line
   comment */
```

▲ **Identifiers** consist of one or more alphabetic letters, decimal digits, underscores ('_') or dollar signs ('$'), and are case-sensitive. The first character may not be a decimal digit.

▲ **Automatic semicolon insertion**. Statements normally end with a semi-colon(';'). If left out, the interpreter will assume one, except within the parentheses of a **for** loop. If a **return** statement with an argument, or an expression with a post-increment('++') or post-decrement ('--') operator is split over two lines, an unexpected semicolon may be inserted.

Conditional Compilation

Microsoft supports a special formatting comment, **@cc**, or conditional compilation. This is intended to allow capable browsers to take advantage of the new features included in JScript.

Keywords	Description
@cc_on	Activates conditional compilation support.
@if, @elif, @end	Conditionally executes a group of statements
@set	Allows creation of variables used in conditional compilation statements.

The following predefined variables are available for conditional compilation. If a variable is not true, it is not defined and behaves as **NaN** when accessed.

Variable	Behavior
@_win32	**true** if running on a win32 system
@_win16	**true** if running on a win16 system
@_mac	**true** if running on an Apple Macintosh system
@_alpha	**true** if running on a Dec Alpha processor
@_x86	**true** if running on an Intel processor
@_mc680x0	**true** if running on a Motorola 680x0 processor
@_PowerPC	**true** if running on a PowerPC
@_jscript	Always **true**
@_jscript_build	Contains the build number of the Jscript scripting engine.
@_jscript_version	Contains the JScript version number in major.minor format.

Literals

Literals are data values embedded directly in a script.

- ▲ **void** is an operator, not a literal.
- ▲ There is no literal representation of the Undefined type's sole value.
- ▲ **null** is the Null type's sole literal value.
- ▲ **true** and **false** are the Boolean type's literal values.

Numeric literals for the Number type may be represented in several ways:

- ▲ **Signed integer**: an optional **+** or **−** leads at least one character instance from the set **0123456789**, but the first may not be **0** (zero) if there is more than one character instance.
- ▲ **Signed decimal**: either a signed integer, **+** , **−**, or nothing, then a **.** (full stop) followed by at least one character instance from the set **0123456789**.
- ▲ **Signed scientific**: a signed decimal followed by one of **eE** followed by a signed integer.
- ▲ **Octal**: a **0** (zero) followed by at least one character instance from the set **01234567**.
- ▲ **Hexadecimal**: a **0x** (zero-x) or **0X** (zero-X) followed by at least one character instance from the set **0123456789abcdefABCDEF**. Therefore hexadecimal numbers are case-insensitive.
- ▲ **NaN and Infinity:** There are no literal representations—see the **global** object for properties with these values.

Numeric literals may not exactly match any computer-representable number. In that case, rounding will occur when interpreted - see Data Types.

String literals for the String type may be represented as follows:

A harmless item is any Unicode character except line terminators, **** (backslash), **'** (single quote) and **"** (double quote).

- ▲ A String literal is a **"** followed by at least zero items from the set of harmless items plus **'** , and then a further **"**.
- ▲ A String literal is a **'** followed by at least zero items from the set of harmless items plus **"**, and then a further **'**.

A String literal may also contain escape sequences. An escape sequence is a **** followed by special characters which together identify a single Unicode character. If a non-special character follows the ****, the **** is ignored. The list of escape sequences is:

Escape Sequence	Name	Unicode value
\b	backspace	\u0008
\t	horizontal tab	\u0009
\n	line feed (new line)	\u000A
\f	form feed	\u000C
\r	carriage return	\u000D
\"	double quote: "	\u0022
\'	single quote: '	\u0027
\\	backslash: \	\u005C
\0DDD (see below)	octal sequence	\u0000 to \u00FF
\xDD (see below)	hexadecimal sequence	\u0000 to \u00FF
\uDDDD (see below)	Unicode sequence	\u0000 to \uFFFF

▲ An **octal escape sequence** is a backslash followed by **0** (zero), followed by an optional character from the set **0123**, followed by one or two characters from the set **01234567**. This is an octal value in the range 0 to 255 (decimal).

▲ A **hexadecimal escape sequence** is a backslash followed by one of **xX**, followed by two character instances from the set 0123456789abcdefABCDEF. This is a case-insensitive hexadecimal number in the range 0 to 255 (decimal).

▲ A **Unicode escape sequence** is a backslash followed by a **u**, followed by four character instances from the set **0123456789abcdefABCDEF**. This is a case-insensitive hexadecimal number in the range 0 to 65535 (decimal).

Data Types

Every data item in a script has a type. Variables can contain any type of data. The standard draws a distinction between the names of types and allowable values for those types - names of types start with an uppercase letter. The standard doesn't say how the values of various types should be output to the user, except for rounding of numbers. See also the Native Objects heading.

Undefined. The type of a variable that hasn't been assigned a value: e.g. **'var x;'**. This type has one value: undefined, with no literal representation.

Null. The type for empty values. This type has one value: null, written **null** literally.

Boolean. The type for truth values. This type has two unique values: true and false, written **true** and **false** literally.

Number. The type for integral and floating point numbers. The Number type is a double precision 64-bit IEEE 754 value, with special values NaN (Not a Number) and positive and negative infinity. Numbers as big as 1×10^{300}, and as small as 1×10^{-300} are possible, as well as their negatives. Roughly 18 significant digits are possible.

Because computers are finite, real numbers such as π cannot always be exactly represented.

> **Special care must be taken to convert those numbers to a human readable format so that they appear as expected–this is a rounding problem.**

Mathematics introduces tiny errors when numbers with multiple digits are operated on. This usually only interests mathematicians and statisticians, and is a general problem with computers. Small integer operations, such as **234 * 12**, are usually unaffected.

> **Some numbers can be represented in more than one way. There are positive and negative zeros, and many different values of NaN. All this is invisible to the scriptwriter.**

String. The type for sequences of Unicode characters. The minimum length is 0; the standard mandates no maximum length. Current implementations allow for strings of at least a Megabyte in size. According to the standard, the String type uses a Unicode 2.0 encoding which covers the whole world of characters. Browsers at version 4.0 or less only support smaller character sets such as ISO 8859-1 (Latin1), which is English ASCII plus Western European characters. So, no Chinese symbols are available without changing the browser's language. The subject of character sets versus character set encodings is a complex one; for more information read the Unicode standard, or investigate on the Web.

Object. The underlying type of all JScript objects. It has no innate values exposed to the script writer's control. Instead it supplies behavior that the script writer can use and that other object types can inherit:

- Properties may be attached to it.
- The **prototype** property may be exploited to support inheritance.
- The **typeof()** method returns **"Object"** for Object type values.

In addition there are Reference, List and Completion type, but these are invisible to the script writer. The Reference type is of some conceptual use to script writers in that it is used to track values of the Object type - see Chapter 1. **void** is not a type, but an operator.

The **typeof()** strings are:

Type operated on	Resulting string
Undefined	**"undefined"**
Null	**"object"**
Boolean	**"boolean"**
Number	**"number"**
String	**"string"**
Object (native object that isn't a function)	**"object"**

Type operated on	Resulting string
`Object` (native object that is a function)	`"function"`
`host object`	No standard. Depends on the specific object.

Type Conversion

The full type conversion story is a complex one. Two specific unusual cases are bit operators and array indices.

 Bit operators temporarily convert their left argument to a 32-bit value, and their right argument to an unsigned 5-bit value.

 Any number value (not string) used as an array element index will be converted to an unsigned 32-bit value.

Operators and Expressions

The JScript operators are:

Operator	Name	Operator	Name
Unary operators			
`delete`	deletes an object	`+`	unary plus
`void`	force the undefined value to be returned	`-`	unary minus
`typeof`	report a value's type	`~`	bitwise **NOT**
`++`	pre- and post-increment	`!`	logical **NOT**
`--`	pre- and post-decrement		
Binary operators			
`*`	multiplication	`<<`	left shift
`/`	division	`>>`	right shift
`%`	modulus or remainder	`>>>`	unsigned right shift
`+`	addition or concatenation		
`-`	subtraction	`&`	bitwise **AND**
		`|`	bitwise **OR**
`<`	less than	`^`	bitwise **XOR**
`>`	greater than		
`<=`	less than or equal	`&&`	logical **AND**
`>=`	greater than or equal	`||`	logical **OR**

Operator	Name	Operator	Name
==	equal		
!=	not equal		
Special operators			
this	refers to the current scope's object	?:	ternary conditional operator; allows 'if' inside an expression
new	construct an object of given type	,	'comma': separates function arguments or sequences of expressions
=	assigns result of right hand expression to left hand variable	( )	delimits function arguments and groups operators in expressions
op= *=,/=,%=, +=,-=,<<= ,>>=,>>>= ,&=,^= or |=	assignment with binary operator applied to old value and new value before final assignment:	[]	Associates a property name with an object in an array-like manner
===, !==	Equal to/not equal to. Jscript special identifiers which will not compare different types	.	Associates a property name with an object

Operator Precedence

Does 1 + 2 * 3 = 1 + (2 * 3) = 7 or does it equal (1 + 2) * 3 = 6?

JavaScript closely follows Java, and Java closely follows C. The table shows precedence with highest at the top, and like operators grouped together. The third column explains whether to read 1+2+3+4 as ((1+2)+3)+4 or 1+(2+(3+(4))).

Operator type	Operators	Evaluation order for like elements
postfix operators	[] () . expr++ expr--	left to right
unary operators	++expr --expr +expr -expr ~ !	right to left
object management or cast	new delete void	right to left
multiplicative	* / %	left to right
additive	+ -	left to right
shift	<< >> >>>	left to right
relational	< > <= >= typeof(expr)	left to right
equality	== !=	left to right
bitwise AND	&	left to right

Operator type	Operators	Evaluation order for like elements
bitwise exclusive OR	^	left to right
bitwise inclusive OR	|	left to right
logical AND	&&	left to right
logical OR	||	left to right
conditional	? :	right to left
assignment	= += -= *= /= %= &= ^= |= <<= >>= >>>=	right to left

Support for Regular Expressions

JScript provides support for string searches by regarding both regular expressions and strings as objects, therefore, providing them with properties and methods as with other objects.

The JScript RegularExpression Object

Regular Expression objects store patterns which are used when searching strings for character combinations. After the Regular Expression object is created, it is either passed to a string method, or a string is passed to one of the regular expression methods. Information about the most recent search performed is stored in the RegExp object.

Unlike other objects, this can be created in two ways with the following pieces of syntax

```
var regularexpression = /pattern/
var regularexpression = /pattern/switch
```

or

```
var regularexpression = new RegExp("pattern")
var regularexpression = new RegExp("pattern","switch")
```

"Pattern" denotes the expression string you want to search for, and is obligatory. **Switch** is optional and denotes the type of search you wish to conduct. Available switches are:

▲ **i** (ignore case)

▲ **g** (global search for all occurrences of pattern)

▲ **gi** (global search, ignore case)

The **RegularExpression** Object has four properties and three methods, as follows:

Property	Description
global	Boolean value denoting whether the global switch (g) has been used.
ignorecase	Boolean value denoting whether the ignore case (i) switch has been used.
lastIndex	Specifies the index point form which to begin the next match.
source	Contains the text of the regular expression pattern.

Method	Description	Return Values	Required Arguments
compile	Compiles a string expression containing a regular expression pattern into an internal format.	(internal conversion)	pattern
exec	Searches for a match in the specified string.	null or array	string
test	Tests whether a pattern exists in a string.	boolean	string

The JScript RegExp Object

The **RegExp** object stores information on regular expression pattern searches. It cannot be created directly–only as a side effect as using the **RegularExpression** object–but is always available for use. Its properties have undefined as their value until a successful regular expression search has been completed.

The **RegExp** object has nine properties and no methods:

Property	Description
index	Returns the beginning position of the first successful match in a searched string.
input	Contains the string against which a search was performed. Read-only Also written as $_ instead of **input**
lastindex	Returns where the last successful match begins in a string that was searched.
lastmatch	Returns the last matched characters. Read only. Also written as $& instead of **lastmatch**
lastParen	Returns the last substring match within parentheses, if any. Read-only. Also written as $+ instead of **lastParen**
leftContext	Returns the input string up to the most recent match. Read-only Also written as $` instead of **leftContext**
multiline	Boolean value specifying whether searching continued across line breaks. Read-only. Also written as $* instead of **multiline**
rightContext	Returns the input string past the most recent match. Read-only. Also written as $' instead of **rightContext**
$1, $2, ... , $9	Returns the nine most-recently memorized strings found during pattern matching. Read-only

Regular Expression Syntax

Special characters and sequences are used in writing patterns for regular expressions. The table that follows details them and includes short examples showing how the characters are used.

Character	Description
\	Marks the next character as special. **/n/** matches the character "n". The sequence /\n/ matches a linefeed or newline character.
^	Matches the beginning of the input or line.
$	Matches the end of the input or line.
*	Matches the preceding character zero or more times. **/zo*/** matches "z" and "zoo."
+	Matches the preceding characters one or more times. **/zo+/** matches "zoo" but not "z."
?	Matches the preceding character zero or one time. **/a?ve?/** matches the "ve" in "never."
.	Matches any single character except a newline character.
pattern	Matches pattern and remembers the match. The matched substring can be retrieved from the resulting Array object elements **[1]**...**[n]** or the **RegExp object's $1**...**$9** properties. To match parentheses characters, (), use "\(" or "\)".
x|y	Matches either x or y. /z|food?/ matches "zoo" or "food."
{n}	n is a nonnegative integer. Matches exactly n times. **/o{2}/** does not match the "o" in "Bob," but matches the first two o's in "foooood."
{n,}	n is a nonnegative integer. Matches at least n times. **/o{2,}/** does not match the "o" in "Bob" and matches all the o's in "foooood." **/o{1,}/** is equivalent to /o+/.
{n,m}	m and n are nonnegative integers. Matches at least n and at most m times. **/o{1,3}/** matches the first three o's in "fooooood."
[xyz]	A character set. Matches any one of the enclosed characters. **/[abc]/** matches the "a" in "plain."
[^xyz]	A negative character set. Matches any character not enclosed. **/[^abc]/** matches the "p" in "plain."
[\b]	Matches a backspace (Javascript only)
\b	Matches a word boundary, such as a space. **/ea*r\b/** matches the "er" in "never early."
\B	Matches a nonword boundary. **/ea*r\B/** matches the "ear" in "never early."
\cX	Where X is a control character. Matches a control character in a string. For example, **/\cM/** matches control-M in a string. (Javascript only)
\d	Matches a digit character. Equivalent to **[0-9]**.
\D	Matches a nondigit character. Equivalent to **[^0-9]**.
\f	Matches a form-feed character.
\n	Matches a linefeed character.

Character	Description
`\r`	Matches a carriage return character.
`\s`	Matches any white space including space, tab, form-feed, and so forth. Equivalent to `[ \f\n\r\t\v]`
`\S`	Matches any nonwhite space character. Equivalent to `[^ \f\n\r\t\v]`
`\t`	Matches a tab character.
`\v`	Matches a vertical tab character.
`\w`	Matches any word character including underscore. Equivalent to `[A-Za-z0-9_]`.
`\W`	Matches any nonword character. Equivalent to c.
`\num`	Matches num, where num is a positive integer. A reference back to remembered matches. \1 matches what is stored in **RegExp.$1**.
`/n/`	Matches n, where n is an octal, hexadecimal, or decimal escape value. Allows embedding of ASCII codes into regular expressions. (Jscript only)
`\o octal` `\x hex`	Where \o octal is an octal escape value or \x hex is a hexadecimal escape value. Allows you to embed ASCII codes into regular expressions.

Statements and Control Flow

Statements are the basic unit of work in the language. Statements are terminated with a semi-colon which can be left out if the line ends after the statement. A block is a collected sequence of statements. Blocks and statements are generally interchangeable.

```
statement-body;    // a statement
```

```
{
   statement;      // one or more statements plus braces equal a block
}
```

break

The **break** statement terminates the current **while** or **for** loop and transfers program control to the statement following the terminated loop. If a label is used in conjunction with the **break**, it will terminate the associated label. The syntax for is:

```
break [label]
```

The optional label argument specifies the label of the statement you are breaking from.

As an example, this simple function breaks out of the loop when the loop count reaches 3, and returns **x** times 3:

```
function testBreak(x) {
var i = 0
    while (i < 6) {
            if (i == 3)
                    break
            i++
    }
return i*x
```

continue

Statement that terminates execution of the block of statements in a **while** or **for** loop, but, unlike **break**, continues execution of the loop with the next iteration. The syntax is:

```
continue [label]
```

As with **break**, **label** is an optional argument that transfers the effect of the **continue** statement to the appropriate labeled statement.

do...while

Carries out the statement until the test condition evaluates to **false**. The statement is always carried out at least once. Syntax is:

```
do
    statement
while(condition)
```

for ...

```
for ( setup-expression; continue-condition; change-expression )
    statement or block
```

or

```
for ( variable in object-variable )
    statement or block
```

Only properties without the **DontEnum** special JScript property attribute are revealed by the second form.

If a block is used it may contain instances of

```
break;
```

or

```
continue;
```

if ... else ...

```
if ( condition )
    statement or block
```

or

```
if ( condition )
    statement or block
else
    statement or block
```

@if Statement

Enables conditional execution of one of a group of statements, depending on the truth value of an expression.

Syntax is

```
@if (expression1)
    statement1
@elif (expression2)
    statement2
...
else
    statementn
@end
```

expression1 and **expression2** are expressions that can give a Boolean result. The statements are evaluated in series, with **statement1** being passed if **expression1** is true, **statement2** only if **expression2** is **true** and **expression1** is **false** and so on. An **@if** statement can be written on a single line. It is also possible to use multiple **@elif** clauses, although they must come before an **@else** clause.

According to the Jscript documentation, the **@if** statement is best used to determine which text among several options should be used for text output, using the **@(platform)** syntax detailed under Conditional Compilation.

labeled

Provides an identifier that can be referred to by **break** or **continue** to indicate whether or not the program should continue execution. Syntax is:

```
label :
    statement
```

statement can be a block of statements.

@set Statement

@set Statement is specific to JScript, and is used to create variables for conditional compilation statements. The syntax is:

```
@set @variablename = term
```

variablename establishes the variable name and must be preceded by the **@** symbol. **term** establishes the variable, and can be composed of a constant, a conditional compilation, or a parenthesized expressions. Note that only Numeric and Boolean variables are supported; strings can't be set. Variables created using **@set** are generally used in conditional compilation statements, but need not be.

switch

Allows a program to evaluate an expression and attempt to match the expression's value to one of several case labels. Syntax is:

```
switch (expression){
    case label :
            statement;
                    break;
    case label :
            statement;
                    break;
                    ...
    default : statement;
}
```

expression is the statement to be evaluated; **label** is the possible result the expression is to be evaluated against. If (and only if) **label** exactly matches the expression result (without a type conversion) then **statement** (which may be a series of statements) will be carried out. **break** is optional, but can be used to jump straight out of the case cycle. **default** is also optional; if it is present, it will be applied if the expression is not matched, but otherwise the program will simply move onto the statements following the **switch.**

while...

```
while ( condition )
    statement or block
```

If a block is used it may contain instances of

```
break;
```

or

```
continue;
```

with ...

```
with ( object )
    statement or block
```

Scope, Functions and Methods

There is always a current object, accessible via the special variable/operator **this**.

Functions are sections of executable script associated with a property name, also called a function name. The name follows the rules for property/variable names. Functions are first declared, then invoked.

Declarations can occur as follows:

```
function example1()
{
// zero or more statements
}
```

or

```
function example2(arg1, arg2)     // as many named variables as needed
{
// zero or more statements possibly using arg1, arg2
}
```

or

```
new Function("a", "b", "c", "return a+b+c");     // a,b,c are arguments
```

or

```
new Function("a, b, c", "return a+b+c");     // a,b,c are arguments
```

or

```
new Function("a,b", "c", "return a+b+c");     // a,b,c are arguments
```

or

```
new Function("return arguments[0]+arguments[1]+arguments[2]");   // no arguments
```

Functions may contain one or more instances of:

```
return;
```

or

```
return expression;
```

Invocation of functions occurs as follows:

```
example1(var1, var2)                          // zero or more arguments
```

or

```
object_variable.method_property_name(var1, var2) // zero or more arguments
```

▲ Any number of arguments can be passed to a function, regardless of its declaration.

▲ All function arguments are passed by value, if they are primitive types, otherwise by reference.

▲ Functions can be called recursively, therefore, care needs to be taken to avoid infinite loops.

▲ The standard does not require that functions be declarable inside other functions.

If a function's body (main statement block) uses the **this** operator, it is said to be a method and must be invoked as a property of an object. Also see the Function object below.

The **caller** property of a function contains a reference to the function that invoked the current function. It is described as **functionname.caller**. It is only defined for a function while that function is executing. If the function is called from the top level of a JScript program, caller contains **null**

Native Objects

Native objects are part of the JScript interpreter. The only built in object is Math.

Objects and their properties commonly form a tree data structure, with the global object at the root of the tree. Because properties and variables can track any object, more general structures than trees are possible. The most general structure possible where objects are tracked with no apparent plan is called a **cyclic directed graph**.

There is a full listing of all the JScript host objects below. Note that because all objects inherit their prototype's properties, objects can call methods and properties of their own using the syntax

```
obj.property()
```

rather than using the full prototype syntax:

```
obj.prototype.property()
```

To aid reference, therefore, only the root name is given here. Where the argument of the property is the current object itself, we have used the keyword **this** to indicate it.

All the objects of JScript have **toString()** and **valueOf()** methods. However, these return different results depending on the object from which they are called, and are so detailed for each object.

Internal Properties

These are the internal properties of all JScript objects. Note that instantiations of particular objects can have these properties read using the **Get** property, but they are internal properties and, therefore, not accessible to the language. However, see Reference Section B for details of JScript mechanisms for doing so.

Property	Parameters	Description
[[Prototype]]	none	The prototype of this object.
[[Class]]	none	The kind of this object.
[[Value]]	none	Internal state information associated with this object.
[[Get]]	(PropertyName)	Returns the value of the property.
[[Put]]	(PropertyName, Value)	Sets the specified property to Value.
[[CanPut]]	(PropertyName)	Returns a boolean value indicating whether a [[Put]] operation with the specified PropertyName will succeed.
[[HasProperty]]	(PropertyName)	Returns a boolean value indicating whether the object already has a member with the given name.
[[Delete]]	(PropertyName)	Removes the specified property from the object.
[[DefaultValue]]	(Hint)	Returns a default value for the object, which should be a primitive value (not an object or reference).
[[Construct]]	a list of argument values provided by the caller	Constructs an object. Invoked via the **new** operator. Objects that implement this internal method are called *constructors*.
[[Call]]	a list of argument values provided by the caller	Executes code associated with the object. Invoked via a function call expression. Objects that implement this internal method are called *functions*.

Global Object

In every case, a **length** property of a built-in function object described in this section has the attributes {**ReadOnly**, **DontDelete**, **DontEnum**} and no others. Note that all objects inherit the methods from the **Global** object:

Property Name	Read/write?	Enumerable?	Description
NaN	Yes	No	Initial value is NaN
Infinity	Yes	No	Initial value is $+\infty$

Method Name	Arguments	Return	Description
eval()	x	string object	Returns either **x** if not a string object, the result of **x** as a program, a runtime error if **x** does not execute as a program or the **undefined** value.
parseInt()	string, radix	integer value	The **parseInt** function produces an integer value by interpreting the contents of the *string* argument according to the specified *radix*. Default radix is 10.

Method Name	Arguments	Return	Description
parseFloat()	string	NaN or number value	Interprets the string value as a decimal literal to give a number.
escape()	string	string	Replaces characters in string with special URL meanings with their corresponding hexadecimal escape sequence.
unescape()	string	string	Translates hexadecimal escape sequences in a string back into characters.
isNaN()	number	True|False	Returns True if the argument is **NaN**, otherwise False
isFinite()	number	True|False	False if the argument is **NaN**, $+\infty$, or $-\infty$, otherwise True.
Object(...)	Value or empty	Object object	If value, must be **null** or **undefined**. Creates a new Object object.
Function(...)	as required	Function object	Creates a new Function object, with the arguments providing formal parameters. The last argument is executable code.
Array(...)	Array items or **length** or empty	Array object	Instantiates an Array object with the arguments as members. Length creates an array of length equal to length, empty creates an empty array.
String(...)	value or empty	string value; empty string	Value returns a string value computed by **ToString(value)**; empty returns " "
Boolean(...)	value or empty	boolean value; **false**	Calculates a boolean value using **ToBoolean(value)**; or simply returns false.
Number(...)	value or empty	Number value; **+0**	Calculates a number value according to **ToNumber(value)**, or returns 0.
Date(...)	see description	string value	Returns a **string** value representing the current time in UTC (GMT)
Math	No	No	It is not possible to call the Math object as a method.

Object

There are no special properties for the Object object, other than those which it inherits from the special built-in prototype object; it does not have an initial **value**:

Property Name	Read/write?	Enumerable?	Description
constructor	Yes	No	Holds the built-in Object constructor

Method Name	Arguments	Return	Description
toString()	this	**String** value	Returns a string for the object of the form "[object ", class, and "]"
valueOf()	this	Object	Returns the object.

Function

The **function** object can be called instead of a function value.

Property Name	Read/write?	Enumerable?	Description
length	No	No	Establishes expected number of arguments as an integer.
arguments	No	No	Value depends on

Method Name	Arguments	Return	Description
toString()	this	String value	Returns an string value representation of the function. Precise whitespacing, formatting etc are left to the implementation.

Array

The **array** object is used to store collections of information in an easily accessible fashion.

Property Name	Read/write?	Enumerable?	Description
Length	Yes	No	This is always numerically greater than the names of all members of the array.

Method Name	Arguments	Return	Description
concat()	(array2)	Array	Combines two arrays to create a new array.
join()	separator see description	string	The array elements are converted to strings, then concatenated with the separator. Default separator is **comma**.
this		Array	Returns a new array object with the elements reversed.
slice()	start, end	Array	Returns a section of an array
sort()	comparefn Function	Array	Sorts the array according to function of a form that establishes ($x>y$ as –ve; $x=y$ as 0; $x<y$ as =ve)

String

The String object can be thought of as a wrapper for a simple string value; the string value passed to the object when it is created becomes in essence an unnamed, implicit, property of the object itself.

Property Name	Read/write?	Enumerable?	Description
`fromCharCode` `(char0, char1...)`	yes	no	Returns a string value containing as many characters as the resulting string.
`length`	No	No	An integer equal to the number of characters in the string; once created, it is unchanging.

Method Name	Arguments	Return	Description
`toString()`	`this`	string value	Returns this String value. Note that the toString method is not generic.
`charAt(pos)`	`number`	string value	Returns character number pos in the string as a string value.
`charCodeAt` `(pos)`	`number`	number	Returns a non negative number that represents, according to Unicode, the character at position **pos**, else **NaN**.
`concat()`	`string2`	string	Combines two strings to create a new string.
`indexOf` `(searchString , position)`	`string,` `number`	Index of rightmost character; -1	Searches string for the next substring, **searchstring** to the right of position **pos**. Returns index position, or −1 if string is not found. Default position is 0.
`lastIndexOf` `(searchString , position)`	`string,` `number`	Index of leftmost character; -1	Searches string for the nearest substring, to the left of position **pos**. Returns index position, or -1 if string is not found. Default position is 0.
`split` `(separator)`	`string`	**Array** object containing substrings.	Splits a string, left to right, by each instance of the **separator**, which are not included in the resulting array. If separator = **'empty string'**, then returns array containing one character per array element, and of a **length** equal to the **length** of the string.
`slice(start, end)`	`number,` `number`	string value	Returns a section of an string
`substring` `(start)`	`number`	string value	Returns a string value beginning at character **start** and running to end of string. If start is NaN or negative, then begins at pos 0.
`substring` `(start, end)`	`number,` `number`	string value	Returns a string value of the characters between start and end positions. Will be reversed if **start>end**; treated as 0 if negative or NaN; as string length if larger than string.

Method Name	Arguments	Return	Description
toLowerCase()	this	string value	Converts entire string to lowercase string value
toUpperCase()	this	string value	Converts entire string to uppercase string value.
valueOf()	this	string value	Returns the string, else runtime error if not a String object.

Boolean

The Boolean object can be seen as a 'wrapper' for a simple Boolean value. When created, the value of the boolean becomes essentially an implicit, unnamed, property of the object

Property Name	Read/write?	Enumerable?	Description
Boolean(value)	Yes	No	returns a boolean value computed by **toBoolean(value)**

Method Name	Arguments	Return	Description
toString()	this	"true" or "false"	Returns a string "true" if **true**, "false" if **false**.
valueOf()	this	**true** or **false**	Returns value of object; generates a runtime error if not a boolean object

Number

Like the String and Boolean objects, the Number object is primarily a wrapper, although it has a number of in built properties that represent significant values for JScript

Property Name	Read/write?	Enumerable?	Description
MAX_VALUE	No	No	The largest possible value, approx $1.7976931348623157e^{308}$
MIN_VALUE	No	No	The smallest positive non-zero value, approx $5e^{-324}$
NaN	No	No	Value is **NaN**
NEGATIVE_INFINITY	No	No	Value is $-\infty$
POSITIVE_INFINITY	No	No	Value is $+\infty$

Method Name	Arguments	Return	Description
toString()	radix	See description	If radix is 10 or not supplied, then a **toString** opration is carried out; if another integer from 2 to 36, the result is an implementation dependent string.
valueOf()	**this**	Number object	Gives error if not a number.

Math

The Math object is unusual in that essentially it provides a number of useful mathematical operations that are accessible through the Math object.

Property Name	Read/write?	Enumerable?	Description
E	No	No	The number value for e, base of the natural logarithms. Approx **2.7182818284590452354**
LN10	No	No	Number value of the natural log of 10, approx. **2.302585092994046**.
LN2	No	No	Number value of the natural log of 2, approx **0.6931471805599453**
LOG2E	No	No	Number value of the base-2 logarithm of 2, which is approx **1.4426950408889634**
LOG10E	No	No	Number value of the base-10 logarithm, which is approx **0.434294481903218**
PI	No	No	The number value for π (ratio of a circle's circumference to its diameter); approx **3.14159265358979323846**
SQRT1_2	No	No	The value for the square root of ½, which is approx. **0.7071067811865476**
SQRT2	No	No	The number value of the square root of 2, which is approx **1.4142135623730951**

Note that every method of the math object first carries out a **toNumber()** operation on each of the arguments, then performs a computation on the resulting value(s). For familiar expressions (eg acos, asin etc) the implementor will use available mathematical libraries, such as those available to C programmers. JScript recommends the use of the freely downloadable Maths library **fdlibm**, available from:

Method Name	Arguments	Return	Description
abs()	x	absolute number	Returns the absolute value of **x**; in general, has the same magnitude as the value but a positive sign.
acos()	x	Number in radians	Approximates the inverse cosine of the argument; expressed in radians.
asin()	x	Number in radians	Approximates the inverse sine of the argument; expressed in radians.
atan()	x	Number in radians	Approximates the inverse tan of the argument; expressed in radians.
atan2()	y, x	Number in radians	Returns the inverse tan of the quotient **y/x** where the argument signs determine the quadrant of the result.
ceil()	x	Integer number	Returns the smallest mathematical integer larger than **x**. If **x** is already an integer, then equal to **x**.
cos()	x	Number in radians	Gives an implementation-dependent approximation of the cosine of the argument.
exp()	x	Number value	Returns an approximation of e to the power **x**.
floor()	x	Number value	Returns the greatest mathematical integer smaller than **x**. If **x** is already an integer, then return is equal to **x**.
log()	x	Number value	Approximates the natural logarithm of **x**.
max()	x,y	**x** or **y**	Returns the larger of the two arguments.
min()	x,y	**x** or **y**	Returns the smaller of the two arguments.
pow()	x,y	x^y	Returns **x** to the power **y**.
random()	None	Number value	Returns a randomly generated number greater than or equal to 0, less than 1.
round()	x	Integer	Returns the closest integer to the argument; rounds up if two are equally close. If **x** is an integer, then return = **x**.
sin()	x	Number in radians	Gives an implementation-dependent approximation of the sine of the argument.
sqrt()	x	Number value	Returns an approximation of the square root of the argument.
tan()	x	Number value	Gives an implementation-dependent approximation of the tan of the argument.

Date

The **date** object contains a number that represents a given time in milliseconds, relative to Midnight, January 1st, 1970. Note that Months are represented by an integer from 0 to 11, inclusive, with 0 being January and 11 being December. Days of the week are integers from 0 to 6, with 0 being Sunday and 6 being Saturday. Note that UTC is Universal Coordinated Time, or GMT.

Property Name	Read/write?	Enumerable?	Description
`length`	No	No	Initial value is **7**

Method Name	Arguments	Return	Description
`parse(`*string*`)`			
`UTC(`*year,* `[`*month,* `[`*date,* `[`*hours,* `[`*minutes,* `[`*seconds,* *ms*`]]]]]]`)`		Number	Creates a date value in UTC, rather than a local time date. Note that arguments can not be 'skipped', and that if date or larger unit is omitted (e.g. month, year) then result is implementation dependent.
`toString()`		String	Implementation dependent, but intended to return a human readable time value. Not generic.
`getTime()`	**Value** stored in date object.	time value	Returns the time value of the object.
`getYear()`	**Value** stored in date object.	19**xx**	Specified only for backward compatibilty; returns two digit year.
`getFullYear()`	**Value** stored in date object.	**xxxx**	Returns four digit year in human readable form. Based on local time.
`getUTCFull_ Year()`	**Value** stored in date object.	**xxxx**	As above; based on UTC.
`getMonth()`	**Value** stored in date object.	0-11	Calculates month, based on local time.
`getUTCMonth()`	**Value** stored in date object.	0-11	Calculates month, based on UTC.
`getDate()`	**Value** stored in date object.	1-31	Calculates date, based on local time.
`getUTCDate()`	**Value** stored in date object.	1-31	Calculates date, based on UTC.
`getDay()`	**Value** stored in date object.	0-6	Calculates day, based on local time.
`getUTCDay()`	**Value** stored in date object.	0-6	Calculates day, based on UTC.
`getHours()`	**Value** stored in date object.	0-23	Calculates hour, based on local time.

Method Name	Arguments	Return	Description
getUTCHours()	**Value** stored in date object.	0-23	Calculates hour, based on UTC time.
getMinutes()	**Value** stored in date object.	0-59	Returns number of minutes past the hour according to local time.
getUTC_ Minutes()	**Value** stored in date object.	0-59	Returns number of minutes past the hour according to UTC time.
getSeconds()	**Value** stored in date object.	0-59	Returns number of seconds past the minute according to local time.
getUTC_ Seconds()	**Value** stored in date object.	0-59	Returns number of seconds past the minute according to UTC time.
getMilli_ seconds()	**Value** stored in date object.	0-999	Returns number of milliseconds past the minute according to local time.
getUTCMilli_ seconds()	**Value** stored in date object.	0-999	Returns number of milliseconds past the minute according to UTC time.
getTimezone_ Offset()		**Integer**	Returns difference between UTC time and local time in minutes.
getVarDate	**Value** stored in date object.		Returns the VT_DATE value stored in the Date object.
setTime(*time*)	time	time	sets date object's value to specified time.
setMilli_ seconds(*ms*)	**integer**	**date** value (integer)	Sets date object's value to specified milliseconds, local time.
setUTCMilli_ seconds(*ms*)	**integer**	**date** value (integer)	Sets date object's value to specified milliseconds, UTC.
setSeconds (sec [, *ms*])	**integer,**	**date** value (integer)	Sets date object's value to specified seconds and milliseconds, local time.
setUTCSeconds (*sec* [, *ms*])	**integer**	**date** value (integer)	Sets date object's value to specified seconds, UTC.
setMinutes (*min* [, *sec* [, *ms*]])	**integer**	**date** value (integer)	Sets date object's value to specified minutes, local time.
setUTCMinutes (*min* [, *sec* [, *ms*]])	**integer**	**date** value (integer)	Sets date object's value to specified minutes, UTC.
setHours(*hour* [, *min* [, *sec* [, *ms*]]])	**integer**	**date** value (integer)	Sets date object's value to specified minutes, local time.
setUTCHours (*hour* [, *min* [, *sec* [, *ms*]]])	**integer**	**date** value (integer)	Sets date object's value to specified minutes, UTC.

Method Name	Arguments	Return	Description
setDate(*date*)	integer	**date** value (integer)	Sets date object's value to specified date, local time.
setUTCDate (*date*)	integer	**date** value (integer)	Sets date object's value to specified date, UTC.
setMonth(*mon* [, *date*])	integer	**date** value (integer)	Sets date object's value to specified month, local time.
setUTCMonth (*mon* [, *date*])	integer	**date** value (integer)	Sets date object's value to specified month, UTC.
setFullYear (*year* [, *mon* [, *date*]])	integer	**date** value (integer)	Sets date object's value to specified full year, local time.
setUTCFull_ Year(*year* [, *mon* [, *date*]])	integer	**date** value (integer)	Sets date object's value to specified full year, UTC.
setYear(*year*)	integer	**date** value (integer)	Sets date object's value to specified year, local time, two digits. Deprecated.
toLocale_ String()	**value** of date object	**string** representation.	Returns a human readable string based on local time & Implementation dependent.
toUTCString()	**value** of date object	**string**	Returns a human readable string based on UTC.
toGMTString()	**value** of date object	**string**	Returns a human readable string based on GMT (Included for backward compatability).

Note that for **set...** methods, where optional arguments (such as [s]) are omitted, they are retrieved using the appropriate **get** method.

The VBArray Object

JScript also provides support for a new kind of object. A **VBArray** provides access to Visual Basic safe arrays. They are read-only, and cannot be created directly. The safeArray argument must have obtained a VBArray value before being passed to the VBArray constructor. This can only be done by retrieving the value from an existing ActiveX or other object.

VBArrays can have multiple dimensions. The indices of each dimension can be different. This object has five methods associated with it.

Method	Description	Required Arguments
dimensions	Returns the number of dimensions in a VBArray	`array.dimensions()`
getItem	Retrieves the item at the specified location	`Array.getItem (dimension1,..., dimn)`
lbound	Returns the lowest index value used in the specified dimension of a VBArray.	`Array.lbound()` `Array.lbound(dimension)`
toArray	Converts a VBArray to a standard JScript array.	`safeArray.toArray( )`
ubound	Returns the highest index value used in the specified dimension of the VBArray.	`Array.ubound()` `Array.ubound(dimension)`

Active Server Pages Object Model

Request Object

Collections	Description
ClientCertificate	Client certificate values sent from the browser. Read Only.
Cookies	Values of cookies sent from the browser. Read Only.
Form	Values of form elements sent from the browser. Read Only.
QueryString	Values of variables in the HTTP query string. Read Only.
ServerVariables	Values of the HTTP and environment variables. Read Only.

Property	Description
TotalBytes	Specifies the number of bytes the client is sending in the body of ths request. Read Only.

Method	Description
BinaryRead	Used to retrieve data sent to the server as part of the POST request

Response Object

Collection	Description
Cookies	Values of all the cookies to send to the browser.

Properties	Description
Buffer	Indicates whether to buffer the page until complete.
CacheControl	Determines whether proxy servers are able to cache the output generated by ASP
Charset	Appends the name of the character set to the content-type header
ContentType	HTTP content type (i.e. **"Text/HTML"**) for the response.

Properties	Description
Expires	Length of time before a page cached on a browser expires.
ExpiresAbsolute	Date and time when a page cached on a browser expires.
IsClientConnected	Indicates whether the client has disconnected from the server
PICS	Adds the value of a PICS label to the pics-label field of the response header.
Status	Value of the HTTP status line returned by the server.

Methods	Description
AddHeader	Adds or changes a value in the HTML header.
AppendToLog	Adds text to the web server log entry for this request.
BinaryWrite	Sends text to the browser without character-set conversion.
Clear	Erases any buffered HTML output.
End	Stops processing the page and returns the current result.
Flush	Sends buffered output immediately.
Redirect	Instructs the browser to connect to a different URL.
Write	Writes a variable to the current page as a string.

The remaining **Response** interface elements can be divided into groups, like this:

Response Items	Description
Write, BinaryWrite	Inserts information into a page.
Cookies	Sends cookies to the browser.
Redirect	Redirects the browser.
Buffer, Flush, Clear, End	Buffers the page as it is created.
Expires, ExpiresAbsolute, ContentType, AddHeader, Status, CacheContol, PICS, Charset	Sets the properties of a page.
IsClientConnected	Checks the client connection

Server Object

Property	Description
ScriptTimeout	Length of time a script can run before an error occurs.

Methods	Description
CreateObject	Creates an instance of an object or server component.
HTMLEncode	Applies HTML encoding to the specified string.
MapPath	Converts a virtual path into a physical path.
URLEncode	Applies URL encoding including escape chars to a string.

Session Object

Collections	Description
Contents	Contains all of the items added to the Session through script commands.
StaticObjects	Contains all of the objects added to the Session with the **<OBJECT>** tag.

Method	Description
Abandon	Destroys a **Session** object and releases its resources.

Properties	Description
CodePage	Sets the codepage that will be used for symbol mapping
LCID	Sets the locale identifier
SessionID	Returns the session identification for this user
Timeout	Sets the timeout period for the session state for this application, in minutes.

Events	Description
OnStart	Occurs when the server creates a new session
OnEnd	Occurs when a session is abandoned or times out.

Application Object

Collection	Description
Contents	Contains all of the items added to the application through script commands
StaticObjects	Contains all of the objects added to the application with the **<OBJECT>** tag

Method	Description
Lock	Prevents other clients from modifying application properties.
Unlock	Allows other clients to modify application properties.

Events	Description
OnStart	Occurs when a page in the application is first referenced.
OnEnd	Occurs when the application ends, i.e. when the web server is stopped.

The ObjectContext Object

Method	Description
SetComplete	Overrides any previous **SetAbort** method that has been called in a script.
SetAbort	Aborts a transaction initiated by an ASP.

Event	
OnTransactionCommit	Occurs after a transacted script's transaction commits.
OnTransactionAbort	Occurs if the transaction is aborted.

Scripting Object and Server Component Methods and Properties

The Dictionary Object

Method	Description
Add	Adds the key/item pair to the **Dictionary**.
Exists	**True** if the specified key exists, **False** if it does not.
Items	Returns an array containing all the items in a **Dictionary** object.
Keys	Returns an array containing all the keys in a **Dictionary** object.
Remove	Removes a single key/item pair.
RemoveAll	Removes all the key/item pairs.

Property	Description
CompareMode	Sets or returns the string comparison mode for the keys. Unavailable in JScript.
Count	Read-only. Returns the number of key/item pairs in the **Dictionary**.
Item	Sets or returns the value of the item for the specified key.
Key	Sets or returns the value of a key.

The FileSystemObject Object

Method	Description
CreateTextFile	Creates a file and returns a **TextStream** object to access the file.
OpenTextFile	Opens a file and returns a **TextStream** object to access the file.

All the methods of **FileSystemObject** can be divided into several categories as shown in the following table:

Category	Methods
File Manipulation	`CopyFile`, `CreateTextFile`, `DeleteFile`, `FileExists`, `MoveFile`, `OpenTextFile`
Folder Manipulation	`CopyFolder`, `CreateFolder`, `DeleteFolder`, `FolderExists`, `MoveFolder`
Path Manipulation	`BuildPath`
Information	`GetAbsolutePathName`, `GetBaseName`, `GetDrive`, `GetDriveName`, `GetExtensionName`, `GetFile`, `GetFileName`, `GetFolder`, `GetParentFolderName`, `GetSpecialFolder`, `GetTempName`

Drive Object

Property	Description
`AvailableSpace`	Returns the amount of space available on specified drive.
`DriveLetter`	Returns the drive letter for the specified drive.
`DriveType`	Returns the value indicating the type of specified drive. Can have one of the following values: 0 = Unknown 1 = Removable 2 = Fixed 3 = Network 4 = CD-ROM 5 = RAM Disk
`FileSystem`	Returns the type of file system for the specified drive. Return types include *FAT*, *NTFS* and *CDFS*.
`FreeSpace`	Returns the amount of free space available on specified drive.
`IsReady`	Returns a boolean value indicating if drive is ready (true) or not (false)
`Path`	Returns the path for specified drive.
`RootFolder`	Returns the **Folder** object representing the root folder of the specified drive.
`SerialNumber`	Returns a decimal serial number used to uniquely identify a disk volume.
`ShareName`	Returns the network share name for the specified drive.
`TotalSize`	Returns the total space (in bytes) of the specified drive.
`VolumeName`	Returns the volume name of the specified drive.

Folder Object

Property	Description
Attributes	Sets or returns the attributes of the folder. Can be combination of the following values: 0 = Normal 1 = ReadOnly 2 = Hidden 4 = System 8 = Volume 16 = Directory 32 = Archive 64 = Alias 128 = Compressed
DateCreated	Returns the date and time when the specified folder was created
DateLastAccessed	Returns the date and time when the specified folder was last accessed
DateLastModified	Returns the date and time when the specified folder was last modified
Drive	Returns the drive letter of the drive on which the specified folder resides
IsRootFolder	Returns boolean value indicating if the specified folder is the root folder (true) or not (false)
Name	Sets or returns the name of the specified folder
ParentFolder	Returns the **Folder** object for the parent of the specified folder
Path	Returns the path for the specified folder
ShortName	Returns the 8.3 version of folder name
ShortPath	Returns the 8.3 version of folder path
Size	Returns the size of all files and subfolders contained in the folder
SubFolders	Returns a **Folders** collection consisting of all folders contained in a specified folder

Method	Description
Copy	Copies the specified folder from one location to another
Delete	Deletes a specified folder
Move	Moves a specified folder from one location to another

Collection	Description
Drives	Read-Only collection of all available drives. Has **Count** and **Item** properties.
Files	Collection of all files within a folder. Has **Count** and **Item** properties.
Folders	Collection of all folders within a folder. Has **Count** and **Item** properties and an **AddFolders** method.

File Object

Property	Description
Attributes	Sets or returns the attributes of file. See description of **Folder** object above
DateCreated	Returns the date and time that the specified file was created
DateLastAccessed	Returns the date and time that the specified file was last accessed
DateLastModified	Returns the date and time that the specified file was last modified
Drive	Returns the drive letter of the drive on which the specified file resides
Name	Sets or returns the name of the specified file
ParentFolder	Returns the **Folder** object for the parent of the specified file
Path	Returns the path for specified file
ShortName	Returns the 8.3 version of file name
ShortPath	Returns the 8.3 version of file path
Size	Returns the size of the file
Type	Returns information about the type of a file

The TextStream Object

Method	Description
Close	Closes an open file.
Read	Reads characters from a file.
ReadAll	Reads an entire file as a single string.
ReadLine	Reads a line from a file as a string.
Skip	Skips and discards characters when reading a file.
SkipLine	Skips and discards the next line when reading a file.
Write	Writes a string to a file.
WriteLine	Writes a string (optional) and a newline character to a file.
WriteBlankLines	Writes newline characters to a file.

Property	Description
AtEndOfLine	**True** if the file pointer is at the end of a line in a file.
AtEndOfStream	**True** if the file pointer is at the end of a file.
Column	Returns the column number of the current character in a file.
Line	Returns the current line number in a file. Both start at **1**.

The Err Object

Method	Description
Clear	Clears all current settings of the **Err** object.
Raise	Generates a run-time error.

Property	Description
Description	Sets or returns a string describing an error.
Number	(Default) Sets or returns a numeric value specifying an error.
Source	Sets or returns the name of the object that generated the error.

The AdRotator Component

Method	Description
GetAdvertisement	Gets details of the next advertisement and formats it as HTML.

Property	Description
Border	Size of the border around the advertisement.
Clickable	Defines whether the advertisement is a hyperlink.
TargetFrame	Name of the frame in which to display the advertisement.

The Content Linking Component

Method	Description
GetListCount	Number of items in the file *list*.
GetListIndex	Index of the current page in the file *list*.
GetNextURL	URL of the next page in the file *list*.
GetNextDescription	Description of the next page in the file *list*.
GetPreviousURL	URL of the previous page in the file *list*.
GetPreviousDescription	Description of previous page in the file *list*.
GetNthURL	URL of the *n*th page in the file *list*.
GetNthDescription	Description of the *n*th page in the file *list*.

The Content Rotator Component

Method	Description
ChooseContent	Retrieves and displays a content string
GetAllContent	Retrieves and displays all the content strings in the Content Schedule file

The Page Counter Component

Method	Description
Hits	Displays the number of times that a specified URL has been opened
Reset	Sets the hit count for a specified page to 0

The Permission Checker Component

Method	Description
HasAccess	Determines whether the user has permissions to access a specified file

The Counters Component

Method	Description
Get	Returns the value of the counter
Increment	Increases the counter by 1
Remove	Removes the counter from the **COUNTERS.TXT** file
Set	Sets the value of the counter to a specific integer

The MyInfo Component

Property	Description
PageType	Returns a number corresponding to the value in the "This site is …" pop-up menu in the Personal Web Server control panel. These are the pop-up menu options with their corresponding numerical values: 1 = About My Company 2 = About My Life 3 = About My School 4 = About My Organization 5 = About My Community
PersonalName	Returns the owner's name.
PersonalAddress	Returns the owner's address.
PersonalPhone	Returns the owner's phone number.
PersonalMail	Returns the owner's e-mail address.
PersonalWords	Returns additional text associated with the owner.
CompanyName	Returns the name of the owner's company.
CompanyAddress	Returns the address of the owner's company.
CompanyPhone	Returns the phone number of the owner's company.
CompanyDepartment	Returns the owner's department name.
CompanyWords	Returns additional text associated with the owner's company.
HomeOccupation	Returns the owner's occupation.
HomePeople	Returns text listing the people the owner lives with.
HomeWords	Returns additional text associated with the owner.
SchoolName	Returns the name of the owner's school.
SchoolAddress	Returns the address of the owner's school.
SchoolPhone	Returns the phone number of the owner's school.

Property	Description
SchoolDepartment	Returns the owner's department or class.
SchoolWords	Returns text associated with the owner's school.
OrganizationName	Returns the name of the organization featured on the site.
OrganizationAddress	Returns the address of the organization.
OrganizationPhone	Returns the phone number of the organization.
OrganizationWords	Returns text describing the organization.
CommunityName	Returns the name of the community featured on the site.
CommunityLocation	Returns the location of the community.
CommunityPopulation	Returns the population of the community.
CommunityWords	Returns text describing the community.
URL(n)	Returns the nth user-defined URL. Corresponds to the nth link description in **MyInfo.URLWords**.
URLWords(n)	Returns a string containing the nth user-defined description of a link. Corresponds to the nth URL in **MyInfo.URL**.
Style	Returns the relative URL (starting with '/') of a style sheet.
Background	Returns the background for the site.
Title	Returns the user-defined title for the home page.
Guestbook	Returns −1 if the guestbook should be available on the site. Otherwise, it returns 0.
Messages	Returns −1 if the private message form should be available on the site. Otherwise returns 0.

The Tools Component

Method	Description
FileExists	Checks for the existence of a file
Owner	Checks if the current user is the site owner (*Macintosh only*)
PluginExists	Checks the existence of a server plug-in (*Macintosh only*)
ProcessForm	Processes an HTML form
Random	Generates a random integer

The Status Component

Property	Description
VisitorsSinceStart	The number of unique visitors (IP addresses or domain names) since the server started up.
RequestsSinceStart	The number of requests since the server started up.
ActiveHTTPSessions	The current number of http connections.
HighHTTPSessions	The highest number of concurrent http connections since the server started up.
ServerVersion	The Personal Web Server version string.
StartTime	The time the server started up.
StartDate	The date the server started up.
FreeMem	The amount of unused memory available to the server.
FreeLowMem	The lowest value for the amount of unused memory available to the server since it started up.
VisitorsToday	Number of unique visitors (IP addresses or domain names) since midnight.
RequestsToday	The number of requests received since midnight.
BusyConnections	The total number of requests that were rejected because the server was already handling the maximum number of connections it can handle.
RefusedConnections	The total number of requests that were refused because authentication was invalid.
TimedoutConnections	The total number of connections that were closed without a request having been received.
Ktransferred	The total number of kilobytes sent by the server since the server started up.
TotalRequests	The total number of requests received since the status counters were reset using the admin tool.
CurrentThreads	The sum of the number active http connections and the number of threads in the connection thread pool that are not currently handling connections.
AvailableThreads	The number of threads in the connection thread pool that are not currently handling connections.
RecentVisitors	An HTML table listing the 32 most recent unique visitors. This table includes each visitor's domain name (or IP address if the domain name is not available) and the number of requests generated by each visitor.
PopularPages	An HTML table listing the 32 most recently visited pages. This table includes each page's URL and the number of requests for each page.

Note. This component is only available on Personal Web Server for Macintosh

Active Database Component Methods and Properties

The Connection Object

Method	Description
Open	Opens a new connection to a data source.
Close	Closes an existing open connection.
Execute	Executes a query, SQL statement, or stored procedure.
BeginTrans	Begins a new transaction.
CommitTrans	Saves any changes made and ends the transaction. May also start a new transaction.
RollbackTrans	Cancels any changes made and ends the transaction. May also start a new transaction.
OpenSchema	For server side scripts, allows the view of database schema, such as tables, columns, etc.

Property	Description
Attributes	Controls whether to begin a new transaction when an existing one ends.
CommandTimeout	Number of seconds to wait when executing a command before terminating the attempt and returning an error.
ConnectionString	The information used to create a connection to a data source.
ConnectionTimeout	Number of seconds to wait when creating a connection before terminating the attempt and returning an error.
CursorLocation	Whether the cursor is located on the client (**adUseClient**) or on the server (**adUseServer**)
DefaultDatabase	Sets or returns the default database to use for this connection.
IsolationLevel	Sets or returns the level of isolation within transactions.
Mode	Sets or returns the provider's access permissions.
Provider	Sets or returns the name of the provider.
State	Returns whether the connection is open or closed. For open connections **adStateOpen** is returned, and **adStateClosed** for closed connections.
Version	Returns the ADO version number.

The Command Object

Method	Description
CreateParameter	Creates a new **Parameter** object in the **Parameters** collection.
Execute	Executes the SQL statement or stored procedure specified in the **CommandText** property.

Property	Description
ActiveConnection	The **Connection** object to be used with this **Command** object.
CommandText	The text of a command to be executed.
CommandTimeout	Number of seconds to wait when executing a command before terminating the attempt and returning an error.
CommandType	Type of query set in the **CommandText** property.
Name	Allows a name to be assigned to a command
Prepared	Whether to create a prepared statement before execution.
State	Identifies whether the current command is open or closed. For an open command **adStateOpen** is returned, and **adStateClosed** for a closed command.

The Parameters Collection

Method	Description
Append	Adds a parameter to the collection.
Delete	Deletes a parameter from the collection.
Refresh	Updates the collection to reflect changes to the parameters.

Property	Description
Count	Returns the number of parameters in the collection.
Item	Used to retrieve the contents of a parameter from the collection.

The Parameter Object

Property	Description
Attributes	The type of data that the parameter accepts.
Direction	Whether the parameter is for input, output or both, or if it is the return value from a stored procedure.
Name	The name of the parameter.
NumericScale	The number of decimal places in a numeric parameter.
Precision	The number of digits in a numeric parameter.
Size	The maximum size, in bytes, of the parameter value.
Type	The data type of the parameter.
Value	The value assigned to the parameter.

The Recordset Object

Method	Description
AddNew	Creates a new record in an updatable recordset.
CancelBatch	Cancels a pending batch update.
CancelUpdate	Cancels any changes made to the current or new record.
Clone	Creates a duplicate copy of the recordset.
Close	Closes an open recordset and any dependent objects.
Delete	Deletes the current record in an open recordset.
GetRows	Retrieves multiple records into an array.
Move	Moves the position of the current record.
MoveFirst, MoveLast, MoveNext, MovePrevious	Moves to the first, last, next or previous record in the recordset, and makes that the current record.
NextRecordset	Returns the next recordset by advancing through a set of commands.
Open	Opens a cursor on a recordset.
Requery	Updates the data by re-executing the original query.
Resync	Refreshes the data from the underlying database.
Supports	Determines whether the recordset supports certain functions.
Update	Saves any changes made to the current record.
UpdateBatch	Writes all pending batch updates to disk.

Property	Description
AbsolutePage	The absolute 'page' on which the current record is located, or specifies the 'page' to move to.
AbsolutePosition	The ordinal position of the current record.
ActiveConnection	The **Connection** object that the recordset currently belongs to.
BOF	Boolean value; True if the current record position is before the first record, False otherwise.
Bookmark	Returns a bookmark that uniquely identifies the current record, or sets the current record to the record identified by a valid bookmark.
CacheSize	The number of records that are cached locally in memory.
CursorLocation	Whether the cursor is located on the client (**adUseClient**) or on the server (**adUseServer**)
CursorType	The type of cursor used in the recordset.
EditMode	The editing status of the current record.
EOF	True if the current record position is after the last record.
Filter	Indicates whether a filter is in use.
LockType	The type of locks placed on records during editing.
MarshalOptions	Sets or returns the records which are to be marshaled back to the server when using client side recordsets.
MaxRecords	The maximum number of records to return from a query.
PageCount	The number of 'pages' of data that the recordset contains.
PageSize	The number of records constituting one 'page'.
RecordCount	The number of records currently in the recordset.
Source	The source for the data in the recordset, i.e. **Command** object, SQL statement, table name, or stored procedure.
State	Returns whether the recordset is open or closed.
Status	Status of the current record with respect to batch updates or other bulk operations.

The Fields Collection

Method	Description
Refresh	Updates the collection to reflect changes to the field values.

Property	Description
Count	Returns the number of fields in the collection.
Item	Used to retrieve the contents of the fields in the collection.

The Field Object

Property	Description
ActualSize	The actual length of the field's current value.
Attributes	The kinds of data that the field can hold.
DefinedSize	The size or length of the field as defined in the data source.
Name	The name of the field.
NumericScale	The number of decimal places in a numeric field.
OriginalValue	The value of the field, before any unsaved changes were made.
Precision	The number of digits in a numeric field.
Type	The data type of the field.
UnderlyingValue	The field's current value within the database.
Value	The value currently assigned to the field, even if unsaved.

Method	Description
AppendChunk	Appends data to a large text or binary field.
GetChunk	Returns data from a large text or binary field.

The Properties Collection

Method	Description
Refresh	Updates the collection to reflect changes to the property values.

Property	Description
Count	Returns the number of properties in the collection.
Item	Used to retrieve the values of the properties in the collection.

The Property Object

Property	Description
Attributes	Indicates when and how the value of the property can be set.
Name	The name of the property.
Type	The data type of the property.
Value	The value of the property.

The Errors Collection

Method	Description
Clear	Removes all of the errors in the collection.

Property	Description
Count	Returns the number of errors objects in the collection.
Item	Used to retrieve the contents of the error objects in the collection.

The Error Object

Property	Description
Description	A description of the error.
HelpContext	Context, as a **Long** value, for the matching help file topic.
HelpFile	The path to the help file for this topic.
NativeError	The provider-specific error code number.
Number	The ADO error code number.
Source	Name of the object or application that generated the error.
SQLState	The SQL execution state for this error.

Active Data Object Constants

To use the constant names in your code, instead of specifying the actual values, you need to include a constants definition file in the page using a Server-side Include (SSI). These files are supplied with ASP, and installed by default in the **ASPSamp/Samples** directory on the server. For VBScript you use **Adovbs.inc**. For JScript, use **Adojavas.inc**. For example, using VBScript:

```
<!-- #include virtual="/Aspsamp/Samples/Adovbs.inc" -->
```

You can copy the file into the application directory instead, and include it using:

```
<!-- #include file="Adovbs.inc" -->
```

See Chapter 1 for more information about using **#include** SSI statements.

CursorTypeEnum Values

Constant	Value	Description
adOpenForwardOnly	0	**Forward-only cursor** (*Default*). Identical to a static cursor except that you can only scroll forward through records. This improves performance in situations when you only need to make a single pass through a recordset. Supports **adAddNew**, **adDelete**, **adUpdate**, **adUpdateBatch**
adOpenKeyset	1	**Keyset cursor**. Like a dynamic cursor, except that you can't see records that other users add, although records that other users delete are inaccessible from your recordset. Data changes by other users are still visible. Supports **adAddNew**, **adDelete**, **adMovePrevious**, **adUpdate**, **adUpdateBatch**.
adOpenDynamic	2	**Dynamic cursor**. Additions, changes, and deletions by other users are visible, and all types of movement through the recordset are allowed, except for bookmarks if the provider doesn't support them. Supports **adAddNew**, **adBookmark**, **adDelete**, **adHoldRecords**, **adMovePrevious**, **adResync**, **adUpdate**, **adUpdateBatch**.
adOpenStatic	3	**Static cursor**. A static copy of a set of records that you can use to find data or generate reports. Additions, changes, or deletions by other users are not visible. Supports **adAddNew**, **adBookmark**, **adDelete**, **adHoldRecords**, **adMovePrevious**, **adResync**, **adUpdate**, **adUpdateBatch**.

CursorOptionEnum Values

Constant	Value	Description
adHoldRecords	&H00000100 (256)	You can retrieve more records or change the next retrieve position without committing all pending changes and releasing all currently held records.
adMovePrevious	&H00000200 (512)	You can use the **MovePrevious** or **Move** methods to move the current record position backward without requiring bookmarks.
adAddNew	&H01000400 (16778240)	You can use the **AddNew** method to add new records.
adDelete	&H01000800 (16779264)	You can use the **Delete** method to delete records.
adUpdate	&H01008000 (16809984)	You can use the **Update** method to modify existing data.
adBookmark	&H00002000 (8192)	You can use the **Bookmark** property to access specific records.
adApproxPosition	&H00004000 (16384)	You can read and set the **AbsolutePosition** and **AbsolutePage** properties.
adUpdateBatch	&H00010000 (65536)	You can use batch updating to transmit changes to the provider in groups.
adResync	&H00020000 (131072)	You can update the cursor with the data visible in the underlying database.
adNotify	&H00040000 (262144)	Not used in ADO.

CursorLocationEnum Values

Constant	Value	Description
adUseServer	2	Use server side cursors.
adUseClient	3	Use client side cursors.

LockTypeEnum Values

Constant	Value	Description
`adLockReadOnly`	1	**Read-only**. You cannot alter the data.
`adLockPessimistic`	2	**Pessimistic locking**, record by record. The provider does what is necessary to ensure successful editing of the records, usually by locking records at the data source immediately upon editing.
`adLockOptimistic`	3	**Optimistic locking**, record by record. The provider uses optimistic locking, locking records only when you call the `Update` method.
`adLockBatchOptimistic`	4	**Optimistic batch updates**. Required for batch update mode as opposed to immediate update mode.

ExecuteOptionEnum Values

Constant	Value	Description
`adRunAsync`	&H00000010 (16)	Not used in ADO.

ObjectStateEnum Values

Constant	Value	Description
`adStateClosed`	&H00000000 (0)	The object is closed.
`adStateOpen`	&H00000001 (1)	The object is open.
`adStateConnecting`	&H00000002 (2)	Not used in ADO.
`adStateExecuting`	&H00000004 (4)	Not used in ADO.

DataTypeEnum Values

Constant	Value	Description
`adEmpty`	0	No value was specified.
`adSmallInt`	2	A 2-byte signed integer.
`adInteger`	3	A 4-byte signed integer.
`adSingle`	4	A single-precision floating point value.
`adDouble`	5	A double-precision floating point value.

Constant	Value	Description
adCurrency	6	A currency value (8-byte signed integer scaled by 10,000).
adDate	7	A **Date** value.
adBSTR	8	A null-terminated character string (Unicode).
adIDispatch	9	A pointer to an **IDispatch** interface on an OLE object.
adError	10	A 32-bit error code.
adBoolean	11	A **Boolean** value.
adVariant	12	An OLE Automation **Variant**.
adIUnknown	13	A pointer to an **IUnknown** interface on an OLE object.
adDecimal	14	An exact numeric value with a fixed precision and scale.
adTinyInt	16	A 1-byte signed integer.
adUnsignedTinyInt	17	A 1-byte unsigned integer.
adUnsignedSmallInt	18	A 2-byte unsigned integer.
adUnsignedInt	19	A 4-byte unsigned integer.
adBigInt	20	An 8-byte signed integer.
adUnsignedBigInt	21	An 8-byte unsigned integer.
adGUID	72	A globally unique identifier (GUID).
adBinary	128	A binary value.
adChar	129	A **String** value.
adWChar	130	A null-terminated Unicode character string.
adNumeric	131	An exact numeric value with a fixed precision and scale.
adUserDefined	132	A user-defined variable.
adDBDate	133	A date value (*yyyymmdd*).
adDBTime	134	A time value (*hhmmss*).
adDBTimeStamp	135	A date-time stamp (*yyyymmddhhmmss* plus a fraction in billionths).
adVarChar	200	A **String** value. (**Parameter** object only).
adLongVarChar	201	A long **String** value. (**Parameter** object only).
adVarWChar	202	A null-terminated Unicode character string. (**Parameter** object only).
adLongVarWChar	203	A long null-terminated string value. (**Parameter** object only).
adVarBinary	204	A binary value. (**Parameter** object only).
adLongVarBinary	205	A long binary value. (**Parameter** object only).

ConnectPromptEnum Values

Constant	Value	Description
adPromptAlways	1	...
adPromptComplete	2	These values are set by the **Provider**.
adPromptCompleteRequired	3	If it supports the **Prompt** property.
adPromptNever	4	...

ConnectModeEnum Values

Constant	Value	Description
adModeUnknown	0	The permissions have not yet been set or cannot be determined.
adModeRead	1	Read-only permissions.
adModeWrite	2	Write-only permissions.
adModeReadWrite	3	Read/write permissions.
adModeShareDenyRead	4	Prevents others from opening connection with read permissions.
adModeShareDenyWrite	8	Prevents others from opening connection with write permissions.
adModeShareExclusive	&HC (12)	Prevents others from opening connection with read/write permissions.
adModeShareDenyNone	&H10 (16)	Prevents others from opening connection with any permissions.

IsolationLevelEnum Values

Constant	Value	Description
adXactChaos	&H00000010 (16)	Indicates that you cannot overwrite pending changes from more highly isolated transactions.
adXactBrowse	&H00000100 (256)	Indicates that from one transaction you can view uncommitted changes in other transactions.
adXactReadUncommitted	&H00000100 (256)	Same as **adXactBrowse**.
adXactCursorStability	&H00001000 (4096)	Indicates that from one transaction you can only view changes in other transactions after they've been committed. (*Default*).

Constant	Value	Description
`adXactReadCommitted`	`&H00001000 (4096)`	Same as **adXactCursorStability**.
`adXactRepeatableRead`	`&H00010000 (65536)`	Indicates that from one transaction you cannot see changes made in other transactions, but that requerying can bring a new recordset.
`adXactIsolated`	`&H00100000 (1048576)`	Indicates that transactions are conducted in isolation of other transactions.
`adXactSerializable`	`&H00100000 (1048576)`	Same as **adXactIsolated**.
`adXactUnspecified`	`&HFFFFFFFF (-1)`	If the provider is using a different **IsolationLevel** than specified, but precisely which cannot be determined, the property returns this value.

XactAttributeEnum Values

Constant	Value	Description
`adXactCommitRetaining`	`&H00020000 (131072)`	Performs retaining commits. Calling **CommitTrans** automatically starts a new transaction. Not all providers will support this.
`adXactAbortRetaining`	`&H00040000 (262144)`	Performs retaining aborts. Calling **RollBack** automatically starts a new transaction. Not all providers will support this.

FieldAttributeEnum Values

Constant	Value	Description
`adFldMayDefer`	`&H00000002 (2)`	Indicates that the field is deferred, that is, the field values are not retrieved from the data source with the whole record, but only when you explicitly access them.
`adFldUpdatable`	`&H00000004 (4)`	Indicates that you can write to the field.
`adFldUnknownUpdatable`	`&H00000008 (8)`	Indicates that the provider cannot determine whether or not you can write to the field.
`adFldFixed`	`&H00000010 (16)`	Indicates that the field contains fixed-length data.
`adFldIsNullable`	`&H00000020 (32)`	Indicates that the field accepts **Null** values.

Constant	Value	Description
adFldMayBeNull	&H00000040 (64)	Indicates that you can read **Null** values from the field.
adFldLong	&H00000080 (128)	Indicates that the field is a long binary field. Also indicates that you can use the **AppendChunk** and **GetChunk** methods.
adFldRowID	&H00000100 (256)	Indicates that the field contains some kind of record ID (record number, unique identifier, etc.).
adFldRowVersion	&H00000200 (512)	Indicates that the field contains some kind of time or date stamp used to track updates.
adFldCacheDeferred	&H00001000 (4096)	Indicates that the provider caches field values and that subsequent reads are done from the cache.

EditModeEnum Values

Constant	Value	Description
adEditNone	&H0000 (0)	No editing operation is in progress.
adEditInProgress	&H0001 (1)	Data in the current record has been modified but not yet saved.
adEditAdd	&H0002 (2)	The **AddNew** method has been invoked, and the current record in the copy buffer is a new record that hasn't been saved in the database.
adEditDelete	&H0004 (4)	The **Delete** method has been invoked and the current record has been marked for deletion.

RecordStatusEnum Values

Constant	Value	Description
adRecOK	&H0000000 (0)	The record was successfully updated.
adRecNew	&H0000001 (1)	The record is new.
adRecModified	&H0000002 (2)	The record was modified.
adRecDeleted	&H0000004 (4)	The record was deleted.
adRecUnmodified	&H0000008 (8)	The record was unmodified.
adRecInvalid	&H0000010 (16)	The record was not saved because its bookmark is invalid.
adRecMultipleChanges	&H0000040 (64)	The record was not saved because it would have affected multiple records.

Constant	Value	Description
adRecPendingChanges	&H0000080 (128)	The record was not saved because it refers to a pending insert.
adRecCanceled	&H0000100 (256)	The record was not saved because the operation was canceled.
adRecCantRelease	&H0000400 (1024)	The new record was not saved because of existing record locks.
adRecConcurrencyViolation	&H0000800 (2048)	The record was not saved because optimistic concurrency was in use.
adRecIntegrityViolation	&H0001000 (4096)	The record was not saved because the user violated integrity constraints.
adRecMaxChangesExceeded	&H0002000 (8192)	The record was not saved because there were too many pending changes.
adRecObjectOpen	&H0004000 (16384)	The record was not saved because of a conflict with an open storage object.
adRecOutOfMemory	&H0008000 (32768)	The record was not saved because the computer has run out of memory.
adRecPermissionDenied	&H0010000 (65536)	The record was not saved because the user has insufficient permissions.
adRecSchemaViolation	&H0020000 (131072)	The record was not saved because it violates the structure of the underlying database.
adRecDBDeleted	&H0040000 (262144)	The record has already been deleted from the data source.

GetRowsOptionEnum Values

Constant	Value	Description
adGetRowsRest	-1	In a GetRows call, get all remaining records.

PositionEnum Values

Constant	Value	Description
adPosUnknown	-1	No current record.
adPosBOF	-2	Before the first record.
adPosEOF	-3	After the last record.

AffectEnum Values

Constant	Value	Description
adAffectCurrent	1	Cancel pending transactions only for the current record.
adAffectGroup	2	Cancel pending transactions for records that satisfy the current **Filter** property setting.
adAffectAll	3	Cancel pending updates for all the records in the **Recordset** object, including any hidden by the current **Filter** property setting.

FilterGroupEnum Values

Constant	Value	Description
adFilterNone	0	Removes the current filter and restores all records to view.
adFilterPendingRecords	1	Allows you to view only records that have changed but not yet been sent to the server. Only applicable for batch update mode.
adFilterAffectedRecords	2	Allows you to view only records affected by the last **Delete**, **Resync**, **UpdateBatch**, or **CancelBatch** call.
adFilterFetchedRecords	3	Allows you to view records in the current cache, the results of the last fetch from the database.
adFilterPredicate	4	Not used in ADO.

PropertyAttributesEnum Values

Constant	Value	Description
adPropNotSupported	&H0000 (0)	Indicates that the provider does not support the property.
adPropRequired	&H0001 (1)	Indicates that the user must specify a value for this property before the data source is initialized.
adPropOptional	&H0002 (2)	Indicates that the user does not need to specify a value for this property before the data source is initialized.
adPropRead	&H0200 (512)	Indicates that the user can read the property.
adPropWrite	&H0400 (1024)	Indicates that the user can set the property.

ErrorValueEnum Values

Constant	Value	Description
adErrInvalidArgument	&HBB9	Invalid argument.
adErrNoCurrentRecord	&HBCD	No current record.
adErrIllegalOperation	&HC93	Invalid operation.
adErrInTransaction	&HCAE	Operation not supported in transactions.
adErrFeatureNotAvailable	&HCB3	Operation is not supported for this type of object.
adErrItemNotFound	&HCC1	Item not found in this collection.
adErrObjectNotSet	&HD5C	Object is invalid or not set.
adErrDataConversion	&HD5D	Data type conversion error.
adErrObjectClosed	&HE78	Invalid operation on closed object.
adErrObjectOpen	&HE79	Invalid operation on opened object.
adErrProviderNotFound	&HE7A	Provider not found.
adErrBoundToCommand	&HE7B	Invalid operation. The recordset source property is currently set to a command object.
adErrInvalidConnection	&HE7D	Invalid operation on object with a closed connection reference.
adErrInvalidParamInfo	&HE7C	Invalid parameter definition.
adErrStillExecuting	&He7f	Not used in ADO.
adErrStillConnecting	&He81	Not used in ADO.

ParameterAttributesEnum Values

Constant	Value	Description
adParamSigned	&H0010 (16)	Indicates that the parameter accepts signed values (*Default*)
adParamNullable	&H0040 (64)	Indicates that the parameter accepts **Null** values.
adParamLong	&H0080 (128)	Indicates that the parameter accepts long binary data.

ParameterDirectionEnum Values

Constant	Value	Description
adParamUnknown	&H0000 (0)	Unknown Type.
adParamInput	&H0001 (1)	Input parameter (*Default*).
adParamOutput	&H0002 (2)	Output parameter.
adParamInputOutput	&H0003 (3)	Input and output parameter.
adParamReturnValue	&H0004 (4)	Return value.

CommandTypeEnum Values

Constant	Value	Description
adCmdUnknown	8	The type of command in the **CommandText** property is not known. (*Default*)
adCmdText	1	Evaluates the **CommandText** as a textual definition of a command.
adCmdTable	2	Evaluates **CommandText** as a table name.
adCmdStoredProc	4	Evaluates **CommandText** as a stored procedure.

MarshalOptionsEnum Values

Constant	Value	Description
adMarshalAll	0	Indicates that all rows are returned to the server (default).
adMarshalModifiedOnly	1	Indicates that only modified rows are returned to the server.

SearchDirection Values

Constant	Value	Description
adSearchForward	0	To search forwards when performing a **Find** method on a **Recordset** object.
adSearchBackward	1	To search backwards when performing a **Find** method on a **Recordset** object.

SchemaEnum Values

Constant	Value	Description
`adSchemaProviderSpecific`	-1	Provider specific information
`adSchemaAsserts`	0	Database asserts
`adSchemaCatalogs`	1	Database catalogs
`adSchemaCharacterSets`	2	Database character sets
`adSchemaCollations`	3	
`adSchemaColumns`	4	Return column details
`adSchemaCheckConstraints`	5	Database constraints
`adSchemaConstraintColumnUsage`	6	Constraint usage for columns
`adSchemaConstraintTableUsage`	7	Constraint usage for tables
`adSchemaKeyColumnUsage`	8	Columns used as key fields
`adSchemaReferentialContraints`	9	Referential integrity constraints
`adSchemaTableConstraints`	10	Table constraints
`adSchemaColumnsDomainUsage`	11	
`adSchemaIndexes`	12	Indexes
`adSchemaColumnPrivileges`	13	Column level privileges
`adSchemaTablePrivileges`	14	Table level privileges
`adSchemaUsagePrivileges`	15	
`adSchemaProcedures`	16	Stored procedures
`adSchemaSchemata`	17	
`adSchemaSQLLanguages`	18	
`adSchemaStatistics`	19	
`adSchemaTables`	20	Database tables
`adSchemaTranslations`	21	Language translations
`adSchemaProviderTypes`	22	
`adSchemaViews`	23	Database views
`adSchemaViewColumnUsage`	24	
`adSchemaViewTableUsage`	25	
`adSchemaProcedureParameters`	26	Stored procedure parameters
`adSchemaForeignKeys`	27	Foreign keys
`adSchemaPrimaryKeys`	28	Primary keys
`adSchemaProcedureColumns`	29	Stored procedure columns

*Those items marked **left blank do** have defined constants in adovbs.inc, but are not exposed to ADO.
Some are accessible to C or C++ programmers, and may be available to ADO in a later release.*

Scripting Library and Remote Scripting

The use of the web as an application development platform has come a long way from the days of just serving up static pages from a web server. One of the constants, though, is the method of interaction between the browser and the web server. When a browser client wants to view information from a web server, it requests that information in the form of a page. This page may be statically stored on the server in a `.html` file. This page could be dynamically created by using a PERL or ASP script. Alternatively, it could be generated by retrieving information from a database or other system. But in each case, the method of interaction is the same:

- Browser requests page from server
- Server locates and/or creates page
- Server sends page to the browser
- Browser displays the entire page

In all interactions between the browser and the server, the information that the client was previously displaying is completely replaced by the new information from the server. While technologies such as frames allow browsers to display information from multiple pages simultaneously, the information from the server must still be stored as a complete page. As web applications move more towards replacing traditional client/server applications, there is some functionality missing from the web world that exists in the client/server world. Since the web is page-based, it is very difficult to retrieve a single piece of information from the server without replacing what the browser is currently displaying. While an astute developer can play tricks with hidden frames and DHTML to try and replicate this type of functionality, it is still very difficult to implement. And with difficult implementation comes a general reluctance to experiment.

Fortunately, Microsoft is working on a solution for this. They have introduced a Technology Preview of the Microsoft Scripting Library. The MSL provides a number of technologies that allow for additional functionality in the interaction between browser and web server. In this appendix we will be taking a look at:

- What the Microsoft Scripting Library consists of
- Where to get the Scripting Library
- The features of the Scripting Library
- Remote Scripting and how it can be used to build applications
- A short case study that uses the power of the Scripting Library

To begin our look at the Microsoft Scripting Library, let's start by looking at what MSL actually is.

What is the Scripting Library?

The Microsoft Scripting Library is a Microsoft technology that will allow you to develop applications in an Internet environment which offer functionality not usually present in Internet applications. The MSL consists of a run-time support library for both the client and the server. The client piece is implemented in JavaScript and Java. This allows it to be used on any platform that supports these technologies. This allows the power of the MSL to be made available to Internet Explorer users, as well as Netscape Navigator and other JAVA enabled browsers.

In the future, we may see the client portion of the scripting library packaged as a run-time library, included with all Microsoft browsers. But, by basing the technology on an open platform such as JAVA, the developer does not have to worry about supporting alternate methods for the same application. As long as the browser supports JAVA and JavaScript, it can support the MSL.

On the server side, MSL is delivered as a set of run-time libraries that provide the support for the execution of remote functions on the server. They also provide support for the other functions that are part of the scripting library. These libraries are delivered in source-code format for inclusion into ASP scripts that will use Remote Scripting. As with the client-side of MSL, we could see the future of the Server-side moving to being part of the web server itself. For now, all that is required is an ASP compliant web server. Next, you will need to know where you can get the scripting library itself.

How to get the Scripting Library

The Scripting Library is currently a work-in-progress. But in the spirit of fostering development and gaining developer's mind share, Microsoft has decided to make it available in its current form. As we stated earlier, it is currently available as a set of both client and server source code. You can find all available information about the Microsoft Scripting Library in the area of the Microsoft web site that is devoted to scripting. You can find it at:

`http://www.microsoft.com/scripting`

When you look at this page in your browser, you will see the following.

The link that is highlighted will allow you to download the latest version of the Microsoft Scripting Library. This will come packaged in a self-extracting executable file called **msl.exe**. Once this file is saved on your computer, you can extract the source files by simply running the executable. The files will need to be saved in the **_scriptlibrary** subdirectory that is underneath the document root for the web server you are installing to.

> *For example, if you have installed your document root using the IIS installation defaults, then your document root will be at* **c:\inetpub\wwwroot**. *This means that you would need to extract the files in the* **msl.exe** *file into the* **c:\inetpub\wwwroot_scriptlibrary** *subdirectory. Once the extraction is complete, these files will be stored in this directory.*

As we mentioned earlier, the Scripting Library is made up of client-side JavaScript functions, a client-side JAVA proxy object, and a server-side script file. These files, containing actually readable source code are stored in this directory. They are:

▲ **rs.htm**, for the client-side JavaScript functions,

▲ **rsproxy.class**, for the client-side JAVA object,

▲ **rs.asp**, for the server-side script file.

The package also includes the source code for the JAVA object in the **rsproxy.java** class, as well as a simple example program in the **simple.htm** and **simple.asp** script files.

At the present time, the Microsoft Scripting Library is distributed in source code format, and needs to be explicitly included in both client and server scripts in order for its features to work correctly. However, this is subject to change in the future. Microsoft, in fact, considers these releases as intermediate versions the purpose of which is to make developers aware of this new technology. By using and studying this implementation of Remote Scripting and the Microsoft Scripting Library you can get started with the technology and be ready to take advantage of it when its finally made available in a released format.

Up to this point, we have focused primarily on one function available in the MSL. The ability to do remote scripting is by far the most powerful aspect of the Scripting Library, but it is by no means the only part. Now, let's take a look at all of the technologies that are part of the Scripting Library.

Scripting Library Features

The Scripting Library brings a rich set of additional features to both the client and server side of ASP and HTML scripting. These features are designed to add additional features to the existing scripting capabilities. The features they add are directed at a single purpose. This purpose is to enable the traditional web browser and server platform to function more as a traditional client/server development platform. As we examine each of the features of the Scripting Library, you will see how each can be used to enhance the connectivity between the browser and the web server application.

Closures

A closure is a programming construct that allows the user to create a "shortcut" to a particular method of an object. It has its roots in functional programming languages, such as LISP. With the advent of object-oriented languages, closures were enhanced to comprise the concept of creating a reference to a specific method of a specific object. For example, if you had an object **objThisIsMyObject**, with a method called **MyMethodToDoSomethingNow**, then to call this method you would have to write:

```
objThisIsMyObject.MyMethodToDoSomethingNow();
```

While this is functionally correct, it is also quite long and tends to clutter up the code. By using closures, we can achieve the following:

```
MyClosure = closure(objThisIsMyObject, "MyMethodToDoSomethingNow");
```

Now, anywhere that we wish to call this method, all that we need to do is write:

```
MyClosure();
```

Even if the method that we were creating a closure took parameters, we can still use that in a closure. Instead of

```
objMyObject.MyMethod(foo, bar, x, y);
```

we can simply use:

```
myClosure2 = closure(objMyObject, "MyMethod");
myClosure2(foo, bar, x, y);
```

A real-life example of using closures is for binding JavaScript event handling functions to HTML Object model events. In traditional JavaScript development, you would create a function for each Object Model event that you wanted to handle. The function would then be associated with the event in one of two ways. In this example, we will see both instances of how this works.

```
<SCRIPT language=JavaScript>
    function handleClick();
    {
            alert("Here is a click");
    }
</SCRIPT>
```

This function will simply display an alert box whenever it is called. To have this function called when the user clicks anywhere on the page, you can do either:

```
<SCRIPT language=Javascript for=document event=onclick>
    handleClick();
</SCRIPT>
```

or you can do this:

```
<SCRIPT language=JavaScript>
    document.onclick = handleClick;
</SCRIPT>
```

When implementing this same functionality using closures, you can gain the benefits of being able to use a method of an object to handle the event. You will first create a method of an object that will handle the event, then create a closure function that encapsulates this method call. By encapsulating this method call within the object, it will not exist globally. You can even use the object that is firing the event to hold the method. Here is an example of how you can use closures in that manner.

```
<INPUT TYPE=INPUT ID='myInput'>
<INPUT TYPE=BUTTON ID='myBtn' VALUE="Add One…">
<SCRIPT language=JavaScript>
    myInput.addOne = function()
            {
                    this.value++;
            };
    myBtn.onclick = closure(myInput, "addOne");
</SCRIPT>
```

Closures are a way to provide a shortcut during coding of an application. By creating a variable that holds a closure function, you can use that variable any place in the code in place of using the method of the object that was used to create the closure.

Object Introspection

JavaScript, as well as most other scripting languages, is a late-bound language. This means that the application exists in source code format until the actual line that the source code is on is executed. What this allows the developer to do is to write applications that dynamically reprogram themselves on the fly.

The source code can be manipulated using the same mechanisms that are used to manipulate a string. Then, through the use of the JavaScript **eval** method, the string can be turned into an executable line of code, which is then executed. This works fine for the source code that the developer can manipulate directly. But there also arises a need for the contents of an object to be manipulated in a string format.

The Microsoft Scripting Library adds an **uneval** method. This method works in the exact opposite method of the **eval** method. Rather than turning an string of code into an executable format, it will convert an executable object into a string. One of the limitations of the **uneval** method is that the string value that is returned cannot be manipulated. It is merely meant to be held until it is passed to an **eval** method. The **eval** method will create an exact duplicate of the object.

One of the new technologies available in IIS 4.0 is support for the Microsoft Message Queue Server. This technology is covered in Chapter 17. In short, this technology is like e-mail for applications. Instead of exchanging human-readable messages between individuals, message queuing allows applications to exchange information in a machine-readable format. While this may sound similar to what DCOM or CORBA perform, message queuing supports store-and-forward routing of messages. This means that if the destination application is not currently running, the message will still get there.

The body of the messages that are sent between applications can either be binary or strings. The **uneval** method can be used to create a string representation of an object, then pass it via a message queue to another application, this then reconstructs the application using the **eval** method. In this manner, the **uneval** and **eval** methods can function as a simple data **marshaller** which can be used to transmit data between systems in a client/server application.

> **Marshalling** *is a technique that is used to efficiently package all of the parameters for a single method call into a package that can be easily transmitted to the remote object that will actually perform the method.*

ADO

In Chapters 7 and 8 of this book, we took a look at the ActiveX Data Objects. These are a powerful mechanism for extracting information from database sources. Along with this power comes a somewhat limited way of manipulating the data. The data is arranged in a tabular format, where the fields represent the columns and the records represent the rows. For many applications, this is sufficient for examining and manipulating. However, in some instances, it may be more effective to manipulate the information in the ADO recordset in an entirely different way.

There are a number of different data aggregation constructs that are available in JavaScript. You can represent a list of data as an array. A list of data can also be represented as an object, with each object property corresponding to each element in the list. A table of data can be represent by a two dimensional array. One dimension of the array represents the list of data for a particular record. The other dimension represents each of the records in the recordset. Up until now, there has not existed an automatic way to convert a Recordset representation of data to one of these representations.

With Microsoft Scripting Library, there are a set of three helper functions that will take the data from a recordset and convert it to another type of data structure. These functions are currently outlined in the white paper that describes the Microsoft Scripting Library. However, there is no support for this functionality that is implemented as of yet. It is anticipated that this will soon be added to the Scripting Library technology preview.

The **RecordSetAsList** object will take an ADO recordset and the name of a field in that recordset. The method will return an array that has the same size as the number of records in the recordset. Each element of the array will contain the value of the field from each record in the recordset. For example, if we had a table that contained the following information:

	X	Y	Z
1	ABC	123	999
2	DEF	456	888
3	GHI	789	777
4	JKL	012	666
5	MNO	345	555

Using ADO, we would create a recordset, **rs**, which represented this table. Then this method:

```
var arRS;
arRS = RecordSetAsList(rs, "Y");
```

This would return an array with the contents:

```
{123, 456, 789, 012, 345}
```

The **RecordSetAsArray** method will take an ADO recordset and create a two dimensional array. The first dimension of the array will represent the records in the recordset. If we use the example recordset from the previous method, there would be 5 elements in the first dimension of the array resulting from this method. The second dimension of the array corresponds to the fields in a particular record. In this example, there would be 3 elements in the second dimension of the array. There will also be a parameter that could be included. This would add the field names as an extra row at the beginning of the array.

The third method is the **RecordAsObject** method. This method will take the current record of the recordset and create an object. There will be a property in this object that corresponds to each field in the record. If the field name will result in an invalid property name, then the **RecordAsObject** method will mangle the name of the property so that is becomes valid. In this example, if the current record of the recordset was record number 3, then the object returned would look like this:

```
myRSObj = RecordAsObject(rs);
myRSObj.X = "ABC"
myRSObj.Y = 123
myRSObj.Z = 999
```

Since an array is also an object, these methods can be looked at as generally taking the information in a recordset and returning an object. If we use this in conjunction with the **uneval** method that we discussed earlier, we now have a powerful mechanism to easily move data between client and server applications. These helper methods prevent us from having to worry about things like persistent objects, threading issues, object lifetimes, and all of the other stuff that concern developers when moving objects from system to system.

Now that we have seen the ways that the Scripting Library makes it easier to package data and move it back and forth between applications and systems, lets look at the mechanism that is actually in place to execute methods on different systems in a client/server environment.

Remote Scripting

The web browser has matured very quickly in the past four years. From only being able to display simple formatted text, then to graphics on through objects such as JAVA Applets and ActiveX controls, the web browser has been quickly advancing down the road towards being a rich user interface. With the recent advent of Dynamic HTML, we now have a great deal of power in being able to manipulate the way that the page is displayed without having to go back to the server. But even Dynamic HTML has its limitations.

Technologies such as the Active Data Connector, which allow for direct interaction between a web page and a server-side database, are fine for applications that are displaying database-type information. But the web server, being a powerful computer in its own right, has the ability to perform a great deal more functionality than simply retrieving information from a database. Active Server Pages are a great example of using the power of the web server to dynamically create pages that can then be displayed in a web browser. But we are still left with one hole in the solution.

When an Active Server Page is created on the server and sent to the client, all the client knows how to do is replace what it is currently displaying with the page that was sent from the server. For many applications, that is OK. But for applications that are being developed to replace existing client/server applications, this is not acceptable.

In traditional client/server applications, the client and the server can freely exchange information. The client can make a request for information or processing on the server, and the server can respond once it has completed the request. The client can then update its display with the results of the request. From a user interface standpoint, this appears to the user as merely one piece of data being refreshed, not the entire user interface being updated. It became obvious that there is a piece of functionality missing if web-based applications were going to reach the power of client/server applications. This missing piece of functionality has been introduced by Microsoft in the form of Remote Scripting technology.

How it works

As we stated earlier in this chapter, Remote Scripting is implemented by using both client-side and server-side pieces. These pieces are packaged into a JavaScript include file that will need to be included in any page that will use remote scripting. The client will also need to create a JAVA object that will handle the communication between the client and server. The user does not need to do anything special with this object, as the JavaScript include file contains all of the necessary functionality to support the object.

On the server side, the ASP script file that contains the remote method will also need to have a script file included as well. By encapsulating all of the plumbing that is needed for Remote Scripting to work, MSL makes it very easy to implement.

While we do not need to delve into a detailed technical discussion of the way that Remote Scripting and MSL is implemented, it would be helpful to look at the architecture of the system. To support a traditional client/server interaction between a web browser and a web server, a combination of JAVA applets and JavaScript code is used.

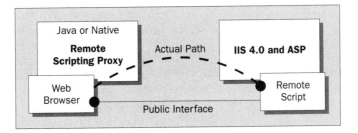

The client page that is using remote scripting will include an HTML source file that contains the JavaScript code as well as the JAVA proxy object. The JavaScript code is used to create a high-level interface to the remote scripting client. This will allow developers to use a simple API call to call a remote scripting function. All of the details of communicating with the JAVA proxy object are encapsulated in this JavaScript source.

> *For a detailed examination of the inner workings of Remote Scripting, and Scriptlet technology in general, check out the Instant Scriptlets book from WROX ISBN – 1-861001-38-X.*

The JAVA proxy object is used to communicate directly with the web server. It is actually communicating with a similar JAVA object running on the web server. It is through these JAVA applets that remote methods can be made available from ASP script pages. These remote methods can be called using the high-level remote scripting APIs that are included in the client-side runtime library. The high-level APIs then communicate with the client proxy object. The client object is responsible for marshalling the parameters for the method call. This marshaled data is then passed to the server-side proxy object, which in turn executes the remote script that is stored in an ASP script file.

In short, this is how remote scripting works. As mentioned earlier, there are other references that explain exactly what happens in the interaction between client and server. In fact, since the MSL is currently distributed in source code format, feel free to dive into the code to understand how it works.

Server Side

When creating the server side of the Remote Scripting call, you will be writing an Active Server Pages script file. Inside this script file will be a block of JavaScript code that serves as the remote scripting function. Within this script block reside methods that can be called remotely. These remote methods can be used to create objects on the server and then use those objects to access databases or other systems. They can also perform processing on the data before it is returned to the web browser.

There are a few constraints that a developer of the server side of Remote Scripting will need to take into consideration when creating these ASP scripts. First, the developer is responsible for initializing the Remote Scripting engine on the server. This is done by a call to **RSDispatch**. This method will be used to locate the proper function to execute based on the call from the JAVA proxy object. This method call needs to be placed at the top of the ASP script file, and will look like this:

```
<% RSDispatch %>
```

The next step that the developer must take is to add the JavaScript helper functions source file as a server-side include. This file contains the **RSDispatch** method, as well as other helper functions that are used in Remote Scripting, and throughout the Scripting Library. This should be added to the ASP script file near the top. The file that will be included is stored in the **_ScriptLibrary** subdirectory off the document root of your web server. Since this is an ASP script, the directory will need to have the scripting access privilege enabled on it.

> *The current version of the* **MSL.exe** *file from Microsoft is a self-extracting file. It will extract to the proper directory by default, but it will not check to make sure that the directory has the proper access privileges set. You should check to make sure that this subdirectory has scripting enabled.*

To add this server-side include to your Remote Scripting server script file, you need to add:

```
<!--#INCLUDE FILE="/_ScriptLibrary/rs.asp"-->
```

The next step that the developer will need to take is to create a Description object. This object will be used to identify all of the publicly available methods contained in the script file. This object is similar to the Description objects that are used with Scriptlets. The Description object will simply consist of a set of properties. There will be one property for each public method in the ASP script file. The name of the property should be identical to the name of the method. After defining the Description object, you will need to create an instance of it and assign a reference to that object to the **public_description** variable.

Since VBScript does not support user-defined objects, the object must be developed using JavaScript. Since the default script processor for ASP scripts is VBScript, you will need to identify that you are using JavaScript as the script language. Furthermore, since the code will exist inside of a **<SCRIPT>** block, you will need to identify that block of code as running at the server by using the **RUNAT=SERVER** parameter when creating the **<SCRIPT>** block. Here is an example of the definition of the Description object and how it assigned to the **public_description** variable.

```
<SCRIPT RUNAT=SERVER LANGUAGE=JAVASCRIPT>

    function Description()
    {
            this.myMethod = myMethod;
            this.myOtherMethod = myOtherMethod;
    }
    public_description = new Description();
```

The final step is to implement the methods for your application. The name of each method needs to be the same as those in the Description object. To pass a value back to the calling application, you will use the return statement along with the desired value. Developers will need to be careful when using the Response and Request objects. Since a JAVA applet is actually calling this ASP script, you cannot use these two objects in the same way as you do with a regular ASP script. All of the work to process the Request information and create the Response information is done in the **rs.asp** include file. If you are interested in what is going on behind the scenes, you can look at the source for this file. But it is safe to say that if you try to use the Response object in your remote scripting functions directly, you will probably not get back the proper response from your function. Here is just an example of a couple method that can be called from a browser using Remote Scripting.

```
    function myMethod()
    {
            return new Date;
    }
```

```
    function myOtherMethod ()
    {
            return new
Array("Monday","Tuesday","Wednesday","Thursday","Friday","Saturday","Sunday");
    }
```

Now that we have developed the server side of the Remote Scripting application, we can move on to the client side code required to call it.

Client Side

The client side of a Remote Scripting call will also be a Dynamic HTML page. It makes little sense to use Remote Scripting if the browser cannot dynamically update the information that is displayed on the screen. The page will need some method of eliciting a user interaction–such as clicking a button or pressing a key on the keyboard. The other necessary part will be some part of the page that will be updateable depending on what information is returned from the server call.

To add Remote Scripting support to a client page, there are a number of steps that a developer must follow as well. The first step is to include the JavaScript helper source file into the page. This include file contains all of the methods that are needed to setup the JAVA proxy object, package the Remote Scripting call into a format that can be transmitted to the server, and interpret the results from the information returned by the server. To add this include file to your HTML file, you will add this to the page source:

```
<SCRIPT LANGUAGE="JAVASCRIPT" SRC="/_ScriptLibrary/rs.htm"></SCRIPT>
```

This statement will cause the browser to read the contents of the **rs.htm** file which is in the **/_ScriptLibrary** subdirectory into a script block on the client. This is a bit different from a server-side include. In a server-side include, the contents of the include file are inserted directly in the response stream that the server sends back to the client. In this method of including a source file, the browser will open another connection with the server and read the contents of the file and dynamically add its scripts to the page being displayed.

Once the include file as been added, the next step is to call the **RSEnableRemoteScripting** method. The source for this method is part of the **rs.htm** file. This method is responsible for inserting the code into the page that will create the JAVA proxy object. To call this method you will add this code after including the **rs.htm** file:

```
<SCRIPT LANGUAGE="JAVASCRIPT">
        RSEnableRemoteScripting();
</SCRIPT>
```

The page is now initialized and ready for Remote Scripting calls. There are a number of ways that Remote Scripting calls can be made. Calls can be made **synchronously**. In this case the browser will pause all other processing until the information is returned from the server. Calls can also be made **asynchronously**. An asynchronous call will return immediately after the browser executes it. Once the server is done processing the method, a method on the client will be called advising it that the function has completed.

Synchronous

A synchronous Remote Scripting call is the easiest type of call to make. The client-side script can call a function, which will return an object containing the status of the function call, and the value returned by the server. To make a synchronous Remote Scripting call, you will use the RSExecute method. This method is defined as:

```
retval = RSExecute(URL, method, p0 … pX);
```

The value of **retval** is an object. This object has five properties. These properties are:

- **status**
- **message**
- **context**
- **data**
- **return_value**

The properties that most concern us are the **status** and **return_value** properties. Since the call to the server may fail for some reason, the return value is not returned directly. The client script must check the value contained in the status property to see if the call was successful. If **retval.status == 'success'** then the Remote Scripting function completed successfully. If this is the case the **retval.return_value** property will contain the information that was returned from the server.

The **URL** parameter will contain the location of the Remote Scripting source file. This can be a relative path to a script file on the same server, or it can be any valid URL that points to a Remote Scripting capable file.

The **method** parameter is a string that contains the name of the Remote Scripting method that the user wishes to call.

The remaining parameters in the method call are the parameters that will be passed to the remote method defined by the **method** parameter.

One of the drawbacks of the synchronous Remote Scripting call is that the **RSExecute** method will not return until the remote script itself has completed. This means that all execution in the browser will be paused until this method returns. Since this is a call to an ASP script file on remote server, there is no guarantee how long it will take to complete, or even if the server can be reached at all. The strength of the synchronous method call is that is very straightforward to use. You will, however, have to balance this ease-of-use against the problems associated with pausing all execution while the remote method is executed.

Asynchronous

The other type of Remote Scripting call is the asynchronous call. Unlike the synchronous call, this type of call will return immediately after it is called. This will allow other processing in the browser to continue. However, it is up to the developer to implement a callback method that will be called when the remote script does return. This callback method will receive the same type of object that is returned from the synchronous call. The advantage of this type of Remote Scripting call is that the browser and application running in the browser will appear to be much more responsive. Other event-handling scripts in the browser can be called while the remote script is processing. This is the exact opposite from a synchronous Remote Scripting call, where no browser processing can take place.

To make an asynchronous Remote Scripting call, you need to use the following method:

```
RSExecute(URL, method, p0 ... pX, callback1);
```

You can see that this looks very similar to the synchronous call. The two differences are that there is no return value and the last parameter is a callback function. Actually, there is a return value, but you don't need to worry about doing anything with it. The callback function will be called when the remote scripting function has completed. The callback function will be passed an object as a parameter. This is the same object that is returned immediately with the synchronous call. Here is an example of how to use the asynchronous Remote Scripting call:

```
RSExecute(URL, method, p0 ... pX, callback1);
...later on in the script
function myCallback(objRetval)
{
    var result;
    if (objRetval.Status == 'success')
    {
            result = objRetval.return_value;
            // do something with the result
    }
}
```

Using the Server Object

In both the synchronous and asynchronous Remote Scripting calls, you see that you need to supply the URL of the remote script as well as the name of the method in the remote ASP script. This is OK if you are making a Remote Scripting call once or twice in a page. If during the processing of a page, you wish to make multiple calls to methods in the same ASP script, then you can use another helper method to streamline your code. There is a method that allows you to get a reference to an object that represents the remote script file. With this reference, you can use standard object-method notation to make both synchronous and asynchronous Remote Scripting calls.

To get a reference to a Remote Scripting source file, you require this method:

```
objServer = RSGetAspObject(url);
```

The url parameter is the same url parameter that is used in the RSExecute method. Once you have retrieved the reference to the remote script source file, you can simply call the method that you are interested in, and it will be executed remotely.

For a synchronous call, you would do this:

```
objServer.myMethod();
```

And for an asynchronous call, you would do this:

```
objServer.myOtherMethod(myCallback);
```

As you can see, in a page that uses multiple Remote Scripting call, using the remote server object will make your code more concise and easier to understand.

Limitations

There are a number of limitations in the current implementation of the Remote Scripting technology. Remember that this is just a technology preview and that as the code matures, some of these limitations may go away. In Remote Scripting, you are able to pass only nonarray intrinsic data types from client to server. This means values like numbers and strings, but no arrays. The remote method can return any data type, including arrays and JScript objects, from the server. This means that you can, even though there is only one return value. This value can be a reference to an array or an object which contains all of the data that you need.

If you make multiple remote script calls to the same object, the Microsoft Scripting Library can't resolve those completely on the receiving client side. This means that you will get a separate instance of the return object for each call that you make. It is important to be aware of this as you are using the library. Since the instances will be different, you cannot simply compare the objects from two different return values. They may have returned the same value, but there is other information stored in the object which will cause them to not be completely identical. In short, you should not rely on being able to compare return value objects to see if they are equal. If you do, you may not get the right answers.

Future Possibilities

As we have said before, this is a technology preview of Remote Scripting. Because of this, everything is delivered in source code format. You will probably find that the current version of Remote Scripting is not shall we say "worthy of prime time." But, with our feedback, Microsoft can hopefully develop a robust version quickly.

One can hope that a future version of the library will relax the restriction on only passing intrinsic data types to the server, and instead allow you to pass arrays and objects to the server. Also, the final version should be in a binary executable format, so that it is not necessary to include the source code on both the client and server. Also, even though JAVA is nice for portability to other browsers an optimized ActiveX version for Internet Explorer would greatly increase performance. But we will have to wait and see as to how and when Microsoft will make Remote Scripting fully functional. But from what we have seen so far, it will quickly become a technology that no developer can do without.

Case Study

The best way to learn about the power of Remote Scripting is to use it in a real-life example. In this example, we will look at how you can use remote scripting to provide an enhanced user experience to a user viewing your site. By allowing the client-side page to interact with the server without the whole page reloading, the user will be presented with a more consistent interaction than if the page reloaded every time that the user entered some information.

One of the strengths of client-side scripting is that it can be used to validate information that is entered into a form. Before the advent of client-side scripting there was no way to check the information that was entered in a form before it was sent to the server for processing. There was no way to ensure that the information that was entered was correct, or was actually even entered, without sending the form to the server for processing.

With client-side scripting, the page itself could hold the business logic that ensured that the proper information was added to each field. This validation could be done as the user entered each piece of information, or could be done before the user submitted the form. The client-side script could check to see that those fields that required certain types of data held that data. It could even be used to make consistency checks between two different fields. For example, if the page was for placing an order, and the user was in state, then a local sales tax percentage must be selected.

While client-side scripting for form validation is powerful, there are some drawbacks. First, all of the logic that is needed to perform the validation has to be part of the client script. Also, since there is no way to update the client script without reloading the entire page, then the business logic is static, and cannot change once the page is loaded. What is needed, therefore, is a way to validate dynamic forms with business rules that can be affected by real-time data. Remote Scripting is a technique that we can use to this.

In this example, we will be simulating a securities trading application. In a security trading application, it is important to have instantaneous access to the prices of a security that is about to be bought or sold. In order to do this from a web page, we will use Remote Scripting in two ways. First, we will use an asynchronous remote scripting call that will be periodically called to return and display the current price of a security. Secondly, we will use a synchronous to lock in a price for a trade and return a trade ID number, which can then be submitted along with the other information for the trade to be completed. When this page is displayed in the browser, it will look like this:

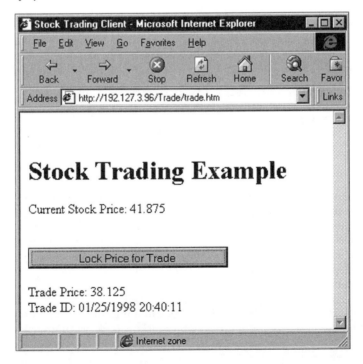

Server Side

On the server side, we will need Remote Scripting methods that will return the current price of the stock and also create a pending trade, which consists of a price and trade ID number that is returned to the client. These methods will be stored in an ASP script file. This script file will be used solely for processing by Remote Scripting. It will not be designed to be called to create a stand-alone HTML page.

```
<%@ LANGUAGE=VBSCRIPT %>
<% RSDispatch %>

<SCRIPT RUNAT=SERVER Language=javascript>
<!--#INCLUDE FILE="rs.asp"-->

    function Description()
    {
            this.GetPrice = GetPrice;
            this.LockPrice = LockPrice;
    }
    public_description = new Description();
```

This Remote Scripting module will expose two methods. These two methods need to be declared by using a **public_description** object. The object will have two properties. Each property will contain a reference to one of the methods exposed by this script file. The description object will allow the server side helper functions that are in the **rs.asp** file obtain a reference to the method that should be called.

```
    function GetPrice()
    {
            var delta, lPrice;
            delta = (Math.random() - 0.5 ) * 2;
            if (Session("lPrice") == NaN || parseFloat(Session("lPrice")) == NaN)
            {
                    lPrice = 30;
            }
            else
            {
                    lPrice = parseFloat(Session("lPrice"));
            }
            lPrice = lPrice + delta;
            lPrice = Math.round(lPrice * 8) / 8;
            Session("lPrice") = lPrice;
            return lPrice;
    }
```

The **GetPrice** method is used to simulate the fluctuating price of a stock. Every time the method is called, the price of the stock is retrieved from a session-level variable. If there is no value stored, then the price will be initialized to 30. A random number between –1 and 1 is used to generate the change in the stock price. The previous stock price is then changed by the delta value. This new price is rounded to the nearest 1/8 of a dollar, which is generally the way that stock prices are represented. This new value is stored in a session-level variable, and then returned to the caller. When we look at the client-side page, you will see how this value is then displayed.

Next, we will look at the method that can be called to lock in a price to process an order. The business rationale behind this function is that a person will want to make a trade when a stock reaches a certain point. At that time, they want to lock in the price. This method will create a database record that records the ID of the person making the trade, the current price of the security, and a unique trade ID that consists of a date/time stamp.

```
function LockPrice(userID)
{
        var objDB;
        var rs;

        objDB = Server.CreateObject("ADODB.Connection");
        objDB.Open("STOCKS");

        rs = Server.CreateObject("ADODB.Recordset");
        rs.Open ("Trade", objDB, 2, 3);
```

This method will use the ActiveX Database Objects to interact with the database. Since we will be adding a record to an existing table, we will be using a dynamic recordset of that table. The database connection is opened and, therefore, links us to the database with the System DSN of "STOCKS." The "Trade" table is opened to enable us to write records to it.

First, the current price of the stock is retrieved. This information is stored in a session-level variable. Since the price could change while we are processing this method, we will cache the value in a local variable.

```
        var curPrice;
        curPrice = Session("lPrice");

        var objDate = new Date();
```

We will then create a date object. This will be used as a timestamp value for the entry that we are making into the database table.

The next step is to add a new record to the database table and set the values of the fields in the table. We will be setting values for the UserID, Price, and TradeID fields. The value that is stored in the TradeID field is a string representation of the date, not an actual date datatype. After the fields have been set, we will update the record in the database and close the table.

```
        rs.AddNew();
        rs.Fields("UserID") = userID;
        rs.Fields("Price") = curPrice;
        rs.Fields("TradeID") = objDate.toLocaleString();
        rs.Update();
        rs.Close();
```

We will be using an array to return information to the calling HTML page. Since there is no direct way to return multiple values, we will create an array that will contain all of the information that we wish to return. The two values that will be returned to the client are the price for the trade along with the date/time stamp that identifies the particular trade. These values are stored in an array. The reference to the array is the value that is returned to the calling function.

```
        var ret = new Array(2);
        ret[0] = curPrice;
        ret[1] =   objDate.toLocaleString();
```

```
                    return ret;
        }
</SCRIPT>
```

Now that we have created the client-side script for this example application, we will turn our attention to creating the client-side HTML pages, along with the script that is needed to interact with the Remote Scripting page.

Client Side

The client side of the example application is a simple page that will perform two functions. First, it will display the current selling price of the security. Since the price is changing frequently, we will be creating an interval timer that will check the price every three seconds. Since we do not want to slow the browser down every time this value is checked, we will make this call asynchronously. This means that we will need to add a callback function as well.

The second function of this example page is to allow the user to lock in a price for a trade. This will take the current price and add it to the database. This allows the user to execute their trade at the exact price that they wish to have. Since we don't want other processing to occur while the trade price is being locked in, we will use a synchronous Remote Scripting call to accomplish this.

```
<HTML>
<HEAD>
<TITLE>Stock Trading Client</TITLE>
</HEAD>
<BODY>
<SCRIPT LANGUAGE="JavaScript" src="/_ScriptLibrary/rs.htm"></SCRIPT>
<SCRIPT LANGUAGE="JavaScript">RSEnableRemoteScripting();</SCRIPT>
```

The first of two initial steps of the example page is to include the JavaScript helper function library, which is stored in the **rs.htm** file in the **/_ScriptLibrary** directory. The next initial step is to call the **RSEnableRemoteScripting** method to setup and initialize the Remote Scripting JAVA proxy application object.

```
<H1>Stock Trading Example</H1>
Current Stock Price: <SPAN ID=StockPrice>30</SPAN>
<BR>
```

The first item that will be displayed is the current stock price. Adjacent to the heading is a **<SPAN>** section that has the ID value of **StockPrice**. By creating this span with an ID, we can use Dynamic HTML later on in the page to change the value that is displayed there. This is where the current price of the stock will be updated whenever the callback function from the asynchronous Remote Scripting method is called.

```
<FORM>
<BR><INPUT TYPE=button NAME=btnRSExecute VALUE="Lock Price for Trade"
onclick="handleRSExecute()" STYLE="width:250;height:25">
</FORM>
<P>
```

The next step is to display a button that the user can press when they wish to lock in the current price for the trade. This is done by using a form button. The button has an **onclick** handler that will fire whenever the button is pressed. In this case, the **handleRSExecute**() method will be called.
As with the display of the stock price, the locked-in price of the trade along with the timestamp of the trade will be displayed for the user. To allow Dynamic HTML to change an area of the screen, we will place that area inside a **<SPAN>** tag and give it an appropriate ID.

```
Trade Price: <SPAN ID=TradePrice></SPAN><br>
Trade ID: <SPAN ID=TradeID></SPAN>

<SCRIPT LANGUAGE="javascript">

    var serverURL = "trade.asp";
    var aspObject;
    var objTimer;

    objTimer = window.setInterval("handleRSExecuteAsync()", 3000);
```

Since we want the stock price display to be updated automatically, we will set up an Interval timer. This will fire every 3 seconds. When it fires, it will call the **handleRSExecuteAsync()** method. The **handleRSExecuteAsync()** method will in turn call the **RSExecute** method. The **RSExecute** method is used to make both synchronous and asynchronous Remote Scripting calls. Since we will not be storing a return value, and will be passing a function reference as the final parameter, this will be an asynchronous call. The **GetPrice** method of the **trade.asp** file will be called. Since this method requires no parameters, there will be no additional parameters in the call to **RSExecute()**.

```
function handleRSExecuteAsync()
{
        RSExecute(serverURL,"GetPrice",PriceUpdateCallBack);
}
```

The **PriceUpdateCallback** method will be called when the asynchronous call to the **GetPrice** method returns. The first job of the callback method is to check the value of the status property of the return object. If the value of that property is 0, then we know that the remote method was executed properly. If it is valid, then we can use the value stored in the **return_value** property of the same object. This new value will be used to replace the existing value inside of the StockPrice **<SPAN>** by using the **innerHTML** property of the StockPrice **<SPAN>** object.

```
function PriceUpdateCallBack(co)
{
        if (co.status == 0)
        {
                document.all("StockPrice").innerHTML = co.return_value;
        }
}
```

The other function of this page is to lock in the price of the stock for a trade. This method will be called when the user clicks the Lock Price for Trade button on the page. Since we don't want any processing to take place while the price is being locked in, we will use a synchronous Remote Scripting call. The call to LockPrice will be made using the **RSExecute** function. Since this method requires a parameter of the user ID, it will be included in the function call. Also, since this is a synchronous call, no callback method is needed.

```
        function handleRSExecute()
        {
                var co = RSExecute(serverURL,"LockPrice", 101);
```

When the call to **RSExecute** returns, we now have a valid return object. We first need to check to see if the remote call returned a valid value. If this is the case, then the status property will be 0, and we can display the information on the page. The return value was actually an array containing two pieces of information. The first element in the array contained the lock-in price, and will be displayed in the **<SPAN>** with the ID of **TradePrice**. The other element of the array contains the generated ID value for the trade, and will be displayed in the **<SPAN>** with an ID of **TradeID**.

```
        if (co.status == 0)
        {
                document.all("TradePrice").innerHTML = co.return_value[0];
                document.all("TradeID").innerHTML = co.return_value[1];
        }

    }
  </SCRIPT>

  </BODY>
  </HTML>
```

This example shows how simple it is to add Remote Scripting to your page. It is also very easy to move client-side validation routines to client/server validation routines through the use of remote scripting. We can only continue to hope that Microsoft will continue to evolve and enrich this technology as time goes on.

Summary

We have basically looked at the features of the Microsoft Scripting Library. This library, currently a work in progress, exists as a set of client-side and server-side scripts and applets that work together to enhance the client/server development capabilities of the IIS 4.0 platform. Specifically, we have seen how to use the Scripting Library to use:

- ▲ Closures, which allow references to methods of objects to be stored in a variable. These references can then be called directly, offering a shortcut during development

- ▲ Object Introspection, which is brought forth through the **uneval** method. This method, which is a converse of the **eval** method, can be used to represent complex objects in a string form. This string form can be passed from system to system, and the original object recreated by calling **eval** on the string.

- ▲ ADO Recordsets. The MSL adds some helper functions that allow for a quick conversion of an ADO recordset into an array. This will allow the data in the recordset to be evaluated using the same techniques that you would use to access an array.

- ▲ Remote Scripting, which provides a mechanism for server-side functions to be called from client applications, without triggering a complete reload of the displayed page. Remote Scripting can be called in both a synchronous and an asynchronous mode, providing a flexible environment for developers.

These technologies will evolve as Microsoft continues work on the Scripting Library. Eventually, we will see them become a built-in part of Internet Explorer and IIS. When these technologies mature, the web will have evolved into a development platform with almost all the power of traditional client/server application architectures whilst retaining all its current advantageous features.

Creating a System Data Source Name

To be able to access databases with ASP on either IIS 4.0 or Personal Web Server, you need to first set up access to the data source by providing the correct **System Data Source Name** (System DSN). Setting up a System DSN allows our database to be accessed by (potentially) all users on the network. This is a simple process, but one which differs slightly depending on the type of database we wish to connect to. We will briefly describe how to set up an Access 97 DSN and then how to set up a SQL Server 6.5 DSN. If you're using a different database system to either of these, then you'll need to select the appropriate ODBC driver. If an entry for it isn't present, you will need to install the driver from your original setup disk, or a disk provided by the database vendor.

Creating an Access 97 System DSN

Launch the 32bit ODBC program by double-clicking on its icon in Windows Control Panel. Click on the System DSN tab in the dialog that appears, to view a list of the currently installed DSNs. If this is the first time you have done this, then this dialog will be empty.

Click on the Add button, to create a new System DSN. To use an Access database, select the Microsoft
Access Driver (***.mdb**) entry from the list and click Finish.

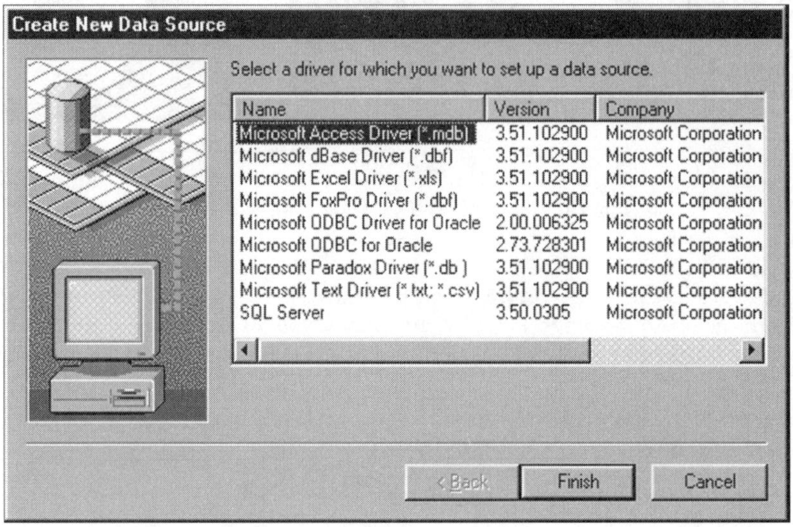

You'll then be presented with the ODBC setup dialog:

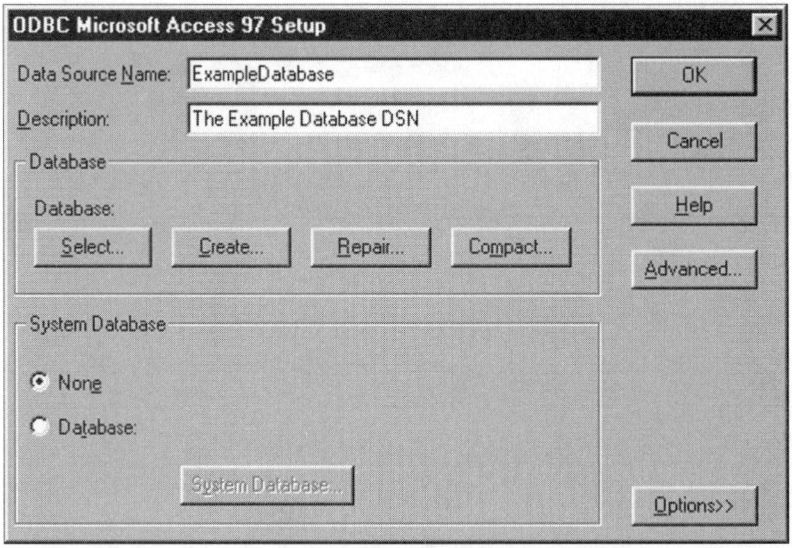

You now have to enter the name of the data source and a description. The Data Source Name provides
the name that our ASP scripts will use as a **Datasource** parameter, and can also be used for ODBC
connections in OLE automation servers. We also need to select the path where our database resides–either
by typing it in directly, or clicking the Select button. Because we're using an Access database, we have the
opportunity to repair and compact the database as well. We can also specify a workgroup (**system.mdw**)
database, to restrict user access if this is required.

When you've entered all the details, click on OK to return to the System Data Sources screen again. The new System DSN will be shown, ready for use:

Creating a SQL Server 6.5 System DSN

If you're using SQL Server, then you'll see a different Setup dialog. The process required to setup a SQL Server 6.5 System DSN is slightly more complex as you need to supply extra details to access the database, such as the server name and network address. We'll quickly go through this process now.

As with Access 97, launch the 32bit ODBC program by double-clicking on its icon in Windows Control Panel. Click on the System DSN tab in the dialog that appears, to view a list of the currently installed DSNs and then click on the Add button, to create a new System DSN. This time to use an SQL Server database, select the SQL Server Driver entry from the list and click Finish. The following dialog will appear:

As with Access 97 you need to supply the name and description, but you also have to supply the SQL Server you need to connect to. You should see the name of the SQL Server in the drop down **Server** list box, in this case it is our own machine. If you don't see anything, then you need to check that the SQL Server is actually visible on the network from your computer. Click on the **Next** dialog when you're able select the Server you want:

Next you need to choose how SQL Server can verify if the login is authorized, if you're using SQL Server authentication, then you can supply an id and password as well in this dialog. If you need to change the method of network communication then click on the Client Configuration button. Otherwise press Next to continue. If the password or id you're using is invalid then you'll receive the following error:

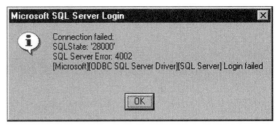

Otherwise you'll be able to progress to the following dialogs, which allow you to create the DSN for the SQL Server and specify where to save the logs, how to perform the character set translation and when to drop stored procedures:

Once you've supplied this information, you are presented with a summary of the configuration:

From this dialog you can test the Data Source to see if it has been set up correctly. If everything works then you should see the following dialog:

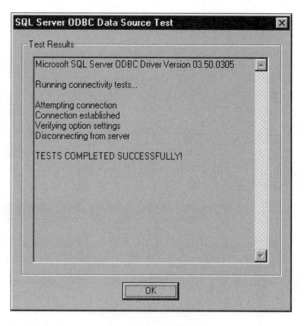

Configuring IIS4

We shall now look at how you can configure the various options in IIS4. This is done via the Properties sheets for the Web Server and the directories.

Configuring Master Properties

We can configure the overall Web server properties by selecting the name of the computer, right clicking and selecting the Properties menu option.

The different types are as follows:

Master Properties

Sets the default properties used by all new and current sites.

WWW Service Properties

Selecting WWW Service and the Edit button generates the default WWW properties – this is the same set of property sheets that we saw earlier when we inspected the properties of a directory.

FTP Service Properties

Selecting FTP Service and the Edit button generates the default FTP properties.

Bandwidth Throttling

▲ *Enable Bandwidth Throttling* – turns bandwidth throttling on / off for all Web and FTP sites – this enables bandwidth to be reserved and made available for other Internet services

▲ *Maximum network use* – specifies maximum bandwidth for all Web and FTP sites as a number of kilobytes per second (KBps)

Computer MIME Map

Sets the Multipurpose Internet Mail Extensions (MIME) mappings - these are names that identify the various file types that the Web service can return to browsers.

Configuring Web Site Properties

We can also configure properties for our specific web site:

There are four main options that can be configured:

Web Site Identification

▲ *Description* – the name that appears in the MMC namespace

▲ *IP address* – the address of the Web Site

▲ *TCP Port* – the TCP port number ; Web browser defaults to port 80

Advanced Multiple Web Site Configurations

Selecting the Advanced button allows multiple identities to be configured for the site. Also, giving the site a Host Header Name enables multiple Web sites to be hosted on the same machine with the same IP address.

Connections

▲ *Unlimited / Limited to* – when enabled, specifies the maximum number of simultaneous connections to the site

▲ *Connection Timeout* – the time in seconds before an inactive user is disconnected

Logging

▲ *Enable Logging* – turns on / off the logging of web site access

▲ *Active log format* – formats available for logged information are: Microsoft IIS Log Format , NCSA Common Log File Format, W^{3}C Extended Log File Format and ODBC Data file

Configuring Operator Properties

The Operators dialog defines which Windows NT user accounts have access to operator functions for management of the Web site.

Configuring Performance Properties

The Performance dialog offers the following options:

Performance Tuning

▲ *Number of expected hits per day* – by setting this to an appropriate value, IIS4 will adjust its internal parameters to provide optimum use of memory

Bandwidth Throttling

▲ *Enable Bandwidth Throttling* – turns bandwidth throttling on / off for this web site – this ensures that bandwidth is available for other Internet services

▲ *Maximum network use* – specifies maximum bandwidth for web site as the number of kilobytes per second (KBps)

Connection Configuration

▲ *HTTP Keep-Alives Enabled*   - turns on / off the ability for the Web server to keep connections to the browser established thus improving performance

Configuring ISAPI Filters Properties

The ISAPI Filters dialog is used to add/remove ISAPI filters. It is also used to edit properties and enable/disable filters.

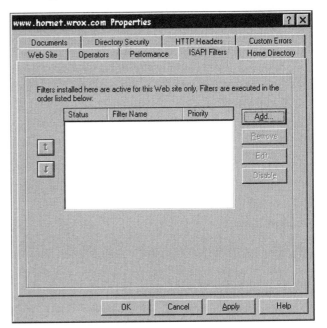

Configuring Home Directory / Virtual Directory / Sub Directory Properties

The Home, Virtual and Sub Directory all use the same dialog.

Since there are quite a few options we will look at them in more detail.

Resource Content Location

The directory may be one of:

 A physical directory located on the same computer as the Web server.

 A physical directory located on another networked computer (option disabled for sub directories) – referenced using the Universal Naming Conventions e.g.\\cobra\marketing.

 Located elsewhere and referenced by another URL – a request for this directory is then redirected.

Access Permissions

 Read – enables permission to read or download files.

 Write – enables permission to change files or upload files.

Content Control

 Log access – when checked, all accesses of Web resources are logged

 Directory browsing allowed – when enabled, a list of sub directories and files will be return if no filename is specified in the URL (this is if no default document has been enabled)

 Index this directory – when checked, Index Server will index the contents of files in the directory

 FrontPage Web – when enabled, the directory will contain information such that the FrontPage explorer can handle Web site management tasks

Application Settings

Used to create applications and enable process isolation. The application permissions specify whether scripts (e.g. ASP files) or executables (e.g. .EXE & .DLL files) located in this directory may be invoked.

If the directory is the start point of an application, another set of property sheets for application configuration can be obtained by selecting the Configuration button.

Extension	Executable Path	Exclusions
.asa	C:\WINNT\System32\inetsrv\asp.dll	PUT,DELETE
.asp	C:\WINNT\System32\inetsrv\asp.dll	PUT,DELETE
.cdx	C:\WINNT\System32\inetsrv\asp.dll	PUT,DELETE
.cer	C:\WINNT\System32\inetsrv\asp.dll	PUT,DELETE
.htr	C:\WINNT\System32\inetsrv\ism.dll	
.idc	C:\WINNT\System32\inetsrv\httpodbc.dll	
.shtm	C:\WINNT\System32\inetsrv\ssinc.dll	
.shtml	C:\WINNT\System32\inetsrv\ssinc.dll	
.stm	C:\WINNT\System32\inetsrv\ssinc.dll	

Application Configuration — App Mappings | App Options | Process Options | App Debugging — Cache ISAPI applications — Application Mappings — Add | Edit | Remove — OK | Cancel | Apply | Help

App Mappings

▲ *Cache ISAPI applications* – when enabled, ISAPI DLLs are cached; should only be disabled when developing/debugging

▲ *Application Mappings* – contains the mapping between file suffix in the URL and the ISAPI extension that will handle the request

App Options

▲ *Enable session state* – turns on / off ASP creating sessions for each user accessing the application

▲ *Session Timeout* – if a sessions is enabled, this specifies the period of time that if no user activity occurs within, the session is deleted

▲ *Enable buffering* – turns on / off the collection of ASP output before sending to the browser

▲ *Enable parent paths* – turns on / off access to parent paths using the relative **..** path notation

▲ *Default ASP language* – language used if not specified within ASP script

▲ *ASP Script timeout* – number of seconds an ASP script can run before an error is flagged

Process Options

▲ *Write Unsuccessful Client Requests to Event Log* – when checked, client access failures are written to NT Event Log

▲ *Enable Debug Exception Handling* – turns on / off detailed error messages being returned when a COM component fails

▲ *Number of Script Engines Cached* – specifies the number of ActiveX Script engines to cache

▲ *Script File Cache* – specifies the number of preprocessed ASP files to cache in order to improve performance.

▲ *CGI Script Timeout* – amount of time a CGI process can execute before an error is flagged

App Debugging

▲ *Enable ASP Server-Side Script Debugging* – turns on / off the ability to use the Script Debugger

▲ *Enable ASP Client-Side Debugging* – ignored

▲ *Send Detailed ASP Error Messages to Client* – turns on / off detailed error messages being returned when ASP errors occur

▲ *Send Text Error Message to Client* – sends a fixed standard message for all ASP errors

Configuring Document Properties

The Document dialog allows you to specify the documents displayed when a user first goes to your site's home page:

Default Documents

▲ *Enable Default Document* – turns on / off the use of a default document; this is the document that is sent if the URL omits a document name.

▲ *List of documents* – contains the list of possible default documents; the directory will be searched for one of these in the order that they appear in the list.

Document Footer

▲ *Enable Document Footer* – turns on /off the addition of a footer on every Web page

▲ *Filename* – full path and name of file containing the footer contents

Configuring Directory Security

The Directory Security dialog allows you to restrict access to certain addresses and domain names:

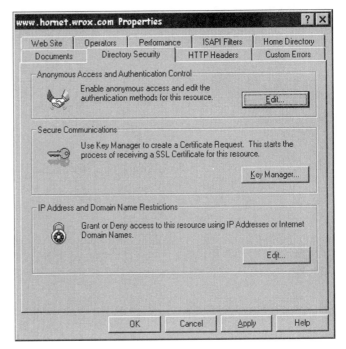

Anonymous Access / Authentication Control

Set authentication methods.

Secure Communications

Invokes Key Manager utility for handling digital certificates – these are needed to implement SSL

IP Address / Domain Name Restrictions

Grants and Denies accessed based on IP address or Domain Name of client

Configuring HTTP Headers

The HTTP Headers dialog allows you to
enable expiry of document content:

Content Expiration

Enable Content Expiry – when enabled, expiry information is included in data sent to the browser and
stored with the item in the cache. The browser uses this information to decide whether to use cached files
or request updates from the Web server. Content can expire:

- Immediately
- After a time period
- At a particular time/date

Custom HTTP Headers

This allows additional information to be appended in the HTTP response headers

Content Ratings

Used to rate Web content according to levels of violence, nudity, sex, and offensive language. This enables
a Web browser to automatically reject information that is unacceptable to the user.

Mime Map

Sets the Multipurpose Internet Mail Extensions (MIME) mappings - these are names that identify the
various file types that the Web service can return to browsers.

Configuring Custom Errors

The Custom Errors dialog allows you to
display your own html files when a
specified a HTTP error occurs:

Error Messages

Allows the customization of the returned error text in any HTTP error responses.

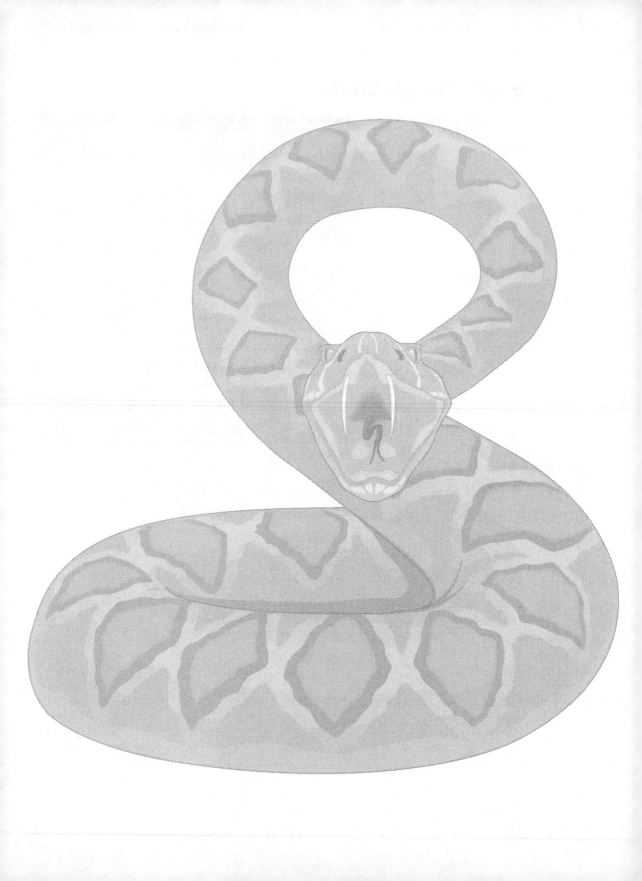

HTTP Server Variables

Variable	Meaning
AUTH_TYPE	User authorization type. **Basic** if the username is authenticated by the server, otherwise omitted.
CONTENT_LENGTH	Number of bytes being sent by the client.
CONTENT_TYPE	Content type when the request is of type **POST**.
DOCUMENT	Current document file name.
DOCUMENT_URI	Virtual path to the current document.
DATE_GMT	Current date, GMT. Can be formatted using **#CONFIG** directive.
DATE_LOCAL	Current date, local. Can be formatted using **#CONFIG** directive.
GATEWAY_INTERFACE	CGI specification of the gateway.
LAST_MODIFIED	Last edit date of the document.
LOGON_USER	Windows NT account details for the user.
PATH_INFO	Additional path information as supplied by client–i.e. the part of the URL after the script name but before any query string.
PATH_TRANSLATED	Value of **PATH_INFO** with any virtual path converted to a physical directory name.
QUERY_STRING	Information following the question mark (**?**) in the URL string.
QUERY_STRING_UNESCAPED	Un-escaped version of the query string.
REMOTE_ADDR	IP address of the client.
REMOTE_HOST	Hostname of the client.
REMOTE_IDENT	Hostname of the client if it supports RFC931 identification.
REMOTE_USER	Client's user name, as authenticated by the server.
REQUEST_METHOD	Request method type sent by client
SCRIPT_MAP	Map used for scripting
SCRIPT_NAME	Name of the script or application to be executed.
SERVER_NAME	Hostname or IP address of server for self-referencing URLs.
SERVER_PORT	TCP/IP port which received the request.
SERVER_PORT_SECURE	Value of **1** indicates the request is on an encrypted port.

Variable	Meaning
SERVER_PROTOCOL	Protocol name and version, usually **HTTP/1.1**. Depends on software on server and client side
SERVER_SOFTWARE	Name and version of the web server software.
URL	Universal Resource Locator address of current page

All other HTTP header information, which isn't parsed into one of the variables listed above, can be obtained using the form **HTTP_<*fieldname*>**, for example:

HTTP_ACCEPT	List of the **MIME** data types that the browser can accept. Values of the HTTP header **ACCEPT** fields are separated by commas in the **HTTP_ACCEPT** variable, i.e.: **ACCEPT: */*; q=0.1** **ACCEPT: text/html** **ACCEPT: image/jpeg** produces the value in **HTTP_ACCEPT** of: **/*; q=0.1, text/html, image/jpeg**
HTTP_ACCEPT_ENCODING	List of encoding types accepted by server
HTTP_ACCEPT_LANGUAGE	List of the human languages that the client can accept.
HTTP_CONNECTION	Type of connection, for example "**Keep-Alive**"
HTTP_USER_AGENT	Product name of the client's browser software.
HTTP_REFERER	URL of the page containing the link used to get to this page.
HTTP_COOKIE	Cookie sent from the client's browser.

You can get values of all HTTP Server Variables by running the following JavaScript program:

```
<!-------------------------------------------------------------------------
                HTTPLIST.ASP - Shows how to iterate through
                     Request.ServerVariables collection
--------------------------------------------------------------------------->
<% @language = JavaScript %>
<HTML>
<HEAD>
 <TITLE>HTTP Server Variables</TITLE>
</HEAD>
<BODY>
 <P ALIGN=center><FONT SIZE=6><B>HTTP Server Variables</B></FONT></P>
 <CENTER>
  <TABLE border>
   <TR><TH>Variable</TH><TH>Value</TH></TR>
   <%
    // create new Enumerator object
    http = new Enumerator(Request.ServerVariables)
   %>
   <%
```

```
   // iterate through collection
   while (!http.atEnd(http)){
   // get one item
   i = http.item()
// show it and it's value
   Response.Write('<tr><td>'+i
               +'</td><td>'+Request.ServerVariables(i)+'</td></tr>')
   // get next item
   http.moveNext()
   }
  %>
  </TABLE>
 </CENTER>
</BODY>
</HTML>
```

HTTP 1.1 Header Codes

Group	Code	Reason Phrase
1 Information		
	100	Continue
	101	Switching Protocols
2 Success		
	200	OK
	201	Created
	202	Accepted
	203	Non-Authoritative Information
	204	No Content
	205	Reset Content
	206	Partial Content
3 Redirection		
	300	Multiple Choices
	301	Moved Permanently
	302	Moved Temporarily
	303	See Other
	304	Not Modified
	305	Use Proxy
4 Client Error		
	400	Bad Request
	401	Unauthorized
	402	Payment Required
	403	Forbidden
	404	Not Found
	405	Method Not Allowed
	406	Not Acceptable
	407	Proxy Authentication Required

Group	Code	Reason Phrase
	408	Request Time-out
	409	Conflict
	410	Gone
	411	Length Required
	412	Precondition Failed
	413	Request Entity Too Large
	414	Request-URI Too Large
	415	Unsupported Media Type
5 Server Error		
	500	Internal Server Error
	501	Not Implemented
	502	Bad Gateway
	503	Service Unavailable
	504	Gateway Time-out
	505	HTTP Version not supported

Listed below is client and server error codes with default explanations, provided by Microsoft Internet Information Server.

Error Code	Short Text	Explanation
400	Bad Request	Due to malformed syntax, the request could not be understood by the server. The client should not repeat the request without modifications.
401.1	Unauthorized. Logon Failed	This error indicates that the credentials passed to the server do not match the credentials required to log on to the server. Please contact the Web server's administrator to verify that you have permission to access the requested resource.
401.2	Unauthorized: Logon Failed due to server configuration	This error indicates that the credentials passed to the server do not match the credentials required to log on to the server. This is usually caused by not sending the proper WWW-Authenticate header field. Please contact the Web server's administrator to verify that you have permission to access to requested resource.

Error Code	Short Text	Explanation
401.3	Unauthorized: Unauthorized due to ACL on resource	This error indicates that the credentials passed by the client do not have access to the particular resource on the server. This resource could be either the page or file listed in the address line of the client, or it could be another file on the server that is needed to process the file listed on the address line of the client. Please make a note of the entire address you were trying to access and then contact the Web server's administrator to verify that you have permission to access the requested resource.
401.4	Unauthorized: Authorization failed by filter	This error indicates that the Web server has a filter program installed to verify users connecting to the server. The authentication used to connect to the server was denied access by this filter program. Please make a note of the entire address you were trying to access and then contact the Web server's administrator to verify that you have permission to access the requested resource.
401.5	Unauthorized: Authorization failed by ISAPI/CGI app	This error indicates that the address on the Web server you attempted to use has an ISAPI or CGI program installed that verifies user credentials before proceeding. The authentication used to connect to the server was denied access by this program. Please make a note of the entire address you were trying to access and then contact the Web server's administrator to verify that you have permission to access the requested resource.
403.1	Forbidden: Execute Access Forbidden	This error can be caused if you try to execute a CGI, ISAPI, or other executable program from a directory that does not allow programs to be executed. Please contact the Web server's administrator if the problem persists.
403.2	Forbidden: Read Access Forbidden	This error can be caused if there is no default page available and directory browsing has not been enabled for the directory, or if you are trying to display an HTML page that resides in a directory marked for Execute or Script permissions only. Please contact the Web server's administrator if the problem persists.
403.3	Forbidden: Write Access Forbidden	This error can be caused if you attempt to upload to, or modify a file in, a directory that does not allow Write access. Please contact the Web server's administrator if the problem persists.
403.4	Forbidden: SSL required	This error indicates that the page you are trying to access is secured with Secure Sockets Layer (SSL). In order to view it, you need to enable SSL by typing "https://" at the beginning of the address you are attempting to reach. Please contact the Web server's administrator if the problem persists.
403.5	Forbidden: SSL 128 required	This error message indicates that the resource you are trying to access is secured with a 128-bit version of Secure Sockets Layer (SSL). In order to view this resource, you need a browser that supports this level of SSL. Please confirm that your browser supports 128-bit SSL security. If it does, then contact the Web server's administrator and report the problem.

Error Code	Short Text	Explanation
403.6	Forbidden: IP address rejected	This error is caused when the server has a list of IP addresses that are not allowed to access the site, and the IP address you are using is in this list. Please contact the Web server's administrator if the problem persists.
403.7	Forbidden: Client certificate required	This error occurs when the resource you are attempting to access requires your browser to have a client Secure Sockets Layer (SSL) certificate that the server recognizes. This is used for authenticating you as a valid user of the resource. Please contact the Web server's administrator to obtain a valid client certificate.
403.8	Forbidden: Site access denied	This error can be caused if the Web server is not servicing requests, or if you do not have permission to connect to the site. Please contact the Web server's administrator.
403.9	Access Forbidden: Too many users are connected	This error can be caused if the Web server is busy and cannot process your request due to heavy traffic. Please try to connect again later. Please contact the Web server's administrator if the problem persists.
403.10	Access Forbidden: Invalid Configuration	There is a configuration problem on the Web server at this time. Please contact the Web server's administrator if the problem persists.
403.11	Access Forbidden: Password Change	This error can be caused if the user has entered the wrong password during authentication. Please refresh the page and try again. Please contact the Web server's administrator if the problem persists.
403.12	Access Forbidden: Mapper Denied Access	Your client certificate map has been denied access to this Web site. Please contact the site administrator to establish client certificate permissions. You can also change your client certificate and retry, if appropriate.
404	Not Found	The Web server cannot find the file or script you asked for. Please check the URL to ensure that the path is correct. Please contact the server's administrator if this problem persists.
405	Method Not Allowed	The method specified in the Request Line is not allowed for the resource identified by the request. Please ensure that you have the proper MIME type set up for the resource you are requesting. Please contact the server's administrator if this problem persists.
406	Not Acceptable	The resource identified by the request can only generate response entities that have content characteristics that are "not acceptable" according to the Accept headers sent in the request. Please contact the server's administrator if this problem persists.
407	Proxy Authentication Required	You must authenticate with a proxy server before this request can be serviced. Please log on to your proxy server, and then try again. Please contact the Web server's administrator if this problem persists.

Error Code	Short Text	Explanation
412	Precondition Failed	The precondition given in one or more of the Request-header fields evaluated to FALSE when it was tested on the server. The client placed preconditions on the current resource meta-information (header field data) to prevent the requested method from being applied to a resource other than the one intended. Please contact the Web server's administrator if the problem persists.
414	Request-URI Too Long	The server is refusing to service the request because the Request-URI is too long. This rare condition is likely to occur only in the following situations: A client has improperly converted a POST request to a GET request with long query information. A client has encountered a redirection problem (for example, a redirected URL prefix that points to a suffix of itself). The server is under attack by a client attempting to exploit security holes present in some servers using fixed-length buffers for reading or manipulating the Request-URI. Please contact the Web server's administrator if this problem persists.
500	Internal Server Error	The Web server is incapable of performing the request. Please try your request again later. Please contact the Web server's administrator if this problem persists.
501	Not Implemented	The Web server does not support the functionality required to fulfill the request. Please check your URL for errors, and contact the Web server's administrator if the problem persists.
502	Bad Gateway	The server, while acting as a gateway or proxy, received an invalid response from the upstream server it accessed in attempting to fulfill the request. Please contact the Web server's administrator if the problem persists.

Please note that Server error message files are placed in `WINNT\HELP\COMMON` folder of Windows NT.

Useful Information

Language Codes supported by Microsoft Internet Explorer 4.0

Language	Abbreviation	Language	Abbreviation
Afrikaans	af	Basque	eu
Albanian	sq	Belarusian	be
Arabic	ar	Bulgarian	bg
Arabic (Algeria)	ar-dz	Catalan	ca
Arabic (Bahrain)	ar-bh	Chinese	zh
Arabic (Egypt)	ar-eg	Chinese (Hong Kong)	zh-hk
Arabic (Iraq)	ar-iq	Chinese (PRC)	zh-cn
Arabic (Jordan)	ar-jo	Chinese (Singapore)	zh-sg
Arabic (Kuwait)	ar-kw	Chinese (Taiwan)	zh-tw
Arabic (Lebanon)	ar-lb	Croatian	hr
Arabic (Libya)	ar-ly	Czech	cs
Arabic (Morocco)	ar-ma	Danish	da
Arabic (Oman)	ar-om	Dutch (Belgian)	nl-be
Arabic (Qatar)	ar-qa	Dutch (Standard)	nl
Arabic (Saudi Arabia)	ar-sa	English	en
Arabic (Syria)	ar-sy	English (Australian)	en-au
Arabic (Tunisia)	ar-tn	English (Belize)	en-bz
Arabic (U.A.E.)	ar-ae	English (British)	en-gb
Arabic (Yemen)	ar-ye	English (Canadian)	en-ca

Table Continued on Following Page

Language	Abbreviation	Language	Abbreviation
English (Ireland)	en-ie	Lithuanian	lt
English (Jamaica)	en-jm	Macedonian	mk
English (New Zealand)	en-nz	Malaysian	ms
English (South Africa)	en-za	Maltese	mt
English (Trinidad)	en-tt	Norwegian (bokmal)	no
English (United States)	en-us	Norwegian (Nynorsk)	no
Estonian	et	Polish	pl
Faeroese	fo	Portuguese (Brazilian)	pt-br
Farsi	fa	Portuguese (Standard)	pt
Finnish	fi	Rhaeto-Romanic	rm
French (Belgian)	fr-be	Romanian	ro
French (Canadian)	fr-ca	Romanian (Moldavia)	ro-mo
French (Luxembourg)	fr-lu	Russian	ru
French (Standard)	fr	Russian (Moldavia)	ru-mo
French (Swiss)	fr-ch	Serbian (Cyrillic)	sr
Gaelic	gd	Serbian (Latin)	sr
German (Austrian)	de-at	Slovak	sk
German (Liechtenstein)	de-li	Slovenian	sl
German (Luxembourg)	de-lu	Sorbian	sb
German (Standard)	de	Spanish	es
German (Swiss)	de-ch	Spanish	es-do
Greek	el	Spanish	es
Hebrew	he	Spanish (Argentina)	es-ar
Hindi	hi	Spanish (Bolivia)	es-bo
Hungarian	hu	Spanish (Chile)	es-cl
Icelandic	is	Spanish (Colombia)	es-co
Indonesian	in	Spanish (Costa Rica)	es-cr
Italian (Standard)	it	Spanish (Ecuador)	es-ec
Italian (Swiss)	it-ch	Spanish (El Salvador)	es-sv
Japanese	ja	Spanish (Guatemala)	es-gt
Korean	ko	Spanish (Honduras)	es-hn
Latvian	lv	Spanish (Mexican)	es-mx

Language	Abbreviation
Spanish (Nicaragua)	es-ni
Spanish (Panama)	es-pa
Spanish (Paraguay)	es-py
Spanish (Peru)	es-pe
Spanish (Puerto Rico)	es-pr
Spanish (Uruguay)	es-uy
Spanish (Venezuela)	es-ve
Sutu	sx
Swedish	sv
Swedish (Finland)	sv-fi
Thai	th
Tsonga	ts
Tswana	tn
Turkish	tr
Ukrainian	uk
Urdu	ur
Vietnamese	vi
Xhosa	xh
Yiddish	ji
Zulu	zu

Some Common MIME Types and File Extensions

MIME Type	Description	File Extention
application/acad	AutoCAD Drawing Files	dwg
application/clariscad	ClarisCAD Files	ccad
application/dxf	DXF (AutoCAD)	dxf
application/msaccess	Microsoft Access File	mdb
application/msword	Microsoft Word File	doc
application/octet-stream	Uninterpreted Binary	bin
application/pdf	PDF (Adobe Acrobat)	pdf

Table Continued on Following Page

MIME Type	Description	File Extention
`application/postscript`	PostScript, encapsulated PostScript, Adobe Illustrator	`ai, ps, eps`
`application/rtf`	Rich Text Format	`rtf, rtf`
`application/vnd.ms-excel`	Microsoft Excel File	`xls`
`application/vnd.ms-powerpoint`	Microsoft Power Point File	`ppt`
`application/x-cdf`	Channel Definition File	`cdf`
`application/x-csh`	C-shell script	`csh, csh`
`application/x-dvi`	TeX	`dvi`
`application/x-javascript`	JavaScript Source File	`js`
`application/x-latex`	LaTeX Source	`latex`
`application/x-mif`	FrameMaker MIF format	`mif`
`application/x-msexcel`	Microsoft Excel File	`xls`
`application/x-mspowerpoint`	Microsoft Power Point File	`ppt`
`application/x-tcl`	TCL Script	`tcl`
`application/x-tex`	TeX Source	`tex`
`application/x-texinfo`	Texinfo (emacs)	`texinfo, texi`
`application/x-troff`	troff	`t, tr, roff`
`application/x-troff-man`	troff with MAN macros	`man`
`application/x-troff-me`	troff with ME macros	`me`
`application/x-troff-ms`	troff with MS macros	`ms`
`application/x-wais-source`	WAIS Source	`src`
`application/zip`	ZIP Archive	`zip`
`audio/basic`	Basic Audio (usually m-law)	`au, snd`
`audio/x-aiff`	AIFF Audio	`aif, aiff, aifc`
`audio/x-wav`	Windows WAVE Audio	`wav`
`image/gif`	GIF Image	`gif`
`image/ief`	Image Exchange Format	`ief`
`image/jpeg`	JPEG Image	`jpeg, jpg, jpe`
`image/tiff`	TIFF Image	`tiff, tif`
`image/x-cmu-raster`	CMU Raster	`ras`
`image/x-portable-anymap`	PBM Anymap Format	`pnm`

MIME Type	Description	File Extention
`image/x-portable-bitmap`	PBM Bitmap Format	`pbm`
`image/x-portable-graymap`	PBM Graymap Format	`pgm`
`image/x-portable-pixmap`	PBM Pixmap Format	`ppm`
`image/x-rgb`	RGB Image	`rgb`
`image/x-xbitmap`	X Bitmap	`xbm`
`image/x-xpixmap`	X Pixmap	`xpm`
`image/x-xwindowdump`	X Windows Dump (xwd) Format	`xwd`
`multipart/x-gzip`	GNU ZIP Archive	`gzip`
`multipart/x-zip`	PKZIP Archive	`zip`
`text/css`	Cascading Style Sheet Source	`css`
`text/html`	HTML File	`html, htm`
`text/plain`	Plain Text	`txt`
`text/richtext`	MIME Rich Text	`rtx`
`text/tab-separated-values`	Text with Tab-Separated Values	`tsv`
`text/x-setext`	Struct-Enhanced Text	`etx`
`video/mpeg`	MPEG Video	`mpeg, mpg, mpe`
`video/quicktime`	QuickTime Video	`qt, mov`
`video/x-msvideo`	Microsoft Windows Video	`avi`
`video/x-sgi-movie`	SGI Movieplayer Format	`movie`

For more information look at: `ftp://ftp.isi.edu/in-notes/iana/assignments/media-types`

Common Codepages

Codepage	Name	Alias
1200	Universal Alphabet	unicode
1201	Universal Alphabet (Big-Endian)	unicodeFEFF
1250	Central European Alphabet (Windows)	windows-1250
1251	Cyrillic Alphabet (Windows)	windows-1251

Table Continued on Following Page

Codepage	Name	Alias
1252	Western Alphabet	iso-8859-1
1253	Greek Alphabet (Windows)	windows-1253
1254	Turkish Alphabet	iso-8859-9
1255	Hebrew Alphabet (Windows)	iso-8859-8
1256	Arabic Alphabet (Windows)	windows-1256
1257	Baltic Alphabet (Windows)	windows-1257
1258	Vietnamese Alphabet (Windows)	windows-1258
20866	Cyrillic Alphabet (KOI8-R)	koi8-r
21866	Ukrainian Alphabet (KOI8-RU)	koi8-ru
28592	Central European Alphabet (ISO)	iso-8859-2
28593	Latin 3 Alphabet (ISO)	iso-8859-3
28594	Baltic Alphabet (ISO)	iso-8859-4
28595	Cyrillic Alphabet (ISO)	iso-8859-5
28596	Arabic Alphabet (ISO)	iso-8859-6
28597	Greek Alphabet (ISO)	iso-8859-7
50220	Japanese (JIS)	iso-2022-jp
50221	Japanese (JIS-Allow 1 byte Kana)	csISO2022JP
50222	Japanese (JIS-Allow 1 byte Kana)	iso-2022-jp
50225	Korean (ISO)	iso-2022-kr
50932	Japanese (Auto Select)	none
50949	Korean (Auto Select)	none
51932	Japanese (EUC)	euc-jp
51949	Korean (EUC)	euc-kr
52936	Chinese Simplified (HZ)	hz-gb-2312
65000	Universal Alphabet (UTF-7)	utf-7
65001	Universal Alphabet (UTF-8)	utf-8
852	Central European (DOS)	ibm852
866	Cyrillic Alphabet (DOS)	cp866
874	Thai (Windows)	windows-874
932	Japanese (Shift-JIS)	shift_jis
936	Chinese Simplified (GB2312)	gb2312
949	Korean	ks_c_5601-1987
950	Chinese Traditional (Big5)	big5

Locale IDs (LCIS)

Country/Region	Language	LCID (Hex)
Albania	Albanian	041c
Algeria	Arabic	1401
Argentina	Spanish	2c0a
Australia	English	0c09
Austria	German	0c07
Bahrain	Arabic	3c01
Belarus	Belarusian	0423
Belgium	French	0813
Belize	English	2809
Bolivia	Spanish	400a
Brazil	Protuguese	0416
Brunei Darussalam	Malay	083e
Bulgaria	Bulgarian	0402
Canada	English	1009
Canada	French	0c0c
Caribbean	English	2409
Chile	Spanish	340a
Colombia	Spanish	240a
Costa Rica	Spanish	140a
Croatia	Croatian	041a
Czech Republic	Czech	0405
Denmark	Danish	0406
Dominican Republic	Spanish	1c0a
Ecuador	Spanish	300a
Egypt	Arabic	0c01
El Salvador	Spanish	440a
Estonia	Estonian	0425
Faeroe Islands	Faeroese	0438
Finland	Finnish	040b
France	French	040c

Table Continued on Following Page

Country/Region	Language	LCID (Hex)
Germany	German	0407
Greece	Greek	0408
Guatemala	Spanish	100a
Honduras	Spanish	480a
Hong Kong	Chinese	0c04
Hungary	Hungarian	040e
Iceland	Icelandic	040f
India	Hindi	0439
Indonesia	Indonesian	0421
Iran	Farsi	0429
Iraq	Arabic	0801
Ireland	English	1809
Israel	Hebrew	040d
Italy	Italian	0410
Jamaica	english	2009
Japan	Japanese	0411
Jordan	Arabic	2c01
Kenya	Swahili	0441
Korea	Korean (Ext. Wansung)	0412
Korea	Korean (Johab)	0812
Kuwait	Arabic	3401
Latvia	Latvian	0426
Lebanon	Arabic	3401
Libya	Arabic	3001
Liechtenstein	German	1407
Lithuania	Classic Lithuanian	0827
Lithuania	Lithuanian	0427
Luxembourg	French	140c
Luxembourg	German	1007
Macau	Chinese	1404
Macedonia	Macedonian	042f
Malaysia	Malay	043e

Country/Region	Language	LCID (Hex)
Mexico	Spanish	080a
Monaco	French	180c
Morocco	Arabic	1801
Netherlands	Dutch	0413
New Zealand	English	1409
Nicaragua	Spanish	4c0a
Norway (Bokmal)	Norwegian	0414
Norway (Nynorsk)	Norwegian	0814
Oman	Arabic	2001
Pakistan	Urdu	0420
Panama	Spanish	180a
Paraguay	Spanish	280a
Peru	Spanish	280a
Philippines	English	3409
Poland	Polish	0415
Portugal	Portuguese	0816
PRC	Chinese	0804
Puerto Rico	Spanish	500a
Qatar	Arabic	4001
Romania	Romanian	0418
Russia	Russian	0419
Saudi Arabia	Arabic	0401
Serbia (Cyrillic)	Serbian	0c1a
Serbia (Latin)	Serbian	081a
Singapore	Chinese	1004
Slovakia	Slovak	041b
Slovenia	Slovene	0424
South Africa	English	1c09
South Africa	Afrikaans	0436
Spain	Basque	042d
Spain	Catalan	0403
Spain (Mod. Sort)	Spanish	0c0a

Table Continued on Following Page

Country/Region	Language	LCID (Hex)
Spain (Trad. Sort)	Spanish	040a
Sweden	Swedish	041d
Switzerland	French	100c
Switzerland	German	0807
Switzerland	Italian	0810
Syria	Arabic	2801
Taiwan	Chinese	0404
Thailand	Thai	041e
Trinidad	English	2c09
Tunisia	Arabic	1c01
Turkey	Turkish	041f
U.A.E.	Arabic	3801
Ukraine	Ukrainian	0422
United Kingdom	English	0809
United States	English	0409
Uruguay	Spanish	380a
Venezuela	Spanish	200a
Vietnam	Vietnamese	042a
Yemen	Arabic	2401
Zimbabwe	English	3009

Useful References and URLs

Here are the URLs of some great ASP pages.

Online tutorials and evening classes, some great discussion of **global.asa** problems, a large free components directory, some sample applications plus much more can be found at:

`http://www.activeserverpages.com`

In-depth articles on programming IIS, ASP and ADSI can be found at:

`http://www.15seconds.com`

One man's deep obsession with ASP has put together an awesome compendium of script libraries, tutorials, components, ASP related articles, lists of consultants, newsgroups and mailing lists. Find them at:

`http://www.asphole.com`

Columns, references and a whole lot of useful links can be found at:

`http://www.aspalliance.com`

Mentioned earlier in this book, Steve Genusa works day and night on component designs to ensure that ASP developers can tackle any task without having to wait 6 months to a year for a specific component. The fruits of his labor can be enjoyed at:

`http://www.serverobjects.com`

The purpose of this expanding site is to provide both expert and novice developers with useful and timely information on the emerging technology of Active Server Pages.

`http://www.asp101.com`

Manohar Kamath's site is devoted to various Internet technologies, specifically those that fall under the umbrella of Microsoft's Active technologies. It covers ASP from a business/technology angle. Check it out at:

`http://www.kamath.com`

Other Useful URLs

You can also get free components and other ASP related information from:

`http://homepages.id.ibs.se/henrik/aspfaq/`
`http://www.tarsus.com`

Support and Errata

One of the most irritating things about any programming book can be when you find that a bit of code you've just spent an hour typing simply doesn't work. You check it a hundred times to see if you've set it up correctly and then you notice the spelling mistake in the variable name on the book page. Grrrr! Of course, you can blame the authors for not taking enough care and testing the code, the editors for not doing their job properly, or the proofreaders for not being eagle-eyed enough but this doesn't get around the fact that mistakes do happen.

We try hard to ensure no mistakes sneak out into the real world, but we can't promise you that this book is 100% error free. What we can do is offer the next best thing by providing you with immediate support and feedback from experts who have worked on the book and try to ensure that future editions eliminate these gremlins. The following sections will take you step by step through how to post errata to our web site to get that help:

- Finding a list of existing errata on the web site
- Adding your own errata to the existing list
- What happens to your errata once you've posted it (why doesn't it appear immediately?)

and how to mail a question for technical support:

- What your e-mail should include
- What happens to your e-mail once it has been received by us

Finding an Errata on the Web Site

Before you send in a query, you might be able to save time by finding the answer to your problem on our web site, **http:\\www.wrox.com**. Each book we publish has its own page and its own errata sheet. You can get to any book's page by using the drop down list box on our web site's welcome screen.

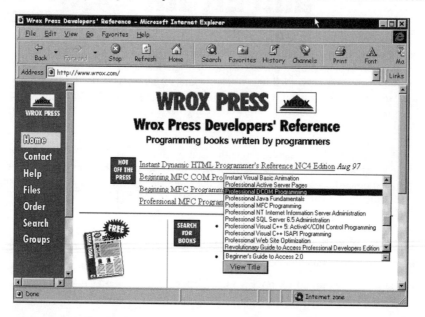

From this you can locate any book's home page on our site. Select your book and click View Title to get the individual title page:

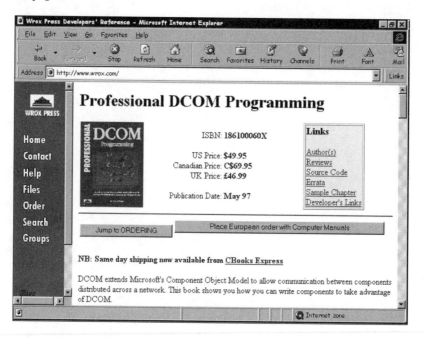

Each book has a set of links. If you click on the Errata link, you'll immediately be transported to the errata sheet for that book:

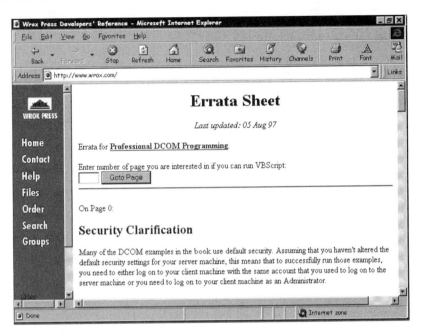

If you're using Internet Explorer 3.0 or later, you can jump to errors more quickly using the text box provided. The errata lists are updated on daily basis, ensuring that you always have the most up-to-date information on bugs and errors.

Adding an Errata to the Sheet Yourself

It's always possible that you may not find your error listed, in which case you can enter details of the fault yourself. It might be anything from a spelling mistake to a faulty piece of code in a book. Sometimes you'll find useful hints that aren't really errors on the listing. By entering errata you may save another reader some hours of frustration and, of course, you will be helping us to produce even higher quality information. We're very grateful for this sort of guidance and feedback. Here's how to do it:

Find the errata page for the book, then scroll down to the bottom of the page, where you will see a space for you to enter your name (and e-mail address for preference), the page the errata occurs on and details of the errata itself. The errata should be formatted using HTML tags - the reminder for this can be deleted as you type in your error.

Once you've typed in your message, click on the Submit button and the message is forwarded to our editors. They'll then test your submission and check that the error exists, and that any suggestions you make are valid. Then your submission, together with a solution, is posted on the site for public consumption. Obviously this stage of the process can take a day or two, but we will endeavor to get a fix up sooner than that.

E-mail Support

If you wish to directly query a problem in the book with an expert who knows the book in detail then e-mail **support@wrox.com**, with the title of the book and the last four numbers of the ISBN in the Subject field of the e-mail. A typical e-mail should include the following things:

the title of the book

the last four numbers of the ISBN

the page number of the errata

the e-mail address

the snail mail address

the phone and fax numbers

We won't send you junk mail. We need details to help save your time and ours. If we need to replace a disk or CD we'll be able to get it to you straight away. When you send an e-mail it will go through the following chain of support;

Customer Support

Your message is delivered to one of our customer support staff who are the first people to read it. They have files on the most frequently asked questions and will answer anything immediately. They answer general questions about the books and web site.

Editorial

Deeper queries are forwarded on the same day to the technical editor responsible for that book. They have experience with the programming language or particular product and are able to answer detailed technical questions on the subject. Once an issue has been resolved, the editor can post the errata to the web site.

The Author(s)

Finally, in the unlikely event that the editor can't answer your problem, he/she will forward the request to the author. We try to protect the author from any distractions from writing. However, we are quite happy to forward specific requests to them. All Wrox authors help with the support on their books. They'll mail the customer and editor with their response, and again, all readers should benefit.

What we can't answer

Obviously with an ever growing range of books and an ever-changing technology base, there is an increasing volume of data requiring support. While we endeavor to answer all questions about a book, we can't answer bugs in your own programs that you've adapted from our code. So, while you might have loved the help desk system examples in our Active Server Pages book, don't expect too much sympathy if you cripple your company with a live application you customized from chapter 12. But do tell us if you're especially pleased with a successful routine you developed with our help.

How to tell us exactly what you think!

We understand that errors can destroy the enjoyment of a book and can cause many wasted and frustrated hours, so we seek to minimize the distress that they can cause.

You might just wish to tell us how much you liked or loathed the book in question. Or you might have ideas about how this whole process could be improved. In which case you should e-mail **feedback@wrox.com**. You'll always find a sympathetic ear, no matter what the problem is. Above all you should remember that we do care about what you have to say and we will do our utmost to act upon it.

INDEX

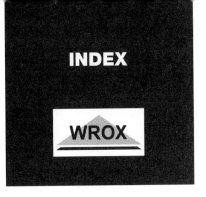

Z

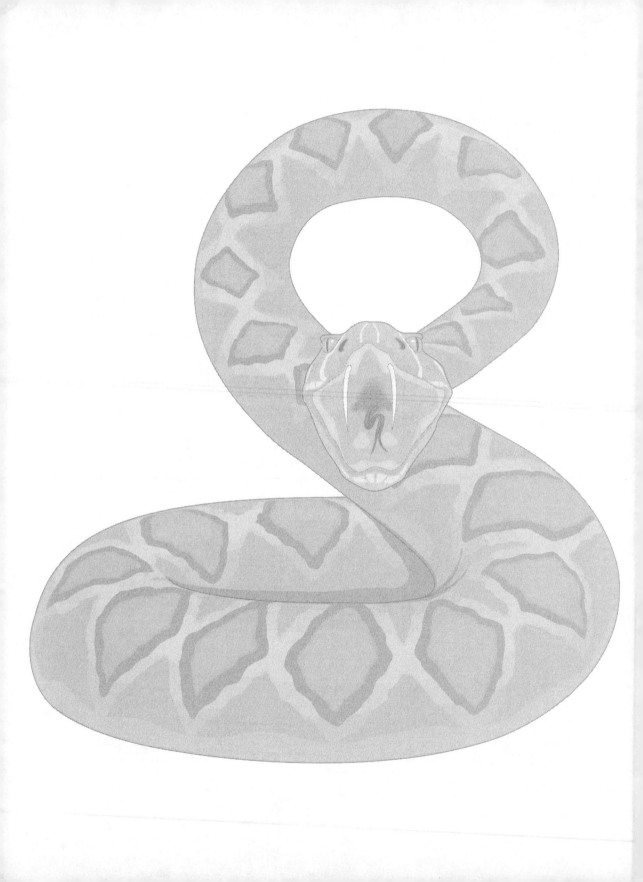

wrox

Wrox writes books for you. Any suggestions, or ideas about how you want information given in your ideal book will be studied by our team. Your comments are always valued at Wrox.

Free phone in USA 800-USE-WROX
Fax (773) 397 8990

UK Tel. (0121) 687 4100   Fax   (0121) 687 4101

Professional Active Server Pages Registration Card

Name _____

Address _____

_____

_____

_____

City_____ State/Region _____

Country_____ Postcode/Zip _____

E-mail _____

Occupation _____

How did you hear about this book? _____

☐ Book review (name) _____

☐ Advertisement (name) _____

☐ Recommendation _____

☐ Catalog _____

☐ Other _____

Where did you buy this book? _____

☐ Bookstore (name)_____ City _____

☐ Computer Store (name)_____

☐ Mail Order _____

☐ Other _____

What influenced you in the purchase of this book?

☐ Cover Design

☐ Contents

☐ Other (please specify) _____

How did you rate the overall contents of this book?

☐ Excellent   ☐ Good

☐ Average   ☐ Poor

What did you find most useful about this book? _____

What did you find least useful about this book? _____

Please add any additional comments. _____

What other subjects will you buy a computer book on soon? _____

What is the best computer book you have used this year? _____

Note: This information will only be used to keep you updated about new Wrox Press titles and will not be used for any other purpose or passed to any other third party.

wrox

NB. If you post the bounce back card below in the UK, please send it to:

Wrox Press Ltd., Arden House, 1102 Warwick Road,
Acocks Green, Birmingham. B27 9BH. UK.

———— *Computer Book Publishers* ————